EXTREMISMS IN AFRICA VOL 3

EXTREMISMS IN AFRICA VOL 3

EDITED BY
ALAIN TSCHUDIN
CRAIG MOFFAT
STEPHEN BUCHANAN-CLARKE
SUSAN RUSSELL
& LLOYD COUTTS

© Good Governance Africa, 2020
All rights reserved. No part of this book may be reproduced or transmitted
in any form or by any means, electronic or mechanical,
including photocopying, recording or any
information storage or retrieval system,
without permission from the copyright holders.

ISBN: 978-0-620-87668-1
e-ISBN: 978-0-620-87704-6

First edition, first impression 2020

Produced on behalf of Good Governance Africa by Bookstorm (Pty) Ltd

Good Governance Africa
11 Cradock Avenue
Rosebank 2196
Johannesburg
South Africa
www.gga.org

Edited by Salome Posthumus
Proofread by Tracey Hawthorne
Cover design by mr design
Book design and typesetting by Triple M Design
Printed by ABC Press, Cape Town

CONTENTS

Contributors — ix
Acronyms and abbreviations — xvii
About Good Governance Africa — xxi
Foreword — xxiii

Chapter 1
The Global Health Threat to Human Security: How Pandemics May Set the Scene for Bioterrorism — CRAIG MOFFAT   1

Chapter 2
The Militarisation of Conservation in Africa — ASHWELL GLASSON   29

Chapter 3
The Potential Impact of Artificial Intelligence on Human and National Security in Africa — FUTHI LUTHANGO   53

Chapter 4
The Terror Business: Assessing the Organised Crime-Extremism Nexus in Africa — RICHARD CHELIN   73

Chapter 5
The Nexus Between Violent Extremism and the Illicit Economy in Northern Mozambique: Is Mozambique Under Siege from International Organised Crime? — LINOS MAPFUMO   96

Chapter 6
Determining What We Know and What We Should Know About What Sustains Violent Extremism in the Horn of Africa – CHARLES GOREDEMA 118

Chapter 7
Kidnapping in West Africa: A Review – MARKUS KORHONEN 135

Chapter 8
The Impact of Terrorism on Business Travellers
– ANNELINE BOOYSE-MOFOKENG 158

Chapter 9
Understanding the Culture of African Partner Forces in the Fight Against Extremism – JAMES ALEXANDER SEDGBEER SMITH 177

Chapter 10
Turning Bullets into Water: Magical Notions and African Armed Groups in the 21st Century Security Environment
– ERICH WAGNER & GERHARDT WAGNER 200

Chapter 11
Neocolonial/Colonial Extremes: Defining Direct Colonialism, Reaction and Resistance in Contemporary Ambazonia and Western Sahara
– MATT MEYER 237

Chapter 12
Fulani and Jihad: The Argument Against Simplistic Narratives in West Africa – MADELINE VELLTURO 262

Chapter 13
Hybridity and Fragmentation: Implications for Regional Security Policy in the Sahel and Beyond – BETHANY L. MCGANN 284

Chapter 14
Using Evidence-Based Research to Directly Improve P/CVE Programming: A Case Study of a Social Network Analysis in Somalia
– FATMA AHMED, LAURA NETTLETON & JEM THOMAS 314

Chapter 15
Disentangling Violent Extremism in Cabo Delgado Province, Northern
Mozambique: Challenges and Prospects
– BLESSED MANGENA & MOKETE PHERUDI   348

Chapter 16
The Libya Crisis and the Need for African Ownership of Peace and Security
Processes on the Continent – LEBOGANG SESHOKA   366

Chapter 17
The Escalation of Extremist Violence in Southern Africa and the Need for More
Collaborative Security Responses – STEPHEN BUCHANAN-CLARKE   383

Index   411

CONTRIBUTORS

FATMA AHMED has considerable international development experience with a focus on stabilisation, countering and preventing violent extremism, strategic communications and civil society engagement, working across Africa, the Middle East and south-east Asia. Fatma currently consults for the United Nations Development Programme, Africa Regional Programme to support the African Union on conflict prevention and peacebuilding. Most recently, she was the Middle East and Africa director at Albany Associates, and is a panel member of the African Union FEMWISE committee.

ANNELINE BOOYSE-MOFOKENG is based in Johannesburg as the security director for Africa for International SOS, and has 17 years' experience in the security industry. As part of the Overseas Security Advisory Council – Africa Regional Committee, Anneline continues to enhance the role of women in security. Prior to her current role, she was a regional security advisor at the Bill & Melinda Gates Foundation, a security specialist for the World Bank, and was involved in the security and manufacturing industries of the South African government, giving her significant experience in the private, public, nongovernmental organisation, and development sectors. She holds several academic qualifications, including a Master's in Security Management from the Wits School of Governance.

STEPHEN BUCHANAN-CLARKE is an independent analyst with several years' experience working in conflict and post-conflict settings in Africa on national security and development issues. He currently serves as lead researcher for Good Governance Africa's National Security Programme, and has been involved in the editing of all three volumes of the *Extremisms in Africa* series, as well as authoring several chapters.

RICHARD CHELIN is a researcher at the Institute for Security Studies focusing on organised crime and its impact on human security. Previously, he was a researcher at the Centre for the Study of Violence and Reconciliation, where he examined issues of transitional justice and terrorism. He was also a conflict analyst for various news channels, commenting on political and security issues in Africa. His research interests are in the fields of organised crime, violent extremism and transitional justice. He holds a Master's (cum laude) in Conflict Transformation and Peace Studies from the University of KwaZulu-Natal.

LLOYD COUTTS is the head of publications at Good Governance Africa. He has an extensive background in journalism and media spanning 36 years. He holds a Bachelor's in Journalism and Media Studies (Honours) from the University of the Witwatersrand, and has worked as a reporter, sub-editor, news editor, assistant editor and acting editor for publications such as *Business Day*, *The Star*, *Business Report* and *Sunday World*. Lloyd also has experience in wire services, notably in the German Press Agency (dpa) and radio (Network Radio News and Classic FM). He has also worked in television news at eNCA.

ASHWELL GLASSON is head of academic policy and sector advancement at the Southern African Wildlife College, a director of Rangers Sans Frontieres, and a member of the executive committee of the Field Guides Association of Southern Africa. He is a graduate of North-West University and is working towards an Honours in Peace and Conflict Studies at Saint Augustine College. His research and policy interests include the militarisation of conservation, the illegal wildlife trade, countering violent extremism and environmental security.

CHARLES GOREDEMA is an independent senior research consultant conducting research into the impact of transnational crime networks on governance in some of Africa's coastal cities. He previously worked on projects in the Transnational Threats and International Crimes division at the Institute for Security Studies. A lawyer by training, Charles's career includes a stint in the prosecution of economic crimes. He subsequently lectured in criminal justice in Zimbabwe and South Africa, while undertaking research and managing research projects on the subject. After joining the Institute for Security Studies in August 2000, Charles focused on studying emerging forms of transnational organised crime and money laundering.

MARKUS KORHONEN is an associate in the political and security risk analysis team at S-RM, a global risk and intelligence consultancy. He previously worked as a lecturer at the Universities of Cape Town and Stellenbosch, and at Webster University's campus in Accra, teaching a variety of political science courses, including international political economy and comparative politics. He also worked as a writer for Africa Check, the continent's first fact-checking organisation. Markus holds a Master's in Research in African Studies from the University of Edinburgh, and a Master's in Politics and International Relations from the University of Aberdeen.

FUTHI LUTHANGO is a graduate of the University of Cape Town, majoring in economics, and has an Honours in Finance. He has worked in the insurance industry but has spent most of his time in the information technology industry, where he has occupied various positions, including chief information officer. He is a certified ISO27001 Information Security Implementer and currently heads up an artificial intelligence, data and analytics practice. He believes that technologies such as machine learning, artificial intelligence and robotic process automation will have a major impact on societies, and that organisations and governments have a primary responsibility to apply these technologies in a way that delivers holistic positive value and contributes to the upliftment of people.

BLESSED MANGENA is a principal researcher and analyst at the Committee of Intelligence and Security Services of Africa and a seasoned diplomat, with extensive experience in the field of international relations and managing peace and security in Africa.

LINOS MAPFUMO, PhD, is a senior foreign-policy analyst in the Zimbabwean Foreign Service, and a research associate at both the N'Zarama Centre for Peacebuilding and the Development Reality Institute. He has over 19 years' practical experience working for government institutions and civil society organisations, wherein part of his work included identifying, profiling and analysing world security threats. His main specialities are counterterrorism, climate change and local governance. He was previously stationed in South Africa as a diplomat, where he worked extensively on promoting bilateral and multilateral cooperation, while at the same time identifying and analysing security threats to the southern African region. Previously, he was an assistant managing editor/administrator with the *Journal of Peacebuilding & Development*, published by the South-North Centre for Peacebuilding and Development. He holds a PhD in administration from the University of KwaZulu-Natal.

BETHANY L. MCGANN serves as research and project manager for the RESOLVE Network, the research component of the Countering Violent Extremism team within the Center for Applied Conflict Transformation at the United States Institute of Peace. Her research focuses on issues of hybrid security governance and non-state actors in sub-Saharan Africa. She has led the design and implementation of multi-year desk and field studies funded by the United States Agency for International Development, which have focused on Sahelian sub-state hybrid armed actors, militias and local security assemblages. She contributed the Africa paper for the 2019 West Point Student Conference on US Affairs. Her most recent research was cited in New America's 2019 Annual Terrorism Assessment. Bethany holds a Master's in Security Policy Studies from George Washington University's Elliott School of International Affairs, and a Bachelor's in Government and International Affairs from Smith College. (The views in this publication are those of the author. They do not necessarily reflect the views of the RESOLVE Network, its partners, the United States Institute of Peace, or any American government agency.)

MATT MEYER is an internationally noted author, historian and organiser elected in 2018 as secretary-general of the International Peace Research Association, the world's leading consortium of university-based professors, scholars, students and community leaders. Matt is the senior research scholar at the University of Massachusetts/Amherst's Resistance Studies Initiative, a position he has held since retiring from more than 30 years as a tenured educator and teacher-trainer for the New York City Department of Education. He also serves as chair of the Financial Advisory Committee of the International Fellowship of Reconciliation, and as Africa support network coordinator for War Resisters' International.

CRAIG MOFFAT, PhD, is a security specialist for Good Governance Africa's National Security Programme. He has more than 17 years' practical experience working for government institutions and multilateral organisations. He was previously employed by the South African Foreign Service, where he worked extensively at identifying and analysing security threats towards South Africa as well as the southern Africa region. Previously, he was the political advisor for the Pretoria Regional Delegation of the International Committee of the Red Cross. He holds a PhD in Political Science from Stellenbosch University.

LAURA NETTLETON is the senior monitoring and evaluation specialist at Albany Associates. She has conducted research in Somaliland, Kenya, Uganda, Tunisia and across the western Balkans. She comes from a communications background and holds a Master's in Conflict, Security and Development from King's College, London, as well as a Bachelor's in Anthropology and Conflict Studies from Exeter University.

MOKETE PHERUDI, PhD, served as a technocrat in the Southern African Development Community mediation processes in Lesotho, Madagascar, the Democratic Republic of Congo and Zimbabwe. He also headed the Early Warning Unit of the Committee of Intelligence and Security Services of Africa in Addis Ababa, where he specialised in early warning, conflict resolution and conflict management in Africa. He recently published a second edition of the book *Governance and Democracy in Lesotho: Challenges faced by SADC intervention, 2007–2017*.

SUSAN RUSSELL is the deputy head of publications at Good Governance Africa. Susan has worked in journalism and media management for more than 30 years in various roles that have included news reporter, sub-editor, section editor, assistant editor, publisher and general manager. After graduating from the University of KwaZulu-Natal, Durban, with a Bachelor's degree in English and Comparative African Government and Administration, Susan joined the *Daily News* as a news reporter. Four years later, she joined *Business Day*, where she spent several years as a hard-news reporter. Moving to the *Sunday Times*, she spent two years as a subeditor before taking over editorship of the *Sunday Times Magazine*, a role she filled for three years before being promoted to *Sunday Times* assistant editor in charge of marketing. It was during this time that she launched the *Sunday Times* travel supplement. Moving into media management at Times Media (formerly Avusa), Susan was promoted to general manager of marketing, and joined the Times Media executive committee. In that role she was subsequently appointed publisher of *The Times*, a weekday sister publication to the *Sunday Times*, as well as publisher of *Business Day*'s *Wanted* magazine and the *Sunday Times* lifestyle supplements.

JAMES ALEXANDER SEDGBEER SMITH served in the police, military and private-military sector for 25 years. He studied post-graduate politics, sociology and history at university, and then joined the police in South Africa, followed by the British army, where he attended the Royal Military Academy in Sandhurst. He was commissioned into the Royal Artillery and served in intelligence, surveillance, target acquisition and reconnaissance, as well as in joint effects. He spent six years training militaries in the Middle East and served as a staff officer in a tactics branch. During his military career he served on operations and training in the Middle East, the Americas, Europe, the Mediterranean and Africa. Currently working in the United Kingdom, he is a qualified cultural advisor, teaches cultural practitioners, and designs cultural understanding courses for United Kingdom defence forces, the North Atlantic Treaty Organization and civilian companies. As a human security and gender advisor, he teaches service personnel courses on conflict-related sexual violence, gender-based violence, protection of civilians, human trafficking, sexual exploitation and abuse, and the protection of children affected by armed conflict.

LEBOGANG SESHOKA holds a Bachelor's in International Relations (Honours) from the University of the Witwatersrand, and has been a career diplomat since 2006. He joined the Department of Foreign Affairs in 2004 and completed his diplomatic training in 2005. He was posted to Senegal between 2006 and 2010 as third secretary, political. Following that posting, he spent 2014 to 2018 in the Kingdom of Lesotho as first secretary, political. He is currently based in the head office of the Department of International Relations and Cooperation. He writes in his personal capacity.

JEM THOMAS is director of training and research at Albany Associates. He has more than 15 years' global experience working in complex and politically divisive communications environments, from the western Balkans to East Africa. He is co-author of *Nature or Nurture: A Crisis of Trust and Reason in the Digital Age*. Originally a qualified engineer officer in the Royal Navy, academically he also has a Master's in Political Sciences from the Universities of Cambridge and St Andrews, and a Postgraduate Diploma in Social Science Research Methods from University College in London.

ALAIN TSCHUDIN, PhD, is executive director of Good Governance Africa (SADC). A registered psychologist with a PhD in Psychology from the University of KwaZulu-Natal, Alain was a Post-doctoral Research Fellow at the University of Cambridge, before returning to studies there, completing an M. Phil. in Divinity and a PhD in Ethics. He has broad research and community-engagement interests, and has worked for universities and non-governmental organisations in Africa and Europe, with the European Commission, and as lead consultant for Save the Children and the United Nations Children's Fund on child protection and emergency coordination in Africa and the Middle East. He is a Honorary Research Associate on the Peacebuilding Programme at the Durban University of Technology, and a visiting professor at the University of the Witwatersrand School of Governance. He is a member of the Institute of Directors, London, and of the Expert Group on the Humanitarian-Development-Peace Nexus for the Office of the Special Adviser on Africa at the United Nations. From May 2020, he will serve as senior advisor to Good Governance Africa.

MADELINE VELLTURO is a research analyst with Stimson's Protecting Civilians in Conflict programme. Her portfolio includes United Nations peacekeeping and multilateral institutions, as well as African geopolitics, with a focus on the Sahel region and an emphasis on pastoralism and herder-farmer conflict. She received a Master's of Public Administration from Columbia University's School of International and Public Affairs, focusing on international security policy and conflict resolution. Madeline lived for several years in Accra, where she founded a series of creative writing workshops for at-risk urban youth. She has also lived and worked in Kenya, Côte d'Ivoire and Uganda with local non-profit organisations in the fields of peacebuilding, literacy, entrepreneurship and public health. Madeline holds a Bachelor's from Bryn Mawr College.

ERICH HENRY WAGNER is a colonel in the United States Marine Corps Reserve. Erich earned a Bachelor's in History from the US Naval Academy and a Master's in International Relations from the Fletcher School of Law and Diplomacy at Tufts University, and is a graduate of the US Army War College. He has published articles on military history and counterinsurgencies in the *Journal of Military History*, the *Journal for the Anglo-Zulu War Historical Society*, the *Marine Corps University Journal*, and for the Joint Center for Operational Analysis, and the Terrorism Research and Analysis Project of the Federal Bureau of Investigation.

GERHARDT STEFAN WAGNER, PhD, is a physician who graduated from Creighton Medical School in Omaha, Nebraska. He is board-certified in the disciplines of neurology and psychiatry, and has a PhD in Immunology and Infectious Diseases from the University of California, Davis. Gerhardt is a primary author or co-author of multiple scientific journal articles and case reports focusing on HIV vaccines, electroconvulsive treatment modalities in patients with severe depression, and the oncogenic potential of phorbol esters.

ACRONYMS AND ABBREVIATIONS

AAH	Asa'ib Ahl Al Haq
ACLED	Armed Conflict Location and Event Data Project
AFRICOM	United States Africa Command
AI	artificial intelligence
AMISOM	African Union Mission to Somalia
AML/CFT	anti-money laundering and combating the financing of terrorism
ANSG	armed non-state group
AQIM	Al-Qaeda in the Islamic Maghreb
ARVN	Army of the Republic of Vietnam
ASG	Abu Sayyaf Group
ASWJ	Alu Sunna Wa-Jama
AU	African Union
BBC	British Broadcasting Corporation
CAR	Central African Republic
CBAG	community-based armed group
CDC	Centers for Disease Control and Prevention
COVID-19	severe acute respiratory syndrome coronavirus 2 (see also SARS-CoV-2)
CPZ	Composite Protection Zone
CRSV	conflict-related sexual violence
CSO	civil society organisation
CT MORSE	Counter-Terrorism Monitoring, Reporting and Support Mechanism

CVE	countering violent extremism
DDRRR	disarmament, demobilisation, repatriation, reintegration and resettlement
DIRCO	Department of International Relations and Cooperation
DRC	Democratic Republic of Congo
EIA	Environmental Investigation Agency
EU	European Union
FARC	Revolutionary Armed Forces of Colombia
FARDC	Forces Armées de la République Démocratique du Congo
FATF	Financial Action Task Force
FID	foreign internal defence
FRELIMO	Frente de Libertação de Moçambique
GGA	Good Governance Africa
GNA	Government of National Accord
GNC	General National Congress
GPS	global positioning system
GSM	Global System for Mobile Communications
GTF	Global Threat Forecast
HACP	High Authority for the Consolidation of Peace
Hawks	Directorate for Priority Crime Investigation
HIV	human immunodeficiency virus
HR	human resources
IED	improvised explosive device
ILO	International Labour Organization
IOM	International Organization for Migration
IPZ	Intensive Protection Zone
IRGC	Islamic Revolutionary Guards Corps
IS	Islamic State
ISGS	Islamic State in the Greater Sahara
ISIS	Islamic State in Iraq and Syria
ISWAP	Islamic State West Africa Province
IUCN	International Union for Conservation of Nature
JAS	Jama'tu Ahlis Sunna Lida'awati wal-Jihad
JNIM	Jama'a Nusrat ul-Islam wa al-Muslimin

Acronyms and Abbreviations

JPZ	Joint Protection Zone
KFR	kidnapping for ransom
LEAP	Law Enforcement and Anti-poaching Strategy
LNA	Libyan National Army
LNG	liquefied natural gas
LRA	Lord's Resistance Army
MERS	Middle East respiratory syndrome
MINUSMA	United Nations Multidimensional Integrated Stabilization Mission in Mali
MISO	military information support operations
MNLA	National Movement for the Liberation of Azawad
MONUSCO	United Nations Stabilization Mission in the Democratic Republic of Congo
MUJAO	Movement for Oneness and Jihad in West Africa
NATO	North Atlantic Treaty Organization
NGO	non-governmental organisation
NISCWT	National Integrated Strategy to Combat Wildlife Trafficking
NOC	National Oil Corporation
NOVACT	International Institute for Nonviolent Action
NSGT	Non-Self-Governing Territories
OCHA	United Nations Office for the Coordination of Humanitarian Affairs
ONLF	Ogaden National Liberation Front
P/CVE	Preventing/Countering Violent Extremism
PFLP	Popular Front for the Liberation of Palestine
PNDS	Nigerien Party for Democracy and Socialism
POCDATARA	Protection of Constitutional Democracy Against Terrorist and Related Activities Act
PRM	Polícia da República de Moçambique
PSYWAR	psychological warfare
REC	Regional Economic Community
RENAMO	Resistência Nacional Moçambicana
RPG	rocket-propelled grenade
SADC	Southern African Development Community

SANDF	South African National Defence Force
SANParks	South African National Parks
SAPS	South African Police Service
SARS	severe acute respiratory syndrome
SARS-CoV-2	severe acute respiratory syndrome coronavirus 2 (see also COVID-19)
SDG	Sustainable Development Goal
SEMG	Somalia and Eritrea Monitoring Group
SNA	Social Network Analysis
SPLA	Sudan People's Liberation Army
SUV	sport utility vehicle
TNC	Transitional National Council
UAE	United Arab Emirates
UK	United Kingdom
UN	United Nations
UNCAC	United Nations Convention against Corruption
UNDP	United Nations Development Programme
UNEP	United Nations Environment Programme
UNHRC	United Nations Human Rights Council
UNODC	United Nations Office on Drugs and Crime
UNPO	Unrepresented Nations and Peoples Organization
UNSC	United Nations Security Council
UNTOC	United Nations Convention against Transnational Organized Crime
UPDF	Uganda People's Defence Force
US	United States (of America)
US AFRICOM	United States Africa Command
USAID	United States Agency for International Development
USSD	unstructured supplementary service data
WHO	World Health Organization
WWF	World Wide Fund for Nature

ABOUT GOOD GOVERNANCE AFRICA

What is Good Governance Africa?
Good Governance Africa (GGA) is an independent and registered non-profit organisation, established to promote better governance in Africa. GGA opened its first centre in Johannesburg in February 2012 to focus on the 16 countries in the Southern African Development Community (SADC). Three years later, GGA opened an office in Accra for English-speaking West Africa: Gambia, Ghana, Liberia and Sierra Leone. This office now also includes several Portuguese-speaking countries: Cabo Verde, Equatorial Guinea, Guinea-Bissau, and São Tomé and Principe. GGA opened its Lagos office in Nigeria in November 2015 to represent Africa's largest population and its largest economy. In 2019, GGA opened an office in Harare, dedicated to Zimbabwe.

In 2020, regional offices were opened in Addis Ababa for East Africa and in Dakar, Senegal with the Gorée Institute to cover Francophone Africa.

GGA's goals
Democracy, accountability and transparency lie at the core of good governance in Africa, without which citizens are unable to track and evaluate government performance.

These go together with the rule of law and respect for human, civil and property rights – principles that GGA emphasises for fostering both economic development and democratic societies. Good governance involves inclusive economic growth and sustainable development, enabled through economic freedom and equal opportunities for all.

With a particular focus on these central areas, GGA aims to promote good governance in Africa through applied research and critical debate. GGA researches, analyses and interprets information to produce fact-based knowledge, represented by *Africa in Fact*, the *Africa Survey*, and other project outputs.

Focal research areas include child development and youth formation, local government, natural resources and state security. GGA is also concerned with the promotion of education, innovation, leadership and social values.

SADC Office, The Mall Offices, 11 Cradock Avenue, Rosebank, 2196
SADC Tel +27 11 268 0479
Nigeria Tel +234 1 4627411-3
West Africa Tel +233 302 672925
Website: www.gga.org
Twitter: @GGA_org
Email: info@gga.org

FOREWORD

Alain Tschudin (PhD)

Governance is concerned primarily with the promotion of societal harmony, prosperity and peace, based on the appropriate allocation of resources. It achieves this through core administrative functions that include defence, economic development, education, fiscal management, health, infrastructure, policing, revenue collection, social development, trade, treasury and transport, among others. However, Book III of the ancient Roman *De Re Militari* cautions us that "if you desire peace, prepare (for) war".[1] The lesson imparted by Vegetius is not a call to arms. Rather, he suggests that if we genuinely seek the promotion of peace and harmony, we need to be prepared to counter those conditions that seek to undermine this, the most extreme case of contrarian conflict being represented by war. War, whether it arises internal to the country as "civil war" or from aggressive forces external to it, represents the gravest threat to governance.

In *The Art of War*,[2] his classical text on strategy, Sun Tzu shares that "to subdue the enemy without fighting is the supreme excellence". The value of pre-emptive measures cannot be underemphasised. His successor, Sun Tzu II,[3] emphasises the importance of psychological strategising. This is a decisive factor recognised by successive major authorities such as Niccolò Machiavelli[4] and Von Clausewitz[5] and, to a lesser extent, others such as Jomini.[6] "Fortune favours the prepared mind" – so says the well-worn motto that tends to serve humanity well. Accordingly, five years ago, Good Governance Africa (GGA) undertook to focus its National Security Programme on a core phenomenon that actively seeks to disrupt, undermine and destroy peace, development and security across Africa. This is the problem of extremisms in Africa – an increasing scourge. These movements are religious, ethnic and race-based in nature, and represent complex and supreme threats to stability.

To better prepare ourselves to understand and engage extremist threats in order to prevent, counter and overcome them, we have plumbed the depths, producing a collection of close on 50 chapters of knowledge in a trilogy of book volumes,[7,8] covering a plethora of topics exceeding a thousand pages on the topic, across regions and countries, and dedicated to markedly diverse themes. Machiavelli, in the *Discourses on Livy*,[9] cites Epaminondas the Theban: "Nothing was so useful and necessary for a commander as to be able to see through the intentions and designs of his adversary, and because it is hard to come at this knowledge directly, the more credit is due to him who reaches it by conjecture."

Machiavelli produces two illustrative examples. First, Tempanius, the Roman centurion, defeater of the Equians, whose success "turned entirely on being the first to be informed of the enemy's condition", continuing that if "two opposed armies shall fall into the same disorder, and be reduced to the same straits; in which case, that which soonest detects the other's distress is sure to come off best". Next, regarding the Florentine defeat of the Venetians retreating from Marradi in 1498, "this victory was wholly due to their having notice of the enemy's movements before the latter had notice of theirs".[10]

The upshot of this is knowledge. In the words of Thomas Hobbes, writing in *Leviathan*, "knowledge is power".[11] It is to the end of being informed, comprehensively, that we have covered the theme of extremisms in Africa from a diverse set of perspectives, employing the skills and experience of academics, practitioners, social scientists, analysts, military and law-enforcement officers, and subject specialists. Comprehensive and credible information enables stakeholders to take appropriate action.

Our conviction from the start was, and remains, that a purely militarised solution is not a solution at all. It addresses the symptoms without tackling the underlying conditions. We use the plural noun 'conditions' here intentionally, as research demonstrates that socio-economics increasingly drive extremist recruitment in Africa. It is simply not the case of a uniform army of zombie-like religious or racist ideologues brainwashed into a fanatical cause.

Conditions of poverty, marginalisation and social exclusion abound. Signing up for a cause often provides alienated young men[12] with money, power and status, a sense of purpose, and an alternative reality to pursue.[13] Of course, radicalisation out of a sense of conviction continues to arise. This latter represents a significant challenge to those working in deradicalisation programmes since, by virtue, appeals to rationality and reason are likely to fail in the face of persistent emotive and extreme zeal.[14]

We have extended our reach way beyond that of the introductory Volume 1, which sought to promote the value of a transdisciplinary and collaborative approach in confronting the phenomenon of extremisms in Africa. Therein, we book-ended chapters on counterterrorism and the value of diplomacy versus military intervention with regional analysis of major extremist groups, and traced key themes and the effects of some of the related fallout. Then, in Volume 2, we ramped up efforts to dive to greater depths, exploring emergent trends such as online recruitment, the role of women as actors, the issues of humanitarian aid, potential ecological drivers and troublesome financial flows, and insights into some of the major players.

Volume 3 of *Extremisms in Africa* evidences an even greater attention to detail on further developments and potential threats. We note with concern current insurgency developments in northern Mozambique and have dedicated substantial page space to discussing this hotspot, which threatens the stability of the entire south-eastern corridor of Africa.

Our authors have engaged the impact of extremisms on business, and the business that is extremist activity, along with considering the crime-extremism nexus and terror financing in Africa's Horn. On the tech and cyber front, our authors speak to the rise of artificial intelligence, as well as social media in relation to trust for extremist groups such as Al-Shabaab in the east. To the north, we look at why Libya remains problematic, to the west, we examine why kidnapping is rife there, and to the south, we review lessons learned for South Africa.

Our contributors reflect on the 'green' militarisation of parks, and from a military-practice point of view, serving officers engage the critical intersection of shared cultural understanding between African and international partner forces striving to combat extremisms, as well as the role that traditional beliefs and superstitions can play in conflicts on the continent.

We consider the impact of extremisms on peoples such as the Fulani, the problem created by colonial and neocolonial extremes in Ambazonia and Western

Sahara, and the notion of hybridity and fragmentation, and the impacts on regional security in the Sahel and beyond.

Topically, given the global COVID-19 pandemic, we attend to the pressing theme of the weaponisation of viruses. Much as it seems that the current outbreak was not laboratory-orchestrated,[15] it reiterates the fact that we ought to be prepared – and remain alert – for non-conventional threats. Extremist groups across Africa have, in some instances, threatened to use viral threats, while others have actively developed such programmes.

Finally, we round out with lessons learnt from the first cycle of GGA's National Security Programme. Here, we highlight the need for greater cooperation and coordination between key stakeholders, within countries and regionally, in order to more effectively address the cross-border challenges arising. This, together with international and inter-agency collaboration, can only serve to strengthen the response in a timely, proportionate and decisive manner.

We have been privileged to work with African and allied law-enforcement services and security forces, with a range of social scientists, and with applied humanities specialists to pull together the most comprehensive offering on this topic from an African base. Beyond our writing, we continue to actively collaborate with our partners to build capacity and develop skills through workshops and training, furthering our mandate to improve governance across Africa. We are delighted to have been invited to join the RESOLVE Network, and look forward to sustained collaboration with our partners.

I would like to thank our contributors, our editorial team and colleagues, and associates for making both this volume and the conclusion of the trilogy a realisable, concrete output, especially in a time of global lockdown and uncertainty. We sincerely appreciate your commitment and flexibility under less than ideal conditions. To our publisher, Bookstorm and Russell Clarke, and editor Salomé Posthumus, thank you.

Thus it is that our next National Security Programme cycle shifts to peace, security and development in Africa, in keeping with both the African Union's Agenda 2063 and the United Nations Sustainable Development Goals for 2030. We trust that the current volume, besides making for informative reading, also makes a seamless transition to highlighting the governance and developmental issues that need to be prioritised 'front and centre'. For it is only by anticipating threats and challenges to security that we are best placed to muster and respond with better governance, which allows for sustained peace and societal harmony in Africa to be realised.

Alain Tschudin, PhD
Executive Director, GGA SADC
Visiting Professor, Wits School of Governance

Endnotes

1. Vegetius. (n.d.). *De re militari*. "*Igitur qui desiderat pacem, praeparet bellum*", otherwise stated as "*si vis pacem, para bellum*".
2. Sun Tzu. (1993). *The Art of War*. Ware: Wordsworth.
3. Sun Tzu, II. (1966). *The Lost Art of War*. Translated by Cleary, T. New York: Harper Collins.
4. Machiavelli, N. (2006). *The Art of War*. Translated by Neville, H. New York: Dover.
5. Von Clausewitz, C. (1987). *On War*. New York: Penguin Classics.
6. Jomini, A. (2007). *The Art of War*. Translated by Mendell, G.H. & Craighill, W.P. New York: Dover.
7. Tschudin, A., Buchanan-Clarke, S., Coutts, L., Russell, S. & Tyala, M. (eds.). (2018). *Extremisms in Africa: Volume 1*. Johannesburg: Jacana/GGA.
8. Tschudin, A., Moffat, C., Buchanan-Clarke, S., Russell, S. & Coutts, L. (eds.). (2019). *Extremisms in Africa: Volume 2*. Johannesburg: Tracey McDonald/GGA.
9. Machiavelli, N. (2007). *Discourses on Livy*. Translated by Thomson, N.H. Chapter XV, p. 303. New York: Dover.
10. Ibid, 304-305.
11. Hobbes, T. (1994). *Leviathan*. Indianapolis: Hackett. Note that Hobbes draws the aphorism '*scientiae potentia est*' from Sir Francis Bacon, who conceived of this notion in his *Sacred Meditations* (1597).
12. Collier, P. (2010). *Wars, guns and votes: democracy in dangerous places*. p.130. London: Vintage.
13. See Tschudin et al (2019).
14. Ibid.
15. Andersen, K.G., Rambaut, A., Lipkin, W.I., Holmes, E.C. & Garry, R.F. (2020). The proximal origin of SARS-CoV-2. *Nature Medicine*, 25, pp. 450-452. https://www.nature.com/articles/s41591-020-0820-9 [accessed 13 May 2020].

CHAPTER 1

The Global Health Threat to Human Security: How Pandemics May Set the Scene for Bioterrorism

Craig Moffat

Introduction

Throughout human history, people have had a need to migrate across oceans and borders, which, due to the opportunistic nature of infectious diseases, has made many a traveller the unwitting carrier of pestilence and plague. While it may be true that outbreaks are continuously erupting in different parts of the world, fortunately not all outbreaks reach pandemic level. A few months ago, much of the world did not know much about SARS-CoV-2. However, today the virus known as COVID-19 has reached almost every country, affecting more than 2 million people, with almost 150,000 deaths.[1] So far, we have witnessed the havoc wreaked on global economies, healthcare systems stretched to breaking point, overcrowded hospitals and emptied-out public spaces. People have been forced into self-isolation, and our everyday lives are organised around avoiding the risk of contagion. This disruption to everyday life is on a scale that most living people have never experienced. Unless the threat is adequately addressed, the chances are that almost everyone will know someone who has been infected.

COVID-19 is a new disease similar to the human immunodeficiency virus (HIV), Middle East respiratory syndrome (MERS) and severe acute respiratory syndrome (SARS). The virus is a zoonotic disease, meaning that it spreads into the human population from an animal host.[2] It is believed that pangolins were the original source.[3] The first transmission occurred in a Wuhan seafood wholesale market in the Hubei Province of China.

The virus is officially called 'severe acute respiratory syndrome coronavirus

2', abbreviated to SARS-CoV-2.[4] COVID-19 is the name of the disease. On 30 January 2020, the International Health Regulations Emergency Committee of the World Health Organization (WHO) declared the outbreak a "public health emergency of international concern". On 11 March, the WHO officially declared COVID-19 to be a pandemic.

The end of the Cold War saw the introduction of a new security agenda by scholars seeking to shift the referent object of security from the state to the individual. The United Nations (UN) was influential in the development of an emerging human security perspective. Human security focuses on a broad understanding of security that not only includes the security of states against external or internal armed threats, but also gives priority to the security of people living within states against non-military threats such as disease, environmental degradation, and economic and social instability.[5]

The United Nations Development Programme (UNDP) took the lead in officially championing the human security perspective. In 1994, the UNDP launched the concept of human security through its Human Development Report, which listed several categories that placed human security at risk, such as food insecurity, economic insecurity, personal insecurity, community insecurity and political insecurity. Following the lead of the UNDP, other international organisations such as the International Monetary Fund and World Bank adopted the concept of human security in their policy frameworks. A number of countries soon followed suit and embraced the concept when defining their national security policies.[6]

The COVID-19 pandemic is categorised as a threat to human security. It is evident that many governments, multilateral agencies and academics have adopted this broadened security perspective. They have raised questions regarding the economic impact of the disease, how the pandemic has the potential to endanger millions of people, whether it has the potential to become a threat to food security, how it contributes to crime, and the implications of the pandemic for governance and economic development.

The ongoing COVID-19 pandemic has gradually moved from the category of a politicised matter to a securitisation concern. The securitisation of the COVID-19 pandemic may be useful in addressing some social ills and strengthening the national response policy to the pandemic.

This chapter is divided into three parts. The first part will give a brief overview of the history of pandemics. The second will discuss the processes related to securitisation, including identifying the actors, factors and dynamics that have a bearing in facilitating this process. Finally, the third will explore a scenario of how extremist organisations could use the ongoing COVID-19 pandemic as a potential design for bioterrorism.

Brief Historical Overview of Pandemics

From time immemorial, human beings have been plagued by diseases and illnesses, exposing our susceptibility to viruses. The development of agrarian communities saw an increase in the spread of diseases by creating communities that made epidemics more possible. Increased trade provided new opportunities for human and animal interactions that sped up such epidemics. Communicable diseases that have had a long history of infecting human beings and making an impact on society are, among others, malaria, tuberculosis, leprosy, influenza and smallpox.[7]

Macro-trends such as urbanisation, industrialisation and globalisation have had a profound impact on the spread of infectious diseases. The modern way of life – with the creation of larger cities, more expansive and exotic trade routes, and expanded contact with different populations of people, animals and ecosystems – acts as a driving force behind pandemics. Ironically, the more civilised the human race becomes, the more vulnerable it becomes to devastating pandemics. Table 1 highlights some of the major pandemics that have occurred over time. (Note that many of the numbers listed in this table are the best estimates based on available research.)

Table 1: Major pandemics[8]

Name	Time period	Type / Pre-human host	Death toll
Antonine plague	165-180	Believed to be either smallpox or measles	5M
Plague of Justinian	541-542	*Yersinia pestis* bacteria (rats and fleas)	30-50M

Japanese smallpox epidemic	735-737	*Variola major* virus	1M
Black Death	1347-1351	*Yersinia pestis* bacteria (rats and fleas)	200M
New World smallpox outbreak	1520 onwards	*Variola major* virus	56M
Italian plague	1629-1631	*Yersinia pestis* bacteria (rats and fleas)	1M
Great plague of London	1665	*Yersinia pestis* bacteria (rats and fleas)	100,000
Cholera pandemics 1-6	1817-1923	V. cholerae bacteria	1M+
Third plague	1885	*Yersinia pestis* bacteria (rats and fleas)	12M (China and India)
Russian flu	1889-1890	Believed to be H2N2 (avian origin)	1M
Yellow fever	Late 1800s	Virus (mosquitoes)	100,000-150,000 (US)
Spanish flu	1918-1919	H1N1 virus (pigs)	40-50M
Asian flu	1957-1958	H2N2 virus	1,1M
Hong Kong flu	1968-1970	H3N2 virus	1M
HIV/AIDS	1981 to present	Virus (chimpanzees)	25-35M
SARS	2002-2003	Coronavirus (bats and civets)	770
Swine flu	2009-2010	H1N1 virus (pigs)	200,000
Ebola	2014-2016	Ebolavirus (wild animals)	11,000
MERS	2015 to present	Coronavirus (bats and camels)	850
COVID-19	2019 to present	Coronavirus (unknown; possibly pangolins)	145,563 (Johns Hopkins University estimate as at 17 April 2020)

Securitisation Approaches

The theory of securitisation is relatively new to the field of security studies. It emerged as a tentative compromise; not a full-scale retreat from realism, but a growing recognition in parts of the inter-state community that states are ultimately made up of individuals and households.[9] An issue is said to be securitised when it is "presented as posing an existential threat to a designated referent object", thus "justifying the use of extraordinary measures".[10]

Securitisation is the form of framing that highlights the existential threat of an issue and undermines the arguments for dealing with it as simply a matter of routine. For some securitising actors[11] it is necessary to securitise COVID-19 because of the human security/developmental approach. This was demonstrated by South Africa's President Cyril Ramaphosa addressing the nation: "As government, we are aware that the lockdown has caused great disruption to all our lives and caused upheaval in our economy. But we all know and agree that this nationwide lockdown is absolutely necessary to save the lives of thousands, even tens of thousands, of our people."[12]

For others, however, the framing of COVID-19 in the language of national security can push the intended response in the wrong policy direction. This was demonstrated by President Yoweri Museveni of Uganda, who announced that the government would be the sole distributor of food and other relief items to vulnerable Ugandans after declaring a 14-day lockdown. He further outlawed politicians distributing relief and food items to different communities in the country, claiming that such people posed a danger of spreading infections to the public, and that they would be "charged with attempted murder" before courts of law.[13]

The language of securitisation is the political instrument used to categorise actors and situations, while also outlining appropriate sets of solutions. The process of securitisation can be described as follows: "Security is the move that takes politics beyond the established rules of the game and frames the issue either as a special kind of politics or as above politics."[14] Understanding the way in which this is carried out is derived from speech act theory.

Speech act theory is an essential component of the securitisation approach as defined by Buzan et al. This approach rests on the premise that "by saying words something is done", meaning that language does not only convey information but also has a constitutive role.[15] In other words, security threats do not exist independently, but are rather socially constructed as such through language.[16] Therefore, policymakers use speech acts as a social activity involving shared understandings, with the objective of framing specific issues as a threat to security.[17]

According to Buzan et al, the defining characteristic of a successful securitisation approach relies on the acceptance by an audience that something is indeed threatening and demands exceptional action.[18] At the global level, it has been demonstrated that the securitising of COVID-19 can be empirically proven by the widespread acceptance of the securitisation claim in multilateral organisations. The WHO officially declared COVID-19 a pandemic on 11 March 2020, and the UN subsequently called the pandemic the world's "most challenging crisis" since the Second World War.

What has been somewhat surprising has been the silence of the UN Security Council (UNSC). In an attempt to elevate the pandemic to the level of the UNSC, Tunisia has proposed a UNSC resolution that would "call the coronavirus pandemic a threat to humanity and to international peace and security", and so call for "an immediate global humanitarian ceasefire to respond to the unprecedented threat posed by COVID-19."[19] The UNSC has twice previously addressed public health emergencies, first the HIV and AIDS pandemic, and secondly the Ebola outbreak in West Africa in 2014, which it declared a threat to international peace and security.[20]

Smith argues that the WHO's emergency declaration was driven mainly by fears of the virus spreading to countries with weak health systems, particularly in Africa.[21] As a result of this risk, the WHO identified 13 African countries (Algeria, Angola, Côte d'Ivoire, the Democratic Republic of Congo, Ethiopia, Ghana, Kenya, Mauritius, Nigeria, South Africa, Tanzania, Uganda and Zambia) as high priorities for support based on the volume of travel from China. The United States (US) Centers for Disease Control and Prevention (CDC) stepped up partnerships with African health ministries, and the Bill & Melinda Gates Foundation committed $100 million to combat the outbreak – half to China, and half to the African Union (AU)'s Africa CDC, underscoring Africa's importance for global containment.[22]

While potentially vulnerable, Africa has abundant experience with and expertise in epidemics.[23] On the one hand, several world leaders have already verbally reiterated the severity of the threat:

- On 11 March 2020, as infections began to rise exponentially in Italy, Germany's Chancellor Angela Merkel claimed that about 70% of her country's population would contract the virus – a sober warning that stood in stark con-

trast to pronouncements from other politicians at the time. Soon afterwards, the chancellor appealed to Germans in a dramatic television address to respect tough restrictions on movement and social contact.[24]
- In Singapore, Prime Minister Lee Hsien Loong also won plaudits for an aggressive testing and tracing campaign that kept the number of infections in the country low – at the time of writing, about 1,000 cases since the beginning of the outbreak. In a recent interview with CNN, Lee asserted that transparency and trust were key to his country's battle against the virus.
- South Korea's President Moon Jae-in, New Zealand's Prime Minister Jacinda Ardern and El Salvador's President Nayib Bukele all received praise for similar decisive and transparent action.[25]

This symbolises a major development in a debate where threats to health are rarely labelled as existential. Only once declared a national security threat does a health threat garner enough attention and resources to address it. On the other hand, other leaders tried to downplay the threat:
- In China, where the illness was first detected in late December 2019, authorities were accused of engaging in a cover-up and punishing doctors who sounded the alarm in the early days of the outbreak – moves which critics said allowed the virus to spread out of the central city of Wuhan to every corner of the globe.
- In the US, President Donald Trump initially downplayed[26] the severity of the threat, predicting that the virus would "disappear" like "a miracle" one day, and dismissing growing concerns over the disease as a "hoax" by his political rivals.[27] He changed tack after polling showed an increasingly worried public, and when modelling predicted that 200,000 people could die in the US in the absence of drastic containment efforts.
- In Brazil, President Jair Bolsonaro dismissed the illness as a "fantasy" and a "little flu".[28] Further instances of denial included Bolsonaro defying the advice of his own health officials to avoid social contact by touring the streets of the capital, Brasilia, in a campaign to get his countrymen back to work.
- Mexico's President Andres Manuel Lopez Obrador continued to hold political rallies late into March 2020, even continuing to kiss his supporters and urging Mexicans to "live life as normal". This was in defiance of medical advice given

by his health minister, calling on citizens to stay home to contain the virus.[29]
- In Indonesia, President Joko Widodo admitted to intentionally suppressing information regarding the outbreak – a strategy he said had been used to prevent panic. In the early days of the epidemic, some of his ministers advised that prayer would keep the disease away, while others stated that the country's warmer weather would slow the spread of the virus.[30]

The initial response to COVID-19 by the Africa CDC was as follows:[31]
- The Emergency Operations Centre and Incident Management System were activated on 27 January 2020.
- The third Incident Action Plan was developed, covering the period between 16 March and 15 April 2020.
- The AU ministers of health gathered in Addis Ababa, Ethiopia, on 22 February 2020 for an emergency COVID-19 meeting, where they agreed on a joint continental strategy and guidance for assessment, movement restrictions, and the monitoring of people at risk for COVID-19, including people repatriated from China.
- Weekly updates were provided to national public health institutes in member states, and working groups were formed for high-priority areas of coronavirus control, including surveillance, laboratory diagnosis, infection prevention and control, clinical care and risk communication.
- Three experts were deployed to Cameroon, and three to Nigeria, to support COVID-19 outbreak response efforts.
- Response simulation exercises (i.e. 'tabletop' exercises for high-level coordination) were initiated, including an initial simulation conducted with a group of 10 West African countries in partnership with the West African Health Organization.
- Africa CDC briefed the AU Permanent Representatives Committee as well as ambassadors from non-member states on the COVID-19 situation in Africa, its response activities and recommendations.

During an AU meeting on 26 March 2020, Ramaphosa, in his capacity as chairperson of the organisation, convened a teleconference of the Bureau of the African Union Heads of State and Government[32] in which he reiterated the human security and development threat that the COVID-19 pandemic represented for the continent.

> "President Ramaphosa underscored the fact that poverty, poor sanitation, an existing disease burden, overstretched health systems and extreme urban population density mean that the pandemic could explode in an even more catastrophic way than has been seen thus far in Africa. Hence the need for urgent action in order to stem the tide. President Ramaphosa emphasised that the AU, Regional Economic Communities (RECs) and all health institutions should direct their efforts at stopping the spread of the virus."[33]

Regionally, the initial response by the Southern African Development Community (SADC) was to host an extraordinary meeting of SADC health ministers on COVID-19 on 9 March 2020.[34] The main purpose of the meeting was to share existing knowledge and information on the COVID-19 outbreak, and to agree on how to harmonise and coordinate the preparedness and response to COVID-19 in the SADC region. In line with the human security/developmental approach, SADC member states were urged to mobilise domestic resources and invest in public health systems to ensure resilience and health security.

States adhering to prominent international declarations of commitment showed that the large audience of UN member states were convinced of the particular security nature of COVID-19. As highlighted above, the compliance of national governments at the international level did not always filter down to the immediate internalisation of the securitisation approach at the domestic level. This meant that in the domestic structures of some states, the securitisation of COVID-19 offered varying outcomes in terms of its assimilation.

Finally, successful securitisation is at its root a political process, but the actual politics of the acceptance are left very underdetermined by this model. Buzan et al make a case that "the issue is securitised only if and when the audience accepts it as such…[it must] gain enough resonance for a platform to be made from which it is possible to legitimise emergency measures."[35] It is precisely the dynamics of this acceptance, this resonance, this politics of consent, that require further unpacking. The Copenhagen School certainly open their model to consideration of the "external, contextual, and social roles and authorised speakers" of the speech act "and, not least, under what conditions (i.e. is the securitisation successful)".[36] However, it must be noted that an omission in the securitisation model is that there is no mechanism to gauge accurately whether the actual securitisation process has been successful or not. McInnes and Rushton attempt to address this limitation by suggesting that "the securitisation is not a binary condition – there is a spectrum from failed to partial to successful securitisation process."[37]

With the COVID-19 pandemic still unfolding, it is too early to definitively conclude where in the securitisation spectrum the process is.

Framing as a Speech Act

Two characteristics need to be present when an issue is to be securitised. First, it must be seen as an existential threat – one that endangers the very physical or cultural continuity of the state or individual – and secondly, this threat must be the kind for which extraordinary, if not extra-legal, measures may be invoked.

Securitisation differs from other framing models because it suggests that this transformation comes about through a speech act. 'Speech act' describes the transformative importance of language in social relations, and Waever explains how speech act statements can work in securitisation: "By uttering 'security', a state representative moves a certain development into a specific area and thereby claims a special right to use whatever means are necessary to block it."[38]

Building on this premise, Buzan et al broke down the security speech act into four constitutive parts. According to them, the following must be present when framing something in terms of security:

1. A securitising actor(s).
2. A specific issue.
3. An existential threat to survival.
4. A referent object.[39]

Following this logic, securitisation is only considered a success when the securitising actor is able to convince a significant audience that something constitutes a threat. Once an issue has been successfully securitised, there is a need for the institutionalisation of the security rhetoric. At this stage, the security argument is enough since the sense of urgency is implicit in the standards of behaviour, principles, policies and bureaucratic processes that were created to tackle the problem.

However, a valid limitation is highlighted by McInnes and Rushton; they point out that, when issues are created as security issues through a speech act, it raises a problem: "who are the actors who, through their speech acts, can create security issues?"[40] Buzan et al also raise the issue that there exists a bias towards certain actors who are "generally accepted voices of security".[41] Therefore, to address this concern, I will adopt the speech act tool developed by McInnes and Rushton. For a speech act to be successful, three facilitating conditions are required in the process of securitisation:

1. It must follow the recognised grammar of security.
2. It must come from an actor in a position of authority to pronounce on security.
3. It helps if the object can be generally said to be threatening.[42]

If one is to adhere to the above conditions, a significant example is an appeal issued on 23 March 2020 by UN Secretary-General António Guterres urging warring parties across the world to lay down their weapons in support of the bigger battle against COVID-19 – the common enemy that was now threatening all of humankind.[43]

This is also best illustrated by the actions taken by several international world leaders such as Cyril Ramaphosa, Angela Merkel, Italian Prime Minister Giuseppe Conte, Spanish Prime Minister Pedro Sanchez, French President Emmanuel Macron, and Indian Prime Minister Narendra Modi, who all acted swiftly by announcing states of emergency or disaster, leading to lockdown measures, and instituting extraordinary movement restrictions on their societies. According to several media reports, more than 3,9 billion people, or half of the world's population, were asked or ordered to stay at home by their governments to prevent the spread of the deadly COVID-19.[44] This measure can be said to be indicative of successfully convincing a significant audience that something constitutes a threat. The extraordinary restrictions adopted included closing down countries domestically, deploying armed forces, unparalleled restrictions on all air travel, confining large tracts and (in some cases) whole populations to their homes, closing schools and universities, and prohibiting religious gatherings. Most international sporting codes were postponed or suspended, including the 2020 Olympic Games in Tokyo, which were postponed to 2021.

Also, in line with the above conditions, in the SADC region the countries in Table 2 adopted states of emergency and/or disaster measures in an attempt to curb the pandemic. Countries that adopted these measures identified the threat in the human security/development approach using the grammar of security. The leaders of these countries can be identified as the securitising actors in a position of authority to pronounce on security and, lastly, the threat posed by COVID-19 was very threatening indeed.

Table 2: Countries in SADC region to adopt lockdown measures (as at 5 April 2020)

Lockdown	Partial lockdown	Not yet announced
Angola	Democratic Republic of Congo	Comoros
Botswana	eSwatini	Malawi
Lesotho	Madagascar	Seychelles
Mauritius	Mozambique	Tanzania
South Africa	Namibia	
Zimbabwe	Zambia	

Interestingly, in response to the securitising move by the UN Secretary-General, a separatist militia group in Cameroon stated that it planned to put down its weapons for a fortnight so that people could be tested for coronavirus. The Southern Cameroons Defence Forces said that its ceasefire would come into effect as "a gesture of goodwill".[45] At the time of writing, it remained the only armed group among several operating in Cameroon's English-speaking regions to have heeded the UN's call for a global ceasefire. The fighters claim that they have been marginalised in the majority French-speaking nation. For the past three years, they have been fighting government forces in the Anglophone regions with the aim of creating a breakaway state called Ambazonia.[46]

The act of securitisation implies the construction of a threat that needs to be reclassified by quick action and, if need be, by extraordinary measures. This securitising act allows for the issue to be raised from the realm of low politics to that of high politics. When securitising an issue, political authorities display it as "an existential threat, requiring emergency measures and justifying actions outside the normal bounds of political procedure".[47] Waever asserts that securitisation consequently has "enormous power as an instrument of social and political mobilisation. Putting something on the security agenda persuades us of the need to furnish urgent and unprecedented responses; it signals imminent danger and is therefore given a high priority."[48]

Security moves beyond the normal working rules of politics. After securitising a threat, the government is positioned to facilitate and carry out the required procedures to help address the threat. In some instances, this process may need to curtail democratic processes. As the government works towards managing a near-threat, it seems only logical to redraw the lines of the legitimating borders of politics and to limit civil and human rights.[49] The state passes new laws, limitations and prohibitions through which it limits the area of politics, and widens that of security, while frightening and subduing the public. As the concept of security is widened, securitisation can narrow the very concept of democracy, and therefore should be handled with care.

Several examples highlight the stringent measures adopted by different countries on the continent, which may limit civil and human rights in an attempt to curb the pandemic. For example, in South Africa it was reported that:

> "within the first days of South Africa's 21-day COVID-19 lockdown, numerous videos emerged allegedly depicting police and soldiers kicking, slapping, whipping and shooting lockdown violators. Security forces were seen discharging water cannons and rubber bullets, and forcing people into humiliating positions…Just five days into the lockdown, by 31 March, police had reportedly killed three people – the same number as COVID-19 at that time. In a period when national unity and trust in the state are vital, such actions could prove disastrous."[50]

A second example comes from Kenya, where President Uhuru Kenyatta issued an apology for violence meted out by police following the declaration of a nationwide curfew to curb the spread of coronavirus. Police were accused of using heavy-handed tactics to enforce the dusk-to-dawn curfew with tear gas, baton charges and live rounds. A 13-year-old boy died in Nairobi after he was shot while standing on his balcony as the police forced people into their homes on the street below.[51]

As has been demonstrated by this section of the chapter, most countries that adopted these measures identified the threat of COVID-19 as a human security/development concern with the potential to impact on national security.

Weaponising Viruses: How Pandemics Can Set the Scene for Bioterrorism

The intrinsic nature of extremist organisations is to disrupt normality and instil a sense of fear in a society. This is carried out by encouraging a state of affairs in which citizens refrain from carrying on with their lives as usual with high levels of personal autonomy and security. It is not far-fetched to imagine a scenario in which a pandemic such as COVID-19 could be found to be useful to potential extremist groups, which may want to use it as a design for future bioterrorism attacks.

Within a few short months, the virus crippled the health services of developed nations such as Italy and Spain, and it continues to wreak havoc on stock markets and threatens to plunge the world into a new economic recession. It is an invisible threat that has relatively healthy people fearing for their lives, while also negatively impacting on community resilience and livelihood sustainability.

Islamic State in Iraq and Syria (ISIS) and other extremist groups have long sought to procure effective bioweapons in the form of a 'poor man's atomic bomb'. To achieve their aim of instilling fear, some extremist groups have focused their strategies on the possibility of controlling deadly global pandemics which could kill or maim a large portion of the world's population, and disrupt economies, governments and technical infrastructures in the world's most developed countries. In a recent article, Means stressed that extremist groups have "access to bioweapon technology; could, relatively easily and cheaply obtain [MERS] or [SARS] or other virulent strains; and figure out human subject-based experiment/refine/distribute systems to launch an attack".[52]

We can envision a scenario in which a particular extremist group had a strategy to launch the current COVID-19 emergency. A particular extremist organisation deploys a devoted, radical, infected follower to potentially carry the virus and launch it in secret, in this instance in Wuhan. As turned out to be the case, the bureaucracy of the People's Republic of China moved at a slow pace to address the epidemic and tried to cover it up, which increased the growth and exposure rate of the disease. Several media outlets have carried news reports uncovering the Chinese government's attempts to silence whistle-blowers, withholding crucial information and downplaying the threat posed by the new coronavirus, in effect permitting an epidemic that has killed thousands to take hold across the country.[53] While this was going on, the crisis could reach critical mass in Wuhan and spread across China and internationally before there was any serious response. As it turned out, this slow response fuelled the spread of the virus domestically in China, while at the same time encouraging the spread of the virus across the globe.

In developing the scenario further, the extremists could replicate the above strategy and go on to spread the virus randomly across the globe with other committed radical insurgents. These acts would be carried out in places and countries that have so far proved impenetrable to major extremist attacks, causing mass hysteria and confusion within many isolated societies. This would achieve their goal of disrupting normality and instilling a sense of fear in a society by encouraging a state of affairs where citizens refrain from carrying on with their lives as usual with high levels of personal autonomy and security. Moreover, radicals hellbent on their mission could infect themselves and knowingly infect others on a massive scale, on a modified suicide mission of sorts.

A more concerning factor in this scenario is that it could be achieved with relatively little funding, as only a small number of radical supporters could cover large distances. Also, extremist operations thrive in secrecy, so the fewer involved, the better for their mission.

Following is a description of possible outcomes, and examples, if the above scenario were carried out.

Economic insecurity: The International Labour Organization (ILO) recently warned of the repercussions of the economic fallout from coronavirus, claiming job losses of up to 25 million. In an initial assessment report on the impact of the coronavirus, the ILO said that "[t]he effects will be far-reaching, pushing millions of people into unemployment, underemployment and working poverty", and that measures for a decisive, coordinated and immediate response were required.[54]

Alarmingly, global economy losses as a result of the 2003 SARS outbreak, for example, run at an estimated $40 billion. As it stands, the number of cases related to the COVID-19 pandemic has already outpaced SARS, and it is predicted to wreak even more economic havoc than SARS.[55] Projections are that the current crisis will dwarf the global financial crisis of 2008.

A recent AU study found that about 20 million jobs may be at risk in Africa alone, as the continent's economies are projected to shrink in 2020 due to the impact of the COVID-19 pandemic.[56]

The Overseas Development Institute estimates that the economic costs for Africa of COVID-19 are likely to be $100 billion (or 5% of gross domestic product).[57] Most African countries have already been hit by collapsing trade and broken supply chains. Several African countries are highly dependent on exports to China, in particular Angola, South Africa and Congo, but also South Sudan, Namibia, Kenya and Rwanda.[58] It is anticipated that countries most impacted will be the resource-rich economies whose oil and other commodities are sold primarily to China. China accounts for about 95% of all of South Sudan's exports, for example, 61% of Angola's, and 58% of Eritrea's.[59] These countries are expected to be the most affected by the collapse in Chinese trade.

Political insecurity: Kenyan President Uhuru Kenyatta's perceived inept handling of the early stages of the COVID-19 crisis, ranging from insufficient preparation at the country's hospitals to the resumption of direct flights from China, resulted in the High Court's intervention to overrule the State House[60] and Kenyans venting their frustrations over the government's response to the virus. A likely outcome if Kenyatta fails to reverse this negative momentum is having to contend with a full-blown political crisis while simultaneously dealing with the pandemic.

The potential for more political confrontations across the African continent remains high. In several countries, opposition parties have been quick to score political points at clumsy government response measures. The opposition Peoples Democratic Party in Nigeria recently attacked President Muhammadu Buhari for neglecting to adequately address the nation's concerns regarding the pandemic, calling it an "absolute leadership failure".[61] Meanwhile, opposition parties in Gabon,[62] Mozambique,[63] South Africa[64] and Zambia[65] wanting to score political points have put forth their own propositions to curb the spread of the virus. In Ghana, the opposition National Democratic Congress advised Ghanaians to "wash your hands thoroughly with soap and running water as if you unexpectedly just touched an NPP T-shirt".[66] (The NPP, or New Patriotic Party, is the ruling party in Ghana.)

Democratic insecurity: Political leaders are usually insulated from major health scares by their wealth and access to private healthcare. However, the coronavirus has defied this logic. Several leaders from across the political spectrum, and from many countries, have become infected with the coronavirus. The first major world leader to contract the virus at the time of writing was Britain's Prime Minister Boris Johnson, who remains in intensive care due to the progression of his case. Britain has no formal succession plan should a prime minister become incapacitated.

On the continent, Burkina Faso's leadership structure has been the most affected, with four senior ministers testing positive for the coronavirus. Minister of Foreign Affairs Alpha Barry, Minister of Mines Oumarou Idani, Minister of Education Stanislas Ouaro, and Interior Minister Simeon Sawadogo have all confirmed their diagnoses.[67] Burkina Faso has experienced bouts of instability in recent years and is currently struggling against an insurgency.

In South Africa, an opposition party, the African Christian Democratic Party, confirmed that its leader, Reverend Kenneth Meshoe, and member of parliament Steve Swart, have tested positive for COVID-19.[68]

Democratic institutions in most developed nations are likely to be robust enough to cope with the short-term incapacity or isolation of their leaders. If necessary, many have tested succession mechanisms in place to select new cabinet members, prime ministers and presidents.

However, the reality may be very different in less-developed nations, where political institutions tend to be weaker and where the illness or death of a leader may lead to a kind of power vacuum that might inspire rival leaders, opposition parties or the military to see it as an opportunity to carry out a power grab. In countries where politics are more personalised, the death of a leader can trigger damaging succession battles which negatively impact on the ruling party and, in the worst cases, might encourage a military coup. Another concern is the rate at which the coronavirus spreads within the political elite in countries where many senior politicians are over 60 years of age, placing them at more risk.[69]

Several African states are scheduled to hold general elections in 2020, including Burkina Faso, Burundi, Côte d'Ivoire, Ethiopia, Guinea, Ghana, Malawi, Niger, Tanzania, the Seychelles, Sudan and Togo. As a result of the pandemic, it is still unknown how many of these elections will go ahead. Of concern is what potential delays might mean for leaders who are at risk of overstaying their welcome. How do opposition movements respond to this current state of affairs? In places such as Burundi, Ethiopia, Côte d'Ivoire and Malawi, where stability is precarious, how much greater will the risk of conflict become?[70]

Social insecurity: Some countries have resorted to hoarding food items to ensure continued supplies for their population as the virus crisis deepens. However, these extreme measures may prove more harmful for poorer developing nations that survive on food imports. This, coupled with shoppers resorting to panic buying and food hoarding, has left food retailers with aisles of empty shelves. The scarcity is more a result of logistical hurdles created by measures to contain the pandemic. "Since most poor countries, many of them in sub-Saharan Africa, are net food importers, sudden price hikes will almost inevitably raise poverty and hunger, because these countries have very limited capacities to respond to shortages and price rises."[71] In some instances, these measures may result in food riots, as was seen in Mozambique a few years ago.[72]

Experts have cautioned about restrictions on the export of wheat and wheat flour as this may cause the price of essential items such as bread to increase, proving lethal for many of the poorer countries in Africa that rely on imported food. Several African countries have fallen victim to high bread prices, which have sparked riots and caused political instability.[73]

Illegal economic gains: Any extremist organisation that controls the speed, locale and effect of the virus could influence the markets in its favour. If any extremist organisation were responsible for releasing the coronavirus, it would have stood to benefit financially from failing economies. This strategy would provide a good source of income for an extremist organisation.

Recent examples of non-radicalised people being arrested for intentionally trying to spread the coronavirus are not only a real concern, but also show that the above scenario may not be as improbable as one might imagine:
- German police arrested a man in Munich after he shared videos online in which he could be seen licking subway ticket machines and handrails, as well

as the handrail of an escalator. He claimed that he wanted to spread the coronavirus.[74]
- A train passenger in Belgium was arrested after he was filmed licking his fingers and wiping them on a vertical handrail. In the video, the man pulled down a face mask he was wearing and then appeared to put his fingers in his mouth and lick them before rubbing them on the handrail.[75]
- A Norwegian man, who resisted arrest for disorderly conduct, spat in the faces of police and threatened that he was infected with the coronavirus. He was convicted and sentenced to 75 days in jail for assaulting police officers, making threats and spreading fear.[76]
- In South Africa, a man who tested positive for COVID-19 and continued running his salon business instead of going into quarantine was charged with attempted murder.[77]
- Finally, in a more frightening example, a video shows a man infected with the coronavirus spitting in the face of another traveller at a Bangkok train station before boarding a train to the southern city of Narathiwat and dying. Authorities conducted tests on his body and claim that the man tested positive for the virus.[78]

In an attempt to curb such acts, US Justice Department Deputy Attorney-General Jeffrey Rosen declared that anyone who intentionally spreads the coronavirus might face criminal charges under the country's terrorism laws. In a memo to top Justice Department leaders, law enforcement agency chiefs and US attorneys across the country, Rosen stated that prosecutors and investigators could come across cases of "purposeful exposure and infection of others with COVID-19…Because coronavirus appears to meet the statutory definition of a 'biological agent'…such acts potentially could implicate the nation's terrorism-related statutes…Threats or attempts to use COVID-19 as a weapon against Americans will not be tolerated."[79] This measure reinforces the potential security threat posed by the COVID-19 pandemic.

An interesting development brought about by the COVID-19 pandemic has seen ISIS issue a directive to its supporters calling for them to stay away from Europe – the epicentre of the pandemic. ISIS also included a full-page infographic on coronavirus prevention in an issue of the group's official weekly *al-Naba* newsletter.[80] From its newsletters, it is evident that ISIS had paid keen attention to the outbreak from early in 2020, with the inclusion of regular updates in the news-briefs section of the newsletter. In January 2020, *al-Naba* stated that "[a] new virus spreads death and terror in China", adding that "communist China is panicking after a new virus has spread" and acknowledging the levels of concern of Chinese officials when discussing the discovery of person-to-person transmission as well as the lockdown of Wuhan. *Al-Naba* further stressed a "growing concern about the spread of the infectious virus", adding that "this could push the World Health Organization into an emergency".[81]

Similarly, ISIS-supporting Quraysh Media also focused on the outbreak by producing and disseminating a poster with a grainy image of a person in a hazmat suit and respirator. "China: coronavirus", the poster stated, adding: "A promise is a debt we must not forget."[82]

In a remarkable turn of events, as the outbreak continued its unabated spread, and perhaps aware that the global reach of the pandemic could also pose a threat to its members or supporters, ISIS criticised the Chinese government for hiding the scope of the coronavirus outbreak.[83]

In February 2020, *al-Naba* published a report on ISIS, noting that while "many Muslims rushed to confirm that this epidemic is a punishment from God Almighty" as a result of China's widescale abuse of the Uyghur population, "the world is interconnected" and transportation "would facilitate the transfer of diseases and epidemics". It warned Muslims to "seek help from God Almighty to avoid illness and keep it away from their countries".[84] This approach can be seen as a securitising move by ISIS in addressing the pandemic.

Conclusion

This chapter has demonstrated that the question of whether the COVID-19 pandemic can be considered a threat will depend on how the disease is framed. Speech act theory demonstrates that COVID-19 can be constructed by securitising actors as a threat through a specific use of language. Also, shifting the pandemic from being a health issue to a security issue creates the need to reframe policies to address the urgency of the threat.

The chapter highlighted the fact that security-studies scholars have identified the need for the concept of security to be expanded beyond the traditional approach, thereby allowing the inclusion of non-traditional security threats into the security debate – in this case, COVID-19. The human security approach has been instrumental in placing the COVID-19 threat onto the agenda of security actors.

However, one may question whether this implies that a large global audience was convinced about the urgency of the threat posed by the pandemic. For instance, when comparing it to other security threats such as international terrorism, the insidious nature of COVID-19 has concealed the actual magnitude and emergency of the security threat. This feature of the securitisation of the COVID-19 pandemic may challenge previous understandings about the determinants of successful securitisation claims.

The scenario presented may indeed make the link between a virus pandemic and bioterrorism sound somewhat far-fetched. Maybe so. But consider this option: if the spread of the coronavirus was indeed at the hands of a terrorist organisation, it would be able to claim the title of the most effective act of non-state terrorism by far in the history of humankind.

There is currently no empirical evidence of any extremist group's direct involvement in global pandemics. However, based on the developed scenario, it is not a far stretch to assume that extremist organisations may see unleashing a pandemic as an opportunity to threaten its adversaries.

However, for the time being, the actual threat of bioterrorism is possibly more psychological than real. "Moreover, unlike conventional 'kinetic' attacks, the consequences of bioterrorism can be substantially reduced by prompt decontamination and treatment."[85] What is required during this time of heightened instability is for security and intelligence services to continue monitoring potential threats, since a weakened state remains an attractive target. We all know and accept that nothing spreads faster than fear.

Select Bibliography

Acheson, I. (2020). Coronavirus and the threat of bio-terrorism. 12 March. Available from: https://capx.co/coronavirus-and-the-threat-of-bio-terrorism/ [accessed 6 April 2020].

African News Agency (ANA). (2020). Coronavirus: Renamo calls for SA-Mozambique border closure. *The South African*, 10 March. Available from: https://www.thesouthafrican.com/news/coronavirus-renamo-calls-for-sa-mozabique-border-closure/ [accessed 31 March 2020].

African Union. (2020a). Press Briefing on the Coronavirus Disease Outbreak. 28 January. Available from: https://au.int/en/videos/20200128/press-briefing-coronavirus-disease-outbreak [accessed 5 April 2020].

African Union. (2020b). Communiqué of the Bureau of the Assembly of the African Union Heads of State and Government Teleconference on COVID-19, Held on 26 March 2020. Available from: https://au.int/en/pressreleases/20200326/communique-bureau-assembly-african-union-heads-state-and-government [accessed 7 April 2020].

Agence France-Presse (AFP) & Tato, L. (2020). Kenya president sorry for coronavirus cop violence. *eNCA*, 1 April. Available from: https://www.enca.com/news/kenya-president-sorry-coronavirus-cop-violence [accessed 5 April 2020].

Alechenu, J. & Nwogu, S. (2020). PDP, APC exchange words over Coronavirus case. *Punch*, 2 March. Available from: https://punchng.com/pdp-apc-exchange-words-over-corona-virus-case/ [accessed 31 March 2020].

Allison, S. (2020). The Covid-19 pandemic is a wildcard that will change politics as we know it. *Mail & Guardian*, 25 March. Available from: https://mg.co.za/article/2020-03-25-the-covid-19-pandemic-is-a-wildcard-that-will-change-politics-as-we-know-it/ [accessed 7 April 2020].

Associated Press. (2020). Proposed UN resolution calls COVID-19 a threat to peace. *Business Standard*, 2 April. Available from: https://www.business-standard.com/article/pti-stories/proposed-un-resolution-calls-covid-19-a-threat-to-peace-120040200310_1.html [accessed 5 April 2020].

BBC. (2020). Cameroon rebels declare coronavirus ceasefire. 26 March. Available from: https://www.bbc.com/news/world-africa-52053738 [accessed 5 April 2020].

Bill & Melinda Gates Foundation. (2020). *Bill & Melinda Gates Foundation Dedicates Additional Funding to the Novel Coronavirus Response*. 5 February. Available from: https://www.gatesfoundation.org/Media-Center/Press-Releases/2020/02/Bill-and-Melinda-Gates-Foundation-Dedicates-Additional-Funding-to-the-Novel-Coronavirus-Response [accessed 8 April 2020].

Buzan, B., Waever, O. & Wilde, J. (1998). *Security: A New Framework for Analysis*. London: Lynne Rienner Publishers.

Chef, R. (2020). Gabon / Coronavirus: Le coup de pub raté de Ping. *Infos Gabon*, 14 March. Available from: https://fr.infosgabon.com/coronavirus-le-coup-de-pub-rate-de-ping/ [accessed 31 March 2020].

Cowie, S. (2020). Deny and defy: Bolsonaro's approach to the coronavirus in Brazil. *Al Jazeera*, 30 March. Available from: https://www.aljazeera.com/indepth/features/deny-defy-bolsonaro-approach-coronavirus-brazil-200330181645501.html [accessed 4 April 2020].

Deutsche Welle. (2020). German man licks ticket machine 'to spread coronavirus'. 23 March. Available from: https://www.dw.com/en/german-man-licks-ticket-machine-to-spread-coronavirus/a-52887069 [accessed 6 April 2020].

Elbe, S. (2006). Should HIV/AIDS be Securitized? The Ethical Dilemma of Linking HIV/AIDS to Security. *International Studies Quarterly*, 50(1), pp. 119-144.

Faull, A. (2020). State abuses could match the threat of COVID-19 itself. Institute for

Security Studies, 2 April. Available from: https://issafrica.org/iss-today/state-abuses-could-match-the-threat-of-covid-19-itself [accessed 5 April 2020].

Gerstein, J. (2020). Those who intentionally spread coronavirus could be charged as terrorists in US. *Politico,* 25 March. Available from: https://www.politico.eu/article/those-who-intentionally-spread-coronavirus-could-be-charged-as-terrorists-in-us/ [accessed 6 April 2020].

Gündüz, Z. (2006). The HIV/AIDS epidemic – What's security got to do with it? Available from: http://sam.gov.tr/wp-content/uploads/2012/02/ZuhalYesilyurtGunduz.pdf [accessed 8 April 2020].

Hayward, A. (2005). Emancipation in the Critical Security Studies Project. In Booth, K. (ed.). *Critical Security Studies and World Politics.* Boulder, Colorado: Lynne Rienner Publishers.

Hernández, J.C. (2020). China Spins Coronavirus Crisis, Hailing Itself as a Global Leader. *The New York Times,* 28 February. Available from: https://www.nytimes.com/2020/02/28/world/asia/china-coronavirus-response-propaganda.html [accessed 31 March 2020].

Johns Hopkins University School of Medicine. (2020). *Coronavirus Resource Centre.* Available from: https://coronavirus.jhu.edu/map.html [accessed 8 April 2020].

Johnson, B. (2020a). ISIS Coronavirus Directives: Do 'Not Enter the Land of the Epidemic,' Cover Your Sneezes. *Homeland Security Today,* 13 March. Available from: https://www.hstoday.us/subject-matter-areas/counterterrorism/isis-coronavirus-directives-do-not-enter-the-land-of-the-epidemic-cover-your-sneezes/ [accessed 1 April 2020].

Johnson, B. (2020b). ISIS Tells Followers to Pray to Avoid Coronavirus, Slams China Over Outbreak Response. *Homeland Security Today,* 10 February. Available from: https://www.hstoday.us/subject-matter-areas/counterterrorism/isis-tells-followers-to-pray-to-avoid-coronavirus-slams-china-over-outbreak-response/ [accessed 1 April 2020].

Kenny, P. (2020). UN body warns of up to 25M job losses due to COVID-19. Available from: https://www.aa.com.tr/en/economy/un-body-warns-of-up-to-25m-job-losses-due-to-covid-19/1771040 [accessed 31 March 2020].

Lam, T.T., Shum, M.H., Zhu, H., Tong, Y., Ni, X., Liao, Y., Wei, W., Cheung, W.Y., Li, W., Li, L., Leung, G.M., Holmes, E.C., Hu, Y. & Guan, Y. (2020). Identifying SARS-CoV-2 related coronaviruses in Malayan pangolins. *Nature.* Available from: https://www.nature.com/articles/s41586-020-2169-0 [accessed 8 April 2020].

LePan, N. (2020). *Visualizing the History of Pandemics.* Available from: https://www.visualcapitalist.com/history-of-pandemics-deadliest/ [accessed 31 March 2020].

Madia, T. (2020). Coronavirus in SA: ACDP's Kenneth Meshoe and Steve Swart test positive. *News24,* 27 March. Available from: https://www.news24.com/SouthAfrica/News/coronavirus-in-sa-acdps-kenneth-meshoe-and-steve-swart-test-positive-20200327 [accessed 7 April 2020].

McInnes, C. & Rushton, S. (2010). *HIV, AIDS and Securitisation.* Paper for 2010 International Studies Association Annual Conference. New Orleans.

Means, G. (2020). *The coronavirus: Blueprint for bioterrorism.* 9 March. Available from: https://thehill.com/opinion/national-security/485921-the-coronavirus-blueprint-for-bioterrorism [accessed 6 March 2020].

Moffat, C.V. (2014). Securitisation of HIV and AIDS in Southern African policy processes: An investigation of Botswana, South Africa and Swaziland, 2000-2008. Doctoral dissertation. Stellenbosch: Stellenbosch University.

Mothata, W. (2020). South Africans call for travel bans due to coronavirus increases. *SABC News,* 15 March. Available from: https://www.sabcnews.com/sabcnews/south-africa-calls-for-travel-bans-due-to-coronavirus-increases/ [accessed 1 April 2020].

News in English. (2020). Latest Corona-related news in brief. 9 April. Available from: https://www.newsinenglish.no/2020/04/06/updates-here-as-corona-rages-on/ [accessed 6 April 2020].

Ng, K. (2020). Coronavirus: Man arrested after licking his fingers and wiping them on pole in train. *Independent,* 11 March. Available from: https://www.independent.co.uk/news/world/europe/belgium-subway-train-passenger-lick-fingers-pole-coronavirus-a9394876.html [accessed 6 April 2020].

Palder, D. & Mackinnon, A. (2020). Coronavirus in the Corridors of Power: Which politicians and senior officials have the coronavirus? *Foreign Policy,* 18 March. Available from: https://foreignpolicy.com/2020/03/18/coronavirus-corridors-power-which-world-leaders-have-covid-19/ [accessed 7 April 2020].

Pandey, A. (2020). Will coronavirus spark a wave of food nationalism? *Deutsche Welle,* 30 March. Available from: https://www.dw.com/en/will-coronavirus-spark-a-wave-of-food-nationalism/a-52952081 [accessed 1 April 2020].

Pangestika, D. (2020). 'We don't want people to panic': Jokowi says on lack of transparency about COVID cases. *The Jakarta Post,* 14 March. Available from: https://www.thejakartapost.com/news/2020/03/13/we-dont-want-people-to-panic-jokowi-says-on-lack-of-transparency-about-covid-cases.html [accessed 5 April 2020].

Peralta, E. (2020). Kenya Criticized for Letting China Flights Land Amid Coronavirus Scare. *NPR,* 3 March. Available from: https://www.npr.org/2020/03/03/811504574/kenya-criticized-for-letting-china-flights-land-amid-coronavirus-scare [accessed 6 April 2020].

Phiri, R. (2020). HH calls for measures to protect Zambians from Coronavirus. *The Mast,* 29 February. Available from: https://www.themastonline.com/2020/02/29/hh-calls-for-measures-to-protect-zambians-from-coronavirus/ [accessed 1 April 2020].

Pulse Ghana. (2020). Wash your hands thoroughly like you just touched NPP T-shirt – NDC advises Ghanaians on coronavirus. 14 March. Available from: https://www.pulse.com.gh/news/local/wash-your-hands-thoroughly-like-you-just-touched-npp-t-shirt-ndc-advises-ghanaians-on/3lw0d58 [accessed 1 April 2020].

Ramaphosa, C. (2020). *Message by President Cyril Ramaphosa on COVID-19 pandemic.* 30 March. Available from: http://www.thepresidency.gov.za/speeches/message-president-cyril-ramaphosa-covid-19-pandemic [accessed 4 April 2020].

Rasheed, Z. (2020). COVID-19 pandemic is testing world leaders. Who's stepping up? *Al Jazeera,* 3 April. Available from: https://www.aljazeera.com/news/2020/04/covid-19-pandemic-testing-world-leaders-stepping-200402201221844.html [accessed 5 April 2020].

Reuters. (2020a). Mexico president defends meeting mother of 'El Chapo'. *Al Jazeera,* 31

March. Available from: https://www.aljazeera.com/news/2020/03/mexico-president-defends-meeting-mother-el-chapo-200330203205037.html [accessed 5 April 2020].

Reuters. (2020b). Africa could lose 20 million jobs due to pandemic. *SABC News*, 6 April. Available from: https://www.sabcnews.com/sabcnews/africa-could-lose-20-million-jobs-due-to-pandemic/ [accessed 6 April 2020].

Rushton, S. (2007). *The Development of HIV/AIDS and Security Discourse: The Role of CSOs*. Case study for the Peter Wall Institute's London Workshop on Civil Society Organisations and Global Health Governance, October 2007.

Sandford, A. (2020). Coronavirus: Half of humanity now on lockdown as 90 countries call for confinement. *Euronews*, 3 April. Available from: https://www.euronews.com/2020/04/02/coronavirus-in-europe-spain-s-death-toll-hits-10-000-after-record-950-new-deaths-in-24-hou [accessed 5 April 2020].

Signé, L. & Gurib-Fakim, A. (2020). Africa is Bracing for a Head-On Collision with Coronavirus. *Foreign Policy*, 26 March. Available from: https://foreignpolicy.com/2020/03/26/africa-coronavirus-pandemic-economic-crisis/ [accessed 7 April 2020].

Singh, K. (2020). KZN man charged with attempted murder for exposing others to Covid-19. *News24*, 25 March. Available from: https://www.news24.com/SouthAfrica/News/kzn-man-charged-with-attempted-murder-for-exposing-others-to-covid-19-20200325 [accessed 7 April 2020].

Smith, D. (2010). UN to hold crisis talks on food prices as riots hit Mozambique. *The Guardian*, 3 September. Available from: https://www.theguardian.com/world/2010/sep/03/un-mozambique-food-prices [accessed 6 April 2020].

Smith, S. (2020). *What the Coronavirus Means for Africa*. Africa Center for Strategic Studies, 4 February. Available from: https://africacenter.org/spotlight/what-the-coronavirus-means-for-africa/ [accessed 6 April 2020].

Southern African Development Community (SADC). (2020). Extra-Ordinary Meeting of SADC Ministers of Health on Covid-19. 9 March. Available from: https://www.sadc.int/news-events/news/extra-ordinary-meeting-sadc-ministers-health-covid-19/ [accessed 5 April 2020].

Ssebwami, J. (2020). COVID-19 CRISIS: Museveni warns politicians distributing relief to communities will be charged with murder, says govt will distribute food to the vulnerable amid total lockdown. *PML Daily*, 30 March. Available from: https://www.pmldaily.com/news/2020/03/covid-19-crisis-govt-to-distribute-food-relief-items-amid-total-lockdown.html [accessed 4 April 2020].

Stepansky, J. (2020). Experts say Trump is wrong to compare coronavirus with flu. *Al Jazeera*, 9 March. Available from: https://www.aljazeera.com/news/2020/03/experts-trump-wrong-compare-coronavirus-flu-200309145951552.html [accessed 1 April 2020].

Taureck, R. (2006). Securitization Theory and Securitisation Studies. *Journal of International Relations and Development*, 9, pp. 53-61.

Te Velde, D.W. (2020). *A $100 billion stimulus to address the fall out from the coronavirus in Africa. Supporting Economic Transformation*, 20 March. Available from: https://set.odi.org/wp-content/uploads/2020/03/A-100-billion-stimulus-to-address-the-fallout-from-the-coronavirus-in-Africa.pdf [accessed 7 April 2020].

The Chronicle. (2020). Man spits in stranger's face then dies. 3 April. Available from: https://www.thechronicle.com.au/news/man-spits-in-strangers-face-then-dies/3988397/ [accessed 6 April 2020].

United Nations News & Dickinson, D. (2020). *COVID-19: UN chief calls for global ceasefire to focus on 'the true fight of our lives'.* 23 March. Available from: https://news.un.org/en/story/2020/03/1059972 [accessed 5 April 2020].

Waever, O. (1995). Securitisation and Desecuritisation. In Lipschutz, R.D. (ed.). (1995). *On Security.* New York: Columbia University Press.

World Health Organization. (2020a). *Zoonoses.* Available from: https://www.who.int/topics/zoonoses/en/ [accessed 8 April 2020].

World Health Organization. (2020b). *Naming the coronavirus disease (COVID-19) and the virus that causes it.* Available from: https://www.who.int/emergencies/diseases/novel-coronavirus-2019/technical-guidance/naming-the-coronavirus-disease-(covid-2019)-and-the-virus-that-causes-it [accessed 15 March 2020].

World Health Organization. (2020c). *The Democratic Republic of the Congo's last Ebola patient discharged.* Available from: https://www.afro.who.int/news/democratic-republic-congos-last-ebola-patient-discharged [accessed 5 April 2020].

Endnotes

1. As of 17 April 2020, there were over 2,159,267 coronavirus cases, according to Johns Hopkins University School of Medicine (2020).
2. A zoonotic disease is an infectious disease caused by bacteria, viruses or parasites that spread from non-human animals (usually vertebrates) to humans (World Health Organization, 2020a).
3. Lam et al, 2020.
4. World Health Organization, 2020b.
5. Moffat, 2014:12.
6. The human security agenda has been primarily associated with 'middle power' countries such as Canada, Australia and Norway. In 1999, a group of states with human security policies launched the Human Security Network. It is currently formed by Austria, Canada, Chile, Costa Rica, Greece, Ireland, Japan, Jordan, Mali, the Netherlands, Norway, Slovenia, South Africa, Switzerland and Thailand. For more on this, see www.humansecuritynetwork.org.
7. LePan, 2020.
8. Ibid.
9. Hayward, 2005.
10. Buzan et al, 1998:21.
11. The securitising actor is the one who puts forward a claim to securitise an issue.
12. Ramaphosa, 2020.
13. Ssebwami, 2020.
14. Buzan et al, 1998:23.
15. Buzan et al, 1998:26; Elbe, 2006:124.
16. Buzan et al, 1998:31.
17. Elbe, 2006:124.
18. Buzan et al, 1998:41.
19. Associated Press, 2020.
20. At the time of finalising this chapter, the UN General Assembly had not met to decide whether to adopt a resolution on COVID-19.
21. Smith, 2020.
22. Bill & Melinda Gates Foundation, 2020.
23. The last Ebola patient in the Democratic Republic of Congo was discharged on 3 March 2020 from a treatment centre in the north-eastern town of Beni. With no more confirmed cases, a 42-day countdown to declaring the end of the world's second-deadliest Ebola epidemic began on 2 March. (World Health Organization, 2020c)
24. Germany has since led the way in Europe with large-scale testing for COVID-19, collecting nearly 1 million samples since the start of the crisis. Also, although the country now ranks fifth among territories with confirmed cases – recording more than 80,000 infections – it has a much lower fatality rate than most. (Note that these numbers were accurate on 3 April 2020.)
25. Rasheed, 2020.
26. Stepansky, 2020.
27. Several tweets by President Trump during March 2020 highlight these instances.
28. Cowie, 2020.
29. Reuters, 2020a.
30. Pangestika, 2020.
31. African Union, 2020a.
32. The Bureau of the African Union Heads of State and Government is chaired by President Ramaphosa and consists of: President Ibrahim Boubacar Keïta of Mali, President Uhuru Muigai Kenyatta of Kenya, President Félix Tshisekedi of the Democratic Republic of Congo, and President Abdel Fattah el-Sisi of the Arab Republic of Egypt. The chairperson of the AU Commission, Mr Moussa Faki Mahamat, and the Director of the Africa CDC, Dr John Nkengasong, also participated in the teleconference.
33. African Union, 2020b.
34. SADC, 2020.
35. Buzan et al, 1998:25.
36. Ibid, 32.
37. McInnes & Rushton, 2010:17.
38. Waever, 1995:55.
39. Buzan et al, 1998:36-37.
40. McInnes & Rushton, 2010:5.
41. Buzan et al, 1998:31.
42. McInnes & Rushton, 2010:5.
43. United Nations News & Dickinson, 2020.
44. Sandford, 2020.
45. BBC, 2020.
46. At the time of finalising this chapter, there has been no indication whether one of the biggest rebel groups, Ambazonia Defence Forces, will follow suit and declare a ceasefire.
47. Buzan et al, 1998:24.
48. Waever, 1995:63.

49 Gündüz, 2006:57.
50 Faull, 2020.
51 AFP & Tato, 2020.
52 Means, 2020.
53 Hernández, 2020.
54 Kenny, 2020.
55 Smith, 2020.
56 Reuters, 2020b.
57 Te Velde, 2020.
58 Signé & Gurib-Fakim, 2020.
59 Ibid.
60 Peralta, 2020.
61 Alechenu & Nwogu, 2020.
62 Chef, 2020.
63 ANA, 2020.
64 Mothata, 2020.
65 Phiri, 2020.
66 Pulse Ghana, 2020.
67 Palder & Mackinnon, 2020.
68 Madia, 2020.
69 Ibid.
70 Allison, 2020.
71 Pandey, 2020.
72 Smith, 2010.
73 Pandey, 2020.
74 Deutsche Welle, 2020.
75 Ng, 2020.
76 News in English, 2020.
77 Singh, 2020.
78 The Chronicle, 2020.
79 Gerstein, 2020.
80 Johnson, 2020a.
81 Ibid.
82 Ibid.
83 Johnson, 2020b.
84 Ibid.
85 Acheson, 2020.

CHAPTER 2

The Militarisation of Conservation in Africa

Ashwell Glasson

Introduction

Our perspectives of African conservation are likely unrealistic and naïve. Protected areas in Africa are heavily contested spaces, whether viewed through physical, social or economic lenses, and this means that many competing needs are jostling for primacy in how these spaces are managed and used.

Much of protected-area conservation in Africa takes place in regions experiencing violent extremism, failed states, porous national borders, human population growth and uneven economic development. Generally, as one moves from southern Africa further northwards, conservation and protected areas have become more tenuous, violence-prone and challenging to manage. North-east African protected areas have a robust culture of law enforcement and community-based approaches to protected-area management.[1] However, the recent regional conflict in the Horn of Africa may have placed pressure on the protected areas in the north-eastern part of Kenya due to displaced persons, refugees, and incursions by insurgent groups and violent extremists. Conservation agencies and their staff in many of these regions have become deterrents against insurgencies and violent extremism, and the parks have become havens for both the displaced as well as violent extremist groups and criminal enterprises. Sadly, one may be a refugee on one day and a poacher the next in order to survive and support one's family. The distinction between poaching for profit and survival remains an unresolved issue for scholars and practitioners on all sides of the debate.

The field of conservation in Africa is a complex nexus of social, political, security and ecological issues that violently collide every day.[2] Geographically, the scale, size and biological diversity of Africa's conservation areas dwarf those of Europe and North America. In many cases, the parks exceed the geographical size of many European countries. Most national parks and protected areas have disproportionately small teams of field rangers and other staff who manage them, when compared to many state law-enforcement agencies in the northern hemisphere.

Conservation and militarisation have become highly contested domains, with scholars and practitioners disputing various strategies and potential solutions for how best to conserve as well as sustainably use natural resources to the benefit of both wildlife (plants, animals and the foundational ecosystems) and all humanity. The latter point emphasises that local communities too – not only privileged tourists, landowners and others with means – should benefit from conservation.

Well-known scholars such as Rosaleen Duffy have raised concerns about the recent 'green militarisation' of conservation, and the language of war used to save species from extinction. Green militarisation is a process by which military approaches and values are increasingly embedded in conservation practice.[3] Green militarisation is not only limited to state conservation agencies, and in many cases has enabled a plethora of other actors – such as conservation non-governmental organisations (NGOs) and private protected-area landowners – to militarise their conservation operations. This has further helped them to rapidly raise funds from various local and international donor organisations to support their day-to-day operations.

Today, green militarisation has become the standard for most parks and conservation agencies across the continent, with varying levels of success. Duffy, however, also adds that it is important that green militarisation does not marginalise vulnerable communities. Instead, local communities should be supported to play a meaningful role in conservation.[4]

Colonial History of Militarisation in Africa
National parks, reserves and forest regions generally became the preserve of colonial settlers.[5] These protected areas were policed and rapidly militarised by colonial administrations, who started to derive an income from selling hunting permits and licences.

Many colonial administrations began to limit the hunting rights of local communities and to establish hunting quotas as well as 'protected areas'. Local communities were virtually excluded from hunting.[6] This strategy became one of the driving reasons to militarise parks: to prevent local communities from hunting and other forms of harvesting. Conservation and colonial administrative authorities were thus directly limiting the rights of local communities to sustainable livelihoods. A review of Verweijen and Marijnen supports this continued exclusion and criminalisation of communities in the Virunga Lakes National Park in the Democratic Republic of Congo (DRC).[7]

Historically, violence and conservation in Africa have gone hand in hand for much of the modern era. During the colonial period, widespread hunting for elephant ivory and other wildlife products was driven primarily by European colonials and, to a certain extent, by Arab and Indian traders.[8] In west, central and east Africa, various local and regional polities were co-opted into the elephant ivory trade, as well as the catastrophic slave trade, which was the fuel that powered the economies of Europe.

The introduction of firearms and gunpowder in the 18th century to west and central Africa hastened the exploitation of elephants, enhancing the indigenous hunting methods of pit-traps, poisoned arrows and other traditional weapons.[9] A by-product of the introduction of firearms to African polities was an enhanced capability to conduct war on a scale previously unthought of against opposing tribes or groups that were blocking access to resources. Firearms brought an uneven advantage to those who possessed them, and this further exacerbated multi-communal conflict and the potential for further conflict, as firearm-owning groups could monopolise the trade routes used to transport wildlife commodities.

As the colonial rush entrenched itself, the European powers competed with one another while suppressing local populations. According to South African History Online,[10] the Berlin conference of 1884 led to an agreement on how best to carve up Africa between the colonial powers. This conference was likely one of the most significant international relations coups ever, the legacy of which continues to have an impact on Africa and its people. The colonial powers were empowered by collective agreement to exploit the continent even further, and the rapid exploitation of ivory and wildlife commodities mushroomed, with wildlife populations crashing rapidly in the 1880s.

Each colonial culture brought its own particular military identity, legal frameworks and national culture. Territorial expansion, state hegemony and the rush for commodities led to the establishment of garrisons, forts and other paramilitary facilities, as well as militarised trading posts that could be defended against other colonial powers and indigenous peoples. These forces could also be used against intractable tribes and to suppress local insurgencies.

The South African experience of apartheid and conservation further entrenched the racial exclusion of black, Indian and coloured communities and individuals from national and provincial parks. Of course, this exclusionary practice excluded black workers who worked in the parks. In South Africa, it was only in the 1980s that protected areas became accessible to 'non-white groups', albeit in a limited fashion via protected areas established by homeland states such as Bophuthatswana, Kangwane, Transkei and Ciskei. For many communities in South Africa, protected areas remained the domain of the 'white man' for 'whiteman holidays'.

In central, east and west Africa, more success was achieved in enabling local communities to access national parks and protected areas to use wildlife for development and conservation purposes.[11] There was a significant shift in approach from the pre-1990s 'fortress conservation' models to community-based natural resource management and participatory techniques. In the late 2000s, however, policy began to swing back towards 'fortress conservation' or militarised models.[12]

Key Pillars of the Militarised Model

The primary model of militarisation that most African conservation organisations and parks have adopted relies on a four-tiered approach, namely boots on the ground, canine support, aerial capabilities and community engagement.[13]

'Boots on the ground' represents the sharp end of the anti-poaching strategy, and focuses on the deployment of highly trained field rangers and specialist anti-poaching operatives. These men and women generally attend formal basic field-ranger training programmes that are usually not shorter than seven weeks and include subjects such as conservation ethics, arrest procedures, firearms training (self-loading and bolt-action weapons), survival, bush-craft, basic combat tactics, patrolling, integrated aerial and ground support operations, radio use, tactical and community intelligence gathering, navigation, combat and animal tracking, and dangerous game animal awareness.[14] Additional skills in wildland first-aid and firefighting round off the skills set of professional field rangers. Many African states, including Zambia, South Africa, Tanzania, Botswana and Namibia, as well as conservation NGOs, operate field-ranger training facilities and programmes at various parks and bases.

The training approach is instructor-driven and paramilitary, focusing on discipline, military drills, teamwork, leadership and physical fitness as critical for selection, as well as an ongoing requirement. Field-ranger teams are generally trained to operate in groups of two to four, with a corporal or sergeant leading the patrol. Many patrols last between 10 and 14 days, with sporadic radio contact with headquarters or regional officials. Unlike pure military training, most rangers are not trained to use hand-held explosives and other incendiary devices. Specialists include rotary and fixed-wing pilots who conduct aerial patrols for carcass detection, poacher suppression, and ranger and canine deployment.

With rapid advances in technology, many rangers now collect information on poaching incidents, tracking and other biological information on live spatio-temporal reporting applications on mobile phones and tablets. These link to information networks, where rapid responses as well as trend data are available at a receiving control centre for analysis and action. Well-known spatial reporting systems such as C-More, Earth Ranger and SMART are deployed in conjunction with intelligence analysis tools to develop poaching hotspot heat maps, geographic information system maps, trend analyses and more. This has meant that many field rangers, particularly in southern and eastern Africa, have needed to upgrade their personal computer and technology skills. In more remote parks in central and western Africa, data collection is still conducted, but it is more reliant on returning to the park offices to upload the datasets. Improvements in radio technology, microwave transmitters and solar-power solutions enable the deployment of transmitters and communication hubs throughout many parks. Internet bandwidth and network data availability are costly enablers for conservation operations in African parks.

In southern and eastern Africa, as field rangers and anti-poaching operatives build experience, a range of specialised training has become available to ensure that they maintain their skills as well as develop new capabilities to enhance their performance. Many organisations offer specialised programmes for patrol leaders, advanced combat and tactics, dog-handler programmes, advanced life support and first aid, and leadership development for promotion and enhanced problem-solving purposes. Unfortunately, countries such as the DRC and Zimbabwe, which lack the budgetary resources for rangers, have curtailed training and development. Organisations such as African Parks, the Peace Parks Foundation and the Wildlife Conservation Society have stepped into the breach and now include field-ranger training in their activities.

Along with the latest technology has been the return of older methods and techniques, specifically canine assets. Very few parks and conservation areas in Africa now operate without anti-poaching and human-tracking canine teams. With the advances made in animal health, dogs can now successfully work in regions with a high risk of disease. Dogs are trained to detect humans, ivory, rhino horn, pangolin and other wildlife products. In many cases, unlike traditional law-enforcement dog training, dogs are trained to operate off the leash and will pursue poachers in a free-running pack of four or five dogs.[15] A handler operating from a vehicle or helicopter tracks the dogs through live global positioning system (GPS) telemetry. The dogs are also trained to work with a variety of handlers and are not limited to one individual. The recent decline in poaching in the Kruger National Park in South Africa has been attributed to several factors, including the additional deployment of dogs – although, sadly, there is also the likelihood that there are fewer rhinos to poach.

The strength of canines lies not only in their ability to detect poachers but also the speed at which they are able to apprehend poachers. Dogs can swiftly outpace their handlers and fleeing poachers, covering distances that a human would struggle to sustain. Ike Phaahla, the communications and marketing manager at the Kruger National Park, states: "Over 90% of the arrests that have been effected thus far in the Kruger National Park since 2011 have been through the assistance of the canine unit."[16] Figures for canine-assisted arrests for other regions in Africa are challenging to obtain at this time.

Light aircraft, both fixed and rotary wing, are increasingly used for conservation. Helicopters used for game counts, animal census and translocation purposes are now being repurposed for anti-poaching patrols and carcass detection. Helicopters provide rapid-response support to ground teams pursuing poachers, they deploy canine assets on standby, and they are also used for evacuating injured rangers and poachers. Light aircraft have become the aircraft of choice because they can hover over carcasses and poachers, are cheaper to run and, in many cases, have been adapted to operate in harsh African conditions – for example, they can operate off short dirt airstrips, which are the norm for many parks in Africa. Many parks in western, central and eastern Africa have upgraded their airfields and built hangar facilities, as light aircraft can cover thousands of kilometres on aerial patrol.

In many instances, light aircraft offer a cheaper option for the larger parks. Meanwhile, other aerial capabilities have arisen from military and civilian drone use. Since most military-grade drones require extensive support and are generally focused on fighting capabilities, those that are focused on intelligence, reconnaissance and surveillance are more applicable to conservation, particularly if they can integrate with park control centres and other sensor technologies. The difference between quality military-grade and civilian drones varies immensely, especially in terms of flight endurance and ability to remain on the station, as well as the quality of their optics. Military-grade drones that use thermal imaging in desert warfare may struggle in a wildlife-rich jungle environment, where a thick canopy and varying levels of heat and humidity are the norm. Differentiating between human beings and other mammals may also be challenging.

The integration of communities, and community beneficiation from conservation, is considered to be a key element in the four-tiered strategy outlined above. Various regions, as well as conservation organisations, have had some success in implementing inclusive and responsible resource-use programmes which enable communities to actively benefit from conservation on a daily basis. However, as leading transfrontier conservation area expert Paul Bewsher has pointed out, community-based strategies have taken a backseat in most of the conservation approaches to poaching and the illegal wildlife trade.[17] Counterinsurgency strategies attempt to build intelligence networks, with community-based informants and other assets reporting on poaching activities, syndicate movements and related criminal activities. These kinds of counterinsurgency strategies do not necessarily result in an overall benefit to a community or conservation partnerships, but rather have law enforcement or prosecution as their end objectives.[18]

The growing use of 'military'-type resources – such as drones, multi-sensor technology, connected live networks, smart fences, and artificial intelligence-driven camera traps – has demonstrated the growing inclusion of technology-driven solutions to the area integrity of parks. However, South African anti-poaching specialist Major-General Johan Jooste cautions that even with some of the best hardware and software available in the fight against poaching, it is still the field rangers, control-room operators, pilots, dog handlers and law-enforcement officials on the frontline who make it all work.[19]

Those employed in anti-poaching operations also face ever-increasing occupational challenges, as Naomi Haupt, a leading field-ranger anthropologist and environmental law-enforcement researcher, has highlighted; she points out that psychological disorders, combat-related stress and institutional issues have become the norm.[20] She goes further, setting out the challenges that are common to those employed by many national parks in Africa as well as in South-East Asia:

- Combat stress, anxiety disorders and psychological trauma due to armed contacts with poachers.
- Ongoing anxiety and concerns over personal safety in their home communities when they are off duty (many rangers live in the same communities as the poachers).
- Direct threats, intimidation and the persecution of rangers' families in their home communities by poachers and members of poaching syndicates.
- Whistle-blowing and a lack of trust within park organisations. Rangers are uncertain of who to trust if they detect corruption or the complicity of park staff in poaching and other crimes.
- The increasing personal risk to life and limb has also meant that danger-pay and other benefits are in demand. Traditionally, public-sector field rangers are paid anywhere between $500 and $1,000 a month, which may exclude other benefits.

Recent media coverage by the British Broadcasting Corporation (BBC) of brutality and the murder of civilians by field rangers has also resulted in a closer analysis of the role that field rangers play in local violence and in the killing and abuse of poachers and other civilians.[21] This trend is similar to what professional soldiers, paramilitaries and militia may experience.

The Militarisation of Conservation in Africa

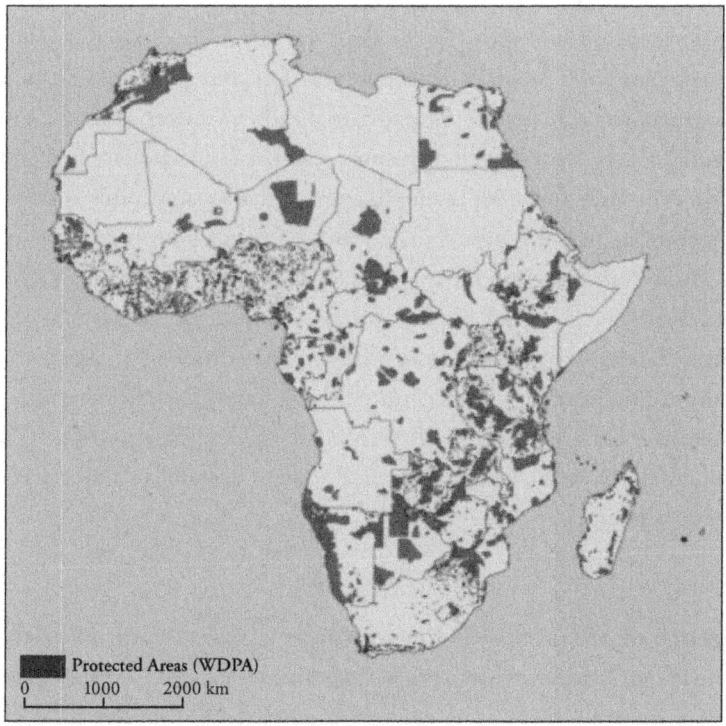

Figure 1: Protected areas in Africa (2015)[22]

With the global explosion of illegal wildlife trafficking, Africa has become the new frontline for a rapacious Asian market for elephant ivory, rhino horn, pangolin scales and a myriad other wildlife products. As noted in Figure 1, Africa has many protected areas, but many of these may only be 'paper parks' – parks that exist on maps but are, in practice, unmanaged regions due to conflict, state capacity and a range of other reasons.

The reality of paper parks and porous borders means that many local communities, as well as insurgencies in sub-Saharan Africa, are able to retreat to national parks and use the available wildlife and other resources to survive and, in many cases, thrive.[23] This factor may continue to underpin the resilience of violent extremist groups and insurgencies, and their chameleon-like capacity to adapt to the changes and rhythms of counterinsurgency, counterterrorism and counter-criminal operations by state forces, inter-regional task forces, paramilitaries, civilian militias and law-enforcement agencies.

Conventional paramilitary forces tend to require extended logistical and deployment support. Most African conservation and protected areas lack the extensive infrastructure needed by traditional military forces. Seasonal rains, lack of navigable roads, disease, lack of potable water, and inadequate fuel and power resources limit large force deployments, which is also observable from counter-terror operations in the Maghreb, the Horn of Africa and in Africa's equatorial forests. These limitations lend themselves to smaller, more easily managed, financially sustainable and logistically supported conservation models that emphasise the current model of operations adopted by many conservation agencies.[24]

For those interested in counterinsurgency and counterterrorism, one can see the similarities between the use of counterinsurgency tools during the colonial period in Africa and the insurgencies and violent extremism that Africa is currently experiencing.[25]

Emergence of Sustainable Development Conservation Models

As a continent, African conservation, together with its supporting sectors such as ecotourism, are seen as socio-economic development drivers for local economies, bringing much-needed infrastructure, local employment and, in some cases, public services such as clinics, schools and roads. For many African states, with competing demands on their fiscus, securing funding and resources for protected-area conservation is challenging at the best of times. Various African countries have keenly felt the influence of multilateral organisations such as the United Nations Environment Programme (UNEP) and the United Nations Office on Drugs and Crime (UNODC), as well as robust conservation NGOs such as the International Union for Conservation of Nature (IUCN) to protect wildlife and put aside dedicated areas for formal conservation.

The growing prevalence of sustainable-development thinking began to take root globally in the 1980s, culminating in the Brundtland Commission definition of sustainable development. This paradigm shift brought social participation and local community beneficiation to the front and centre of development and conservation practice. To be considered a triple-bottom-line (economic, social and environmental) or sustainable-development institution meant that conservation organisations had to rethink their strategies.[26] Traditional security thinking, from an international relations perspective, expanded to include the definition of environmental security which, according to Homer-Dixon,[27] examined how human-induced environmental pressure affects conflict and the scarcity of resources.

A melting pot of terms like 'food security', 'water security' and 'human security' have emerged as key concerns for many states, especially with the spectre of climate change, resource depletion, human population growth and the uncertainty of global markets. Terms such as 'community-based natural resource management' became a standard language in the conservation world to specifically address the legacy of exclusion and social injustice perpetrated by conservation agencies and colonial administrations. Community-based natural resource management also went further to make the case that conservation can, and does, occur outside of the formally protected-area networks of various states. The need for community-based participatory approaches remains a persistent challenge for many conservation agencies, with or without the spectre of poaching, as they strive to have a 'social compact to operate' – these include organisations such as South African National Parks (SANParks) and the iconic Kruger National Park.

Bewsher explains that before the 2014 World Parks Congress in Sydney, Australia, the pendulum was swinging towards the role that empowered communities could play in protecting Africa's wildlife and natural resources. This role included their active participation in conservation decision-making structures in parks and conservation agencies. Various workshops, panel discussions and launches focused on innovative and exciting approaches to placing communities at the forefront of conservation and wildlife-management initiatives.[28]

Bewsher points out that successful community-based natural resource management programmes from the Southern African Development Community (SADC) region were globally heralded as best practice.[29] Various awareness and sensitisation programmes were promoted in other regions globally to share information and create a community of best practice in the emerging field of community-based natural resource management.

However, much of this was undone by the growing spectre of poaching and illegal wildlife trafficking as it began to take centre stage in Africa, with elephant and rhino poaching growing exponentially from 2008 onwards. Where previously local communities were seen as partners, law-enforcement elements began to see them in a new and ominous light. Ongoing insurgencies, the rapid growth in violent extremism, and multi-communal violence in regions such as the Horn, central, west and north Africa have also potentially contributed to a dire socio-ecological nexus where poachers cannot be discerned from violent extremist groups and vice versa. In many cases, this has led to 'shoot-from-the-hip', reactive policies that may isolate and alienate local communities that have legitimate sustainable-livelihood needs from conservation.

Communities could improve biodiversity conservation in their homes, in agricultural practice and in communal life, and enhance food, water and public-health security. With the recent outbreak of COVID-19 from Wuhan in China, the latter point may have some salience, since evidence that the pangolin was a vector (or intermediary host) has illustrated that the illegal wildlife trade and consumption of certain species have significant public-health consequences. China's recent ban on the consumption of wild-animal meat may signal to the illegal wildlife trade market the inherent risks attached to eating wildlife. However, inconsistent political and media messaging regarding the ban seems to be an ongoing issue that creates further confusion, as illustrated by recent media reports emanating from China.[30]

From the perspective of the militarisation of conservation, this short-term ban may suppress demand for wildlife products. Still, the illegal wildlife trade is a highly complex socio-cultural as well as economic phenomenon that has defied analysis and predictions. What the ban is likely to do is to extend the need for better intelligence-gathering and social-network analysis of transnational criminal syndicates, by allowing resources outside of the conservation agencies – such as criminal intelligence services, law-enforcement agencies, regional task forces and other related organisations – to conduct surveillance and arrest players involved in illegal wildlife trafficking. These players would include point-of-origin local bosses, transporters, higher-level syndicate members and, of course, corrupt officials.

Internal corruption in conservation agencies is the elephant in the room, and dealing with internally enabled crime is an ongoing challenge for most protected-area agencies. For example, a highly respected regional ranger from the Kruger National Park was arrested by a subordinate just after he had poached rhino in 2016, and the court case continues. Haupt has noted that corruption in state conservation agencies is a leading concern that undermines park, institutional, national and regional anti-poaching strategies.[31]

What is clear from the Mozambican, South African and Botswanan experiences is that a clear separation of powers and roles needs to be implemented to ensure that conservation agencies, law-enforcement agencies, private-sector organisations, conservation NGOs and other officials do not interfere with one another's activities. The need for greater inter-agency coordination has increased over time, but concerns regarding trustworthiness and credibility remain between the private- and public-sector players. The legislative mandate and roles of the public agencies, especially in crime intelligence and criminal investigations, have been reinforced with the private sector and non-profits through various forums to ensure clarity.

The South African Approach

The National Integrated Strategy to Combat Wildlife Trafficking (NISCWT), developed by South Africa's security cluster departments in 2017, has provided the policy framework to direct the various state agencies in their strategies to counter illegal wildlife trafficking. Several vital departments collaborated to produce the strategy as an extraordinary response to illegal wildlife trafficking. As Major-General Jooste highlights, a cohesive plan was needed to buy time for the rhino.[32] Although enhanced militarisation and law-enforcement strategies were the chosen toolkit, further critical work was required to reduce demand, change end-user behaviour and incorporate local communities into the solutions.

In the case of the Kruger National Park, this resulted in a holistic strategy to develop zones in the park, intensify field rangers' training, and improve detection, interdiction and case management. Additional aerial support and canine resources have been introduced to enhance the effectiveness of boots-on-the-ground anti-poaching operations. Also, closer cooperation with the South African Police Service's stock-theft unit, as well as with the priority-crimes unit known as the Hawks, was established to speed up investigations, process cases, and enhance crime intelligence and law-enforcement operations outside the park, where rangers are unable to operate. This task-force-based approach allowed for better management of shared resources as well as collaboration in dealing with priority suspects and syndicates. Similarly, the Kruger National Park and the South African Department of Environmental Affairs expanded their relationships with their Mozambican counterparts to address the cross-border nature of poaching and the illegal wildlife trade.

The Kruger National Park was divided into three zones, based primarily on the density of the rhino population and the prevalence of poaching:[33]

- The Intensive Protection Zone (IPZ), where 71% of the rhinos reside, and where the park is, to a large extent, surrounded by communities that may be housing potential poachers. In this zone, various technologies are implemented to support anti-poaching operations.
- The Joint Protection Zone (JPZ), where 26% of the rhinos live, and where the park is surrounded by other reserves that serve as buffer areas. Here, the focus is on human intelligence and communication between surrounding private reserves.
- The Composite Protection Zone (CPZ), where only 3% of the rhinos live. Here, the focus is on cross-border operations and local-community involvement, with an emphasis on rhino guardianship.

The IPZ is located in the southern part of the park and features advanced sensor-detection systems and other enhanced anti-poaching resources to deter poaching. There are densely populated rural communities on either side of the park boundaries, where local bosses and poaching syndicates recruit many of the local poachers. In the early stages of what has become known as the rhino poaching crisis, poachers were drawn largely from Mozambique across the border. This has changed over time, with the bordering western community region outside of the park now also a poacher point of origin. In military terms, the Kruger National Park has faced poaching on several fronts – from the east, west and south.

The JPZ is located due north of the IPZ; here, the rhino population is smaller, and the terrain and topography are easier to traverse. The Kruger National Park recognised the need for enhanced collaboration with private reserves. To this end, the Greater Kruger Environmental Protection Foundation was formed to build and enhance relationships, coordinate best practice, and support information- and intelligence-sharing between the private-sector reserves and state conservation agencies, including the Mpumalanga Parks and Tourism Agency. While much has been said about the rhino poaching crisis in state conservation areas, there has also been a significant amount of rhino poaching on private reserves in southern Africa, including Mozambique, Namibia, Botswana, eSwatini and South Africa. Information on rhino herd numbers has been less forthcoming from the private sector, so initiatives such as the Greater Kruger Environmental Protection Foundation have provided a valuable bridge to connect the private and public sectors in their common goal of rhino protection. This has meant that the private security industry, as well as private conservation management services, has also militarised.

The third zone, the CPZ, is in the northern part of the Kruger National Park, where the borders of Zimbabwe, South Africa and Mozambique meet. This zone has a small rhino population but, interestingly, has begun to experience an increase in elephant poaching for ivory.

The wildlife security zoning concept has provided a set of criteria that allows conservation agencies to prioritise their efforts based on sound evidence-based thinking.[34] It was this critical insight by Major-General Jooste and his SANParks colleagues that blended biological and rhino population census data with proper military planning and law-enforcement solutions. In the process, Jooste and South Africa's Department of Environmental Affairs identified the need for comprehensive guidelines for anti-poaching operations that would address critical doctrine, standards, technology, training and related requirements. This guideline would enhance standardisation and consistency as well interoperability between anti-poaching services in different organisations. *The Guideline to Inform Decisions on the Establishment of Anti-Poaching Related Systems and Services*[35] was developed and is now being implemented primarily by South African state conservation agencies, with a strong focus on interoperability and ultimately improved public- and private-sector coordination.

As the Kruger National Park anti-poaching strategy began to gain traction, other regions in South Africa were also struggling to contain rhino poaching. In 2016, South Africa's then minister of environmental affairs, Edna Molewa, asked SANParks to assist Ezemvelo KZN Wildlife – the provincial conservation agency responsible for the public protected areas in the KwaZulu-Natal province – with guidance on addressing poaching and illegal wildlife trafficking in its reserves.

This ongoing collaboration has resulted in improved anti-poaching performance in KwaZulu-Natal by building on its provincial strategies and reserve-level plans. Structured networks and communities of practice have been formed to further share best practice and new learnings across the provincial conservation agencies.

The NISCWT strategy acknowledges that illegal wildlife trafficking is a serious transnational organised crime and a national security threat.[36] The latter point firmly brings illegal wildlife trafficking into the realm of security considerations. The NISCWT has three strategic objectives:

1. Improving law enforcement, supported by the whole of government and society, to effectively investigate, prosecute and adjudicate wildlife trafficking as a form of transnational organised crime. The strategy outlines the necessary steps the police and other relevant government and non-government entities should take to increase and enhance law-enforcement capacity in the country, focusing specifically on the investigation and prosecution of wildlife trafficking syndicates. This includes significantly increasing wildlife trafficking investigation resources (both human and technological); changing current policies, which will make the South African Police Service the lead department in combating wildlife trafficking; increasing investigations and prosecutions with regard to the link between corruption and wildlife trafficking; improving intelligence gathering and analysis; strengthening collaboration between the South African Police Service and other government departments, as well as with non-government entities that play a role in wildlife and conservation; and consolidating law-enforcement initiatives to investigate wildlife trafficking.

2. Increasing the government's ability to detect, prevent and combat wildlife trafficking in South Africa and beyond. The strategy outlines the necessary initiatives government should take to expand its ability to detect and prevent wildlife trafficking, especially in the border-management environment. This includes a significant expansion of detection resources in and around the country's ports and borders; reducing the risk of corruption at these ports; increasing and centralising wildlife compliance and enforcement resources; and increasing crime-prevention initiatives in and around poaching hotspots.

3. Increasing national, regional and international law-enforcement

collaboration and cooperation on combating wildlife trafficking. The strategy outlines the necessary initiatives government should take to expand international law-enforcement collaboration to improve its ability to prevent, combat and investigate the entire illicit value chain of wildlife trafficking in South Africa. This includes, among others, joint law-enforcement and intelligence operations between South Africa and law-enforcement agencies from transit and market countries; increasing South African participation in international wildlife trafficking combating forums; and benchmarking effective wildlife trafficking practices.

The Southern African Development Community Approach

In the case of SADC, growing recognition of illegal wildlife trafficking and poaching led to the development of a Law Enforcement and Anti-poaching Strategy (LEAP) for 2016–2021. Member states recognised that the illegal killing of and trade in wildlife had become a global issue and had rapidly metastasised into a regional challenge.

On 3 October 2013, the SADC ministers responsible for the environment and natural resources gathered in Maputo, Mozambique, to draft a proactive strategy to respond to the growing illegal wildlife trade crisis. The SADC region resolved to:

- Develop and adopt a comprehensive anti-poaching strategy.
- Establish a coordination unit within the secretariat whose primary role would be to coordinate natural resources related to law enforcement and monitoring illegal harvesting of the resources.
- Invest in a robust education and communication programme to engage communities effectively to participate in national and cross-border efforts to fight poaching.
- Strengthen institutional capacity at national levels for efficient and effective enforcement.
- Take advantage of existing opportunities through transfrontier conservation areas, national action plans and relevant agreements to eliminate the illegal harvesting and unregulated exploitation of wildlife in SADC member states.

As noted in the South African NISCWT and the SADC LEAP strategies, law-enforcement approaches have been prioritised to combat poaching in the past few years. Although there was a critical acknowledgement that communities had to be harnessed in the combating of illegal wildlife trafficking and poaching, there has been a struggle to differentiate between commercial poaching and poaching for sustainable-livelihood purposes.

To evaluate the implementation of the SADC LEAP and South African NISCWT strategies, one has to understand the limitations of both. The LEAP strategy requires regional collaboration between member states, their law-enforcement agencies and conservation authorities. Much of the reporting on successes is completed at the national and provincial level, which is then fed back into the SADC secretariat via the designated country representatives and political executives. As this chapter is being written, the SADC LEAP strategy is under review and will likely be reconfigured; the consultation and review process has begun between member states.

Therefore, as community-centric approaches began to take a backseat, paramilitary responses swiftly became mainstream policy, and were integrated into public governance structures and policy decisions by various states and regional organisations such as SADC. As Jaspero points out, paramilitary responses to poaching and illegal wildlife trafficking essentially became missions for the militaries of Botswana, Gabon, Mali, Mozambique and Tanzania.[37] Policy decisions placed militarisation at the centre of several African states and their responses to poaching. Within a short period, western military support began to respond to the need for advanced training, and soon British troops were deployed to train anti-poaching forces in Gabon, Kenya and Malawi. The United States Africa Command (AFRICOM) and the United States (US) marines trained and collaborated with anti-poaching and military forces in Gabon, the Congo, Chad and Tanzania. Capabilities in anti-poaching, patrolling, operational planning and related activities were prioritised, all of which have the hallmarks of militarised approaches, especially counterinsurgency approaches.

A critical concern for some social development specialists, conservation professionals and local communities is the growing presence of private military corporations, contractors and military veterans in African conservation. Drawn from a myriad wars in Iraq, Afghanistan, Syria and further afield, military veterans can further use their war experience and skills in the African context. Concerns revolve around the likelihood that private military contractors will use counterinsurgency-type strategies to mitigate poaching and illegal wildlife trafficking in their areas of operation and in local communities.

There are also concerns that the competence, skills set and experience of non-African military veterans will directly affect the quality of training and advice, and any operations in which they participate against low-level poachers. Another concern is that the rules of engagement promoted by private military contractors for anti-poaching activities may be opaque. Furthermore, in a brutally honest appraisal, the temptation to use excessive force against poachers in remote regions remains a likely eventuality.

Conservation NGOs such as African Parks, the Peace Parks Foundation, the Wildlife Conservation Society, Fauna and Flora International, and the World Wide Fund for Nature (WWF), together with other conservation organisations, play intimate roles in securing conservation areas throughout Africa. Most of these organisations have adopted the sustainable-development approach, acknowledging and embracing the need for community-based inclusion, or what one may term 'inclusive conservation'. Nonetheless, many of the above-mentioned organisations, such as African Parks, have also accepted that their role in law enforcement provides a broader non-conservation benefit to many local communities, particularly in central and western Africa, where national parks become refuges for externally and internally displaced people. These groups are fleeing multi-communal violence, warlords, state repression, natural disasters and other injustices.

Protected areas in Africa are rapidly militarising, and in many cases they are already focal points for what military experts would consider paramilitary operations; plans generally focus on securing protected-area integrity. Explicitly, the protected-area boundaries – such as national parks, state-declared forestry reserves, and provincial game reserves such as those found in South Africa – are militarised.

The formation of regional socio-economic development and political institutions such as the East African Community and SADC brought issues regarding peace, security and transnational crime into the spotlight. Furthermore, these regional institutions also promote regional socio-economic development and, in many cases, recognise the role that transfrontier conservation areas play in cross-border tourism, the movement of goods and economic integration. Transfrontier Conservation Areas build on the concept of Peace Parks, which focus on creating mutual benefits for conservation areas, communities and wildlife, particularly for former foes, such as South Africa and Mozambique.

What is not always noticed is that in the case of countries with more liberal land-ownership rights, private game reserves also undertake similar militarised measures, including those in Namibia, South Africa, Botswana and Zimbabwe. Small and large private reserves employ field rangers to protect their wildlife from poaching.[38]

Everyday activities such as establishing area-integrity and resource-management plans are critical foundational activities that protected-area management agencies undertake at early stages. These agencies are generally connected to secure international and local funding sources, ranging from NGOs to private institutions that sponsor aircraft, personal equipment, sensor technology, firearms, canine assets, training and more.[39]

Conclusion

The militarisation of parks in Africa has been driven by many factors in the past 10 years or so. Undoubtedly, the growth in illegal wildlife trafficking, commercial poaching and transnational criminal syndicates has been the defining factor. Also, many African states have pursued more open policies for local economic development by encouraging ecotourism and hospitality organisations to establish lodges, hotels and other tourism infrastructure. Mozambique, for example, has focused explicitly on diversifying its tourism from beach and coastal tourism to photographic safaris and hunting tourism. In the case of Kenya and Tanzania, revenue from tourism plays a significant role in their financial health and their concerns about the impact of wildlife trafficking and poaching. In SADC, which is home to the largest population of rhino and, possibly, elephant in Africa, these concerns abound. Central and western Africa face a range of state governance, capacity and other pressing issues, including ongoing violent extremism, legacy conflicts and insurgencies.

Given all of these challenges, the green militarisation of African conservation is here to stay, and has become the standard for most African parks and conservation agencies, with varying levels of success. However, the critical need for local community ownership, socio-economic development, and a meaningful stake in conservation for local communities remains a massive challenge and requires other strategies to address the demand, cultural and economic aspects of the illegal wildlife trade. It is in this context that green militarisation remains a short- to mid-term approach that must not be seen as the solution. In the words of Major-General Jooste:

> "Green militarisation, I think, despite the one-sided criticism, it's a reality. If there is any alternative, then one must consider it. You first go to your own forces, your police forces – but police in the bush, it's not a good fit. The army is conventionally trained. It's not a good match either. In Africa, these forces have other priorities – crime-fighting and peace-support operations. So now you're back to the rangers. Yes, militarisation is certainly not the preferred option in the bigger scheme of things. But what must we do to make sure that it doesn't last a day longer than it must? One would like a discourse on that, to say, 'Let's make sure that this necessary intervention doesn't last another 20 or 30 years.'"[40]

Select Bibliography

African Parks. (2020). Park Protection | African Parks. Available from: https://www.african-parks.org/our-work/park-protection [accessed 21 February 2020].

Balt, M. (2019). Case against former ranger to resume. *The Lowvelder*, 13 April. Available from: https://lowvelder.co.za/476339/case-against-former-ranger-to-resume/ [accessed 2 February 2020].

BBC. (2019). WWF accused of funding guards who torture and kill in poaching war. 4 March. Available from: https://www.bbc.com/news/world-47444297 [accessed 3 February 2020].

Bewsher, P. (2020). The militarisation of conservation in Africa – transfrontier conservation consultant. Personal interview, 14 February.

Deng, S. & Westcott, B. (2020). China has made eating wild animals illegal after the coronavirus outbreak. But ending the trade won't be easy. Available from: https://edition.cnn.com/2020/03/05/asia/china-coronavirus-wildlife-consumption-ban-intl-hnk/index.html [accessed 4 March 2020].

Department of Environmental Affairs. (2019). *Guideline to Inform Decisions on the Establishment of Anti-Poaching Related Systems and Services.* Pretoria: Department of Environmental Affairs.

De Rosner, C. (2020). The militarizsation of conservation in Africa – antipoaching service provider. Personal interview, 3 March.

Dickerman, K. (2018). Inside the effort to save Africa's elephant. *The Washington Post*, 8 August. Available from: https://www.washingtonpost.com/news/in-sight/wp/2018/08/08/inside-the-effort-to-save-africas-elephant-population/ [accessed 3 February 2020].

Duffy, R. (2014). Waging a war to save biodiversity: The militarized conservation. *International Affairs*, July.

Galula, D. (1964). *Counterinsurgency warfare – theory and practice.* London: Praeger Security International.

Glasson, A. (2019). The rhino rifle syndicates. In Jurgens, R. (ed.). (2019). *Africa in Fact.* Johannesburg: Global Governance Africa.

Gorman, J. (2020). China's Ban on Wildlife Trade a Big Step, but Has Loopholes, Conservationists Say. *The New York Times*, 27 February. Available from: https://www.nytimes.com/2020/02/27/science/coronavirus-pangolin-wildlife-ban-china.html [accessed 4 March 2020].

Haupt, N. (2020). The militarisation of conservation in Africa – environmental anthropologist. Personal interview, 12 February.

Heuser, B. & Shamir, E. (2016). *Insurgencies and counterinsurgencies, national cultures and strategic cultures.* Cambridge: Cambridge University Press.

Homer-Dixon, T. (1999). *Environment, scarcity, and violence.* Princeton: Princeton University Press.

International Ranger Federation. (2016). *Anti-poaching in and around protected areas: A training guideline for field rangers.* Melbourne: The Thin Green Line Foundation.

International Union for Conservation of Nature (IUCN). (2015). Protected Areas in Africa in the World Database on Protected Areas. Available from: https://www.iucn.org/theme/protected-areas/our-work/world-database-protected-areas [accessed 12 February 2020].

Jaspero, C. (2018). *Wildlife trafficking and poaching: Contemporary context and dynamics for security cooperation and military assistance.* Newport: CIWAG Case Studies 17.

Jooste, J. (2020). The militarisation of conservation in Africa, Head of Special Projects – South African National Parks. Personal interview, 19 February.

Kopylova, S. & Danilina, N. (2011). *Protected Area Staff Training: Guidelines for Planning and Management.* Gland, Switzerland: International Union for Conservation of Nature (IUCN).

Lindeque, B. (2020). Meet the dogs being trained to combat poaching in South Africa. Available from: https://www.goodthingsguy.com/environment/dogs-combat-poaching-south-africa/ [accessed 3 March 2020].

Murphree, M. & Hulme, J. (2001). *African wildlife & livelihoods: The promise & performance of community conservation.* Oxford: James Curry Ltd.

Somerville, K. (2016). *Ivory: Power and poaching in Africa.* London: C. Hurst & Company.

South Africa. (2017). *National Integrated Strategy to Combat Wildlife Trafficking (NISCWT)*. Version 4. Pretoria, South Africa.

South African History Online. (2019). The Berlin Conference. Available from: https://www.sahistory.org.za/article/berlin-conference [accessed 7 March 2020].

Southern African Development Community (SADC). (2015). Law enforcement and anti-poaching strategy 2016-2021. Gaborone: SADC Secretariat.

Southern African Development Community (SADC). (n.d.). Transfrontier Conservation Areas. Available from: https://tfcaportal.org/sadc-tfcas [accessed 27 February 2020].

Southern African Wildlife College. (2020). Wildlife Guardianship. Available from: https://wildlifecollege.org.za/wildlife-guardianship/ [accessed 12 March 2020].

Verweijen, J. & Marijnen, E. (2016). The counterinsurgency/conservation nexus: Guerrilla livelihoods and the dynamics of conflict and violence in the Virunga National Park, Democratic Republic of Congo. *The Journal of Peasant Studies*, 45(2).

Endnotes

1. Murphree & Hulme, 2001:67.
2. This violent nexus has nonetheless created positive opportunities for conservation and communities. African Parks, considered to be one of the leading private conservation agencies in Africa, has been a trendsetter by entering into bilateral agreements with various states to manage, fundraise and re-establish park integrity. These agreements include agenda-setting with local communities for local employment, ecotourism and other sustainability practices. African Parks has set an ambitious vision to manage 20 different parks in Africa. At present, African Parks manages 15 parks with a total area of 10,5 million hectares, protected by approximately 1,000 field rangers (Glasson, 2019:62). The Kruger National Park in South Africa, by comparison, has around 500 field rangers protecting the 2,2 million hectares of the park. African Parks has adopted a law-enforcement approach to its conservation strategy across all parks. Furthermore, it states: "In 2017 alone, our rangers conducted almost 113,159 ranger patrol days, up 33% from 2016; 501 arrests were made; over 48,151 snares [were] removed and more than 54,493 confiscations were made across all the parks. In Odzala in Congo, our rangers confiscated 31 tonnes of bushmeat and 53 firearms. In Garamba in the DRC and Chinko in the [Central African Republic], our [field] rangers are often the first and at times the only responders protecting refugees fleeing from conflict or from more insidious forces like the Lord's Resistance Army or other regional terrorist groups." (African Parks, 2020)
3. Duffy, 2014:1-2.
4. Ibid, 5-6.
5. Somerville, 2016:26.
6. Ibid.
7. Verweijen & Marijnen, 2016:7-8.
8. Somerville, 2016:12.
9. Ibid, 14.
10. South African History Online, 2019.
11. Murphree & Hulme, 2001:1.
12. Duffy, 2014:5-6.
13. African Parks, 2020; Department of Environmental Affairs, 2019; Southern African Wildlife College, 2020.
14. International Ranger Federation, 2016.
15. Southern African Wildlife College, 2020.
16. Lindeque, 2020.
17. Bewsher, 2020:1.
18. Galula, 1964:24-27.
19. Jooste, 2020.
20. Haupt, 2020:4.
21. BBC, 2019.
22. African Parks, 2020; Verweijen & Marijnen, 2016:1-13.
23. African Parks, 2020; Verweijen & Marijnen, 2016:1-13.
24. Kopylova & Danilina, 2011:1-3.
25. Heuser & Shamir, 2016:12.
26. Murphree & Hulme, 2001:1-2.
27. Homer-Dixon, 1999:3-5.
28. Bewsher, 2020:1.
29. Ibid, 2.
30. Deng & Westcott, 2020; Gorman, 2020.
31. Haupt, 2020:3.
32. Jooste, 2020.
33. Department of Environmental Affairs, 2019:15-16.
34. Ibid.
35. Ibid.
36. South Africa, 2017:13.
37. Jaspero, 2018:9.
38. De Rosner, 2020:3.
39. Ibid, 1.
40. Jooste, 2020.

CHAPTER 3

The Potential Impact of Artificial Intelligence on Human and National Security in Africa

Futhi Luthango

Introduction

Advances in artificial intelligence (AI), which make it possible for machines to learn from experience, adjust to new inputs and perform human-like tasks, will in the coming years impact on virtually all spheres of life. The use of machine learning, deep learning and other transformative AI technologies will drive change across industries, and has the potential to help humanity address some of its most pressing challenges, from healthcare and medicine to food insecurity and climate change.

However, while the potential positive applications of AI technologies are great, there is also the possibility that AI technologies could disrupt the international peace and security architecture, and be misused and exploited by negative forces.

To date, policy and regulation have been unable to catch up with or get ahead of the rapid progress made in the development of automated weapons systems and other AI-enabled military technologies. This means that, in their current form, regulatory bodies and international laws are insufficient to answer even the most fundamental questions posed by these technologies, such as: to what degree should weapons systems that can kill be autonomous? How do we establish accountability when autonomous weapons systems are used in the execution of war crimes?

Although there are as yet no recorded instances of extremist groups in Africa using AI to attack targets, the speed and sophistication with which they have adopted innovations such as the internet and social media to, for example, disseminate propaganda and recruit members serves as a warning that it is not a question of if so much as when.

A December 2016 British Broadcasting Corporation (BBC) report quoted

United States (US) military sources as saying that groups were already using drones for surveillance, and were even fitting them with small bombs:

> "Fitting a drone with weapons still requires some technical skill but it is being made easier with cheap add-ons intended for hobbyists, such as a kit which allows any drone to drop a hundred-gram toy bomb filled with powder. In August [2016], Hezbollah released a video showing small bombs dropped from commercial drones."[1]

The Islamic State in Iraq and Syria (ISIS) has also used commercially available drones, as US counterterrorism analyst Daveed Gartenstein-Ross pointed out in an article for the website *Defense One*:

> "In the 2017 battle for Mosul, for example, the Islamic State dispatched small and agile consumer drones armed with grenades to harry the Iraqi forces assembled to retake the city. These uses of social media, encryption, and drones illustrate a key pattern: as a consumer technology becomes widely available, terrorists will look for ways to adapt it. Artificial intelligence will almost certainly end up fitting into this pattern."[2]

Driverless motor vehicles are another innovation that could prove to be a potent weapon if abused.

Establishing new norms and regulations to encourage the positive use of AI, while discouraging its misuse and abuse, is essential to harnessing the potential this technology holds. AI is currently in its pre-infancy in Africa, and the continent is therefore well positioned to formulate policies that will encourage and guide positive development in the field and serve as an example globally.

This chapter will define and provide a brief history of AI before looking at how this technology is challenging the international peace and security architecture, and driving changes in different industries. The inherent vulnerabilities AI creates will be examined, as well as the potential benefits it could provide to human and national security. Finally, with a focus on Africa, recommendations will be provided on how we can aim to make the journey towards adopting and implementing AI technologies safer through policy and planning.

History of Artificial Intelligence

The study of mechanical or 'formal' reasoning can be seen in the work of the classical philosophers and mathematicians of antiquity. However, it was only in the 20th century that AI, in its modern form, was conceived.

In 1936, in a bid to solve a puzzle known to mathematicians as the *Entscheidungsproblem*, the British polymath Alan Turing invented the Universal Turing Machine – a mathematical model of computation that defines an abstract machine. This model was able to determine whether any given mathematical statement could be shown to be true or false by following a step-by-step procedure – which is what we today call an algorithm. Turing suggested that a machine, by shuffling symbols as simple as 0 and 1, could simulate any conceivable act of mathematical deduction. In 1950, in his seminal paper 'Computing Machinery and Intelligence', Turing discussed how to build intelligent machines and how to test their intelligence, premised on the idea that if humans use available information and reason to solve problems and make decisions, then machines should be able to do the same.[3]

In 1956, the term 'artificial intelligence' was first coined, and the field was formally founded at a conference at Dartmouth College in Hanover, New Hampshire, in the US. Conference presentations were made by Allen Newell, Cliff Shaw and Herbert Simon on their computer program, Logic Theorist, which was designed to mimic the problem-solving skills of a human and is considered by many to be the first AI program.[4]

The proof of concept provided by the Logic Theorist program, and the discussion generated by this conference, led to an increase in funding and interest in the field. Up until this point, computers lacked a key prerequisite of intelligence: they had no memory and therefore could not store commands; they could only execute them. Computing was also expensive, affordable only to large corporates and prestigious universities. Additional investment in the field, however, meant that computers became cheaper and more accessible. Advances also meant that computers were able to store information and compute much faster. More algorithms were written and improved on, and researchers in the field got better at selecting the right algorithm to apply to a problem.

By 1974, due to a combination of high expectations and slow progress in achieving an artificially intelligent being, government and corporate funding

– and interest in the field – began to wane. In fact, the period between 1974 and 1980 is known as the 'AI winter'.[5] It was only in the 1980s that interest and funding in the field returned, driven in part by Japan's efforts to automate its industries and the competition this generated among other nations.

During this time, there was an expansion of the algorithmic toolkit. John Hopfield (a physicist) and David Rumelhart (a psychologist) popularised 'deep-learning' techniques that allowed computers to learn using experience. It was also during this period that Edward Feigenbaum, a computer scientist working in the field of AI, introduced 'expert systems'. These systems imitated the decision-making processes of a human expert. The program would ask an expert in a field how to respond in a given situation, and once this was learned for virtually every situation in a given field, non-experts could receive advice from the program. These databases of expert knowledge quickly became widely used in industries. However, this period of progress and funding in the field of AI was short-lived. The stock market crash of 1987 and the subsequent recession ushered in another AI winter, which lasted from 1987 to 1993, slowing funding and the growth of early general-purpose computers.[6]

It was not until the 1990s that key landmark goals in AI were achieved. The most notable and publicised of these was in 1997 when IBM's Deep Blue, a chess-playing computer program, became the first computer to beat the reigning human chess champion, Russian grandmaster Garry Kasparov. This was a significant step in creating an artificially intelligent decision-making program that could surpass a human at a particular mental task. What made this landmark goal possible were advances in hardware, which impacted computer storage and processing speed.

Artificial Intelligence Today

Today, we are in the age of big data. The constraints of computer storage and processing speed have been overcome, and only now are we really starting to realise the potential of AI. The algorithm toolkit has not changed much, but the vastness of data, and the ability of computer programs to process it, has made AI prevalent in many areas of our lives. AI has evolved to be much broader than its initial pursuit of human-like intelligence; it has become a technology used in the fields of banking (think fraud detection), marketing (the tailored marketing of goods and services to you online), the medical industry, and in military applications, to name a few.

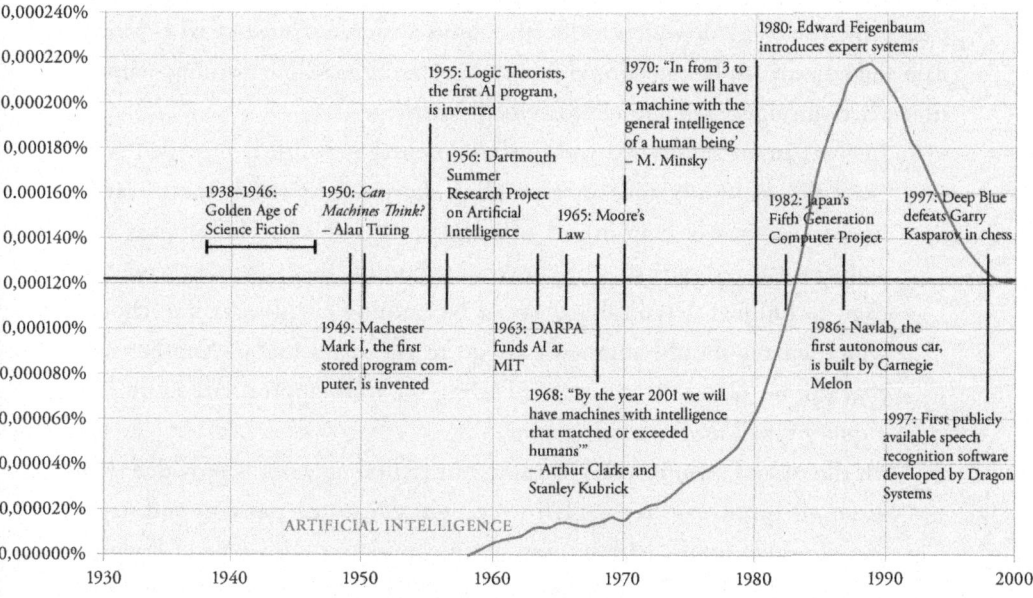

Figure 1: AI development timeline[7]

Today, modern AI can be described as the simulation of human intelligence behaviour by a computer system. It includes three processes, namely:
1. Learning, which involves acquiring real-world information, and algorithms (rules) that define the learning process relating to that information.
2. Reasoning, which allows the computer system to reach a conclusion based on the information and the information rules.
3. Self-correction.

Machine learning, as an approach to achieve AI, needs vast amounts of data to learn from. Artificial neural networks – algorithms inspired by the networks of neurons that make up the human brain – use layers of algorithms to process data. Information is passed through each layer, with the output of the previous layer providing input for the next, expounding its reasoning and self-correcting as it processes more information. This is a branch of machine learning called deep learning. The deep-learning algorithm will perform a task repeatedly, each time tweaking itself slightly to improve the outcome.

Currently, the ways in which artificial neuron structures interact with source data and stimuli can be categorised into three types of machine learning, namely supervised, unsupervised and reinforcement learning.[8]

1. In the case of supervised learning, the neural network is provided with examples of inputs and corresponding desired outputs. It then 'learns' how to accurately map inputs to outputs by adjusting the weights and activation thresholds of its neural connections. This is the most widely used technique. A typical use would be training email servers to choose which emails should automatically go to the spam folder. Another task that can be 'learnt' in this way is finding the most appropriate results for a query typed into a search engine.
2. In the case of unsupervised learning, the neural network is provided with example inputs and is then left to recognise features, patterns and structure in these inputs without any specific guidance. This type of learning can be used to cluster the input data into classes on the basis of its statistical properties. It is particularly useful for finding things of which you do not know the form, such as as-yet-unrecognised patterns in a large dataset.
3. Finally, in the case of reinforcement learning, the neural network interacts with an environment in which it must perform a specific task, and receives feedback on its performance in the form of a reward or a punishment. This type of learning corresponds, for example, to the training of a network to play computer games and achieve high scores.[9]

The culmination of the achievements in AI discussed above means that today we have artificial neural networks with the ability to learn, and vast amounts of real-world data for these programs to draw on. These can be run on computers with exceptionally fast computing power and little memory constraints.

Vulnerabilities of Artificial Intelligence

Over the past three centuries, technological evolutions have shaped the rise and decline of nations, corporations, and sometimes entire industries. AI is already used in industries to aid expert systems, speech recognition and machine vision.[10] The countries which lead this new revolution will share the global economy in the coming decades. China, for example, has already made significant advancements in the field, and a combination of cultural and social factors, together with an abundance of capital, puts the country in a strong position to lead the AI revolution.[11] Machine learning requires a vast amount of data to learn from. The Chinese government has considerable access to readily available citizen data, and this presents a great advantage for the country's technology firms when developing their AI programs.

Today, most aspects of our lives are touched by AI in one way or another, from deciding which books or flights to buy online, to whether our job applications are successful, whether we receive a bank loan or not, and even what treatment we receive for cancer. There are, however, weaknesses and vulnerabilities in AI systems. The algorithms that have been designed are not perfect. They are not 100% accurate, and often the data we feed into an AI system is imperfect, which introduces a margin of error in the answers that AI machines provide and the decisions they make.

The decision-making processes we embark on based on AI output must be cognisant of the margin of error inherent in its systems, and appropriate additional scrutiny must be applied. As Nogrady[12] argues: "Since we are building artificial intelligence in our own image, it is likely to be both as brilliant and as flawed as we are." These vulnerabilities can be further augmented by bias. As many as 85% of all AI projects are expected to have errors due to either bias in the algorithm, biased programmers, or bias in the data used to train them.[13]

AI is effectively a computer program-based learning system. Therefore, like other computer systems, it is vulnerable to attack by a malicious program and must be secured. An attack can be designed to make a learning system produce unintended or incorrect results, or to produce a targeted outcome designed by the attacker. A learning system can also be corrupted to learn sensitive information about individuals.

This leads us to another challenge with AI learning programs: given the vastness of the data and the complex algorithms used in an artificial neural network, it is very difficult to open it up and identify where and how it may have gone wrong. Put simply, it is near impossible to work out exactly why an AI system does what it does, so where we choose to apply AI requires considerable discernment of potential consequences. AI can be used as an enabler of security, or it can be misused to attack, posing a threat to security. As AI systems continue to be further integrated into society, these AI attacks represent an emerging and systematic vulnerability, with the potential to have a significant effect on human and state security.[14]

Artificial Intelligence and the International Peace and Security Architecture

Like many other technologies, AI can be used for good or misused to harm, and it is thus able to play the dual role of creating security in some contexts and insecurity in others. To understand the impact of AI on security and insecurity in the context of nations and their societies, we must first look at today's international peace and security architecture, which largely came into being after the Second World War and has continued to evolve since then through the codification of international laws and treaties, and cooperation between states. Garcia outlines three pillars, which together constitute this paradigm:

> "The first pillar is the regulation of war and the prohibition of the use of force with the accompanying global norm of peaceful settlement of disputes between states and, increasingly, other actors. The second pillar is composed of the dense network of global norms that constrain and guide the behaviour of states. This includes an extensive array of treaties that form numerous governance regimes and comprise an elaborate framework of transparency, confidence building, and security mechanisms put in place to maintain peace and security. The third pillar is built upon a structure that fosters cooperation in cultural, economic, social, and environmental matters that affect all humanity and tackle problems that must be solved collectively."[15]

While imperfect, achieving and sustaining this current peace and security architecture between nations has taken an enormous amount of time and resources. It has required transparency, trust-building, security mechanisms such as treaties, alliances, arms control agreements, nuclear weapons non-proliferation agreements, joint operations among states, disarmament, conflict resolution, restraint and arbitration. The militarisation of AI to create lethal AI could fundamentally destabilise this architecture in various ways, and such weapons would represent the third major transformation in the nature of war and how it is fought – the first being gunpower, and the second nuclear weapons.

Over time, the threshold for use of force by nations against other nations has largely come to be understood and accepted globally. This threshold has been high given the requirement to mobilise troops and the loss of life that could result. Automated weapons could lower this threshold due to the reduced involvement of humans in their deployment and the ability to use force from long distances. The disintegration of such threshold norms, which have been carefully crafted by international laws since the founding of the United Nations, could destabilise fragile peace and conflict situations. Already, autonomy has been an official component of US national security strategy since the 2012 release of the Department of Defense's Directive 3000.09. This policy was the first of its kind and allows for semi-autonomous systems to engage targets pre-selected by human operators, as well as for fully autonomous weapons to select and engage targets after senior-level approval in the Department of Defense.[16]

The militarisation of AI also threatens the current norms and behaviours that guide the behaviour of states. Today, these behavioural norms are underpinned largely by rules relating to the international protection of human rights and international humanitarian law. However, for these norms and rules to work effectively, there has to be accountability. An autonomous system, be it in our daily lives or in the case of national security, undermines traditional thinking around accountability. For example, if a self-driving vehicle on its way to fetch a client knocks over a child in the street, or an automated weapons system engages a target, establishing a chain of responsibility can be difficult.

South Korea has become a strong player in the development of lethal automated weapons systems and the world leader when it comes to autonomous sentry weapons.[17] The country has deployed these weapons, which automatically survey, target and fire using sensors, to the demilitarised zone between South Korea and its neighbour, North Korea. While South Korea is one of the first, many other countries have invested in, and are likely to continue to invest in, automated weapons systems for their national security. However, the dissonance between advancing technology and retreating political commitments to allies is a threat to international peace. AI and other technological advancements will not compensate for these commitments, or for the abandonment of important bilateral and multilateral partnerships.

The third pillar of peace and security today is embraced by the efforts to promote cooperation in cultural, economic, social and environmental matters that affect all humanity, and to tackle problems that can only be solved collectively. This becomes difficult to realise when there is a situation of 'haves' and 'have nots', especially when 'not having' exposes you to national insecurity.

Already, one can see the beginnings of an AI weapons race between nations. As discussed, autonomy is already an integral part of US national security strategy. Russia plans to have autonomous systems guarding its weapons silos by 2020, and have 30% of its combat power partially or fully autonomous by 2030, while the country's autonomous Uran-9 robotic tank has already been deployed to Syria.[18] In China, President Xi Jinping has called for the country to become a world leader in AI by 2030, and has placed military innovation firmly at the centre of the programme, encouraging the People's Liberation Army to work with start-ups in the private sector, and with universities.[19]

Finally, like the first industrial revolution, in the age of AI the population size of a country will become less important with regard to national military power. Small countries that develop a significant edge in AI technology will be able to punch far above their weight. This could, for example, bring about a change in the member countries that sit on the United Nations Security Council, causing some multinational treaties and alliances to become ineffective, or leading to the creation of new ones.

Current developments and advances in AI will have both positive and negative effects on the international security landscape by driving changes in military superiority, information superiority and economic superiority. For example, adversarial AI – or the malicious development and use of advanced digital technology and systems that have intellectual processes typically associated with human behaviour – is already a threat which several nations have experienced. The informational superiority that AI brings in terms of the collection and analysis of data is immense. The use of AI systems to learn from past experience, discover meaning from complex data, and exploit these findings in the form of information warfare, is suspected to have played a role in the 2016 US presidential elections. Evidence suggests that in the build-up to the elections, a vast amount of information on the country's electorate was harvested from social networks (without their knowledge), and exploited to customise and shape advertising messaging that would favourably influence voters.[20]

The use of AI in facial recognition and surveillance systems is already having profound consequences. AI is fundamentally changing surveillance from a passive to an active type of security measure. AI programs are able to recognise and tag individual faces (facial recognition). Video analytics, which allow computers to 'understand' what is going on in a video, means that modern surveillance systems can, for example, detect when a person or vehicle enters a forbidden area. They can count people or cars. They can detect when luggage is left unattended, or when previously unattended luggage is picked up and removed. They can detect when someone is lying down, running, or loitering in a given area. Increasingly, they can detect particular actions by people, flag people based on their clothing or behaviour, identify people's emotions through body language and behaviour, and find people who are acting 'unusually' when compared to the population around them.

Facial recognition technology is improving all the time, aided by the vast number of images posted by people on social media platforms, and governments' collection of identification cards and driver's licence photographs.[21] Governments are already starting to use this technology in respect of security measures to counter terrorism, improve policing, and shorten response times to incidents. China is using data from its mass AI-enabled surveillance system in the 'social credit' system that is currently being piloted in select provinces. However, constant surveillance can potentially also create modifications in social behaviour, giving rise to less public social interaction and generating more concealed security threats.

The fundamental ingredient of any AI learning system is data. The way data is collected, stored and used (and by whom, why and when) are questions that policy needs to address. In this regard, AI policymakers must effectively support the interests of government and businesses so as not to jeopardise national security or economic development, while also considering the interests of citizens and the prevention of AI's potential misuse by these parties.

Developing policy around the use of AI is especially difficult as there is no standardised way to develop it: the algorithm toolkits are different, the applications are continuously learning from new data, and there is no industry standard in terms of testing. Nonetheless, more effort is required with regard to auditing and validating AI outcomes when they are applied in critical areas, since this may result in conflict. There must also be public oversight of the use of emerging semi- and fully autonomous weapons systems.

To preserve the stability of global and regional security dynamics, some argue for a 'preventative security governance' approach. This approach is premised on the precautionary principle of international law, and on previous cases where prevention brought stability to all countries, for instance, nuclear weapons non-development and proliferation. It encourages states to adopt preventative prohibition on the weaponisation of AI.

However, if one looks at the current stance of members of the United Nations Security Council on the weaponisation of AI systems, and the rapid advancements already made in AI weaponisation, it seems that prohibition may be too late. For example, China has announced that it wishes to ban the battlefield use of AI-powered automation systems, but not their development and production. Russia has fully embraced a militarised AI system and has initiated programmes to achieve its deployment. The US is pursuing an America-first foreign policy stance and is already heavily invested in the development and deployment of AI weapons systems. France and Germany,[22] to their credit, have advocated the use of the Convention on Certain Weapons process to develop 'possible guiding principles' as a code of conduct to encourage lethal AI weapons development to stay within the ambit of current international law.[23]

These divergent approaches to AI weaponisation illustrate the emerging challenge that AI poses to the international peace and security architecture, and the distance that needs to be travelled before the majority of states accept the new norms that need to be formed for conducting international relations and the peaceful resolution of disputes in the context of these new weapons systems.

Artificial Intelligence in Africa

Historically, Africa has lagged behind developed nations in the investment, development and adoption of new technologies. This has had its advantages and disadvantages. For example, in terms of telecommunications technology and industry, we have seen Africa leapfrog the traditional lifecycle experienced by developed countries – moving directly from very low penetration levels of fixed-line services to very high penetration levels in mobile communications. This has helped Africa advance quickly in terms of the improvement of banking services which mobile connectivity has made possible.

The GSM Association estimates that 84% of sub-Saharan Africa's one billion people will have access to a SIM connection by 2025 – a 3,7% increase from 2017.[24] About 35% of these will be linked to smartphones. The data generated by the creation and transmission of this data will help to fuel AI in Africa in the coming years.

A number of global technology companies have invested in Africa. Google has opened an AI lab in Ghana, Microsoft has built two cloud data centres in South Africa, and Facebook has provided funding and training in a number of African countries.

In South Africa, President Cyril Ramaphosa is the first leader to emphasise the importance of adapting to the fourth industrial revolution and place focus on supporting AI technology development. In 2019, Ramaphosa established the Presidential Commission on the Fourth Industrial Revolution to develop an integrated national response strategy.[25] The commission is composed of representatives of tech start-ups, academia, cybersecurity specialists, researchers, social scientists, trade unionists, and other representatives from key economic sectors. The focus of the strategy is to leverage technology and AI to facilitate economic growth and competitiveness, and to skill (and re-skill) labour to engage with technology and not be left behind.

High levels of population growth and rapid urbanisation have tasked African governments with enormous service delivery challenges, especially in quickly growing metropolitan areas, which may already experience high crime levels, food insecurity, poor healthcare facilities and political instability. If leveraged correctly, AI could go a long way in helping governments and policymakers to address these challenges and augment state capacity where it is lacking.

In healthcare, for example, AI solutions can help scarce personnel and facilities do more with less by speeding up initial processing, triage, diagnosis and post-care follow-up. IBM Research Africa is using AI to determine the optimal methods for eradicating malaria in specific locations, and is using game theory and deep-learning data analytics to diagnose pathological diseases. Rwanda became the first country to incorporate drones into its healthcare system, using autonomous air vehicles to deliver blood for transfusions to remote regions.

In agriculture, automated drones are already used to monitor livestock and crops, and to collect visual information on their location and condition. AI applications have enabled farmers to optimise the scheduling of work that needs to be done on farms, such as pruning, picking, weeding, watering, and spraying for pests in the right areas.

A number of structural challenges undermine the rapid adoption and implementation of AI on the continent. Inadequate basic and digital infrastructure seriously erodes efforts to activate AI-powered solutions as it reduces crucial connectivity. In some cases, though, this limitation has fuelled innovative solutions for the challenges of connectivity, like unstructured supplementary service data (USSD). Sometimes referred to as quick codes or feature codes, USSD is a communications protocol used by Global System for Mobile Communications (GSM) cellular telephones to communicate with a mobile network operator's computers.

As technology leaders seek to scale their businesses across borders, they can be hampered by the continent's high linguistic diversity – between 1,500 and 2,000 languages are spoken daily in Africa. However, AI itself could potentially offer solutions to this challenge, with constant improvements in automated language translation software.

A lack of flexible and dynamic regulatory systems frustrates the growth of a digital ecosystem that favours AI technology. Similarly, the lack of adequate investment in research and development is a major obstacle to the adoption and implementation of AI solutions on the continent. Africa must develop innovative financial instruments and public-private partnerships to fund human-capital development, including a focus on industrial research and innovation hubs that bridge the gap between higher education institutions and the private sector to ensure the transition of AI products from lab to market.

In certain cases, governments have been reluctant to support technologies that seem to threaten existing jobs, especially as job creation for the continent's burgeoning youth population is a priority in most African countries. However, AI technologies, if used correctly, can grow an economy and replace low-skilled service jobs with higher-skilled ones. A lack of relevant technical skills, particularly among young people, is a growing threat to Africa's adoption and implementation of AI. This skills gap means that those who would otherwise have been at the forefront of building AI are left out, preventing the continent from harnessing the full potential of transformative technologies and industries.[26]

As discussed, Africa has much to gain from the positive use of emerging AI technology. However, AI is a double-edged sword, and the potentially deleterious effects when exploited by negative forces cannot be ignored. There is also the potential for AI technologies to lower the cost associated with violence by both state and non-state actors, whether it be the use of enhanced cyber-intelligence gathering techniques, augmented small arms or weaponised drones. AI technologies can also be used to further one's political goals in other ways, such as the fabrication and rapid dissemination of a news story designed to denigrate an opposition party, or as a recruitment tool for extremist organisations. Governments can use it to spread misinformation, monitor political opposition, or marginalise minority voices. For example, with the assistance of China, the Zimbabwean government has begun collecting individual facial imagery to be used by current monitoring and facial recognition applications. These applications have human rights advocates worried about potential misuse once the system comes online.[27]

Africa is in its AI pre-infancy stage and is, therefore, in a better position to put policies in place that will encourage and guide positive development in the field. In November 2018, the African Union Commission presided over the 7th Internet Governance Forum on the theme of Development of the Digital Economy and Emerging Technologies in Africa. The meeting focused on several key areas, including protecting human rights while harnessing the potential of internet-enabled economies.[28] Such forums should be given more impetus to drive the development of common technology-related frameworks.

The African Union, and other such regional organisations, can play a pivotal role in establishing a common framework for the effective governance of internet-enabled technologies, by promoting the positive and forbidding the negative use of the internet, data and AI applications. Furthermore, South Africa, Ghana, Nigeria, Rwanda and Kenya are currently the frontrunners in the development of AI technologies on the continent, and are thus best positioned to influence the course taken by the rest of Africa.

Conclusion

AI technology has the potential to help solve some of the continent's most enduring challenges, such as those relating to human and national security, economic security, food security, healthcare and inclusive growth. However, it will be up to Africans to ensure that this powerful technology is not exploited to drive further ethnic and religious divisions, or to strengthen authoritarian systems.

Select Bibliography

Allen, G. & Chen, T. (2017). Artificial Intelligence and National Security. Belfer Center Study. Cambridge, Massachusetts: Belfer Center for Science and International Affairs, Harvard Kennedy School. Available from: https://www.belfercenter.org/sites/default/files/files/publication/AI%20NatSec%20-%20final.pdf [accessed 27 February 2020].

Anyoha, R. (2017). Can Machines Think? Blog, Special Edition on Artificial Intelligence – The History of Artificial Intelligence, 28 August. Available from: http://sitn.hms.harvard.edu/flash/2017/history-artificial-intelligence/ [accessed 7 March 2020].

Bendett, S. (2017). Red Robots Rising: Behind the rapid development of Russian unmanned military systems. *The Strategy Bridge*, 12 December. Available from: https://thestrategybridge.org/the-bridge/2017/12/12/red-robots-rising-behind-the-rapid-development-of-russian-unmanned-military-systems [accessed 7 March 2020].

Besaw, C. & Filitz, J. (2019). Artificial Intelligence in Africa is a double-edged sword. One Earth Future, 16 December. Available from: https://cpr.unu.edu/ai-in-africa-is-a-double-edged-sword.html [accessed 16 March 2020].

Bode, I. & Huelss, H. (2018). Autonomous weapons systems and changing norms in international relations. *Review of International Studies*, 44(3), pp. 393-413.

Braunstein, J. & Laboure, M. (2018). The AI advantage of nations in the fourth industrial revolution. *Global Policy*, 17 April. Cambridge, Massachusetts: Belfer Center for Science and International Affairs, Harvard Kennedy School. Available from: https://www.belfercenter.org/publication/ai-advantage-nations-fourth-industrial-revolution [accessed 7 March 2020].

Brooks, M. (2014). Turing's Oracle: The computer that goes beyond logic. *New Scientist*, 16 July. Available from: https://www.newscientist.com/article/mg22329780-400-turings-oracle-the-computer-that-goes-beyond-logic/ [accessed 7 March 2020].

Buckley, C. & Mosur, P. (2019). How China uses high-tech surveillance to subdue minorities. *The New York Times*, 22 May. Available from: https://www.nytimes.com/2019/05/22/world/asia/china-surveillance-xinjiang.html [accessed 7 March 2020].

Chan, M.K. (2019). China and the US are fighting a major battle over killer robots and the future of AI. *Time*, 13 September. Available from: https://time.com/5673240/china-killer-robots-weapons/ [accessed 7 March 2020].

Cole, C. (2017). Harm to Global Peace and Security. In Acheson, R., Bolton, M., Minor, E. &

Pytlak, A. (eds.). *The Humanitarian Impact of Drones*. Women's International League for Peace and Freedom, pp. 48-59, Available from: https://reliefweb.int/sites/reliefweb.int/files/resources/humanitarian-impact-of-drones.pdf [accessed 27 February 2020].

Comiter, M. (2018). Attacking Artificial Intelligence: AI's security vulnerability and what policy makers can do about it. August. Cambridge, Massachusetts: Belfer Center for Science and International Affairs, Harvard Kennedy School. Available from: https://www.belfercenter.org/publication/AttackingAI [accessed 28 February 2020].

Convention on Certain Weapons (CCW) Group of Government Experts. (2018). Report of the 2018 Session of the Group of Governmental Experts on Emerging Technologies in the Area of Lethal Autonomous Weapons Systems. Geneva: United Nations. Available from: https://www.unog.ch/80256EDD006B8954/(httpAssets)/20092911F6495FA7C125830E003F9A5B/$file/CCW_GGE.1_2018_3_final.pdf [accessed 2 March 2020].

Dixon, W. (2018). What is adversarial artificial intelligence and why does it matter? *Global Policy*, 23 November. Available from: https://www.globalpolicyjournal.com/blog/23/11/2018/what-adversarial-artificial-intelligence-and-why-does-it-matter [accessed 28 February 2020].

Edmeades, A. (2017). International Law Perspectives. In Acheson, R., Bolton, M., Minor, E. & Pytlak, A. (eds.). *The Humanitarian Impact of Drones*. Women's International League for Peace and Freedom, pp. 101-114. Available from: https://reliefweb.int/sites/reliefweb.int/files/resources/humanitarian-impact-of-drones.pdf [accessed 27 February 2020].

Foote, K.D. (2017). A brief history of deep learning. Dataversity, 7 February. Available from: https://www.dataversity.net/brief-history-deep-learning/ [accessed 28 February 2020].

Future of Life Institute. (2015). Autonomous weapons: An open letter from AI and robotics researchers. 28 July. Available from: https://futureoflife.org/open-letter-autonomous-weapons/?cn-reloaded=1 [accessed 28 February 2020].

Garcia, D. (2014a). The case against killer robots – why the United States should ban them. *Foreign Affairs*, 10 May. Available from: https://www.foreignaffairs.com/articles/united-states/2014-05-10/case-against-killer-robots [accessed 28 February 2020].

Garcia, D. (2014b). Governing guns, preventing plunder: International cooperation against illicit trade by Asif Efrat. Book Review. *Political Science Quarterly*, 129(3).

Garcia, D. (2016a). The lethal artificial intelligence problem. *Global Policy*, 14 April. Available from: https://www.globalpolicyjournal.com/blog/14/04/2016/lethal-artificial-intelligence-problem [accessed 28 February 2020].

Garcia, D. (2016b). Future Arms, Technologies and International Law: Preventative Security Governance. *European Journal of International Security*, 1(1), pp. 94-114.

Garcia, D. (2018). Lethal Artificial Intelligence and Change: The Future of International Peace and Security. *International Studies Review*, 20(2), pp. 334-341.

Gartenstein-Ross, D. (2018). Terrorists are going to use artificial intelligence. *Defense One*, 3 May. Available from: https://www.defenseone.com/ideas/2018/05/terrorists-are-going-use-artificial-intelligence/147944/?oref=d-river [accessed 10 April 2020].

Gartner. (2018). Gartner says nearly half of CIOs are planning to deploy artificial intelligence. 13 February. Available from: https://www.gartner.com/en/newsroom/press-releases/2018-02-13-gartner-says-nearly-half-of-cios-are-planning-to-deploy-artificial-intelligence [accessed 28 February 2020].

GSM Association (GSMA). (2020). The Mobile Economy 2020. Available from: https://www.gsma.com/mobileeconomy/ [accessed 10 April 2020].

Hambling, D. (2016). How Islamic State is using consumer drones. *BBC*, 9 December. Available from: https://www.bbc.com/future/article/20161208-how-is-is-using-consumer-drones [accessed 10 April 2020].

Haner, J. & Garcia, D. (2019). The artificial intelligence arms race: Trends and world leaders in autonomous weapons development. *Global Policy*, 10(3).

History-Computer.com. (n.d.). Logic Theorist. Available from: https://history-computer.com/ModernComputer/Software/LogicTheorist.html [accessed 27 February 2020].

Horowitz, M.C. & Levendusky, M.S. (2011). Drafting support for war: Conscription and mass support for warfare. *The Journal of Politics*, 73(2), pp. 524-534.

Human Rights Watch. (2018). Eradicating ideological viruses – China's campaign of repression against Xinjiang's Muslims. 9 September. Available from: https://www.hrw.org/report/2018/09/09/eradicating-ideological-viruses/chinas-campaign-repression-against-xinjiangs [accessed 5 March 2020].

IntelliVision. Real-time AI Video Analytics Processing. Available from: https://www.intellivision.com/intelligent-video-analytics/ [accessed 5 March 2020].

Keats, J. (2016). How Alan Turing Found Machine Learning in the Human Mind. *New Scientist*, 29 June. Available from: https://www.newscientist.com/article/mg23130803-200-how-alan-turing-found-machine-thinking-in-the-human-mind/ [accessed 5 March 2020].

Lewis, T. (2014). A brief history of artificial intelligence. *LiveScience*, 4 December. Available from: https://www.livescience.com/49007-history-of-artificial-intelligence.html [accessed 5 March 2020].

Lufkin, B. (2017). Why the biggest challenge facing AI is an ethical one. BBC Future, 17 March. Available from: https://www.bbc.com/future/article/20170307-the-ethical-challenge-facing-artificial-intelligence?referer=http%3A%2F%2Fsitn.hms.harvard.edu%2Fflash%2F2017%2Fhistory-artificial-intelligence%2F [accessed 5 March 2020].

Marr, B. (2018). What is deep learning AI? A simple guide with 8 practical examples. *Forbes*, 1 October. Available from: https://www.forbes.com/sites/bernardmarr/2018/10/01/what-is-deep-learning-ai-a-simple-guide-with-8-practical-examples/#694c015b8d4b [accessed 5 March 2020].

Microsoft. (2017). AI and Security. Presented at the Microsoft Research Faculty Summit 2017. Available from: https://www.microsoft.com/en-us/research/wp-content/uploads/2017/07/AI_and_Security_Dawn_Song.pdf [accessed 27 February 2020].

Mizokami, K. (2018). Russia's tank drone performed poorly in Syria. *Popular Mechanics*. Available from: https://www.popularmechanics.com/military/weapons/a21602657/russias-tank-drone-performed-poorly-in-syria/ [accessed 25 February 2020].

Mnih, V., Kavukcuoglu, K., Silver, D., Rusu, A.A., Veness, J., Bellemare, M.G., Graves, A.,

Riedmiller, M., Fidjeland, A.K., Ostrovski, G., Petersen, S., Beattie, C., Sadik, A., Antonoglou, I., King, H., Kumaran, D., Wierstra, D., Legg, S. & Hassabis, D. (2015). Human-level control through deep reinforcement learning. *Nature*, 518.

Moor, J. (2006). The Dartmouth College Artificial Intelligence Conference: The Next Fifty Years. AI Magazine, 27(4).

New Scientist. (2020). Alan Turing: 23 June 1912 – 7 June 1954 – Alan Turing helped crack Nazi codes and established the field of artificial intelligence. Available from: https://www.newscientist.com/people/alan-turing/#ixzz6F2pcm73G [accessed 2 March 2020].

Nissenbaum, D. & Strobel, W. (2019). Mideast Insurgents Enter the Age of Drone Warfare. *The Wall Street Journal*, 2 May. Available from: https://www.wsj.com/articles/mideast-insurgents-enter-the-age-of-drone-warfare-11556814441 [accessed 25 February 2020].

Nogrady, B. (2016). The real risks of artificial intelligence. BBC Future, 10 November. Available from: https://www.bbc.com/future/article/20161110-the-real-risks-of-artificial-intelligence [accessed 25 February 2020].

Petropoulos, G. (2017). Machines that Learn to Do, and Do to Learn: What is Artificial Intelligence? *Global Policy*, 5 May. Available from: https://www.globalpolicyjournal.com/blog/05/05/2017/machines-learn-do-and-do-learn-what-artificial-intelligence [accessed 25 February 2020].

Ramaphosa, C. (2020). A national strategy for harnessing the Fourth Industrial Revolution: The case of South Africa. Brookings, 10 January. Available from: https://www.brookings.edu/blog/africa-in-focus/2020/01/10/a-national-strategy-for-harnessing-the-fourth-industrial-revolution-the-case-of-south-africa/ [accessed 16 March 2020].

Robles, P. (2018). China plans to be a world leader in artificial intelligence by 2030. *South China Morning Post*, 1 October. Available from: https://multimedia.scmp.com/news/china/article/2166148/china-2025-artificial-intelligence/ [accessed 2 March 2020].

Schneier, B. (2019). AI has made video surveillance automated and terrifying. *Vice*, 13 June. Available from: https://www.vice.com/en_us/article/bj93z5/ai-has-made-video-surveillance-automated-and-terrifying [accessed 2 March 2020].

The Moscow Times. (2014). Battle robots to guard Russian missile silos by 2020. 18 August. Available from: https://www.themoscowtimes.com/2014/08/18/battle-robots-to-guard-russian-missile-silos-by-2020-a38460 [accessed 25 February 2020].

Travaly, Y. & Muvunyi, K. (2020). The Future is Intelligent: Harnessing the Potential of Artificial Intelligence in Africa. Brookings, 13 January. Available from: https://www.brookings.edu/blog/africa-in-focus/2020/01/13/the-future-is-intelligent-harnessing-the-potential-of-artificial-intelligence-in-africa/ [accessed 16 March 2020].

Turing, A.M. (1950). Computing Machinery and Intelligence. *Mind*, 49.

United States Department of Defense. (2012). Directive 3000.09. Available from: https://www.esd.whs.mil/Portals/54/Documents/DD/issuances/dodd/300009p.pdf [accessed 27 February 2020].

Endnotes

1. Hambling, 2016.
2. Gartenstein-Ross, 2018.
3. *New Scientist*, 2020.
4. Lewis, 2014.
5. *New Scientist*, 2020.
6. Ibid.
7. Anyoha, 2017.
8. Petropoulos, 2017.
9. Ibid.
10. 'Machine vision' is the use of a camera or multiple cameras to inspect and analyse objects automatically. The resulting data goes to a computer which, using algorithms, learns to identify the images collected.
11. Braunstein & Laboure, 2018.
12. Nogrady, 2016.
13. Gartner, 2018.
14. Comiter, 2018.
15. Garcia, 2016a.
16. United States Department of Defense, 2012.
17. Garcia, 2014a.
18. Bendett, 2017; *The Moscow Times*, 2014.
19. Chan, 2019.
20. Dixon, 2018.
21. Schneier, 2019.
22. Germany is not a permanent member of the United Nations Security Council.
23. Convention on Certain Weapons (CCW) Group of Government Experts, 2018.
24. GSMA, 2020.
25. Ramaphosa, 2020.
26. Travaly & Muvunyi, 2020.
27. Besaw & Filitz, 2019.
28. Ibid.

CHAPTER 4

The Terror Business: Assessing the Organised Crime-Extremism Nexus in Africa

Richard Chelin

Introduction

Organised crime and terrorism have traditionally been perceived as two distinct concepts in terms of their conceptual definitions and the motivations of the individuals involved in these entities. With the evolving threat of transnational terrorism, the international community gradually started to focus on the existence of the linkages between organised crime and terrorism. Reflecting this development, the United Nations Security Council (UNSC) has adopted various resolutions on this issue.

In fact, for the past few decades, the international community's approach to defeating terrorism has been premised on the need to isolate and deny terrorists any support or benefits they could acquire from both their immediate environment and the international community as a whole. In Resolution 1267 (1999), adopted under Chapter VII of the United Nations (UN) Charter, the Council indicts the Taliban and all those who provide any form of support, directly or indirectly, to Al-Qaeda. This resolution imposes an obligation on all states to implement an asset freeze, travel ban and arms embargo against individuals, groups and entities blacklisted by the Council.[1] This practice has been strengthened in a series of resolutions adopted by the UNSC between 1999 and 2019.[2]

Most recently, in Resolution 2482 (2019), the Council expresses "its concern that terrorists can benefit from organised crime, whether domestic or transnational, as a source of financing or logistical support...". In Africa, the organised-crime and terrorism linkages were acknowledged in the 2004 Protocol of the Algiers Convention as "the links between terrorism and mercenarism, weapons of mass destruction, drug trafficking, corruption, transnational organised crimes, money laundering, and the illicit proliferation of small arms as increasing prevalent risks associated with terrorism".[3]

Despite the numerous resolutions recognising the evolving relationship between organised crime and terrorism, the nexus between the two continues to pose significant challenges to the international community and Africa more specifically. One of the most prevalent limitations in this regard is the lack of consensus on the definitions of terrorism and organised crime. Despite the challenge posed by the lack of an adequate and all-encompassing definition of terrorism, terrorist groups have been identified, and recognition of what a terrorist act constitutes has been detailed in various regional instruments and communities. Generally, there exists some form of concurrence on what constitutes a terrorist activity, namely, an act that involves "political motivations through intimidation, coercion and violence towards a civilian population and/or a government".[4]

In the absence of an international definition of terrorism, scholars and regional organisations have attempted to define the concept. The European Union's Counter-Terrorism Monitoring, Reporting and Support Mechanism (CT MORSE), for instance, defines terrorism as "the unlawful use of violence and intimidation, especially against civilians, in the pursuit of political aims".[5] While Makarenko[6] defines terrorism as "the conduct of premeditated violent acts or the threat of violence that is perpetrated by members of an organised group, designed to create fear in an adversary or specific segment of society", counterterrorism scholar Bruce Hoffman[7] labels it as "the deliberate creation and exploitation of fear through violence or the threat of violence in the pursuit of political change". Despite the plethora of definitions, this chapter adopts the UNSC Resolution 1566 of 8 October 2004 working definition of terrorism as:

> "Criminal and violent acts, including those against civilians, committed with the intent to cause death or serious harm, or taking of hostages, with the purpose to provoke a state of terror in the general public or in a group of persons or particular persons, intimidate a population or compel a government or an international organisation to do or to abstain from doing any acts, which constitute offences within the scope of and as defined in the international conventions and protocols relating to terrorism."[8]

The United Nations Convention against Transnational Organized Crime (UNTOC) does not provide a definition of organised crime due to the ever-changing criminal activities that can exist in numerous markets and be undertaken under the guise of legitimate enterprises; semi-legal, state activities; or purely in the criminal domain. Nonetheless, UNTOC describes organised crime as serious crime under national law, whereby the conduct is transnational and involves an organised criminal group. Furthermore, an organised criminal group is, according to UNTOC, "a structured group of three or more persons, existing for a period of time and acting in concert with the aim of committing one or more serious crimes or offences…in order to obtain, directly or indirectly, a financial or other material benefit".[9]

UNTOC is further supplemented by three protocols on crimes often carried out by organised criminal groups: the Protocol to Prevent, Suppress and Punish Trafficking in Persons, Especially Women and Children (Trafficking in Persons Protocol); the Protocol Against the Smuggling of Migrants by Land, Sea and Air (Smuggling of Migrants Protocol); and the Protocol Against the Illicit Manufacturing of and Trafficking in Firearms, their Parts and Components and Ammunition (Firearms Protocol). The United Nations Convention against Corruption (UNCAC), adopted in 2003, specifies and recognises different forms of corruption, and provides a legal framework to criminalise and combat a crime widely committed by organised criminal groups globally.

Distinguishing Between Terrorism and Organised Crime

Theoretically, the distinction between terrorism and organised crime lies in their respective objectives and modalities, as shown in Table 1. Terrorist groups seek political change through violence, or the threat of violence, based on an ideological inclination as a means to deliberately challenge the state. Terrorist groups need resources to achieve their goals, rather than resources being the goal itself. By contrast, organised criminal groups have no interest in influencing or affecting public opinion or political change but are rather interested in material satiation and personal financial gain. For these groups, profit is the ultimate goal.

At a legal level, terrorism and transnational organised crime may sometimes overlap and sometimes differ. Terrorism and organised crime often share the characteristics of being perpetrated by structured groups, involving serious national law offences and a transnational element. The key difference, as previously mentioned, lies in the specific requirement of a financial or material benefit in determining the overlap or differentiation between terrorism and transnational organised crime.

Table 1: Differences and similarities between organised-crime groups and transnational terrorist groups[10]

	Organised-crime groups	Transnational terrorist groups
Differences	Are motivated by economic gain and greed	Are motivated by political ideology and grievance
	Have a status-quo orientation	Have a revolutionary orientation
	Shun media attention	Seek media attention
	Do not legitimate their actions	Claim legitimacy for their actions
	Deny responsibility for their acts	Accept responsibility for their acts
	Develop working relations with state organisations	Rarely develop working relations with state organisations
Similarities	Are rational actors	
	Use or threaten severe violence	
	Use kidnapping, assassinations and/or extortions	
	Act clandestinely	
	Act illegally under national and international law	
	Pose an asymmetrical threat to states	
	Are highly adaptable and resilient organisations	
	Often act in sympathetic environments	
	Profit from globalisation and new technologies	
	Increasingly develop networks	
	Are particularly strong if operating from safe havens	

For instance, terrorist groups often finance themselves and their operations through serious criminal activities either directly or indirectly, such as the trafficking of arms, people, drugs and cultural artefacts, extortion, kidnapping for ransom (KFR) and the illicit trade of natural resources, inter alia, which will be discussed further below. However, it is important to note that there are instances where organised criminal groups may pursue political strategies and strategically use violence to enable and protect their illicit businesses, either to keep state institutions at bay or to co-opt the state through corruption and patronage networks. To this end, what constitutes a terrorist group or an organised criminal entity becomes increasingly blurred. Cognisant of this, scholars have attempted to develop frameworks to explain this issue more clearly, in what is often termed the organised crime-terrorism nexus, or the nexus in short.

Organised Crime and Terrorism Nexus

The concept of the nexus finds its genesis in the 1970s and 1980s, when scholars began to uncover the connection between terrorism and organised crime. In an attempt to label the terrorist acts perpetrated by drug trafficking organisations in Latin America, the then United States (US) ambassador to Colombia proposed the term 'narco-terrorism'.[11] Since then, the nexus has grown in complexity and scope. In a bid to assess and explain the complex relationship of the nexus, scholars developed a framework known as the crime-terror continuum. The continuum consists of terrorist groups on the one end of the spectrum and organised-crime entities on the other, and it can be divided into four phases.

The first is the alliance phase, where both organised crime and terrorist groups form alliances to promote their respective interests. These alliances can be either tactical, in that there is a once-off deal or a short-term negotiation, or strategic, where it lasts for a longer period, depending on the interests of the actors involved.[12]

Phase two, the appropriation stage, is where one entity adopts the other's methods and tactics and vice versa, featuring the employment of operational tactics by both terrorist and organised-crime groups. As such, terrorists engage in criminal activities as a means to fund their cause, while organised-crime entities employ "selected and calibrated violence to destroy competitors or threaten counter-narcotic authorities".[13] The first two phases can be categorised as the transactional nexus due to the collaboration between the two entities to fulfil certain specific operational requirements.

Convergence is the third phase, where the relationship between the two groups extends beyond mere cooperation and/or alliance. In this phase, the groups merge into a single hybrid entity, displaying similar characteristics and motivations, making it almost impossible to distinguish one from the other. A hybrid group will display ideological and economic motivations by perpetrating acts of terrorism and engaging in organised crime for profit maximisation. These types of entities often present the biggest challenge to the state, as difficulties in defining their nature can result in them being overlooked by both law-enforcement and counterterrorism agencies.

The last phase is the transformation phase, which refers to the evolution of the aim and motivation of a single group to the extent that it results in a drastic change in the nature of the group. In other words, it occurs when a terrorist group fuses (organisationally and operationally) into an organised-crime entity or vice versa. The last two phases constitute the organisational nexus whereby terrorist groups and organised-crime entities occupy the same space and time.

Factors Influencing the Nexus

Having examined the nature of the crime-terror continuum, it is of the utmost importance to understand the context that promotes the emergence of these networks. The development and success of the crime-terror relationship include a state of chaos, protracted conflicts, and regions possessing shadow economies, which are further strengthened when both terrorist groups and organised criminals are allowed to operate freely in spaces over which governments have little or no control.[14] In such spaces, instability and the need to prolong the conflict become primary motives for both entities to facilitate their operations. Unstable environments often lead to poor border security, weak law enforcement, corrupt public officials and established smuggling networks. Countries such as Afghanistan, Sierra Leone, Pakistan, Thailand, Somalia, northern Mali and, most recently, the greater Sahel region are key examples.

It is in the context of conflict and post-conflict that the nexus is at its most interactive phase. Given a context of instability, neither criminal nor terrorist groups display any innate loyalty or ascribe any form of legitimacy to the state. As mentioned above, maintaining instability is crucial in diminishing the legitimacy of the government, thus creating conditions conducive for criminal activities and recruitment into terrorist groups. For example, the 2012 Tuareg rebellion in northern Mali provided the perfect context for various extremist groups – such as Al-Qaeda in the Islamic Maghreb (AQIM), Ansar Al Dine and the Movement for Oneness and Jihad in West Africa (MUJAO) – to capitalise on the situation for recruitment and conducting criminal activities.

With regard to transitional states, there have been several variations of transactional and organisational displays of the nexus, with hybrid and transformational entities being the most prevalent. Poor border security, weak law enforcement, corrupt public officials and established trafficking networks have facilitated the emergence of hybrid groups. Corruption is one of the crucial aspects that organised-crime and terrorist groups exploit as a way to enhance the crime-terror nexus. Their aim is to create a situation where corruption becomes widespread and endemic, leading to a loss of authority by the state, which is then perceived as a "predator instead of a protector".[15] Facing a loss of legitimacy among the people, governments can do very little to prevent terrorist and organised-crime groups from expanding the nexus. It is therefore not surprising that organised-crime and terrorist groups "gravitate towards regions of the globe with high levels of corruption".[16]

Transitional and conflict states are not the only operational grounds for the nexus, as there have also been manifestations of the nexus in politically stable states. However, organised criminals and terrorists are mostly involved in the transactional manifestation of the nexus. This usually takes the form of terror cells that engage in crime as a source of financing. A growing body of evidence shows that extremist groups are recruiting individuals with criminal backgrounds into their operations. For example, Abdelhamid Abaaoud, the leader of the Paris November 2015 attacks, Ahmed Coulibaly, a key figure in the Charlie Hebdo attacks, and numerous other terrorists were involved in various forms of criminality before becoming jihadists.[17]

While this is mostly witnessed in Europe, there is little evidence of such in Africa and it remains a trend to explore in future. In recruiting criminals, terrorist groups gain access to individuals who can provide criminal expertise and links to organised criminal networks, which can be useful in helping to fund their operations. This also creates the dilemma of homegrown terrorism, and challenges law enforcement to distinguish between petty crimes, which facilitate terrorist funding, and crimes that are part of a politically stable country.

Overview of the Nexus in Africa

The challenges associated with examining the organised crime-terrorism nexus are highly prevalent in Africa. The multiplicity of different groups itself presents a unique challenge on its own, notwithstanding the contrasting models, ideologies and implications of these entities. Although most groups in operation on the continent tend to affiliate themselves with international terrorism brands, their operations and targets are predominantly within their local community and region. Furthermore, with regard to financing, most groups tend to benefit from international illicit flows.[18]

The Sahel and Sahara regions have long been marked as a source of instability, due predominantly to the tribal conflicts, porous borders and fragile states that characterise this expansive location. Criminal and terrorist groups alike have infiltrated the historic trade routes across countries such as Algeria, Libya, Mali and Mauritania, partly as a result of weak state institutions and widespread corruption. This, in turn, has presented the perfect opportunity for criminal and terrorist groups to translate their activities into political influence and military and financial power.

The porousness of the region has made it an ideal location for the movement of illicit goods and other forms of organised crime, such as KFR, counterfeit goods and drug smuggling. Such criminal activity has often been carried out by long-standing commercial and social networks based around local tribes and communities specialising in trade through informal arrangements across the region. Tensions among these local tribal communities have long reinforced the instability of the region, with tactical alliances proving necessary for organised criminal and terrorist networks to operate. The conflict dynamics in the area directly contribute to the muddling of lines between groups seeking financial and material benefits and those primarily driven by political motives. Such groups may be characterised as opportunistic, rearranging their alliances once doing so becomes opportune to promote their political, ideological or business interests.

It is within this context that radical terrorist groups have capitalised on regional dynamics to promote their ideologies and fund their operations. For example, with its roots in Algeria, AQIM espouses Salafist jihadism dogma with regionally resonant elements. The group formed tactical alliances with indigenous tribes such as the Tuareg and Berabiche, through marriage and other means, providing it with a recruitment source and allowing it to become intimately involved in their criminal activities to fund its operations.[19]

Apart from West Africa and the Sahel, in the east, the Horn of Africa has also seen an interchange between terrorism and organised crime. The vast coastlines, failing state institutions and weak borders have enabled the region to become a hub for organised criminal activities. Al-Shabaab, which focuses its operations primarily on Somalia and Kenya, has demonstrated a strong interdependence and has been officially identified as both a terrorist and organised criminal group, with an estimated annual turnover of nearly $70 million.[20] In addition to its terrorist activities, Al-Shabaab has reportedly been linked to a number of illicit activities ranging from extortion to charcoal trafficking and wildlife crime.

Typologies of Organised Crime Associated with Terrorism

There are a number of typologies of criminal behaviour associated with terrorism. The types of crimes associated with terrorism chosen below are based on existing literature and UNSC Resolution 2482 (2019), which expresses the concern:

> "…that terrorists can benefit from organised crime, whether domestic or transnational, such as the trafficking in arms, drugs, artefacts, cultural property and trafficking in persons, as well as the illicit trade in natural resources, including gold and other precious metals and stones, minerals, charcoal and oil, illicit trafficking in wildlife and other crimes that affect the environment, as well as from the abuse of legitimate commercial enterprise, non-profit organisations, donations, crowdfunding and proceeds of criminal activity, including but not limited to kidnapping for ransom, extortion and bank robbery, as well as from transnational organised crime at sea."[21]

Examined below are the crime-terrorism linkages as they play out through the following activities: drug trafficking; trafficking in small arms and light weapons; human trafficking; trafficking in cultural property and antiquities; counterfeit goods; KFR; and exploitation of natural resources.

Terrorism and Drug Trafficking
The links between drug trafficking and terrorism are the strongest when compared to other forms of transnational organised crime. There have been instances in which terrorist groups directly produce or traffic drugs themselves. More commonly, terrorist groups may generate revenue by taxing illicit drug production, transport or distribution by others. Terrorist groups may protect this revenue base by also providing protection for drug facilities, producers and traffickers. Groups such as AQIM have been known to offer 'protection' to drug cartels originating primarily in Latin America for passage across the harsh terrain of the Sahel and onward to Europe.[22] Al-Shabaab has also been linked to heroin trafficking, moving product through port towns and onward to Europe, along with cocaine transported as sugar or rice aboard trucks into Kenya.[23]

Terrorist groups have also used illicit drugs as currency, as demonstrated in the Madrid train bombings in 2004, where drugs were swapped and sold for explosives, and a known drug trafficker was convicted in Morocco for his part in the operation.[24] The Taliban maintained "opium warehouses across Afghanistan's southern poppy heartland where Taliban commanders [could] deposit and later withdraw quantities of the drug as if using an ATM", and used such drugs to purchase other supplies and commodities.[25] Terrorist groups may use revenue from drug trafficking to buy weapons, pay bribes to key individuals, fund propaganda and recruitment, and sustain operations and networks. Following the crime-terror continuum mentioned above, terrorist groups originally inspired by political, religious or ideological aims may transform over time into organised criminal groups focusing on drug trafficking, captured by a trade initially used to finance their political goals. Conversely, over time, drug cartels may seek to violently exert political influence.

The links between terrorism and drug trafficking may be spread across multiple countries, following the complex routes of supply, transport and distribution. For example, a Malian national was convicted in the US in 2011 for material support for terrorism, as he transported cocaine through west and north Africa with the intent to supply Al-Qaeda.[26] Consequently, as terrorist groups become more fixated on the financial benefits of the drug trade, they slowly drift from their original *raison d'être* to share similarities with drug cartels, as drugs and terrorism coexist across the globe in a marriage of mutual convenience.

Terrorism and Weapons Trafficking

It is evident that terrorist organisations rely on a supply of weapons to carry out their attacks. Small arms and light weapons are among the most commonly used, and the most readily available. They are also unregulated by the existing sectoral counterterrorism treaties. While terrorists will often use lawfully obtained firearms – particularly in states without strict controls – the illicit production and traffick of firearms account for a significant portion of terrorist caches.

The phenomenon of arms trafficking is one laden with complexities. For instance, a terrorist buys small arms and light weapons on both the grey and black markets. In the case of the Revolutionary Armed Forces of Colombia (FARC), weapons would be bought with profits from its drug trade. On the black market, the entire transaction – the sale, distribution and final destination – is illegal because it involves unauthorised actors or channels. This would take the form of state officials illegally transferring military stocks; stocks remaindered after conflicts, as in the case of Libya post-Gaddafi; and arms made in factories. Arms can also be obtained on the domestic black market from local traffickers connected to international traffickers, or from corrupt security or corporate personnel.

Conversely, on the grey market the initial sale and distribution are undertaken through legal channels, by an authorised state or private actor, but the final destination is an illegal actor. Grey-market sales include weapons from the diversion of surplus foreign-state military weapons by corrupt officials working through illegal trafficker intermediaries, as well as the movement of arms from the other country's domestic private market, often using false identification documents.

In Africa, the destabilisation of Libya has also been a major component in the instability of the north African region, and has contributed to terrorist and organised-crime operations. The fall of the Gaddafi regime established the perfect setting for regional volatility, including providing impetus for a proliferation of weapons in the Sahel-Sahara region. Libyan arms obtained by AQIM and other forces have been smuggled to groups such as Boko Haram and Al-Shabaab, emboldening and enabling them to mount more deadly attacks and further their illicit activities. In the east, Al-Shabaab has taken advantage of porous borders with Kenya and South Sudan to coordinate with local criminal networks to smuggle weapons into neighbouring countries, further undermining state institutions, security and stability in the region.

Terrorism and Human Trafficking
The links between human trafficking and terrorism can be difficult to identify because of the clandestine nature of both crimes. Human trafficking may be attractive to terrorists for three reasons: It can generate revenue, supply fighters, and intimidate enemy populations.[27] In reality, there is some evidence of human trafficking by terrorist groups. For example, the Taliban in Afghanistan abducted women and girls for forced marriage, sexual slavery in brothels, to use as concubines by officers, for domestic servitude, or for sale into sexual slavery in Arab countries.[28] Boko Haram in Nigeria has abducted more than 2,000 people, including kidnapping young girls and forcing them into marriage, domestic servitude, labour or sexual slavery.[29] There have been reports of terrorist groups, such as Al-Shabaab in Somalia and Boko Haram in Nigeria, forcibly recruiting children. The UNSC has also condemned human trafficking by terrorist groups such as the Islamic State (IS), Boko Haram and the Lord's Resistance Army (LRA).[30]

Terrorism and Trafficking in Cultural Property and Antiquities
A four-stage network supply-chain model, premised on geography, laws, economy and cultural views on antiquities, can be used to understand the global trafficking of antiquities.[31] The stages are:
1. Looting – this occurs most often in an area where conflict exists or that is economically depressed.
2. Early-stage middlepersons/intermediaries specialising in the procurement and transit of illicit antiquities/cultural property work with organised criminal groups to traffick the objects from the source countries.
3. A late-stage intermediary launders the objects after transit, creates export licences and false provenance, and then brings the objects to the legitimate global market.

4. The objects enter the legal market via international brokers in the transit country, or arrive in the hands of the collector.

Terrorist groups seem to have increasingly taken up trafficking in illicit antiquities and cultural property to fund their operations, support recruits and acquire weapons. Antiquities are not only a source of revenue generation for terrorists, but they also have symbolic value. By destroying and/or removing symbolic representations of culture, terrorist groups effectively undermine the state/nationalism and attack the morale of local populations through a type of 'cultural cleansing'. This latter aspect, also termed cultural terrorism, has been a feature of contemporary conflicts.

In Mali in 2012, fundamentalist religious militants destroyed around 40,000 ancient manuscripts and 16 Sufi mausoleums, while the Taliban in Afghanistan notoriously blew up the Bamiyan Buddha statues. On a larger scale, IS has destroyed cultural property in Syria, Iraq and Libya, including mosques, shrines, tombs, churches, monasteries, museums and ancient ruins. Its targets have included Shiites, Sufis, Assyrians, Chaldeans, Armenians and Yazidis. IS also seriously damaged the World Heritage Site of ancient Palmyra. It has also taxed the looting and smuggling of artefacts, and dealt directly in stolen and fake antiquities.[32]

Terrorism and Counterfeit Goods
The money obtained through narcotics and other forms of smuggling is often channelled towards the purchase of weapons. Another form of illegal activity through which terrorist groups financially benefit is counterfeit goods, especially cigarette smuggling. Some groups have even become professionals in the domain of cigarette smuggling. The smuggling of narcotics still remains a primary form of revenue for some criminal groups, as typified by Mokhtar Belmokhtar, a former commander of AQIM, who was so successful in smuggling cigarettes that he was subsequently given the moniker 'Mr Marlboro'.[33] Furthermore, it is important to note that cigarette smuggling was the original operation of the organised-crime network in the Sahel, and it contributed immensely to the subsequent emergence of the practice and networks that have solidified the growth of drug trafficking into its present state.

One of the reasons that terrorists engage in counterfeit trade is because it has a low risk profile. Furthermore, terrorists engage in counterfeit operations in two ways: either directly or indirectly. Direct involvement means the group is personally engaged in the production, distribution and sale of the illicit goods, and the funds obtained are redirected towards financing the operation of the group. Groups such as AQIM and IS are directly involved in illicit activities such as counterfeit goods trafficking rather than operating through third parties. As such, terrorist organisations with direct involvement include groups that resemble or behave more like organised criminal groups than traditional terrorist organisations.

Terrorism and Kidnapping for Ransom
From 1970 to 2010, kidnapping incidents represented 6,9% of all terrorist attacks. However, through 2016 the percentage of kidnappings jumped significantly to 15,8%. A number of terrorist groups in Africa have raised substantial funds in this way, namely MUJAO, Boko Haram and Ansaru in Nigeria, as well as the most notable of them all, AQIM. The former leader of Al-Qaeda in the Arabian Peninsula, Nasser al-Wuhayshi, referred to kidnapping as "an easy spoil … a profitable trade and a precious treasure".[34]

Between 2008 and 2014, Al-Qaeda and its direct affiliates made at least $125 million in revenue from kidnappings, $66 million of which was collected in 2013.[35] It is estimated that AQIM received $75 million in ransom payments between 2010 and 2014.[36] AQIM uses historic trade routes and strategic alliances to facilitate KFR, which is its most lucrative source of funding. Estimates relating to the amount of revenue that AQIM generates from KFR varies, but figures suggest that in the period between 2003 and 2012 alone, the group brought in nearly $89 million, focusing on nationals of countries (particularly Europe) known to be willing to pay ransoms.[37] Similarly to AQIM, Boko Haram has garnered a large portion of its funding through KFR.[38] Since KFR activities have proven to be a lucrative source of income for many extremist groups, it would not be surprising to see an increase in kidnapping by various groups in the near future.

Terrorism and Exploitation of Natural Resources
Some terrorist groups have financed themselves by illicit trafficking in natural

resources, or the taxation of trafficking by others, both of which can also cause serious environmental damage. One example is the illicit logging and trade in timber or charcoal by Al-Qaeda, the Haqqani network, Al-Shabaab, and various groups in the Virunga National Park in Uganda/Rwanda.[39] For instance, charcoal smuggling by Al-Shabaab has proven especially lucrative, with the UN estimating that the organisation makes in the region of $15 million to $50 million per year from this illegal trade.[40] Al-Shabaab exploited charcoal smuggling routes by taxing coal bags en route to Somali harbours, forcing traders to pay multiple taxes and bribes before reaching port. In addition to charcoal, Al-Shabaab has identified major sugar smuggling routes and has charged up to $1,000 per truck. In 2011, the illicit sugar trade generated between $400,000 and $800,000 for the group.[41]

While there are presumed linkages between illegal wildlife poaching, such as rhinoceros or elephant for ivory, and a variety of terrorist organisations, these claims have gone largely unsubstantiated. One group that is pertinent with regard to wildlife poaching and trafficking, especially in ivory, is the LRA. Originally, the reason behind the poaching of elephants by the LRA was to exchange bushmeat and ivory with the local population around Garamba for agricultural and manufactured goods, including medicines. What started as a need for survival evolved into a business partnership in which the group started trading ivory with foreign business people for food and arms.[42]

Illegal mining and the export of minerals such as gold or diamonds and precious metals, or the illicit production of and trade in oil, are other forms of resource exploitation through which terrorist groups obtain financing. There have been reports indicating Al-Shabaab's involvement in illegal mining and the export of minerals in East Africa in conjunction with a Ugandan militant group.[43] Gold mines in the Sahel provide jihadists with a new source of funding, and even terrain on which to recruit. These groups have capitalised on informal networks in the region to become increasingly involved in smuggling the precious metal. Gold also contributes to the growth of international money-laundering networks.

In the north of Niger and Mali, several important artisanal gold-mining entrepreneurs are major players in narco-trafficking.[44] Traffickers frequently purchase gold above the market price to export it via smuggling networks. The trafficking in oil is another example of how terrorist groups accrue their funds. IS also generates vast revenues through its exploitation of the oil and gas sector, taking over wells and refineries inside Syria and Iraq, and smuggling oil to Turkey, with estimates of earnings reaching up to $3 million a day.[45]

Conclusion and Recommendations

The evolution of the relationship between organised crime and terrorism, and the widespread discord on its very nature, has translated into confused responses from policymakers and practitioners seeking to address this threat. Thus far, international and regional responses to the organised crime-terrorism nexus have remained limited in that they tend to focus on 'traditional' terrorist activities (such as the financing of terrorism) at the expense of organised crime (or vice versa), rather than tailoring efforts that acknowledge and address the nexus itself.

Additionally, while the relationship between organised crime and terrorism is often political in nature and a product of the local context, efforts to counter this phenomenon have remained largely tactical and reactive in nature. Responses are driven primarily by law-enforcement objectives. While such responses are no doubt important, they lack strength in addressing the root causes of the increasingly interlinked roles of criminals and terrorists. In other words, such interventions thus far have failed to address why terrorists and criminals are increasingly becoming one and the same.

To address this phenomenon, policymakers and practitioners will be required to move beyond traditional law-enforcement methods to adopt a more nuanced, phased and multi-sector approach. For instance, the responses around countering the financing of terrorism, which are often coupled strategically with those to prevent money laundering, are advanced and well documented, with extensive guidance for financial institutions, law-enforcement bodies, global and national regulators, and states to follow and oversee. These are, however, far more effective for those contexts where money is moved through an institutionalised financial system. As a growing number of Financial Action Task Force (FATF) reports have acknowledged, an increasing amount of money is moving through the informal *hawala* financial system, or through non-traditional means such as crypto-currencies or even social media channels and networks.[46] There has been little response to addressing such challenges with the informal money system.

Another limitation is the lack of responses available to address the ability of local groups to extort or tax local populations, businesses and revenue flows, which have been identified in the case studies as a major means by which contemporary terrorist groups raise funds. There has been some work, albeit limited, on breaking cycles of criminal extortion and mafia-style behaviour. It can be argued that approaches to break cycles of criminal extortion may also be applicable in cases where terrorist groups also levy protection taxes to resource their causes.

Furthermore, the responses to the nexus have largely overlooked the social and economic capital and legitimacy that criminal and/or terrorist groups have managed to garner with their local communities, for which technical responses are poorly suited. At the point at which criminal and/or terrorist groups are presenting an alternative governance model, the strategic response would need to be tailored to breaking down their influence and rebuilding that of a legitimate state, as exemplified in the FARC peace process in Colombia.

The predominant factors contributing to both criminal and terrorist recruitment are the failure of state service delivery and the inability to provide economic opportunities. Based on this, a long-term strategy would be for state actors and policymakers to work to address large-scale contributors to the nexus by implementing interventions aimed at issues such as improving the rule of law, enhancing transparency and boosting economic opportunities. Additionally, there is a need to raise awareness among key policymakers of the types of factors that raise the risk of radicalisation and criminalisation, and of potential measures to address these vulnerabilities. The state may also put measures in place to carefully monitor vulnerable communities and people who are on terrorism watch lists to allow for early and supportive action, while keeping in mind the need to respect an individual's right to privacy.

Community-led responses, in collaboration with law-enforcement practices that allow individuals the opportunity to voice and address their grievances, may be effective in reducing the vulnerability of local populations more broadly. Furthermore, there is a need to move beyond focusing on the financing of terrorism to focusing on specific areas, such as the role of women and youth (as both proponents and victims of terrorism and organised crime) as well as the operation of illicit economies and local businesses. Strategies should focus on local engagement to build social resilience through a multi-sectoral approach with actors from all areas of society to dispel any narratives that attempt to make terrorism and organised crime a viable option. Lastly, it is arguably the case that principles of good governance, anti-corruption, and countering impunity, social marginalisation and exclusion are critical to breaking down the strategic objectives and capacities for leverage of both criminal and terrorist groups, regardless of their manifestation.

In conclusion, it is important to reiterate that responses to the organised crime-terrorism nexus have focused largely on addressing issues related to the financing of terrorism, strengthening the practices through which illicit money can be earned, transferred and procured. In the light of the evolving nature of the nexus, however, there is a need to develop effective and appropriate responses to the organised-crime and terrorism phenomena that address the underlying causes of the convergence at regional, national and local levels, based on a strong evidence base, engagement with local actors, enhanced service delivery and, most importantly, the principle of good governance.

Select Bibliography
Action on Armed Violence (AOAV). (2017). Sources of funding (including self-funding) for the major groupings that perpetrate IED incidents – al Shabaab. 25 May. Available from: https://aoav.org.uk/2017/sources-funding-including-self-funding-major-groupings-perpetrate-ied-incidents-al-shabaab/ [accessed 1 April 2020].
Adepelumi, P. (2015). The Root Causes of Human Trafficking in Nigeria. African Center for Advocacy and Human Development, Nigeria. Presentation at the High-level Event on the UN Trust Fund for Victims of Trafficking in Persons, 13th UN Crime Congress, Doha, Qatar, 13 April. Available from: https://www.unodc.org/documents/congress/workshops/workshop2/Presentation_P_Adepelumi_African_Center_.pdf [accessed 31 March 2020].
African Union (AU). (2004). Protocol to the OAU Convention on the Prevention and Combating of Terrorism, 8 July.
Associated Press. (2006). Madrid bombing probe finds no al-Qaida link: Two-year investigation concludes that terrorists were homegrown radicals. *NBC News*, 9 March. Available from: http://www.nbcnews.com/id/11753547/ns/world_news-terrorism/t/madrid-bombing-probe-finds-no-al-qaida-link/#.XoRVhIgzZPY [accessed 1 April 2020].
BBC News. (2016). Chibok girls: Kidnapped schoolgirl found in Nigeria. 18 May. Available

from: https://www.bbc.com/news/world-africa-36321249 [accessed 1 April 2020].

Bøås, M. (2014). Guns, Money and Prayers: AQIM's Blueprint for Securing Control of Northern Mali. *Combating Terrorism Center (CTC) Sentinel*, 7(4). Available from: https://www.ctc.usma.edu/guns-money-and-prayers-aqims-blueprint-for-securing-control-of-northern-mali/ [accessed 1 April 2020].

Breuer, L.A. (2011). Questions and Answers: Questions for the Record. In Combating International Organized Crime: Evaluating Current Authorities, Tools, and Resources. Testimony of the Assistant Attorney-General Criminal Division to the Subcommittee on Crime and Terrorism of the Committee on the Judiciary, 1 November.

Callimachi, R. (2015). ISIS Enshrines a Theology of Rape. *The New York Times*, 13 August. Available from: https://www.nytimes.com/2015/08/14/world/middleeast/isis-enshrines-a-theology-of-rape.html [accessed 31 March 2020].

Campbell, P.B. (2013). The Illicit Antiquities Trade as a Transnational Criminal Network: Characterizing and Anticipating Trafficking of Cultural Heritage. *International Journal of Cultural Property*, 20(2).

Center for Security Studies (CSS). (2013). Kidnapping for Ransom as a Source of Terrorism Funding. *CSS Analysis in Security Policy*, 141, October. Zurich: CSS. Available from: https://www.files.ethz.ch/isn/170968/CSS-Analysis-141-EN.pdf [accessed 1 April 2020].

Costa, A.M. (2007). Europe's Cocaine Problem is a Curse ... and not only for Europe. Speech presented at the Conference on Cocaine, Madrid, 15 November. Available from: https://www.unodc.org/unodc/en/about-unodc/speeches/2007-11-15.html [accessed 31 March 2020].

Cottee, S. (2016). Reborn Into Terrorism: Why are so many ISIS recruits ex-cons and converts? *The Atlantic*, 25 January. Available from: https://www.theatlantic.com/international/archive/2016/01/isis-criminals-converts/426822/ [accessed 31 March 2020].

Daase, C. (2010). Terrorism and Organized Crime: One or Two Challenges? In Benedek, W., Daase, C., Dimitrijević, V. & Van Duyne, P. (eds.). *Transnational Terrorism, Organized Crime and Peace-Building: Human Security in the Western Balkans*. New York: Palgrave Macmillan, pp. 54-65.

Dishman, C. (2001). Terrorism, Crime, and Transformation. *Studies in Conflict & Terrorism*, 24(1), pp. 43-58.

Doward, J. (2013). How cigarette smuggling fuels Africa's Islamist violence. *The Guardian*, 27 January. Available from: https://www.theguardian.com/world/2013/jan/27/cigarette-smuggling-mokhtar-belmokhtar-terrorism [accessed 1 April 2020].

Duffy, M. (2015). The Sahel, Libya, and the Crime-Terror Nexus. *Foreign Policy Journal*. Available from: https://www.foreignpolicyjournal.com/2015/10/30/the-sahel-libya-and-the-crime-terror-nexus/ [accessed 1 April 2020].

Faiola, A. & Mekhennet, S. (2015). The Islamic State creates a new type of jihadist: Part terrorist, part gangster. *The Washington Post*, 20 December. Available from: https://www.washingtonpost.com/world/europe/the-islamic-state-creates-a-new-type-of-jihadist-part-terrorist-part-gangster/2015/12/20/1a3d65da-9bae-11e5-aca6-1ae3be6f06d2_ story.html [accessed 31 March 2020].

Financial Action Task Force (FATF). (2013). The role of *hawala* and other similar service providers in money laundering and terrorist financing. FATF report, October. France: FATF.

Financial Action Task Force (FATF). (2014). Financial flows linked to the production and trafficking of Afghan opiates. FATF report, June. France: FATF.

Financial Action Task Force (FATF). (2015). Financing of the Terrorist Organisation Islamic State in Iraq and the Levant (ISIL). FATF report, February. France: FATF.

Financial Action Task Force (FATF). (2016). Terrorist Financing in West Africa. FATF report, October. France: FATF.

Freeman, C. (2016). Boko Haram demands '$50m ransom' for release of kidnapped Chibok schoolgirls. *The Telegraph*, 9 April. Available from: https://www.telegraph.co.uk/news/2016/04/09/boko-haram-demands-50m-ransom-for-release-of-kidnapped-chibok-sc/ [accessed 1 April 2020].

Fuchs, D. (2004). Spain Says Bombers Drank Water From Mecca and Sold Drugs. *The New York Time*s, 15 April. Available from: https://www.nytimes.com/2004/04/15/world/spain-says-bombers-drank-water-from-mecca-and-sold-drugs.html [accessed 1 April 2020].

Heibner, S., Neumann, P.R., Holland-McCowan, J. & Basra, R. (2017). Caliphate in Decline: An Estimate of Islamic State's Financial Fortunes. March. London: The International Centre for the Study of Radicalisation and Political Violence. Available from: https://www.start.umd.edu/publication/caliphate-decline-estimate-islamic-states-financial-fortunes [accessed 1 April 2020].

Hoffman, B. (1998). *Inside Terrorism*. New York: Columbia University Press.

International Crisis Group. (2019). Getting a Grip on Central Sahel's Gold Rush. Crisis Group Africa Report N° 282, 13 November.

Keatinge, T. (2014). The Role of Finance in Defeating Al-Shabaab. Whitehall Report 2-14. London: The Royal United Services Institute for Defence and Security Studies. Available from: https://rusi.org/sites/default/files/201412_whr_2-14_keatinge_web_0.pdf [accessed 31 March 2020].

Keller, A. (2015). Documenting ISIL's Antiquities Trafficking: The Looting and Destruction of Iraqi and Syrian Cultural Heritage: What We Know and What Can Be Done. Press statement at The Metropolitan Museum of Art, 29 September. Available from: https://2009-2017.state.gov/e/eb/rls/rm/2015/247610.htm [accessed 31 March 2020].

Luengo-Cabrera, J. & Moser, A. (2016). Transatlantic drug trafficking – via Africa. Paris: European Union Institute for Security Studies. Available from: https://www.iss.europa.eu/content/transatlantic-drug-trafficking-%E2%80%93-africa [accessed 31 March 2020].

Makarenko, T. (2012). Europe's Crime-Terror Nexus: Links between terrorist and organised crime groups in the European Union. Brussels: Directorate-General for Internal Policies, Policy Department C: Citizens' Rights and Constitutional Affairs, European Parliament.

McGirk, T. & Plain, S. (2002). Lifting the Veil on Taliban Sex Slavery. *Time*, 10 February.

Available from: http://content.time.com/time/magazine/article/0,9171,201892,00.html [accessed 31 March 2020].

Nellemann, C., Henriksen, R., Raxter, P., Ash, N. & Mrema, E. (eds.). (2014). The Environmental Crime Crisis – Threats to Sustainable Development from Illegal Exploitation and Trade in Wildlife and Forest Resources. United Nations Environment Programme Rapid Response Assessment. Nairobi and Arendal: United Nations Environment Programme and GRID-Arendal.

Picarelli, J.T. (2012). Osama bin Corleone? Vito the Jackal? Framing Threat Convergence Through an Examination of Transnational Organized Crime and International Terrorism. *Terrorism and Political Violence*, 24(2), pp. 180-198.

Reitano, T., Clarke, C.P. & Adal, L. (2017). Examining the Nexus between Organised Crime and Terrorism and its Implications for EU Programming. Brussels: CT MORSE Consortium. Available from: https://icct.nl/wp-content/uploads/2017/04/OC-Terror-Nexus-Final.pdf [accessed 31 March 2020].

Rhode, D. (2014). Column: Did America's policy on ransom contribute to James Foley's Killing? *Reuters*, 20 August. Available from: https://www.reuters.com/article/rohde-foley/column-did-americas-policy-on-ransom-contribute-to-james-foleys-killing-idUSL2N0QQ23920140820 [accessed 31 March 2020].

Sampaio, A. (2015): Shifts in heroin trafficking highlight organised crime threats in East Africa. Bahrain, London, Singapore, Washington: International Institute for Strategic Studies.

Shabelle Media Network. (2013). Somalia: Kenya Lists Al-Shabaab As Organized Crime Gang. *AllAfrica.com*, 31 August. Available from: https://allafrica.com/stories/201308310553.html [accessed 1 April 2020].

Shelley, L. (2005). The Unholy Trinity: Transnational Crime, Corruption, and Terrorism. *The Brown Journal of World Affairs*, 11(2), pp. 101-111.

Shelley, L. (2014). ISIS, Boko Haram, and the Growing Role of Human Trafficking in 21st Century Terrorism. *The Daily Beast*, 26 December. Available from: https://www.thedailybeast.com/isis-boko-haram-and-the-growing-role-of-human-trafficking-in-21st-century-terrorism [accessed 31 March 2020].

Titeca, K. & Edmond, P. (2019). Outside the Frame: Looking Beyond the Myth of Garamba's LRA Ivory-Terrorism Nexus. *Conservation & Society*, 17(3), pp. 258-269.

United Nations (UN). (2004). United Nations Convention Against Transnational Organized Crime and the Protocols Thereto. Adopted 15 November 2000, entered into force 29 September 2013. Vienna: United Nations Office on Drugs and Crime.

United Nations (UN). (2010). *Digest of Terrorist Cases*. Vienna: United Nations Office on Drugs and Crime.

United Nations (UN). (2017). *World Drug Report 2017: The Drug Problem and Organized Crime, Illicit Financial Flows, Corruption and Terrorism. Booklet 5*. Vienna: United Nations Office on Drugs and Crime.

United Nations Human Rights Council (UNHRC). (2016). Report of the Independent International Commission of Inquiry on the Syrian Arab Republic. A/HRC/31/68, 11

February. Available from: https://www.refworld.org/docid/56d6b3843ea.html [accessed 1 April 2020].

United Nations Security Council (UNSC). (1999). Resolution 1267. Available from: https://www.un.org/securitycouncil/sanctions/1267/resolutions?page=4 [accessed 19 December 2019].

United Nations Security Council (UNSC). (2004). Resolution 1566: Establishment of a working group to consider measures to be imposed upon individuals, groups or entities other than those designated by the Al-Qaida/Taliban Sanctions Committee. Available from: https://documents.un.org/prod/ods.nsf/home.xsp [accessed 19 December 2019].

United Nations Security Council (UNSC). (2014a). Resolution 2195: Threats to international peace and security. Available from: http://unscr.com/en/resolutions/2195 [accessed 1 April 2020].

United Nations Security Council (UNSC). (2014b). The Monitoring Group's final report on Somalia. S/2014/726, 13 October. Available from: https://www.securitycouncilreport.org/atf/cf/%7B65BFCF9B-6D27-4E9C-8CD3-CF6E4FF96FF9%7D/S_2014_726.pdf [accessed 1 April 2020].

United Nations Security Council (UNSC). (2015a). Statement by the President of the Security Council. S/PRST/2015/25, 16 December. Available from: https://undocs.org/S/PRST/2015/25 [accessed 1 April 2020].

United Nations Security Council (UNSC). (2015b). Resolution 2242. Available from: https://www.securitycouncilreport.org/atf/cf/%7B65BFCF9B-6D27-4E9C-8CD3-CF6E4FF96FF9%7D/s_res_2242.pdf [accessed 1 April 2020].

United Nations Security Council (UNSC). (2015c). Somalia report of the Monitoring Group on Somalia and Eritrea submitted in accordance with resolution 2182. S/2015/801. Available from: https://www.undocs.org/S/2015/801 [accessed 1 April 2020].

United Nations Security Council (UNSC). (2019). Resolution 2482: Threats to international peace and security caused by international terrorism and organized crime. Available from: https://www.un.org/sc/ctc/news/document/s-res-2482-2019-threats-international-peace-security-caused-international-terrorism-organized-crime/ [accessed 1 April 2020].

Van der Merwe, J. (2014). The Crime-Terror Continuum: The Case of Africa. Toronto: Aberfoyle International Security. Available from: http://www.aberfoylesecurity.com/?p=778 [accessed 31 March 2020].

Wang, P. (2010). The Crime-Terror Nexus: Transformation, Alliance, Convergence. *Asian Social Science*, 6(6), pp. 11-20. Available from: https://www.foreignpolicyjournal.com/2015/10/30/the-sahel-libya-and-the-crime-terror-nexus/ [accessed 31 March 2020].

Williams, P. (1994). Transnational criminal organisations and international security. *Survival*, 36(1), pp. 96-113.

Endnotes

1. UNSC, 1999.
2. The UNSC has adopted over 40 resolutions addressing different aspects of the links between terrorism, violent extremism and organised crime, notably: 1267 (1999), 1333 (2000), 1363 (2001), 1388 (2002), 1390 (2002), 1452 (2002), 1455 (2003), 1526 (2004), 1617 (2005), 1624 (2005), 1735 (2006), 1989 (2011), 2083 (2012), 2129 (2013), 2133 (2014), 2161 (2014), 2170 (2014), 2178 (2014), 2354 (2017), 2388 (2017), 2467 (2019) and 2482 (2019).
3. African Union, 2004.
4. Reitano et al, 2017.
5. Ibid.
6. Makarenko, 2012.
7. Hoffman, 1998.
8. UNSC, 2004.
9. UN, 2004.
10. Daase, 2010.
11. Williams, 1994.
12. Dishman, 2001; Wang, 2010.
13. Dishman, 2001:45.
14. Shelley, 2005.
15. Picarelli, 2012.
16. Ibid.
17. Cottee, 2016.
18. UN, 2017; Reitano et al, 2017.
19. Bøås, 2014; Duffy, 2015.
20. Shabelle Media Network, 2013; Reitano et al, 2017.
21. UNSC, 2019:1.
22. Luengo-Cabrera & Moser, 2016.
23. Van der Merwe, 2014; Sampaio, 2015.
24. Costa, 2007; UN, 2010:49 (in 2008, Hicham Ahmidan was sentenced to a 10-year prison term in Morocco); Fuchs, 2004; Associated Press, 2006.
25. FATF, 2014:42-43.
26. Breuer, 2011:37.
27. Shelley, 2014.
28. McGirk & Plain, 2002.
29. Adepelumi, 2015.
30. UNSC, 2015a; UNSC, 2014a (expressing concern that terrorists benefit from transnational organised crime in some regions, including from trafficking); UNSC, 2015b (concerned that acts of sexual and gender-based violence are part of the strategic objectives and ideology of certain terrorist groups).
31. Campbell, 2013:20.
32. UNHRC, 2016, para. 138-140; Keller, 2015.
33. Doward, 2013.
34. Rhode, 2014.
35. Callimachi, 2015.
36. UNSC, 2014b.
37. CSS, 2013.
38. BBC News, 2016; Freeman, 2016.
39. Nellemann et al, 2014:48.
40. AOAV, 2017.
41. UNSC, 2015c.
42. Titeca & Edmond, 2019.
43. Keatinge, 2014.
44. International Crisis Group, 2019.
45. Heibner et al, 2017.
46. FATF, 2013; FATF, 2015; FATF, 2016.

CHAPTER 5

The Nexus Between Violent Extremism and the Illicit Economy in Northern Mozambique: Is Mozambique Under Siege from International Organised Crime?

Linos Mapfumo

Introduction

Since October 2017, Mozambique's northernmost province of Cabo Delgado has been under sustained militant attack from the Islamist extremist group Alu Sunna Wa-Jama (ASWJ), resulting in thousands of people being either killed, kidnapped or displaced, while their properties have been destroyed. These incidents have reportedly escalated every year, with the group changing tactics from night-time attacks on isolated targets to more nuanced and well-coordinated daylight attacks. These attacks have targeted mainly installations and employees of multinational companies such as the American oil company Anadarko Petroleum Corporation (now Total) and government security departments such as the Polícia da República de Moçambique (PRM).

The growing popularity of ASWJ among the people of Cabo Delgado indicates worrying social cleavages and the growing rift between the general populace and the ruling elite. This social alienation and disillusionment are happening at the same time that northern Mozambique is quickly emerging as a hub and transit route for an illicit economy dominated by drug trafficking, poaching and illegal trading in timber, rubies and ivory. In fact, the towns and ports of Pemba, Nacala, Mocímboa da Praia and their surrounding environs have become nerve centres of illicit trading, organised crime and transit points for illicit consignments into southern Africa and beyond. The same ports and towns are also used to export illicit timber and wildlife products such as ivory to Asia. Indications are that ASWJ is financing its operations through proceeds derived from this illicit trade. As a result, the Cabo Delgado province has now evolved into a melting pot for violent extremism, and a major illicit trading and transit hub, due to its neglect by the central government.

A general assessment of the conflict situation within the province shows that grievances are driven primarily by feelings of exclusion among the local population in the exploitation of the state's natural resources. Despite its resource abundance, Cabo Delgado is the least developed province in Mozambique. The province is dominated by dilapidated infrastructure, high poverty rates and a lack of access to social services. The situation is further compounded by a complicated series of underlying factors, such as conflict over land, controversy over a resettlement programme, as well as communities' distrust of their local political actors.

Moreover, while the region is awash with rich mineral resources, locals are at the economic periphery in terms of both employment opportunities and profit sharing. Instead, the process of awarding concessions is murky. For instance, in several cases where natural resources have been found, the indigenous population has been unilaterally driven off their land without fair and just compensation. Meanwhile, only a small percentage of profits from resource extraction finds its way back to the province, as successive Frente de Libertação de Moçambique (FRELIMO) governments have structurally weakened local governance structures. This has led to a widespread perception that the Mozambican government and multinational companies are not only exploiting the north's resource base, but are also causing insecurity within the region – as shall be highlighted later in this chapter.

The security situation in northern Mozambique suggests a need for the Southern African Development Community (SADC) to intervene, in particular, and the international community, in general. This assistance would aim to arrive at speedy and extensive countermeasures that not only address the conflict situation, but also help the local populace to participate in the exploitation of natural resources.

This chapter will therefore unpack, and discuss the impact of, the intricacies of Cabo Delgado's political economy in the face of violent extremism and the illicit economy. The growing insecurity has hampered development and service delivery to the province, leading to further underdevelopment. It has also affected food security in the province, as locals now have restricted access to their crops and livelihoods. If not well managed, the constellation of violent extremism and the illicit economy could result in regional insecurity, with serious consequences.

The Application of Collaborative Governance and 'Absence-of-Trust' Governance Theories in Cabo Delgado

International experiences of collaborative governance have brought about new perspectives, norms and models of governance that place citizenry inclusion at the core of governance and economic development. This chapter adopts the collaborative governance and 'absence-of-trust' governance theories to argue that community participation, accountability and trust in governance processes and systems are of paramount importance if society is to develop and achieve peace. These theories are particularly important within the fields of peacebuilding and development due to a greater emphasis on accountability and 'soft' indicators such as citizen- and user-satisfaction targets, as well as an increased demand for information on performance in relation to 'governance' as a whole in a bid to enhance public administration.[1]

Therefore, this chapter will argue that the escalation of acts of terrorism in northern Mozambique is a result of the decreasing level of trust in government and its detrimental effects on governance, development and social cohesion. It further argues that both improving the quality of governance and enforcing transparency in the use of natural resources (resource nationalism) will result in Cabo Delgado's residents expressing higher levels of satisfaction and trust in government.

The Emergence of ASWJ in Cabo Delgado and the Internationalisation of the Insurgency

Northern Mozambique has always been a vortex of struggle and conflict, dating back to the advent of the liberation war against Portuguese rule when FRELIMO insurgents attacked a Portuguese garrison at Chai, northern Mozambique, on 25 September 1964. The attack marked the genesis of the Mozambican war of independence and the emancipation of the people of Mozambique from Portuguese colonial rule. Furthermore, with the formation of FRELIMO in 1962 in Dar es Salaam, Tanzania, and due to its proximity to Tanzania, northern Mozambique became accustomed to being a trailblazer and leader in the struggle towards universal suffrage and freedom.

The majority of the founding members of FRELIMO were from the north, predominantly from the Makonde ethnic group. In fact, the war of independence between 1964 and 1974 was fought mainly in Cabo Delgado.[2] The first landmines were laid in 1965 at Muidembe, Cabo Delgado,[3] and in 1970 roads and bridges south of Rio Messalo were mined with FRELIMO's launch of Operation Estrada.[4] The province battled to recover from the impact of the war, which was one of the reasons it began to lag developmentally when compared to other provinces.

Inspired by the teachings of the late radical Kenyan preacher, Sheikh Aboud Rogo Mohammed, and a Tanzanian cleric, Abdul Chacur, ASWJ emerged in 2015 as a fundamentalist religious movement.[5] The group continued to follow Rogo's radical teachings even after he was killed in 2012 in Mombasa by unknown assailants.

The origins of ASWJ can be traced to Kibiti, Tanzania, where its followers were initially based. These followers would later trek south, where they finally settled in Cabo Delgado. Once firmly established in northern Mozambique, and using two mosques in Cabo Delgado, ASWJ began to spread its brand of Islam, which was shaped by the radical views of Rogo and Chacur.[6] Their teachings were predicated on Wahhabism and the assumption that the Islam propagated in Mozambique was corrupted and not in line with the dictates of Prophet Muhammad.

Consequently, Rogo followers began attacking traditional mosques, with the aim of forcing other Muslims to follow their radical Wahhabist beliefs, while at the same time preventing them from going to hospitals or attending schools. They considered these hospitals and schools as 'anti-Islamic' and secular in nature. ASWJ proponents also convinced local communities not to recognise the authority of the Mozambican government. Instead, they encouraged them to implement sharia law and to strive for the creation of an Islamic caliphate within Mozambique. To achieve this, Rogo's followers began to organise themselves into armed groups, and formed secret camps in the districts of Macomia, Mocímboa da Praia and Montepuez.

Kibiti, Tanzania, has also featured prominently in the radicalisation of northern Mozambique. Several extremists from the region have used marriage to entrench themselves across the border in northern Mozambique. Once entrenched, locals have been encouraged to join the jihad, train for military operations, and listen to sermons by Rogo and other radical religious figures.[7]

The spread of external Wahhabism also coincided with the emergence of opportunistic criminals and army defectors, who helped swell the ASWJ ranks. It is likely that this religious ideology is providing the organisation with a justification to take up arms and recruit new members. Wahhabism was introduced in Mozambique in the 1960s by graduates from Saudi Arabia and religious schools in other Gulf states, who began challenging the country's traditional and more tolerant Sufi customs.[8] The status quo was destabilised in the 2000s when the Islamic Council tapped Gulf non-governmental organisations to provide scholarships for students to study abroad, particularly in Qatar and Saudi Arabia. Upon return, these graduates joined the ASWJ ranks and began challenging local Sufi customs.[9]

ASWJ first gained notoriety when it attacked a police station in Mocímboa da Praia on 5 October 2017, which resulted in the police temporarily losing control of the town. The raid was led by 30 armed insurgents who managed to kill 17 people. Among the dead were two police officers and a community leader. During the raid, ASWJ stole arms and ammunition, and incited local residents to not pay taxes to the Mozambican government. ASWJ terrorists used the stolen weapons in Maluku, Columbe, Pemba, Mutumbate and Maculo a few weeks later.[10] Cumulatively, these attacks left more than 60 people dead, including women and children, while hundreds were injured.

In 2018 there was an escalation in the number of attacks within Cabo Delgado province. The first occurred on 13 January when, in an evening raid, ASWJ militants stormed the town of Olumbi in Palma district.[11] The attack targeted a market and a government administrative building, and left five people dead. More incidents were to follow in Chitolo, Manilha, Diaca Velha and Mangwaza, which suffered three successive attacks. In all these incidents, houses were looted and burned, and it is estimated that hundreds of civilians lost their lives.[12]

Little progress was made against the group in 2019, and Cabo Delgado recorded more than 55 attacks across several villages and towns. Meanwhile, at the time of publication, 33 attacks had been recorded in nine out of Cabo Delgado's 16 districts in 2020, one of which was the 22 March storming of the strategic town of Mocímboa da Praia. The attack resulted in the insurgents seizing control of the small but strategic town's air base, port and police stations, with ASWJ raising its flag at all these key points.

To date, more than 100,000 people have been displaced due to ASWJ attacks. Killings and displacements are projected to increase, since ASWJ has officially been accepted as a member of the Islamic State in Puntland, an affiliate of Islamic State (IS). In fact, the United Nations Security Council notes that the Islamic State in Puntland now operates as a command centre for IS affiliates in the Democratic Republic of Congo (DRC) and Mozambique. The aim of the Islamic State in Puntland is to consolidate a triad connection of IS affiliates in East Africa, central Africa and southern Africa.[13]

Early on, ASWJ attacks targeted mainly security forces. However, this has changed within a relatively short period of time, as evidenced by multiple attacks on civilians within the province as early as 2018. The strategy was to attack villages or isolated homes, which were either partially or completely burnt down. From 27 May 2018 onwards, the group's *modus operandi* began to include extreme acts of violence – methods such as beheading, kidnapping for ransom and, at times, rape. The beheadings were accompanied by the burning down of hundreds of houses.[14]

The group also changed from night-time attacks to coordinated daylight attacks against specific high-profile targets, such as foreigners employed by Anadarko, the American oil company, which was leading a $20 billion liquefied natural gas (LNG) project before it was bought out by Total. Areas that have experienced serious attacks thus far include the villages of Monjan in the Palma district, Rueia in Macomia, and Namaluco in the Quissanga district. In 2019, the scorched-earth policy, accompanied by beheadings, continued unabated, with multiple attacks and beheadings recorded in Piqueue, Nacate, Ntapuala, Banga-Vieja, Ida, Ipho, Nangade and Mitopy.[15] The attack at Mitopy was a defining moment in the history of ASWJ, as this marked the first time that IS claimed responsibility.

The Spread of Islamist Ideology in the North

In recent years, Cabo Delgado has seen a rapid increase in the number of radical Islamist preachers, and a spread in the popularity of their teachings, especially among young men from the largely disenfranchised Mwani ethnic group. The attraction of this new brand of Islamic teaching, and the rejection of established Islamic scholars in the region, points to a generational conflict led by younger, more radical religious actors against the older, more established Muslim Council in Cabo Delgado.

Certain clerics have played an important role in the growing influence of ASWJ in the province. One of these clerics (and a recruiter) was Nuro Adremane, who received his religious education in Somalia after travelling by road through Tanzania and Kenya. Adremane actively sought out recruits in the Montepuez and Mocímboa da Praia districts – areas deeply aggrieved by the activities of international mining companies and the Mozambican government. As a result, he managed to transform local grievances into narratives of conflict and revenge. Some young men from the region have been recruited though the promise of loans, given scholarships to study at Qur'an schools in East Africa and the Middle East, or sent for military training in East African countries such as Tanzania and Somalia.[16]

Adremane and other clerics have reinforced ideology introduced into Cabo Delgado in recent years by those who received scholarships from Saudi Arabia, Sudan and other Gulf states, and have stressed the need for violent jihad among their recruits. These teachings are completely at odds with the Sufi-inspired religious practices which have long been seen in Mozambique. Adremane and other radical preachers have operated largely from two mosques in Mocímboa da Praia (closed in October 2017 after the police station attack) from where they managed to spread their brand of Islam across the province.

Ethnic and Political Divisions

The actions of the post-independence ruling party, FRELIMO, have exacerbated ethnic tensions in the north, which has also helped radical actors gain traction in the region – especially among the Mwani ethnic group, who have helped to swell ASWJ's ranks. In Cabo Delgado, the Mwani are still the largest ethnic group in terms of population size, followed by the Makonde. While the Mwani are the original inhabitants of the province, they are economically, politically and socially marginalised by the Makonde. The Makonde dominate the Mozambican political space and have benefited the most since independence, often at the expense of the Mwani. To make matters worse, the Makonde are Christian, while the Mwani are predominantly Muslim. This has added a further ethno-religious dimension to the challenges facing the province.

The marginalisation of the province's Mwani ethnic group has historical roots. As initially highlighted, the most prominent operational theatre of the 1964-74 war of independence was Cabo Delgado. The largely Christian Makonde aligned themselves with FRELIMO, while the Muslim Mwani sided with their Portuguese colonial masters. This explains why the Makonde continue to receive preferential treatment from the Mozambican government; they have even been rewarded with pensions and political concessions. The Mwani, on the other hand, fought on the side of the Portuguese and even remained in Portuguese camps. FRELIMO has not forgotten this, and after independence the FRELIMO government sidelined the Mwani in favour of the Makonde and other ethnic groups. Even today, the Mwani are treated with disdain and are commonly considered to be uneducated criminals, spurned for their prior support for the Portuguese and, later, the Resistência Nacional Moçambicana (RENAMO).

While the Mwani dialect is a mixture of Swahili and a local Makhuwa language, it is considered 'foreign' and the result of having been 'Swahilised'. These longstanding ethnic tensions meant that when Wahhabism was introduced to the province by outside actors, it found fertile ground among the Mwani, who had long felt alienated and discriminated against by the Makonde. Furthermore, the province has a sizeable population of people who came from neighbouring Tanzania and other East African states. As a result, a large segment of the population often feels a stronger connection to southern Tanzania and East Africa than to regions within Mozambique. This is further compounded by the fact that the province is located far from the capital, Maputo, and has largely been neglected by the central government, the net effect of which has been extraordinarily high poverty rates, pitiable infrastructure and a lack of access to social services. While the province's residents have tried to elevate these concerns, they are rebuffed by the central government, which accuses the local population of pushing a RENAMO agenda.

Coincidentally, the underdevelopment of Cabo Delgado coincided with a decline in support for FRELIMO. However, the loss of support for FRELIMO did not translate into increased support for RENAMO, which is not regarded as an alternative. Instead, support has gone to ASWJ. Thus, it is clear that both local and regional factors have contributed to the expansion of the group. The support for ASWJ is an expression of historical tensions between the north and south, while active recruitment among the Mwani is ASWJ's instrumentalisation of more local ethnic divides.[17]

The political dynamics within FRELIMO do not help matters, and in many cases simply serve to entrench ethnic divides. For example, during his tenure as president of Mozambique and leader of FRELIMO, Armando Guebuza, who is from Cabo Delgado and a Makonde, spearheaded many development projects within the province as a strategy to win the hearts and minds of the people, enabling him to retain leadership of the party. However, the projects only benefited the Makonde, to the total exclusion of the Mwani. This affirmative action also saw the Makonde appointed to influential positions, such as board membership and chief executives of large corporations. Makonde-owned companies were also given lucrative mining concessions. Little has changed under the current president, Felipe Nyusi, who is also a Makonde from Cabo Delgado. Rather, his presidency has only served to fuel resentment among the Mwani, who feel continually marginalised.

Economic Marginalisation and the Role of the Extractive Industries
Many analysts maintain that there is a direct link between the surge in violent attacks in the region and the exploitation of minerals, oil and gas. Cabo Delgado is endowed with abundant natural resources, especially petroleum and natural gas, as well as the world's largest ruby and pink-sapphire deposits. Regrettably, these discoveries have not translated into a marked improvement in the living standards of the local population, as all the concessions have been awarded to foreigners and people from outside the province. The exploitation of natural resources has in fact led to further underdevelopment and the widespread eviction of locals, as they have been driven off their land with little to no compensation. In addition, only a very small proportion of the profits have found their way back to the province, in part due to the central government's many years of neglect,

resulting in weak local administrative and governance structures.

Mozambique's northernmost province can aptly be described as the country's forgotten province – where little government support has led to wide-scale poverty, dilapidated infrastructure and a lack of social delivery. In a September 2019 publication by the Mozambican Instituto de Estudos Sociais e Económicos (Institute of Social and Economic Studies), the triple challenges of poverty, unemployment and lack of education were identified as the primary push factors that helped ASWJ attract recruits.[18] Local male youth are totally emasculated, unable to afford to marry, and see little or no employment opportunities. Although the province has, in the past few years, received considerable investments in infrastructure to support the extraction of natural resources, it has not resolved unemployment challenges, since most of the jobs available have been given to foreigners, mainly Zimbabweans. Investment has also seen the expropriation of land without proper compensation, and foreign companies have generated further tensions by committing human rights abuses. For example, the United Kingdom-based company Gemfields has been accused of forcibly expropriating land without proper compensation, and its security personnel have been accused of using violent force when dealing with locals.

Unsurprisingly, ASWJ has been immensely successful in recruiting youths in the Montepuez district, where the Gemfields Montepuez Ruby Mining Limitada is domiciled. In fact, some scholars[19] have argued that the human rights violations by the private security companies hired by Gemfields were the triggers that fuelled ASWJ's first attacks in Mocímboa da Praia in October 2017. These private military contractors would destroy the property of locals and artisanal miners, torturing and killing some to force them out of the concession areas of multinational companies.

In addition, there has been anger among the local populace over the manner in which their land was expropriated to make way for multinational companies such as Anadarko (now Total) and the Canadian-based petroleum company Wentworth. Residents were violently uprooted by the development plans. Moreover, they have lamented the rushed legal processes and their compensation, which has been below market value. Livelihoods were also disturbed, especially within farming and fishing communities, and locals felt either cheated or abandoned as Mozambican government officials tended to side with multinational companies. For example, in February 2018, while aggrieved residents were feeling economically marginalised, the country's labour minister travelled to Cabo Delgado to lay the groundwork for receiving 2,000 foreign workers who were earmarked to work for Anadarko after the company received authorisation to build an onshore LNG plant in Palma.

Anadarko's construction of what will be one of the world's largest LNG plants, as well as a port capable of accommodating large vessels especially designed to ferry LNG, has necessitated the resettlement of thousands of fishermen and farmers on the Afungi Peninsula in Palma. Despite companies such as Anadarko pouring billions of dollars into the region, there is a widely held perception among local communities that they have received, and will continue to receive, little benefit. Rather, negative sentiment continues to grow as complaints multiply with regard to inadequate restitution, lack of compensation for their investment in fruit-producing trees, dissatisfaction over the manner in which the resettlement programme is being implemented, and suspicions that funds intended to assist them are being diverted. Locals have been particularly irked by the resettlement programme itself, as resettled households were mixed with communities they did not know. Communities that used to rely on fishing were settled in the hinterland, resulting in the loss of their livelihood.

Collectively, the spread of Islamist ideology in the region, as well as the economic, social and political drivers outlined above, has immensely benefited ASWJ. The population in Cabo Delgado has largely lost faith in local politics, creating pools of disgruntled and unemployed youth who are easily recruited with a promise of employment opportunities and better living conditions.

The Internationalisation of the Insurgency

ASWJ's strategies and tactics, including the use of beheadings, kidnapping and rape, are largely influenced by Islamist terrorist groups such as IS. While the local presence of IS was for a time contested among analysts, in 2019 the group claimed responsibility for an attack against Mozambican security forces in Cabo Delgado, and has claimed responsibility for several attacks since. Furthermore, IS is now including ASWJ in its promotional videos, and has placed the group under the operational command of its central African Wilayat, or administrative division.

So far, a limited number of its leaders have been identified, and these have included both Mozambicans and international members.[20] While most Mozambican recruits are drawn mainly from the Mocímboa da Praia, Palma and Macomia districts, evidence suggests that foreign nationals come from a variety of countries, including Tanzania, Chad, Kenya, Somalia, Sudan, Saudi Arabia and even Russia. The presence of international members elevates the group's status and helps to generate support from both IS and other Islamist actors in Russia, Tanzania, Uganda, Sudan and Saudi Arabia. ASWJ is also receiving support from organised-crime groups, foreign sympathisers and like-minded groups in the region.

Due to its growing internationalisation, several governments have joined forces with the Mozambican government in an attempt to bring an end to the insurgency. Russian intervention, for example, is premised on the January 2017 Russia-Mozambique military and technical cooperation agreement which, among others, provides for the supply of arms and military equipment, as well as other military-oriented products, spare parts and components as part of the war on terrorism. Resultantly, on 25 September 2019, Russian military hardware in the form of Mi-17 helicopters were delivered via a Russian Air Force An-124 (registration RA-82038) transport aircraft, which landed at Nacala.

The Role of Northern Mozambique's Illicit Economy

The illicit economy in Mozambique has been growing exponentially side-by-side with the recent upsurge in terrorist activity. While the illicit economy has been thriving in Cabo Delgado for years, ASWJ has, of late, been directly profiting from the activity through taxes received from the illicit traffickers. Martin[21] and Berry et al[22] have outlined direct linkages between terrorism and organised crime in Cabo Delgado, while Haysom[23] argues that a significant local heroin-trafficking economy has developed in the region, largely off the radar, complemented by wildlife trafficking, human trafficking, illegal timber felling and gemstone smuggling. These illicit activities have flourished, particularly within the precinct of Mocímboa da Praia, due to corruption and an attitude of indifference within the political establishment, and has seen the port of Mocímboa da Praia emerge as a hotbed of criminal activity where the arms trade and human trafficking thrive.

There are well-established trafficking routes in Cabo Delgado that are used to transport drugs into Mozambique en route to South Africa and Europe. One of the most trafficked commodities is heroin, usually brought into Mozambique from Pakistan by dhows (seaworthy motorised sailing ships). Once on shore, this heroin is repackaged for onward transportation into the southern African hinterland, primarily to South Africa.[24]

Northern Mozambique is a favoured transit route due to its largely unpatrolled and unprotected coastline, which traffickers use to move drugs into southern Africa. Drugs, such as heroin, are usually brought into Mozambique either through beaches or via container freight traffic, especially at the ports of Pemba and Nacala in neighbouring Nampula province. These ports are popular because they are virtually controlled by traffickers, who bribe port and government officials. There are also frequent allegations that traffickers have relationships with local politicians, who sustain their political careers through this illicit trade.

The ports, especially the port in Pemba, are also popular with traffickers of timber and wildlife products, such as ivory headed for Asia. ASWJ also profits from the proceeds of human and drug trafficking through the ports of Mocímboa da Praia and Pemba, and ruby and gem smuggling from Montepuez and Mueda, as well as from the general insecurity in northern Mozambique. However, while these income streams are relevant, the majority of ASWJ funding comes from donations and protection money.

With growing insecurity in the region, and the government clampdown on trafficking routes in Tanzania, northern Mozambique has become the transit route of choice. Cabo Delgado provides a unique set of environmental circumstances that allows the illicit economy to thrive. Weak law-enforcement systems are in place to deter criminal activity, and there are high levels of corruption in local government as well as a weak and compromised police force. Alleged drug kingpins such as Mohamed Bachir Suleman have corrupted state institutions and wield influence among certain political and religious elites within Cabo Delgado, further undermining public trust in government and garnering support for ASWJ.

The illicit economy in Cabo Delgado is linked to international criminal enterprises, and many of its markets in northern Mozambique are controlled by citizens from Tanzania, Mali, Ethiopia, the DRC, Rwanda, Somalia, Nigeria,

Cameroon, China, Thailand and other south Asian countries.[25] For example, south Asians control the heroin trade, while the Chinese control the timber and ivory market, and the Thais control the gem market.

It can be argued that the shaping and architecture of northern Mozambique's illicit economy are symptoms of the region's neglect by the state, the prevailing impunity, and the intertwined nature of the illegal and legal economies. The major beneficiaries of heroin trafficking and the illicit timber trade have often been politicians, who receive protection money from the leaders of organised crime. In her report on transnational organised crime, Haysom[26] refers to the numerous links between FRELIMO and drug traffickers. Politicians provide protection from checks at ports and on the road to ensure that traffickers pursue their criminal enterprises under cover of legal commercial activities. It is well known that these highly profitable and internationally linked illicit activities are protected by criminal-political connections within the Mozambican political establishment. For example, Haysom points to the existence of a protective arrangement nexus whereby criminal enterprises have paid FRELIMO officials large amounts of money in exchange for legal protection.[27]

Similar arrangements can be seen in the illicit ivory and timber trade, where mostly Asian networks have been able to conduct their business unhindered. Evidence suggests that officially licensed Chinese companies illegally export large quantities of illicit timber and ivory with the protection of politicians and police. The Environmental Investigation Agency (EIA) has established that in 2012 up to 48% of Chinese timber imports from Mozambique were illegal.[28] The EIA also reveals the close relationship between Mozambican officials and Chinese timber companies. Similarly, in 2017, the illegal activities of the Shuidong syndicate in Mozambique were exposed; this syndicate was smuggling ivory into Asia, facilitated by bribes.[29]

Hanlon[30] argues that loosely organised networks of criminal actors, located in strategically less-relevant places, are exercising authority and playing an important role in the illicit trade. They are influential locally in illegal activities such as logging or mining for gemstones, as they both provide investment in local infrastructure and employ locals.

In addition to the activities outlined above, recent large investments in oil and gas exploitation near the Rovuma Valley in the north, and in mining rubies and other minerals and gems near Montepuez and Mueda, have helped to grow the illicit economy by drawing in foreign workers or assisting to mask the generation of illicit wealth.

Challenges and the Way Forward

The Mozambican government is failing to dismantle ASWJ because of the terror group's diversified funding portfolio and its ability to raise money through transnational organised crime. The country has limited capacity to adequately investigate financial flows, and as such cannot comprehensively tackle ASWJ's funding mechanisms. This is further compounded by the fact that the province's economy is cash based and is also highly informalised. This makes it extremely difficult for the Mozambican authorities to effectively track illicit financial flows into ASWJ.

The membership and leadership structure of ASWJ remains unclear, making targeted counterterrorism operations difficult to carry out. Meanwhile, the terrain and the isolated nature of the five districts – Macoma, Nangande, Mocímboa da Praia, Palma and Quissanga – provide ample safe-haven opportunities for ASWJ. To further compound the situation, the province's road and communication network is very poor, making the movement and coordination of security forces extremely challenging.

To date, the Mozambican government's response to the insurgency has been very heavy-handed. A widespread curfew has been implemented in Cabo Delgado, mosques have been closed, and citizens have been arbitrarily detained, tortured and, in some cases, executed on suspicion of being ASWJ members. There has also been a media blackout, and various media organisations have been barred from visiting the province. In some cases, the security forces have either detained or arrested journalists who have managed to sneak into Cabo Delgado. For example, one journalist, Amade Abubacar, was unlawfully detained and subsequently subjected to torture. He was only released on bail after 107 days in detention. As a result of this media blackout, there has been a general lack of information about the conflict. Furthermore, the Mozambican security forces' use of brutal tactics has served to alienate a population that was already disillusioned, and garnered additional support for ASWJ. As observed by Bester,

Johnson, Omeni and Ukeje et al,[31] terrorist attacks generally escalate following indiscriminate security crackdowns – as seen in Somalia, the Lake Chad Basin, the Sahel and the Maghreb.

The Mozambican government, therefore, needs to immediately review its counterinsurgency tactics and prioritise addressing the socio-political and religious dynamics behind the insurgency. If these are not addressed, the attacks are very likely to continue. Already, the conflict has had a debilitating effect on the citizens of Cabo Delgado. The province is already at food insecurity stress levels (IPC-2) because locals have restricted access to their crops and livelihoods due to the violence, while the continued insecurity and displacement are negatively impacting local economic development within the region.

Security services, especially the police and private security companies, must be trained on how to carry out their responsibilities in ways consistent with international humanitarian law in conflict settings. In this regard, legal provision must be made and systems put in place aimed at holding security forces accountable for human rights violations.

The Mozambican government should develop an amnesty system for youths who have been recruited into ASWJ. The amnesty programme should be accompanied by an offer of rehabilitation, vocational skills training and employment opportunities.

Improving relationships between the local civilian population and security forces is also key to improving the efficacy of counterterrorism operations. ASWJ's use of guerrilla tactics, melting into the local populace after an attack, has led security forces to indiscriminately target whole villages, creating new grievances against the state and distrust towards the police and military. Since a large proportion of ASWJ militants are natives of the Cabo Delgado communities, residents are already reluctant to provide information which would help security officials to combat ASWJ. Currently, ASWJ lacks a charismatic leader and, as such, there is potential for the government to exploit internal weaknesses to its advantage. Active measures can also be taken to target this leadership vacuum through strategic communications and counter-narratives.

There is an urgent need to find common ground from which to build trust among communities. This will require facilitated community dialogues among a broad spectrum of faith-based, traditional and community leaders, including women, the youth and government officials. Increased community participation is paramount for effective conflict resolution. Government officials must be trained and equipped with good communication skills to properly engage with communities and, conversely, for communities to feel respected and consulted. Similarly, there is also a need for the media, especially community radio stations, to play a part in promoting social cohesion, public participation and inclusivity.

The problem in northern Mozambique is in large part economic. As such, there is a need for an equitable distribution of wealth, employment and inclusive economic participation. The communities of Cabo Delgado should also enjoy part of the wealth generated, and steps must be taken to ensure that the local population has access to training and employment opportunities, particularly in the fields of health, agriculture, aquaculture and education.

The Mozambican government should also consider establishing a comprehensive stakeholder commission populated with strong representation from affected communities, including representatives from both the Muslim and Christian faiths. The aim of the commission should be to examine the allegations of abuse by multinational corporations in all sectors within Cabo Delgado and, where appropriate, offer compensation to citizens. The commission could also serve as a truth and reconciliation mechanism and a grievance and solutions platform.

Meanwhile, the Mozambique government must combat the influence of criminal organisations on the political system. Legislation should thus be enacted that makes the financing of political parties and election campaigns more transparent. In the interim, individual cases of corruption should be publicised to create the pressure to act. Moreover, there should be a total revamp of law enforcement, and the regular rotation of law-enforcement personnel countrywide. Also, to the extent possible, the unregulated informal sector in northern Mozambique should be brought into the formal sector and promoted.

Collaboration between regional governments is key to addressing the insurgency, and the Mozambican government should approach SADC and its neighbours with a view to establishing consensus and a joint action plan aimed at border cooperation, especially in tackling any illicit financing.

Conflict in Cabo Delgado is driven by a range of underlying drivers and a complex set of factors. As such, there is a need for a comprehensive and integrated strategy which aims to address the insurgency in a more holistic manner, rather than simply using heavy-handed security responses. In this regard, the government must stop downplaying the situation by calling it 'banditry'. Rather, using the aegis of SADC, the African Union and the United Nations, the Mozambican government should comprehensively brief the international community on the nature and form of the threat so that resources towards countering the threat can be mobilised.

Select Bibliography

Alibegović, D. & Slijepčević, S. (2018). Attitudes towards Citizen Participation in the Local Decision-Making Process: A Comparative Analysis. *Društvena istraživanja: časopis za opća društvena pitanja*, 27(1), pp. 155-175.

Berry L., Curtis, G.E., Gibbs, J.N., Hudson, R.A., Karacan, T., Kollars, N. & Miró, R. (2003). Nations hospitable to organized crime and terrorism. Washington, D.C.: Library of Congress Congressional Research Service.

Bester, P.C. (2019). Emerging challenges in terrorism and counterterrorism: A national security perspective. Paper presented on 17 January at The Hague University of Applied Sciences, Faculty of Public Management, Law and Safety, The Hague.

Bouckaert, G. & Van de Walle, S. (2003). Comparing measures of citizen trust and user satisfaction as indicators of 'good governance': Difficulties in linking trust and satisfaction indicators. *International Review of Administrative Sciences*, 69(3), pp. 329-343.

Bryden, M. & Bahra, P. (2019). East Africa's terrorist triple helix: The Dusit Hotel attack and the historical evolution of the jihadi threat. *Combating Terrorism Center Sentinel*, 12(6), pp. 2-11.

Chiovelli, G., Michalopoulos, S. & Papaioannou, E. (2019). Landmines and Spatial Development Appendix I History of Conflict. Available from: https://land-mines.com/pdf/paper/appendices/01_cw_hist_dec19.pdf [accessed 2 April 2020].

Chome, N. (2019). From Islamic reform to Muslim activism: The evolution of an Islamist ideology in Kenya. *African Affairs*, 118(472), pp. 531-552.

Chome, N. (2020). The political role of Islam. In Cheeseman, N., Kanyinga, K. & Lynch, G. (2020). *The Oxford Handbook of Kenyan Politics*. Oxford: Oxford University Press.

Dang, L. (2019). Violent Extremism and Community Policing in Tanzania. United States Institute of Peace Special Report, 442. Available from: https://www.usip.org/sites/default/files/2019-03/violent-extremism-and-community-policing-in-tanzania-sr_442.pdf [accessed 2 April 2020].

Environmental Investigation Agency (EIA). (2013). *First class connections: Log smuggling, illegal logging, and corruption in Mozambique*. London: EIA.

Faleg, G. (2019). Conflict prevention in Mozambique: Can there be peace after the storm? European Union Institute for Security Studies, 10 April. Available from: https://www.iss.europa.eu/content/conflict-prevention-mozambique [accessed 2 April 2020].

Florea, A. (2020). Rebel Governance in De Facto States. *European Journal of International Relations*, 24(2).

Global Initiative Against Transnational Organized Crime. (2020). Civil Society Observatory of Illicit Economies in Eastern and Southern Africa. *Risk Bulletin*, Issue 4, 30 January. Available from: https://globalinitiative.net/esaobs-risk-bulletin-4/ [accessed 2 April 2020].

Hanlon, J. (2018a). Running Mozambique's heroin trade with WhatsApp. London School of Economics, Centre for Africa, 3 July. Available from: https://blogs.lse.ac.uk/africaatlse/2018/07/03/running-mozambiques-heroin-trade-with-whatsapp/ [accessed 2 April 2020].

Hanlon, J. (2018b). The Uberization of Mozambique's heroin trade. Working Paper Series 2018, No. 18-190, July. London: London School of Economics.

Haysom, S. (2018). *Where Crime Compounds Conflict. Understanding Northern Mozambique's Vulnerabilities*. Geneva: Global Initiative Against Transnational Organized Crime.

Herráez, P.S. (2019). Revista del Instituto Español de Estudios Estratégicos. Sumario/Summary. *Journal of the Spanish Institute for Strategic Studies*, 14.

Hübschle, A. & Faull, A. (2017). Organised environmental crimes: Trends, theory, impact and responses. *South African Crime Quarterly*, 60, pp. 3-7.

Johnson, P.L. (2019). The Crime and State Terrorism Nexus: How Organized Crime Appropriates Counterinsurgency Violence. *Perspectives on Terrorism*, 13(6), pp. 16-26.

Liu, B., Wang, X., Xia, N. & Ni, W. (2018). Critical Success Factors for the Management of Public Participation in Urban Renewal Projects: Perspectives from Governments and the Public in China. *Journal of Urban Planning and Development*, 144(3).

Mabera, F. (2019). A Roundup of Strategic Developments and Trends in Africa in 2019. Institute for Global Dialogue. Available from: https://www.africaportal.org/publications/roundup-strategic-developments-and-trends-africa-2019/ [accessed 2 April 2020].

Mahadevan, P. (2018). *Islamism and Intelligence in South Asia: Militancy, Politics and Security*. London: Bloomsbury Publishing.

Maier, F.X. (1974). *Revolution and terrorism in Mozambique*. New York: American African Affairs Association.

Martin, G. (2013). Terrorism and Transnational Organized Crime. In Albanese, J. & Reichel, P. (2013). *Transnational Organized Crime: An Overview from Six Continents*. New York: Sage Publications.

Martin, V.B. (2019). *Survival or Extinction? How to Save Elephants and Rhinos*. New York: Springer Nature, pp. 355-366.

Massimaculo, A., Oliveira, D.D. & Do Nascimento Durães, T.F. (2019). Violências do estado e segurança pública em Moçambique pós-independência. *Revista de Políticas Públicas*, 23(2), pp. 883-906.

Matsinhe, D.M. & Valoi, E. (2019). The genesis of insurgency in northern Mozambique. Institute for Security Studies. Available from: https://issafrica.org/research/southern-africa-report/the-genesis-of-insurgency-in-northern-mozambique [accessed 2 April 2020].

Meyer, K. (2019). Building State Resilience. A Response to Terrorism in Southern and Eastern

Africa. *Accord: Conflict Trends* 2019/3, p. 111. Available from: https://www.accord.org.za/conflict-trends/building-state-resilience/ [accessed 2 April 2020].

Morier-Genoud, E. (2018). Mozambique's own version of Boko Haram is tightening its deadly grip. *The Conversation*, 11 June. Available from: https://theconversation.com/mozambiques-own-version-of-boko-haram-is-tightening-its-deadly-grip-98087 [accessed 2 April 2020].

Müller, M. & Vorrath, J. (2019). Mozambique still at risk: Despite the peace process, a serious crisis looms. German Institute of International and Security Affairs, September. Available from: https://www.swp-berlin.org/10.18449/2019C36/ [accessed 2 April 2020].

Nabatchi, T. & Jo, S. (2018). The future of public participation: Better design, better relations. In Gerard, C. & Kriesberg, L. (eds.). *Conflict and Collaboration: For Better or Worse*. United Kingdom: Taylor & Francis Group.

Niedziałkowski, K., Komar, E., Pietrzyk-Kaszyńska, A. Olszańska, A. & Grodzińska-Jurczak, M. (2018). Discourses on Public Participation in Protected Areas Governance: Application of Q Methodology in Poland. *Ecological Economics*, 145, pp. 401-409.

Omeni, A. (2019). *Insurgency and War in Nigeria: Regional Fracture and the Fight Against Boko Haram*. London: Bloomsbury Publishing.

Oxford Analytica. (2018a). Mozambican attacks will raise renewed security fears. Emerald Expert Briefings, 17 January.

Oxford Analytica. (2018b). Mozambique government will try to ease terrorism fears. Emerald Expert Briefings, 30 May.

Radtke, J., Holstenkamp, L., Barnes, J. & Renn, O. (2018). Concepts, Formats, and Methods of Participation: Theory and Practice. In Holstenkamp, L. & Radtke, J. (eds.). *Handbuch Energiewende und Partizipation*. Wiesbaden: Springer VS, pp. 21-42.

Rasheed, A., Bakar, H. & Rahman, N.A. (2018). Democracy needs civic participation: A critical review. SMMTC Postgraduate Symposium 2018, 18-19 March, Universiti Utara Malaysia.

Reisman, L. & Lalá, A. (2012). Assessment of Crime and Violence in Mozambique & Recommendations for Violence Prevention and Reduction. Open Society Initiative for Southern Africa and Open Society Foundations. Available from: https://issuu.com/osisa/docs/cvpi_mozambique_report_-_final_engl [accessed 2 April 2020].

Reitano, T., Jesperson, S. & De Lugo, B.R. (2017). *Militarised Responses to Transnational Organised Crime: The War on Crime*. New York: Springer.

Rousseau, D.M., Sitkin, S.B., Burt, R.S. & Camerer, C.F. (1998). Not so different after all: A cross-discipline view of trust. *The Academy of Management Review*, 23(3), pp. 393-404.

Shaw, M., Haysom, S. & Gastrow, P. (2018). The heroin coast: A political economy along the eastern African seaboard. ENACT, 2 July. Available from: https://enactafrica.org/research/research-papers/the-heroin-coast-a-political-economy-along-the-eastern-african-seaboard [accessed 2 April 2020].

Shen, M. (2020). *Rural Revitalization Through State-led Programs*. New York: Springer, pp. 9-32.

Ukeje. C., Toga, D. & Boukhars, A. (2019). State of Peace and Security in Africa 2019. Tana

High-Level Forum on Security in Africa. Available from: https://www.africaportal.org/publications/state-peace-and-security-africa-2019/ [accessed 2 April 2020].

Vicente, P.C. & Vilela, I. (2019). Preventing Violent Islamic Radicalization: Behavioral Evidence from Northern Mozambique. Available from: https://novafrica.org/wp-content/uploads/2019/05/PedroVicente_Preventing-Violent-Islamic-Radicalization.pdf [accessed 2 April 2020].

Endnotes

1. Alibegović & Slijepčević, 2018; Nabatchi & Jo, 2018:75; Radtke et al, 2018; Liu et al, 2018; Niedziałkowski et al, 2018; Rasheed et al, 2018:78; Shen, 2020; Rousseau et al, 1998; Bouckaert & Van de Walle, 2003.
2. Maier, 1974.
3. Chiovelli et al, 2019.
4. Ibid.
5. Alu Sunna Wa-Jama is loosely translated to mean 'adepts of the prophetic tradition'. The group is also sometimes referred to as Ahlu Sunna Wa-Jama, Ansar al Sunna or Al-Shabaab.
6. Meyer, 2019; Matsinhe & Valoi, 2019.
7. Bryden & Bahra, 2019; Meyer, 2019; Mabera, 2019; Dang, 2019; Herráez, 2019:203.
8. Chome, 2020:150; Vicente & Vilela, 2019; Faleg, 2019; Chome, 2019.
9. Chiovelli et al, 2019.
10. Ibid.
11. Johnson, 2019.
12. Oxford Analytica, 2018a.
13. Florea, 2020.
14. Morier-Genoud, 2018.
15. Oxford Analytica, 2018b.
16. Mahadevan, 2018.
17. Meyer, 2019.
18. Massimaculo et al, 2019.
19. Meyer, 2019; Matsinhe & Valoi, 2019.
20. Atanasio M'tumuke, Bernadino Rafael, Abdul Rahmin Faizal, Abdul Remane, Abdul Raim, Nuno Remane, Ibn Omar, 'Salimo' and Abdul Aziz are some of the members who have been identified.
21. Martin, 2013:163.
22. Berry et al, 2003.
23. Haysom, 2018.
24. Reisman & Lalá, 2012.
25. Reitano et al, 2017; Hübschle & Faull, 2017.
26. Haysom, 2018.
27. Ibid.
28. EIA, 2013.
29. Martin, 2019; Hanlon, 2018a.
30. Hanlon, 2018b.
31. Bester, 2019; Johnson, 2019; Omeni, 2019; Ukeje et al, 2019.

CHAPTER 6

Determining What We Know and What We Should Know About What Sustains Violent Extremism in the Horn of Africa

Charles Goredema

Introduction

> "Many experts, both in government and the private sector, admit that the chances of detecting terrorists' funds in a bank sufficiently far in advance of a planned attack that it can be prevented are incredibly small."[1]

Terrorism is conventionally understood as the commission of violent criminal acts that are intended or calculated to provoke a state of terror in the general public, a group of people or particular people, for illegitimate political purposes.

Terrorism exists in at least three forms in the Horn of Africa. The first comprises violent acts committed by internal insurgent groups and which are directed towards governmental authorities in the targeted country. The second consists of violent acts committed by organisations which are based outside the region, and which are directed at countries within the region. The third consists of violent acts committed by an organisation within the region that are aimed at a neighbouring country.[2]

Any financial or logistical support that is afforded to an organised armed formation that commits atrocities against civilians to further political aspirations amounts to terrorist financing. The essence of terrorist financing is the provision of resources to support terrorism and any other forms of violent extremism. Such financing may be deliberately provided or occur because of the lack of diligence by individuals or institutions that should prevent it. While some legal systems are still either silent or ambiguous on this, it would appear to be logical to regard anyone who wilfully provides resources – whether directly or indirectly, and whether in monetary or logistical terms – to carry out a terrorist act as guilty of financing terrorism. This would include the dealer in small arms and light weapons, the shipping agent through whom the consignment of weapons is shipped, the operator of the vessel used to move the weapons, and the transport operator on whose trucks the weapons are moved overland from the port.[3]

Generally speaking, the financing of terrorism moves through five stages:

1. **Acquisition:** During the first stage, the funds or commodities are procured. The providers may do so intentionally, or may benefit from a lack of diligence on the part of persons or institutions with whom they interact. Acquisition may involve predicate processes such as the conduct of lawful or illicit business activities, or the exchange of goods.
2. **Aggregation:** Relatively small amounts of the collected funds or goods are pooled together into a larger resource base.
3. **Transmission to terrorist organisations:** The aggregated funds are transmitted or moved to a central location or repository which is managed by the terrorist organisation.
4. **Transmission to operational cells:** The funds or commodities are distributed to the cells (individuals or groups) responsible for terrorist activities.
5. **Conversion or utilisation:** The received funds or commodities are exchanged for end-use goods and services. End-use goods and services could include weapons, travel, training, communications equipment, food, accommodation, falsified documents, recruitment, propaganda, bribes and compensation.[4]

As has occasionally been illustrated, terrorist financing can involve the use of formal, reputable financial institutions.[5] It is probably for this reason that global policymakers have lumped together measures to curb terrorist financing with anti-money-laundering processes. Subsequent experience has shown, however, that while they share in common the accumulation and use of money, there are differences between them in respect of the sources of funds and the direction of financial flows. It is not always as necessary to seek to legitimise the 'accumulation' and 'use' of money in the financing of terrorism as it is in money laundering.

Furthermore, the intensified focus on financial institutions as potentially particularly susceptible to being abused to channel funds to terrorists may have forced a shift to the use of alternative avenues. Nevertheless, there is no question that terrorist organisations continue to access resources to continue their activities. This raises numerous questions about the adequacy of what is known about terrorist financing.

What Do We Know About the Financing of Terrorist Activities in the Horn of Africa?

Knowledge of the drivers of terrorism is important to the inquiry about sources and routes of terrorist financing in the Horn of Africa. After all, curbing the funding of terrorism is only part of the larger task of preventing and combating terrorism.

It is established that terrorism in the Horn of Africa has for a long time taken advantage of ethnic, language, cultural and religious differences. As in other parts of post-colonial Africa, inherited legacies of inequality of distribution of resources and development have tended to fuel simmering tensions. Examples from disparate environments such as Uganda, Ethiopia and Kenya underscore the utility of these cleavages to ambitious political agitators. It is a relatively simple matter for them to exaggerate the sense that incumbent political regimes deliberately accord the distribution of access to scarce resources on ethnic or religious lines – and that only violent destruction of the status quo can rectify things. The sense of grievance and marginalisation rooted in the inherited skewed order has been worsened by the perception, in some cases justifiable, that incumbent regimes easily collude with former colonial powers in managing the illicit and exploitative flow of resources out of African communities.[6] Political agitation has invariably yielded violent extremism. At the core of the political agitation is a desire for power and control over resources.

The artificial borders that have long divided different states, as well as regions within states, serve to create sources of support for cross-border insurgencies. This manifests itself in the interconnectedness of most indigenous, homegrown terrorism. The resulting conflict produces the displacement of communities, and refugee flows in various directions. It also frequently leads to support for a dissident group in one country by a neighbouring country. Historically, this support has, in turn, provoked reciprocal antagonism, with the affected country supporting a dissident organisation in conflict with the neighbouring state.

Funding for Terrorist Activities from State Sources and Criminal Entrepreneurship

Funds to support terrorist activities are derived from various sources. They may be provided by third parties (financiers and supporters). In several instances, these third parties are governments sympathetic to the cause pursued by the extremists they support, or, equally often, motivated by strategic considerations or animosity to the governments targeted by the terrorists.

At different points in time, Ethiopia, Uganda and Eritrea have supported the Sudan People's Liberation Army (SPLA) against Khartoum, at a time when the SPLA was regarded as a terrorist organisation by Sudan and its allies. In retaliation, Sudan backed the Lord's Resistance Army (LRA) against Uganda,[7] the Oromia Liberation Front against Ethiopia, and the Eritrean Islamic Jihad against Eritrea. Following the 1998–2000 Ethiopian-Eritrean war, Eritrea has supported the Oromia Liberation Front against Ethiopia. Ethiopia responded by supporting a coalition of Eritrean dissidents against Eritrea. The exchange of hostile actions in the region has sustained state-funded terrorism at least since the mid-1990s.[8]

Resolution 1907 of the United Nations Security Council (UNSC) is pertinent. Paragraph 15(b) of the resolution seeks to prohibit Eritrean support to armed opposition groups that have been implicated in destabilising the Horn of Africa, specifically by conducting military attacks in Somalia and Ethiopia. Paragraph 15(d) prohibits Eritrea from "harbouring, financing, facilitating, supporting, organising, training, or inciting individuals or groups to perpetrate acts of violence or terrorist acts against other states or their citizens in the region".[9]

Since 2009, Eritrea has been accused of supporting groups engaged in armed conflict in Ethiopia and South Sudan. Kenya, whose troops form part of the regional contingent confronting Al-Shabaab in Somalia, has also criticised Eritrea. The South Sudanese allegations pertain to alleged links with the Sudanese People's Liberation Movement in Opposition, led by the former vice-president, Riek Machar. In allegations made to the Somalia and Eritrea Monitoring Group

(SEMG) of the United Nations (UN), Eritrea was accused of facilitating and in some cases providing weapons to three armed groups in South Sudan, the others being George Athor Deng's rebel forces and the David Yau Yau group. The SEMG received information from senior government officials in South Sudan that Eritrea delivered military equipment to Machar's forces on four occasions in 2014.

In respect of Ethiopia, SEMG reported that Eritrea supported armed opposition groups, notably the Somalia-based Ogaden National Liberation Front (ONLF), the Tigray People's Democratic Movement, and Ginbot Sebat. It was alleged that funds were transferred from Eritrea to an ONLF bank account in Dubai in three ways: using a bank account, through the *hawala* system, and by cash couriers.

The *hawala* is a value transfer system rooted in traditional methods of moving money in India and some Arab countries. It involves the transfer of the equivalent or accepted transfer value of a given amount of money between two or more places that are in different jurisdictions. The sender requests an agent (hawaladar) in the country from which he or she intends to make a transfer, and once a rate of exchange and transfer fee is agreed, hands over the money to be transferred. The *hawaladar* contacts a *hawaladar* in the country to which the funds are to be transferred, with whom he or she has a business relationship, with instructions as to the sum to be transferred and sufficient particulars to enable the identification of the recipient. The latter is subsequently able to receive transfer of the equivalent value of the funds transferred by contacting the receiving *hawaladar*.

The *hawala* has proved resilient partly because it is a rapid means of transferring value, is comparatively inexpensive and relatively informal, and offers rates of transfer that are better than those offered by commercial financial institutions.[10] The services of *hawaladars* are also available in areas that are poorly served by formal banking institutions.

The ONLF bank account was controlled by ONLF deputy chair Mohamed Ismail, who was based in Australia, but registered under the name of Abdi Shakur Mohammed Nur. From Dubai, the money was dispatched to Somalia through *hawala* transfers. In its 2014 report, the SEMG concluded that there was credible evidence of continuing support for the Tigray People's Democratic Movement, which was in conflict with the Ethiopian government.[11]

Eritrea consistently denied allegations that it had violated the UNSC resolution, and called on the UNSC to lift targeted sanctions imposed on the country. At the same time, Eritrea also denied the SEMG entry into Eritrea to verify or contradict the allegations. Following an SEMG report in April 2017, sanctions were renewed. A shift in Eritrea's position has since occurred, which is discussed below.

Funding could also be mobilised by terrorists from their own economic and commercial activities, some of them lawful and others patently illegal. In this respect, the commodities in which terrorists trade to raise funds vary according to geographic locality, availability, ease of access and movement, as well as the exigencies of the situation. Experience shows that the most commonly traded goods are narcotics, ivory, sugar, charcoal,[12] and precious extractive commodities such as gold and fuel. In some instances, commodities are exchanged for money, but sometimes they are at the centre of barter transactions for firearms and explosives.[13] Some insurgents supplement their income by committing armed robbery in host communities, robbing food convoys, carrying out crimes against businesses, and targeted extortion.

This is partly the reason for the focus of the UN's Global Counter-Terrorism Strategy on a range of activities directed at the financing of terrorism. The strategy urges member states:

> "To strengthen coordination and cooperation among states in combating crimes that might be connected with terrorism, including drug trafficking in all its aspects, illicit arms trade, in particular of small arms and light weapons, including man-portable air defence systems, money laundering and smuggling of nuclear, chemical, biological, radiological and other potentially deadly materials."[14]

The plea to focus on the trafficking of small arms and light weapons represents a logical appreciation of the scope of support for violent extremism. Modern terrorism depends on, and is increasingly committed to, the use of such weapons. In the Horn of Africa, there is ample evidence of shifts that have occurred in the past few years in the channels by which small arms and light weapons enter the region. Whereas Eritrea used to be the entry point for weapons used by some insurgent groups, this has changed, particularly following the 'normalisation' of relations between Eritrea and its neighbours. The indications are that Djibouti has emerged as the new entry point. Between September 2019 and mid-March 2020, several significant arsenals of weapons were intercepted that landed in Djibouti and were destined for Ethiopia.[15] The March 2020 incident was still under investigation at the time of writing, but initial indications were that it was consistent with earlier trends.

Regarding the parties complicit in the movement of weapons destined to perpetuate regional violent extremism, risk analysis consultancy EXX Africa has alleged that "senior Djiboutian military officials, government officials and heads of state-owned enterprises have ties with companies involved in the funding and facilitation of arms trafficking into the Horn of Africa."[16] While the report does not explore the combination of factors that could be facilitating this, it is conceivable that this may reveal:

- The corruption of the public officials concerned.
- The absence of mechanisms for tracking and monitoring the transport of weapons through the country.
- The absence of effective collaboration and information-sharing in the management of the border between Djibouti and its neighbours.

As the transition from Eritrea to Djibouti as the source or transit territory has occurred, there has also been an escalation in the role of Persian Gulf and Middle Eastern power struggles, alliances and agendas in inter- and intra-state conflicts in the region. Discernible influences are those emanating from Saudi Arabia, the United Arab Emirates (UAE), Turkey and Qatar. The Saudis and the UAE are in a strong alliance over shared interests, distinguished and characterised by Saudi Arabia's antipathy towards Iranian influence in the region and the UAE's determination to counter political Islam. In both priorities, they are joined by the United States (US) and Israel, and to a lesser extent by Egypt. Qatar pursues a different agenda, with the support of Turkey and Iran. Ironically, both sides of the divide claim to be acting to negate violent extremism. They have increasingly sought to pursue their diametrically opposed aspirations across the Horn of Africa. As a region that already has an unfortunate legacy of cross-border and internal armed conflict, maritime and land-based piracy, human trafficking and money laundering, this is bound to worsen insecurity and human security in the Horn of Africa.[17]

The intensity of the interest of foreign Middle Eastern powers in the region is evident in Somalia and Ethiopia. In the former, at different stages, Saudi Arabia and Qatar have lent their support to the current government in its continuing conflict with Al-Shabaab, while Turkey maintains one of the largest military bases in the region, just outside Mogadishu.

Indicators That Prevailing Knowledge is Inadequate

Al-Shabaab is affirmed to be the most prominent current threat to regional stability in East Africa. It controls territory in parts of southern and central Somalia, and continues to accrue resources and fighters. It is not known to be receiving any resource support from any government, in the region or elsewhere. There is reasonable cause for apprehension that this may change, given the probability of ethnic friction and contests for power prompted by the reconfiguration of some countries in the region.

This risk is apparent in Ethiopia, one of the largest and most influential states in the region. It arises from a combination of the expected further stratification of Ethiopia into additional federal sub-structures,[18] and the risk of newly created minority communities in some border areas being subjected to victimisation, and becoming susceptible to radicalisation and recruitment to violent extremism.

The animosity harboured by Al-Shabaab towards Ethiopia is, after all, a matter of public record. The formation of Al-Shabaab has been traced and attributed to the entry of Ethiopian troops into Somalia in 2006, and its subsequent occupation between 2006 and 2009. Prominent among the analysts behind the allegation is American-based academic Alemayehu Mariam.[19] He contends that the 'invasion' was prompted by two factors – the intention of Ethiopia's former leader, Meles Zenawi, to thwart the emergence of an Islamic fundamentalist regime in neighbouring Somalia (which could be an inspirational example to Islamic elements in his own backyard), and his determination to attract the support of the US by portraying Ethiopia as a bulwark against radical Islamic structures.

The factors that have a bearing on future terrorism necessarily also have a bearing on future types of terrorist funding. The imbalances and inequalities of economic development within different parts of each country – which, in several instances, preceded the advent of sovereign statehood in East African countries – persist and in some instances are worse. Examples can be found in the greater development of the coastal areas in Tanzania compared to the hinterland, and the disparity in development between major cities and rural areas in Ethiopia.

Furthermore, the emerging interest in hegemony over the Somali coast and the regional hinterland by Gulf states and Turkey, which is yet to take definite shape, might have a bearing on the forms of politically inspired violent conflict in the future. Several realities raise concern. The first is the fierce rivalry among the most powerful Gulf states, which pits Saudi Arabia and the UAE against Turkey and Iran. This rivalry could spawn conflict in the Horn of Africa at the instance of, or as a proxy, conflict between these emerging powers, as it has already done in Yemen. In this regard, the conflict in Yemen has already prompted Eritrea and Sudan to take sides with Saudi Arabia and the UAE against Iran.

The risk that economic inequalities can be exploited by domestic agitators and by foreign agents of regime change is universally recognised. As Chatterjee puts it: "The link between poverty and violent extremism is compelling, and means that if we want to address extremism, we must fight inequality too."[20]

The danger, as far as the future of violent extremism in the Horn of Africa is concerned, is that there are ambitious political actors in the region who could be spurred on by money and influence emanating from one Middle Eastern camp or another to promise support, in exchange for support in the contest for influence and access to resources in the region.[21] It is likely that the external support will be offered as being ostensibly directed at improving the opportunities of marginalised communities within certain countries. Such alliances and deals – which echo the strategic relationship that used to tie Jonas Savimbi's National Union for the Total Independence of Angola movement to apartheid South Africa – have precipitated state support for violent extremism and terrorism at the hands of the LRA in Uganda. They can fuel local conflicts and unsettle regional and internal politics.

In instances where state support is given to terrorist structures and extremist groups, support is often rendered conditionally. The insurgent group receives support on condition that it fights or disrupts the operations of a government or organisation that it is in opposition to, or that is considered inconvenient to the aspirations of the state. This was the case with the LRA, which, as a quid pro quo for Sudanese support, had to show that it could sustain its conflict against the Ugandan government.[22] The existence and cost of state support for terrorist organisations can be concealed in the military budget of the state, as part of the 'ordinary' defence budget. The secretive nature of defence budgeting in several countries, including countries that have been implicated, makes it problematic to determine how much financing of terrorist activities flowed from Sudan to the LRA.

The role and importance of safe havens for conducting various commercial activities should not be underrated. For terrorist organisations to generate resources to sustain their activities, they need 'liberated' spaces in which to conduct income-earning activities. In the case of the LRA, this was in the form of regions, such as Kafia Kingi and Darfur, secured from their opponents by the government supporting them. In these regions, the organisation could store ivory for occasional sale.

In the case of Al-Shabaab, for a while this was the role that the port of Kismayo played, as it was from there that the organisation could levy 'taxes' for permitting commodity trading to be conducted through the port. As Freeman and Ruehsen explain, the optimal context for mobilising funding for terrorism is one in which significant volumes of commodities can be traded or moved, with minimal risk of detection and interception, conveniently, expeditiously and at low cost.[23] Liberated spaces offer such contexts in that commodity movements and payments can occur beyond the gaze of regulatory and law-enforcement agencies. Just as important is that payments can be made anonymously without using formal banking systems, which have increasingly come under tight regulatory monitoring.

Financing is important in supporting recruitment to the ranks of any extremist organisation. Parallels can be drawn between the manner in which youths are recruited during electoral political contests, and their radicalisation and recruitment into terrorist organisations. The Horn of Africa is replete with instances that indicate that there are important similarities. A study has shown that some youth become part of terrorist organisations because of the prospect of earning money, which is promised to them by recruiters.[24] In the recruitment process, some money may indeed be used.

Funds in the hands of a terrorist organisation could also be used to corrupt public officials responsible for border management or tasked with other regulatory functions. One of the risks is that, once compromised, a corrupted official is unable to terminate the relationship with the individual or organisation that bribed him or her, and becomes susceptible to future collaboration. Corruption becomes a tool for securing the collusion of public officials in facilitating commodity trafficking, as well as unimpeded border crossings. Accusations of this nature continue to dog security officials in Kenya.[25]

How Useful Are AML/CFT Frameworks in Tackling Existing and Future Terrorist Financing?

Containing the financing of Al-Shabaab has proved particularly problematic, and may be treated as a test case. Some of the major activities to which its resources have been attributed include taxation of the trades in charcoal, sugar smuggling, road tolls and fees, donations and external assistance, kidnapping and ransom, khet taxes and drug smuggling, and wildlife trafficking. Most of the funding mechanisms depend on the organisation's ability to exercise territorial control. Correspondingly, frameworks relating to anti-money laundering and combating the financing of terrorism (AML/CFT) can only work when exercised in a context in which there is effective regulatory enforcement and low levels of corruption. The effectiveness of such enforcement in some areas from which Al-Shabaab is believed to source funding is questionable.

Notwithstanding the use of AML/CFT compliance-assessment processes, undertaken when mutual evaluations occur in the various countries in the region, it is up to each country to ensure the effective implementation of its own AML/CFT framework. In most parts of the region, the most glaring deficiencies are in weak coordination and the leadership of their respective regimes against money laundering and terrorist financing. Some countries still do not have any AML/CFT national strategy around which to mobilise the efforts of disparate agencies and institutions. In the absence of a national strategy, it is unclear who should lead the implementation of AML/CFT measures. It is even less clear how their effectiveness and impact should be measured, and when.[26]

Law enforcement is further complicated by corruption within agencies, which is a challenge for countries in the Horn of Africa. There, in both business and politics, corruption slows efficiency and undermines policies and procedures, from regulation to enforcement. Accusations of complicity against some armed forces in the military alliance that is supposed to combat Al-Shabaab have been made, and unconvincingly refuted. It is well established that corruption facilitates other illicit activities.

A major result of the instability in Somalia and Yemen is distrust in their economies, resulting in, and manifested by, their loss of access to the formal global banking sector. In both instances this has prompted the emergence of a widespread black market revolving mainly around fuel and money exchanges. Transactions on the black market in these and other commodities are largely undocumented and beyond regulation, which means that they are exploitable to fund criminality and terrorism. It is well established that "untracked money transfers from anonymous individuals enables radical organisations to garner the resources necessary to launch terrorist attacks".[27] In several parts of the region, these sorts of transfers are evident in the funding of structures that are mainly used for religious instruction, but that have also been abused to spawn ideas that are inimical to governance structures.[28] The latest assessment of Yemen is that it has strategic deficiencies in its AML/CFT regime, but the current security situation negates any on-site inspection of the efficacy of the measures adopted on paper.

In the case of South Sudan, illegal logging is at the centre of fund mobilisation from and for violent conflict during which acts of terrorism are committed. Illegal logging plays an integral role in perpetuating war, and in money laundering and terrorism financing. The conviction of Liberian timber baron Guus Kouwenhoven for trading arms in return for natural resources and permits for timber extraction is an example of the link between illegal logging and violent conflict in African countries.

In spite of the frequently expressed relief at the decline of state-supported terrorism elsewhere, for the Horn of Africa the spectre of state-supported violent extremism persists. It is driven in no small measure by the emerging trend of supporting proxy conflicts, as discussed above. It has added to the causes of violent extremism, which are relatively well known. Uneven development within countries, in turn, feeds the radicalisation and militarisation of the youth.

The success of contemporary measures to negate support for violent extremist groups turns on the extent to which they contribute to addressing both long-established and emerging sources of support, as well as the drivers of disillusionment that affect vulnerable sectors of society. Countries can step up efforts to influence the self-generated support for violent extremism by enhancing the opportunities for marginalised communities and groups to participate in their economies. It is in this regard that ongoing debates around the link between illicit financial flows and worsening inequalities loom large. The causative connection between corruption and illicit financial flows is well known. Illicit financial flows, however, have more complex and deeper causes than corruption. As is the case between different countries, uncoordinated approaches, or even competitive tendencies, play a significant role.

At a regional level, contests between neighbours in attracting investment from foreign sources often present opportunities for unscrupulous exploitation by investors who are keen to benefit from regulatory and taxation arbitrage. Disaffected sectors such as the youth experience the adverse impact of inequitable growth, as the small ventures through which they sustain themselves are displaced by condominiums and gleaming hotels that offer them no employment. Just as it is doubtful whether it is within the competence of governments in the Horn of Africa to impact on the participation of foreign sources of support for conflict, so too is their readiness to collaborate across borders to stem illicit financial flows.

The persistence of these threats points to the weakness of existing initiatives to pre-empt, minimise or suppress violent extremism in the Horn of Africa. It may well be that the capacity of governments to achieve this is inadequately supported by failures in resource governance. The improvement of resource mobilisation and use requires further attention.

Resource mobilisation should be focused on strengthening resource-derived taxation, targeting the following spheres:

1. **Harmful inter-state tax competition:** Reduce such competition, partly by harmonising policies and practices on incentives offered to potential investors;
2. **Tax evasion and tax avoidance:** Prioritise the use of data on beneficial ownership of corporate and related legal entities;
3. **Corporate transparency and accountability in the extractive sector:** Align

policies to encourage the domestication and implementation of the normative frameworks set by the Extractive Industry Transparency Initiative and the Africa Mining Vision;
4. **Public debt management:** Ensure that governments do not borrow beyond certain limits at the expense of current and future generations. Such a programme should seek to empower legislatures and civil society organisations to monitor this obligation, by raising their awareness of the guidelines to sovereign indebtedness contained in regional protocols on finance and investment, where such instruments exist;
5. **Institutional and programmatic capacity of regional civil society organisations:** Enhance the capacity of such organisations to play a more effective role with, and on behalf of, the general public in monitoring compliance by governments and global corporations to fiscal obligations.

Conclusion

Examples from other parts of the world, such as countries in the Organisation for Economic Co-operation and Development, highlight the value of regional approaches that are expressed in transnational instruments. To be effective, initiatives should be adopted by member states of the East African Community and the Intergovernmental Authority on Development. These two organisations have some overlapping membership in Kenya, Uganda and South Sudan. Activities will be conducted by regional structures that derive their mandates from these economic communities. Advocacy against practices that are conducive to illicit financial flows should be central, in order to persuade national legislatures and policymakers to adopt and implement improvements to the legal and institutional frameworks through which public resources are produced and/or collected. Implicit in that premise is the conviction that the African Union's Regional Economic Communities develop policies, laws and frameworks to guide their membership, to be reinforced by peer pressure and, if necessary, enforced through various instruments such as protocols and conventions.

Public information-dissemination initiatives should simultaneously support civil society as an important sector of 'rights holders' to monitor what governments do. The expectation is that standardised regional positions stand a better chance of achieving effective, sustainable improvements in resource mobilisation than individual state initiatives. As Sene has observed, the African Union "could address the issue at a political level by putting in place a common continental strategy on which national strategies will be anchored, and by advocating for the strengthening of international cooperation in combating tax evasion, money laundering, crime, corruption, false invoicing and mispricing of imported or exported goods practices".[29]

Select Bibliography
Ali, A.M. (2017). Radicalization Process in the Horn of Africa – Phrases and Relevant Factors. Available from: https://www.files.ethz.ch/isn/87744/ispsw.pdf [accessed 12 April 2020].
Chatterjee, S. (2017). Driven to extremes – Poverty fuels violent extremism. 17 October. Available from: https://www.ke.undp.org/content/kenya/en/home/blog/2017/10/17/Driven-to-extremes-Poverty-fuels-violent-extremism.html [accessed 12 April 2020].
ECADF Ethiopian News. (2019). Ethiopia seizes large illegal weapons cache in sting operation. 25 September. Available from: https://ecadforum.com/2019/09/25/ethiopia-seizes-large-illegal-weapons-cache-in-sting-operation/ [accessed 12 April 2020].
Faber, P. (2017). Sources of Resilience of the Lord's Resistance Army. CNA Analysis and Solutions. Available from: https://www.cna.org/cna_files/pdf/DOP-2017-U-015265-Final.pdf [accessed 20 December 2019].
Fabricius, P. (2016). Is the LRA rising again? *ISS Today*, 16 July. Available from: https://issafrica.org/iss-today/the-lra-rising-again [accessed 19 December 2019].
Freeman, M. & Ruehsen, M. (2013). Terrorism Financing Methods: An Overview. *Perspectives on Terrorism*, 7(4). Available from: http://www.terrorismanalysts.com/pt/index.php/pot/article/view/279/html [accessed 2 February 2020].
Hellsten, S. (2016). Radicalisation and terrorist recruitment among Kenya's youth. Nordic Africa Institute, Policy Note #1. Available from: http://nai.diva-portal.org/smash/get/diva2:906144/FULLTEXT01.pdf [accessed 12 April 2020].
Mariam, A.G. (2016). The "Fantastic Somalia Job". *Huffington Post*, 12 June. Available from: https://www.huffpost.com/entry/the-fantastic-somalia-job_b_792234 [accessed 12 April 2020].
RFI. (2018). Djibouti emerges as arms trafficking hub for Horn of Africa. 16 September. Available from: http://www.rfi.fr/en/africa/20180915-djibouti-emerges-arms-trafficking-hub-horn-africa [accessed 12 April 2020].
Sene, L.J.M. (2018). Mobilization of Domestic Resources: Fighting against Corruption and Illicit Financial Flows. April. African Union Commission: Department of Economic Affairs. Available from: https://au.int/sites/default/files/newsevents/workingdocuments/34086-wd-dea_paper_stc_2018_mobilization_of_domestic_resources_fighting_against_corruption_iff_english_0.pdf [accessed 12 April 2020].

Shetret, L. (2019). *Striking the Balance: Practical AML/CFT Risk Mitigation in Cash-Based Economies in The Horn Of Africa*. European Union.

Shinn, D.H. (2003). Terrorism in East Africa and the Horn: An Overview. Available from: https://journals.lib.unb.ca/index.php/jcs/article/view/218/376 [accessed 12 April 2020].

The Economist. (2005). *Looking in the wrong places: Hindering flows across international financial networks is costly and does not stop terrorists' primary activity.* 20 October. Available from: https://www.economist.com/special-report/2005/10/20/looking-in-the-wrong-places [accessed 13 April 2020].

Thompson, E. (2011). *Trust is the Coin of the Realm: Lessons from the Money Men in Afghanistan*. Oxford: Oxford University Press.

United Nations. (2014). *Yearbook of the United Nations, 2014*. Volume 68. New York: United Nations Department of Global Communications. Available from: https://unyearbook.un.org/node/1026 [accessed 13 April 2020].

United Nations General Assembly. (1999). International Convention for the Suppression of the Financing of Terrorism (A/RES/54/109).

United Nations General Assembly. (2006). The United Nations Global Counter-Terrorism Strategy (A/RES/60/288). Available from: https://undocs.org/A/RES/60/288 [accessed 13 April 2020].

United Nations Security Council (UNSC). (2009). *Resolution 1907: Peace and security in Africa.*

Endnotes

1. *The Economist*, 2005.
2. Shinn, 2003.
3. For a general discussion, see Freeman & Ruehsen (2013).
4. Freeman & Ruehsen, 2013.
5. The infamous atrocities committed in the US in September 2001 were funded by the use of several financial institutions, including Western Union, Standard Chartered Bank, Union Bank of California, Royal Bank of Canada, Citibank, Bank of America and MoneyGram. None of these institutions were aware of the intended terrorist activities as funds passed through their systems.
6. Insurgencies in the Sahel are in some instances based on this sense of grievance, for example, the palpable anger at the arrangements facilitating the extraction of uranium from Niger by French companies.
7. Fabricius, 2016.
8. Shinn, 2003.
9. UNSC, 2009.
10. Thompson, 2011:203.
11. UN, 2014:377.
12. The funding of Al-Shabaab has been attributed to sugar imports and charcoal exports.
13. This trend is also evident in the Sahel region, in which various jihadist structures are engaged in armed conflict with governmental authorities in Mali, Niger, Burkina Faso and Nigeria.
14. United Nations General Assembly, 2006.
15. The September 2019 interception was reported in the Afar region bordering Djibouti. See ECADF Ethiopian News (2019).
16. RFI, 2018.
17. Shetret, 2019.
18. In November 2019, a referendum held in the southern region decided in favour of the establishment of a new state to be dominated by the Sidama ethnic community. If the result is endorsed by the federal legislature, the new state will be the 10th constituent structure in the federal republic.
19. Mariam, 2016.
20. Chatterjee, 2017.
21. There are indications that one such charismatic ethnic-political leader has received sympathy and support from a Gulf state in exchange for promising to support it should he assume power.
22. The relationship between the LRA and Sudan dates from 1994, when former Sudanese President Omar Hassan al-Bashir provided guns and ammunition in exchange for LRA attacks on the South Sudanese rebels, the SPLA, and the Ugandan army.
23. Freeman & Ruehsen, 2013.
24. Hellsten, 2016.
25. Hellsten, 2016:4-5.
26. This point is often exposed when training initiatives are undertaken with different law-enforcement and regulatory practitioners.
27. United Nations General Assembly, 1999.
28. Ali, 2017.
29. Sene, 2018.

CHAPTER 7

Kidnapping in West Africa: A Review

Markus Korhonen

Introduction

When analysing kidnapping trends in West Africa,[1] or anywhere else for that matter, attempts at statistical accuracy are wisely abandoned at the outset. For a variety of reasons, which will be discussed in detail in this chapter, kidnapping data is incomplete at the best of times. This is not to say that we can know nothing or learn nothing, or that we should discard attempts at better understanding the nature of the kidnapping threat. Instead, we should glean from known cases what information we can, and accept that we are looking at an incomplete and potentially unrepresentative sample.

From the risk-management perspective – which, since I work in the industry, will indubitably colour my assessment – as uncertainty increases, it is prudent to impose a concomitant increase on the risk rating. Risks should always be assessed on a case-by-case basis, and there is no mathematical formula into which variables can be plugged to arrive at an answer. It follows, then, that where there are significant unknowns, it can be methodologically justified to increase a moderate risk rating to a high one, for instance. A similarly conservative approach is also sensible from an analytical or academic point of view.

Having presented this notable caveat, we know that West Africa has recently seen a number of high-profile kidnappings, with emerging indications that kidnappings are becoming more organised and systematic, and increasingly associated with extremist and criminal groups. Nigeria remains the African hotspot for kidnapping for ransom, with notable recent cases elsewhere in the region in the likes of Cameroon, Benin and Ghana. Many of the reported cases, particularly those affecting foreign nationals, are maritime kidnappings in the Gulf of

Guinea. As multinational and coordinated anti-piracy efforts in the Horn of Africa have reduced the threat there, maritime kidnapping in the Gulf of Guinea has become an increasingly frequent occurrence in recent years.

But who is doing the kidnapping, and why? Understanding the drivers behind kidnapping in West Africa is central to developing measures to mitigate the risk in both the long and short term, and in terms of response, which will have an impact on how kidnapping negotiations are conducted. Whether kidnappers have purely criminal motivations, purely extremist motivations, in which kidnappings are used to send ideological messages and show power, or whether they are a funding stream for terrorist organisations, will directly inform responses. The motivations of kidnappers in the region are complex, and the perpetrators do not fall neatly into a criminal-extremist divide.

For academics and practitioners alike, an improved understanding of the nature of kidnapping in West Africa can be valuable. This chapter will begin by looking at kidnapping more broadly: what is it, who does it, and how does it work? The chapter then presents insights into the observable and emerging trends of this activity in West Africa. Despite the known unknowns, to borrow Donald Rumsfeld's phrasing, my hope is that in pulling together the data that does exist, we can get a step closer to understanding both the logic and the *modus operandi* of kidnappers in this part of the world.

Kidnapping: What we Know and What we do not Know

The focus of this chapter will be on kidnap for ransom, and will therefore exclude child abductions and kidnapping motivated by human trafficking, for instance. I neither engage with these crimes in my professional capacity, nor do they fit analytically into the same category as kidnap for ransom. Instead, what I discuss below relates to incidents where humans are forcefully captured and held against their will, and where the kidnappers enter into a transactional negotiation over the lives and/or liberty of the victims (typically with the families or employers of the victims).

Strictly speaking, 'negotiation' is an inaccurate depiction of the process during a kidnap or extortion case because it is carried out under an element of substantial threat. A more apt term would be 'coercive bargaining', because as one experienced crisis responder puts it: "The reality is that when a life is at stake few, if any, of us would ever choose to walk away."[2] However, for the purposes of this chapter, and in recognition of the use of the term in common parlance, I will refer to the kidnappers' coercive bargaining as negotiation.

Money Talks
Kidnapping is (probably) a big industry. It is impossible to put an exact figure on the total amount of ransoms paid out. Estimates vary, but annual turnover may be as high as $1,5 billion.[3] The discrepancy results from uncertainty in two key variables. First, we do not know for certain the total number of kidnappings that take place (I will return to this in more detail later). Second, even in known cases, the exact sums paid out might not be made public. There are some very good reasons for this, not the least of which is that it can be quite personal information: effectively, a ransom payment demonstrates the victim's personal wealth. This applies equally whether the victim has insurance or not. A core principle of kidnap insurance is that claims are paid out retrospectively; you have to come up with the money first (by, for example, emptying savings accounts and selling property) and then claim it back on your insurance.[4] This means that there is a genuine incentive to reduce the ransom, which makes the negotiation credible.

It is in the kidnappers' interests to extract the maximum amount possible from a negotiation. Of course, there are other considerations, such as time. The longer a kidnapping continues, the higher the chances that something will go wrong – the kidnappers are found, or the hostage falls ill, for example. However, the fundamental purpose of a kidnapping is to extract a reward, whether monetary or otherwise, and the higher the reward, the more it compensates for the substantial risk in carrying out a kidnapping.

Economic Versus Politically Motivated Kidnapping
Although some kidnappers are driven by cultural or religious motives, for example, broadly speaking we can draw a distinction between kidnappers driven by economic goals and those driven by political ones.

Since individuals or companies cannot offer political concessions, negotiations involving the latter will inevitably involve states, at least indirectly. In recent years, one of the best examples of this type of organisation is Asa'ib Ahl Al Haq

(AAH), an Iranian-backed militia group operating in Iraq. AAH has carried out several high-profile kidnappings of foreigners in Iraq, including citizens from the United States (US), United Kingdom (UK), Turkey and Qatar.[5] However, AAH is funded and equipped by Iran, and generously so. In 2014, AAH was estimated to be receiving between $1,5 million and $2 million a month from Iran.[6] A 2017 Amnesty International report on paramilitary groups in Iraq suggested that Iran was still a "major military sponsor" of AAH, among others.[7] In addition to monetary support, the firm ties between AAH and Iran have also extended to training and armaments, predominantly through the Islamic Revolutionary Guards Corps (IRGC) and one of its units, the Quds Force.[8] AAH is therefore unlikely to be motivated by monetary incentives, and has instead pushed for political concessions when it has conducted kidnappings. Of the four high-profile kidnappings between 2007 and 2016 in which AAH was implicated, three were resolved through negotiated political concessions, including prison swaps. The terms of release of the fourth victim were unclear.

Economically motivated kidnappers, typically but not exclusively members of criminal organisations, practise kidnapping as a means of generating revenue – in other words, kidnapping is a business. It is motivated not by religious or political zeal, but by the same logic that most of us apply to our own employment: We expect our labour and enterprise to be remunerated.

In Mexico, for example, which has one of the highest per capita kidnap rates in the world, the perpetrators are predominantly criminal groups that use revenue from kidnapping to fund other activities such as the illicit drug trade. In 2018, the Mexican government recorded 1,480 kidnappings. This number is likely to be significantly lower than the actual number of kidnappings, as an estimated 90% of cases go unreported in Mexico.[9] While ransom demands can be upwards of $300,000 for wealthier victims, quick turnaround, lower-reward kidnapping is also increasingly prevalent in the country. This type of kidnapping, known as express kidnapping, whose duration is measured in hours rather than days, requires a lot less planning and can be completed at a higher frequency. In 2019 there was an 800% year-on-year increase in the number of express kidnappings reported in the country.[10] While the payments received are much smaller, the pool of targets is much larger – you are more likely to find victims able to pay hundreds of dollars than ones able to pay hundreds of thousands.

There is not always a clear-cut delineation between politically and economically motivated kidnapping. Unlike better-funded groups such as AAH, some terrorist organisations carry out kidnappings to indirectly enable the pursuit of political objectives. Instead of demanding political concessions for the return of kidnap victims, they demand ransom payments, which can then be put towards political activities. The Abu Sayyaf Group (ASG), which operates in the southern Philippines, is a good example. In 2019, ASG was implicated in at least four high-profile kidnappings of foreign nationals.[11] Groups such as ASG may not even perceive kidnapping as inherently criminal, but see it as a component of their political activity, "[justifying] the use of crime as being part of a legitimate act as long as it hurts the 'enemy'".[12] Kidnap for ransom and extortion are the group's primary sources of funding, but not its *raison d'être*.[13] Its ultimate goal is the establishment of an independent Islamic state in Mindanao and the Sulu Archipelago – funds from kidnapping are directed towards this purpose.[14] The practice can be lucrative. In 2014, ASG kidnapped two German tourists near Mindanao and held them captive for seven months, before releasing both in exchange for a $5,6 million ransom.[15]

These distinctions have practical applications. The kidnappers' motivations should inform the response; if concessions are to be granted, who has the authority to grant them? The motivation of a group can also provide vital information about likely targets, and thereby allow states, companies and individuals to take appropriate preventative or protective measures. The attractiveness of a target, for instance, is a vital component of a thorough threat assessment, and this can only be determined when the potential victim is considered in the light of the typical *modus operandi* of kidnapping groups operating in a particular geography.

Negotiating with Kidnappers
When called to assist in resolving a kidnapping incident, professional responders are guided by three basic tenets:
1. Secure the safe and timely release of the victim.
2. Protect the best interests of the victim, the victim's family and/or the victim's employer.
3. Act within the law.[16]

In attempting to achieve this, some form of negotiation must take place. The negotiation requires a balancing act which "both satisfies the kidnappers and is affordable (and ethically acceptable) for the victims' representatives."[17] Comfortingly, this balance is achieved in the vast majority of cases: if the key consideration in kidnapping situations is the safe return of victims, professional crisis responders have a remarkable success rate of more than 97%.[18] Arguably, when dealing with economically motivated kidnappers, this process is more straightforward: it is a question of money, and while it may be laborious and financially detrimental for the victim's representatives to raise the money, the loss is measurable and easily defined.[19]

Political concessions are much more complicated, not least because they can only be granted by states. Politically motivated kidnappers will, more often than not, be associated with terrorist organisations. The US government, for example, has designated AAH a terrorist organisation.[20] This can make negotiations more complicated, since different states have different policies on whether they negotiate with terrorists or not. Yet, even those governments that have a stated policy of not negotiating with terrorists (such as the US)[21] still do so, as demonstrated by the prisoner swaps mentioned above: "Governments routinely declare that they will not negotiate with terrorists, and regularly (if not routinely) do so nonetheless."[22] Other countries, such as Spain, aim to achieve the release of hostages "at all costs".[23] However, even a government willing to negotiate must weigh up the interests of an individual victim against the interests of the wider public. As Rachel Briggs notes in a UK Foreign Policy Centre paper: "In these cases, the hostage is taken as a representative of their country or the ideological system to which they belong, and so concessions have ramifications far beyond the immediate case."[24] A prisoner swap might be an acceptable cost for the safe return of a kidnap victim, but no government is likely to make major foreign-policy concessions.

We may justifiably ask whether giving in to kidnappers' demands merely encourages them to undertake further kidnapping. On a basic level, the answer is obvious: of course it does – if it did not, kidnapping would not take place. Underlying this dynamic is that, when faced with a genuine threat to the life of a loved one, as opposed to a theoretical discussion, most of us would willingly pay. However, putting ethical quandaries aside, it is impractical to suppose that there could be a collective global decision to refuse ransom payments. The deterrent effect of individual states' policies to not negotiate with kidnappers is unclear.[25] Workable deterrents are more likely to be found through other means, such as improved law-enforcement capabilities.

The Difficulties of Data Collection

Some estimates suggest that around 10,000 kidnappings take place globally each year[26] but, with a large number of unreported cases, the real figure may well be higher. Kidnappings are also recorded differently, as organisations and officials have varying definitions and methodologies for tallying the data in the first place, and they also report on that data in different ways. For instance, in the last quarter of 2019, private security and risk management company S-RM recorded at least 128 kidnapping victims taken in 10 separate incidents in West Africa.[27] Between November and December 2019, Constellis recorded 57 kidnappings of foreign citizens in the region,[28] while Control Risks recorded nine cases of "special risks", including kidnapping, between October and December.[29] While all three datasets speak to the same issue in the same geography, the data points are varied and comparable only in limited ways. All three risk-management firms are no doubt capable of producing comprehensive and detailed reports specific to a given region, based on the analysis their regional teams produce, but their outputs are driven by commercial considerations that do not necessarily align. Herein lies the first challenge for developing comprehensive analyses of kidnapping data.

As with all criminal enterprises, there is significant uncertainty associated with almost all aspects of kidnapping. For several of the stakeholders involved, keeping (at least some) information about kidnapping under wraps makes sense. For instance, the kidnap insurance industry operates on the premise of imperfect information: "If the kidnappers know who's insured and who's not, they may run up their ransom demands accordingly. If they know what strategies the insurers employ, they may adapt. And since most of the time it's employers insuring employees, the employees also shouldn't know they've been insured – lest they behave more recklessly or divulge information to the kidnappers."[30] For companies offering kidnap insurance, it therefore makes sense to contain details about their products, including how much has been paid out in ransom fees.

The families of kidnap victims may have other reasons to practise discretion. It has been estimated, for instance, that at least 90% of kidnappings in Mexico go unreported.[31] The hesitance to go to the authorities stems from, at least in part, a justifiable distrust of the police, with members of the Mexican police force themselves implicated in numerous kidnapping cases in recent years.[32] Mexico is by no means alone. In both the Philippines and Nigeria, for instance, police involvement in kidnapping incidents is common. Pervasive corruption and poorly resourced police forces go a long way towards explaining the temptation for officers to accept bribes or become involved in criminal activities. In Nigeria, police recruits earn less than $400 per annum, while in Mexico a 2018 police survey found that officers were so poorly resourced that 48% of respondents had to pay for their own boots, while 23% had bought their own ammunition for their service firearms.[33] Little wonder, then, that in some jurisdictions the police may be the last people you would want to approach to assist in addressing a kidnapping.

A kidnapping transaction takes place when the two sides recognise the basic premise of the activity: the victim's family believes that the victim will be released if they comply with the kidnappers' demands, and harmed if they do not. Therefore, a final point on the limits of available information is the risk to the victim if kidnappers specifically warn against involving the authorities or making cases public. It is a justifiable fear, and although the overwhelming majority of kidnap victims are released alive (as noted above), the practice contains an inherent element of violence. Publicly available information on kidnapping must therefore be incomplete.

Kidnapping in West Africa
Kidnapping in West Africa appears to be a growing threat, both on land and at sea. In its latest annual report on maritime crime, the International Maritime Bureau recorded 103 maritime kidnapping incidents off the coasts of West African countries in 2019.[34] The report further notes: "The Gulf of Guinea accounts for over 90% of global crew kidnappings and has increased more than 50% year on year – with 121 crew taken in 2019 compared to 78 in 2018."

Maritime kidnapping and other piracy incidents have been reported on widely, but on land, too, there were a number of high-profile incidents in West Africa in 2019, including in Ghana, Nigeria, Burkina Faso, Senegal, Côte d'Ivoire, Benin and Burkina Faso.[35] Following several kidnappings in the country in 2019, including that of an Estonian diplomat and two Canadian non-governmental-organisation workers, Ghana's President, Nana Akufo-Addo, expressed his concern over the growing kidnapping threat, saying: "We do not know if ransoms are being paid, and we do not know if Ghana is now becoming a hub for these kidnappers."[36]

For several years, Nigeria has been a kidnapping hotspot in sub-Saharan Africa, but most kidnapping activity has been focused in the southern, oil-rich parts of the country. In the past few years, this kidnapping threat has become more pronounced elsewhere, prompting some observers to dub it a "growing kidnapping crisis".[37] In Burkina Faso, a deteriorating security environment over the past few years has been accompanied by a growing threat of kidnapping incidents.[38] Militant groups have targeted predominantly foreign nationals working in the mining and humanitarian sectors in the country.

As the descriptions above suggest, West Africa's size and its social and political complexity mean that there is a range of drivers of the kidnapping threat. Perpetrators, methods and motives are varied. Aside from the inevitability of some overlap between different types of kidnapping groups, I have separated the discussion below into criminal, militant and maritime kidnapping in West Africa. The purpose is not to extensively discuss any individual groups, their motivations, or the root causes of the circumstances that have prompted them to undertake kidnapping activities. Instead, what I offer are observations and trends from various actors from a more practical perspective. When responding to kidnapping incidents, practical threat intelligence is paramount. Understanding who might be responsible, what they are likely to ask in return for the safe release of a victim, and how they tend to operate can help in resolving a kidnapping quickly and safely.

Criminal Groups
Rachel Briggs refers to kidnapping as a "rational problem with rational causes".[39] This depiction of kidnapping applies particularly well to economically motivated kidnappers. Kidnapping is run as a straightforward business operation, and

the factors that determine the viability of that business are the same as for any legitimate business. Businesses function for the purpose of making profit, and business owners make decisions about operating strategy based on a calculation of the approaches and practices that are likely to yield the highest returns. Briggs notes that kidnapping happens under the following conditions:[40]

1. There is a presence of organisations that are able and willing to enact kidnappings.
2. The calculation of the risks and rewards in a given jurisdiction is favourable for the kidnappers.
3. There exist sufficient opportunities in an operating environment to make the activity worthwhile.

Very simply, then, we could apply this template to explain differences in kidnapping rates between jurisdictions. In an operating environment with few criminal organisations, but a well-resourced law-enforcement framework, potential kidnappers are likely to be caught and prosecuted. Under these conditions, despite the ample opportunity for kidnapping as a result of few people taking precautions to guard against it, the rate of kidnapping is likely to be low. In contrast, kidnapping will be much more common in places where security forces are under-resourced or corrupt, where there are sufficient levels of wealth to compensate for the risks that do exist, and where kidnappers are, on balance, able to overcome protective measures that potential victims have put in place.

In Nigeria, there is a wide variety of groups that actively participate in kidnapping, including organised and semi-organised criminal gangs, militants and pirates. In its January 2020 report, Constellis notes that kidnapping across Africa is on the rise: "Poor security infrastructure and corruption are two of the main factors perpetuating the ability of criminal groups across the region to carry out kidnapping. This is particularly evident in Nigeria, where the kidnap risk is among the highest in the world."[41] Already in 2011, commentators were noting the commodification of kidnapping in Nigeria: "The crime has become a veritable commodity in the hands of its perpetrators who apparently have now made a multi-million naira business out of it."[42] In line with Briggs's characterisation above, Osumah and Aghedo note the lack of an adequate legal framework stemming from a weak state, the existence of ample but unequally distributed wealth, the existence of criminal and militant gangs, and a police force that can only "whimper" in response to rising crime. Little surprise, then, that they conclude: "A state that is largely unresponsive to the genuine and legitimate needs and aspirations of its youth is likely to elicit violence and anti-state engagements, such as commodified kidnapping."[43]

However, kidnapping dynamics have not remained static in Nigeria, nor in other parts of West Africa. What we have seen is that economically motivated kidnappings in West Africa reflect a global trend of shorter captivity times, where perpetrators pursue high volumes of quick, lower-value ransom payments. This suggests an increasingly business-like approach to kidnapping. A Control Risks report notes that the duration of the average kidnapping worldwide decreased from 29 days in 2011 to only five days in 2018.[44] This trend fits with the logic described above. If we accept that kidnapping is a rational pursuit, it makes sense that kidnappers would adjust their *modus operandi* to reflect the best market information. It appears, therefore, that the better operating model is a "...high turnover, rapid settlement strategy where [kidnappers] seek to maximise profits through high volumes of victims as opposed to large profits attained over extended durations."[45] While by far the most incidents reported take place in Nigeria, there have been similar kidnappings in Senegal and Ghana in the past few years.[46]

The dynamics of kidnapping as set out above provide a useful framework for explaining the high incidence rates of kidnap for ransom in Nigeria, and provide clues as to the conditions under which criminal kidnapping elsewhere in the West African region may become more frequent. From a practitioner's point of view, knowing that reducing the opportunity for kidnapping can counter the effects of the first two features can, and should, inform the degree of practical measures that can be applied to reduce exposure.

Militant Groups

As discussed above, the motivation for militant groups to engage in kidnapping can be informed either by the desire for profit or for political concessions. Kidnapping can also be conducted to make a political statement. For instance, the Islamic State (IS) militant group claimed responsibility for the January 2019 kidnapping and subsequent killing of Canadian geologist Kirk Woodman in

Burkina Faso. The reports of IS involvement were met with scepticism.[47] The group has a history of claiming responsibility for a range of terrorist incidents in which its involvement is questionable. There are a number of reasons why it and other militant groups might wish to lay claim to kidnappings, which provide some insights into the potential benefits they perceive to be gained. Soliev and Siyech write about the politics of IS claiming responsibility for certain terror attacks, whether it was involved in them or not, and suggest: "By acknowledging its responsibility publicly, the group sends a political message to the targeted audience about its motives and identities."[48]

However, if the only purpose of kidnapping is to send a political message, negotiating conditions for release can be challenging, if not impossible. That said, the fundamental equation for explaining kidnapping need not change. Perpetrators may still deem those incidents to be rational, as per the framework explained above: a group can perceive kidnappings to be worthwhile, and the 'reward' of publicity to outweigh the risks it takes on. While this does happen occasionally,[49] more frequently militant groups will demand ransom payments for the release of kidnapping victims. In most high-profile kidnappings in West Africa over the past few years, militant groups have used kidnapping as a means, either directly or indirectly, for financial gain. Victims have been returned after ransom payments were made, or they have been 'sold' to other militant groups. Across the Sahel, but also elsewhere in West Africa, militant groups have turned to kidnapping as a means of financing their operations. High-profile kidnappings linked to a variety of militant groups have taken place in at least Burkina Faso, Mali, Senegal, Niger, Benin and Nigeria.[50]

The rise in Islamist militancy across West Africa, and the general deterioration in the security environment since at least 2015, has been written about extensively.[51] Poverty, dissatisfaction and political instability have created ideal circumstances for a variety of extremist Islamist militant groups to exploit. Against this background, it is little surprise that militant groups vying for power and influence have used kidnapping as one tool by which to further their agendas.

It appears that kidnappings perpetrated by militant groups in West Africa are more likely to be driven by pragmatic considerations than ideological ones. The end result may be the same: the group gains the means by which to pursue broader goals, but the kidnappings themselves are not necessarily political acts.

Already in 2014, Boko Haram had reportedly shifted its previous perception of kidnapping as a "dirty business" to a practical means by which to expand its coffers.[52] That position appears to be held by other groups too. In Burkina Faso, for instance, Jama'a Nusrat ul-Islam wa al-Muslimin (JNIM), Islamic State in the Greater Sahara (ISGS) and Ansaroul Islam are likely to be responsible for most kidnapping incidents targeting foreign nationals, but those attacks are often opportunistic in nature as opposed to being an integral component of the groups' strategies.[53]

Maritime Kidnapping and Piracy

Perhaps the most widely discussed feature of West African kidnapping in recent years has been the proliferation of maritime kidnappings in the Gulf of Guinea. The pirate threat off Africa's east coast appears to have abated almost entirely. The International Maritime Bureau did not record a single attack off the coast of Somalia and Gulf of Aden in 2019.[54] While this should not be taken to mean that the threat of piracy there has disappeared, it is remarkable that eight years previously there were as many as 160 incidents in a single year.[55] In contrast, in 2019 off the coast of Nigeria alone, there were 35 attacks with a total of 44 crew members reported kidnapped.[56] These numbers, as concerning as they are, are most likely incomplete: "The situation is actually worse than the statistics depict, because, it is believed, unlike in other regions, only about half of the incidents of piracy in the Gulf of Guinea are actually reported by ships' masters and operators for fear of reprisal during their next visit."[57]

The West African region as a whole has seen a dramatic increase in maritime attacks and kidnappings. A One Earth Future report calculated that piracy cost West Africa $818 million in 2017 in terms of naval activity, counter-piracy programmes, insurance payments, stolen goods and contracted security services, among others.[58] Given the year-on-year increase in kidnapping and other incidents, this figure is likely to be significantly higher now, not least because, as the risks of being attacked or kidnapped have become widely known, shipping operators may find it increasingly difficult to recruit willing staff to crew ships.

So, what explains this relatively rapid growth in the number of maritime incidents in the Gulf of Guinea? The answer, unsurprisingly, lies in the circumstances onshore. The same drivers that explain criminality and militancy onshore in West

Africa go a long way in explaining the increase in piracy incidents. As Siebels notes, with reference to piracy in the Gulf of Guinea: "Kidnappings of seafarers are an extension of land-based problems."[59]

Nigerian groups dominate the offshore kidnapping market as they dominate the onshore one: "Nigeria stands out as the epicentre of Gulf of Guinea piracy and as the primary piracy enclave."[60] The Niger Delta, in particular, is a stronghold of piracy. Groups stationed there make use of high-powered speed boats to approach and board vessels, before returning to the difficult-to-navigate waterways of the delta. Criminal and militant groups who may have previously relied on oil theft from operators onshore in the Niger Delta have subsequently turned to offshore robberies and kidnappings. World oil prices dropped significantly between 2014 and 2015, and despite a slight resurgence, have remained at a new lower level. As a result, some criminal organisations have shifted to what they perceive to be a more lucrative source of income: kidnapping.[61]

Returning to the notion of the kidnapper as a rational actor, this same logic will drive maritime kidnappers in the other major kidnapping hubs on the Gulf of Guinea: Benin and Togo. Benin recorded 35 maritime kidnappings in 2019, and Togo seven.[62] An interesting development in Benin has been the targeting of ships in port, where vessels are usually presumed to be safe from harm. While these attacks have taken place since at least 2011,[63] it is worth noting that there were three incidents of ships being attacked in port in 2019 in Benin.[64]

The Togolese government has blamed the proliferation of maritime kidnapping on the lack of coordination among West African states; Togo's minimal coastline of only 56 km means that its naval forces cannot pursue suspected pirates for very long before having to hand the pursuit over to other countries.[65] However, widespread poverty[66] in Togo may drive criminal actors with maritime capabilities to attack potentially lucrative targets transiting the waters off its coast. It should also be remembered that not all maritime attacks undertaken in Togolese or Beninese waters are perpetrated by Togolese or Beninese actors – Nigerian-based pirates have conducted several kidnap-for-ransom operations across the Gulf of Guinea.[67] Kamal-Deen notes that since 2009, the activities of Nigeria-based militants "expanded beyond the southern and western coasts of Nigeria, [with] westerly swarms targeting vessels off the coast of Benin, and those to the south attacking ships off Cameroon and the neighbouring coast".[68]

The success of maritime attacks, including kidnappings, in the Gulf of Guinea suggests that perpetrators have sufficient capability to make the endeavour worthwhile: the rewards are worth the risks, and the targets present sufficient opportunities. The pirates are well prepared;[69] they usually arrive in high-powered speedboats[70] that allow them to both approach target vessels and escape from naval responders. The pirates are also well-armed and use a range of weapons, from knives and firearms (including assault rifles) to rocket-propelled grenades (RPGs). Kidnapped crew members are taken ashore and held in generally poor conditions until ransom negotiations are concluded.

The duration of captivity can vary. While the same logic will apply as in land-based kidnappings, there are indications that, in maritime kidnappings in the Gulf of Guinea, the trend for a shorter duration of captivity may not apply in the same way, and may in fact be getting longer.[71] One explanation for this may be the limited pressure that kidnappers, especially in the Niger Delta, feel in terms of discovery or capture – the extant geography affords them a degree of cover that is not necessarily available to most kidnapping groups. This ties in with Lawson's observation that "longer case durations tend to occur in jurisdictions where a lack of governance, reach, capability or competence allow kidnappers to extend the length of an incident with relative impunity and hold out for bigger concessions (whether financial or non-financial)".[72] However, there is a limit to this. The generally poor conditions of detention can have a deleterious effect on the health of victims, particularly in the tropical regions. As one report notes: "Ironically, the unhygienic conditions may act as a brake on the duration of kidnaps. The kidnappers are very aware of the impact of these conditions on their hostages and they likely understand that it is not in their interests to have seriously ill hostages on their hands – it does not suit their business model."[73]

And that is the crux of it: as long as the targeting of vessels and crew in the Gulf of Guinea fits into the business models of the perpetrators, and remains lucrative, it will continue. The long-term solutions to achieving a significant reduction in maritime attacks need to extend beyond increased naval patrols or offshore security services. While countries around the Gulf of Guinea would surely benefit from improved cooperation and coordination efforts for their maritime security, this will not have the desired effect without a concomitant focus on resolving the criminal and militant networks onshore. Whether the perpetrators' motives are criminal, political or a hybrid of the two, West African kidnapping will be informed by a universal calculus: is the risk-reward ratio in my favour? On the one hand, there are the risks of detection, countermeasures and prosecution, which must be weighed up against the rewards of lucrative ransom payments on the other. Based on the evidence, in West African nations the latter currently tend to outweigh the former.

Conclusion

In the preceding text, I have attempted to shed some light on the nature of kidnapping, both in general terms and specifically in the West African context. To this end, while the findings and conclusions presented here are premised on the evidence, the kidnapping business by its very nature tends to obscure much of the detail. Data-collection methods vary, as does the reliability of the data itself – and that is only when the data is available. Many of the details of past kidnapping incidents are unknown, and this will continue to be the case. Kidnappers, kidnap victims, victims' families and employers, kidnap responders, governments and law-enforcement agencies all have valid reasons to keep some (though not always the same) parts of the operational details of kidnapping incidents confidential. Despite these limitations, we can still identify some core truths that help us to better understand and respond to kidnapping incidents when they happen.

At its core, kidnapping is nothing more than a business transaction, albeit a distasteful one. Both parties aim to get the maximum reward and limit their costs. The concept of 'reward' can vary. For economically motivated kidnappers, the aim is to get the highest possible monetary value from each victim. Approaches to attaining this goal can vary. Some actors will commit a larger number of kidnappings but be willing to release captives for lower fees. For others, higher payouts for fewer victims will be the more lucrative method.

For politically motivated kidnappers, the prize is not monetary, but the logic remains the same: what concessions can I realistically achieve in return for my victim? Groups seeking political concessions in return for releasing their victims will find their negotiating counterparts severely narrowed. Only states can directly grant political concessions (although companies may attempt to influence state decisions), and states' approaches to these situations vary. Some states willingly engage with kidnapping groups, while others, at least in theory, will resist making any concessions under duress. While we can debate the ethics of negotiating with kidnappers (whether criminal or militant), we must acknowledge that negotiation is successful in the vast majority of known cases, with victims eventually released alive.

West Africa presents an interesting case study, or set of case studies, on kidnapping. Kidnapping, both on land and offshore, is increasingly prevalent in this part of the world. The complexity and diversity of the region does not lend itself to simplistic explanations for why kidnapping might be on the rise. However, when looked at from the perspective of kidnapping being a rational action pursued by rational actors, we can begin to search for reasonable and practical solutions to the problem. Militants in Burkina Faso, criminal gangs in Nigeria, and pirates off the coast of Benin can all be understood through the framework of rational actors. We can account for the prevalence (or not) of kidnapping in a particular jurisdiction by establishing the presence of groups willing to engage in kidnapping, weighing up the respective risks and rewards in the environment, and assessing the opportunities available for carrying out kidnappings. Furthermore, we can use this approach, at least at the strategic level, to identify the interventions most likely to mitigate against the risk in the short term, and those most likely to address the root causes of kidnapping in the long term.

For policymakers, law-enforcement officials and commercial operators, the prevalence of kidnapping in West Africa is of notable concern. With existing data suggesting the problem is getting worse, both the economic and human costs associated with operating in the region are likely to rise. Consequently, the better we understand the drivers behind kidnapping, the groups involved in the activity, and the methods they employ, the better we are placed to address and respond to the threat kidnapping poses in the region.

Select Bibliography

Africa Renewal. (2016). Briefing: The new Jihadist strategy in the Sahel. 4 February. Available from: https://www.un.org/africarenewal/sahel/news/briefing-new-jihadist-strategy-sahel [accessed 1 April 2020].

Al Jazeera. (2019). Nigerian police battle a growing kidnapping crisis. 24 August. Available from: https://www.aljazeera.com/news/2019/08/nigerian-police-battle-a-growing-kidnapping-crisis-190824124410317.html [accessed 1 April 2020].

Amnesty International. (2017). Iraq: End irresponsible arms transfers fuelling militia war crimes. 5 January. Available from: https://www.amnesty.org/en/latest/news/2017/01/iraq-end-irresponsible-arms-transfers-fuelling-militia-war-crimes/ [accessed 1 April 2020].

Asociación Alto al Secuestro. (n.d.). Estadísticas 2020. Available from: http://www.altoalsecuestro.com.mx/estadistica [accessed 1 April 2020].

Australian National Security. (2018). Abu Sayyaf Group (ASG). Commonwealth of Australia. Available from: https://www.nationalsecurity.gov.au/Listedterroristorganisations/Pages/AbuSayyafGroup.aspx [accessed 1 April 2020].

Boe, S. (2019). 2018 kidnapping trends in review. 21 March. London: Control Risks. Available from: https://www.controlrisks.com/our-thinking/insights/2018-kidnapping-trends [accessed 1 April 2020].

Briggs, R. (2001). *The Kidnapping Business*. London: Foreign Policy Centre.

Causa en Común. (2018). Qué piensa la policía? Available from: http://causaencomun.org.mx/beta/wp-content/uploads/2018/12/Presentaci%C3%B3n-Encuesta-2018.pdf [accessed 1 April 2020].

Chulov, M. (2014). Controlled by Iran, the deadly militia recruiting Iraq's men to die in Syria. *The Guardian*, 12 March. Available from: https://www.theguardian.com/world/2014/mar/12/iraq-battle-dead-valley-peace-syria [accessed 1 April 2020].

Constellis. (2020). Kidnap + Ransom Insight: Global Summary. January 2020 report. Virginia, United States: Constellis. Available from: https://constellis-production-tmp.s3.amazonaws.com/uploads/document/file/132/CONSTELLIS_-_Global_Kidnap_for_Ransom_Report_-_JANUARY_2020.pdf [accessed 1 April 2020].

Control Risks. (2020). The Special Risks Report. January. Available from: https://www.controlrisks.com/ [accessed 1 April 2020].

Counter Extremism Project. (2020). Abu Sayyaf Group (ASG). Available from: https://www.counterextremism.com/threat/abu-sayyaf-group-asg [accessed 1 April 2020].

El Universal. (2019). At least two hundred people are kidnapped in Mexico every day. 19 May. Available from: https://www.eluniversal.com.mx/english/least-two-hundred-people-are-kidnapped-mexico-every-day [accessed 1 April 2020].

Engler, S. (2014). The U.S. Does Negotiate With Terrorists. *Foreign Policy*, 3 June. Available from: https://foreignpolicy.com/2014/06/03/the-u-s-does-negotiate-with-terrorists/ [accessed 1 April 2020].

Ferdman, R.A. (2013). 99% of kidnappings in Mexico went unreported last year. *Quartz*, 3 October. Available from: https://qz.com/131408/99-of-the-more-than-100000-kid-

nappings-in-mexico-last-year-went-unreported/ [accessed 1 April 2020].
Graham-Harrison, E. (2016). Three Americans kidnapped in Baghdad freed and transferred to US embassy. *The Guardian*, 16 February. Available from: https://www.theguardian.com/world/2016/feb/16/three-americans-kidnapped-in-baghdad-freed-and-transferred-to-us-embassy [accessed 1 April 2020].
Ibukun, Y. (2019). Pirates Thriving Off West Africa Show Disunity, Togo Leader Says. *Bloomberg*, 17 November. Available from: https://www.bloomberg.com/news/articles/2019-11-17/pirates-thriving-off-west-africa-show-disunity-togo-leader-says [accessed 1 April 2020].
International Institute for Applied Systems Analysis (IIASA). (2009). Negotiating with Terrorists: A Mediator's Guide. IIASA Policy Brief, 6 March. Available from: https://iiasa.ac.at/web/home/resources/publications/IIASAPolicyBriefs/pb06-web.pdf [accessed 1 April 2020].
International Maritime Bureau. (2020). Piracy and Armed Robbery Against Ships: Report for the Period 1 January – 31 December 2019. January. London: International Maritime Bureau. Available from: https://www.icc-ccs.org/reports/2019_Annual_Piracy_Report.pdf [accessed 1 April 2020].
Islam, S. (2020). Held to ransom: Kidnapping and extortion in the extractive sector. S-RM. Available from: https://insights.s-rminform.com/kidnapping-and-extortion-in-the-extractive-sector [accessed 1 April 2020].
Jenkins, B.M. (2017). *Does the U.S. No-Concessions Policy Deter Kidnappings of Americans?* California, United States: RAND Corporation.
JLT. (2019). Burkina Faso's recent kidnappings of foreign nationals. 1 February. Available from: https://www.jlt.com/en-hk/insurance-risk/credit-political-security-risk/insights/burkina-fasos-recent-kidnappings-of-foreign-nationals [accessed 1 April 2020].
Kaledzi, I. (2019). Ghanaians worried by rising number of kidnappings. *Deutsche Welle*, 12 June. Available from: https://www.dw.com/en/ghanaians-worried-by-rising-number-of-kidnappings/a-49155602 [accessed 1 April 2020].
Kamal-Deen, A. (2015). The Anatomy of Gulf of Guinea Piracy. *Naval War College Review*, 68(1), Winter, pp. 93-118.
Lawson, D. (2020). Two very different transactions: Physical versus cyber extortion. Cyber Incident Response: Perspectives from Inside the Risk Ecosystem. 11 March. Available from: https://insights.s-rminform.com/physical-versus-cyber-extortion?utm_campaign=Vectors_of_Response&utm_source=website&utm_medium=unbounce&utm_content=Extortion [accessed 1 April 2020].
Louw-Vaudran, L. (2014). Kidnap for ransom: to pay or not to pay? *Daily Dispatch*, 20 February. Available from: https://issafrica.s3.amazonaws.com/site/uploads/2014-02-18-Daily-Dispatch.pdf [accessed 1 April 2020].
Osumah, O. & Aghedo, I. (2011). Who wants to be a millionaire? Nigerian youths and the commodification of kidnapping. *Review of African Political Economy*, 38(128), June, pp. 277-287.
Pigeon, M., Sadic, E., Duncan, S., Ridgway, C. & Soeth, K. (2018). The State of Maritime

Piracy 2017: Assessing the Economic and Human Cost. Broomfield, United States: One Earth Future. Available from: http://oceansbeyondpiracy.org/sites/default/files/one_earth_future_state_of_piracy_report_2017.pdf [accessed 1 April 2020].

Reid, G. (2019). Burkina Faso: A New Kidnapping Frontier. 13 June. Available from: https://gsi.s-rminform.com/articles/burkina-faso-a-new-kidnapping-frontier [accessed 1 April 2020].

Reuters. (2019). Islamic State, without evidence, claims killing of Canadian in Burkina Faso. 3 April. Available from: https://www.reuters.com/article/us-buburkina-kidnapping-is-claim/islamic-state-without-evidence-claims-killing-of-canadian-in-burkina-faso-idUSKCN1RF0B2 [accessed 1 April 2020].

Reva, D. (2018). Ten years on, is Somali piracy still a threat? 7 November. Pretoria: Institute for Security Studies. Available from: https://issafrica.org/iss-today/ten-years-on-is-somali-piracy-still-a-threat [accessed 1 April 2020].

Risk Intelligence. (2019). Long-term perspective on West Africa and Gulf of Guinea piracy. 12 November. Available from: https://riskintelligence.eu/articles/long-term-perspective-west-africa-and-gulf-guinea-piracy [accessed 1 April 2020].

Shortland, A. (2017). Governing kidnap for ransom: Lloyd's as a "private regime". *Governance*, 30(2), pp. 283-299.

Shortland, A. (2019). Inside the ransom business – why kidnapping rarely pays. *The Conversation*, 8 February. Available from: http://theconversation.com/inside-the-ransom-business-why-kidnapping-rarely-pays-110678 [accessed 1 April 2020].

Siebels, D. (2019). Fighting piracy in the Gulf of Guinea needs a radical rethink. *The Conversation*, 18 November. Available from: https://theconversation.com/fighting-piracy-in-the-gulf-of-guinea-needs-a-radical-rethink-127032 [accessed 1 April 2020].

Simon, J. (2019). The business of kidnapping: inside the secret world of hostage negotiation. *The Guardian*, 25 January. Available from: https://www.theguardian.com/news/2019/jan/25/business-of-kidnapping-inside-the-secret-world-of-hostage-negotiation-ransom-insurance [accessed 1 April 2020].

Singh, B. (2018). Crime-Terror Nexus in Southeast Asia: Case Study of the Abu Sayyaf Group. *Counter Terrorist Trends and Analyses*, 10(9), pp. 6-10.

Soliev, N. & Siyech, M.S. (2016). Terrorist Attacks: The Politics of Claiming Responsibility. *Counter Terrorist Trends and Analyses*, 8(8), pp. 17-21.

Spross, J. (2019). The weird world of kidnapping insurance. *The Week*, 7 June. Available from: https://theweek.com/articles/840360/weird-world-kidnapping-insurance [accessed 1 April 2020].

S-RM. (2019). Bad Cops: Global case studies of police involvement in kidnap for ransom and extortion. 22 July. Available from: https://insights.s-rminform.com/global-kidnap-bulletin-july-2019 [accessed 1 April 2020].

S-RM. (2020). Expert Insights: Kidnap and Extortion. 15 January. Available from: https://insights.s-rminform.com/kidnap-and-extortion-expert-insights [accessed 1 April 2020].

Sulemana, M. (2015). Islamism in West Africa: Context and Enabling Factors. *Counter Terrorist Trends and Analyses*, 7(2), pp. 19-23.

UK P&I Club, UK War Risks, Hellenic War Risks Club & Terra Firma Risk Management. (2016). Risk focus: Kidnap and ransom: Anatomy of West African maritime kidnappings – a guide for seafarers. Available from: https://www.hellenicwarrisks.com/fileadmin/uploads/hellenic/Docs/PDFs/Risk_Focus_2016_-_K_R.pdf [accessed 1 April 2020].

United Nations Office on Drugs and Crime (UNODC). (2006). UNODC launches manual of best practices to counter kidnapping. 26 April. Available from: https://www.unodc.org/unodc/en/press/releases/press_release_2006_04_26.html [accessed 1 April 2020].

United States Department of State. (2001). International Terrorism: American Hostages. 31 July. Available from: https://2001-2009.state.gov/s/ct/rls/fs/2001/4337.htm [accessed 1 April 2020].

United States Department of State. (2020). State Department Terrorist Designations of Asa'ib Ahl al-Haq and its leaders, Qays and Laith al-Khazali. 3 January. Available from: https://translations.state.gov/2020/01/03/state-department-terrorist-designations-of-asaib-ahl-al-haq-and-its-leaders-qays-and-laith-al-khazali/ [accessed 1 April 2020].

Weiss, M. (2014). Trust Iran Only as Far as You Can Throw It. *Foreign Policy*, 23 June. Available from: http://foreignpolicy.com/2014/06/23/trust-iran-only-as-far-as-you-can-throw-it/ [accessed 1 April 2020].

World Bank. (2019). The World Bank In Togo. 18 October. Available from: https://www.worldbank.org/en/country/togo/overview [accessed 1 April 2020].

Endnotes

1. For the purpose of this chapter, West Africa comprises Benin, Burkina Faso, Cape Verde, Côte d'Ivoire, Gambia, Ghana, Guinea, Guinea-Bissau, Liberia, Mali, Mauritania, Niger, Nigeria, Senegal, Sierra Leone and Togo.
2. Lawson, 2020.
3. Shortland, 2017.
4. See, for example, Simon (2019).
5. Graham-Harrison, 2016.
6. Chulov, 2014.
7. Amnesty International, 2017.
8. Weiss, 2014.
9. S-RM internal database. Country-specific kidnapping data can be accessed on the Global Security Insight platform at https://gsi.s-rminform.com.
10. Asociación Alto al Secuestro, n.d.
11. S-RM internal database.
12. Singh, 2018.
13. Counter Extremism Project, 2020; Australian National Security, 2018.
14. Singh, 2018.
15. Counter Extremism Project, 2020.
16. S-RM, 2020.
17. Shortland, 2019.
18. Shortland, 2019; Simon, 2019.
19. This is not to say that the experience of being kidnapped is straightforward. It can be incredibly stressful for both the victim and his or her family. It may involve mental and physical abuse, and can have significant psychological impacts even after the incident has been resolved. Detailed accounts of kidnappings do not make for pleasant reading.
20. United States Department of State, 2020.
21. The United States Department of State (2001) notes on its website: "The US government will make no concessions to terrorists holding official or private US citizens hostage. It will not pay ransom, release prisoners, change its policies, or agree to other acts that might encourage additional terrorism." For more on the contradictions within this policy, see Engler (2014).
22. IIASA, 2009.
23. Simon, 2019.
24. Briggs, 2001.
25. Jenkins (2017) notes that the evidence does not support the claim that the US's non-concession policy deters kidnappers, who may not be "…aware of US policy, do not believe it, or may not care".
26. Briggs, 2001; UNODC, 2006.
27. S-RM internal database.
28. Constellis, 2020.
29. According to the case breakdown provided by Control Risks (2020), "special risks" refer to incidents of kidnap, threat, extortion, international problems, cyber extortion and detention.
30. Spross, 2019.
31. See, for example, El Universal (2019) and Ferdman (2013).
32. S-RM, 2019.
33. Causa en Común, 2018.
34. International Maritime Bureau, 2020.
35. S-RM internal database.
36. Kaledzi, 2019.
37. Al Jazeera, 2019.
38. See, for example, Reid (2019) and JLT (2019).
39. Briggs, 2001.
40. Ibid.
41. Constellis, 2020.
42. Osumah & Aghedo, 2011.
43. Ibid.
44. Boe, 2019
45. S-RM, 2020.
46. S-RM internal database.
47. See, for example, Reuters (2019).
48. Soliev & Siyech, 2016.
49. For instance, following the killing of IS leader Abu Bakr al-Baghdadi in a raid in Syria in October 2019 by the US, Islamic State West Africa Province (ISWAP) militants in Nigeria reportedly killed 11 Christian hostages previously abducted from Maiduguri, Borno State and Damaturu, Yobe State. The group released a video claiming to show the executions. The killings were reportedly an act of vengeance for al-Baghdadi. (S-RM internal database)
50. S-RM internal database.
51. See, for example Sulemana (2015) and Africa Renewal (2016).
52. Louw-Vaudran, 2014.
53. Gabrielle Reid, quoted in Islam (2020).
54. International Maritime Bureau, 2020.
55. Reva, 2018.

56 International Maritime Bureau, 2020.
57 Kamal-Deen, 2015.
58 Pigeon et al, 2018.
59 Siebels, 2019.
60 Kamal-Deen, 2015.
61 UK P&I Club, 2016.
62 International Maritime Bureau, 2020.
63 Kamal-Deen, 2015.
64 International Maritime Bureau, 2020.
65 Ibukun, 2019.
66 World Bank (2019) figures for 2015 suggest that Togo has a national poverty rate of 55,1%.
67 S-RM internal database.
68 Kamal-Deen, 2015.
69 A good description of pirates' capabilities is presented in Kamal-Deen (2015).
70 Reports suggest that some pirate vessels are equipped with 200-horsepower engines and have an extensive range of up to 170 nautical miles from the coast. See, for example, UK P&I Club (2016) and International Maritime Bureau (2020).
71 Risk Intelligence, 2019.
72 David Lawson, as quoted in S-RM (2020).
73 UK P&I Club, 2016.

CHAPTER 8

The Impact of Terrorism on Business Travellers

Anneline Booyse-Mofokeng

Introduction

The impact of terrorism on the business traveller is vast and far reaching, not just from a financial point of view, given the loss of business deals and operations, but also dealing with mental health afterwards, such as fear, anxiety and depression. On the financial front, there are also the consequences of changes to flights and loss of productivity. Ultimately, the cost associated with safe and secure travel and implementing travel-risk management policies is significant.

The aim of the case studies and terrorism incidents discussed in this chapter is to demonstrate how violent extremism impacts on business travellers worldwide, and to highlight some of the different strategies and targets that extremists have used over the past two decades. This chapter aims to demonstrate that it is not only counterterrorism that will assist in minimising the impact of violent extremism, but also a wide range of additional approaches, starting from staff training to socio-political changes that need to be implemented to support safe international travel. To this end, this chapter also looks at the 'duty of care' principle, which opens up the discussion that terrorism is but one of the elements that can have an impact on a business traveller.

Impact of Terrorism on Business Travellers

Terrorism has a direct impact on a country's ability to attract and maintain business development and investment.[1] While countries such as the United States (US) spend millions of dollars on enhancing domestic protection, the country has done little to protect its citizens when they travel abroad, with scant consideration given to how international threats can affect the global economy. Research into the effects of transnational terrorist attacks on international commerce found that these events did reduce bilateral trade flows. However, the indicators for terrorism were measured at a country level, not internationally. This has limitations because there has been a shift in extremists' *modus operandi*, from travelling from one country to another to execute an attack, to local assailants committing attacks against international targets in their own country.[2]

As governments tighten security at public sites, business locations have become more attractive terrorist targets, with important implications for the operations and performance of multinational companies. Also, while violent extremism has been substantially studied, there has been little research into the distinctive challenges it poses for international business.[3]

Terrorism has transitioned significantly from its traditional methods and motives in its convictions, intentions, strategies and the territorial aspirations of its actors. There has been a shift from acts such as kidnapping, suicide bombings (human and vehicle-borne), hostage taking, improvised explosive devices (IEDs) and armed assaults, to unbalanced warfare, cyber warfare, cultural rivalry, aircraft-borne suicide bombings, lone-actor terror attacks. and genocidal and fratricidal attacks.[4]

These new forms of terrorism have substantially altered the way the security industry responds to terror attacks simply because they impact the political and territorial landscape of states and international political systems. Gunaratna[5] highlights the fact that the global terrorism threat has become more decentralised, unpredictable, difficult to detect, and resilient with regenerative capacities. Both Islamic State (IS) and Al-Qaeda have become more subversive in their networks, which allows them to sustain themselves for longer and carry out more violent attacks.

After the 11 September 2001 attacks (9/11 attacks) in the US and the Madrid bombings in 2004, it was evident that the stock exchanges in both North America and Europe were affected (the Dow declined by 14,4% and the European Dow Jones Stoxx 600 declined by 2,67%). In these circumstances, investors almost certainly flee the market in search of safer financial mechanisms, and this is often accompanied by panic selling.[6]

Although no sector has been immune to violent extremism, terrorist threats can generally be classified into two groups. The first is based on the type of target that is involved, such as military installations, churches or government buildings. The second group is described by the *modus operandi* of the attacks, such as kidnappings, simultaneous attacks or suicide bombings.

Glaeser and Shapiro[7] point out that, historically, large-scale violence has impacted on cities in three ways. First, concentrations of people have an advantage in defending themselves from attackers, making cities more appealing in times of violence. Second, cities often make attractive targets for violence, which creates an incentive for people to disperse. Third, since warfare and terrorism are often specifically targeted at modes of transport, violence can increase the effective cost of transportation, which will usually increase the demand for density. Evidence from wars and cities in the 20th century suggests that the effect of wars on urban form can be great but, more commonly, neither terrorism nor wars have significantly altered urban form.

The first point made by Glaeser and Shapiro[8] has certainly evolved. Violent extremists now specifically target large gatherings in cities, such as markets, entertainment shows and events, where they know there will be a large number of people, offering the potential of a greater impact. Cities, therefore, remain appealing locations for terrorist attacks. The second point bases its assumption on the panic and chaos associated with, and created by, an act of terror, which leads companies to either take robust steps to ensure secure travel to these locations, or potentially restrict travel to these locations. This has had a significant impact on business, including broad risk management and travel security with regard to, for example, lodging and ground transportation. Therefore, the points made by Glaeser and Shapiro[9] remain relevant, but the dynamics of the impact of these events have been significantly transformed since the terrorist attacks in the 20th century referred to above.

Even though governments issue regular travel advisories and warnings, some travellers do not pay much heed to these until it is too late. Kidnapping remains a reality when travelling to some countries, such as certain parts of Nigeria. In conservative countries such as Saudi Arabia, India and the Philippines, where it is frowned upon for a woman to be seen in a bar with male counterparts, women are also often not allowed to move around unaccompanied. There are also some places in Asia where white women are perceived to be 'available' due to differences in dress code and appearance. In cases such as these, female travellers have a different risk profile when travelling compared to their male counterparts, and the organisational support policy needs to take this into consideration when support plans are designed. Considerations such as these have a direct impact on job performance and satisfaction. It is also evident that larger corporates provide greater levels of support than smaller ones.[10]

Just as companies apply different models to justify the class of travel, the grade of accommodation and a variety of policy directives to manage international travel, so should the same principles be applied to countries of travel based on their security-risk rating.

Cost Associated with Travelling to a Country with a Medium to High Terrorism Risk

Listed below is a summary of significant terror incidents that have influenced business travellers. These events did not only force companies to review their travel policies, but also, to a certain extent, compelled them to understand the 'duty of care' principle and just how widely this responsibility needs to be implemented.

Albers-Miller, Straughan and Prenshaw[11] indicate that the impact of terrorism and how it affects the business traveller may, in some instances, be the difference between who survives and who does not. An analysis of business travel indicates that the sector represents as much as 50% of travel-industry revenue. Although there is a clear difference between business and leisure travellers, the concept of bleisure[12] travellers creates a new challenge for international travel. It is estimated that approximately 14% of all travel expenditure comes from international travel.[13]

Figure 1 indicates that the number of terrorism-related incidents worldwide saw a rapid increase after 2011. However, it should be noted that the Middle East and North Africa account for the majority of these incidents. The number of fatalities has, likewise, been on the rise since 2011.[14] The purpose of Figure 1 is to illustrate that the number of fatalities per incident prior to 2011 was significantly lower than after 2011, which signifies that terrorist attacks have a broader impact.

Overleaf are some of the incidents that are reflected in Figure 1.

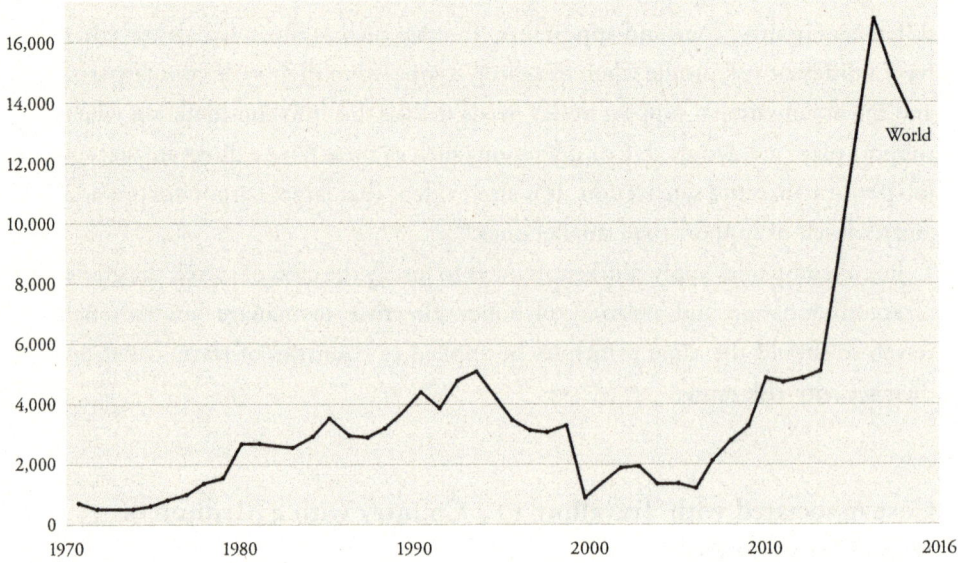

Figure 1: Number of terrorism-related incidents worldwide[15]

- In 1996, a suicide bomber rammed into the front of the Sri Lanka Central Bank in Colombo, killing 88 people and injuring 1,400.
- In 2000, a vehicle in a parking lot at the Jakarta Stock Exchange exploded, killing 15 and injuring many others.
- 11 September 2001 will remain one of the most significant events in the history of terrorism when the attack on the World Trade Center in New York City killed about 3,000 people and injured thousands more. The cost of collateral damage remains in the billions of dollars.
- In Bangladesh, four cinemas were bombed in 2002, killing 17 people and wounding about 300.
- In the same year, explosions rocked Bali and Indonesia, causing 202 deaths and hundreds of injuries.
- Approximately 120 theatregoers died during a rescue attempt when terrorists occupied a theatre in Moscow, Russia in 2002.
- In March 2004, almost simultaneous bombs on four trains in Madrid killed 193 people and injured around 2,000.

The Impact of Terrorism on Business Travellers

- In Kenya, 71 people were killed and more than 200 injured during the terror attack of 21 September 2013.
- The Radisson Blu attack in Mali on 20 November 2015 left 20 dead and 170 people taken hostage.
- In April 2019, three churches and three luxury hotels were bombed in Sri Lanka, killing 290 people and injuring several hundred others.

This list is not exhaustive, but includes some of the most significant global terror attacks in recent history. However, contrary to assumptions that the 9/11 attacks might have negatively impacted on business travel, research indicates that the volume of staff travelling for work was largely unaffected, despite the advances made in electronic communication, such as email and video-conferencing. A 2002 American Express study indicated that business people maintained or increased their business travel the year after the 9/11 attacks because they believe that some business transactions cannot be done electronically and are preferably handled in person.[16]

As companies become more geographically dispersed and their activities more global, the need for international movement increases. Group and regional meetings, staff briefing sessions, joint training sessions, product development meetings and cross-border projects are just some of the activities associated with a company with an international footprint. All these activities are internal. External activities include negotiating sales deals and contracts; selling products, services and solutions; attending conferences and fairs; engaging with alliance partners; subcontracting; and foreign supplies and logistics. Welch and Worm[17] argue that the nature of modern globalised firms, which are geographically dispersed, and have global production divisions and complex supplier networks, requires physical travel if an employee seeks to be an effective executive, manager or sales person. Taking into consideration the growing number of employees travelling around and across the world, organisations should be able to account for the risks involved when their staff travel to potentially hazardous environments, and be in a position to assist and support them in the event of a medical or security emergency.

Countering Terrorism: Risk Management Methodologies that will Answer to the 'Duty of Care' Principle

Research indicates that there is a significant difference between business and leisure requirements when it comes to motivation for international travel. Leisure travellers are more concerned about the experience and consumption, whereas business travellers make their decisions based on convenience and comfort.

Amenities such as modern business equipment, high-tech features and entertainment spaces are some of the overarching factors in deciding where business events take place. Research has also revealed the growing phenomenon of combining business with a few days of leisure. Safety, cleanliness and a healthy environment also appear to be factors for both business and leisure travellers, although of less importance when bookings are made.

There is also a financial incentive for organisations to minimise risks for travelling staff. While it is difficult to calculate the total costs associated with workplace injuries and illness, it is safe to say that accidents represent a drain on an organisation's resources. According to Boyle[18] there have been cases where companies have had to close down due to the death or injury of key personnel, or when key assets were damaged. It makes good business sense, therefore, for organisations to mitigate the risks associated with business travel.

According to International SOS, travellers are exposed to a number of threats and risks. Listed below are some examples.[19]

- Lost during a terrorist attack: An engineer from the United Kingdom was due to stay at a Mumbai hotel that was attacked by terrorists. A flight delay caused him to miss his connecting flight and he arrived in India a day late. Unable to track his travel itinerary, his company was unable to ascertain his whereabouts for more than 24 hours.
- Airplane hijacking: One passenger was killed and several were injured when terrorists hijacked an Air India plane en route to Delhi from Kathmandu. On board were several volunteers of a large non-governmental organisation who were working in the area. The passengers were released six days later.
- Mortal remains: A South African construction worker hired by a British firm was one of the casualties in an ambush outside of Fallujah, Iraq. His remains had to be repatriated to Johannesburg.

The list below provides a more extensive overview of situations in which international travellers can find themselves. This list is based on the case-management system and client engagement statistics used by International SOS, and specifically focuses on international assignees and business travellers.[20]

- Terrorism, kidnapping, hijacking and piracy.
- Lawlessness, violent crime, threats, opportunistic crime, organised crime and imprisonment.
- War, insurgency, political upheaval, coups and civil unrest.
- Natural disasters such as hurricanes, floods, tornados, storms, mudslides, earthquakes, tsunamis, snowstorms, extreme weather conditions and drought.
- Infectious diseases and pandemics such as influenza, severe acute respiratory syndrome (SARS), avian flu and H1N1 (commonly known as swine flu).
- Travel-related infections such as malaria, respiratory infections, hepatitis, typhoid fever, dengue fever and other medical emergencies.
- Lack of air quality, rural isolation, and language and cultural estrangement.
- Vehicle accidents and airline catastrophes.
- Hotel fires.
- Common travel problems such as lost luggage; invalid, expired or forgotten passports; pickpockets; and scheduling delays.
- Lack of legal or administrative compliance (such as immigration and visa challenges).

Countering terrorism has become a costly exercise. Since the 9/11 attacks, one can only imagine how airport security has been impacted. Even though corporate security enjoys a large portion of company resources, in some instances the security allocation is influenced by time, manpower, company size, industry, geographical location, international activities, symbolical value, and the probability and ease of being a target.[21]

Industry security can only be as strong as the support offered by government or the mandates that exist within the security industry itself to protect a particular sector, and these mandates may differ from country to country. Compliance to industry security guidelines remains a challenge as very few companies implement sanctions. Further complicating the matter is employees who do not obey company-posted security measures and, therefore, expose company defence mechanisms to further weaknesses.

As previously mentioned, the global terrorism threat has become more regionalised, volatile, difficult to detect, and resilient with regenerative capacities, according to Gunaratna.[22] We see this phenomenon especially in countries such as Somalia, Kenya and Mozambique, where localised grievances provide a breeding ground for jihadists to recruit. We also see that the prediction that was made by the Global Threat Forecast (GTF) in 2018 that IS would transform from a "caliphate-building" entity into a global terrorist movement has manifested itself in Mozambique, and in attacks on places of worship in Sri Lanka, for example. The GTF has also forecast that IS will expand its presence in Africa, which is evident in the current security situation in the Maghreb and Sahel, West Africa and East Africa.

Joni[23] raises the concern that while much research has been conducted on the safety of tourism and other global risks, not much has been done with regard to risk management for international business travellers. What research has revealed is that travel-approval processes to high-risk countries, inaccurate or misleading traveller information, incomplete information, and changes in itinerary were just some of the challenges that make it difficult to trace, track and locate a traveller during a crisis. These elements can easily be resolved by collaborating with travel agencies and hotels to ensure the validity of data and information. Additionally, larger organisations have their own particular ways of managing the risks associated with both domestic and international business travel, although there is little available academic research on the subject.

Countering Terrorism
According to Rineheart,[24] counterterrorism is a difficult concept to define, especially for western democracies. Rineheart quotes the US Army Field Manual, which defines counterterrorism as "operations that include the offensive measures taken to prevent, deter, pre-empt and respond to terrorism".[25] It is important to take into consideration that counterterrorism operations are subject to change according to the nature of the threat.

De Graaf[26] underscores that counterterrorism takes into consideration elements such as how the threat is defined, and what measures are implemented to make objectives attractive, which places counterterrorism in the broader socio-political context of political decision-making processes. These are influenced by elements such as existing political practices and institutions, and cultural traditions.

Counterterrorist policies may involve taking direct actions against extremists or their sponsors. These initiatives are regarded as proactive and may include the destruction of terror groups and training camps, gathering intelligence, infiltrating terrorist groups, reacting against state-sponsored terrorism and freezing terrorist assets.[27]

Prevention is the ideal proactive policy in dealing with terrorists and their assets, and in restraining subsequent terrorist operations. Defensive policies include technological barriers, as seen at airports, and securing borders. The aim of these measures is to deter an attack by limiting the likelihood and possibility of a successful attack in a specific location. This often results in displacing the attack to other venues, or in modes of attack that may have a lesser impact or casualties.

It is evident from research reports that terrorism has migrated and transformed itself into many different guises. Unfortunately, counterterrorism techniques have not changed at the same rate. International politics take place in an increasingly fluid environment in which people, goods and services cross borders with little difficulty.

State actors are forced to engage with a range of non-state actors to address transnational threats and vulnerabilities within a framework of international, regional and global governance. Intergovernmental organisations, multinational enterprises, international financial institutions, media networks and the United Nations (UN) are some of the non-state entities that create a "multicentric world" that states need to navigate when making decisions on counterterrorism policies.[28] This is evident in the current insurgency situation in Mozambique. There, a number of actors are involved – the government of Mozambique, the Southern African Development Community (SADC) security cluster, the African Union (AU), and international actors such as the French and Russian governments. The situation is further complicated by the presence of mercenaries and private security companies.

It is also important to understand that counterterrorism has changed over the past four decades because the nature of terrorism has changed. Following July 1968, when three members of the Popular Front for the Liberation of Palestine (PFLP) hijacked a commercial plane from Rome to Tel Aviv, international terrorism has been a serious problem. Events such as this resulted in what is referred to as 'hard' and 'soft' power in counterterrorism. This has involved, on the one hand, a struggle against terrorism in military terms, where armed forces are responsible for developing counterterrorism strategies, and, on the other hand, the criminal justice model, defending the rule of law and democratic values.[29]

Lum and Koper[30] make reference to the fact that the most promising counterterrorism approach may lie outside the criminology purview and expertise, involving instead international diplomacy, economic or political sanctions, technology or military solutions, or the transformation of religious institutions. When terror attacks are rare, and with large intervals in between, crime-prevention techniques may even become irrelevant and endanger counterterrorism initiatives.

However, criminal justice agencies are responsible for engaging the perpetrators and victims of terrorism, and this probably makes the justice sector the most relevant area for prevention strategies to be researched and developed. These crime-prevention researchers study individuals – their social, psychological and economic backgrounds, including their life course – in an attempt to ascertain the possibility of later criminality. The same approach could possibly be used to research why some juveniles are susceptible to militant recruitment or activities and, ultimately, extremist violence. The multidisciplinary tradition of criminology levels up well with the knowledge and skills developed by the study of terrorism, and we see a move towards the overlapping of research fields.

Understanding the Concept of 'Duty of Care'

Business travel is growing in range and frequency, with the need to seek new markets and lower production costs in ever more remote places.[31] International work and travel are an integral part of the daily operations of a multinational corporation. Multinational corporations seeking growth opportunities and lower costs of production have embraced globalisation, and increasing numbers of employees are required to work outside their countries of residence as expatriates or international business travellers. This exposes both employees and employers to greater risk. Away from familiar surroundings, employees may encounter precarious environments, presenting added and unfamiliar threats to their health, safety and security. This heightens the corporate liability of employers, who have a legal, fiduciary and moral duty of care for their employees.[32]

The term 'duty of care' refers to the principle that directors and officers of a corporation, in making all decisions in their capacities as corporate fiduciaries, must act in the same manner as a reasonably prudent person in their position would. Courts will generally adjudge lawsuits against directors' and officers' actions to meet the duty of care under the business judgement rule. The business judgement rule refers to the principle that courts will not second-guess the business judgement of corporate managers, and will find that the duty of care has been met, so long as the fiduciary executed a reasonably informed, good-faith, rational judgement without the presence of a conflict of interest. The burden of proof lies with the plaintiff to prove that this standard has not been met. If the plaintiff meets the burden, the defendant fiduciary can still meet the duty of care by showing fairness, meaning both that a fair process was used to reach the decision, and that the decision produced a substantively fair outcome for the corporation's shareholders.[33]

International SOS defines duty of care as the presumption that individuals and organisations have legal obligations to act towards others and the public in a prudent and cautious manner to avoid the risk of reasonably foreseeable injury to others. This obligation may apply to acts of both commission and omission. Duty-of-care requirements may be imposed by statute (legislation) and common law. They are also the result of cultural and social expectations of acceptable standards of care. In that sense, employers have a moral as well as a legal responsibility and obligation for the health, safety and security of their employees. Breaching duty of care may give rise to an action alleging negligence, and may result in damages or in the criminal prosecution of the employer.[34]

According to International SOS, duty of care should be classified into three broad categories: the legal perspective, the corporate social responsibility view, and a cost-benefit analysis. Common law with regard to negligence requires employers to exercise reasonable care to prevent or mitigate the impact of foreseeable hazards. If they fail to take reasonable steps to prevent these risks, they will be found in breach of duty of care.

Challenges with Regard to Duty of Care

The International Labour Organization (ILO) has not done much to clarify the requirements for duty-of-care principles and implementation, primarily because countries apply different labour laws. Although employers' duty of care for the safety of their employees is explicit in the relevant ILO conventions and protects all workers, these conventions do not specifically elaborate on the safety of workers on assignments abroad, whether as business travellers or international assignees. Uncertainties around duty of care are as follows:[35]

- **Duty of care is not a duty:** A duty is an obligation, and in private law (of which the law of negligence is a part) duties are obligations owed to other people, which correlates with a claimed right which the person has against the duty-holder. This right or action arises only if and when the defendant's unreasonable risk creation results in an interference with a legally protected interest of the claimant, such as a broken limb or a dented rear bumper. Damage is the '"gist" of negligence, "an essential ingredient not merely of recoverability but of the cause of action itself", so that time starts to run for limitation purposes not from the moment of the defendant's 'breach of duty', but from the moment the claimant suffers damage recognised by law, and disputes about the causation of such damage go to liability not quantum.[36]

- **Duty-of-care scepticism is not inconsistent with a rights-based analysis of negligence law:** The failure of many proponents of a rights-based conception of negligence to distinguish between duty of care and global primary obligations, which they believe are imposed by negligence law, is a good example of the confusion sown by the duty-of-care concept, and a reminder of the oddity and incoherence of separating out one element of a cause of action and labelling it 'duty'.

- **The duty-of-care concept has a dual role in negligence law:** The third point is that the duty-of-care device plays a dual role in the modern law of negligence, in that there are two different duty-of-care questions: First, whether damage to someone in the claimant's position was a reasonably foreseeable consequence of the defendant's negligence (the factual duty question), and second, whether there is a rule of law that either allows or bars recovery in this category of case; in other words, the legal or 'notional' duty question.

- **The final point is that the duty-of-care question is not analytically anterior to the question of fault.**

Table 1 illustrates the cost-benefit components of duty of care, and how a lack of these components can have a major financial impact on an organisation or company. Larger corporates may be able to absorb the costs associated with these elements, but smaller organisations and businesses may be unable to do so, and in some cases this may cause the company to close down or redirect its operations. Ensuring that these elements are involved, not just in the human resources (HR) protocols and policies but, ultimately, in the budget, may be critical to ensure the continuation of the business and its operations.

Table 1: Duty-of-care cost-benefit components[37]

Cost component	Benefit component
Costs of a lack of duty of care	Maintenance of employee wellbeing (health, safety and security, and life)
Cost of an incident or injury to the victim(s) (such as loss of life, emotional distress and lost earnings)	Better trained and prepared workforce
Cost of medical expenses, treatment, evacuation and repatriation	Avoidance of expensive incidence costs
Cost of sick pay for employee	Possibility of greater bonuses for managers and employee profit-sharing (if applicable)
Cost of diversion of resources (financial and human)	Insurance-premium discounts if the appropriate risk-management measures are in place
Cost of extensive executive resources to deal with the situation	Greater legal compliance
Property and economic damage	Avoidance of litigation
Cost of business interruptions, downtime and/or closure of a site	Increased ability to attract and retain employees
Cost of employment litigation	Increased ability to attract customers and investors
Cost of damages resulting from liability	Improved corporate social responsibility reputation
Cost of fines and penalties under relevant laws	Improved productivity
Cost of insurance premiums rising as a result of the incident	Increased morale
Cost of morale and productivity loss	Increase reputation and employment brand

Cost of loss of potential employees who cannot be recruited
Cost of replacing employees who leave (recruitment and onboarding)
Potential for bankruptcy
Cost of the loss of goodwill
Prevention costs
Cost of developing a risk management plan
Cost of compliance and training
Cost of insurance coverage
Cost of vendors

Cortina et al[38] highlight that, even though health and safety laws differ from country to country, which underlines the inconsistencies in the application of these principles, the UN's Sustainable Development Goals (SDGs) of 2015, Goal 3[39] and Goal 8[40], help corporates and businesses to achieve an environment in which employee safety and security can be implemented as part of the duty-of-care objective.

International SOS lists the following employer-related, duty-of-care obligations on the part of the employer:[41]
- Physical and mental health.
- Work injuries and accidents.
- Consequences of job workload and stress.
- Repetitive strain injuries.
- Spread of communicable diseases.
- Safety (including tools, equipment and the workplace).
- Security.
- Workplace bullying, harassment and discrimination.
- Corporate fleet management.
- Travel for work purposes.
- Car rentals, employees' use of personal vehicles, travel to and from work, traffic accidents, driver fatigue, etc.
- Accommodations for employees while travelling for work.
- Corporate events away from the workplace (travel, drinking, accidents, etc.).

- Pre-employment selection (fit for work).
- Negligent hiring (sex offenders, violent personalities, etc.).
- Accuracy of job references for former employees.
- Security and confidentiality of employees' personal data.
- Fiduciary duties of board members/directors.
- Selection of insurance providers.
- Management of employees' benefits.
- Due diligence in acquisitions.

Conclusion
As detailed above, the after-effects of terrorist attacks on the business community, and the financial strains that accompany some of the decision-making that is associated with such attacks, are profound. Companies must start thinking about the duty-of-care principle and how this can help them prepare for and minimise the impact of terror attacks on business travellers.

The cost associated with a business traveller going to a high- or medium-risk country is but one element that needs to be taken into consideration when business trips are undertaken. Terrorism will remain on our radar for much time to come, and the dynamics of travel will continue to be influenced by tangible elements such as terrorism, and intangible elements such as pandemics, meaning that companies need to be more flexible and vigilant in how they respond to these phenomena.

Select Bibliography
Alexander, D.C. (2004). *Business Confronts Terrorism: Risks and Responses.* Wisconsin: University of Wisconsin Press.
Arce, D.G. & Sandler, T. (2005). Counterterrorism: A Game-Theoretic Analysis. *The Journal of Conflict Resolution*, 49(2), pp. 183-200.
Boyle, T. (2015). *Health and Safety: Risk Management.* 3rd ed. New York: Routledge.
Cilliers, J. (2003). Terrorism and Africa. *African Security Review*, 12(4), pp. 91-103.
Clarke, R. (2011). *Crime-Terror Nexus in South Asia: States, Security and Non-State Actors.* Oxon: Routledge.
Claus, L. (2009). Duty of Care of Employers for Protecting International Assignees, their Dependents, and International Business Travelers. International SOS White Paper Series. Singapore: International SOS.

Cortina, L.M., Magley, V.J., Williams, J.H. & Langhout, R.D. (2001). Incivility in the workplace: Incidence and impact. *Journal of Occupational Health Psychology*, 6(1).
Crelinsten, R. (2013). *Counterterrorism*. New York: John Wiley & Sons.
Czinkota, M., Knight, G.A., Liesch, P. & Steen, J. (2010). Terrorism and international business: A research agenda. *Journal of International Business Studies*, 41(5), pp. 826-843.
De Graaf, B. (2012). *Evaluating Counterterrorism Performance: A Comparative Study*. Oxon: Routledge.
Falode, A.J. (2018). Terrorism 4.0: A Global and Structural Analysis. *Open Political Science*, 1(1), pp. 153-163.
Ganor, B. (2011). *The Counter-Terrorism Puzzle: A Guide for Decision Makers*. Herzliya, Israel: The Interdisciplinary Center for Herzliya Projects.
Geistfeld, M. (2001). Reconciling Cost-Benefit Analysis with the Principle that Safety Matters More than Money. *New York University Law Review*, 76(1), pp. 114-189.
Glaeser, E.L. & Shapiro, J.M. (2002). Cities and Warfare: The Impact of Terrorism on Urban Form. *Journal of Urban Economics*, 51(2), pp. 205-224.
Goslin, C.E. (2017). *Understanding Personal Security and Risk: A Guide for Business Travellers*. Boca Raton, Florida: Taylor & Francis Group.
Gunaratna, R. (2018). Global Threat Forecast. *RSIS Counter Terrorist Trends and Analysis*, 10(1). Singapore: Nanyang Technological University, S. Rajaratnam School of International Studies (RSIS), pp. 1-6.
Joni, J. (2018). *Contemporary methods in business travel risk management: A comparison of industry best practices*. Finland: Laurea University of Applied Sciences.
Larobina, M.D. & Pate, R.L. (2009). The Impact of Terrorism on Business. *The Journal of Global Business Issues*, 3(1), pp. 147-156.
Legal Information Institute. (n.d.). Duty of Care. New York: Cornell Law School. Available from: https://www.law.cornell.edu/wex/duty_of_care [accessed 31 March 2020].
Lum, C. & Koper, C.S. (2011). Is Crime Prevention Relevant to Counterterrorism? In Forst, B., Greene, J. & Lynch, J. (eds.). *Criminologists on Terrorism and Homeland Security*. Cambridge: Cambridge University Press, pp. 129-150.
Mahmood, S. & Basit, A. (eds.). (2018). *RSIS Counter Terrorist Trends and Analysis*, 10(1). Singapore: Nanyang Technological University, S. Rajaratnam School of International Studies (RSIS).
Mason, K.J. (2005). Observations of fundamental changes in the demand for aviation services. *Journal of Air Transport Management*, 11(1), pp. 19-25.
National Consortium for the Study of Terrorism and Responses to Terrorism (START). (2018). Trends in Global Terrorism: Islamic State's Decline in Iraq and Expanding Global Impact; Fewer Mass Casualty Attacks in Western Europe; Number of Attacks in the United States Highest since 1980s. Maryland, Virginia: University of Maryland.
Nolan, D. (2013). Deconstructing the Duty of Care. *Law Quarterly Review*, 129, pp. 559-588.
Nte, N.D. (2011). *The dynamics of global terrorism, multilateralism and counter terrorism efforts: Prospects, challenges and implications for Nigeria's national security*. Nigeria: Rivers State University of Education.

Papatheodorou, A. (2018). The impact of terrorism on European tourism. *Annals of Tourism Research*, 75, pp. 1-17.
Qayyum, M.T. (2016). *The ISIS Footprint in Pakistan: Myth or Reality*. Islamabad, Pakistan: National Defence University.
Richardson, H.W., Gordon, P. & Moore, J.E. (eds.). (2009). *Global Business and the Terrorist Threat*. Cheltenham: Edward Elgar Publishing.
Richter, L.K. & Waugh, W.L. (1986). Terrorism and tourism as logical companions. *Tourism Management*, 7(4), pp. 230-238.
Rineheart, J. (2010). Counterterrorism and Counterinsurgency. *Perspectives on Terrorism*, 4(5), pp. 31-47.
Steward, T. (2014). The Strategic Importance, Causes and Consequences of Terrorism: How Terrorism Research Can Inform Policy Responses. Presentation. Available from: https://docplayer.net/4570135-The-strategic-importance-causes-and-consequences-of-terrorism.html [accessed 31 March 2020].
Welch, D.E. & Worm, V. (2006). International business travellers: A challenge for IHRM. In Stahl, G.K. & Björkman, I. (eds.). *Handbook of Research in International Human Resource Management*. Cheltenham: Edward Elgar Publishing, pp. 283-301.
Williams, A. (1974). The cost-benefit approach. *British Medical Bulletin*, 30(3), pp. 252-256.
Woodside, A.G. & Martin, D. (eds.). (2008). *Tourism Management: Analysis, Behaviour and Strategy*. Wallingford, United Kingdom and Cambridge, Massachusetts: CABI Pub.

Endnotes

1. Larobina & Pate, 2009.
2. Richardson et al, 2009.
3. Czinkota et al, 2010.
4. Clarke, 2011.
5. Gunaratna, 2018.
6. Larobina & Pate, 2009:147.
7. Glaeser & Shapiro, 2002.
8. Ibid.
9. Ibid.
10. Welch & Worm, 2006.
11. Quoted in Woodside & Martin, 2008.
12. Bleisure travellers are travellers who travel for business and take a few days off on the same trip to engage in some leisure or tourist activities. In some cases, travellers take leave while doing business in a country, and then shift from being a business traveller to a leisure traveller.
13. Teachers Insurance and Annuity Association of America, quoted in Woodside & Martin, 2008:186.
14. National Consortium for the Study of Terrorism and Responses to Terrorism, 2018.
15. Our World in Data, ourworldindata.org.
16. Mason, 2005.
17. Welch and Worm, 2006:284.
18. Boyle, 2015:22.
19. Claus, 2009:5.
20. Ibid.
21. Alexander, 2004:12.
22. Gunaratna, 2018:2.
23. Joni, 2018.
24. Rineheart, 2010.
25. Ibid, 32.
26. De Graaf, 2012.
27. Arce & Sandler, 2005.
28. Crelinsten, 2013.
29. Rineheart, 2010.
30. Lum and Koper, 2011.
31. Claus, 2009.
32. Ibid.
33. Legal Information Institute, n.d.
34. Claus, 2009:8.
35. Nolan, 2013.
36. Ibid, 562.
37. Claus, 2009:27.
38. Cortina et al, 2001:64.
39. Good health and wellbeing.
40. Decent work and economic growth.
41. Claus, 2009:9.

CHAPTER 9

Understanding the Culture of African Partner Forces in the Fight Against Extremism

James Alexander Sedgbeer Smith

Introduction

Understanding the culture of African militaries cannot be underestimated if international partner forces, the United Nations (UN), the North Atlantic Treaty Organization (NATO), the European Union or any other multinational coalition and non-aligned armies are to train, advise, assist, accompany and enable their African partners in the fight against violent extremist organisations.

The aim of this chapter is not to stereotype any country, culture, society or military. Rather, it is to provide an insight into the cultural dynamics that international armies and other organisations should analyse before, during and after their partnership with African armies to ensure success.[1] Without this awareness, and a deeper comprehension of the culture of African partner forces, any international efforts to assist them in stabilising and preventing conflict in their countries will be nugatory, and defeat will be the default outcome.

Historically, partnering forces have failed to prosecute conflicts effectively or successfully when they have been unable to establish or develop cohesive and effective relationships based around intercultural communication, deep cultural understanding, mutual trust and rapport. The United States (US) experience in Vietnam with the Army of the Republic of Vietnam (ARVN)[2] and its lack of understanding of the language, religion, sensitivities, etiquette, politics and broader hidden culture of the population are illustrative of this failure.[3] Alternatively, the British experience in the Sultanate of Oman during the Dhofar Rebellion of 1962 to 1976[4] was successful largely because of the intimate rapport and relationship that developed between the British and its

Omani partner forces and the local population.[5]

Historical examples of partnering in Africa in the decolonisation and post-colonial 'bush war' conflicts abound. Equally successful and disastrous counterinsurgency campaigns and interventions in Anglophone (Kenya and Tanzania), Francophone (Chad, Djibouti and Kolwezi[6])and Lusophone (Angola, Portuguese Guinea-Bissau and Mozambique) Africa, as well as interventions by mercenaries in the Congo in the 1960s and in Angola in the 1970s, were tantamount to failures by colonial and post-colonial armies to understand the African culture where they operated, which often led to military and ethical failures as well as human rights violations. That said, later campaigns by international armies or private military companies, like Executive Outcomes[7] in Angola in 1993-1995 and Sierra Leone in 1995-1997,[8] in conjunction with African partners, exhibited greater success, largely because the mentors had developed a better understanding of their counterparts.[9] The evidence supports the argument that to successfully prosecute a campaign, international armies must develop this deep cultural understanding quickly, and make sure that it is enduring and persistent.

To train the African partner force effectively, the international mentor needs to become acutely aware of the deeper sub-surface cultural nuances and complexities, and avoid accepting everything at face value or allowing their biases, prejudices and stereotypes to control their initial perceptions. These hidden cultural triggers are often intangible and cannot be easily accessed by international officers and soldiers,[10] largely because of an intrinsic polarity between different geographical cultures that developed in post-industrialised, individualist, hierarchically flatter, more liberal societies, and the less industrialised, agrarian or pastoralist, collectivist, hierarchically steep and conservative societies. It is important here to emphasise both Africa's cultural heterogeneity and the varied levels of economic development across the continent's 55 countries. Some African nations or organisations could, for example, fall more into the former category than the latter, and would thus pose less of a challenge in terms of establishing cohesive and effective relationships based around intercultural communication. This chapter, however, will focus primarily on cultures which developed from the latter context.

In cases where there are large cultural differences between cultures, and when people from these cultures are placed under conditions that include an amalgamation of stress and a lack of mutual cultural awareness and understanding, compounded by poor communication and preconceived bias and stereotypes, they will inevitably clash or fail to work effectively together in the contested environment of the battlefield. So, what is the answer to a seemingly impossible task of getting polar-opposite cultures to work together without being tripped up by cultural sensitivities?

The answer is multifaceted and complex but not beyond resolving, or at least mitigating. These differences and frictions can be analysed through a number of dimensions, lenses and theories.

Undoubtedly, without deep, enduring, persistent, high-context, personalised communication and rapport-based relationships, this is difficult to achieve. International post-industrialised individualists, who make up most international armies, almost invariably maintain low-context communication and distant relationships based around short-term, task-oriented, professional behaviours that are not conducive to more traditional, collectivist, pre-industrial agrarian or pastoralist, deeper, more intimate personal relationships that are designed to endure over long periods and are based around mutual trust and friendship.

Consequently, there is a critical requirement to teach international armies and organisations to understand the importance of high-context communicative relationships with their African partners before conducting any tasks or professional business. A failure to do so will lead the African partner force to perceive this as a lack of interest in developing the relationship beyond what the partner wants to achieve.[11]

The answer to these issues often lies in education and training for both the trainer and partner force. Each must understand the other, or it will potentially result in failure. Without this targeted education, both sides of the partnering project will be at an immediate disadvantage. The 'how' this is done requires considerable understanding in the analysis and design of this training. Undoubtedly, for the international trainer, a combination of communications and applied behavioural studies, welded or blended together with basic effective teaching skills, social sciences and psychology, is necessary, as well as more bespoke historical, political, economic and cultural training to create a holistic view of the intricacies of the partner force.[12] Coupled with this should be an understanding of the values, standards and beliefs of the partner force. Concepts and behaviours that international armies take for granted may not be perceived or practised in the same way by the partner culture, exposing both parties to the risk of undermining cohesion and trust.[13]

The Problem of Understanding Power Distances

The first dimension that international armies find difficult to deal with is the difference between flatter, modern international military hierarchies, which have moved away from steeper autocratic military rank-based privilege and hegemonic decision-making systems, to systems where decision-making is devolved and decentralised down to the lowest tactical level to increase tempo. In ever-changing, fast and asymmetric battle spaces, understanding the commander's intent, the mission and main effort, and being trusted and empowered with the freedom of action to carry out that intent without recourse, are critical. It is encouraged in international armies. However, this is not the case in more traditional and steeper African post-colonial military models, where the all-powerful senior officer has centralised all decision-making in one commander, and there is little independent action by subordinates, who accept this without question.

Historically, there is evidence to suggest that armies that constantly have to be told what to do fail to adapt to ever-changing circumstances on battlefields, and armies that cannot make or communicate decisions quickly to react to, or pre-empt, the enemy's decisions and actions are invariably at risk of defeat. This lack of decentralised decision-making and empowerment – accepting the status quo and, invariably, one's place in the system – makes these armies unable to work effectively, especially when trying to counter insurgencies against flatter guerrilla organisations which, unhindered by traditional hierarchies, can make decisions quickly.

Unlike the international mentor, who is close in terms of power to their commanders and empowered to make decisions, their African counterparts – even if they want to and recognise the value of mission command[14] and decentralised, devolved action – cannot change this as it is intrinsically woven into the fabric of their culture and the military.

As their position in their militaries is often reliant on the favour of a benevolent patriarch, any attempt to change this would undermine the authority and position of that benefactor and invariably be seen as a threat to their benefactor's status and position. Until this cultural anchor is changed, African militaries are unlikely to change as well. The consequence of this is that subordinates who would normally be required to make quick tactical decisions cannot do so for fear of undermining their superiors. The fear of failure is used as a means of control and maintaining power. This power gap, and the inability or lack of will to make decisions, is the source of cultural risk between African and international partners. It becomes a point of frustration for international advisors who need partner forces to react quickly when in fact they cannot. Largely, this is because their culture prohibits them from doing so, and if they did it would put them in an untenable position of undermining the authority of the hierarchy. At the tactical and operational levels, this can increase the risk of being outmanoeuvred. Ultimately, unless there is a cultural shift towards independent decision-making and responsibility at all levels within the partner force (something which is contingent on changes in the culture of the society and would, therefore, take time), this problem is unlikely to be resolved quickly.[15]

That said, through concerted education and training, the partner force can be taught to carry out this style of decision-making, which over time may encourage institutional change to occur. International mentors must be educated and trained to think around this problem to give the partner force the best chance of making decisions in their own way and thus adapt to the demand for a higher tempo and decentralised decision-making.

The Two Most Powerful Warriors are Patience and Time

Cultural differences between international armies and their African partners are often compounded by a lack of understanding – on both sides – of the other's perception of, and attitudes to, time.[16] Post-industrialised international armies, which tend to emphasise strict adherence to monochronic linear time, are strictly future-planning oriented and value quick solutions and being kept busy. Often, this typically western, north European, Anglo-Saxon attitude to time will clash with the more traditional approach of some African cultures who, as polychronic people, prefer a multidimensional, even cyclical approach to time, focusing on family time and activities that strengthen interpersonal relationships.

International armies, which tend to be monochromes, perceive time as the most important aspect in prioritising events and sequencing tasks. They are often content to provide any solution quickly, even if it is incomplete and does not address the problem completely, rather than miss a deadline. Polychronic people, on the other hand, prioritise the event, and the relationships between people at the event, over the time – even at the expense of the task and a deadline. Often, the time they afford to the event and task may be subdivided with their other personal, family, network, kin and business interests.

This quickly becomes an issue, both in training polychronic partner forces, and in planning for and accompanying them on operations. This, then, poses a threat for any campaign. The African partner might not have put a timeline on the crisis or the war they are expected to face or fight. The international partner's government officials, often in isolation from the operational area, have already decided on a timeline – related to budget – without setting foot in the country, or understanding the deeper implications of the partner forces' understanding of time and the almost insurmountable constraints they face. These include the challenge of managing their forces, understanding the threat and planning, providing logistics, endemic corruption, and a vulnerable civilian population. Applying an international 'time-based' solution to an African 'time-agnostic' problem will fail if it is designed with a single culture-specific timeline that does not include the partner force's perception of time.

Me Versus We: The Clash of Individualism and Collectivism

The cultural dynamic of individualism versus collectivism often presents further risk to partner-force cohesion, due largely to a lack of comprehension of what it is like to grow up and live in a collectivist or an individualist society. The risk manifests itself in military partnerships where international officers and soldiers are individualists – the US, United Kingdom (UK), Australia, New Zealand and some north-western European nations – and cannot perceive what a collectivist African society (and military) is like.[17] The same can be said for the African officers and soldiers of their individualistic counterparts.

The fundamental issue that international soldiers fail to understand is the degree of interdependence a society maintains among its collectivist members.

It has to do with whether people's self-image is defined in terms of 'I' or 'we'. People in individualist societies are supposed to look after themselves and their direct family only. In collectivist societies, people belong to 'in-groups' that take care of them in exchange for loyalty;[18] it is the same for African armies drawn from collectivist societies. This is manifest in a close, long-term commitment to the member group, be that an ethnic group, a clan, a family or extended family, kin or extended relationships. Loyalty is paramount in a collectivist society and overrides most other societal rules and regulations. The society fosters strong relationships wherein everyone takes responsibility for fellow members of their group. In collectivist armed forces, offence leads to shame and loss of face.[19] Officer-soldier relationships are perceived in moral terms (like a family link), and recruitment and promotions take account of the officer or soldier's in-group and familial connections.

Hence, international soldiers find it confusing when a group of partner-force soldiers will defend or support one of their own even when they know that he or she has erred or failed to do what is required. The acceptance of unprofessional military behaviour to save the face of the individual and the collective is seen as paramount to overall peace rather than pinning responsibility on that individual. This affects the collective application of discipline by group punishment as opposed to individual liability. This form of punishment is not new to international armies, and was used in the past, but modern military law, individual responsibility and guilt-based international societies have moved away from this practice. Today, it is anathema to the modern soldier.

I Took My Revenge After a Hundred Years, and I Only Regret That I Acted in Haste
The consequences of a lack of understanding of the collectivist attitude, especially loss of face, can result in everything from benign disengagement and the end of training to extreme incidents of 'green-on-blue' shootings (when a member of the partner force shoots at the mentor).[20]

Examples of these incidents have occurred in Afghanistan, Jordan and Iraq. Failure to understand the severity of cultural sensitivities evidentially resulted in numerous green-on-blue revenge attacks in Afghanistan during a period when multinational forces were training the Afghanistan national army and police. The examples may be specific to central Asia and the Middle East, as well as extreme and rare, but loss of face, and a desire for revenge, is inevitable if international partners continue to misunderstand the importance of shame in collectivist societies and armies.[21]

Competition Versus Caring
How do militaries that value winning and the pursuit of individual excellence help those that value group satisfaction and collective peace?

International armies that come from extremely competitive and traditionally masculine societies,[22] such as the UK, the US, Canada, Australia and New Zealand, tend to be driven by achievement and success, with success defined by the winner; it is a value system that starts in school and continues throughout organisational life. However, military organisation within certain African societies, such as the Zulus for example, also demonstrates hyper masculine and competitive warrior traits.

Many African societies, although not all, tend to exhibit values in society where caring for others (within their 'in-group') and quality of life are placed above winning competitions and individual success. This is typical of collectivists: quality of life is a sign of success, and standing out from the crowd is not admirable. International advisors tend to come from militaries that demand very high standards and are extremely competitive. For these militaries, this is an easy mechanism for motivating people. Caring, nurturing, empathy, patience and sympathy are not traits that are valued in the average international soldier during training or operations. This is not to say that they do not empathise with the partner force or those affected by conflict, but these are not the typical competitive traits synonymous with the successful prosecution of the contact battle. If they were, it is unlikely that one would win or remain alive very long in war.

That said, to build rapport with African soldiers who exhibit less competitive traits, the international soldier must be trained and educated to develop an understanding of what motivates the partner force. International soldiers who exhibit masculine traits tend to 'live to work', where leaders are expected to be decisive and assertive, and the emphasis is on equity, competition and performance. Conflicts are resolved by fighting them out. African soldiers and officers who come from less competitive societies may avoid competition and conflict, and may prefer to maintain the established status quo rather than upset the equilibrium. The questions international forces need to ask are: What are the partners trying to achieve? Can the partner force articulate their goals and, if not, what do they want or expect from their international partners? without these difficult conversations, both partners will flounder in uncertainty.

Uncertainty and the Partner Force

One of the key components of successful partnering is understanding how the partner force deals with uncertainty. When planning, training and operating with an African force, the international partner must educate themselves to understand how the other deals with the fact that the future can never be known, i.e. either accepting or avoiding uncertainty. Both partners should be asking the question of the other: should we try to control the future (with planning, training, shaping, etc.) or just let it happen (fatalism)?

One needs to determine the concerns of the partner force and what they are confident about. This ambiguity brings anxiety with it, and different cultures have learnt to deal with this anxiety in different ways. The extent to which the members of a culture or army feel threatened by ambiguous or unknown situations, and consequently have created beliefs, protocols and institutions that try to avoid these, will be reflected in their flexibility to adapt and improvise as the situation changes.

International militaries, with a high propensity to see doctrine as an aid to thinking and not dogma or direction, tend to plan in a collegial manner. They devolve and decentralise command, control and decision-making to the lowest level, encouraging flexibility to situational change, and amending plans as new information comes to light, thereby easily dealing with uncertainty. Militaries that are comfortable in ambiguous situations or with 'muddling through' tend to be flexible and adaptive; they learn from their mistakes and become better at the execution of the plan. There are generally not too many rules in these militaries, but those that exist are there to be adhered to within reason, and if unsuitable to circumstances, they are seen as guidance and can be changed accordingly.

In military terms, this results in planning that is not too detail-oriented but where intent or the overarching mission will be clear.[23] The detail of how the mission is achieved will be light, and the actual process fluid and flexible to the changing environment. Planning horizons will also be shorter and, most importantly, the combination of a highly individualist and curious mindset, a high level of creativity, and a strong need for innovation is perfect for a fast-paced manoeuvre style of campaigning. Diverse thought and flexibility are encouraged. This emerges throughout the military in its humour, innovation, creativity, desire to learn, and pursuit of high standards. All of these traits are very typical of a north-west European and North American approach. While this is a strength within their own militaries, it can pose a risk, or a threat, when dealing with cultures that have a propensity for rigidity and rules to avoid uncertainty.

Some African partner forces may exhibit a preference for avoiding uncertainty. These militaries, which tend to maintain rigid codes of belief and behaviour, can be intolerant of novel or unorthodox ideas, doctrine and tactics. In these military cultures, there is an emotional need for rules, even if the rules mean failure to achieve the main effort or mission. Innovation may be resisted, and security is an important element in individual motivation. The military may rely heavily on convention and religion, which provides a comfort zone of structure and the 'well known'. Their ability to adapt and remain flexible to fast-changing situations may be severely limited. Furthermore, these militaries may be incapable of devolving decision-making to the lowest level, and command and control that is vested in hierarchy can be ineffectual.

Consequently, a flexible, malleable and innovative international partner force may struggle to work with a military force steeped in dogma, hierarchy and convention, and which is inflexible and avoids uncertainty. Time spent training and educating the partner force may pay dividends and even change the culture within the military. This, however, will not be a 'quick-impact' project and will take much longer than some international forces are content to accept. Over time, a partner force may respond well to clear planning that considers their avoidance of uncertainty and provides them with detail that alleviates or mitigates this. This, however, will be a complete culture change, which may be very difficult to institutionalise. Here, "presence, patience and persistence" is the key.[24]

Understanding the Past, the Present and the Future

"If you want to know the end, look at the beginning."
– African proverb

Every culture, within both society and the military, has to maintain some links with its own past while dealing with the challenges of the present and future. Some cultures prioritise these two existential goals differently. Normative societies, for example, prefer to maintain time-honoured traditions and norms while viewing any change with suspicion. These cultures accept their own norms and do not question why something is the way it is. Militaries that exhibit this sort of behaviour are not adaptive, and repeat failures without learning from lessons. Militaries that take a more pragmatic approach encourage critical thought and innovation, and place emphasis on efforts to educate everyone to be able to make decisions and plan and prepare for the future.

Some African militaries tend to exhibit conservative and change-resistant behaviours, meaning that their internal cultures are normative instead of pragmatic. Officers and soldiers in these militaries have a strong concern about establishing the absolute truth. Heavily reliant on past written doctrine, they are normative in their thinking. Invariably they exhibit great respect for surface-level traditions and may be discouraged from engaging in critical thinking for fear of punishment by leadership, resulting in the prioritisation of quick, visible and tangible results over long-term planning and conceptualisation.

Herein lies a source of conflicting opinions and approaches between partners. If international partners intend to introduce change, they need to consider how to 'sell' new ideas within the context of normative thinking. This is no easy task, and gently persuading them to have a deeper understanding of the culture and hierarchy that shapes this type of behaviour takes time. Education in communication styles, and influencing key leaders on how to anticipate the behaviour of the partner force, is key to success. International military personnel must be taught to change their approach from 'telling' to one of measured diplomacy, 'asking' the partner force for their ideas and previous experience and, over time, 'coaching' and developing the appropriate analysis and critical thinking to plan the solution with the partner force. Empowering the partner force with their own strategic, operational and tactical solutions is the key to solving localised problems. Delivering international solutions designed for international contexts invariably will fail. Fundamental to this process is the ability of the international partner to conduct intercultural communication with their African partner.

Intercultural Communication

"You have two ears and one mouth. Listen twice as much as you speak."
– Epictetus, 55 BC

In the conduct of training and operations, the only mechanism whereby officers and soldiers from both international and African partners perceive and try to make sense of one another is through intercultural communication and the resultant understanding. Unfortunately, unless both partnered armies have invested heavily in understanding the other partner's culture, there are no guarantees that military personnel will be respectful of the differences they encounter in this process. It is fundamental that both partners seek to understand one another's intentions in non-evaluative ways. For that reason, intercultural communication incorporates particular strategies that encourage us to attribute equal humanity and complexity to people who are not part of our own group.[25] This is especially difficult for militaries that see themselves in a mentoring role rather than an equal partnership; humility becomes the watchword. Any xenophobia, assumptions, preconceptions, biases and stereotypes need to be dispelled early through education and training, or the individual must be removed, as this will undermine the mission and potentially become a self-induced risk or threat to force protection.

The context of situations can become an issue when international militaries and their African partners communicate. Many post-industrialised northern European and international cultures tend to be low-context communicators who are more explicit, direct, removed and formal because they are not expected to know one another's histories, age, status, backgrounds, families or kinship, and communication is not necessarily shaped by long-standing relationships between speakers.[26] Since low-context communication concerns more direct messages, the meaning of these messages is more dependent on the words being spoken than on the interpretation of more subtle or unspoken cues. Low-context communicators invariably want to get straight to the point and on with the task immediately, rather than go through the niceties of rapport-building, and they tend to invest lightly in getting to know the person they are dealing with. Low-context communicators also place less emphasis on non-verbal cues, status, the hierarchical sequence of speakers, and information they deem to be superfluous to the task at hand. This, invariably, can be difficult for high-context communicators, who are more focused on relationships, status and events, and for whom the task is not as important as building rapport.

For African partners who are from high-context cultures, the rules of communication are transmitted primarily through the use of contextual elements such as body language, a person's status, tone of voice or age, and are not explicitly stated. This is in direct contrast to many international militaries in which information is communicated primarily through direct language, and rules are explicitly spelled out. This can be problematic unless both parties clearly understand the intricacies of the style of communication the other party uses. For international militaries, this requires a concerted effort to educate their personnel to observe and try to understand the peculiarities of status, influence and etiquette, and the choreography of communication with the high-context culture, and to switch to building rapport through a more invested approach.[27] In turn, the African partner force needs to be made aware of this, otherwise they will not understand why the international partner tends to want to get on with the task at hand without significant and timely pleasantries.

It is important to note that no culture is completely high context or low context, since all societies contain at least some parts of both. For example, while the UK is a low-context culture[28] in terms of direct, straightforward and concise communication in military interaction, they tend to be high context in business, politics, economics, education, family gatherings and relaxed social events.

Members of high-context cultures usually have close relationships that last for an extended period of time. As a result of these years of interacting with one another, the members know what the rules are, how to think and how to behave, so the rules do not have to be explicitly stated. This makes high-context cultures difficult to navigate for those who do not understand the unwritten rules.

The most common tactical goal of intercultural communication is to inform the partner force of adaptations in training or on operations in multicultural or multi-ethnic environments. In those cases, international partners need to recognise cultural differences that are relevant to short-term communication, to predict misunderstandings that may arise from those differences, and to adapt their behaviour as necessary to participate appropriately in cross-cultural communication, training and operations. Central to this application is having a good system for identifying cultural differences that are relevant to communication. Whatever system is used, the outcome of employing tactical intercultural communication is generally to reduce the stereotyping of cultures encountered, improve knowledge of cultural differences, and broaden the behavioural repertoire of the adapters. This may be done through interpreters, the development of a library of translation nuances, a repository of standard operating procedures in communications for both sides, and additional mutual language training. Language may not afford you an understanding of deep hidden cultural practices, but it certainly aids in communicating intent. Coupled with an in-depth knowledge of sensitivities, etiquette, humour and peculiarities, intercultural communication can be improved over time.

A more substantial practical goal of intercultural communication between militaries is to contribute to the success of projects by transferring knowledge, building long-term relationships, or effecting change through specific development projects at every level of the partner force.

Building trust over time through high-context communication cannot be underestimated when partnering with African armies. Unfortunately, it is not a quick process for international armies, and it requires a shift in cultural mindset. The mantra 'progress not perfection' illustrates this perfectly.

Understanding Gender When Partnering in African Conflicts

The use of 'weaponised' sexual violence in armed conflict and post-conflict theatres is one of the most serious human security challenges due to its scale, prevalence and profound impact. Its prevalence in African conflicts, among other theatres of war, cannot be disputed. The UN's ad hoc tribunals for Rwanda and the former Yugoslavia, and the Special Criminal Court for Sierra Leone, all contained cases where sexual violence against civilians formed part of convictions for genocide, crimes against humanity, and war crimes. In 2008, the UN Security Council adopted Resolution 1820,[29] recognising sexual violence as a tactic of war, and subsequent resolutions have established the conflict-related sexual violence

(CRSV) framework to combat CRSV through prevention, coordinated response and accountability within the broader framework of the UN Security Council's Resolution 1325 on women, peace and security.[30]

Gender-based violence, CRSV, human trafficking, sexual abuse and exploitation, children affected by armed conflict, and gender targeting as a 'weapon of war' are now considered crimes against humanity, and the UN has classified them as punishable under international human rights law, international humanitarian law and international criminal law.

These gender-based violations are frequently and deliberately used to target vulnerable populations, as part of ethnic cleansing, to inflict psychological trauma, and to humiliate, displace and perpetuate violence. Unless this cycle is broken, new generations will grow up conditioned to accept this as the norm rather than the exception. The long-term effects of this will be a reliance on violence to maintain conflict economies and the status quo of power held by those who wield the monopoly on violence.

Gender-based violence, CRSV and sexual abuse are no longer seen as an inevitable by-product of war, and constitute crimes that are preventable and punishable. Men, women, boys and girls are targeted in different ways by violent extremist organisations, including the use of all genders in armed conflict for sexual, logistic and combative functions. For example, armed groups in the Central African Republic have engaged in the rape of men and boys as a way of 'shaming' them for refusing to join their ranks or assisting the enemy.[31] Sexual violence is not a new phenomenon and provides the violent extremist organisation with a 'softer' option designed to break down the very fabric of society and to perpetuate violence through its normalisation. Civilian soft targets also provide violent extremist organisations with a quick and easy means of catching the media's attention.

Undoubtedly, gender-based violence and sexual exploitation are not solely committed by violent extremist organisations; armed forces, security forces and non-governmental organisations (NGOs) have also committed them. With this in mind, international forces must develop a clear understanding of how their partners perceive violence against civilians, training and educating them against unacceptable and unprofessional military behaviour. The difficulty lies in understanding what the tolerance threshold is for violence and unacceptable behaviour, reducing this perception, and educating against it, while developing the partner's mindfulness of international humanitarian law.

There are several examples of important strides made in Africa in terms of championing women in peace and security operations on the continent, encapsulated by initiatives such as the African Union (AU) Strategy on Gender Equality and Empowerment, African Women's Decade, and the AU Solemn Declaration on Gender Equality in Africa, to name a few. The challenge to the international partner is how to train and educate partner forces that may still be resistant to championing women in peace and security, developing gender mainstreaming in their organisations, and diversifying their personnel to ensure that they engage with women affected by conflict. This is a difficult task, especially when one considers that some cultures are more conservative in their approach to the emancipation and inclusion of women in the military and security forces.[32]

International partner forces must train their personnel and the partner force to understand and plan for the reality of gender issues in their mission. Unlike in their own developed economies, the African civilian population which the international partner may encounter might be at risk purely by carrying out their daily economic and domestic practices and pattern of life. Women, men, boys and girls are more vulnerable to the threat of violence purely because their more traditional agrarian and domestic roles – be it collecting water and firewood, going to school or working in fields – expose them to the risk of gender-based violence and ethnic targeting.

At the strategic, operational and tactical level, planners must consider the African gender perspective if they are to have a positive effect on stemming human rights violations. At the strategic level, planners must analyse the operational value of having a diverse gender range sewn into the force to be deployed, especially in countries where the female population is larger and more vulnerable to gender targeting. The presence of international female officers and soldiers provides the force with the ability to train and operate alongside women in the partner force, as well as adapt and flex to engage with, protect and interact with the female population. Women as a force multiplier cannot be underestimated. Victims of gender-based violence and CRSV are anecdotally less likely to approach male soldiers than they are female soldiers.

The UN Security Council has specifically mandated UN peacekeeping operations and signatories to Resolution 1325 to address CRSV. Along with other mission entities, the military component is responsible for proactively preventing and deterring perpetrators, protecting civilians (especially women and children), and neutralising potential, impending and ongoing CRSV threats. To help peacekeepers, police and the military in carrying out these mandated tasks, the UN-CRSV Specialised Training Materials package was developed. These materials familiarise militaries with the concept of CRSV, clarify roles and responsibilities, and equip them with the required tools to proactively address CRSV in their operational environment. It is the international partner's responsibility, as a signatory, to engage with the African partner force (some of which are themselves signatories) and provide training to educate, prevent, deter, report and manage the response to CRSV.

Psychological Implications of Partnerships Between International and African Armies

The psychological implications of partnering between international and African armies are fraught with frictions from the onset. To simplify the psychology of partnering, and to understand how partners should behave, is imperative to the success of a partnership mission. The potential for an initial failure to build rapport between military partners lies in the fact that the basic quick instincts of reticence, survival and emotions often precede the slower, more calculated, analytical thinking that allows one to accept a new partner over time. The fear of the unknown, and of dealing with different people, ideas, perspectives, cultures, doctrines, methodology and perceptions, can be damaging if not quickly overcome. Partners on both sides of the spectrum need to be educated to be aware of these if they are to have any chance of success. Indeed, the key to overcoming the initial reticence of any partner in a new relationship is a slow and steady 'winning over' of the partner by breaking down barriers, emotional intelligence, respect, and understanding what makes partners behave the way they do.

Both partners need to determine each other's goals, expectations and visions of success or failure, or 'what good looks like'. Failure to do so will affect their attitudes, stress, leadership, and the management of training and operations. What international mentors deem to be required to achieve a mission or task may not be synonymous with what the partner force thinks or requires. Cooperation between normative and pragmatist thinking will need to be at the forefront of planning for a successful partnering campaign or mission.

Practice Makes Performance: Training International Partner Forces
Despite the very real difficulties of military partnering, the challenge is not insurmountable. Pre-deployment training must incorporate significant conceptual education, blended with real-life simulated intercultural communication scenarios in contested and stressful environments. International officers and soldiers can conduct these with either the partner force or actors to reflect the same cultural environment – or even with people from a similar culture. These real-life simulated scenarios will introduce the international force personnel to the difficulties and complexities of working with key leaders, who will have influence over issues such as decision-making, planning, logistics and training. Instructors must guard against expatriate bias and parochial cultural theatre if actors are used. Pre-deployment training must emulate conditions of cultural stress so that the international mentors gain sufficient understanding of effective methods and appropriate behaviour, even when confronted with adversity or when dealing with uncomfortable issues with the partner force.

This blended learning, coupled with country-specific cultural education, and applied behavioural sciences training and techniques for teaching international learners, is designed to ensure that every member of the partnering force understands their own culture as much as the African culture with which they will be integrating. It reduces the effect of their own presence and behaviours, and of their own subconscious, on their normal daily interactions with the partner force. It provides international soldiers with the necessary 'risk reduction' to ensure that they are not shocked by their first immersion in the new culture.

Pre-deployment training may also reduce the effect of 'culture shock' on the international partner force. Culture shock is an experience soldiers may have when they operate in a cultural environment significantly different from their own. Individuals may feel disoriented experiencing an unfamiliar way of life when dealing with the partner force in different social, training and operational environments.

If the soldier is incapable of adjusting and adapting to the new environment,

Understanding the Culture of African Partner Forces

this can present a risk to the integrity of the mission. Culture shock may cause anxiety when differences between the international and African military cultures become apparent. The initial novelty of the deployment may eventually give way to unpleasant feelings of frustration and anger as one continues to experience unfavourable events perceived as strange, offensive, or completely opposite to one's normal military and cultural attitude to training and conduct. Language barriers, stark differences in military discipline, field and camp hygiene, training safety, and food accessibility and quality may heighten the sense of disconnection from the partner force. The effects of these factors, and the level of risk they pose to the mission and international mentors, need to be mitigated. This can be done through either retraining or removing the mentor from the situation until the cultural shock wears off. One cannot mitigate the effect of the environment by attempting to change the culture of either partner force. Undoubtedly, this would be a mistake.

Working with an African partner force may put additional pressure on the international partner's leadership and management of personnel, logistics, training and communication, as well as test their tactical knowledge, skills and experience. In addition, there are practical difficulties to overcome, often because the partner force's own personnel, training, and operational and logistical support may be significantly different or even non-existent.

Still, the most important change remains communication. The language barrier may contribute to, or become a major obstacle in, creating new relationships. To reduce culture shock, special attention must be paid to the African partner's culturally specific body language, subtle social signs, tone of conversation, linguistic nuances and customs. Interpreters can help train personnel to overcome these issues as well as prevent any *faux pas*.

As the international partner becomes accustomed to the African partner's culture, they will inevitably develop synergies and routines. Over time, the international partner will learn what to expect in most situations, and as cultural barriers break down and the proverbial ice melts, the African partner force's culture no longer feels as difficult to address as it may have done. Basic daily business becomes more 'normal' and cultural shock becomes less acute. Both partners will experience this and begin to develop problem-solving skills for dealing with the other's culture. Each will begin to accept the other's cultural ways with a more positive approach, and may even assimilate some aspects of the other's culture.

The culture begins to make sense in its own environment, and negative reactions and responses are reduced. At this stage, the international partner is able to be conscious of and avoid sensitivities, train effectively, and participate comfortably with the African partner's military and societal culture.

Conclusion

International military partnerships between armies that are culturally obtuse remain one of the most difficult missions to successfully deliver. Both partners must learn to understand one another's deeper cultural dynamics, and at the same time exploit valuable training and preparation time to conduct operations against violent extremist organisations. All of this needs to be done in a collegial manner, despite the numerous constraints and complexities confronting all parties. Without this deep cultural awareness and comprehension of how each partner plans and makes decisions, success will be difficult to achieve.

The fundamental values, standards and mindsets of one's own culture must also be studied and learned. Understanding the complexities of one's own culture will already help to reduce potential risk and friction in a relationship. Leaders on both sides must seek out commonality, and focus on shared values and acceptable behaviours to align the interests of the partners. Understanding must go beyond surface differences. It must include a mastery of the perception of time, collectivism, communication, normative or pragmatic thinking, of engaging and influencing key leaders and the local populace – and negotiating within the context of the partner's culture to find a shared and locally influenced solution.

Select Bibliography

All Survivors Project. (2018). "I don't know who can help": Men and boys facing sexual violence in Central African Republic. February 2018. Available from: https://reliefweb.int/sites/reliefweb.int/files/resources/ASP-Central-African-Republic.pdf [accessed 8 April 2020].

Barlow, E. (2016). *Composite Warfare: The conduct of successful ground force operations in Africa*. Pinetown: 30° South Publications.

Barlow, E. (2018). *Executive Outcomes. Against All Odds*. Pinetown: 30° South Publications.

Gardiner, I. (2006). *In the Service of the Sultan: A first-hand account of the Dhofar Insurgency*. United Kingdom: Pen and Sword Military.

Hall, E. (1976). *Beyond Culture*. Doubleday Garden City, New York: Anchor Press.
Hall, E. (1985). *Hidden Differences: Studies in International Communication*. Hamburg: Grunder and Jahr.
Herring, G. (2017). How not to 'win hearts and minds'. *The New York Times*, 19 September. Available from: https://www.nytimes.com/2017/09/19/opinion/vietnam-war-americans-culture.html [accessed 8 April 2020].
Hofstede, G. (1984). *Culture's Consequences: International Differences in Work-Related Values (Cross Cultural Research Methodology)*. California: Sage Publications.
Hofstede, G. (2001). *Culture Consequences: Comparing Values, Behaviours, Institutions, and Organizations Across Nations*. 2nd edition. California: Sage Publications.
Kluckhohn, F. & Strodtbeck, F.L. (1961). *Variations in Value Orientations*. Evanston, Illinois: Row, Peterson & Co.
O'Connell, A. (2017). *Our Latest Longest War: Losing Hearts and Minds in Afghanistan*. Chicago: University of Chicago Press.
Ronen, S. & Shenkar, O. (1985). Clustering countries on attitudinal dimensions: A review and synthesis. *Academy of Management Review*, 10(3), pp. 435-454.
Samovar, L.A., Porter, R.E. & McDaniel, E.R. (2012). *Communication Between Cultures*. California: Wadsworth Publishing.
Schwartz, S.H. (1994). Cultural dimensions of values: Towards an understanding of national differences. In Kim, U., Triandis, H.C., Kagitcibasi, C., Choi, S.C. & Yoon, G. (eds.). *Individualism and Collectivism: Theoretical and Methodological Issues*. California: Sage Publications, pp. 85-119.
Simpson, H. (2014). UK Sponsored Stabilisation and Reform in Sierra Leone 2002-2013. RMAS Occasional Paper No 19.
Trompenaars, F. (1993). *Riding the Waves of Culture: Understanding Diversity in Global Business*. Chicago, Illinois: Irwin.
United Nations Development Fund for Women (UNIFEM). (2010). Addressing Conflict-Related Sexual Violence – An Analytical Inventory of Peacekeeping Practice. UNIFEM, United Nations Department of Peacekeeping Operations, and UN Action Against Sexual Violence in Conflict. Available from: https://www.unwomen.org/en/digital-library/publications/2010/1/addressing-conflict-related-sexual-violence-an-analytical-inventory-of-peacekeeping-practice [accessed 8 April 2020].
Van Heerden, R. & Hudson, A. (2012). *Four Ball One Tracer: Commanding Executive Outcomes in Angola and Sierra Leone*. United Kingdom: Helion and Company.

Endnotes

1. While Geert Hofstede's work will primarily be drawn on, several authors using a variety of frameworks have shown that national cultural values relate to workplace behaviours, attitudes and other organisational outcomes. See, for example, Kluckhohn & Strodtbeck (1961), Hall (1976), Trompenaars (1993), Schwartz (1994) and Ronen & Shenkar (1985).
2. The ARVN began as a post-colonial army trained by and closely affiliated to the US army during the Vietnam War. Initially it was conceived as a 'blocking force', but it later developed a more modern conventional role using helicopter deployments in combat. During the US intervention, the role of the ARVN was marginalised to a defensive one, with incomplete modernisation, and transformed again most notably following Vietnamisation as it was geared up, expanded and reconstructed to fulfil the role of the departing US forces. By 1974, it had become much more effective. However, the withdrawal of US forces through Vietnamisation meant that the armed forces could not effectively fulfil all the aims of the programme, and had become completely dependent on US equipment, given it was meant to fulfil the departing role of the US. Unique in serving a dual military-civilian administrative purpose, the ARVN had, in addition, become a component of political power and suffered from continual issues of political-loyalty appointments, corruption in leadership, factional infighting, and occasional open internal conflict.
3. Herring, 2017.
4. The Dhofar Rebellion, also known as the Dhofar War, was waged from 1962 to 1976 in the province of Dhofar against the Sultanate of Muscat and Oman. The war began with the formation of the Dhofar Liberation Front, a faction of the People's Front for the Liberation of the Arabian Gulf, which aimed to create an independent state in Dhofar, free from the rule of Sultan Said bin Taimur. The rebels also held the broader goals of Arab nationalism, which included ending British influence in the Gulf region. The war initially took the form of a low-level insurgency, with guerrilla warfare used against Omani and British forces in the country. A number of factors, such as the British withdrawal from Aden, and support from China and the Soviet Union, brought the rebels greater success, with the communists controlling the entirety of the Jebel region by the late 1960s. The 1970 Omani coup d'état led to the overthrow of Sultan Said bin Taimur by his reformist son Qaboos bin Said, who was backed by a major British military intervention in the conflict. The British initiated a 'hearts and minds' campaign to counter the communist rebels, and began the process of modernising Oman's armed forces while simultaneously deploying the Special Air Service, the Royal Marines and a number of other conventional units to conduct counterinsurgency operations against the rebels. This approach led to a string of victories against the rebels. Intervention by the Shah of Iran in the conflict boosted support for the sultanate in 1973. The war ended with the final defeat of the rebels in 1976.
5. Gardiner, 2006.
6. The Battle of Kolwezi was an airborne operation by French and Belgian airborne forces that took place in Zaire in May 1978 during the Shaba II invasion of the country by the Front for the National Liberation of the Congo. It aimed at rescuing European and Zairian hostages held by rebels from the Front for the National Liberation of the Congo after they conquered the city of Kolwezi. The operation succeeded with the liberation of the hostages and light military casualties.
7. Executive Outcomes was a private military company founded in South Africa by Eeben Barlow, a former officer in the pre-1994 South African Defence Force. It was contracted to provide training support to the armed forces of the governments of Angola and Sierra Leone.
8. Van Heerden & Hudson, 2012.
9. Barlow, 2018.
10. Hofstede, 2001:29.
11. Ibid, 30.
12. Ibid, 19.

13 Ibid, 24.
14 'Mission command' is a style of military command, derived from the Prussian-pioneered mission-type tactics doctrine, which combines centralised intent with decentralised execution, and promotes freedom, speed of action and initiative, within defined constraints. Subordinates – understanding the commander's intentions, their own missions and the context of those missions – are told what effect they are to achieve and the reason why it needs to be achieved. They then decide, within their delegated freedom of action, how best to achieve their missions. Orders focus on providing intent, control measures and objectives, allowing for greater freedom of action by subordinate commanders. It is advocated, but not always used, by the militaries of the US, Canada, Netherlands, Australia and UK. Mission command is compatible with modern military net-centric concepts, and less centralised approaches to command and control in general.
15 Hofstede, 2001:29.
16 Ibid, 30.
17 Ibid, 29.
18 Ibid, 30.
19 Within the Pashtunwali code of conduct, *badal*, or revenge, is considered the foremost, dominant and most important of all Pathan traits. The urge to take revenge on an enemy is infused in the very psyche of a Pathan from birth.
20 'Green on blue' is a phrase used to describe attacks on NATO forces by members of the Afghan security forces.
21 Hofstede, 2001:29.
22 Ibid.
23 Gardiner, 2006:150.
24 O'Connell, 2017:270.
25 Hall, 1985:91.
26 Ibid.
27 Samovar et al, 2012:215.
28 Hall, 1985:91.
29 Resolution 1820, adopted by the UN Security Council on 19 June 2008.
30 UNIFEM, 2010.
31 All Survivors Project, 2018.
32 UNIFEM, 2010.

CHAPTER 10

Turning Bullets into Water: Magical Notions and African Armed Groups in the 21st Century Security Environment

Erich Wagner (Col, USMCR) and Gerhardt Wagner (MD, PhD)

Introduction

As skirmishes waged across the age-old battlefields of Libya in 2010, Colonel Muammar Gaddafi fought to retain the power he had held since 1969 against combined rebel and North Atlantic Treaty Organization (NATO) forces. At the conflict's outset, Libyan television interviewed a sub-Saharan witchdoctor who threatened NATO and assured the dictator that jinns were fighting alongside him.[1] Gaddafi evidently considered 'magic' as a secondary intelligence apparatus, allowing him to spy on Libyan officials and leaders.[2]

Occult signs were ubiquitous. One rebel brandished a belt of amulets and charms used for sorcery taken from a regime mercenary,[3] while another hailed the work of specially assigned imams to counter the strongman's wizards, and yet another blamed 'magic' for the resilience of his die-hards.[4] Gaddafi's witch-doctors, the rebel asserted, "thwarted our attacks with their magic. Every time we launched an offensive, a sand storm whipped up to blind us. When our imams on the frontline started to recite from the Qur'an, the witchdoctors' spells were broken."[5] Regime defector Colonel Saleh al-Obeidi reported that Gaddafi resorted to using African shamans from Mali, Mauritania, Nigeria, Gambia and Morocco in his desperate attempt to prolong his 41-year reign. Gaddafi trained and deployed magicians on the battlefield to provide his military with talismans that would ensure loyalty in an attempt to counteract widespread desertion.[6] The dictator himself summoned their power. One fighter claimed he took "a bag full of amulets" from Gaddafi prior to his execution,[7] while the first doctor to examine the dictator's corpse noticed an *Ihdjab* knotted into his hair – an amulet made of paper, blood and various other items.[8] This charm would supposedly shield the dictator against weapons and detection.[9] Two magicians from Sudan and Chad were among the dead in his last contingent.[10] A reporter identified Chadian witchcraft charms in some abandoned weapons depots,[11] while counter-regime fighters passively attributed the discovery of amulets found on Gaddafi's mercenaries to "magic…Africa".[12]

Now, head south to sub-Saharan Africa. In 2002, the Special Court for Sierra Leone was established to try 'those who bear greatest responsibility' for crimes against humanity committed during that country's decade-long civil war (1991-2002). Six years later, this court found Allieu Kondewa guilty on four counts of war crimes, crimes against humanity and serious violations of international humanitarian law, and sentenced him to 20 years in prison. Kondewa was the high priest of the civil defence forces and its largest militia, the Kamajors, a Sierra Leonean pro-government paramilitary organisation involved in armed conflict against the combined rebel forces of the Revolutionary United Front and the Armed Forces Revolutionary Council. In reality, Kondewa was an illiterate witchdoctor[13] and national hero who motivated thousands of irregular Kamajors to commit ritualistic cannibalism, rape and mutilation to render them bullet-proof.[14] Kondewa's conviction educated the world on not only the horrific nature of African conflicts, but also the facilitating and often misunderstood nature of African religions that coexist with Christianity or Islam, and through which the melodrama of war was, and is, refracted.

Today, in increasingly unstable African environments characterised by religious, ethnic and sectarian strife, it is statistically likely that foes will not only be armed with AK-47s and rocket-propelled grenades (RPGs), but also be emboldened by paranormal convictions.

As the 21st century progresses, policymakers, military and police professionals, and intelligence specialists are constantly trying to stay ahead of a rapidly changing security environment to better quell insurgencies and kill, capture or convert their perpetrators. Similarly, humanitarian organisations in these conflict and post-conflict environments vie to positively impact affected communities. Academics have struggled to establish a definition that recognises the unique yet varied character of today's battlefields. "Conceptualising war accurately and effectively is essential," as a recent treatise explains, "for along with trying to define these conflicts successfully...western military establishments...need to fully comprehend events on the ground."[15]

For decades, Africa was arguably the most overlooked continent, with American military involvement apportioned among three combatant commands with only episodic engagement. In the early hours of the new millennium, Africa rapidly appeared on the world's radar as to the role it might play in the new 'War on Terror' as a result of its many unstable nation states and vast ungoverned areas. Sub-Saharan Africa is the second-fastest growing region of the world today, trailing only Asia.[16] Additionally, the continent is home to massive untapped mineral resources and energy reserves, eagerly eyed by foreign investors. The potential for conflict looms as multinational companies vie for dominance and control. The ensuing violence, as David Crane, the chief prosecutor of the Special Court for Sierra Leone, has remarked, often emanates tales "of horror, beyond the gothic into the realm of Dante's inferno".[17]

In the context of belligerent groups in Africa, the requisite for sophisticated approaches in defusing volatile tensions under duress is critical. Decision-makers must understand as fully as possible the enemy's nature. Combatants are more and more of an ambiguous, 'non-state' character such as illegal armed groups, insurgents, guerrillas, terrorist organisations, and transnational organised crime networks that operate sub-nationally to transnationally in failing and failed states or ungoverned areas.[18] Collectively, this disparate group of irregular and comparatively untrained combatants can be termed 'armed non-state groups' (ANSGs). ANSGs are usually outmatched in materiel, resources, finances, population and firepower by the domestic or foreign state forces opposing them.

The literature is voluminous on comparing and contrasting the multiplicity of differences between conventional and irregular warfare, and published thought on how to be victorious in such environments is prolific. However, one persistent element has been virtually overlooked in contemporary discussions: the recurring, often bizarre, yet persistent presence in many cultures of occult practices influencing armed conflict.[19] These elements cannot be easily explained and are often ignored in traditional courses taught at military academies worldwide.[20] And nowhere is this phenomenon more apparent than in Africa.

So What?

Following 9/11, religion emerged at centre stage of scholarly discourse and analysis in an attempt to conceptualise the entanglement between theology and violence. Depending on the conflict, the religious aspects motivating ANSGs tend to be met with more scepticism than other aspects, quickly relegated to the realm of the irrational, arising from a people's backwardness. For westerners emerging from an Enlightenment heritage, religion and magic are signs of primitive intellects. Anthropologists have studied the meshing of the spiritual world with perceptions of power and legitimacy, but few have addressed the interplay on military conflicts where ANSGs invoke supernatural beliefs into fighting cultures. Historical studies of combatants fighting under magical notions are not uncommon, but these focus mainly on detailing behaviour rather than instrumentality in addressing the prevalence in today's current operational environment.

The strategists' "So what?" question centres on the varying effects of different methods to alter a combatant's mindset. When preparing for conflict, campaign planners attempt to deduce the enemy's freedom of action, physical strength and will to fight. In evaluating the enemy, however, analysts sometimes fail to look at the nucleus of the opponent's nature. Warfighting, Patrick Porter reminds us, is a manifestation of a protagonist's culture, umpired through contact with environment, inhabitants and opponents.[21] To extrapolate the particular character of the conflict, its context and its participants, intelligence analysts must not ignore the effects of traditional rituals incorporating supernatural notions. A 1964 United States (US) army treatise on paranormal combat argued that to adequately "exploit the psychological potential of superstition", the counterinsurgent "must be able to compile and analyse a large quantity of specific and detailed information embracing the entire spectrum of superstitious beliefs and other values of the specific ethnic group with which he is concerned".[22]

Strategist Ralph Peters illustratively outlines the direction of such critical components during the decision-making process:

"We take great pains to develop our intelligence preparations of the battlefield, studying the terrain, the enemy's order of battle, his doctrine and his leaders. As we work in the developing world, we must do the equivalent sort of analysis of the client's (or, sometimes, enemy's) spiritual terrain: What does he believe? What frightens him? What lines won't he cross? What taboos must we avoid transgressing? Which can be turned against him? How can we leverage his beliefs to achieve our desired ends? We don't have to participate in blood rituals, but we had better know if one of our actions might create the need to appease the local spirits personified by the shaman."[23]

Familiarisation with the psychological underpinnings of the enemy's nature will aid multilateral efforts in understanding, countering and exploiting enemy actions and intents. Dr Nathalie Wlodarczyk, one of the few scholars who has taken a trenchant look into the effects of magic notions on contemporary African battlefields, feels this gap "needs to be bridged by showing how religious beliefs can be a source of military tactics".[24]

The importance of cultural anthropology to contemporary internecine conflict is understood. At the outset of operations in Iraq and Afghanistan, David Petraeus acknowledged: "We did not have the depth and breadth and sheer number of experts on local circumstances."[25] With an ethnographic understanding of potential adversaries prior to hostilities, security forces can increase their ability to preserve and protect the innocent while destroying insurgents. Islamic magic scholar Dawn Perlmutter emphasises:

"Knowledge of local myths, customs, and magical beliefs can present unique opportunities for diplomacy as well as warfare, but westerners do not know how to deal with belief in supernatural phenomena, continually applying a rational, scientific approach to cultures that engage in magical thinking and refusing to acknowledge the political significance of these beliefs. Currently, US policymakers cannot even publicly acknowledge that acts of terrorism are based on Islamist religious ideologies, much less give credence to jinn."[26]

If the essence of manoeuvre warfare is defeating the enemy's will rather than his ability to fight, then a solid comprehension of a group's internal dynamic is vital.[27] Understanding what drives combatants, physically as well as mentally, is, as the late Colin Gray suggested, "of greater significance" in irregular warfare because of its unpredictability. "If we do not know much about those beliefs and values, we are unlikely to register much progress in persuasion, except by accident."[28] Since ANSGs are inherently disadvantaged, they seek to increase strength by any asymmetric means available. Wlodarczyk advocates that "differentiating between motivations that drive behaviour – whether to correctly identify the relative threat...or to access the most suitable means of engaging with armed groups to promote peace – is paramount".[29] Invulnerability notions are such a driver. If such notions are used to make fighters do something contrary to human nature, then tacticians must account for the sometimes-bizarre behaviour of such actors on battlefields. Understanding local culture and social processes could help explain how warlike practices morph.[30]

In complex environments where normative behavioural rules are alien to peacekeepers of different socio-cultural backgrounds, life and death decisions are beclouded. Claudia Baisini accurately assesses that, in such scenarios, "intuition would be based on experiences, patterns and dynamics that generate from, and are applicable to, his own social context, but not necessarily applicable to the context in which he is deployed."[31] Ability to decipher what is happening and not happening, and to respond to such cultural clues, is vital.

Ethnic and religious components comprise most African struggles, which frequently exhibit fragmentary, partial adoption of modern practices concomitantly coexisting with pre-colonial, warfighting *modus operandi*.[32] African conflict trends portray a canvas dominated by cultures with long traditions of supernatural entanglement with violent politics. These provide clues to decode some puzzling aspects of these wars while producing disproportionate effects.[33]

It is beyond our scope to address the current panoply of war magic in African factionalism, or its historical precedents. However, in order to present a snapshot of the contemporary picture, we will examine Boko Haram, the Lord's Resistance Army (LRA) and Al-Shabaab. This treatise suggests how counter-ANSG elements can use an understanding of an opponent's supernatural milieu to increase military effectiveness, and how practical, applied aspects can influence various levels of warfare.

The Psychology of Invulnerability Notions

"Men in war are among the most superstitious of people..."
– Scott Anderson, *Lawrence in Arabia*

Magic has been defined as cultural beliefs and practices, deeply rooted in a society's traditions and moral foundations, which "provide coherent and systematic means to influence the world".[34] For this study, we are concerned with the use of this power to affect battlefield events, and the beliefs addressed herein revolve around two perceived classes of power: sorcery and witchcraft. Sorcery relies on power gained from spirits, while witchcraft relies on an ability to control people or events, sometimes effected through potions, talismans and charms. While doctrinally different, we are addressing both under the collective rubric of 'magic' to investigate "where people evoke and enact supernatural, liminal, or divine power, on the one hand, to perpetuate violence and, on the other, to resist harm" in contemporary African conflicts.[35]

In an effort to understand how ethnographic magic affects African warfare, we draw on Pierre Bourdieu's complex concept of *habitus*.[36] Bourdieuan *habitus* can be understood as the socially acquired, culturally ingrained relationship between people's actions and the contexts in which they occur. At the heart of this study is the question of how the *habitus* of mystically imbued fighters impacts tactics and battlefield comportment. For many in sub-Saharan Africa, the condition of existence is one of constant, continual warfare and struggle to survive. It is not the authors' assumption that a customised solution to the multidimensional reality of magic warfare can be reached, but rather that this study stimulates discussion on a prominent aspect of these complex environments. Many of the examples presented here stretch the human capacity for fantastical beliefs, yet only the naïve and those unaccustomed to such warfare would dismiss them. It is impossible to credibly interpret events in unfamiliar settings without an understanding of the cultural context within which they flourish.

Approaching battle, a soldier's confidence in luck plays a significant role in overcoming fear, and emboldening him, as General George Patton said, "a minute longer".[37] Many African societies perform preparatory combat rituals, some lasting days or weeks. Obviously, these methods have the unconcealed purpose of shielding the warrior from harm and death while concurrently motivating him. Generating invulnerability feelings assists this pre-battle mindset, whether gained through rituals, amulets, incantations, drugs or other consumables, and they provide individual and communal energy toward the desired outcome, while helping the warrior cope with uncertainty and the fates' whims. "Soldiers find some measure of comfort behind the flimsiest of cover if it makes them feel less exposed," writes William Miller, "even though in fact it provides no protection whatsoever."[38]

Past conquering armies procured substances believed to embolden soldiers. Pharaohs' magicians beseeched warriors' blessings through magical prayers and charms.[39] Persians chewed pomegranates for protection and carried spears adorned with the fruit.[40] Aristotle allegedly convinced Alexander to undertake an expedition to ensure the supply of aloe to immunise his army.[41]

Various beliefs influence individuals' risk perceptions and willingness to face them. Donald Horowitz identifies a major theme of ethnic conflict as risk reduction, lowering inhibitions for violent engagement. We are interested in activators that suppress inhibitors through the invocation of supernatural powers. Usually, magic enheartens fighters by providing at least one of the following: (1) the ability to perform great feats; (2) increased lethality; (3) the ability to control enemy actions; and (4) invulnerability. While all of these conditions affect risk calculations, foremost they are invulnerability beliefs.[42]

Using the occult facilitates control when traditional military discipline is absent. Perceived group immunity has a considerable effect in environments where chaos, fog, friction and chance reign, and where collective behaviour differs from organised behaviour. The Kamajors – poorly equipped and trained, but "immunised" – so impressed one general that he "wished he could have elements of that calibre of bravery and tenacity in the rank and file of his western and sophisticated army".[43]

Cultures fusing indigenous religious beliefs and formal religious systems – syncretistic groups[44] – are found predominantly in the 'third' and 'fourth' world, which account for three quarters of the globe's population. These cultures routinely incorporate spiritual beliefs into wartime behaviour,[45] and it is not uncommon for them to invoke medicine men to administer esoteric concoctions to enhance warriors' martial efforts. Many societies use talismans, tokens and various rituals as pre-battle 'medicine' substitutes. In some cases, the spiritual dimension fills this void left by a dearth of such materiel and training.[46]

Jean and John Comaroff identify ritualistic practices as a means for people to empower themselves and to "assert a measure of control over worlds often perceived to be rapidly changing".[47] The resurgence of magical repertoires is particularly strong where secular state apparatus is dysfunctional. Religion in these areas is used to counter modernity, which is often viewed as the causation of social ills.[48] In cases where spiritual mediums use their powers to bring order from chaos, they are capable of attracting politically important followings.[49] The spiritual realm is therefore a logical capital for activity that requires power, such as violent conflict. As a result, Wlodarczyk notes that "enemy activity is often associated with the 'evil' use of spiritual power whereas the own side's appeal to the same is considered positive and constructive".[50]

The Question of Rationality
"An amulet has power the way a prayer has power. It's holy because you believe in it."
– Itai Suissa, victim of a terrorist bombing

Western rationalism begs the question: how do human beings succumb to such irrational notions? Anthropologist Roderick Aya argues:

"To call an action 'rational' is to say the actor expects it to gain his goal…The guts of a rational-choice explanation are what the actors want and think they must do to get it, not one's own evaluation of their goals or credence in their ideas about what they can do and what will be the consequence to alternative courses of action."[51]

Mau-Mau scholar Rob Buijtenhuijs asserts that magic would be rational if people believed it worked. "Are such adherents 'sane' people who expect to gain their goals by magical devices, or 'hallucinated' lunatics no longer in touch with reality?"[52] Western rationality cannot be used as a metric when analysing different ethno-social calculations that enable violent actors. Obviously, if there was no culturally shared belief in magic efficacy, then groups would have no reason to pursue it.

Magic becomes a resource for fighters because of the cosmological interconnection of the people and their *habitus*. To illustrate the function and logic of supernatural beliefs and their role in warfare, Wlodarczyk developed a framework for analysis: (1) know what practices and beliefs are incorporated in warfare and (2) understand the meanings they provide in order to (3) identify the functions they serve, and in extension (4) connect them to the means-ends logic of strategy.[53] We are focused on the roles and functions of magic rituals, the 'why' and 'how' actors use such practices in warfare, and to what extent these rituals affect combat and belligerents.

Common Characteristics

One does not need to be a modern-day Clausewitz to understand the functional logic from a combat leader's perspective of instilling invulnerability notions among soldiers. However, the means-ends relationship does not end with this. David Francis concludes: "[T]he use of oracular deities, juju[54] warriors and the spirit world…should also be understood from the perspective of the military and the psychological dimension of asymmetrical warfare."[55]

The *modus operandi* for conferring invulnerability is as varied as the notions themselves. The use of medicines (compounds of natural ingredients/body parts) is one method. Once prepared, such medicines are applied by secret societies by a variety of means, ranging from ingestion, inhalation, injection or incision. Former Liberian combatant Joshua Milton Blahyi, more commonly known by his nom de guerre, General Butt Naked, recalls: "[W]e would do different rituals. Sometimes I would put my blood in with the blood of the other animals or humans that we have, and I would make them drink it."[56] Protections can be worn on specific clothing or physically carried on the body in amulet form. Invulnerability can also be conferred through trances or songs.[57]

While the methods of conveyance differ vastly, the outcome is generally the same: protecting the immunised from harm and granting them supernatural powers. Contemporary warfare scholar Anthony Vinci has identified three basic requirements an ANSG must meet to be effective: people who will fight, a means of force, and the ability to exercise direction.[58] Spiritual immunisations serve all of these particular functions to include:

1. Morale and intimidation.
2. Recruitment and retention.
3. Discipline and the failure of magic.
4. Finances.

Morale and Intimidation

One of magic's most valuable functions is the motivation of one side's fighters and, conversely, the intimidation of the opposition who share similar belief systems. Wlodarczyk understands that "creating myths of invincibility is perhaps the most potent of both intimidation strategies and combat motivation".[59] Proving the superiority of certain magic over others is vital to success, and examples abound.

Some groups expend great efforts to remove their own casualties to convince opponents that their magic has failed.⁶⁰ When Liberians battling Charles Taylor's forces proclaimed, "We eat human heart to be strong," it served a dual purpose: feeding the belief that cannibalism of the enemy made the fighter powerful, while also petrifying the enemy.⁶¹ In 1964, when Congolese Simba rebels descended on Stanleyville led by cavorting witchdoctors, government resistance disintegrated.⁶² Rape is repeatedly exercised by Mai-Mai militias based in the Democratic Republic of Congo (DRC) to empower magic while simultaneously intimidating the populace.⁶³ The result is that sexual violence is accentuated by its understood supernatural effects, an experience shared by both agents and victims.⁶⁴

Recruitment and Retention
Availing local beliefs and securing the backing of key religious personnel are vital to recruiting efforts, promoting solidarity, and providing psychological and structural platforms for mobilisation. "The reason that the deal with the mediums was sought and that once struck was perpetuated year after year," observes David Lan, an historian of the 1970s Zimbabwean conflicts, "was that the mediums could deliver the goods...and the goods in this case were the people."⁶⁵ Employing spiritual *habitus* for many ANSGs results in mass recruitment. Further, it helps screen applicants and reinforces the credibility of their loyalty. In a sense, the spiritual fetishes function as a token of membership and forge a bond between irregulars, often drawn from the marginalised elements of villages.

Today, more than half of Africa's population was born in the 21st century. Children are especially susceptible to invulnerability notions. Psychologists indicate that youth might be more strongly influenced by superstition, as they have less social stakes and experiences.⁶⁶ One study, for example, found that paranormal beliefs tend to be lower in late adulthood.⁶⁷ "The commanders would wear certain pearls and said that guns wouldn't hurt us," former child soldier Ishmael Beah recalled, "and we believed it."⁶⁸ The Kondewa case judge determined that "no enlistment [of] children under the age of 15 years into the Kamajor armed group could take place...if they were not initiated into the Kamajor society and immunised by [Kondewa]".⁶⁹

Most African soldiering 'careers' begin as forcefully recruited youth. It is estimated that about 300,000 children, both male and female and under the age of

18, participate in conflicts worldwide, as either combatants or auxiliaries.[70] Thirty to forty percent are female.[71] In the DRC alone there are an estimated 31,000 children, more than a third girls.[72] A Mai-Mai commander recognised that children "are extremely obedient to orders...make few demands which are easy to satisfy and many of them join as virgins which help us preserve the [magic] rituals as children perform these on adults".[73] Further, children's comparative agility, their small size, and the ease with which they can be physically and psychologically controlled are advantages.[74] Amnesty International's Rhona Keen believes that vulnerable youth "are...easier to control than adults; and they can be misled into thinking they are invulnerable".[75] Children are raised to follow instructions and trust adults, and are, by nature, inexperienced and therefore more expendable than veterans. As a result, ANSGs often employ children as cannon fodder, increasing their casualty rates.[76] When magic inevitably fails, children are taught to blame themselves by manipulative leaders.[77]

Magic indoctrination stifles desertion, which, as Roman general Vegetius noted, can be more harmful than slaughter in battle.[78] Leaders from the Mozambican Resistência Nacional Moçambicana (RENAMO) warned soldiers that spirits would hunt defectors.[79] Former LRA soldiers said their magical indoctrination served numerous purposes, including making them "unable to escape" and causing them to "forget home".[80]

Discipline and the Failure of Magic
Immunised recruits are ordered to strictly follow rules to ensure magic's functionability. The requirements for effectiveness often share familiar patterns. Foremost, recruits are told their faith must be absolute for the magic to work. If the immunised obey the mediums' prohibitions, they will meet with success.[81] Failure in the mechanism of magical protection is almost always explained by the non-observance of the countless rules of behaviour imposed. The death of an LRA member, for example, is blamed on that member's lack of faith or improper use of amulets and prayers, or that the spirits were punishing him.

From a command and control perspective, the rules of behaviour for invulnerability effectiveness serve the dual purpose of becoming essentially a code of conduct or rules of engagement. In the ethnologies of many African ANSGs, "these beliefs and practices serve instructional purposes for the implementation of tactics and discipline".[82] Leadership, with a veneer of supernatural respectability, can harness subservience by arbitrarily prohibiting virtually anything that, through their explanation, harms the effectiveness of the initiation and, in turn, the group. Exclusions span certain foods, alcohol or tobacco, to personal grooming standards. Sexual abstinence is most common in many such societies, as intercourse is believed to diminish energy and the ability to fight. Former Congolese militiamen recalled: "In order not to break the pact that was concluded during initiation, we [Mai-Mai] had to respect certain rules during combat: not to steal, not to touch women, not to have coins in our pockets, not to eat meat unless it was grilled, never to eat pumpkin, never to run away from the enemy or turn our backs to it, [to] shout with triumph every time we won a battle, etc."[83]

Violators are often killed as 'Jonahs' for cursing the entire group. One Kamajor testified he was warned the laws must be followed lest he "be subjected to collective punishment by Kamajors themselves and other relevant authorities".[84] Psychologist Elisabeth Schauer, during testimony against warlord Thomas Lubanga, explained: "[Spirit possession] instils more fear and more hierarchy. If you think that your chief commander is a supernatural man, probably you obey better."[85]

Finances
Often, those endorsing violence use the administration of war medicine to profit financially, by preaching the need for violence at the same time as they confer invulnerability, usually for a fee.[86] Often, those who administer such magic come from afar and are talented swindlers. Kamajor initiates, for example, had to pay immunisation fees to Kondewa, and wealthy elites contributed funds for community initiation rites.[87] The invulnerability-tier 'level' a Kamajor purchased had a corresponding impact on the degree of commitment he exhibited and the amount of command and control that could be exercised by leadership.[88] Charlatans often quickly exit the communities for their own safety after the reality of their farce is recognised.

War Magic in Contemporary African Conflicts

"You call them medicine men, but you have your own armour in western armies and sometimes it does not work, which is the same with us. Sometimes we get hurt and sometimes we get killed, but that doesn't mean it doesn't work."

– Former Sierra Leonian Deputy Defence Minister Chief Sam Hinga Norman[89]

"Magical practices, witchcraft, and warfare in the African continent during the 19th and 20th centuries offer interesting opportunities towards a better understanding not only of African societies," writes Dr Beatrice Nicolini, "but most of all, of their historical role in numerous political and military conflicts and also within peace-building processes..."[90] The US army's Special Operations Research Office argued that there exists an "ingrained quality of superstition throughout... Africa".[91] African spiritual beliefs impact politics and political action at every societal level.[92] Similarly, Dr Erik Gilbert indicates: "There is a growing awareness that magic and witchcraft have played a role in many [of Africa's] conflicts and that resolving these conflicts requires knowledge of the role of witchcraft in sustaining warfare."[93] Polymorphous beliefs, however, vary vastly between ethnic groups.

Africa is the only continent where members of the world's two largest faiths, Christianity and Islam, live in roughly equal numbers. In the past century, Africa's religious demographics have undergone an incredible metamorphosis. In 1900, less than a quarter of the population was either Christian or Muslim (11 million Muslims lived in sub-Saharan Africa and seven million Christians). Today, at 631 million adherents, there are more Christians living in Africa than any other continent, accounting for 45% of the population. Muslims, at 446 million, account for about 41%.

Despite these staggering numbers, Bjørn Møller notes that "indigenous beliefs exhibited a remarkable resilience and stickiness".[94] Syncretism is common in sub-Saharan Africa, with sizeable percentages of both Christians and Muslims – a quarter or more in many countries – believing in magic's protective power. Seventy-six percent of the continent's inhabitants still follow African traditional religions of one sort or another. Various elements of these religions, to include the "inextinguishable appeal of magic",[95] survived and were incorporated into Christian and Islamic beliefs.

As in the colonial era, spiritually imbued tactics continue to play an ever-prominent role in Africa's long list of 'un-civil' wars. Belligerents invoking magical rituals are ubiquitous, influencing regional conflicts and the African ANSGs waging them. War ceremonies that existed in pre-colonial and colonial times were revived and adapted during the civil wars of the late 20th century and today. State-based violence and non-state conflicts (conflict fought between two non-state actors), many of which are religious in nature, are increasing.[96] According to Uppsala's Conflict Data Programme, some 15,000 Africans perished in violent confrontations in 2018, the last year for which figures are available.[97] While far from inclusive, hotspots of conflict in Africa include Burkina Faso, the Central African Republic (CAR), Chad, Côte d'Ivoire, Ghana, Libya, Mali, Mozambique, Nigeria, Senegal, Sierra Leone, Somalia, Sudan, as well as the Great Lakes regions of Rwanda, Uganda, the DRC and Burundi. More than 130 armed groups operate in the eastern DRC alone.[98] Such groups, with their galaxy of acronymic names, routinely morph and switch sides, making group taxonomy extremely difficult. The following three examples provide a snapshot of how ANSGs weaponise occult powers in contemporary Africa.

The Lord's Resistance Army

For 33 years, the LRA's terror rampage has plagued vast, remote regions of central Africa, humiliating African governments by displacing an estimated 2,5 million people and killing more than 100,000.[99] In 2001, the US listed the LRA on its Terrorist Exclusion List, and in 2011 joined the hunt for the LRA's elusive leader, Joseph Kony. The LRA become the deadliest militia in Congo – killing, raping and mutilating victims in their wake by cutting off ears, noses and appendages as a warning to others. At the peak of Kony's power, many, including some commanders of the Uganda People's Defence Force (UPDF), believed he had mystical powers. Considering their experiences with Kony, these assertions were difficult to reject.[100]

The LRA, like many other such groups, has bizarre origins. In October 1987, Ugandan prophetess Alice Lakwena claimed to be possessed by the spirit of a dead Italian army officer and created the Holy Spirit Mobile Forces to liberate the world from sin and bloodshed. Fusing animistic and Christian beliefs, she attracted some 10,000 hymn-singing adherents by persuading them to smear their bodies with nut oil and take magic potions to convert bullets into water and stones into grenades.¹⁰¹ When defeated by government forces, her cousin, Joseph Kony, a semi-illiterate, former Catholic altar boy, forged the LRA from its ashes. This accomplished guerrilla has been variously described as "[v]oodoo, harems, barbarism, and magic…every primitive cliché rolled into one" and a "'social' bandit, a monstrous criminal, or quite simply, a madman with the capacity to wreak untold horrors on the innocent…".¹⁰² Kony is said to function not in his own capacity, but as a mouthpiece of the spirits possessing him,¹⁰³ as God's tool to destroy "evil using fire".¹⁰⁴ He claims he was visited by a multinational host of 13 spirits, including a Chinese phantom.¹⁰⁵

Magical notions are a defining characteristic of the group.¹⁰⁶ LRA commanders invoke supernatural spirits for three pragmatic reasons: to maintain discipline, raise morale and legitimise military outcomes. Magical rites variously known as 'baptising', 'injecting' or 'vaccinating' include ritual cutting; the injection of powder, paste and oils; and the use of amulets.¹⁰⁷ Initiation turns recruits into *malaika* (angels),¹⁰⁸ and Kony's child soldiers are taught prayer songs with lyrics such as "God, God, God, you come and help us, we have prepared to come to you", and are required to clap hands while singing to bulletproof themselves. Failure to sing would cause a bullet to hit their mouths, and failure to advance, their legs.¹⁰⁹ Recruits are prohibited from smoking or drinking, and eating mutton or pork, as Kony considers pigs to be ghosts.¹¹⁰ Strategic decisions and behavioural codes are often attributed to witchcraft as a way to mask the near complete inability of commanders to control outcomes.

Today, after having spent billions chasing Africa's most wanted warlord, western interest has waned. While the LRA has been reduced to a few dozen people, Kony endures, while simply struggling to survive and remaining one of the region's enduring sources of terror.¹¹¹ Understanding how LRA behaviour is shaped by mystical beliefs is an important step in understanding the reasons why remaining members have yet to defect.

Boko Haram
Northern Nigeria's Islamic State West Africa Province (ISWAP), more commonly known as Boko Haram, first emerged in 2007, tapping into a legacy of violent jihad dating back to the 14th century. Styling itself as Islamic defenders with a goal of a fundamentalist state in northern Nigeria, the ANSG was, at the height

of the insurgency in 2015, the deadliest terror organisation in the world. While the etymology of the moniker Boko Haram has been debated, linguists suggest *boko* is actually derived from the Hausa word for 'magic', 'deception' or 'superstition', *boka*, and that it was this western deception that its founder, Mohammed Yusuf, believed was *haram* (blasphemous).[112] (See also the chapter by Graham Furniss in *Extremisms in Africa: Volume 1* for an extensive definitional debate.)

Boko Haram operationalises magic as it needs to recruit non-Salafists joining for other motivations. Paradoxical to its Salafist strictness, the organisation cannot escape the regional belief systems. Yusuf superstitiously drew adherents with fetishes promising spiritual protection.[113] Exemplifying the syncretism of its elements, some members believe in black magic, especially prevalent in recruits from neighbouring countries. One former member recounted:

"…we used to drink what one could call spiritual water because it is not ordinary water. We also used to receive strange visitors who were not equally ordinary humans. We receive the visitors in a strange way, our leaders used to summon them: they used to instruct us to recite some passages in the Qur'an and whenever we do that, the visitors would appear to us during those unholy hours. They could come in three or four. They appeared like humans but they are not humans. We know they are not humans. They usually fortify us with charms for the task before us. They used to instruct us to be strong and fight."[114]

He further described the ritual of taking spiritual water, which "fortifies us against gunshots", and being issued a "mystery ring from our leaders", which provided almost anything asked from it.[115]

Fighters have been observed distributing amulets, assuring locals of protection against government forces.[116] Some captured ISWAP members revealed that commanders forced them to drink the blood of victims and, in some cases, eat them.[117] Consuming blood was believed to prevent the deceased's ghost from haunting the killer's dreams.[118] Warlord Ibrahim Tada Ngalyike, notorious for kidnapping the Chibok girls in 2014, is known for sporting charms that ward off bad spirits and make him invisible.[119] The Nigerian army has discovered various fetishes at abandoned camps, along with condoms and hard drugs.[120]

Some Boko Haram abductees described a certain "magic book" used for indoctrination. These youth were kidnapped on the assumption that they were influential in their communities or had access to charms and amulets. Allegedly, the ANSG has used a spiritual book called *Guduma* (Hausa for hammer) to brainwash newly abducted people. An escapee narrated how, even before his abduction, he had heard about *Guduma*: "People would say it is a magic book where Boko Haram members derive supernatural powers from, and keep captives under spells and essentially brainwashed." Other abductees recounted threats of subjection to the "magic book…so we can be hypnotised for suicide missions or as soldiers".[121]

Traditional Nigerian mystical practices play a large role.[122] Members from Niger are reportedly particularly superstitious, believing, for example, that desertification is the result of sinister women and infidels rather than nature.[123] The mystical is even physically used to camouflage weapons. The bodies of suicide bombers have been found bedecked with "all manner of charms or amulets",[124] while one foiled 2012 attacker used an improvised explosive device (IED) disguised as an amulet.[125]

Grassroots counterinsurgency remains an important dimension in Nigeria's operational environment. Boko Haram's 2014 abduction of the schoolgirls ignited international action. US President Barack Obama joined the effort to rescue these women. Interestingly, so did hundreds of traditional Nigerian hunters armed with homemade guns, poisoned spears and amulets who were "eager to use their skills and…supernatural powers".[126] The hunters demonstrated their talents as follows:

"Cow horn trumpets echoed eerie war cries from the screaming and chanting men as they twirled knives and swords with dexterity, occasionally stabbing and cutting themselves with no apparent harm. The hunters claimed their magic charms prevented any blood being drawn. They also trust amulets of herbs and other substances wrapped in leather pouches as well as cowrie shells, animal teeth and leather bracelets to protect them from bullets."[127]

One elder asserted: "We are seasoned hunters, the bush is our culture and we have the powers that defy guns and knives; we are real men of courage, we trust in Allah for protection, but we are not afraid of Boko Haram."[128] An entrepreneurial 74-year-old commenced a booming enterprise selling amulets to these 11,000 vigilantes.[129] Similarly, Cameroon's President Paul Biya advised his citizens to use witchcraft against Boko Haram in 2017. Not everyone endorsed this in a country that outlaws black magic. "It is not up to a head of state to advocate practices of black magic in a theatre of operations where it is the weapons that must inflict defeat on Boko Haram, not magicians or sorcerers. This is very serious for the morale of the troops," editorialised one analyst.[130]

Al-Shabaab

Somalia has been plagued by cycles of violence and suffering for decades. Since its inception in 2006, Al-Qaeda's Somalia-based affiliate Al-Shabaab has battled Mogadishu's government, and more recently, has conducted attacks transnationally in Kenya. Facing an onslaught from African Union Mission to Somalia (AMISOM) forces in 2012, Al-Shabaab promulgated black magic myths to fund operations and recruits.

To raise money, the ANSG authorised the sale of hyena meat in the port city of Kismayo, which it controlled.[131] Notwithstanding that Somali clerics had for centuries considered this act *haram*, Al-Shabaab assured inhabitants that eating the scavengers' meat protected against illness and evil spells.[132] While some residents complained that it was against Somali tradition to consume hyenas, the price skyrocketed and quickly became affordable only to wealthy people.[133]

A recent study tackled why Al-Shabaab was so successful at recruiting youth. In addition to drugs, several Somalis alleged that Al-Shabaab recruited through magic. One Mogadishan emphasised: "[Al-Shabaab] poured perfume on you that convinces you to join…They use black magic." Others added: "[The perfume] puts a person under a spell."[134] Some Somalis alleged mind control through black-magic-contaminated food handouts.[135]

Al-Shabaab financing also turned to piracy, both by imposing taxes on prizes and commissioning its own sea bandits, who turned to magically imbued protection. By 2015, European Union (EU) and NATO flotillas had virtually put Somali pirates out of business. Some, therefore, turned to sorcerers to identify lucrative targets and predict outcomes. Magicians could reportedly earn thousands of dollars and be rewarded with luxury sport utility vehicles (SUVs) for accurately divining shipping targets that promised high-value booty.[136] Locals were also infuriated by rumours that sorcerers had instructed pirates to sacrifice young children and post-menopausal women after their comrades were killed on the seas. While pirates admitted sacrificing rabbits or crocodiles to avert seagoing calamities, one woman complained: "[M]others [are] worried about their babies.

They say they were being hunted by pirates who now believe human killings may be more powerful than slaughtering wild animals."[137]

Tactical Implications of Paranormal Notions

Magically imbued effectiveness is most impactful at the tactical level. Psychologists generally agree that humans have four natural, automatic, inborn responses when faced with danger: (1) stay and fight; (2) flee; (3) posture to intimidate; or (4) submit. When preparing battle plans, most military staff analyse the enemy's 'most probable' courses of action, derived partly from intelligence predictions of an opponent's proclivity towards these options. How, then, can planners use social science to exploit war magic to defeat insurgents? Can strategists more correctly frame the environment through contextual sensitivity to spiritually imbued warfare?

Imbued combatants often display an altered, unnatural, non-rational predisposition towards aggression and exhibit a significant lack of empathy. When the 'fight or flight' response is activated, the resulting response is abnormally weighted towards the 'fight' option. Invincibility encourages aggression. The paramount requirement of defeating the opponent's mind – his will to fight – is correspondingly much more difficult, if not impossible. Factors contributing to his "killing-enabling process" – a term measuring a soldier's psychological enablement to kill, coined by David Grossman in his book *On Killing* – are unpredictable. Attempting to outwit abnormally confident fighters and cultivate submission or flight responses diminishes, and tactical procedures must be modified if the goal is to disable resistance by means other than kinetic.

Supernatural notions also alter the combatant's risk-to-reward analysis. Horowitz says:

"A major theme of the violent enterprise is risk reduction. Angry or aroused people are not necessarily heedless of risk. An impressively wide range of variables affects…calculation of risk. Among these are supernatural beliefs in invulnerability…[which lower] inhibitions on violent behavior…"[138]

The utter disregard of risk creates more violent and dangerous battlefield environments, and makes peaceful outcomes more distant. The mannerisms of actors who share the invulnerability *habitus* will often exhibit a "type of display which tends to be more obvious and specifically intended to convey and exert power".[139] Warriors with reduced inhibitions are less predictable, more pugnacious, and more reluctant to surrender. Brave acts by 'bulletproof' troops during operations will be more commonplace than in engagements with similar ethnographic, unimbued combatants.

Spirit mediums often acquire high organisational rank, have their own staff, and even accompany columns on campaign. Applying social networking can assist in mapping leadership. In Mozambique, Uganda, Congo, Zimbabwe and Sierra Leone, priests and mediums were deeply involved in battles – leading, planning and advising – and often retained a high degree of control over commanders.[140] In Zimbabwe, mediums knew the land intimately and could guide guerrillas through the dense forests.[141] Mai-Mai doctors, often children, follow warriors when they go to war, sprinkling them with water and chanting '*mayi-mayi*'.[142] Simba witchdoctors led attacks against Belgian paratroopers, just as Ashanti priests had a century earlier in the Anglo-Ashanti Wars.[143]

Inoculated belligerents increase the likelihood of battlefield unpredictability and place opposing forces at greater harm. They can exhibit any of the following characteristics: a heightened proclivity to take risks and disregard self-preservation; abnormal perceptions of pain; an increased religious conviction; decreased empathy; extremely aggressive tendencies; erratic behaviour; exaggerated strength; and increased mental alertness. Such an aggressive psyche, heightened by ubiquitous drugs, produces "angry violence", which deviates from the standard military professional's call of duty motivation.[144] As a result, violence levels can escalate abnormally and desensitise perpetrators, blinding them to everything but destructive goals. One LRA ex-combatant described how, through magic, he "[saw] people as animals".[145]

Like the saying that 'tracers work both ways', so do cultural influences. Cross-cultural influencing is a dynamic process. A 2011 US army report cautioned that because of the proclivity of drug-plagued indigenous forces, western commanders must remain vigilant in checking their soldiers for use and noticing behavioural changes.[146] Similarly, Peters astutely cautions that, albeit unlikely, "marines and soldiers we send to train developing-world militaries" might be "susceptible to psychological manipulation by local shamans". As Peters stresses:

"Leaders…need to pay special attention to any alteration in the behaviour of a subordinate in such environments. Undetected psychological vulnerabilities could play havoc with a mission. The exotic and esoteric can be fatefully alluring to certain personalities – sometimes unexpectedly. If any subordinate shows undue interest in local practices, get him under control immediately. Some human beings are naturally drawn to unusual spiritual environments – and their identities are not always predictable. Don't lose control of a subordinate because you 'don't believe in all that crap'."[147]

Such leadership considerations are important for those conducting security-force assistance missions, as these require "adaptive units led by well-informed, culturally astute leaders".[148] This resonates, as millennials are assumed to be the most culturally appreciative and find value in "living like a local",[149] while concomitantly representing 71% of those on active duty.[150]

An understanding of the potential secondary and even tertiary effects of mystically imbued warriors is fundamental to crafting branches – or pre-planned options that allow militaries to respond to expected changes in the operational environment. To address these changes, planners must examine the potential consequences of friendly actions as well as those resulting from enemy actions and reactions. A case in point: the presence of large numbers of children on African battlefields will impact the existing 'warrior code' of western armies with regard to the ability and proclivity to engage in kinetic action.

In sub-Saharan Africa, children, who comprise the bulk of many militias, believe in their leaders' spiritual power and are taught that life depends on spirit-appeasement.[151] While magic can spur children to do unspeakable things, killing children creates a conflict between morality and necessity. Potential hesitation to kill could have the same harmful outcomes for today's counterinsurgent as it did for French Legionnaires facing female warriors of the Dahomey kingdom in 1890; some Legionnaires delayed killing women, resulting in their own casualties.[152] Similarly, US soldiers during the Battle of Mogadishu (1993) were reluctant to engage women who were used as human shields, or attack them.

There is no doubt that western militaries will continue to encounter child soldiers in Africa, and will face the 'lose-lose' conundrum of engagement (and the images that will emerge in world media) or jeopardising force protection. Psychological preparation for troops, and those responsible for counselling them after these encounters, must be implemented. Operations will require more role-play scenarios for combat-bound units on the possibility – nay, likelihood – of using lethal force on youthful adversaries. One example is the Battle of Bangui that took place from 22 to 24 March 2014 when the South African National Defence Force (SANDF) engaged Seleka rebels, who used progressive waves of child and youth fighters before sending in adult combatants, causing the CAR national army and others to flee. The SANDF sustained losses and inflicted heavy casualties before a ceasefire and negotiated surrender.[153]

Interviewing and Interrogating
ANSGs and the occult must not be viewed solely as a military problem, but also as a shared inter-agency opportunity, as such notions span the blurred crime-war continuum. Relegating the implications and effects of this battlefield reality solely to the military spectrum will retard the development of solutions and inhibit imaginative thought for this transnational, multi-agency, multi-dimensional threat.

Understanding the psychological impact of mysticism can assist interrogators in designing and navigating interviews. It may impact preparations, developing rapport, moulding themes, managing resistance, understanding motivations and detecting deception. Special Forces interrogators are urged to "be an actor!" and "think outside the box" to develop suspect rapport-building.[154] Coupling this advice with even a cursory understanding of supernatural mindsets could result in more truthful and reliable results that other interrogation strategies miss.

Operational Considerations of Paranormal Notions

"To be successful on the frontier, a man has to deal with the hearts and minds of the people, and not only with their fears."
– Thomas Henry Thorton[155]

How do invulnerability beliefs resonate operationally? As on the tactical side of military engagements, there are corresponding implications on higher echelons of war as well. A better conceptualisation of opponents' superstitions in operational arenas can assist in reaching strategic ends more efficiently and effectively.

"*Habitus*," Laure Paquette notes, "need not be an obstacle…[but] one of the forces that strategy can tap. A new definition of strategy and tactics, and all that they imply, cannot be used without some awareness of *habitus*."[156] In other words, strategy, like tactics, needs to be informed by a deep understanding of the ethnographic setting. Fighting *habitus* "is a waste of time for those of us with practical missions to accomplish", recognises Peters.[157] French army captain Antoine Camus echoed this view in 2011 when he admonished his soldiers in Côte d'Ivoire "to respect the gris-gris" versus wasting their time attempting to change local beliefs.[158]

The United States Africa Command (USAFRICOM) currently has no programme educating security cooperation teams deployed on foreign internal defence (FID) missions[159] about the mystical beliefs of the environments to which they are assigned. However, the challenges of prevailing supernatural perceptions must be acknowledged when assisting host-nation forces. One USAFRICOM officer posed the conundrum: "How do you 'train-the-trainer' to train invulnerability notions out of them?"[160] It is vital to address *habitus* during the disarmament, demobilisation, repatriation, reintegration and resettlement (DDRRR) process, when fighters from a mosaic of militias are massaged into a national army.

For example, as Mai-Mai forces continue to integrate into the Congolese national army – the Forces Armées de la République Démocratique du Congo (FARDC) – harmful Mai-Mai behaviours have a high probability of manifesting in FARDC units if not addressed. As of 2009, three quarters of those convicted of rape in the Congo were in the military.[161] Illustratively, FARDC officers have been known to advocate sexual violence by telling recruits that raping a virgin will make them unassailable.[162] In May 2013, the United Nations Stabilization Mission in the Democratic Republic of Congo (MONUSCO) reported gross human rights violations committed by the FARDC, asserting that it had raped more than 135 displaced women.[163] This was of particular concern to USAFRICOM, since a US-trained battalion was identified in the area of responsibility during the period. Can less be expected when the FARDC and the Mai-Mai spring from the same *habitus*?

Unlike demobilised soldiers, those reintegrated into the army receive little to no rehabilitation. Rising levels of sexual violence committed in civilian communities are often attributed to an increase in ex-combatant reintegration without adequate rehabilitation.[164] Congolese-born Emmanuel Muhozi assisted

USAFRICOM on FID missions and discussed this challenge of relating to and, more effectively, instructing such soldiers while communicating tactical ideas. Muhozi stressed the pre-deployment significance of "educating-the-trainer" to comprehend the ubiquitous nature of mystical-thinking Africa.[165] Trainers' education must be tailored to the individual tribal culture of those they are going to assist. Further, westerners must accept that they will be unable to train animistic beliefs out of their protégées. One FARDC major recalled getting into trances and being transformed into air, wind and grass to make himself invulnerable, while another officer still advocated *'maji's'* protective power, asking an USAFRICOM trainer how to protect himself from getting shot on the right side of his body, since he was already invulnerable on the left. Muhozi remembered that the advisor did not know how to respond and therefore dismissed the question. Before teaching tactics – how to properly 'react to an ambush', for example – there needs to be an awareness of local culture, which will lead to mutual trust and understanding. Practical applications then follow; otherwise the message is often lost. Finally, Muhozi lamentably often observed trainers only teaching but never being taught – a vital trait for successful security cooperation.[166]

Facing talisman-induced foes should alter mission planning. "How far this war of the spirits makes a difference in the eventual resolution of a conflict is virtually impossible to assess," acknowledges Paul Sturges. "However, the spiritual element might sometimes be decisive. For example, it is sometimes suggested the Biafran secessionists collapsed during the Nigerian civil war (1967-70), not when starvation and shortage of materiel became acute, but when spirit mediums attached to military units were deprived of their positions of influence."[167]

To attain costless advantages over adversaries and to influence their attitudes and behaviour, counterinsurgent forces must take full advantage of information operations to delegitimise occult ideology. Counterinsurgents must ask themselves: what collective behaviour are we attempting to get the populace to engender? The answer should help shape operational design, particularly with respect to the civil information portion of the campaign. Military information support operations (MISO) should message evidence that fighters are not impervious to physical laws. Invulnerability should be aggressively challenged by MISO, spearheaded by indigenous forces engaging with community leaders.

Turning Bullets into Water

Anna Catherine de Laine, in her study of Sierra Leone's Kamajors, acknowledges the value of such:

"It could be worthwhile looking into the much less researched area of why so many eligible men didn't join the Kamajors. A few reasons have appeared in the data, though in a non-systematic way: individuals more embedded in established religion were suspicious of the use of 'heathen' magic, some were preoccupied with studies or work in a way considered acceptable to Kamajors; others were wary about rumours of human sacrifice and cannibalism, and others again found protection with other groups."[168]

MISO needs to magnify internal differences through local civic and religious authorities to delegitimise medicine men. Shaping civilian perceptions may mould willingness to assist friendly forces or, conversely, not assist insurgents. Wlodarczyk argues for the benefits of propaganda and psychological campaigns tailored to influence emotions and behaviours.[169] Such campaigns can help break myths, dilute beliefs and divert local support, while highlighting the adverse medical repercussions of ingesting toxic medicaments. In such a manner, the Rhodesian government dropped leaflets with appeals from prominent spirit mediums to stop aiding the rebels during Zimbabwe's 15-year war for independence (1964-79), one stating that "the ancestral spirits do not want bloodshed in this country. I shall work with the government. I shall not die helping terrorists".[170]

Using information campaigns to discourage a fight or to minimise an ANSG's ability to recruit by dispelling invulnerability notions should be *de rigueur* operational planning in African environments. Action reports from units engaged with spiritually emboldened combatants need to be emphasised post-conflict and used to build a knowledge database for inter-agency awareness.

At times, the goal of diminishing the phantasm of invulnerability can stifle intelligence collection, as demonstrated by an inflation of Mai-Mai casualties by opposition forces in 1998.[171] Additionally, the desire to prove scientific rationalism can sometimes result in over-zealous security forces slaughtering peaceful citizens on the pretext of crushing such notions. Atrocities in such conflict zones are often linked to spiritual beliefs. One commander thought it necessary to publicly execute a captured Mai-Mai boy with a rocket grenade in full view of his men to vanquish their fear of Mai-Mai powers.[172]

Myths that shape a society may be effectively exploited in psychological warfare (PSYWAR) campaigns by both insurgents and counterinsurgents. A US army's extraordinary 1964 strategy paper gave instructions for "exploitation of enemy vulnerabilities provided by superstitions and deeply held traditional beliefs". Titled Witchcraft, Sorcery, Magic, and Other Psychological Phenomena and their Implications on Military and Paramilitary Operations in the Congo, the report is a treatise on paranormal combat, discussing "counter-magic" against rebels motivated by witchdoctors and fetishes.[173] Famous American clandestine commander Edward Lansdale argued that the key asset of the psychological combatant is a thorough understanding of the target culture's beliefs and mores for effective PSYWAR operations. Strategic planners should incorporate anthropological realities in plans. As the report argued, to adequately "exploit the psychological potential of superstition", the counterinsurgent "must…compile and analyse a large quantity of specific and detailed information embracing the entire spectrum of superstitious beliefs and other values of the specific ethnic group…concerned".[174]

Likewise, when attempting to divine what course an insurgency may take and mitigate risk, regional supernatural beliefs provide clues. The adoption of spiritual rhetoric on both sides of a conflict escalates the spiritual dimension of the struggle.[175] The willingness of tribal-group members to respond to courage-inducing schemes can be deduced through cultural competency and historical memory. In the past, government claims to have inscrutable powers often served to subdue rebellions. Sometimes, magical notions transcend group lines, potentially influencing susceptive government forces, as in the Congo's Simba rebellion. Magical practices were "effective in conditioning dissident elements and their followers to do battle with government troops. Rebel tribesmen…[were] persuaded that they can be made magically impervious to Congolese army firepower. Their fear of the government has thus been diminished and, conversely, fear of the rebels has grown within army ranks."[176]

From a Machiavellian viewpoint, an ANSG's dependence on magic can be a source of vulnerability when it comes at the expense of tactics and leadership. One of the age-old quandaries of colonial generals was a fear that the enemy would not 'come out and fight'. Of course, guns and bullets are no respecter of people, and spiritual beliefs can be counter-weaponised. The late Mike Hoare, one of history's most famous mercenaries, remembered the ease of destroying Simba formations because they would charge straight into the guns. In Angola, it is believed that a mutilated body cannot enjoy an afterlife. The Angolan government capitalised on this fear during the 1961 rebellion as rebels fearlessly charged machine guns but thought "twice about attacking anyone armed with a machete".[177]

Conclusion

Understanding the strategic functions of war magic within the African milieu provides tools for undermining ANSGs. Counterinsurgents need to comprehend how the enemy sees the world, not only to understudy how they are able to exploit mysticism but, more importantly, to conceptualise how they operate to more efficiently and effectively defeat them.

To summarise our conclusions for understanding ANSGs in Africa and what portents and opportunities their beliefs indicate:

- Magically imbued warfare is characteristic of 21st century African conflict.
- *Habitus* varies with the ethnographic area, yet elements may overlap cultures.
- Supernatural invocations are used to recruit, motivate, maintain discipline, and structure units.
- Magically imbued warfare influences both the tactical and operational levels of war.
- Understanding how ANSGs weaponise magic can assist in identifying probable courses of action and counter-action.
- Belligerent belief in war magic may indicate opportunities for information operations.
- Traditional beliefs constitute potent psychological-operations tools for both insurgents and counterinsurgents.

Magical notions in a people's *habitus* encourage groups who might otherwise avoid an armed confrontation to engage in violent acts. A socio-cultural knowledge of invulnerability rituals could have a plethora of effects on regional warfare and the DDRRR process by assisting in reducing kinetic operations, increasing situational awareness, decreasing/destroying attacks, intelligence analysis, campaign planning, counter-messaging, FID training and humanitarian assistance efforts.

As shown, invulnerability perceptions play a fundamental role in creating a state of mind in individuals to kill or to self-destruct, while fuelling violence because of the combat advantages they portend. They contribute to breaking down will and abetting subjugation to a cause or an act contrary to human nature. The manipulation of supernatural discourse has been shown to motivate people to fight and to demoralise like-minded opponents. Knowledge of *habitus* and control of magical *legerdemain* have significant political worth. A superstitious population presents opportunities to communicate fear, apprehension or awe, and to exert influence. In Africa, these beliefs often come to dominate conflicts, shaping the course of the aggression while overshadowing the legitimate socio-economic and security grievances that originally sparked them.

Select Bibliography

Abuja Daily Trust. (2016). Nigeria; Plenty Used Condoms, Narcotics Found at Insurgents Camp. 2 June.

Adesanya, O. (2014). Boko Haram: Nigerians Buy Arms and Bullet Proofs to Defend Themselves. *Kaduna Today*, 29 June.

African Development Bank. (2017). Africa Remains World's Second-fastest Growing Region. 24 May.

Ahmed, A. (2011). Colonel Gaddafi using "African magic" to prolong his reign. *Asharq Al-Awsat*, 1 July.

Ahmed, M. & Sheikh, A. (2011). Somali Islamists Want to Do Ransom Deals on Board. *Reuters*, 28 February.

AIRVIBEZ.Net. (2014). Body of Suspected Suicide Bomber of Abuja Bomb Blast Identified. 16 April.

Al-Sudani (Khartoum). (2011). Al-Qadhafi's Son Reportedly being Sheltered by Sudanese Rebels. 24 October.

Anderson, S. (2014). *Lawrence in Arabia: War, Deceit, Imperial Folly and the Making of the Modern Middle East*. New York: Anchor Books.

ANSAmed. (2011). Libya: Gaddafi Calls Up Shamans Against Rebels. 1 July.

Asharq Al-Awsat. (2011). Colonel Gaddafi Using 'African Magic' To Prolong His Reign – Libyan Rebel Officer. 1 July.

Associated Press. (2014). Traditional Nigerian Hunters Want to Find Girls. 19 May.

Aya, R. (1990). *Rethinking Revolutions and Collective Violence: Studies on Concept, Theory and Method*. Amsterdam: Het Spinhuis.

Baaz, M. & Stern, M. (2010). The Complexity of Violence: A critical analysis of sexual violence in the Democratic Republic of Congo (DRC). The Nordic Africa Institute, 18 May.

Baisini, C. & Nyce, J. (2010). Lethal Theory: Some Implications. *Military Intelligence*, April-June.

Basedau, M. & Schaefer-Kehnert, J. (2019). Religious Discrimination and Religious Armed Conflict in Sub-Saharan Africa: An Obvious Relationship? *Religion, State and Society*, 47(1), pp. 30-47.
Bassett, T. (2003). Dangerous Pursuits: Hunter Associations (Donzo Ton) and National Politics in Côte d'Ivoire. *Africa*, 73(1).
BBC News. (2008). Spying Accused 'Used Black Magic'. 23 October.
Behrend, H. (2000). *Alice Lakwena and the Holy Spirits: War in Northern Uganda, 1985-97*. Athens: Ohio University Press.
Bhatia, M. (2008). *Terrorism and the Politics of Naming*. London: Routledge.
Blahyi, J. (2017). Interview with Joshua Blahyi. Monrovia, Liberia, 23 July.
Boehland, N. (2015). The People's Perspectives: Civilian Involvement in Armed Conflict. Report. Washington, D.C.: Center for Civilians in Conflict.
Bourdieu, P. (1990). *The Logic of Practice*. Cambridge: Polity.
Brabazon, J. & Stack, J. (2004). Liberia: An Uncivil War. Discovery.
Bradfield, E. (2011). Interview with Edward Bradfield. 24 February, Stuttgart, Germany.
Buijtenhuijs, R. (1996). The Rational Rebel: How Rational, How Rebellious? Some African Examples. *Afrika Focus*, 12(1-2-3).
Campagne, J. (2011). Imams Break Gathafi's Spell. *Middle East Online*, 17 June.
Camus, A. (2012). Interview with Antoine Camus. 24 October, Washington, D.C.
Coalition to Stop the Use of Child Soldiers. (2004). Child Soldiers: Global Report 2004. London: Coalition to Stop the Use of Child Soldiers..
Comaroff, J. & Comaroff, J. (1993). *Modernity and its Malcontents: Ritual and Power in Postcolonial Africa*. Chicago: University of Chicago Press.
Combs, M. (1996). *The Tragic Tale of the Mayi-Mayi*. Associated Press.
Crane, D.M. (2005). Dancing with the Devil: Prosecuting West Africa's Warlords: Building Initial Prosecuting Strategy for an International Tribunal after Third World Armed Conflicts. *Case Western Reserve Journal of International Law*, 37(1).
Crick, M. (1979). Anthropologists' Witchcraft: Symbolically Defined or Analytically Undone? *Journal of the Anthropological Society of Oxford*, 3, pp. 139-146.
Cringle, V. (2003). Child Soldiers – A Global Issue. *British Army Review*, 131, Spring.
Danjibo, N. (n.d.). Islamic Fundamentalism and Sectarian Violence: The 'Maitatsine' and 'Boko Haram' Crises in Northern Nigeria. Ibadan: Institute of African Studies, University of Ibadan.
Dassie, R. (2009). Men on Men Rape Cases in Dr Congo: The Ordeal of 'Bush Wives'. *Afrik-News*, 13 August.
De Laine, A.C. (2008). Civil Militia & The Power to Rule: A Case Study of The Microdynamics of War in Bo District, Sierra Leone. Master's thesis. Utrecht: University of Utrecht.
Dempsey, M. (2009). FM-3-07.1: Security Force Assistance. Washington, D.C.: Department of the Army.
Der Spiegel. (2011). Gadhafi Legacy a Lasting Burden for Libya. 24 October.
Dumas, L. (2003). *Wounded Childhood: The Use of Children in Armed Conflict in Central Africa*. Washington, D.C.: International Labour Organization.

Farmer, B. & Jawad, B. (2011). Libya: The Battle of Bin Jawad. *UK Telegraph*, 29 March.
Farrer, D. (ed.). (2016). *War Magic: Religion, Sorcery, and Performance*. New York: Berghahn.
Fisher-Thompson, J. (2004). Strong U.S. Religious Base Seen Key to Effective Aid to Africa; Authors Discuss Power of Faith in Africa at CSIS Meeting. 22 November. Washington, D.C.: State Department.
Flint, C. (2006). *The Geography of War and Peace*. Oxford: Oxford University Press.
Francis, D. (2005). *Civil Militia: Africa's Intractable Security Menace?* Burlington: Ashgate.
Future Foundation. (2016). Millennial traveller report: Why millennials will shape the next 20 years of travel. Available from: https://www.foresightfactory.co/wp-content/uploads/2016/11/Expedia-Millennial-Traveller-Report-Final.pdf [accessed 4 April 2010].
Gettleman, J. (2007). The Perfect Weapon for the Meanest Wars. *The New York Times*, 29 April.
Ghana News. (2013). Ex-Boko Haram Member Speaks to a Gathering of Christians. 11 August.
Gray, C. (2007). Irregular Warfare, One Nature, Many Characters. *Strategic Studies Quarterly*, Winter.
Grossman, D. (1994). Defeating the Enemy's Will: The Psychological Foundations of Maneuver Warfare. In Hooker, R. (ed.). *Maneuver Warfare: An Anthology*. Novato: Presidio Press.
Grossman, D. (1995). *On Killing*. New York: Little, Brown.
Hamblin, W. (2006). *Warfare in the Ancient Near East to 1600 BC*. London: Routledge.
Harsch, E. (2020). Silencing the Guns. *Journal of Good Governance Africa*, January-March.
Harvard Humanitarian Initiative. (2015). Indoctrinate the Heart to Impunity: Rituals, Culture and Control within the Lord's Resistance Army. 24 November.
Haug, K. & Maaø, O. (2011). *Conceptualizing Modern War*. London: Hurst.
Hedlund, A. (2010). Anthropology of Rape in War: Sexual Violence and Magical Beliefs in the Congo War. EASA Conference, Ireland, August.
Heitman, H.R. (2013). How deadly CAR battle unfolded. *Sunday Independent*, 31 March. Available from: https://www.iol.co.za/sundayindependent/how-deadly-car-battle-unfolded-1493841 [accessed 6 April 2020].
Hentz, J. & Solomon, H. (eds.). (2017). *Understanding Boko Haram*. New York: Routledge.
Herbert, D. (2017). Billions of Dollars Later, Joseph Kony Remains at Large and the First World has Lost Interest in Bringing Him to Justice. *QZ.com*, 27 April.
Hills, A. (1997). Warlords, Militia and Conflict in Contemporary Africa: A Re-Examination of Terms. *Small Wars & Insurgencies*, 8(1), pp. 35-51.
Hoare, M. (2008). *Congo Mercenary*. Boulder: Paladin.
Holmes-Eber, P. & Salmoni, B. (2008). *Operational Culture for the Warfighter*. Quantico: Marine Corps University.
Horowitz, D. (2001). *The Deadly Ethnic Riot*. Berkeley: University of California Press.
Howden, D. (2008). The Deadly Cult of Joseph Kony. *UK Independent*, 8 November.
Howe, N. & Strauss, W. (2000). *Millennials Rising: The Next Great Generation*. New York: Vintage.

Hubbard, J. (1969). Ashanti Military Affairs in the Nineteenth Century. Master's thesis. Madison: University of Wisconsin.
Human Rights Watch. (1997). The Scars of Death. Children abducted by the Lord's Resistance Army in Uganda. Human Rights Watch/Africa Children's Right Report, 18 September.
Human Rights Watch. (2007). State of Anarchy: Rebellion and Abuses against Civilians. *Human Rights Watch*, 19(14a), 14 September.
Internal Displacement Monitoring Centre. (2013). LRA-Related Displacement in Central Africa: An End to the Emergency, but Not to IDPs' Needs. September.
International Criminal Court (ICC). (2009). Case against Thomas Lubanga Dyilo, Hearing – Open Session. Trial, ICC-01/04-01/06, 7 April.
Kilcullen, D. (2007). Religion and Insurgency. *Small Wars Journal*, 12 May.
Lan, D. (1989). *Guns & Rain: Guerrillas & Spirit Mediums in Zimbabwe*. Berkeley: University of California Press.
Levinson, C. & Boudrewau, R. (2011). Rebel Gains Fail to End Siege of Libyan City. *The Wall Street Journal*, 26 April.
Lilley, K. (2016). The Millennials have Taken Over: A Primer for the Military's Generational Shift. *Army Times*, 31 July.
Locka, C. (2017). Cameroon Uses Witchcraft to Fight Boko Haram. *GlobalPost*, 12 January.
Makongo, V. (1998). Naked Mai Mai Fight Rebels. *Kinshasa Le Palmares*, 24 September.
McConnan, I. (2000). Child Soldiers and Children Associated with the Fighting Forces: Draft Report of a Desk Study. February. London: Save the Children UK.
McGreal, C. (2007). Christians Live in Dread as New, Local Taliban Rises in the North. *The Guardian*, 3 May.
McGregor, A. (2011). Rebellion Without Reason: The Strange Survival of Joseph Kony and the Lord's Resistance Army. *Jamestown Foundation*, 2(11), November.
Mellen Press. (2009). Studies in Witchcraft, Magic, War and Peace in Africa. Available from: www.mellenpress.com/mellenpress.cfm?bookid=6769&pc=9 [accessed 5 April 2020.]
Miller, W. (2000). *The Mystery of Courage*. Cambridge: Harvard University Press.
Misser, F. (2020). River of Arms. *Journal of Good Governance Africa*, January-March.
Møller, B. (2006). Religion and Conflict in Africa: With A Special Focus on East Africa. Report. Danish Institute for International Studies.
Muhozi, E. (2013). Interview with Emmanuel Muhozi. 20 May, Stuttgart, Germany.
Mullenix, P.A. (2014). Interrogation: Theme Selection for Jihadist Combatants. *Special Warfare*, April-June.
Nduwimana, D. (2013). Reintegration of Child Soldiers in Eastern Democratic Republic of Congo: Challenges and Prospects. IPSTC Peace and Security Research Department, Occasional Paper Series, 4(2), Karen, Kenya.
Ngugi, T. (2012). Joseph Kony's Biblical Master Plan for The World. *Africa Review*, 12 December.
Nicolini, B. (2006). *Studies in Witchcraft, Magic, War and Peace in Africa: Nineteenth and Twentieth Centuries*. Lewiston: Edwin Mellen.
Ogwu-Chinuwa, S. (2012). Attempt to Bomb Lagos Church Fails. *The Moment*, 25 April.

Organized Crime and Corruption Reporting Project (OCCRP). (2018). Trekking Through Hell to Flee From al-Shabab. 1 October.
Osborne, H. (2013). Hyena Burger? Saudi Taste for Wild Meat Threatens Species Extinction. *IBTimes* UK, 21 June.
Palitza, K. (2011). Rehabilitating Former Child Soldiers Who 'Liked' Killing. Inter Press Service, 2 November.
Paquette, L. (2009). *Counterinsurgency and the Armed Forces: How to Prepare to Face New Threats*. Canada: Lakehead University.
Patton, G. (2013). Courage is fear holding on a minute longer. In Charlton, J. (ed.). *The Military Quotation Book*. New York: Thomas Dunne.
Perlmutter, D. (2013). The Politics of Muslim Magic. *Middle East Quarterly*, 20(2).
Peters, R. (2007). Rising from Strategic Ashes: African Phoenix. August. Quantico: Center of Emerging Threats and Opportunities, Marine Corps Combat Development Command.
Petraeus, D. (2009). Counterinsurgency Leadership in Afghanistan, Iraq, and Beyond. Speech at National Press Club, Washington, D.C., 23 September.
Porter, P. (2009). *Military Orientalism: Eastern War through Western Eyes*. London: Hurst.
Price, J. & Jureidini, P. (1964). Witchcraft, Sorcery, Magic, and Other Psychological Phenomena and their Implications on Military and Paramilitary Operations in the Congo. Special Operations Research Office, 8 August.
Reuter, C. (2011). Shedding Light on How Moammar Gadhafi Died. *Der Spiegel*, 1 November.
Ronan, P. & Titecamarch, K. (2020). Kony's Rebels Remain a Threat, but They're also Selling Honey to Get By. AfricanArguments.org, 10 March.
Sabahi Online. (2012). Al-Shabaab Resorts to Selling Hyena Meat to Fund Military Operations. 25 August.
Schweizer, M. (1994). *Aloe Vera: The Health and Healing Plant*. 4th edition. Paris: APB.
Skelton, T. & Allen, T. (1999). *Cultural and Global Change*. London: Routledge.
Sturges, P. (2011). The Role of Spirit Messages in African Conflicts: The Case of Joseph Kony and the Lord's Resistance Army in Uganda. *The Open Information Science Journal*, 3.
The Nation (Nigeria). (2014). Boko Haram Kills Over 150, Injures 164 in Abuja. 14 April.
The Prosecutor of the Special Court v. Sam Hinga Norman Moinina Fofana Allieu Kondewa. (2006). Transcript, case no. SCSL-2004-14 T, 5 October, Trial Chamber I.
The Prosecutor v. Moinina Fofana, Allieu Kondewa (the CDF Accused). (2007). SCSL-04-14-T, Special Court for Sierra Leone, 2 August. Available from: www.unhcr.org/refworld/docid/46e123dc2.html [accessed 4 April 2020].
Tobacyk, J., Pritchett, G. & Mitchell, T. (1988). Paranormal Beliefs in Late-Adulthood. *Psychological Reports*, 62, pp. 965-966.
Torgler, B. (2007). Determinants of Superstition. *Journal of Socio-Economics*, 36(5), October, pp. 713-733.
Tripodi, C. (2009). 'Good for One but Not the Other': The 'Sandeman System' of Pacification as Applied to Baluchistan and the North-West Frontier, 1877-1947. *Journal of Military History*, 73(3), pp. 767-802.
Twum-Danso, A. (2000). The Limits of Individualism: What Constitutes an Effective Form

of the Reintegration and Rehabilitation of Child Soldiers into Society after Civil War? Dissertation. London: London School of Economics.

Ukwu, J. (2016). How Boko Haram Threaten Us with 'Magic Book' – Escapees. NAIJ.com, 3 July.

Van Acker, F. (2004). Uganda and the Lord's Resistance Army: The New Order No One Ordered. *African Affairs*, 103(412).

Vinci, A. (2006). The 'Problems of Mobilization' and the Analysis of Armed Groups. *Parameters*, Spring.

Wagner, E. (2010). Making Bullets Dance: Drug Use among Insurgents and Terrorists in the Current Operational Environment. November. Washington, D.C.: FBI's Terrorism Research and Analysis Project.

Walker, P. (2011). Gaddafi's Son Mutassim 'Held' in Sirte Onslaught. *UK Independent*, 13 October.

Wanzala, J. (2020). The Art of War. *Journal of Good Governance Africa*, January-March, pp. 112-117.

Waring, R. (1961). *The War in Angola – 1961*. Lisbon: Silvas.

Williams, P. (2011). *War & Conflict in Africa*. Cambridge: Polity.

Wlodarczyk, N. (2009). *Magic and Warfare: Appearance and Reality in Contemporary African Conflict and Beyond*. New York: Palgrave Macmillan.

Wollacott, M. (2000). Sierra Leone: Special Report. *The Guardian*, 6 June.

Worth, R. (2011). Qaddafi's Faustian Bargain. *New York Times* Blogs, 21 October.

Yalman, N. (1972). Magic. Excerpted from Sills, D. (ed.). (1972). *International Encyclopedia of the Social Sciences*, 9. New York: Macmillan.

Young, C. (2002). Deciphering Disorder in Africa: Is Identity the Key? *World Politics*, 54(4), July.

Zenn, J. (2012). Interview with Jacob Zenn. 20 June.

Zenn, J. (2014). Boko Haram and the Kidnapping of the Chibok Schoolgirls. *CTC Sentinel*, 7(5), March 2014.

Zenn, J. (2020). *Unmasking Boko Haram*. Boulder: Lynne Rienner.

Endnotes

1. *Jinns* are supernatural, unseen spirits, sometimes called 'genies' in the West (ANSAmed, 2011).
2. Asharq Alawsat, 2011.
3. Farmer & Jawad, 2011.
4. Levinson & Boudrewau, 2011.
5. Campagne, 2011.
6. Ahmed, 2011.
7. *Der Spiegel*, 2014.
8. Reuter, 2011.
9. Al-Sudani (Khartoum), 2011.
10. Reuter, 2011.
11. Worth, 2011.
12. Walker, 2011.
13. In the halls of academe there is a long-standing debate on the efficacy of the semantic use of the term 'witchdoctor'. The authors acknowledge this; in this chapter we use various terms interchangeably to represent the spiritual mediums who act as intermediaries between the human and spirit worlds. For a scholarly discussion on terminology, see Crick (1979).
14. The Prosecutor v. Moinina Fofana, Allieu Kondewa (the CDF Accused), 2007.
15. Haug & Maaø, 2011.
16. African Development Bank, 2017.
17. Crane, 2005.
18. Bhatia, 2008; Hills, 1997.
19. Flint, 2006:242.
20. Wlodarczyk, 2009:2.
21. Porter, 2009:1.
22. Price & Jureidini, 1964.
23. Peters, 2007:259.
24. Wlodarczyk, 2009:6.
25. Petraeus, 2009.
26. Perlmutter, 2013:80.
27. Grossman, 1994:142.
28. Gray, 2007:44.
29. Wlodarczyk, 2009:4.
30. Hedlund, 2010.
31. Baisini & Nyce, 2010:48.
32. Kilcullen, 2007; Wanzala, 2020.
33. Young, 2002:547.
34. Yalman, 1972:527.
35. For a detailed terminological discussion, see Farrer (2016:2).
36. While a complex concept, *habitus* in its simplest usage can be understood as an inclination towards a particular way of behaving, a system of dispositions. Religious beliefs incorporating magic can be placed in the *habitus* categorisation. (Bourdieu, 1990:53)
37. "Courage is fear holding on a minute longer" (Patton, 2013:13).
38. Miller, 2000:215.
39. Hamblin, 2006:418.
40. Herodotus 7.41.
41. Schweizer, 1994:15.
42. Horowitz, 2001:100.
43. The Prosecutor v. Moinina Fofana, Allieu Kondewa (the CDF Accused), 2007.
44. Holmes-Eber & Salmoni, 2008:193-194.
45. Skelton & Allen, 1999:232.
46. Wlodarczyk, 2009:78.
47. Comaroff & Comaroff, 1993:xiv.
48. Danjibo, n.d.:18.
49. Bassett, 2003:1.
50. Wlodarczyk, 2009:25.
51. Aya, 1990:32.
52. Buijtenhuijs, 1996:12.
53. Wlodarczyk, 2009:8.
54. 'Juju' is a West African term for magic attributed to, or associated with, fetishes, charms, amulets or supernatural powers.
55. Francis, 2005:36.
56. Blahyi, 2017.
57. Horowitz, 2001:100.
58. Vinci, 2006:51.
59. Wlodarczyk, 2009:37.
60. Ibid.
61. Brabazon & Stack, 2004.
62. Hoare, 2008:23.
63. Hedlund, 2010.
64. Ibid.
65. Lan, 1989:14.
66. Torgler, 2007.
67. Tobacyk et al, 1988.
68. Gettleman, 2007.
69. The Prosecutor v. Moinina Fofana, Allieu Kondewa (the CDF Accused), 2007.
70. Coalition to Stop the Use of Child Soldiers, 2004.
71. ICC, 2009:12.
72. Palitza, 2011.
73. Nduwimana, 2013:7.
74. McConnan, 2000.
75. Twum-Danso, 2000.
76. Cringle, 2003:20.
77. Dumas, 2003:45.

78 Vegetius: *De Re Militari*, iii, 378.
79 Wlodarczyk, 2009:38.
80 Harvard Humanitarian Initiative, 2015:28.
81 Lan, 1989:4.
82 Wlodarczyk, 2009:39.
83 Dumas, 2003:45.
84 The Prosecutor of the Special Court v. Sam Hinga Norman Moinina Fofana Allieu Kondewa, 2006.
85 ICC, 2009:68.
86 Horowitz, 2001:98.
87 The Prosecutor v. Moinina Fofana, Allieu Kondewa (the CDF Accused), 2007.
88 Wlodarczyk, 2009:80.
89 Hinga Norman quoted in Wollacott (2000).
90 Nicolini, 2006:4.
91 Price & Jureidini, 1964.
92 Fisher-Thompson, 2004.
93 Mellen Press, 2009.
94 Møller, 2006:6.
95 Peters, 2007:3.
96 Basedau & Schaefer-Kehnert, 2019.
97 Harsch, 2020:15.
98 Misser, 2020:106.
99 Internal Displacement Monitoring Centre, 2013.
100 Author's conversations with UPDF officers, March 2012.
101 Behrend, 2000. See also Sturges (2011:78).
102 Sturges, 2011:78. See also Herbert (2017).
103 Van Acker, 2004:348.
104 Ngugi, 2012. Interestingly, Kony has been observed wearing a Muslim *kanzu* and created his own Qur'anic-inspired Ten Commandments.
105 Howden, 2008.
106 Harvard Humanitarian Initiative, 2015:27.
107 Ibid, 26.
108 Williams, 2011:142.
109 Human Rights Watch, 1997.
110 McGregor, 2011:12.
111 Ronan & Titecamarch, 2020.
112 Zenn, 2020:2.
113 Hentz & Solomon, 2017:26.
114 *Ghana News*, 2013.
115 Ibid.
116 McGreal, 2007.
117 Hentz & Solomon, 2017.
118 *Ghana News*, 2013.
119 Zenn, 2014:5. See also SOCAFRICA Native Prospector: East Bridge, NG-110, Navanti Group (11 March 2014).
120 *Abuja Daily Trust*, 2016.
121 Ukwu, 2016.
122 Zenn, 2012.
123 Zenn, 2012. Many Muslims (and Christians) in the north have trouble reconciling the level of violence that Boko Haram is inflicting, believing that leaders must be using charms to entice recruits.
124 *The Nation* (Nigeria), 2014. The charms and amulets are typical of those used by members of the terrorist group. See also AIRVIBEZ. Net (2014).
125 Ogwu-Chinuwa, 2012.
126 Associated Press, 2014.
127 Ibid.
128 Ibid.
129 Adesanya, 2014.
130 Locka, 2017.
131 Sabahi Online, 2012.
132 Ibid.
133 Osborne, 2013.
134 Boehland, 2015:81.
135 OCCRP, 2018.
136 Ahmed & Sheikh, 2011.
137 Ibid.
138 Horowitz, 2001:526-527.
139 Wlodarczyk, 2009:90.
140 Wlodarczyk, 2009:74; Lan, 1989:53.
141 Lan, 1989:148.
142 Hedlund, 2010:4.
143 Hubbard, 1969:11-13.
144 Wagner, 2010:422.
145 Harvard Humanitarian Initiative, 2015:28.
146 Afghan CDR AAR Book 2011, Task Force Duke, 3-1 IBCT, RC-E (Khost, Paktia, Ghazni), OEF 11-12.
147 Peters, 2007:259. Such a case was reported in 2008 involving a soldier from the United Kingdom accused of spying for Iran who testified that he used "black magic" to protect his NATO commander from the Taliban (BBC News, 2008).
148 Dempsey, 2009.
149 Howe & Strauss, 2000; Future Foundation, 2016.
150 Lilley, 2016.
151 ICC, 2009.
152 Grossman, 1995:175.
153 For a media report, see Heitman (2013).
154 Mullenix, 2014:14.

155 Tripodi, 2009.
156 Paquette, 2009.
157 Peters, 2007:259.
158 Camus, 2012.
159 FID is a broad, 'whole of government' support mission which the US provides to enable other governments to field viable internal defence and development programmes addressing security threats.
160 Bradfield, 2011.
161 Dassie, 2009.
162 Baaz & Stern, 2010:49.
163 Available from https://monusco.unmissions.org/.
164 Baaz & Stern, 2010:46.
165 Muhozi, 2013.
166 Ibid.
167 Sturges, 2011:77.
168 De Laine, 2008.
169 Wlodarczyk, 2009:142-143.
170 Lan, 1989:196.
171 Makongo, 1998:8.
172 Combs, 1996. For additional examples of prisoner executions based on magic, see Human Rights Watch (2007).
173 Price & Jureidini, 1964.
174 Ibid.
175 Wlodarczyk, 2009:33.
176 Price & Jureidini, 1964.
177 Waring, 1961:27.

CHAPTER 11

Neocolonial/Colonial Extremes: Defining Direct Colonialism, Reaction and Resistance in Contemporary Ambazonia and Western Sahara

Matt Meyer

Introduction

Though it has become fashionable in academic circles to proclaim that 'recent' experience around the world provides evidence of the defining importance of resistance and liberation movements,[1] in fact there have been few periods over the past two centuries lacking in significant radical civilian uprisings.[2] Debates regarding strategies, tactics and ideology – especially argued among both academics and practitioners of the global north – have taken particularly dichotomised forms over the past century, corresponding to the modern era of decolonisation.[3]

The term 'decolonisation' was applied after the Second World War, as Marshall[4] points out, to the winning of independence and recognition of indigenous national governments by former colonial rulers. Decolonisation, in this sense, was synonymous with formal national liberation and was understood as an achievement in the public domain of politics, often at the behest of the colonial power.[5] However, in the late 20th century, decolonisation took on different meanings. Rather than being understood as a formal event initiated at the centre of colonial power, decolonisation was perceived as a process internal to the colonised that promised, as Ghana's first post-colonial president, Kwame Nkrumah, put it, "the fuller redemption and realisation of a people".[6]

Contemporary concerns regarding 'decolonising' theory and practice in the post-colonial era often skip the deeper, older and more striking root lessons of the late 20th century national liberation movements and corresponding subsequent cultural, political, economic, geographic, gendered and related anti-oppression struggles.[7] The neocolonialism predicted by Nkrumah, even as the concept itself was being implemented in his own native Ghana, has now overtaken the African continent and the world in ways barely imaginable even a quarter of a century ago. The more extreme cases of continuing direct colonialism, however, have become both symbolically and strategically important in developing a contemporary discourse on social change. It should be no surprise that ongoing, unresolved anti-colonial and anti-occupation movements often search for these deep lessons in their own practice and study of the last decades of real-world examples. The African experiences of Cameroon-Ambazonia and Morocco-Western Sahara provide perfect evidence regarding the neocolonial/colonial resistance extremes. For the peoples of those regions, working out effective and concrete survival strategies is a life-and-death, future-focused endeavour.

21st Century Colonialisms, Strictly Speaking

To frame a conceptual space for these 'ongoing', 'unresolved' peoples and movements, it is necessary to examine, from both a descriptive and definitional perspective, the various on-the-ground conditions faced in such settings. This need is foundational, as much for the emergence of a practical space for dialogue and sharing as it is for the construction of theoretical models for 21st century liberation. A praxis growing out of such an international, multi-disciplinary, grassroots-based approach may prove most effective in supporting long-term progressive, anti-oppression outcomes. Perhaps the greatest historic lesson needed in setting such a conceptual context is that rigid lines of separation and division are rarely useful, either for intellectual analysis or for organisers' pursuits of effective coalitions.

The connections between land, freedom, sovereignty and self-determination have been established as universally significant to the life of a people.[8] Since the founding of the United Nations (UN) in 1945, when questions of extermination and genocide were undoubtedly prescient, subjugated people – imprisoned by external powers and occupying military forces – were given new hope.[9] Perhaps the most cited definition and listing of which peoples are and are not 'free' comes from the UN, itself a complicated and problematic actor not disinterested in its own relationship to powerful stakeholders. Nonetheless, the UN Committee of 24 (the Special Committee on Decolonisation) worked and works to monitor the process, methods and progress of Non-Self-Governing Territories (NSGT).[10] Though the assertions of the committee are consistently ignored by the UN General Assembly and Security Council, its annual reports are still used by occupied peoples to assert their self-determination rights.[11]

Although the right of all peoples to exercise self-determination continues to be articulated – including the rights of a people to select their own government leaders as well as the means to achieve such governance – a UN definition of colonialism has still not wholly been developed or agreed upon. The 'third decade' of UN decolonisation, lasting until the end of 2020, was declared by the UN, but the methods of implementing a freedom process for the generally acknowledged two million people living under some form of occupied force have hardly been specified. This lack of basic agreement has led to intense confusion and dispute regarding the UN compilation and maintenance of its NSGT lists.

As of 2019, the UN decolonisation listing of NSGT included in Africa only Western Sahara and Saint Helena (a tiny British-controlled island). Europe's listing is solely Gibraltar, while North America includes Anguilla, Bermuda, the British Virgin Islands, the Cayman Islands, Montserrat, the Turks and Caicos Islands, and the United States (US) Virgin Islands. South America, according to the UN lists, has only the Falkland Islands, while the Oceania/Asia/Pacific region includes French Polynesia, New Caledonia, Tokelau, the Pitcairn Islands (population: 49), American Samoa, and Guam.[12]

On the face of it, this list is highly problematic on at least two levels. First, it omits many peoples whose colonised and occupied status is evident *a priori* given any classic or modern definition of the word. Second, several territories on this list exist in a substantially harmonious relationship with their 'colonising host' – sometimes evident in agreed-upon legal frameworks of autonomy, sovereignty and partial independence (Gibraltar being a classic example).[13] Thus, the political nature of this list suggests its inadequacy, particularly exempting from scrutiny the dominant permanent Security Council members the US, China and France.[14]

There is an additional UN decolonisation list, something of a parallel structure, which includes "Trust and NSGT" peoples who have experienced changes

of status over the past seven decades.[15] This list includes:[16]
- **Africa:** Reunion.
- **Asia:** Cocos, Portuguese Macau, British Hong Kong.
- **North America:** Greenland, Guadeloupe, Martinique, St Pierre and Miquelon, Netherlands Antilles, Alaska, Panama Canal Zone, Puerto Rico.
- **Oceania:** French Polynesia, New Caledonia, Hawaii, Northern Mariana Islands, Cook Islands, Niue.
- **South America:** French Guiana.

Though this list does include still-disputed territories, and some peoples included have technically resolved their struggles from a strictly military and legal perspective, the cases still hold deep political, socio-cultural and economic issues between colonised and colonising powers. Some of these issues relate to the problem of still-unclear definitions of the concept of self-determination; others to the influence of superpowers within UN structures.[17]

Because the island archipelago of Puerto Rico has technically held referendums on the colonial question, the US successfully called for its removal from the first list in 1953 (with a UN General Assembly vote of only 40% in favour of removal winning out once substantial abstentions weighed in from US benefactors). The ongoing nature of unresolved issues on all levels of Puerto Rican life, including active armed movements and massive unarmed civil resistance campaigns held over the past half century, led to the creation of a unique, unprecedented UN status: in 1972, the question of Puerto Rico's status was formally reopened, with annual hearings taking place to this day. Puerto Rico is thus an NSGT under UN Decolonisation Committee review, despite placement on the official list of NSGT in only asterisked form.[18] Along similar lines, it is worth noting that in 2018, the government of Vanuatu began an effort within the UN to have Indonesia's colony of West Papua added to the NSGT list.[19] In all of these cases, so many of which most adversely affect peoples of African origin, the fundamentally destructive dynamic described by Tunisian intellectual Albert Memmi in the classic *The Colonizer and the Colonized* (1965)[20] holds true.

The Unrepresented Nations and Peoples Organization (UNPO)

In the context of these controversies, and following the widely popular sweep of independence and national liberation movements through the 1950s to 1970s, talk of a non-governmental formation led to the founding of the Unrepresented Nations and Peoples Organization (UNPO) in 1991. Breaking the UN Security Council stranglehold, at least by China, early founders of the UNPO included Tibetan leader Lodi Gyaltsen Gyari Rinpoche, His Holiness the Dalai Lama's special envoy to the US, and the Dalai Lama's international law advisor, Michael van Walt van Praag. Thus, Tibet, omitted from UN consideration, has been a central force within the UNPO from the outset. Furthermore, as a voluntary membership organisation, the UNPO makes no claims to be globally inclusive of all 'unrepresented', colonised or occupied peoples, only to bring together a key grouping of those concerned and like-minded on these issues.[21]

At the same time, desires to gain and maintain US governmental support has meant that US colonial holdings such as Puerto Rico have not received much focused attention. Ironically, more central to the UNPO work in North America has been an ongoing spotlight on the District of Columbia (DC). A 2019 UNPO report on the US, however, submitted to the 36th session of the UN Universal Periodic Review of Human Rights, calls out the US for "longstanding denial of voting and representation rights" for the peoples of the US Capitol District of Columbia and the "five permanently inhabited, unincorporated US territories (Puerto Rico, Guam, US Virgin Islands, American Samoa, and the Northern Mariana Islands)".[22]

One of the UNPO's most significant contributions has been the creation of a clear set of definitions, not designed to determine all peoples under occupation, but to create criteria whereby those peoples so inclined can come together for dialogue and joint work. Five such criteria bind together UNPO members, as enduring principles enshrined in their covenant:

- That all peoples have the right to self-determination, thus the right to freely determine their political status and freely pursue their economic, social and cultural development.
- That UNPO members adhere to internationally accepted human rights standards, including those set forth in the Universal Declaration of Human Rights.
- That UNPO members adhere to the principles of democratic pluralism and the rejection of intolerance.

- That UNPO members are dedicated to the promotion of non-violence, and the rejection of terrorism and violence as instruments of policy.
- That UNPO members are dedicated to the protection of the natural environment.[23]

Indigenous nations also play a role in UNPO proceedings, though they have had uneven participation over the years. The US-based Lakota nation, for example, served as a member from 1994 to 2007, and the Canadian-based Buffalo River Dene nation from 2004 to 2009, but sovereignty issues within and outside the UNPO have been difficult to compare and track alongside those of more nationalist struggles. As the centrality of the nation state gives way to regional sub-imperial powers, noted most pointedly by Bond and Garcia,[24] and political economies become increasingly significant to the issues of sovereignty, noted by Xing[25] and others, the questions of autonomous regional interdependence reviewed by the UNPO are likely to become more significant in the years to come.

As of the end of 2019, the peoples represented as members of the UNPO included: Abkhazia, Acheh, Afrikaners, Ahwazi, Ambazonia, Assyria, Balochistan, Barotseland, Batwa, Belah People, Brittany, Catalonia, Chameria, Chittagong Hill Tracts, Crimean Tartars, District of Columbia (Washington, D.C.), East Turkistan, Gilgit Baltistan, Haratin, Hmong, Iranian Kurdistan, Kabylia, Khmer-Krom, Latin American Indigenous Peoples (Project), Lezghin, Medhesh, Nagalim, Ogaden, Ogoni, Oromo, Rehoboth Basters, Savoy, Sindh, Somaliland, South Moluccas, Southern Azerbaijan, Southern Mongolia, Sulu, Taiwan, Talysh, Tibet, West Balochistan, West Papua and Western Togoland.[26]

Scepticism regarding the work of the UNPO and its membership structure has been raised at times, when even UN-acknowledged Western Sahara did not at first play a role in its structures. In addition, criticism regarding the inclusion of such groups as the Afrikaner Freedom Front Plus, a South African-based political party founded by one of the racist apartheid regime's top military commanders, suggests a western or Eurocentric organisational bias. Nevertheless, the UNPO continues to provide a unique and consistent voice to those most often left out of the mainstream international arena.

Ambazonia, Palestine, Kashmir and the Question of Timing and Strategy

It is striking that none of these extensive lists include the peoples of Palestine or Kashmir, or other substantial struggles for liberation, survival, solidarity and recognition. Palestine, whose historical interactions with the UN as both a trust territory and a recognised liberation movement, was checked off the lists in November 2012 when General Assembly Resolution 67/19 formally granted Palestine status as a "non-member observer state", the same status granted to the Holy See (the Vatican).[27] In the years following 2012, with the continuation and intensification of Zionist settler colonialism and the ensuing *Nakba*, as has been chronicled by Khalidi,[28] it is evident that no resolution to the problem has been found.

Similarly, though it has been argued that in the 1940s, during the partition of India and Pakistan, the peoples of Kashmir (or some of their leaders) opted to accept some forms of autonomy within the structures of Indian federalism, it has been clear that occupation and colonial repression have been the order of the day in the decades since[29] – with especially fierce violence and the stripping of legal rights since 2019. Thus, any project focused on civilian resistance looking at including occupied peoples must not fail to include the peoples of Palestine and Kashmir, even as we may choose to focus on more neglected and overlooked struggles in Africa.

That said, a brief examination of the question of negotiation and timing is in order. If, at a given historic moment, a people or their represented liberation leaders choose to engage in, suggest or accept some forms of accommodation or compromise, it is not the role of outsiders or solidarity activists to sit in judgment of those decisions or disengage in support work because of them. Though outside critique may be useful, it is still important to adhere to the principles of self-determination. A long-term view of decolonisation, which includes political, economic and cultural forms, must include a stalwart solidarity which leaves room both for tactical shifts from within the frontlines of struggle, and for continued material aid beyond a moment of victory; reformist, revolutionary or otherwise. This is the very *raison d'être* of self-determination. In the case of Ambazonia (what is sometimes referred to locally as Anglophone Cameroons), for example, it can be understood that the movement's decision to agree to incorporation into a federal republic of Cameroon must be accepted along with that same movement's decision to reverse that decision once Cameroon's actions made it clear that no such true or equitable republic would be allowed to exist.[30]

In a similar light, regions and areas that are essentially devoid of conflict at one moment might still merit consideration and reflection in case of a future breakdown of accepted de facto autonomy. Such might be most striking in states such as Transnistria and the Commonwealth for the Democracy and Rights of Nations, also known as the Commonwealth of Unrecognised States. These east European, Soviet-influenced territories exist with sometimes significant autonomy but also with great fragility; Transnistria has its own unique currency, functioning immigration system, national postal and automobile licensing institutions, and industries. It is simply not recognised by the UN and only tacitly accepted by bordering Ukraine and Moldavia. Without support from Russia, it is doubtful that these local and regional acceptances would hold.

In addition, micro-states – recognised and unrecognised – make up another problematic category, as their regional strategic influences may wax and wane given geopolitical factors outside of their control.[31] Tiny San Marino, fully surrounded by Italy and fully accepted as a UN member-state, may be unlikely to ever cause world headlines (other than as a tax and personal shelter for the extremely wealthy),[32] but unrecognised though fully autonomous Somaliland in the Horn of Africa might.[33] Though the Oromo ethnic-political group based in the Horn is included on some of the lists, the current power shifts within Ethiopia (including the 2019 Nobel Peace prize selection of Prime Minister Abiy Ahmed) make it unlikely that the Oromo peoples will be pushing for even greater separatist recognition or autonomy in the near future.[34]

Stateless Nations and Contemporary Attempts at Academically Comprehensive Lists

Since the question of self-determination and people's freedom is both an existential and essentially grassroots-based phenomenon, it is likely that academic inquiry will always be a step behind in figuring out the common or divergent issues worthy of further examination. Perhaps the most ambitious attempts at creating a comprehensive, non-ideologically biased framework come from those using the concept of 'stateless nations' and working to define the factors which separate these peoples from, say, partially recognised peoples or ethnic groups living with full rights within multi-ethnic nation states. The stateless-nations groupings, as Minahan[35] describes, tend to recognise a common issue of domination, sometimes using the designation of 'fourth world' to describe the status of these peoples. Recognising also the ongoing impact of colonisation, imperialism and migration, the generally accepted defining elements of stateless nations include peoples who:

- Have no sovereign state of their own.
- Do not form a majority within any existing sovereign state.
- Have at least one active autonomist, independence, decolonising or secessionist movement.
- Are not recognised by the UN, or by many or most UN member-states.
- Are more than simply a sub-group of an existing nation.[36]

These last two categories raise the greatest potential problems, as regional cooperation now tends to encourage support for decolonisation struggles within local contexts (i.e. Vanuatu for West Papua, Algeria for Western Sahara, Cuba for Puerto Rico, etc.). As serious consideration of issues of 'internal colonialism' within existing empires begins to gain wider acknowledgement, as the work of Kly, Falk and others gain critical attention, the definitions of 'sub-groups' might also undergo significant shifts.[37]

The question of New Afrika within the US empire, for example, is already undergoing a period of greater intellectual examination.[38] In this apparently far-fetched case, which has nonetheless gained enough supporters to claim control of the mayor's office in the capital city of Jackson, Mississippi,[39] advocates of a "provisional government of the Republic of New Afrika" have set up land areas across the US southern 'black belt' regions of Alabama, Mississippi, New Orleans, Georgia and South Carolina where representatives call for a referendum of citizenship separate from the US.[40] As of 2020, however, the basic premise set forth by the general criteria of 'stateless nations' seems most useful for current investigation.

Strategy, Tactics and the Developing Struggle for Sovereignty in Western Sahara

On the morning of 26 February 2018, in the refugee camps on the far western border of Algeria and Morocco that most Sahrawi displaced people call home, there was a certain sense of foreboding: a nasty sirocco, or sandstorm, was apparently on its way. Still, there was also an anxious anticipation, as an historic resistance action was about to take place: on the eve of the 42nd declaration of a still-unrecognised Sahrawi Arab Democratic Republic, and after 136 years of Spanish colonialism and Moroccan occupation, people from all walks and areas of Western Saharan life were about to assert themselves as a united people by voting in a symbolic but highly representative referendum for full independence as a nation. The people of Western Sahara were not waiting for colonialists, neo-colonialists, or an unresponsive global community to grant them what they are in the business of building for themselves.[41]

One should not have to be a human rights expert, a lawyer specialising in international border policy, or a modern-day pan-Africanist to know that colonialism has long been declared a crime against humanity. However, more than 70 years after the UN founding documents, which allude to this principle, only a small handful of concerned people outside of the Sahara region of north-west Africa seem to concern themselves with or even know about the plight of this colonised North African nation. The dramatic non-violent action and the accompanying 'Sahara Rise' conference at the end of February 2018 brought about the beginnings of a shift in the Sahrawi freedom movement, which hopes to extend knowledge of this new phase of struggle well beyond the region.[42]

The hundreds who gathered were a tiny cross-section from dozens of affiliated Sahrawi organisations, communities and geographic areas. Groups of women adorned in traditional dress sang, shouted and waved the national flag with the word 'liberty' written across it in Arabic and Catalan. Lines of people signed in, were handed a voting card, and cast their ballot for a free, independent and united Western Sahara. The action was symbolic and simple, but clearly deeply emotional for all those involved. The referendum results were also clear; the international legal and humanitarian consensus is evident.

In the middle of the desert west of Algeria lie three interrelated yet distinct territories. Western Sahara itself, recognised by the UN since 1963 as a non-self-governing territory, is split in two. Most of it is occupied by Morocco, which has taken total control of its land and natural resources. "The rich Sahrawi phosphate reserves were essentially stolen by the Moroccans," says noted legal scholar Magdalene Moonsamy, a former South African member of parliament close to the Sahrawi movement.[43] Moonsamy, an attendee of Sahara Rise, also reported that South Africa's High Court made a significant international judicial ruling on 23 February 2018, namely that the valuable minerals now mined by international corporations "have never belonged to Morocco, and are owned by the Sahrawi Arab Democratic Republic".[44] Morocco's exploitation of Western Sahara represents one of the last – and geographically the largest – direct examples of colonialism left in the world.

The second geographic area, which is part of Sahrawi territory, is a liberated zone, long governed by the Sahwari liberation movement known as the Polisario Front. Polisario has controlled this rural region since 1975 when Morocco gained military control over all but this section of Sahrawi national land. The liberated zone is inhabited largely by traditionally nomadic people, who join with Polisario combat units to protect the small communities that have developed close to the waterways, which serve as a partial political oasis in the desert.

Finally, outside of Western Saharan territory, on the western tip of the Algerian border (which disputedly belongs to Morocco), is a series of six huge refugee villages, potentially housing more than 100,000 Sahrawi people who have been forced off their land. In a stable and supportive relationship between Polisario and Algeria, these lands are run by a Sahrawi government structure in exile – the perfect place to hold a large coming-together of those living under the occupation, those spread out in the diaspora, those living in the camps themselves, plus a few international solidarity workers. Perhaps the most historic aspect of the 2018 resistance referendum was the coming together of all these groups in a united, national display.

NOVA, a youth movement committed to non-violence made up of Sahrawi activists across these borders, has emerged as a major force of change throughout the region.[45] "Our strategy is to continue the peaceful struggle, which began at the very beginning of colonialism and continues right up to today," stated Maglaha Hamma, president of NOVA, at the opening session of the Sahara Rise conference,[46] which took place in the refugee village of Smara from 25 to 27 February 2018.

The conference included Polisario leadership and a broad cross-section of Sahrawi civil society, and focused on building coordination of a global work plan of civil resistance. Brahim Dahane, a former political prisoner still living in Moroccan-held territory and representing Sahrawis under occupation, asserted that "one of the greatest victories of peaceful resistance has been our ability to speak as one people, empowered to build bridges across borders".

Mohamed Elouali Akeik, the Polisario Minister for the Occupied Territories and the Diaspora, echoed that perspective, emphasising that the essential goal of the resistance is to "regain the rights of all of our identity as a people". Noting that resistance was growing significantly every day, Akeik said that "we are all prisoners so long as there are any prisoners", and added that all those concerned with human rights must "oppose the legitimacy of Morocco's occupation by all peaceful means".[47]

It is noteworthy that all sectors of Western Saharan society make little distinction between the significance of the armed actions of the past and the embracing of radical non-violence today. There are no significant divisions between peoples and groups based on these different approaches and ideological strains. As one local Smara activist put it: "We started with armed resistance and have now come to peaceful resistance. We have a huge heritage of resistance."

That resistance will surely continue to take many forms and has already included numerous acts of creative civil disobedience. Elder organiser Deida Uld El Yazid, known as the Sheikh of the Intifada for his participation in countless sit-ins, protests and meetings, was one of the first to pull together the 30,000-person Gdeim Izik encampment of 2010, taking back a small part of the land that had long been Sahrawi. A new generation, dynamically committed to building across pan-Arab and pan-African lines, had already taken the lead by the time of El Yazid's death in January 2018.

Abdeslam Omar Lahsen, coordinator of the Sahara Rise action and conference, is one such leader. He was also a co-founder of the Pan-African Nonviolence and Peacebuilding Network in 2014, which shares best practices and support to its affiliates in 35 countries from every region of the continent.[48] At Sahara Rise, the spirit of solidarity with the ideals of peaceful change and Sahrawi independence was evident, especially from neighbouring Tunisia, which was represented in part by the 2015 Nobel Peace laureate organisations whose fundamental principles include dialogue and coalition-building. Tunisian organiser Ines Tlili, who works with the International Institute for Nonviolent Action (NOVACT), put it this way in an interview with this author: "One of the main advantages of nonviolent resistance is that it opens the door for the participation of everyone."[49]

Well into the night, with fears of a worse storm in the days to come, the Sahrawi activists discussed strategies and tactics. These included potential plans for a major boycott and divestment effort spotlighting the Moroccan occupation; for human rights campaigns focused on the repression and political imprisonment faced by many of their human rights defenders; and for increased work around the protection of natural resources. Through it all, the sentiments expressed by National Union of Sahrawi Women leader Fatma Mehdi summed up the mood and understanding: "Organisation is a crucial factor in resistance."[50]

Fighting Françafrique and for Ambazonian Freedom

The central African country of Cameroon, whose tourist slogan for years was "all of Africa in one country", presents itself as a unifier of diverse environments, languages and cultures in this nation located in the centre-west of the continent.[51] Recent headlines out of Cameroon, however, suggest the worst of conflict, corruption and colonialism, relating primarily to the country's intensifying repression against the English-speaking minority in the region of Ambazonia, little-known even to Africanists and anti-colonial academics from the global north. Despite the efforts of Ambazonian scholars based throughout the diaspora, and a trickle of not-always-helpful information from Amnesty International, Human Rights Watch and the British Broadcasting Corporation (BBC), the escalation of military violence since 2018, and especially a new 'scorched earth' burning of entire villages and escalating massacres of civilians since May 2019, has gone largely unchecked.[52]

The sparks of the contemporary crisis began on the evening of 11 July 2018, when five students were separated during a round-up by government military forces at the University Centre in the town of Bambili, allegedly for not having identification cards. Bambili is a university town in the north of Ambazonian territory. Though the BBC reported on the incident,[53] it did not make the connection to a pattern of attacks on Ambazonian students, activists and community leaders, which had worsened over the previous year. Three days later, 10 more unarmed Ambazonians and one Ghanaian pastor, who was working with them, were killed in the town of Batibo.

Though this news may never have surfaced if not for the connection to clergy in Ghana, organisations such as the Central African Human Rights Defenders Network[54] began to analyse, document and report on these incidents. Several pan-African groups, including affiliates of the prominent Network of African National Human Rights Institutions (which share a collegial relationship with the Pan African Nonviolence and Peacebuilding Network),[55] raised growing concerns about violence, instigated by the government and perpetrated by the military in the area, which makes up the southern border of Cameroon and Nigeria.

Historically, non-violence has been the overriding and committed strategy and philosophy of choice among the Ambazonian leadership and civil society, with the decades-long freedom slogan focused on the logic of winning Ambazonia freedom by "the force of argument not the argument of force". In 1961, the UN Trust Territory of Southern Cameroons voted for full independence from colonial Great Britain, and neighbouring Francophone Cameroon quickly incorporated the territory into its own 'United Republic' of Cameroon. Since that time, a mass, unarmed civil resistance movement has declared its desire for full independence, given its distinct languages (English and Indigenous African), culture, history and geographic base. In 1984, when Cameroon President Paul Biya removed the 'United' from the official name of the country, an even more intense crisis ensued. "All this time, however, from the 1960s until 2017," noted Eben Egbe, US facilitator of the Ambazonia Prisoners of Conscience Support Network, "barely a single stone was thrown as part of our resistance. Armed resistance was never a tactic we engaged in."[56]

Following a series of lawyer-led uprisings, which began on 1 October 2016, escalating non-violent civil resistance and a massive general strike in September 2017, which was met with gunfire from Cameroon government helicopter gunships, some Ambazonians did initiate an armed struggle, declaring independence and setting up a government in exile.[57] Cooperation between the governments of Nigeria and Cameroon has played a negative role in the aspirations of

Neocolonial/Colonial Extremes

Ambazonians, as Nigeria handed over some who were taking refuge there, and who now make up a growing political-prisoner population in Cameroon.

Nigeria's inability to resolve its 'Boko Haram problem' – the Islamist fundamentalist military movement with close ties to Iraq – also plays a role. Nigeria can push Boko Haram forces across the border into Cameroon, and Cameroon in turn attacks both Boko Haram military units and Ambazonian independence activists as if they represented the same 'nuisance' to the common people. It is the ordinary civilian, however, who is most caught up between governments, militaries and borders.[58] A horrifying July 2019 video of Cameroon soldiers murdering two women, a young child and a baby, apparently because their families allegedly had ties to Boko Haram, went viral and gained the condemnation and temporary attention of Amnesty International and much of the international human rights community. In an eerie flashback to words uttered 50 years ago in Vietnam at the My Lai massacre, one soldier can be heard asking his commanding officer: "Are we going to kill the children too?"[59]

Beyond Boko Haram and the realpolitik manoeuvres between Cameroon and Nigeria, the regional Nigerian authorities in charge of the Cross River State, which borders most of Ambazonian territory, have been fairly welcoming and somewhat supportive of the streams of refugees who have entered their territory over the past two years. Flying into Calabar, the capital of Cross River State, one can sometimes see women and men in bright purple shirts: the design of Mawuh Global Solutions, a Canadian-based Nigerian non-governmental organisation, which helps coordinate aid for the refugees and displaced people pouring over from the east. The national, regional and local leaders of Mawuh, it is important to note, are not in fact Nigerian: they are all from Ambazonia, leading efforts in their newly adopted country that can only be categorised as self-help. Mawuh coordinates skills-based training in dozens of areas, as well as looking after housing, healthcare and education efforts.[60]

Though the Nigerian government is generally tolerant of these efforts, there are some who stand out as exemplary solidarity chiefs. The Nigerian presidency has developed a National Commission for Refugees, Migrants and Internally Displaced Persons. Akintunde R Oyasanya, as zonal coordinator for south-south relations, serves as an informal and highly dedicated ambassador between the people of Cross

River and the Ambazonians in a world of confused and contested borders.

The Ambazonian spokespeople living in Calabar and Cross River are clear: their stay as exiles in Nigeria will be neither permanent nor long. Just as they situate in their new locations, they continue to develop plans to go back to their homeland. The youthful and dynamic Mawuh director, Dr Sama Sylveinus, puts it this way: "We will use our time here productively, building capacity and empowerment among the people. But we are always planning to return to our sovereign home, preparing for the long haul. After all, when you give people fish, they will eat for one day. But when you teach people how to fish, they will be set for life."[61]

Reports from within the occupied territory itself have been thwarted by clampdowns from the Cameroon government which, as of 2020, continues to prevent independent fact-finding missions, even from the United Nations Human Rights Council (UNHRC). Significantly and tragically, even Amnesty International – widely seen as the unquestioned expert on human rights in the region – has been slow and significantly misguided in reporting the facts of events in the region. An incredibly detailed and well-documented critique of the June 2018 Amnesty International report on 'Anglophone Cameroon' spotlights ways in which the respected organisation has misunderstood and distorted the reality of Ambazonian life and struggle.[62] The popular refrain that there 'is violence on both sides' not only gives too much emphasis to the very limited armed struggle, dismissing decades of previous history, but also ignores the fact that the past two years have seen a sharp increase in the breadth and scope of non-violent civic engagement on the part of Ambazonians, both in the territory and in the diaspora. An entire network of home-front media producers has congealed around a Southern Cameroons TV project,[63] and dozens of diaspora organisations have formed and successfully pressed for attention from local and national politicians. The Southern Cameroons Congress of the People was also formed as a political party, and a veritable social media army has begun to link refugees, political prisoners and their supporters, home-front organisers, and those living abroad.[64]

Independent internationalists might be especially confused by the 19 July 2018 briefings and commentaries issued by Human Rights Watch. On the one hand, its poignant report, titled 'These Killings Can Be Stopped', recounts in 59 detailed pages how the area "is slipping into a protracted human rights crisis in the largely Anglophone north-west and south-west regions that border Nigeria".[65] It documents how the Cameroon government has responded to demonstrations, legal challenges and unarmed protests with "heavy clampdowns", "repression and arrest" and "abuse", which likely caused a radicalisation on the part of the Ambazonian freedom movement.

On the other hand, in Human Rights Watch's summary press release sent out the same day, titled 'Cameroon: Killings, Destruction in Anglophone Regions', the organisation misleadingly and inaccurately asserts that "in response to protests and violence by armed separatists, government forces have killed civilians, used excessive force against demonstrators, tortured and mistreated suspected separatists and detainees, and burned hundreds of homes in several villages".[66] Want to find evidence that the Human Rights Watch summary press release is inaccurate? It can be found by carefully reading the Human Rights Watch full report! This poor attempt to be 'even-handed' sadly dilutes Human Rights Watch's basic good point: these killings *can and must* be stopped by support for justice-seeking, non-violent campaigners and a condemnation of government-based military violence and oppression.

The crisis in Ambazonia, like so many anti-colonial crises that seem to be escalating in the age of neocolonialism, cannot easily be resolved, especially by traditional military or diplomatic means. As grassroots women's and social groups inside the country, organised refugees on the border in Nigeria, and supporters or allies in the diaspora continue to put pressure on the colonial regime, unarmed civil resistance seems to be the main hope for lasting change. However, change cannot take place without clear, pro-justice, international attention and support, which so far have been egregiously lacking.

Despite the lack of widespread knowledge or recognition, Ambazonia most surely exists – with a defined land mass, a distinctive and long history and culture, and, most especially, a visionary and dedicated people. Though one would be hard-pressed to find it on any map, or even in most accounts of modern Africa or topical prose extolling peaceful change, it is a centre point of contemporary strategic movements fighting against 21st century colonialism.

Towards a Decolonising Resistance and a Congress of Occupied Peoples

Between the extremes of violence perpetrated by local bandits out for personal profit and power, and the vastly greater but much more cloaked and invisible structural violence of continuing colonialism often enforced via neocolonial regimes, the struggles of Ambazonia and Western Sahara stand out. On the continent of Africa in particular, these movements spotlight the ways in which direct colonialism continues to haunt the process of freedom, which, Tanzania's Julius Nyerere liked to remind people, was little more than "flag independence".[67] In the case of France, through its extensive Françafrique control over currencies, manufacturing, natural resources, arms and the military, as well as cultural-political norms, we see Cameroon as a regional power broker, part of a network of neocolonial states barely attempting to meet the basic needs of their people.[68] For Morocco, the myths of pan-Arab liberalism and Muslim solidarity are laid bare in its continued occupation of Western Sahara – but both its isolation in the Maghreb and recent debates regarding its readmission into the African Union show that the spaces for struggle and solidarity are still wide open.[69]

Taking account of the histories, criteria and current realities faced by those on the frontlines, it might be both appropriate and strategic that a network or congress of occupied peoples in struggle be formed, to share common concerns and strengths, setbacks and lessons learned, support mechanisms – and occasionally coordinated efforts among those still facing direct colonialism. In July 2019, in Bogotá, Colombia, the beginnings of such a grouping took place in meetings that included leaders from Ambazonia, Palestine, Puerto Rico, West Papua and Western Sahara. Solidarity/support people from Australia, Haiti, Israel, South Sudan and the US also took part. This group agreed that criteria for inclusion would remain open to further discussion, and that, in general, there would be three or four categories of involvement. Those most affected, living under military occupation or direct colonialism, would make up the core leadership of the network, including – in addition to those peoples mentioned – the struggles of Kashmir, Kurdistan/Rojava and Tibet. Those working in direct solidarity would be welcome, as would those who have experienced and recently come out of a decolonising process (such as representatives of the movements of South Sudan and East Timor). Finally, those working for conditions of autonomy, sovereignty or greater human rights (without necessarily struggling for full independence as defined by member-state status at the UN) would also be given space. In this final category, First Nation/indigenous peoples, Maroon societies and other unrepresented peoples may be included.[70]

The common principles and experiences evident in *all* the peoples already represented in the occupied peoples' group are as follows:

1. Each is working for self-determined, decolonised political status, the freedom to pursue economic, social and cultural development, and a withdrawal of outside occupying armed forces, which will bring about substantial demilitarisation to the affected locales.
2. Each has a decades-long history of significant civil resistance, with substantial armed and unarmed components, and with contemporary leaders willing to discuss strategies and tactics, including non-violent direct action.
3. Each has mass-based organisations and/or mobilisations that easily affect large numbers and/or extensive majorities of their peoples, and which have worked steadfastly for an end to continued colonialism/occupation.

How, then, to expand and understand these concepts such that academics and human rights advocates alike recognise the urgent tasks ahead?

First, it will be important for the larger human rights, pro-democracy and peace communities to more sharply acknowledge the ways in which direct colonialism still (and neocolonialism more than ever) causes terror and violence throughout the modern world. The construct that colonialism is a crime against humanity has long been held – first used to describe Leopold's stranglehold over the people and land of the Congo – but is still not enshrined in contemporary international human rights law. Furthermore, the fact of still-existing direct colonialism, as laid out in this chapter and typified by Western Sahara and Ambazonia, is neither widely understood nor collectively addressed within global human rights or solidarity institutions. As noted, even the UN Decolonisation Committee has, at best, an uneven record concerning still-colonised peoples.

Second, both the unique and common features of the few still-existing direct colonies need to be more rigorously examined and discussed outside of their own particular regions, and their freedom struggles more intensively supported. It is no coincidence that both the Western Saharan and Ambazonian resistance movements of the past few years have struggled to define strategies and tactics that include massive 'people's power': unarmed civil resistance and non-violent mass mobilisation. They have also addressed issues of armed struggle, with even the military wing of Western Sahara's Polisario Front carefully and critically reviewing how effective military means might be at this juncture. Ambazonia's young militants, while reintroducing minor armed defence into their freedom struggle, suggest that no strict tactic is off limits, even while unarmed resistance appears a current preferred form. There is a clear need for greater, more fluid and truly safe global spaces for occupied peoples to share and collectively strategise, along with dedicated academic and activist solidarity workers.

Third, the deep connections between land, climate, cultural survival, personal and political health, economic equity and human rights – and the everyday resistance activities so often required to maintain them – need to be more sharply articulated in both academic and community activist circles. In this instance, indigenous peoples, both among still-colonised peoples and among those living in states of semi-autonomy, contested or otherwise, may take the lead in understanding the land-health-freedom connection. As Marshall described in her pioneering study of Hawai'ian sovereignty struggles:

"At the turn of the twentieth century, [a] deeper meaning of decolonisation was occurring at the intimate level of the body and soul and collectively at the level of community…Native Hawai'ians in the late twentieth century grasped the concept that decolonisation was based upon healing, and they revived ways of understanding health and disease that had been outlawed and suppressed by colonial rule. Most significantly, they understood that decolonizing and healing meant recovering historical and ancestral memory and reasserting the primacy of mana, love, and dependence between humans, the environment, and the divine. But the assertion of ancestral land historical memory in Hawai'i was not simply about understanding the past, it was about creating the means for a different, decolonised future."[71]

Finally, as both Sahrawian and Ambazonian struggles suggest, a new discourse around the praxis of ideology, strategy, tactics and civil society development is long overdue. International relations and the study thereof are stuck in largely rhetorical and vaguely ineffective cycles of their own construct. If effective reforms are to be developed using innovative methods of conflict resolution, mediation and negotiation, non-violent communication, and related forms of social progress, this impasse needs to be urgently approached through an interdisciplinary approach to contemporary research. Descriptions of modern civil society and government – which lack the nuanced, dialectic and multi-faceted nature of our complex times, presenting tired and incomplete accounts of falsely dichotomised popular movements – not only fail to explain important global phenomena; they hinder critical engagement with the world, perhaps satisfying the fundamental intent of such flat and unimaginative scholarship: upholding and bolstering the status quo. The point, as was well noted almost two centuries ago, is not merely to accurately interpret the world, but indeed also to change it.

Select Bibliography

Aharone, E. (2016). *The Sovereign Psyche: Systems of Chattel Freedom Vs. Self-Authentic Freedom.* 1st edition. Bloomington: AuthorHouse.

Ambazonia Prisoners of Conscience Project. (2018). An Open Letter to Amnesty International: 'A Turn for the Worse'. Available from: https://www.ambazoniapocs.net/node/12 [accessed 22 January 2020].

Ambazonia Prisoners of Conscience Support Network. (2018). #Cameroon Soldiers Murdering in Cold Blood. Twitter. Available from: https://twitter.com/apocsnet/status/1018086829696933888 [accessed 29 January 2020].

Amin, S., Arrighi, G., Frank, A.G. & Wallerstein, I. (1990). *Transforming the Revolution: Social Movements and the World-System.* 1st edition. New York: Monthly Review Press.

BBC News Africa. (2018). BBC Radio 1. 13 July, 22:00. Available from: https://drive.google.com/file/d/15jOaYMlARJMBVKezfYld62LosCf6zlKX/view [accessed 5 April 2020].

Bond, P. & Garcia, A. (eds.). (2015). *BRICS: An Anticapitalist Critique.* 1st edition. Chicago: Haymarket Books.

Bosco, D. (2009). *Five to Rule Them All: The UN Security Council and the Making of the Modern World.* 1st edition. Oxford: Oxford University Press.

Bronner, E. & Hauser, C. (2012). UN Assembly, in Blow to US, Elevates Status of Palestine. *The New York Times*, 15 November.

Central African Human Rights Defenders Network. (2019). REDHAC Statement to the 64th ordinary session of the African Commission on Human and Peoples' Rights. Available from: https://africandefenders.org/achpr64-statement-by-the-central-african-human-rights-defenders-network/ [accessed 26 January 2020].

Dudouet, V. (2009). *From War to Politics: Resistance/Liberation Movements in Transition.* Berlin: Bergof Research Center for Constructive Conflict Management.

Egbe, E. (2019). Interview with APoCSN founder Eben Egbe by Matt Meyer. 1 September.

Egbe, E. & Dalton, A. (2019). History & Context: The Ambazonia Crisis and Africa's

Unending Nightmare of Francafrique. Available from: https://www.ambazoniapocs.net/node/16 [accessed 29 January 2020].

Flint, J. (1983). Planned Decolonization and its Failure in British Africa. *African Affairs*, 82(328), pp. 389-411.

Ghazoul, F. (2007). *Edward Said and Critical Decolonization*. Revised edition. Cairo: The American University in Cairo Press.

Global Initiative to End Cameroons Colonial Conflict. (2019). Gather the Facts on the Ground to Pave the Way for Peace. Available from: https://globalinitiative3c.org/ [accessed 29 January 2020].

Gold, P. (1994). *A Stone in Spain's Shoe: The Search for a Solution to the Problem of Gibraltar*. 1st edition. Liverpool: Liverpool University Press.

Guttenplan, D.D. (2017). Is This the Most Radical Mayor in America? Chokwe Antar Lumumba has an audacious plan to make Jackson, Mississippi, the 'most radical city on the planet'. Available from: https://www.thenation.com/article/archive/is-this-the-most-radical-mayor-in-america/ [accessed 22 March 2020].

Human Rights Watch. (2018). Cameroon: Killings, Destruction in Anglophone Regions. Available from: https://www.hrw.org/news/2018/07/19/cameroon-killings-destruction-anglophone-regions# [accessed 29 January 2020].

International Justice Resource Center. (2017). Following Three Decades of Isolation, Morocco Rejoins African Union. Available from: https://ijrcenter.org/2017/02/06/following-three-decades-of-isolation-morocco-rejoins-african-union/ [accessed 29 January 2020].

International Peace Research Association. (2019). Symposium on Occupied Peoples. International Peace Research Association in conjunction with IFOR, SweFOR and SERPAJ. Bogota, International Peace Research Association.

Khalidi, R. (2020). *The Hundred Years' War on Palestine: A History of Settler Colonialism and Resistance 1917-2017*. 1st edition. New York: Metropolitan Books.

Kly, Y.N. & Kly, D. (2012). *The Right to Self Determination: Collected Papers and Proceedings of the First International Conference on the Right to Self Determination and the United States*. 1st edition. Atlanta: Clarity Press.

Lubin, A. (2014). *Geographies of Liberation: The Making of an Afro-Arab Political Imaginary*. 1st edition. Chapel Hill: University of North Carolina Press.

Maass, G. (2016). A Pearl in the Desert: The Group NOVA in Western Sahara. Stockholm: NOVA, AFAPREDESA and SweFOR. Available from: https://krf.live.afonso.se/wp-content/uploads/2019/04/External-evaluation-NOVA-2016.pdf [accessed 20 January 2020].

Marshall, W. (2011). *Potent Mana: Lessons in Power and Healing*. 1st edition. Albany: State University of New York Press.

Mawuh Global Solutions. (2019). Providing Hope for the Under-privileged. Available from: https://www.mawuhsolutions.org/ [accessed 29 January 2020].

Mbaku, J.M. & Takougang, J. (2003). *The Leadership Challenge in Africa: Cameroon Under Paul Biya*. 1st edition. Trenton: Africa World Press.

Mbulu, M. (2019). *America in Black: From Africa to New Afrika*. 1st edition. Jackson: Asset Books.

Memmi, A. (1965). *The Colonizer and the Colonized*. 1st English edition. New York: Beacon.

Meyer, M. (2008). *Let Freedom Ring: A Collection of Documents from the Movements to Free U.S. Political Prisoners*. 1st edition. Montreal: Kersplebedeb.

Meyer, M. (2012). New Pan-African Nonviolence Network Formed. Available from: https://wagingnonviolence.org/2012/08/new-pan-african-nonviolence-network-formed/ [accessed 20 January 2020].

Meyer, M. (2018a). Violence and Nonviolence Intensify in Ambazonia. Peacenews. Available from: http://peacenews.org/2018/07/22/violence-and-nonviolence-intensify-in-ambazonia-for/ [accessed 22 January 2020].

Meyer, M. (2018b). Western Sahara Calls for Independence in Historic Symbolic Referendum. Available from: https://wagingnonviolence.org/2018/03/western-sahara-independence-referendum/ [accessed 20 January 2020].

Meyer, M. (2019). Moving in the Direction of Freedom: En route to Ambazonia. Available from: https://www.forusa.org/2019/04/10/moving-in-the-direction-of-freedom-en-route-to-ambazonia/ [accessed 29 January 2020].

Mills, G., Hartley, R. & Nwokolo, M. (2019). Somaliland: New Ways of Doing Things in a Rough Neighborhood. *Daily Maverick*, 12 September. Available from: https://www.dailymaverick.co.za/article/2019-09-12-somaliland-new-ways-of-doing-things-in-a-rough-neighbourhood/ [accessed 23 January 2020].

Minahan, J. (2016). *Encyclopedia of Stateless Nations: Ethnic and National Groups Around the World*. 2nd edition. Westport: Greenwood.

Moonsamy, M. (2018). Interview by Matt Meyer for Waging Nonviolence. 26 February. Available from: https://wagingnonviolence.org/2018/03/western-sahara-independence-referendum/ [accessed 20 January 2020].

Moore, C. (2014). Cable Network News Travel: 'All Africa in One Country': Cameroon Wants its Place on the Tourist Map. Available from: https://www.cnn.com/travel/article/all-africa-one-country-cameroon/index.html [accessed 24 January 2020].

Network of African Human Rights Institutions. (2018). NAHRI Our History and Constitution. Available from: https://www.nanhri.org/our-history/ [accessed 26 January 2020].

Nkrumah, K. (1973). *Neo-colonialism: The Last Stage of Imperialism*. 2nd edition. New York: International Publishers.

Obadele, I. (1984). *Free the land!: The true story of the trials of the RNA-11 in Mississippi and the continuing struggle to establish an independent Black nation in five states of the Deep South*. 1st edition. Detroit: House of Songhay.

Pedneault, J. & Human Rights Watch. (2019). These Killings Can Be Stopped: Abuses by Government and Separatist Groups in Cameroon's Anglophone Regions. Available from: https://www.hrw.org/report/2018/07/19/these-killings-can-be-stopped/abuses-government-and-separatist-groups-cameroons [accessed 29 January 2020].

Potapkina, V. (2020). *Nation Building in Contested States: Comparative Insights from Kosovo, Transnistria, and Northern Cyprus*. 1st edition. Stuttgart: Ibidem Press.

Quane, H. (1998). The United Nations and the Evolving Right to Self-Determination. *The International and Comparative Law Quarterly*, 47(3), pp. 537-572.

Radio New Zealand News. (2019). Vanuatu PM calls for UN action on West Papua. Available from: https://www.rnz.co.nz/international/pacific-news/399952/vanuatu-pm-calls-for-un-action-on-west-papua [accessed 14 February 2020].

Sahara Rise. (2018). Sahara Rise International Conference for Civil Resistance. Available from: https://sahararise.org/en/sahara-rise-manifest/ [accessed 20 January 2020].

Sari, U.C. (2019). Daily Sabah: Ethiopia's Dilemma: A Peace Award But No Peace. Available from: https://www.dailysabah.com/op-ed/2019/11/13/ethiopias-dilemma-a-peace-award-but-no-peace [accessed 23 January 2020].

Shah, F. (2013). *Of Occupation and Resistance: Writings from Kashmir*. 1st edition. Delhi: Westland and Tranquebar Press.

Southern Cameroons Broadcasting Corporation. (2018). About Us: SCBC-TV Background. Available from: https://scbctv.com/about-us/ [accessed 29 January 2020].

Sutherland, B. & Meyer, M. (2000). *Guns and Gandhi in Africa: Pan African Insights on Armed Struggle, Nonviolence and Liberation*. 1st edition. Trenton: Africa World Press.

Tlili, I. (2018). Interview by Matt Meyer for Waging Nonviolence. 27 February. Available from: https://wagingnonviolence.org/2018/03/western-sahara-independence-referendum/ [accessed 20 January 2020].

Turtle, M. (2019). The World's Oldest Sovereign State: Visiting San Marino. Available from https://www.timetravelturtle.com/visiting-san-marino-oldest-country/ [accessed 23 January 2020].

United Nations. (2016). Special Committee on Decolonization Approves Text Calling upon United States Government to Expedite Self-Determination Process for Puerto Rico. GA/COL/3296. Available from: https://www.un.org/press/en/2016/gacol3296.doc.htm [accessed 29 February 2020].

United Nations Department of Public Information. (2019). The United Nations and Decolonization. Available from: https://www.un.org/dppa/decolonization/en/nsgt [accessed 15 February 2020].

Unrepresented Nations and Peoples Organization (UNPO). (2019a). About UNPO. Available from: https://unpo.org/section/2 [accessed 17 January 2020].

Unrepresented Nations and Peoples Organization (UNPO). (2019b). Unrepresented People of the USA. Geneva, UNPO Submission to the UN OHCHR, 36th Session.

Unrepresented Nations and Peoples Organization (UNPO). (2019c). Compromised Space: Bullying and Blocking at the UN Human Rights Mechanisms. Oxford: UNPO and the University of Oxford.

Western Sahara Resource Watch. (2018). SA Court confirms: Morocco has no ownership over Saharawi phosphates. Available from: https://www.wsrw.org/a249x4098 [accessed 20 January 2020].

Wilmot, P. (2018). Ambazonians Struggle for Independence from Cameroon Amid Military Takeover. Available from: https://wagingnonviolence.org/2018/06/ambazonians-struggle-independence-cameroon-military-takeover/ [accessed 20 January 2020].

Xing, L. (2014). *The BRICS and Beyond: The International Political Economy of the Emergence of a New World Order*. 1st edition. Surrey: Ashgate Publishing Limited.

Yacoubi, Y. (2007). Edward Said, Eqbal Ahmad, and Salman Rushdie: Resisting the Ambivalence of Postcolonial Theory. In Ghazoul, F. (ed.). *Edward Said and Cultural Criticism*. Cairo: University of Cairo Press, pp. 193-218.

Endnotes

1. Dudouet, 2009.
2. Amin et al, 1990.
3. Ghazoul, 2007.
4. Marshall, 2011.
5. Flint, 1983.
6. Nkrumah, 1973.
7. Yacoubi, 2007.
8. Aharone, 2016.
9. Lubin, 2014.
10. United Nations Department of Public Information, 2019.
11. See, for example, Meyer (2008).
12. United Nations Department of Public Information, 2019.
13. Gold, 1994.
14. Bosco, 2009.
15. General Assembly of the United Nations, Transmission of Information under Article 73e of the Charter: https://www.un.org/en/ga/search/view_doc.asp?symbol=A/RES/66%28I%29&Lang=E&Area=RESOLUTION
16. General Assembly of the United Nations, Trust and Non-Self-Governing Territories (1945-2002): https://www.un.org/en/decolonization/nonselfgov.shtml
17. Quane, 1998.
18. United Nations, 2016.
19. Radio New Zealand News, 2019.
20. Memmi, 1965.
21. UNPO, 2019a.
22. UNPO, 2019b.
23. UNPO, 2019c.
24. Bond & Garcia, 2015.
25. Xing, 2014.
26. See https://unpo.org/nations-peoples.
27. Bronner & Hauser, 2012:1.
28. Khalidi, 2020.
29. Shah, 2013.
30. Meyer, 2018a.
31. Potapkina, 2020.
32. Turtle, 2019.
33. Mills et al, 2019.
34. Sari, 2019.
35. Minahan, 2016.
36. Ibid.
37. See Kly & Kly (2012).
38. Mbulu, 2019.
39. Guttenplan, 2017.
40. Obadele, 1984.
41. Meyer, 2018b.
42. Sahara Rise, 2018.
43. Moonsamy, 2018.
44. Western Sahara Resource Watch, 2018.
45. Maass, 2016.
46. Meyer, 2018b.
47. Ibid.
48. Meyer, 2012.
49. Tlili, 2018.
50. Meyer, 2018b.
51. Moore, 2014.
52. Ambazonia Prisoners of Conscience Project, 2018.
53. BBC News Africa, 2018.
54. Central African Human Rights Defenders Network, 2019.
55. Network of African Human Rights Institutions, 2018.
56. Egbe, 2019.
57. Wilmot, 2018.
58. Egbe & Dalton, 2019.
59. Ambazonia Prisoners of Conscience Support Network, 2018.
60. Mawuh Global Solutions, 2019.
61. Meyer, 2019.
62. Ambazonia Prisoners of Conscience Project, 2018.
63. Southern Cameroons Broadcasting Corporation, 2018.
64. Global Initiative to End Cameroons Colonial Conflict, 2019.
65. Pedneault & Human Rights Watch, 2019.
66. Human Rights Watch, 2018.
67. Sutherland & Meyer, 2000.
68. Mbaku & Takougang, 2003.
69. International Justice Resource Center, 2017.
70. International Peace Research Association, 2019.
71. Marshall, 2011.

CHAPTER 12

Fulani and Jihad: The Argument Against Simplistic Narratives in West Africa

Madeline Vellturo

Introduction

Islamist extremism is on the rise in West Africa, with violent extremist attacks doubling every year since 2015.[1] International terrorist organisations such as Al-Qaeda and Islamic State (IS) are teaming up with local fighters and jihadist leaders to control large swathes of territory in this fragile region. Many foreign-policy experts have noted in recent years that the epicentre of global terrorism is shifting from the Middle East to Africa, with West Africa and the Horn of Africa the most significant theatres[2] and the south-eastern corridor a rising threat.

In West Africa, the Fulani are a powerful and diverse collection of ethnically affiliated groups. Commonly associated with Islam and with the herding of livestock, Fulani communities have long been powerful players in the social and political lifeblood of West African societies. In addition, Fulani are commonly perceived to be strongly associated with the history of jihad in the region, both by academics and by local civil society.[3]

For many, evidence of strong ties between Fulani groups and jihad are well rooted in history. Fulani leaders, often from elite tribes and backgrounds, played significant roles in many of the jihadist revolutions that swept the region in the 18th and 19th centuries.[4] One of the most successful of these, Uthman Dan Fodio's jihad that established the Sokoto caliphate in what is now Nigeria, is commonly known as the Fulani Jihad.[5]

Today, many continue to highlight links between Fulani groups and terrorist organisations as evidence of an inherent connection between the two. Some argue that the Fulani are at higher risk of joining jihadist movements than other ethnic groups.⁶ In some cases, extremist groups themselves seem to be operating under this assumption and are using recruitment strategies that specifically target Fulani fighters.⁷ In some areas of the region, practitioners and experts report a growing narrative among civil society that Fulani are equivalent to extremism.⁸

Yet others opine how erroneous, and harmful, these assumptions are. False equivalencies between Fulani and jihad have led to security forces and vigilante militias targeting innocent civilians in their attempts to root out terrorists.⁹ This phenomenon has even exacerbated the terrorist threat, as extremists play on impunity for these attacks to recruit those who feel that they have been wrongfully targeted.

This chapter aims to set the record straight. It does not deny the important role that many Fulani groups played in the West African jihadist movements of the 18th and 19th centuries, nor does it ignore the role that many Fulani individuals currently play as leaders and fighters in modern-day terrorist organisations in the region. Instead, it places these observations in a broader historical and political context. It places past and present jihadist movements in the region in comparison with one another, and interrogates the roles that Fulani did and did not play in these movements. In doing so, it attempts to shed light on findings that may be useful in informing policy and efforts aimed at reducing violence in the region.

Who Are the Fulani?

The Fulani – also commonly referred to as the Fulbe or the Peuhl[10] – are an ethnically delineated grouping of peoples residing in many countries across West Africa. Fulani typically have several common characteristics, including that they share dialects from a common linguistic family (Fulfulde), are typically Muslim, and tend to be livestock herders or otherwise deal in the trading and rearing of livestock as a source of livelihood.[11] It is important to note, however, that many Muslims and many pastoralists in West Africa are not Fulani.

Historians and anthropologists believe that the Fulani emerged around the turn of the first millennium along the south-western fringes of the Sahara Desert. Fulfulde is a member of the Niger-Congo linguistic lineage, and the Fulani also show strong influences from outlier Berber peoples.[12] Estimates of their population size range from 5 million to 65 million,[13] spanning east to west from Senegal through Chad and into Sudan, and extending south as far as northern Côte d'Ivoire and Benin, across Nigeria and northern Cameroon, and into the Central African Republic and even northern Democratic Republic of Congo.[14]

Population estimates vary so greatly in part because there is little scholarly consensus regarding the definition and boundaries of the Fulani ethnicity. Experts debate whether the Fulani in fact constitute a single ethnic group or rather many distantly related sub-groups. Some scholars cite that members of Fulani groups espouse a common socio-ethnic identity with one another, despite their geographic and cultural diversity. Victor Azarya described the Fulani as "a large group of people, several millions in number, attributing themselves to the same collective identity".[15] Roger Blench argues that there is substantively greater unity among the Fulbe communities of west and central Africa than across pastoralist communities in East Africa.[16]

At the same time, Fulani groups' social and political structures and predominant economic activities vary greatly throughout the various states and territories they occupy. Katherine Homewood writes:

"[C]ontemporary Fulani, although identified by their common language, have thus come to comprise a broad array of economics, sub-ethnic groups and social forms, from the primarily agricultural or agropastoral Fulani of the Senegal Valley, to the mobile pastoral Wodaabe sub-clan of the Mbororo Fulani, to more settled, centralised, socially and politically differentiated Fulani livestock trading communities in Nigeria."[17]

Azarya notes that internal Fulani social structures create many divides among groups, including that "wealthier Fulbe are differentiated from poorer kinsmen, latecomers from earlier migrations, sedentary political office holders from religious specialists, etc."[18]

This intra-group diversity is so vast that some have argued that the divergence across various sub-groups that are called Fulani is greater than any common ethnic lineage or linguistic thread that bonds them. Some evidence the fact that the many dialects of Fulfulde are highly diverse, and that this linguistic diversity speaks to a broader socio-ethnic diversity.[19] Even within Fulani groups, their own definition of 'Fulaniness' can differ – Breedveld notes that higher-class Fulani tend to use a narrower definition of 'Fulani' than lower castes.[20]

Some have argued that 'Fulani' and other terms for them are driven by the need of outside communities to assign them a common identity. Burnham notes that "different stereotypes of Fulbe-ness are stressed by different groups under different circumstances".[21] Abu-Manga notes that "the only common element left among the Fulbe of Sudan is the term attributed to them, and even that is shared with other groups who migrated from West Africa".[22] However, he notes that it is precisely the external prescribing of the term 'Fulani' to these diverse groups that has allowed them to affiliate with a common, albeit externally defined, ethnic identity.

Thus, the Fulani present a problematic grey area for social scientists attempting to conduct ethno-centric studies, and for policymakers searching to draw parallels between Fulani behaviour and other ethnic groups. The Fulani seem to exist somewhere in between a cohesive and identifiable ethnic group, like the Hutus and Tutsis of Africa's Great Lakes region, and a broadly defined grouping of distantly related socio-linguistic peoples, like the broader Bantu-speaking peoples spread across east and southern Africa. This fuzzy picture has led people to make problematic assumptions and come to simplistic conclusions regarding the Fulani, assuming more cohesion and common identity across communities than perhaps exist.

Fulani and Jihad in Historical Context

Eric Hobsbawm described the late 18th and early 19th centuries as the 'age of revolution' across the Atlantic world.[23] While Haiti and the United States (US) fought vicious wars of independence in the Americas, social and industrial revolutions challenged existing monarchies and governments in western Europe. Less explored in historical study are the corresponding revolutions that took place during this period in West Africa, despite that West Africa is, and was, a key region in the Atlantic world. Across West Africa, during this 'age of revolution', states and empires rose and fell, many due to mass revolutionary movements by large swathes of West African civil society. Many of these revolutions took the form of Sufi jihadist movements.

The jihadist revolutions in West Africa first manifested at the very end of the 17th century in the Bundu plateau, now in western Senegal. Following the example of Nasir al-Din, a Berber jihadist in Mauritania, a Muslim cleric named Malik Sy waged jihad in 1690 to bring about Fuuta Bundu, an Islamic state in Senegambia. Between 1727 and 1728, Muslim leaders in the highlands region of what is now Guinea waged jihad and established the Imamate of Fuuta Jalon. This trend extended to northern Senegambia in 1775 with the establishment of the Fuuta Toro Imamate. In 1804, Islamic preacher Uthman Dan Fodio waged jihad in Nigeria and established the Sokoto caliphate. Between 1817 and 1818, Sheku Amadu broke away from Sokoto to found the Macina caliphate in what is now Mali. In 1860, Omar Tall established the Toucouleur empire, a jihadist state that endured until the end of the century. By 1835, "West Africa had come under the dominance of jihad regimes".[24]

Fulani leaders played key roles in many of these jihads.[25] The leaders of the jihadist revolutions that founded Fuuta Bundu, Fuuta Jalon, and Fuuta Toro – Malik Sy, Karamokho Alfa, and Sulayman Baal, respectively – are all identified by historians as ethnic Fulbe.[26] Uthman Dan Fodio, founder of the Sokoto caliphate, was also Fulani, and his Islamic movement has often been known among scholars as the 'Fulani Jihad' (although some scholars tout that Fodio also identified as Hausa).[27] Sheku Amadu, who founded the Macina empire, too, was ethnically Fulani,[28] as was Omar Tall, the founder of the Toucouleur empire, who came from the Fulbe-speaking Toucouleur ethnic group.[29]

Some of these leaders drew on their ethnic identities to recruit other Fulani fighters for their campaigns, and as a result these revolutions are often associated heavily with Fulani groups. Lovejoy writes that by the end of the 18th century, "jihad had become fully associated with the Fulbe", and that ethnic Fulani were "particularly influent" in West African jihadist movements.[30] This is confirmed for the Macina empire by Johnson, who writes that the Fulani were the "dominant people of the Macina theocracy",[31] and by Shillington, who writes that Sheku Amadu's jihad had "ardent support from Fulani pastoralists".[32] Philips writes that the majority of Dan Fodio's flagbearers were Fulani, and that most of the civil servants and councillors appointed in the Sokoto caliphate were also Fulani.[33] Lovejoy also notes that the term 'Fuuta' indicated a Fulani-led state, demonstrating the strength of the Fulani people in the jihadist movements of the region.[34]

However, the core driving forces of these jihadist movements were broader and more global than ethnic grievance. The social and economic upheavals of the transatlantic slave trade and other increased interaction between Europe, Africa and the Americas were major drivers of the spread of jihad in West Africa at this time.[35] The wealth that flooded into West Africa as a result of increased trade with Europe and the Americas, both of goods and of people, allowed new entrepreneurs and business people to flourish, disrupting the status quo.[36] As opportunities for trading cattle expanded, Fulani herdsmen and other pastoralist groups considerably improved their financial position, but this was not always reflected in their political or social capital under the ruling empires of the day.[37] This imbalance bred resentment and fed revolutionary jihadist ideologies.

Many jihadist movements at the time were also motivated by aspirations to reduce the number of Muslim Africans captured and sold into the transatlantic slave trade. Lovejoy notes that "the Muslim interior of West Africa was underrepresented in terms of the number of slaves who moved as part of the transatlantic migration", due in no small part to the efforts of jihadist states like Fuuta Jallon and others to protect practising Muslims from capture.[38] Philips writes that eventually the concern over the illegal enslavement of Muslims became the *casus belli* of Dan Fodio's jihad.[39]

Considering the broader social nature of the drivers, jihadist narratives were often based on a broader ideology than ethnic affiliation and loyalty. Lovejoy notes that the jihads of the day were not an ethnic phenomenon.[40] Waldman notes of Dan Fodio that ethnic sympathy played only a minor role in his articulation of grievances, and that "identity was not essential to the success of his movement".[41] Dan Fodio warned that "to believe that every Fulani is Muslim" was "false and an illusion".[42]

As a result of this broad narrative that transcended ethnic identity, not all fighters in these jihadist movements were Fulani. Several scholars highlight that the various jihadist movements throughout this period attracted fighters and supporters from all segments of the population, across a range of identities and ethnic backgrounds.[43] Hill notes that Dan Fodio was supported by Hausa peasants,[44] and Aremu points out that the lingua franca under the Sokoto caliphate was Hausa, not Fulfulde.[45] In 1789, non-Fulani Muslim Mahdi Fatta attempted to wage jihad in Moria, though his efforts were unsuccessful.[46] Philips writes "the history of Islam in West Africa is littered with the remains of minor

Islamic revolts...only the revolts which involved the Fulani to some extent were successful", implying that there were many Islamic movements that were not led by Fulani.[47]

Moreover, support for these jihads among Fulani populations was far from universal. Azarya notes that there were groups of Fulani who took little part in the jihads, or even opposed them, highlighting that these groups continued to live at the margins of the new caliphates and grew increasingly differentiated from the ruling Fulani sub-clans.[48] Waldman writes that a large number of Fulani did not rally to Dan Fodio's side, and that not even all Muslims agreed to fight with him, citing that Dan Fodio was "constantly forced to appeal for help from them and others".[49] Philips writes that the jihad was not a totally Fulani affair anywhere in Hausaland, noting that in one province, only six of the 12 Fulani clans supported the jihad.[50] Some Fulani spied against Dan Fodio for the neighbouring Ningi.[51]

Some jihadist leaders were antagonistic towards other Fulani leaders and communities. In Macina, when Amadu assessed that many Fulani chiefs were declaring loyalty out of self-interest rather than religious ideology, he "overthrew them one by one",[52] despite their shared ethnic affiliation. Johnson also notes that Amadu established his caliphate in part by driving out fellow Fulani leader Galadio.[53] Philips reports that Dan Fodio did not hesitate to attack Fulani with whom he disagreed.[54]

It is also important to point out the limitations of much of the literature available on the details of these jihadist movements. Much of the historical and anthropological study that catalogues the history of jihadist movements in West Africa was conducted about half a century ago in the 1960s and 1970s. More recent study would surely benefit our understanding of the historical context in which these jihads occurred, allowing for advances in historical and social scientific study to improve the quality of the analysis. Moreover, in some cases the reliability of the primary source material on which these accounts and studies are based, often collected through oral historical accounts, has been called into question. For example, Gomez challenges some of the foundational studies recounting the formation of Fuuta Bundu, highlighting that many of the interviewees are anonymous, and of those who are traceable, many originate from outside the borders of the empire in question. Gomez points out that oral history in the region has often been "designed to appeal more to the popular" audience than to historians.[55]

Once again, we are left with an unclear picture. There can be no doubt that Fulani leaders played significant roles in the majority of jihadist movements in the 18th and 19th centuries in West Africa, and that their followings likely included significant numbers of Fulani fighters and supporters. Yet drivers of these revolutions were complex and global, incorporating economic and political dynamics that extended well beyond ethnic grievances. Some scholars report that jihadist ideological narratives did not play particularly heavily on ethnicity, instead seeking to include non-Fulani individuals and groups in their calls for revolution. While many jihadist fighters were Fulani, many others were not, and some Fulani opposed these movements altogether.

Fulani and Terrorism in the 21st Century

The tradition of jihad has once again risen to prominence in some regions of West Africa in the 21st century. This phenomenon has been placed in a broader global context of growing Islamic extremism and the global War on Terror led by western states and supported by many others. At the same time, regional experts continue to highlight that many of the drivers of these movements are rooted in local dynamics and grievances.

Moreover, once again the Fulani have been placed front and centre in the narrative of contemporary West African Islamic extremism. Following a brief summary of the current terrorism landscape in West Africa, this section interrogates alleged links between modern jihadist movements and Fulani communities. It finds that, just as was true in the 18th and 19th centuries, links between the Fulani and terrorism in the 21st century are complex.

West Africa's Current Terrorism Landscape

Over the past decade, the growth of violent Islamic extremist movements in West Africa has accelerated at an alarming rate. The region has experienced the most rapid increase in militant Islamist group activity of any region in Africa in recent years, with extremist-group violence doubling every year since 2015.[56] This growth has not necessarily been consistent, and extremist groups have experienced victories and setbacks as they battle with state security forces and with local populations. However, the rise of Islamic extremist activity in West Africa in recent years has been significant, and threats posed by jihadist violence now permeate most facets of social, political and economic life in many countries in the region.

Contemporary West Africa is home to a complex constellation of jihadist movements, some of which have been homegrown and others imported from abroad. This landscape is fluid and constantly evolving, with groups frequently allying with one another and with other insurgencies when it is opportune to do so, and fracturing as a result of internal power struggles or external shocks. At the time of writing, there are three terrorist organisations of particular import operating in central and West Africa: Boko Haram, Islamic State in the Greater Sahara (ISGS) and Jama'at Nasr al-Islam wal Muslimin (JNIM).

Boko Haram (which has been loosely translated as 'western education is forbidden' in a mix of Arabic and Hausa) began as a homegrown jihadist movement in 2002 aimed at purifying Islam in northern Nigeria. In 2009, after the execution of Boko Haram's founder, Mohammed Yusuf, by Nigerian authorities, Abubakar Shekau took over as leader. Under Shekau's leadership, Boko Haram rose to international notoriety for its gruesome attacks and tactics, especially in the wake of the group's kidnapping of 276 schoolgirls from Chibok, Borno State, in 2014.

In 2015, Shekau pledged allegiance to the IS leader Abu Bakr al-Baghdadi and the group was given the new moniker 'Islamic State in West Africa Province' (ISWAP). A year later, the group fractured, with many senior leaders splitting off from Shekau and forming their own movement under the leadership of Mamman Nur and Abu Musab al-Barnawi. This faction was recognised by the IS leadership and became ISWAP, while Shekau's faction reassumed the group's original name, Jama'tu Ahlis Sunna Lida'awati wal-Jihad (JAS). In 2018, an internal dispute within the ISWAP faction led to the execution of Nur and the ascendance of Abu Abdallah al-Barnawi as leader of ISWAP. Thus, there are currently two distinct factions of Boko Haram operating independently from, and sometimes in competition with, one another.[57]

ISGS was formed in 2015 when leader Adnan Abu Walid al Sahrawi broke from an Al-Qaeda-affiliated terrorist group in northern Mali (Al-Mourabitoun, led by Belmokhtar) and pledged allegiance to IS. Sahrawi had been a jihadist fighter for many years, including a commander with Al-Qaeda in the Islamic Mahgreb (AQIM), and a leader in the founding of the Movement for Oneness and Jihad in West Africa (MUJAO) in October 2011.[58]

JNIM is a conglomerate of four of the most powerful jihadist organisations in the Sahel region of Africa: AQIM, Ansar Dine, Al-Mourabitoun, and Katiba Macina. In 2017, these groups created an alliance under the leadership of Ansar Dine leader Iyad Ag Ghali. Although it is not an operational entity, JNIM facilitates communications and coordination among its affiliated groups, mitigates infighting, and shields individual leaders from unwanted attention.[59] Although ISGS is not a part of JNIM, reportedly these two groups communicate regularly with one another and are not subject to the broader antagonism that exists between Al-Qaeda and IS in the Middle East.[60]

These major terrorist organisations and conglomerates operate across two distinct geographical theatres. JNIM and ISGS operate in the Sahel region, particularly in central Mali, Burkina Faso and western Niger. Boko Haram's two factions operate in the Lake Chad Basin region at the intersection of northeastern Nigeria, northern Cameroon, Chad and Niger. However, in recent years, the distance between these two theatres has narrowed, as jihadist movements in the Sahel expand their territory further south and west, and as the IS leadership has made attempts to connect ISGS and ISWAP activities.[61]

As was the case in the 18th and 19th centuries, current jihadist trends in West Africa are driven in large part by socio-economic dynamics. A Centre for Humanitarian Dialogue/United Nations Development Programme survey of perceptions in the Sahel region found that "77,5% of the respondents perceive radicalisation as being driven by socio-economic forces while only 14,8% see it as a religious phenomenon".[62] Estelle highlights that poor social and economic conditions in Burkina Faso have made populations vulnerable to jihadist efforts.[63] In Nigeria, Mahmood and Ani report that underdevelopment, unemployment and other socio-economic drivers are "chief among the factors enabling the rise of Boko Haram",[64] while Evans and Kelikume find that poverty, unemployment and inequality are among the strongest drivers of violence in the region, including the rise of Boko Haram.[65]

However, contemporary jihadist movements in West Africa differ from their

18th and 19th century counterparts in several important ways. For example, while most jihadist movements during the 'age of revolution' were waged under the Sufi tradition,[66] contemporary Islamic extremism in the region is overwhelmingly Salafi. Whereas Sufi jihad advocates an inclusive form of Islamic tradition, interpreting Islamic law in a holistic and at times flexible way, Salafi tradition advocates a stricter form of Islam, including a highly literal interpretation of Islamic text and puritanical approaches to enforcing Islamic practice.[67]

Another distinction is that there is more ethnic diversity across jihadist leaders in modern-day West Africa than there seems to have been during the 'age of revolution'. JAS leader Shekau and ISWAP leader Al-Barnawi are ethnic Kanuri. Sahrawi, leader of ISGS, comes from the Sahrawi ethnic group, a mixed Arab-Berber group in western Sahara and Morocco. Among the JNIM groups, Ghali is ethnically Tuareg, and AQIM's Abdelmalek Droukdel and Al-Mourabitoun's Belmokhtar are Arab fighters from Algeria. Katiba Macina's Amadou Koufa is the sole ethnic Fulani among the main modern jihadist leaders.

Yet the ethnic identity of leaders may not be as important in contemporary jihadist movements as it was in the 18th and 19th centuries. This is because, while current movements are often led by elites who came from wealthy and socially significant backgrounds, the ethos of these modern movements heavily focuses on non-elite fighters. Katiba Macina privileges non-elite pastoralists and calls for social change that will free herders from the yoke of the domination of elites.[68] Estelle writes of Ansarul Islam that "sermons focus on equality between the minority elites and the majority underclass...this narrative aims to mobilise lower classes and youth against traditional elites".[69]

This stands in contrast to the region's historical jihadist movements, where elites played a key role in the instigation and success of the movements.[70] For example, while 18th and 19th century jihads tended to be driven by more sedentary, educated and aristocratic Fulani sub-clans,[71] in recent movements nomadic communities are overrepresented among Fulani jihadist fighters, with settled and elite Fulani being more exposed to attacks and intimidation from jihadist elements.[72]

Interrogating Links between Fulani and Contemporary Terrorism
Contemporary analysts have noted the appearance of strong Fulani elements in

many modern West African jihadist movements. Benjaminsen and Ba report that Fulani have "joined jihadist groups in central Mali in larger numbers than any other ethnicity".[73] Nsaibia finds that Fulani desire to join terrorist groups as a method of self-protection against other ethnic militias that were supported by the government, which "likely enabled the growth of ISGS".[74] Hoije and Sangare report that it was the recruitment of Fulani by jihadist groups that prompted other ethnic groups like the Bambara and Dogon to set up their own militias in Mali.[75] Sangare notes that modern jihadist propaganda "finds a more 'natural' echo among the Fulani than other ethnic groups".[76]

Links between Fulani and modern-day jihadist movements appear to be more prevalent in the Sahelian theatre. JNIM affiliates Katiba Macina and Ansar Dine, as well as ISGS, have all been reported to recruit heavily from Fulani groups. Katiba Macina, led by Amadou Koufa, operates in the Mopti region of central Mali and reportedly draws on narratives of reviving the Macina caliphate, designing its outreach efforts around the discontent of Fulani communities.[77] Ansarul Islam – the Burkina Faso branch of Ansar Dine, which was led by Fulani preacher Ibrahim Malam Dicko until his death in May 2017 – mobilised the Fulani population around a sense of shared grievance, at times actively targeting non-Fulani groups with violence.[78] ISGS is also reported to heavily recruit from the Fulani community.[79] Moreover, some analysts highlight that these three groups have been primarily responsible for the growth of extremist violence in the region, including roughly two-thirds of the extremist attacks in the Sahel theatre from 2015 to 2019.[80] This could mean that Fulani-led groups are responsible for a disproportionately large amount of jihadist impact in current-day West Africa.

However, there is also evidence of Fulani populations that do not support these jihadist movements. Several writers note that groups such as Katiba Macina, Ansarul Islam and ISGS lack deep local support, and that supporters for these groups represent a "tiny fraction of the population",[81] even in regions with large Fulani populations.[82] In his analysis on Katiba Macina, Diallo writes that support for the group is "far from unanimous among the Fulani of central Mali".[83] Sangare says that in Nigeria, many Fulani militias remain autonomous from jihadist movements.[84] In some instances, jihadist groups have attacked or actively targeted Fulani communities.[85]

Furthermore, there are many regions in West Africa where Fulani are prominent minorities but where jihadist groups have not spread or manifested. Guinea – the only country where Fulani make up the largest ethnic minority at 38% of the population – is not affected by jihadism, and the Fulani there "are not and have not been particularly involved in violent conflicts".[86] In northern Ghana, Bukari et al assess that Fulani and non-Fulani exist as 'cultural neighbours' and cooperate more frequently than they conflict with one another.[87]

Moreover, there is also evidence of jihadist groups in West Africa catering to non-Fulani communities. Estelle says that Ansarul Islam has recruited non-Fulani individuals by appealing to them on the basis of class.[88] Crisis Group reports that ISWAP recruits heavily from the Kanuri and Buduma ethnic groups.[89] ISWAP has reportedly dug wells, distributed seeds and fertilisers to farmers, and revitalised farming and fishing markets.[90] Considering that Fulani are traditionally pastoralists, this practice could indicate that ISWAP is catering not only to Fulani but to a variety of constituents across a range of livelihoods and ethnic affinities. The fact that most jihadist propaganda is conducted in Arabic or Hausa,[91] not in Fulfulde, also indicates that the intended audience is broader than Fulani.

It is important to note, however, that not all recent allegations accusing the Fulani of being terrorists are tied to jihad. Some of the most common accusations come from Nigeria's Middle Belt region, which is outside the area of operation of Boko Haram or any of the region's other major jihadist organisations. In this region, centuries-old conflicts between sedentary farming communities and nomadic herders – typically Fulani – have escalated in recent years. Many Nigerian commentaries refer to Fulani in this region as 'Fulani terrorists' or otherwise accuse them of extremism or terrorist activity.[92] These references are not necessarily a commentary on a group's religious or ideological objectives, but rather on the vicious, extreme and terror-inspiring tactics of some armed actors. The Global Terrorism Index designates a separate category for Fulani extremists, distinct from other jihadist movements operating in West Africa.

However, Nigeria is a country with chronic and internecine conflict between Muslim and Christian populations that is struggling with a significant jihadist threat. This context has impacted dynamics and narratives in other regions of the country. Some local informants link Fulani fighters in the Middle Belt with Boko Haram, despite the fact that this territory is outside the area in which the group's factions operate. The fact that Fulani are typically Muslim, and that they played such a strong leadership role in the Sokoto caliphate, has also driven narratives that 'killer herdsmen' seek to wage jihad, establish sharia law, or otherwise Islamise the Middle Belt region.[93]

The literature and information available regarding Fulani participation in contemporary jihadist movements are also quite limited and may have significant gaps. Due to the security situation in the region, rigorous academic and scientific study has been curtailed and stifled in recent years. Most direct information on the situation comes from news outlets and humanitarian reports. These sources are often aimed at a general audience, and may simplify certain aspects of local social dynamics for the purpose of communicating a clear story or analysis. Additionally, reporters are not always well-educated regarding ethnic nuances, and may neglect or misinterpret important local social dynamics in their analyses or reporting.

The Risks of False Equivalencies

Allegations of robust links between Fulani groups and jihadist movements are difficult to substantiate due to the dynamic, complex nature of the regional context. The social, economic and geographic diversity within Fulani groups, the Salafi tradition touted by most 21st century jihad movements in West Africa, the ethnic diversity among contemporary jihadist leaders in the region, and the predominantly socio-economic drivers of jihad in West Africa (both in the past and in the present) all complicate attempts to draw direct links between Fulani communities and modern jihadist movements. In this shifting landscape, and considering the flaws inherent in the research and information available, the value that highlighting such links can bring to efforts to fight terrorism in the region is extremely limited.

Conversely, the risk that such narratives will yield false equivalencies between Fulani communities and jihadist movements presents significant threats to efforts to combat the spread of Islamic extremism in West Africa. The deliberate ethnic targeting of Fulani by security and counterterrorism forces, which is taking place across the region, will breed resentment and grievance among Fulani communities, including those who originally stood opposed to jihad.[94]

This has already happened. In central Mali, Diallo writes that:

"during the redeployment of state institutions in 2013, Malian security forces clamped down on pastoral communities, leading to mass detention and extrajudicial killings...based more on the false equivalency of Fulani pastoral communities and terrorists, than on the proven culpability of the arrested. Disaffection towards the state and the mass appeal of non-state armed groups, especially Islamist-leaning, were the consequences of this security crackdown."[95]

In Burkina Faso, Dicko's attempts to begin a jihadist movement in his home province of Soum were initially unsuccessful because many Fulani community members, especially elites, were not supportive. Instead, Dicko was forced to travel to neighbouring Mali to recruit and conduct jihad. In November 2016, the Burkinabe security forces enacted a state of emergency in Soum to root out jihadists who had crossed the border from Mali. During this campaign, these state forces humiliated several local elders and traditional chiefs – actions which, according to Le Roux, Dicko was able to exploit to garner more support for his cause in his home province.[96]

When security forces or political actors overestimate the importance of ethnicity in driving jihadist activity, they may contribute to the toxic hardening of ethnic divides, often with violent consequences. For example, the perceived link between the Fulani community and Ansarul Islam in Burkina Faso drove the rise of ethnic self-defence militias in Mossi communities, known as *Koglweogo*. Le Roux reports that *Koglweogo* have inflicted violent punishments on innocent people in their pursuit of 'jihadists'.[97]

This dynamic contributes to the arguably more threatening security challenge facing West Africa today, which is escalating identity-based violence and the growing risk of atrocities, including crimes against humanity and genocide. The US Holocaust War Memorial Museum has warned that ethnic violence involving Fulani and non-Fulani groups in central Mali poses a high risk of atrocities,[98] and the United Nations has triggered an investigation into a Fulani massacre in 2019, believing it could constitute a crime against humanity.[99] In Nigeria, Christians continually accuse Fulani of committing genocide against them.[100] In the Central African Republic in 2016, contestation of power between Fulani and non-Fulani groups fuelled vicious identity-based violence that demonstrated the early warning signs of genocide.[101]

In this context, many communities, both Fulani and non-Fulani, join or support jihadist groups not out of any common religious or ideological belief, but because those jihadists are armed and can keep them safe from the escalating cycles of retaliatory violence.[102] They also protect livelihoods and access to services as growing instability threatens rural areas, key roads and markets. This self-reinforcing cycle will be difficult to disrupt, especially if policymakers continue to privilege ethno-centric narratives.

Conclusion

The goal of this chapter was to set the record straight regarding alleged links between Fulani and jihad, examining cases in both the past and the present. As it turns out, the record is not straight at all. It is jagged and gnarled and twisted around itself.

Fulani groups played significant roles in the Sufi jihads that erupted in West Africa in the 18th and 19th centuries, and Fulani individuals continue to play influential roles in some of the Salafi jihadist movements prevalent in the region today. Yet throughout both eras, jihadist recruitment strategies frequently engaged a broad range of individuals across a diverse array of ethnic identities, and in both periods there are many examples of Fulani communities that did not support the jihadist movements. This is, in part, because the apparent links between Fulani and jihad are complicated by a dynamic political, economic and social context, the complexity of which far surpasses the simplistic, though admittedly appealing, narrative of a direct and linear relationship between the Fulani and jihad.

Thus, the value of such a narrative in informing actions aimed at reducing violent extremism in the region is far outweighed by its risks. False equivalencies between Fulani and jihad, which are already common, have fuelled and will continue to fuel actions against innocent civilians based on ethnic identity, which in turn breeds resentment and grievance on which jihadists can draw in their attempts to recruit new fighters for their causes.

The relationship between Fulani groups and jihadist movements in West Africa is, and has always been, extremely complex. Narratives implying a simple relationship are harmful, both to efforts to combat the spread of violent extremism, and to broader policies and programmes aimed at stabilising and developing the region. Scholars, policymakers and practitioners interested in reducing violence in the region should avoid ethnic narratives and focus instead on understanding and addressing the political and economic drivers of the phenomenon.

Select Bibliography

Abu-Manga, A. (1999). Socio-cultural, Socio-economic, and Socio-linguistic Diversity Among the Fulbe of the Sudan Republic. In Azarya, V., Breedveld, A., De Bruijn, M. & Van Dijk, H. (eds.). (1999). *Pastoralists Under Pressure? Fulbe Societies Confronting Change in West Africa*. Netherlands: Brill Publishers.

Akpor-Robaro, M.O.M. & Lanre-Babalola, F.O. (2018). Nomadic Fulani Herdsmen Turn Terrorists? Exploring the Situation and the Security Implications for Nigeria. *Journal of Humanities and Social Science*, 23(7).

Al Jazeera. (2017). UN Sees Early Warning Signs of Genocide in CAR. 8 August. Available from: https://www.aljazeera.com/news/2017/08/sees-early-warning-signs-genocide-car-170807215828039.html [accessed 26 March 2020].

Aremu, J.O. (2011). The Fulani Jihad and its Implications for National Integration and Development in Nigeria. *African Research Review*, 5(5), serial no. 22, October.

Azarya, V. (1996). Pastoralism and the state in Africa: Marginality or incorporation? *Nomadic Peoples*, 38, Nomads and the State.

Azarya, V. (1999). Introduction. In Azarya, V., Breedveld, A., De Bruijn, M. & Van Dijk, H. (eds.). (1999). *Pastoralists Under Pressure? Fulbe Societies Confronting Change in West Africa*. Netherlands: Brill Publishers.

Benjaminsen, T.A. & Ba, B. (2018). Why do pastoralists in Mali join jihadist groups? A political ecological explanation. *Journal of Peasant Studies*, June.

Blench, R. (1999). Why Are There So Many Pastoral Groups in Eastern Africa? In Azarya, V., Breedveld, A., De Bruijn, M. & Van Dijk, H. (eds.). (1999). *Pastoralists Under Pressure? Fulbe Societies Confronting Change in West Africa*. Netherlands: Brill Publishers.

Boukhars, A. (2019). The Paradox of Modern Jihadi Insurgencies: The Case of the Sahel and Maghreb. Al Jazeera Centre for Studies, 15 July. Available from: https://carnegieendowment.org/2018/07/15/paradox-of-modern-jihadi-insurgencies-case-of-sahel-and-maghreb-pub-76875#:~:text= [accessed 10 March 2020].

Breedveld, A. (1999). Prototypes and Ethnic Categorization: On the Terms Pullo and Fulbe in Maasina (Mali). In Azarya, V., Breedveld, A., De Bruijn, M. & Van Dijk, H. (eds.). (1999). *Pastoralists Under Pressure? Fulbe Societies Confronting Change in West Africa*. Netherlands: Brill Publishers.

Brown, W.A. (1968). Towards a Chronology for the Caliphate of Hamdullahi (Masina). *Cahiers d'Etudes Africaines*, 8(31).

Bukari, K.N., Sow, P. & Scheffran, J. (2018). Cooperation and Co-Existence Between Farmers and Herders in the Midst of Violent Farmer-Herder Conflicts in Ghana. *African Studies Review*, 61(2), July.

Burnham, P. (1999). Pastoralists Under Pressure? Understanding Social Change in Fulbe Society. In Azarya, V., Breedveld, A., De Bruijn, M. & Van Dijk, H. (eds.). (1999).

Pastoralists Under Pressure? Fulbe Societies Confronting Change in West Africa. Netherlands: Brill Publishers.

Centre for Humanitarian Dialogue/United Nations Development Programme. (2016). Radicalization, violence and (in)security: What 800 Sahelians have to say.

Crisis Group. (2019). Facing the Challenge of the Islamic State in West Africa Province. *Africa Report*, 273, 16 May.

Curtin, P.D. (1971). Jihad in West Africa: Early Phases and Inter-relations in Mauritania and Senegal. *Journal of African History*, XII(1).

Diallo, O.A. (2017). Ethnic Clashes, Jihad, and Insecurity in Central Mali. *Peace Review: A Journal of Social Justice*, 29, 16 August.

Echenberg, M.J. (1969). Jihad and State-building in late Nineteenth Century Upper Volta: The Rise and Fall of the Marka State of Al-Kari of Bousse. *Canadian Journal of African Studies*, 3(3), Autumn.

Encyclopaedia Britannica. (n.d.). Tukulor. Available from: https://www.britannica.com/topic/Tukulor [accessed 31 March 2020].

Estelle, E. (2019). How Ansar al Islam Gains Popular Support in Burkina Faso. Critical Threats, 9 May. Available from: https://www.criticalthreats.org/analysis/how-ansar-al-islam-gains-popular-support-in-burkina-faso [accessed 17 March 2020].

European Council on Foreign Relations (ECFR). (2019). Mapping Armed Groups in Mali and the Sahel. Available from: https://www.ecfr.eu/mena/sahel_mapping/katibat_macina [accessed 30 March 2020].

Evans, O. & Kelikume, I. (2019). The Impact of Poverty, Unemployment, Inequality, Corruption and Poor Governance on Niger Delta Militancy, Boko Haram Terrorism, and Fulani Herdsmen Attacks in Nigeria. *International Journal of Management, Economics, and Social Sciences*, 8(2).

Gilbert, L. (2019). An Unrecognized Genocide in Nigeria. Hudson Institute, 19 January.

Global Terrorism Index. (2019). Global Terrorism Index 2019: Measuring the Impact of Terrorism. Institute for Economics and Peace.

Gomez, M.A. (1985). The Problem with Malik Sy and the Foundation of Buundu. *Cahiers d'Etudes Africaines*, 25(100).

Heras, N.A. (2015). May 2015 Briefs. Militant Leadership Monitor, 6(5). The Jamestown Foundation, 31 May. Available from: https://jamestown.org/brief/may-2015-briefs/ [accessed 31 March 2020].

Hill, M. (2009). *The Spread of Islam in West Africa*. Freeman Spogli Institute for International Studies. Stanford: Stanford University.

Hobsbawm, E. (1962). *The Age of Revolution: 1789-1848*. London: Wiedenfeld & Nicolson.

Hoije, K. & Sangare, B. (2019). Islamist Insurgencies Feed Age-Old West African Conflicts. *Bloomberg*, 21 March. Available from: https://www.bloomberg.com/news/articles/2019-03-21/islamist-insurgencies-fuel-age-old-west-african-ethnic-conflicts [accessed 18 March 2020].

Homewood, K. (2008). *Ecology of African Pastoralist Societies*. London: James Curry Ltd.

Ibrahim, I.Y. & Zapata, M. (2018). Regions at Risk: Preventing Mass Atrocities in Mali. US

Holocaust Memorial Museum, Early Warning Country Report, April.

Idowu, A.J. & Okunola, B.T. (2017). Pastoralism as a New Phase of Terrorism in Nigeria. *Global Journal of Human Social Science*, H Interdisciplinary, 17(4).

Inemugha, N. (2018). Is Fulani Herdsmen Menace in Nigeria an Act of Terrorism? 12 November. Available from: https://ssrn.com/abstract=3283286 or http://dx.doi.org/10.2139/ssrn.3283286 [accessed 11 April 2020].

Ivey, K. (2018). JNIM: The New Terrorist Threat from the Sahel. *Geopolitical Monitor*, 17 September. Available from: https://www.geopoliticalmonitor.com/jnim-the-new-terrorist-threat-from-the-sahel/ [accessed 18 March 2020].

Johnson, M. (1976). The Economic Foundations of An Islamic Theocracy – the Case of Masina. *Journal of African History*, XVII(4).

Kelly, F. (2019). At least 157 people were killed and 65 injured in the attack by dozo hunters from the Dogon ethnic group, MINUSMA said. *Defense Post*, 3 May. Available from: https://www.thedefensepost.com/2019/05/03/mali-ogossagou-massacre-crime-against-humanity-minusma/ [accessed 31 March 2020].

Le Roux, P. (2019a). Responding to the Rise in Violent Extremism in the Sahel. Africa Center for Strategic Studies, 2 December. Available from: https://africacenter.org/publication/responding-rise-violent-extremism-sahel/ [accessed 17 March 2020].

Le Roux, P. (2019b). Ansaroul Islam: The Rise and Decline of a Militant Islamist Group in the Sahel. Africa Center for Strategic Studies, 29 July. Available from: https://africacenter.org/spotlight/ansaroul-islam-the-rise-and-decline-of-a-militant-islamist-group-in-the-sahel/ [accessed 17 March 2020].

Le Roux, P. (2019c). Exploiting Borders in the Sahel: The Islamic State in the Greater Sahara. Africa Center for Strategic Studies, 10 June. Available from: https://africacenter.org/spotlight/exploiting-borders-sahel-islamic-state-in-the-greater-sahara-isgs/ [accessed 17 March 2020].

Lévy, B. (2019). The New War Against Africa's Christians. *The Wall Street Journal*, 20 December. Available from: https://www.wsj.com/articles/the-new-war-against-africas-christians-11576880200 [accessed 31 March 2020].

Lounnas, D. (2018). The Transmutation of Jihadi Organizations in the Sahel and the Regional Security Architecture. Middle East and North Africa Regional Architecture, Future Notes No. 10, April.

Lovejoy, P.E. (2016). *Jihad in West Africa: During the Age of Revolutions*. Athens, Ohio: Ohio University Press.

Mahmood, O.S. & Ani, N.C. (2018). Response to Boko Haram in the Lake Chad Region: Policies, Cooperation and Livelihoods. Institute for Security Studies, July.

Nmah, P.E. & Amanambu, U.E. (2017). 1804 Usman Dan Fodio's Jihad on Inter-group Relations in the Contemporary Nigerian State. *International Journal of Religion & Human Relations*, 9(1), June.

Nsaibia, H. (2018). Targeting of the Islamic State in the Greater Sahara (ISGS). ACLED, 21 March. Available from: https://acleddata.com/2018/03/21/targeting-of-the-islamic-state-in-the-greater-sahara-isgs/ [accessed 17 March 2020].

Odeigah, T.N. & Mawere, M. (2018). Herdsmen, Farmers and the National Security under Threat: Unveiling the Farmers and Fulani Herdsmen Violence and Conflicts in the Niger Delta Region of Nigeria. In Mawere, M. (ed.). (2018). *Development Naivety and Emergent Insecurities in a Monopolised World: The Politics and Sociology of Development in Contempora*. Langaa RPCIG.

Paquette, D. & Warrick, J. (2020). Al-Qaeda and Islamic State groups are working together in West Africa to grab large swaths of territory. *The Washington Post*, 22 February.

Philips, J.E. (2017). Causes of the Jihad of Usman Dan Fodio: A Historiographical Review. *Journal for Islamic Studies*, 36.

Postings, R. (2019). Islamic State puts the Sahel in West Africa – for now. *The Defense Post*, 30 May. Available from: https://thedefensepost.com/2019/05/30/islamic-state-greater-sahara-west-africa/ [accessed 17 March 2020].

Rodney, W. (1968). Jihad and Social Revolution in Futa Djalon in the Eighteenth Century. *Journal of the Historical Society of Nigeria*, VI(2), June.

Salkida, A. (2019). Special Report: Why Troops are Losing Ground to ISWAP. Sahara Reporters, 2 January. Available from: https://saharareporters.com/2019/01/02/special-report-why-troops-are-losing-ground-iswap [accessed 10 March 2020].

Samuel, M. (2019). Economics of terrorism in Lake Chad Basin. Institute for Security Studies, 10 July. Available from: https://issafrica.org/iss-today/economics-of-terrorism-in-lake-chad-basin [accessed 18 March 2020].

Sangare, B. (2019). Fulani people and Jihadism in Sahel and West African countries. Fondation pour la Recherche Strategique, March.

Shillington, K. (ed.). (2004). *The Encyclopedia of African History. Hamdallahi Caliphate, 1818-1862*. London: Routledge.

Souza, S.M.D. & Routray, B.P. (2020). Surging Jihadist Wave in Western Africa: Conflict Spillover – Analysis. *Eurasia Review*, 13 February. Available from: https://www.eurasiareview.com/13022020-surging-jihadist-wave-in-western-africa-conflict-spillover-analysis/ [accessed 18 March 2020].

The Economist. (2018). The fight against Islamic State is moving to Africa. 14 July. Available from: https://www.economist.com/middle-east-and-africa/2018/07/14/the-fight-against-islamic-state-is-moving-to-africa [accessed 18 March 2020].

Waldman, M.R. (1965). The Fulani Jihad: A Reassessment. *Journal of African History*, VI(3).

Woodward, M., Umar, M.S., Rohmaniyah, I. & Yahya, M. (2013). Salafi Violence and Sufi Tolerance? Rethinking Conventional Wisdom. *Perspectives on Terrorism*, 7(6), December.

Zajac, A.K. (2014). Between Sufism and Salafism: The Rise of Salafi Tendencies after the Arab Spring and Its Implications. *Hemispheres*, 29(2).

Zenn, J. (2015). The Sahel's Militant 'Melting Pot': Hamadou Kouffa's Macina Liberation Front (FLM). *Terrorism Monitor*, 13(22), November. Available from: https://jamestown.org/program/the-sahels-militant-melting-pot-hamadou-kouffas-macina-liberation-front-flm/ [accessed 31 March 2020].

Endnotes

1. Le Roux, 2019a.
2. *The Economist*, 2018.
3. Lovejoy, 2016; Azarya, 1996.
4. Lovejoy, 2016; Azarya, 1999.
5. Waldman, 1965.
6. Benjaminsen & Ba, 2018.
7. Estelle, 2019; Postings, 2019; Le Roux, 2019a; Diallo, 2017; Sangare, 2019; Boukhars, 2019.
8. Inemugha, 2018; Odeigah & Mawere, 2018; Sangare, 2019; Idowu & Okunola, 2017; Ivey, 2018; Akpor-Robaro & Lanre-Babalola, 2018.
9. Diallo, 2017; Le Roux, 2019b.
10. In this chapter, the terms 'Fulani', 'Fulbe' and 'Peuhl' are used interchangeably.
11. Lovejoy, 2016.
12. Homewood, 2008.
13. Homewood, 2008; Sangare, 2019.
14. Homewood, 2008.
15. Azarya, 1999.
16. Blench, 1999.
17. Homewood, 2008:24.
18. Azarya, 1999:18.
19. Homewood, 2008.
20. Breedveld, 1999.
21. Azarya, 1999:8.
22. Ibid, 7.
23. Hobsbawm, 1962.
24. Lovejoy, 2016:13. See also Echenberg (1969), Rodney (1968), Brown (1968) and Curtin (1971).
25. Azarya, 1999.
26. Gomez, 1985; Rodney, 1968; Lovejoy, 2016.
27. Philips, 2017.
28. Johnson, 1976.
29. Encyclopaedia Britannica, n.d.
30. Lovejoy, 2016:45.
31. Johnson, 1976:488.
32. Shillington, 2004:614.
33. Philips, 2017.
34. Lovejoy, 2016.
35. Lovejoy, 2016; Waldman, 1965; Rodney, 1968; Johnson, 1976.
36. Rodney, 1968; Curtin, 1971.
37. Rodney, 1968; Philips, 2017.
38. Lovejoy, 2016:50.
39. Philips, 2017:52.
40. Lovejoy, 2016.
41. Waldman, 1965:334.
42. Philips, 2017:44.
43. Lovejoy, 2016; Echenberg, 1969; Waldman, 1965.
44. Hill, 2009.
45. Aremu, 2011.
46. Philips, 2017; Lovejoy, 2016.
47. Philips, 2017:39.
48. Azarya, 1996.
49. Waldman, 1965:353.
50. Philips, 2017:47.
51. Philips, 2017.
52. Shillington, 2004.
53. Johnson, 1976.
54. Philips, 2017.
55. Gomez, 1985:539.
56. Le Roux, 2019a.
57. Crisis Group, 2019.
58. Heras, 2015; Le Roux, 2019c.
59. Lounnas, 2018; Ivey, 2018.
60. Paquette & Warrick, 2020.
61. Postings, 2019.
62. Centre for Humanitarian Dialogue/United Nations Development Programme, 2016:5.
63. Estelle, 2019.
64. Mahmood & Ani, 2018:3.
65. Evans & Kelikume, 2019.
66. Lovejoy, 2016; Woodward et al, 2013.
67. Lovejoy, 2016; Zajac, 2014.
68. Benjaminsen & Ba, 2018.
69. Estelle, 2019.
70. Lovejoy, 2016; Azarya, 1996.
71. Azarya, 1999.
72. Diallo, 2017.
73. Benjaminsen & Ba, 2018:12.
74. Nsaibia, 2018.
75. Hoije & Sangare, 2019.
76. Sangare, 2019:8.
77. Zenn, 2015; ECFR, 2019.
78. Estelle, 2019.
79. Postings, 2019; Le Roux, 2019c.
80. Le Roux, 2019c; Lounnas, 2018.
81. Le Roux, 2019b.
82. See also Centre for Humanitarian Dialogue/United Nations Development Programme (2016).
83. Diallo, 2017:302.
84. Sangare, 2019.
85. Hoije & Sangare, 2019.
86. Sangare, 2019:11.
87. Bukari et al, 2018.

88 Estelle, 2019.
89 Crisis Group, 2019.
90 Salkida, 2019; Crisis Group, 2019; Samuel, 2019.
91 Crisis Group, 2019.
92 Idowu & Okunola, 2017.
93 Lévy, 2019; Sangare, 2019; Odeigah & Mawere, 2018; Nmah & Amanambu, 2017.
94 Centre for Humanitarian Dialogue/United Nations Development Programme, 2016.
95 Diallo, 2017:301.
96 Le Roux, 2019b.
97 Ibid.
98 Ibrahim & Zapata, 2018.
99 Kelly, 2019.
100 Gilbert, 2019.
101 Al Jazeera, 2017.
102 Boukhars, 2019.

CHAPTER 13

Hybridity and Fragmentation: Implications for Regional Security Policy in the Sahel and Beyond

Bethany L. McGann

Introduction

Of the global milestones reached as 2019 drew to a close, none was more sobering than the events in the Sahel, witness to the most rapid increase in violence of any region for the year.[1] Over the past decade, the Sahel – an ecoclimatic, biogeographic zone of transition stretching from the Atlantic Ocean to the Red Sea – has experienced the near collapse of the Malian state, the proliferation of diffuse and adaptable armed groups with ties to global terrorist organisations, and a startling increase in intercommunal violence driven by ethnic militias.

Despite the myriad challenges driving the regionalisation of insecurity, and numerous experts citing poor resource management, underdevelopment, and climate change (to name a few) as drivers of conflict, western policymakers continue to focus on extremist groups and radicalising ideologies as the chief threats to Sahelian states, and increased militarisation of the region through counterterrorism and peacekeeping missions as the one-size-fits-all solution. Unfortunately, the blood and resources committed to military intervention have yet to make a significant impact on the crisis, despite more than 20,000 international and local personnel deployed, and it could be argued that such interventions have actually made things worse, given the unceasing attacks on civilian targets.[2]

The spiralling violence and insecurity have decoupled longstanding formal and informal authority structures between communities and the state, and disrupted patterns of relatively peaceful coexistence between tribal groups (for example, those in Burkina Faso),[3] underscoring the capacity of militant groups to take advantage of vulnerable political seams within and across state borders. This was perhaps best put in a recent brief by the Armed Conflict Location & Event Data Project (ACLED): "[T]hese dynamic [re]arrangements are actively reconfiguring the political geography of states at a time when ideologies and alliances are in flux across the Sahel."[4] As such, the Sahel, which was once described in the context of shared geographies and human terroir, is now best framed as a zone of conflict and ambiguity centred on three states: Mali, Niger and Burkina Faso.

Although the armed groups and cascading violence are an appropriate and worthy subject of investigation and evaluation, widening the analytical aperture reveals a complex system of relationships, bargains and concessions that, prior to 2012, held up the facade of state consolidation and stability, and has over the past decade fragmented into the morass of competing actors and priorities we see today. All political arrangements, from the lowest system of organisation to the highest levels of multilateral cooperation, are hybrid orders built on coalitions and power-sharing agreements.

The Sahel Summit of January 2020, called by President Emmanuel Macron of France, convened the heads of state of Chad, Niger, Mali, Burkina Faso and Mauritania (known as the G5 Sahel),[5] laying bare a clear example of the macro-level dynamics of geopolitical hybridity at play. France, concerned about rising anti-French speech spreading across Sahelian states, wanted the African heads of state to make clear their support for the continued French military presence and counterterrorism mission – even if such declarations might weaken the already fraught political positions of said heads of state at home. Worse, the death toll for which jihadist groups were responsible (859) versus national security forces (597) for Burkina Faso in 2019 (with similar trajectories in its regional neighbours) speaks to the challenge created by the state's pernicious exercise of violence, which undermines its counterterrorism mission through the creation of civilian suffering and an increased recruitment opportunity for terrorist organisations.[6] By the end of 2019, at least 2,000 civilians had been killed in the area where the borders of Mali, Niger and Burkina Faso meet.[7]

This example is one lens through which to understand the broad-spectrum insecurity within and between polities with vested interests in the Sahel, demonstrating the benefit of a systems approach to understanding the context in which the broader region has descended into violence and instability. It also raises the question of what, given the evidently tenuous nature of the hybrid environment, 'stability' in the region looked like prior to this context of collapse. Given that the actors remain largely the same, what characterises the current context of a collapse as opposed to the pre-context,[8] which evidenced similar levels of intercommunal conflict-based security challenges? Is it enough to claim, as do circles in the Sahelian public discourse, that the parochial agendas of jihadists and western powers alike were the tipping point? Systems and complexity-aware approaches[9] are promoting a local-first approach to intervention, but policy solutions – such as counterterrorism missions and security coordination – remain at the high political/geopolitical level. What can be gained from looking at the foundation, the very human social domain, upon which these low and high politics rest?

In this chapter I will investigate the extent to which hybridity[10] in governance and security has contributed to the rapidity of collapse, what specific dynamics within these orders trend toward fragility and vulnerability, and which might be leveraged for better policy. Understanding hybrid orders is critically important, as security strategy drives interventionism and policy related to public and state authority, especially in the transhumance areas of the Sahel where non-state actors, including jihadists,[11] have – as a result of a largely absent and/or predatory state – taken on security and justice provision roles.

This chapter will begin with a review of the current security landscape, followed by a discussion of hybridity, situating the Sahel within the conceptual framework of multi-layer hybrid security governance. The final sections will illuminate the dynamics of micro-, meso- and macro-level fragmentation of these hybrid orders, using examples mainly from Mali and Niger, with some coverage of Burkina Faso and other states, and discuss implications for counterterrorism and security policy as regional and international actors seek to halt the flow of terrorism south and westward from the Sahel.

Origins of Regional Insecurity and Vulnerability

To understand the expansion of the terrorist threat in West Africa and the Sahel, one must look to some of the core factors undergirding regional instability and vulnerability. This section discusses how the nature of the state, the experiences of communities affected by insecurity, and histories of conflict have created a fertile security environment for opportunistic violent and criminal actors.

The border region of Mali and Niger, one of several regional hot zones, has housed an array of separatist, criminal and insurgent networks for decades. Two events in particular have contributed to the insecurity of the region, in addition to the large swathes of under-governed and low-access territories across both states' neighbouring countries: the Algerian civil war (1992-2002) and the collapse of Libya in the aftermath of the intervention by the North Atlantic Treaty Organization (NATO) in 2011.[12]

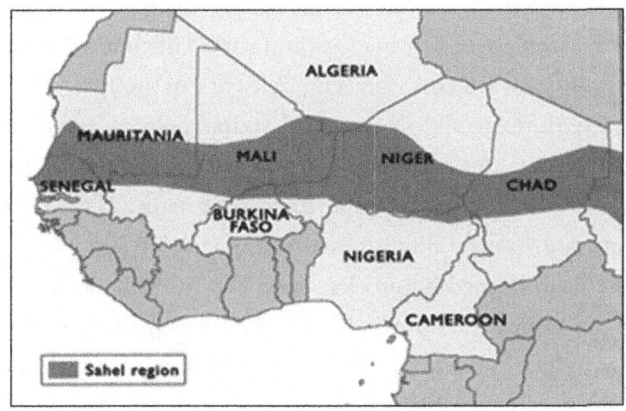

Figure 1: Map of West Africa Sahel Region[13]

The 2012 military coup in Mali further destabilised the region, with the spillover of arms and fighters from Libya reviving the longstanding Tuareg rebellion. Though long viewed by security partners in the west as a reliable bulwark against violent actors and extremists in the Sahara, particularly after the successful peace agreement of 2005, the contemporary collapse of the Malian state has contributed to the proliferation of militant fighters and violent extremists operating in the broader Sahel.[14]

Of the numerous active insurgencies and criminal organisations in the region, Al-Qaeda in the Islamic Maghreb (AQIM), Jama'at Nusrat al-Islam wal-Muslimin (JNIM) and Boko Haram top the long list of violent actors contributing to regional instability, presenting the greatest threat to states and communities, and increasingly articulated in terms relating to the security interests of the United States (US) and Europe.[15] Each of these groups has engaged in transnational activities, clustered in the border regions of the Lake Chad Basin (Cameroon, Chad, Niger and Nigeria), and in the intersection of Mali, Niger and Burkina Faso. Their positioning lends directly to lucrative smuggling and trafficking initiatives, both within the region and across the Sahel, to Mediterranean ports and European markets. Though the smuggling of goods and peoples exiting the continent has been a chief focus of international actors, the transregional movement of goods is a historic and critical component of local and regional economies. The illicit movement of goods within Africa complicates efforts to institutionalise border controls, strengthen licit markets and curtail illicit flows. Last, intergroup interactions with local armed actors lend to a cycle of group consolidation, fracturing and indiscriminate violence as social capital, political capital and resources produce fertile opportunities for competition and collaboration.

Nigeria serves as a pertinent example of how the nature of the state has a direct impact on creating vulnerability to the development of violent extremist organisations and empathetic communities. Historically, Nigeria's security services, both police and military, have adjudicated their role in the context of communal ethnic and religious composition, which is further impacted by competition for federal and local government resources and services. The state has violently suppressed popular movements expressing grievances against national economic and development policy. The ongoing crisis in the country's Niger Delta is yet another example of state excess driving further insecurity. Lack of trust between communities and security actors has resulted in a culture of impunity on the security-actor side, and resentment on the community side. These dynamics directly led to the spark that transitioned Boko Haram from a civil society religious organisation to the virulent and violent extremist actor it is today.[16]

While state capacity and security orientations, as well as citizen and community perceptions of both, range to either extreme of the example provided by Nigeria, similar dynamics exist across and within the impacted states in the region. The countries in the Sahel have long ranked towards the bottom of development indices. Social and economic marginalisation and deprivation, particularly centre-periphery inequalities, are a key driver of grievance and vulnerability to extremist and separatist narratives in Sahelian states. Described as "frontiers of discontent", poverty, political exclusion and socio-economic exclusion lead to participation in informal and illicit economic activity, and dependence on contraband and trafficking for daily subsistence.[17] Reliance on the illicit movement of goods and the networks operating informal trade contributes to a sense of shared experience and identity that transcends state loyalty, which can easily be shifted into outright antipathy.

The broader region is a priority for international development organisations due to its complex security situation, vulnerability to climate change, resource insecurity, high poverty rates, and weak governance and institutions.[18] Though development needs remain high, funds earmarked by international partners to assist Sahelian countries focus largely on security cooperation or outright economic coercion,[19] a trend reflected in other regions impacted by terrorist violence.[20] Unfortunately, focus on the security rather than the economic dynamics of grievances in the region does little to resolve perceptions of deprivation, and thus misses the root conditions driving communities into the arms of terrorist and other armed groups.

Current Threat Landscape: Terrorism, Non-State Actors and Sectarianism

Understanding the threat landscape requires both horizontal and vertical analysis of the dynamics of localised and community insecurity, state capacity and predation, and the inherently transnational nature and objectives of violent terrorist and criminal organisations. Levels of deprivation, both contextual and relative, further inflame grievances leveraged by these groups.[21] Across the continent, and particularly in Sahelian West Africa, localised conflicts and insecurity in areas largely bereft of a functional, formal institutional presence in some cases lend to protracted isolation and vulnerability. In areas characterised by limited or alternative governance, challenges presented by population movements, food and water security shocks, or the encroachment of foreign actors can quickly move from manageable to intractable crises. These factors drive community mobilisation processes, including armament, self-protection and resource competition, which in turn generate greater levels of violence, deepen inter- and intra-communal feuds, and ultimately create fertile ground for terrorist groups to mobilise and recruit in pursuit of revisionist and ideologically driven objectives.

The cycle of localised, state-wide and transnational fragility and violence has played out in predictable and, to date, largely unstoppable ways in Mali, Niger, Nigeria, Cameroon and Burkina Faso. Though this section describes three categories of non-state security actors emerging from and influencing conflict and grievance dynamics, it must be noted that these group types are dynamic and fluid, intersecting and overlapping, and they take on similar roles within the context of local, state and international narratives and interventions.

Terrorism

As the Islamic State in Iraq and Syria (ISIS) and Al-Qaeda lose territory in the Middle East and seek new bases, criminally oriented outshoots and ideological affiliates have made marked gains in the Sahel, capitalising on the vulnerabilities articulated above and grievances fostered by state predation and incapacity.

In 2018, the JNIM leadership issued a call for the Fulani people to commit to jihad across West Africa, calling out Cameroon specifically.[22] That country has been racked with internal discord between Anglophone and Francophone populations as it combats the cross-border insurgency of Boko Haram, and it presents fertile ground for violent extremist groups to take advantage of the chaos and expand their regional presence. ISIS militants based in the region have also laid claim to attacks in Burkina Faso and Mali, and continue to operate with near impunity across the impacted territories.[23]

Despite repeated claims of victory by the Nigerian government,[24] Boko Haram remains a critical threat to security in the north-east of the country and across borders in Chad, Niger and Cameroon. Boko Haram's declaration of allegiance to ISIS in 2015, and the later-stage fracturing of the group into two competing extremist organisations, demonstrates the sustainability of the foothold the groups have in the region.[25] Figure 2 displays the extent to which terrorist activity expanded in the Sahel/West Africa in 2017 alone, and the cross-border contagion effect of localised insecurity.

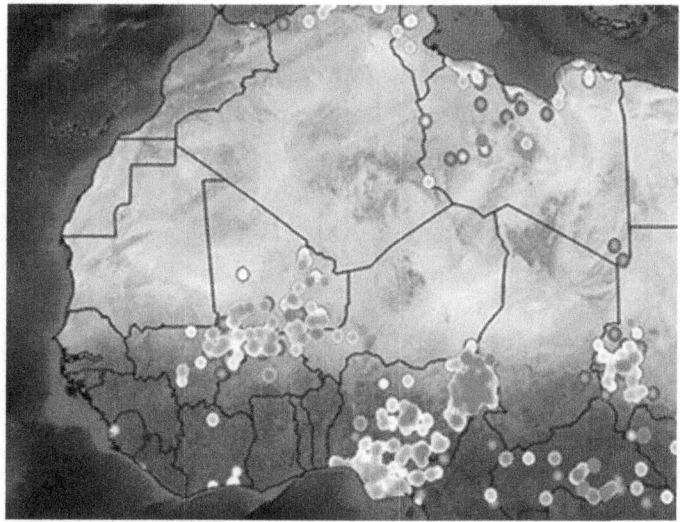

Figure 2: Regional snapshot of terrorist attacks in 2017[26]

Non-State Actors and Community-Based Armed Groups

Community-based armed groups (CBAGs) is a new name for an old phenomenon in Africa. CBAGs vary by their purpose, mission, historical origins, operational focus, deployment of violence, risks and measures of success. Although non-state actors, CBAGs are not necessarily antagonistic to the state and sometimes cooperate with it. Groups form and proliferate in places where communities experience limited governance, historical inter- and intracommunal conflicts or enmity, marginalisation, or deprivation in relation to the state security apparatus.[27] In other cases, CBAGs form to counter localised violent extremist and insurgent threats. Relationships and affiliations to the state and the community, including sources of legitimacy, funding, and socio-cultural norms around the exercise of violence, define and transform CBAGs over time. The inherent tensions embedded in shifting bounds of legitimacy versus illegitimacy in the state-society relationship are central to the CBAG phenomenon.

These groups present an opportunity to expand collaboration outside the formal state to further secure outlying areas. At the same time, the potential for malignant external actors to leverage these groups against the state is equally perilous. Money and arms placed in the hands of militias, vigilantes and other armed groups could lay the foundation for conflict, particularly in areas with valuable natural resources. The conflict in the Central African Republic is one example of how foreign actors can exploit and deepen existing insecurity.[28] An encroaching China and Russia, one bringing money and the other muscle (each with questionable ethical standards), have the potential to disrupt tenuous relationships between state actors and the CBAGs that have proliferated due to deepening insecurity and the rise of jihadists across the Sahel and Lake Chad Basin.[29]

Outside the reach of the state, responsibilities that would be handled by formal security actors are filled by armed non-state actors, only some of whom bear political or ideological animus toward the international entities. Many others are fixtures of local communities, with deep knowledge of the terrain, and of intelligence, surveillance and reconnaissance capabilities, which many militaries – domestic or international – lack the ability to obtain in any period of time. As security, and often securitised, actors, CBAGs play an integral role in the overall security environment, having the potential to be leveraged by domestic and foreign actors, and to serve as a bellwether for understanding the overall state of security-sector governance in both functioning and fragile countries.

Sectarianism, Separatists and Insurgents
Separatist and insurgent groups, much like CBAGs, come in many forms and exercise violence in different ways. Some are holdovers from the colonial period, while others mobilised in the crucible of independence movements following the Second World War. Many other separatist and insurgent groups have emerged as contemporary states struggle to address social and political marginalisation, corruption, and the capture of resources by elites. These groups are perhaps best viewed as manifestations of shared identity and sovereignty, with revisionist narratives placing identity-based communities in opposition to predatory or marginalising state governance strategies.

The Tuareg groups of Mali have held one of the longest-standing coordinated separatist movements in the region, engaging in four major uprisings since the 1960s.[30] Following the collapse of the 2005 peace agreement (the fifth of its kind) and a surge of violence across the country in 2012, the contemporary security environment is characterised by numerous insurgent and self-protection groups competing for territory, access to lucrative smuggling routes, and the influence and arms that come with opportunistic alliances with violent extremist groups.[31] The strongest and most prestigious rebel insurgent group is the National Movement for the Liberation of Azawad (MNLA), which has been known to associate with transnational terrorist groups such as AQIM.

The involvement of radical Islamists, transnational organised crime and international terrorist organisations in the Malian conflict has drawn regional and international attention and resources, including military support. Since May 2014, the rebels have managed to hold as much as three-quarters of Mali's landmass.[32] Both bilateral French-supported campaigns and the United Nations Multidimensional Integrated Stabilization Mission in Mali (MINUSMA, a peacekeeping mission led by the African Union) have failed to stabilise the country, as ongoing conflict limits the ability of internal and external stakeholders to reconsolidate the state outside of urban areas near the capital.

Approaching the threshold of a full-blown insurgency, the Anglophone-Francophone conflict in Cameroon has driven internal displacement and civilian casualties, and has ramped up militarised state security tactics.[33] Beginning in 2016, aggrieved Anglophone Cameroonians began advocating against perceived policies of political and economic marginalisation by the Francophone government. A heavy-handed response to protests, including jailing some English-speaking activists and sympathisers, has mobilised the broader Anglophone population to support armed separatist groups.[34] The state's focus on suppressing Anglophone actors rather than the broader threats presented by Islamic State West Africa Province (ISWAP) and Boko Haram serves only to further inflame conflict dynamics. As one of the region's largest economies and an important security partner for French, British and American interests, the dual insurgent threat in Cameroon has the potential to become the next flashpoint in the region.

As demonstrated through these examples, the surge in sectarianism, terrorism and armed community mobilisation throughout West Africa and the Sahel must be viewed at the intersection of local, regional and global conflict and security dynamics. Historic and contemporary state governance, longstanding grievances, political and socio-economic grievances, and securitisation narratives and practices emerging from bilateral and international governance schemas must also be taken into account towards generating a nuanced understanding of the scope of the threat.

It is at this point that it is most useful to shift the frame to an analysis of hybrid orders, and how contestations between and within these transregional orders have led to the wicked challenges presented and perpetuated by indigenous and international armed groups.

1. Hybrid Orders as Areas of Ambiguity

In establishing why Sahelian states can be described as hybrid orders, it is important to reiterate that all political arrangements – from the lowest systems of organisation to multilateral cooperation – are hybrid orders built on coalitions and power-sharing agreements. Most state-based political orders contain elements of pluralism, expressed through elite brinkmanship, party politics, labour unions and so on. The Sahelian states, like other fragile governance environments, have state institutions that are more likely to be centralised with authoritarian tendencies and a pluralised security governance landscape, progressively more so towards the periphery and border areas.

It is important to historicise hybridity in the Sahel, understanding it as a perpetual condition[35] that has to date served as a facade concealing the failure to achieve substantive state consolidation – but not as the diametric opposite of consolidation. For instance, in the dichotomy of customary versus formal governance, there might be some opposition, but there is also, more importantly, complementarity and some kind of continuation of status, service, and flows of legitimacy between the community and the state. The customary continues the formal governance in areas where the latter institutions have failed to grow. In considering the Sahelian states as embodying constantly shifting zones of ambiguity rather than static state-like apparatchiks, the act of constructing sustainable and effective policy must evolve from a short-term, one-size-fits-all affair to a nuanced, adaptive and holistic strategy that negotiates political, security and economic determinants across multiple layers of human and physical terrain.

The particulars of Sahelian hybridity are legible across political, economic and security frames. The presence of customary and traditional justice and service-provision mechanisms viewed by the polity as equally valid as state-based institutions constitutes one layer. These states feature intentionally blurred boundaries between state and non-state regulation, as opposed to the state functioning in a role that defines boundaries and authority. In Mali, informal systems exist parallel to the state, whereas in Niger the role of traditional authorities in conflict resolution and local governance is formally integrated into state political mechanisms.[36] For both states, centre-periphery identity politics are a key area of contestation in consolidating state power – "since independence, in Mali and to a lesser extent in Niger, state power, which has its political and social bases in the southern parts of both these countries, is struggling to establish legitimacy in the north".[37] Mali and Niger have chosen different routes in managing the distribution of authority and assets,[38] and the sometimes violent exchanges between the governors and the ungoverned.

> "The states of Mali and Niger have used seemingly similar procedures for 'peacemaking', although Niger appears much more advanced through an integrated political framework and an innovative tension control and conflict prevention tool: the High Authority for the Consolidation of Peace (HACP)."[39]

In short, hybrid governance in Mali has stronger strains of failed consolidation, whereas Niger demonstrates an intentional hybridisation that has, to date, better managed contestation at the periphery, where nefarious actors have proven deft at mobilising communities on the margins.

An analysis of hybrid market governance[40] and the nexus of licit and illicit trade crossing the Sahel[41] could fill volumes. From artisanal mining and informal market vendors living at the margins, to large-scale narco-, arms and human trafficking,[42] the diversity of currencies of interest motivate just as varied political and criminal agendas. State authority, whether complicit or controlling, has an impact on the exercise and expression of economic transhumance across the region. Insecurity has ratcheted up the conflict dynamics over economic assets in the past several years, especially in border areas.[43] The levels of violence track with the ways Niger and Mali have diverged in their manifestations of hybridity:

> "Unlike in Mali, where competition for control over drug trafficking routes fuels violence between armed groups, drug trafficking violence in Niger has been relatively contained, thanks in part to political efforts to calm flare ups and manage their fallout."[44]

These political efforts, part and parcel of the intentional integration of traditional authorities into statutory authorities, act "as a social safety valve".[45]

> "...the grey economy can produce integration when it is controlled by a small circle which channels the involvement of autonomous actors, or even co-opts and retains them. This configuration, which is fragile and risky in the medium/long-term, is a short-term element of social peace."[46]

The precarious state of politics and economics impacts the manifestation of 'security', lending to a "particularly pernicious form of state power in which political and economic leaders on both the 'left' and the 'right' [or opposition and empowered] consciously enable violent groups to proliferate in order to protect their perks and maintain control".[47] These groups come in the form of CBAGs for self-defence and policing,[48] identity-oriented militias that manage (sometimes violently) contested resources and terrain, warlords, transnational criminal groups, and proxy forces aligned to political actors.[49]

Given the numerous intersecting actors (some described in the previous section on the security landscape), interests and systems of governance, one can appreciate the difficulty of identifying key nodes of authority when attempting to implement local, national and geopolitical policy. In the Sahel, sovereign governance, from a conventional Westphalian standpoint,[50] is often only skin deep, with a glacier of local conflict and contestation taking place outside the capital cities.

2. Strategic Hybridity: (Un)governing at the Nexus of Continuity and Complementarity

Having described what these orders are and given examples of how hybridity manifests in Sahelian contexts, one might rightfully ask how these orders came to be in the context of the dynamics shaping and conditioning the zones of ambiguity and fragility therein. Decades of elite bargains,[51] exchanges, and political and communal concessions set up precarious governance environments.[52] The necessity of these bargains[53] to secure territorial and political control across numerous ethnic, tribal, language and religious groups conditions the inherent fragility of the semi-consolidated state. The state – a euphemism for empowered elites and their allies – relies on negotiated and coercive bargains between groups rather than a statutory social contract and monopoly on violence.[54] These relationships, though in some cases contributing to stability (notably, not functionality) within the state apparatus, are nonetheless necessarily short-term. The balance of power is constantly subject to pressure from local political economies, identity politics and social support bases, as well as an enduring realpolitik rendering those local relationships and political economies more unstable, insecure and increasingly violent.[55] As a result, policy that does not take this instability into account will necessarily be as short-termed and as precarious.

Hybridity survives under the guise of a coexistence between fixed formal written law and evolving informal customary law, a delicate balance that manages inherent vulnerability – but only to an extent. In this section, I explore these vulnerabilities, and how internal and external actors leverage them. In understanding the zones of ambiguity characterising the sub-national, regional and geopolitical organs of governance, the dynamics of their potential for fragmentation become legible.

Hybrid governance met its nadir at the hands of development actors lionising the conceptual shift from good governance to 'good enough' governance, in their efforts to strengthen fragile and weak governments emerging from war or struggling to achieve various development goals and markers of statehood.[56] At the same time, security practitioners have traditionally expressed concern about involving non-state actors in reformation and consolidation projects because they violate the western-centric Weberian conception of the state monopoly on service provision and defence. This is perhaps a contradiction, as the process of peace and reconciliation has continually included a platform for inclusion of armed groups and other non-state contestants in the violent state-building processes of the past decades. These convergences and divergences of the external-actor perspective on the practical role of non-state actors create challenges in programming in insecure, conflict-affected environments that can be characterised as hybrid orders.[57]

Hybrid orders, though pluralistic in theory, contain actors straddling multiple boundaries, and creating/formalising governance linkages between them can "disrupt, strengthen or weaken governing mechanisms within the state in unpredictable ways".[58] Though deft at creating seams where cleavages between the state and community would otherwise exist, these orders are not built to manage complex emergencies and collective-action challenges. Violent extremism, climate change and resource management, and competition over political, security and economic resources, each contribute to the buckling of these fragile structures.

Hybrid orders also present the challenge of legitimacy at the same time as seeking to dispense legitimacy as a currency to those most deft at wielding it – both inside and outside the state. If all actors are equally valid or influential, or dependent on a specific political contextual moment, who determines who has most legitimacy in decision-making, governance processes or resource distribution? The core assumption of positive hybridity is that non-state actors have more legitimacy in local communities than state actors, but it leaves open the question as to which is most appropriate to engage in achieving the broader goal of state institutional strengthening and governing capacity.

Many African states play host to numerous non-state actors, including international non-governmental organisations, regional multilateral platforms and programmes, and peacekeeping and stabilisation missions. They are also sites of deep civil society engagement. While it is assumed that non-state actors have more legitimacy in communities than state actors, the following questions remain: is legitimacy about the exercise of violence, service provision or both? How do external actors fit into the legitimacy ecosystem?[59] According to international development specialist Kate Meagher and colleagues, "hybrid arrangements with dubious non-state orders may create low-cost solutions to governance problems in the short run, but [they] risk eroding local legitimacy and consent in the long run", and "may strengthen or weaken elements within the state in unpredictable ways".[60]

3. Dynamics of Fragmentation: Triggers and Trajectories

Having established what hybridity looks like, and the inherent vulnerabilities presented by the bonds of formal and informal agreements uniting pluralistic entities, the chaos of the Sahel brings into clarity the dynamics of fragmentation as these hybrid orders collapse upon themselves. Where and how these fractures occur can also explain to some extent the different trajectories of insecurity exhibited by Mali, Niger and Burkina Faso, and cast into relief what the trajectories of their southern and western neighbours might be if similarly triggered.

Micro Level

At the community level, fragmentation is most readily seen in the reduced capacity of traditional authorities to manage conflict resolution and intercommunal relationships, and the relative vanishing of whatever local state authority existed in these spaces.

In Niger, the role of state and traditional authority is vested in traditional chiefs, who have been targeted and kidnapped to cow their communities into acceding to armed-actor agendas. In Mali, without a process integrating traditional authorities into statutory governance, customary bodies are subject to top-down and bottom-up pressures seeking to leverage their legitimacy for area access (humanitarian groups), intelligence (military missions), or territorial control and recruitment (armed groups). In Burkina Faso, mass displacement has contributed to sharp increases in intercommunal distrust. With the state moving to support mass armed community mobilisation through the creation of village-based vigilante groups,[61] the micro-dynamics of fragmentation lead to a potential increase in intercommunal violence. In each setting, the absence of systems to manage conflict leads local communities to pull further apart, eroding the possibility of the reconstitution of local political orders to support access to state authority and governing resources.

Meso Level

In assessing cross-border dynamics, the disparate treatment of ethnic groups on a state-by-state basis creates a meso-dynamic of fragmentation of hybridity. The treatment of the Tuareg in Mali versus Niger is one example, lending to the ability of armed actors to mobilise ethnic communities as the situation demands. The Fulani are another cross-regional group whose treatment at the hands of state and non-state actors contributes to the fragmentation of regional economies and relationships, and increased contestation between settled and nomadic peoples (see Madeline Vellturo, this volume).

The growing focus on border policing and security by G5 missions and their partners increases the presence of violent state authority in areas previously open to transhumance communities, disrupting local political economies and bargains that both criminal and civilian communities relied upon. The mass displacement of people, just as it impacts trust at the local level, also disrupts cross-border relationships because the increased presence of 'strangers' makes it easier for nefarious groups to operate, and more difficult for security actors to protect their own forces or identify targets.

Macro Level
External actors, be they western states,[62] transnational criminal organisations, or internationally linked jihadist groups, have complicated the hybridised security environment with competing parochial agendas that have the unfortunate shared result of limiting or reducing the legitimacy of the central state as a key contributor to providing solutions to the insecurity racking the region.[63] Western-actor bilateral support to struggling state actors is contrasted with the predation carried out on local communities by criminals and terrorists, further pulling the constituencies apart and making policy addressing governance and security concerns at the same time all but impossible.

Projecting the Spread
Many West African states share, to some extent, the micro, meso and macro characteristics of Sahelian states that contribute to their vulnerability to collapse and insecurity. In projecting ahead to the next cases, watchers should be focusing on: shoring up states with similar fault lines and seams in pluralistic governance environments; indications of failed consolidation, especially predatory elites and security actors operating with increasing impunity at the threat of terrorism; and the potential for highly armed mobilisation and the presence of numerous armed groups. Countries that have been largely 'ignored' by external actors in terms of the provision of security coordination and assistance might be the highest on this list, all else given equal consideration.[64]

When ignorance turns to attention under the guise of strategic urgency, the vacuum tends to be filled by deposits of currency and political legitimacy into the central state, eliding the underlying dynamics that contributed to its weakness in the first place. The injection of securitised cash and programming, which featured prominently under the Countering Violent Extremism (CVE) framework (led by the US), has the potential to be replicated as the nation and its multilateral partners move to implement new strategies aimed at shoring up fragile and weak states.[65] Countries in West Africa, hungry for support and the benefits of strategic engagement with the west, should be cautious of such a bellwether, and work intentionally to ensure that the distribution of funding provides services to those most at risk of being targeted by nefarious actors for the purpose of undermining the state's capacity to respond to complex challenges, including violent extremism.

4. Implications for Policy and Practice

Looking ahead to the next stages of conflict within the zones of contestation and ambiguity that characterise the Sahel, where can policymakers and relevant stakeholders be most effective in identifying key leverage points to resist short-termism, mitigate the role of armed actors within pluralistic security landscapes, and support the reconstitution of functioning coalitions for effective and stable governance? This section will discuss policy developments to watch for and potential tripwires to avoid, and make specific recommendations for the development of a holistic framework to address contemporary security challenges in Sahelian West Africa.

External Actors and Global Coordination
As demonstrated in previous sections, external actors acting without coordination have the potential to disrupt tenuous political economies of governance and violence. Despite the challenges and expanding insecurity, the appetite of external actors for intervention in the region remains complicated in its articulations and in situ response dynamics. In early March 2020, the US general in charge of American troops in the region warned that terrorist organisations are "on the march". At the same time, US domestic policymakers are discussing whether to reduce their troop presence in the Sahel, which is currently 1,000 boots on the ground providing intelligence support to French missions as well as training regional security actors. The potential departure of the US forces has alarmed France, which has pushed forward with its kinetic counterterrorism activities

despite political consternation within regional partners.

Contributing to the uncertainty surrounding America's commitment to the region, the US State Department has appointed a special representative to the region, charged with "combating the growing threat of violent extremism by boosting fragile governments in the region, their security forces and their legitimacy and control over their territory".[66] The focus on security forces, in particular, runs a high risk of further consolidating elite power bases through injections of cash rather than supporting the extension of governing authority and legitimacy in vulnerable areas – at the cost of effective security-sector governance and stabilisation missions. A recent World Bank report assessed whether increases in service provision – including security provision – resulted in an increased perception of state legitimacy, and found that it did not.[67] In the case of the Sahel, the goals of bilateral and multilateral external-actor coordination, on the face of it, seem prescriptive, but they run the risk of further inflaming local dynamics by perpetuating a top-down approach to addressing the hyper-localised drivers of conflict and insecurity.

Further Hybridisation

One of the main challenges facing Sahelian states will be reconstituting political constituencies and collective (or elite) bargaining mechanisms that have been polarised by the widespread identity-based conflict and intercommunal violence. The tactics Niger used to integrate different ethnic groups into government and the security forces might not work. Traditional chiefs might not want to be associated with the state, breaking the continuity of legitimacy between customary and formal governance. Some of this has already been witnessed, especially in Mali, where customary authorities are caught between jihadists, ethnic militias and state security actors. The spate of kidnappings and killings targeting traditional authorities reflect how aware violent actors are of the positive potential these leaders have as bridges between the community and the state, and the roles they often play on the frontlines as bearers of the most in-depth knowledge of armed-group movements.[68]

In the interest of self-protection, as insecurity progresses, and in the absence of a reliable state partner, we may see an increase in hybridisation and decoupling from the central state. This may mean an expansion of illicit activities undertaken for survival. As stated in an International Crisis Group report, "policies seeking to tackle trafficking as a driver of insurgency or terrorism should consider how informal/illicit economies, if managed well, may alternatively provide much-needed forms of economic and political stability".[69] In the short term, pockets of stability may indeed appear, but in the long term the presence of non-statutory armed groups and authorities will make reconciliation and reformation of national identity more difficult.

Recommendations for a New Approach

Given the low returns on military-based approaches to address and mitigate the spread of terrorism and violent extremism in the Sahel, a different method might prove more fruitful. The following section seeks to provide recommendations to both state and international partners based on this author's conceptual Prevent, Disrupt, Deny framework, with the goal of achieving both short- and long-term strategic priorities in addressing the threat of terrorism across the region. Where complementary efforts exist, they should be supported. Where capacity slows the rate of implementation, there should be support through funding and technical assistance. Where state actors are complicit, mechanisms to improve legitimacy and social accountability should be viewed as a top priority for governments and partners in institutional strengthening.

Prevent

Violence – political, communal and extremist – is endemic in the region. One way to prevent the proliferation of terrorist organisations in the Sahel is to increase local-level resilience and state-level institutional capacity. Communities in rural and border areas are of particular concern. These areas are difficult to police, making them logical routes for illicit trafficking, and havens for the opportunists and corrupt officials who benefit from criminal activity. Although the state is often unable to effectively reach these areas, the communities themselves have mechanisms that development partners can strengthen to reduce their vulnerability. Customary justice and security providers, if given the proper training and social accountability mechanisms,[70] can provide both intelligence on groups using the areas for nefarious purposes as well as a rule-of-law-informed process for dealing with the low-level criminality that often serves as a precursor to more able groups.

Rather than relying solely on security provision and kinetic counterterrorism assistance, foreign governments should revive development funding, particularly for democracy, rights and governance programming. Improving community resilience to environmental challenges and food insecurity, as well as other efforts to reduce poverty, will provide a long-term runway to stability for the region.

Disrupt
Jihadi and insurgent groups in the Sahel survive largely off local-level criminality (extortion and community predation), transnational criminal networks (smuggling people, cigarettes, etc.) and the less material benefits of being public participants in global jihad. Conducting catastrophic attacks against western, state and civilian targets is a means of demonstrating how lethal they are and their commitment to causes promoted by international terrorist groups – a potent tool for recruitment and fundraising from empathetic audiences. Disrupting the capability of insurgents to amass the resources and personnel to conduct illicit business and terrorist attacks is critical for near- and long-term counterterrorism goals.

It is difficult for foreigners to counter local criminality which, to some extent, can be addressed through some of the prevention mechanisms discussed above. Interrupting and curtailing the flow of illicit financing is crucial in the short term. Impeding a group's ability to make money, or benefit from the diversion of arms, can reduce the lustre of participating in the organisation for those more likely to be involved due to financial incentives as opposed to true believers. A smaller threat is more easily contained.

Unfortunately, groups that feel pressure from counterterrorism or other security operations are more likely to attempt increasingly devastating attacks to regain prestige and reputation. This is where the final 'D' in the framework comes in.

Deny
Denying territory can be a near impossible task in countries like Niger or Mali. Weak or predatory centralised governments have little capacity to deploy troops into rural border communities, and when they do, they are often party to abuses and violence that stoke additional grievances and drive communities into the

arms of terrorist groups. Reducing access to recruits and resources can move groups to escalation and, potentially, miscalculation through overexposure. The conflict with Boko Haram is a clear example of the complexity of combating an insurgency that relies on captive or empathetic communities. As discussed above, empowering local interlocutors to conduct policing and limited military activities can provide desperately needed formalised coverage in under-governed and low-access areas. These actors can also provide crucial on-the-ground insights and intelligence that military forces can leverage.

Once communities are stabilised and the capacity of groups to recruit members and conduct illegal business is reduced, it is then up to state security actors and the partners assisting them to deny these groups access to territory and communities. At this point, aggressive military action can be restricted to tactical deployment against insurgent leadership and core personnel.

In the final stages of the framework, once local communities are secured through legitimate interactions and the insurgents reduced to a limited set of actions, tried-and-tested kinetic counterterrorism tools can be used to their greatest effect. This is where western weapons platforms and personnel are most effective – targeted strikes, verified through the assistance of local knowledge brokers, with the goal of neutralising the leadership and enemy disruption.

Conclusion

There is a dire need to reframe our approach, from looking at jihadists and militant armed actors as drivers of insecurity, to forming a systemic and symptomatic response which accepts that fragility is not something that merely 'happens' to countries but is inherent in states that have failed to consolidate the monopoly of violence and consensus-based social contract in post-colonial construction. The key is to understand how to manage the inherent vulnerabilities of hybrid orders, how to identify fulcrum points in the trajectories of hybridity, and how to develop pluralistic and inclusive capacity, while keeping the house of cards from collapsing under the weight of illegitimacy. The complex dynamics on the ground that facilitate transnational criminal networks and state predation might also contain localised areas of resistance and resilience that make it equally difficult for jihadis to achieve long-term strategic goals as it is for weak and fragile states to deter them.

A holistic (top down and bottom up) approach to counterterrorism and broader insecurity might provide the Sahelian states and their security partners with a means of sustainably managing and mitigating the threat from both existing theatres and future outbreaks. Focusing on grievance reduction; increasing human security; strengthening multilateral institutions; and using military tools for strategic, targeted missions are the ingredients for achieving short- and long-term objectives. As long-term efforts provide increased returns on security and stability at both the state and regional levels, the perception and reality of the threat will hopefully decrease.

With decades of lessons available on what works and does not work in African counterterrorism engagements, as well as those prosecuted in other locales impacted by terrorism, it is imperative that all stakeholders move forward with a clear-eyed understanding of what mechanisms are most important to fund, and which efforts most important to prioritise. Looking ahead to the next stages of the conflict, the question remains as to who has the will (within the state and the general populace), who has the capacity, and who has neither.[71]

Select Bibliography

Africa Center for Strategic Studies. (2020). Threat from African Militant Islamist Groups Expanding, Diversifying. 18 January. Available from: https://africacenter.org/spotlight/threat-from-african-militant-islamist-groups-expanding-diversifying/ [accessed 3 April 2020].

Africa Faith & Justice Network. (2018). U.S. Military Presence and Activity in Africa: Sahel Region. 23 July. Available from: http://afjn.org/u-s-military-presence-and-activity-in-africa-sahel-region/ [accessed 3 April 2020].

Agbiboa, D.E. (2019). Origins of Hybrid Governance and Armed Community Mobilization in Sub-Saharan Africa. Community Based Armed Group Series, October. RESOLVE Network and United States Institute of Peace. Available from: https://resolvenet.org/system/files/2019-10/RSVE_CBAGs_Origins_Agbiboa_Oct2019.pdf [accessed 4 April 2020].

Alliance for Peacebuilding. (2020). Global Fragility Act. Available from: https://allianceforpeacebuilding.org/globalfragilityact/ [accessed 4 April 2020].

Ariotti, M. (2019). Mali's government collapsed. Here's what that tells us about parliamentary coalitions in Africa. *The Washington Post*, 14 June. Available from: https://www.washingtonpost.com/politics/2019/06/14/malis-government-collapsed-heres-what-that-tells-us-about-parliamentary-coalitions-africa/ [accessed 3 April 2020].

Armed Conflict Location & Event Data Project (ACLED). (2020a). Dashboard. Available from: https://www.acleddata.com/dashboard/ [accessed 4 April 2020].

Armed Conflict Location & Event Data Project (ACLED). (2020b). Tag Archives: Mali. Available from: https://www.acleddata.com/tag/mali/ [accessed 4 April 2020].

Armstrong, H. (2019). Behind the Jihadist Attack in Niger's Inates. International Crisis Group, 13 December. Available from: https://www.crisisgroup.org/africa/sahel/niger/behind-jihadist-attack-inates [accessed 3 April 2020].

Armstrong, H.R. (2020). 4. Unlike in #Mali, where competition for control over drug trafficking routes fuels violence between armed groups, drug trafficking violence in Niger has been relatively contained, thanks in part to political efforts to calm flare-ups and manage their fallout. Twitter, 6 January. Available from: https://twitter.com/brkinibeachriot/status/1214240677820850182 [accessed 3 April 2020].

BBC News Africa. (2020a). Violence in the region left just under one million people displaced at the end of 2019 with over 500,000 fleeing their homes in Burkina Faso alone. Twitter, 13 January. Available from: https://twitter.com/BBCAfrica/status/1216733554513719297 [accessed 3 April 2020].

BBC News Africa. (2020b). Jihadist violence is not the only reason for the high death toll in the Sahel. National security forces & other armed groups have also been responsible for the large numbers of casualties in Burkina Faso, Mali & Niger. Twitter, 13 January. Available from: https://twitter.com/BBCAfrica/status/1216733549308665858 [accessed 3 April 2020].

Boukhars, A. (2018). The Maghreb's Fragile Edges. Africa Security Brief, 34, 19 March. Africa Center for Strategic Studies. Available from: https://africacenter.org/publication/maghreb-fragile-edges/ [accessed 3 April 2020].

Chauzal, G. & Van Damme, T. (2015). The roots of Mali's conflict: Moving beyond the 2012 crisis. Chapter 2: Rebellion and fragmentation in northern Mali. CRU Report, March. The Hague: Clingendael – the Netherlands Institute of International Relations. Available from: https://www.clingendael.org/pub/2015/the_roots_of_malis_conflict/ [accessed 3 April 2020].

Cocks, T. (2018). Anglophone Cameroon's separatist conflict gets bloodier. Reuters, 1 June. Available from: https://www.reuters.com/article/us-cameroon-separatists/anglophone-cameroons-separatist-conflict-gets-bloodier-idUSKCN1IX4RS [accessed 4 April 2020].

Cooke, J.G. (2016). Militancy and the Arc of Instability: Violent Extremism in the Sahel. Center for Strategic & International Studies, 6 June. Available from: https://www.csis.org/analysis/militancy-and-arc-instability [accessed 3 April 2020].

Devermont, J. (2019). U.S. Counterterrorism Priorities and Challenges in Africa. Center for Strategic & International Studies, 17 December. Available from: https://www.csis.org/analysis/us-counterterrorism-priorities-and-challenges-africa [accessed 3 April 2020].

Dewast, L. (2020). France Summit: Sahel Crisis in Danger of Slipping out of Control. *BBC News*, 13 January. Available from: https://www.bbc.com/news/world-africa-51061229 [accessed 3 April 2020].

Fessy, T. (2013). Mali and Tuareg Rebels Sign Peace Deal. *BBC News*, 18 June. Available from: https://www.bbc.com/news/world-africa-22961519 [accessed 3 April 2020].

Finnegan, C. & McLaughlin, E. (2020). Terrorist Groups 'on the March' in West Africa and the Sahel, US General Warns. ABC News, 10 March. Available from: https://abcnews.go.com/Politics/terrorist-groups-march-west-africa-sahel-us-general/story?id=69511422 [accessed 3 April 2020].

Foreign Assistance. (2020). Map of Foreign Assistance Worldwide. Available from: https://www.foreignassistance.gov/explore [accessed 4 April 2020].

Freeman, C. (2018) Revived Boko Haram Makes Mockery of Nigerian Army. *The Telegraph*, 16 December. Available from: https://www.telegraph.co.uk/news/2018/12/16/boko-haram-gain-support-nigeria-move-away-killing-civilians/ [accessed 3 April 2020].

Friend, A.H. (2018). U.S. National Security and Defense Goals in Africa: A Curious Disconnect. Center for Strategic & International Studies, 13 February. Available from: https://www.csis.org/analysis/us-national-security-and-defense-goals-africa-curious-disconnect [accessed 3 April 2020].

Grant, A. (2018). Cashing in on Fragility: Al-Qaida in the Islamic Maghreb and Crime in the Sahelo-Saharan Region. In Thachuk, K.L. & Lal, R. (eds.). (2018). *Terrorist Criminal Enterprises: Financing Terrorism through Organized Crime*. Santa Barbara, California: Praeger.

Hauer, N. (2018). Russia's Favorite Mercenaries. *The Atlantic*, 27 August. Available from: https://www.theatlantic.com/international/archive/2018/08/russian-mercenaries-wagner-africa/568435/ [accessed 3 April 2020].

Idrissa, R., Lyammouri, R. & Schmauder, A. (2019). Legitimacy of Traditional Authorities: Mali, Niger and Libya. 30 September. The Hague: Clingendael – the Netherlands Institute of International Relations. Available from: https://www.clingendael.org/publication/legitimacy-traditional-authorities-mali-niger-and-libya [accessed 3 April 2020].

International Crisis Group. (2020). Managing Trafficking in Northern Niger. 6 January. Available from: https://www.crisisgroup.org/africa/sahel/niger/285-managing-trafficking-northern-niger [accessed 3 April 2020].

Kishi, R. (2020). Ten Conflicts to Worry About in 2020. Armed Conflict Location & Event Data Project (ACLED), 27 February. Available from: https://acleddata.com/2020/01/23/ten-conflicts-to-worry-about-in-2020/ [accessed 3 April 2020].

Kleinfeld, R. (2018). *A Savage Order: How the World's Deadliest Countries Can Forge a Path to Security*. 1st edition. New York: Pantheon Books.

Lawrence, M. (2017). Security Provision and Political Formation in Hybrid Orders. *Stability: International Journal of Security and Development*, 6(1), p. 10. Available from: https://www.stabilityjournal.org/articles/10.5334/sta.554/ [accessed 3 April 2020].

Lebovich, A. (2020). "More Coordination" Won't Fix the Sahel. European Council on Foreign Relations (ECFR), 10 January. Available from: https://www.ecfr.eu/article/commentary_more_coordination_wont_fix_the_sahel [accessed 3 April 2020].

Leroux-Martin, P. & O'Connor, V. (2017). Systems Thinking for Peacebuilding and Rule of Law: Supporting Complex Reforms in Conflict-Affected Environments. United States Institute of Peace, 5 December. Available from: https://www.usip.org/publications/2017/10/systems-thinking-peacebuilding-and-rule-law [accessed 3 April 2020].

Lewis, D. (2012). Analysis: Mali Coup Shakes Cocktail of Instability in Sahel. *Reuters*, 24 March. Available from: https://www.reuters.com/article/us-mali-sahel-instability/analysis-mali-coup-shakes-cocktail-of-instability-in-sahel-idUSBRE82N07120120324 [accessed 3 April 2020].

Madowo, L. (2018). Should Africa Be Wary of Chinese Debt? *BBC News*, 3 September. Available from: https://www.bbc.com/news/world-africa-45368092 [accessed 3 April 2020].

Mahmood, O.S. & Ani, N.C. (2018). Factional Dynamics within Boko Haram. Institute for Security Studies, 6 July. Available from: https://issafrica.org/research/books-and-other-publications/factional-dynamics-within-boko-haram [accessed 3 April 2020].

McAllister, E. (2018). Cameroon Insurgency Drains Life from Once Vibrant Towns. *Reuters*, 5 October. Available from: https://af.reuters.com/article/topNews/idAFKCN1MF17R-OZATP?feedType=RSS&feedName=topNews [accessed 3 April 2020].

McCullough, A. & Papoulidis, J. (2020). Why We Need to Rethink Our Understanding of State Legitimacy to Address Fragility. World Bank, 28 January. Available from: https://blogs.worldbank.org/dev4peace/why-we-need-rethink-our-understanding-state-legitimacy-address-fragility [accessed 3 April 2020].

Meagher, K., De Herdt, T. & Titeca, K. (2014). Unravelling Public Authority: Paths of Hybrid Governance in Africa. IS Academy.

Menastream. (2018). #Mali: #JNIM announced forthcoming (official) release of video entitled "Go forth, whether light or heavy", featuring first audiovisual speech (as part of JNIM) by Katiba Macina founder Amadou Kouffa, calling on the Fulani in West Africa and Cameroon to wage "jihad". Twitter, 7 November. Available from: https://twitter.com/MENASTREAM/status/1060183246846246912 [accessed 3 April 2020].

Ministère de l'Europe et des Affaires étrangères. (2019). G5 Sahel Joint Force and the Sahel Alliance. France Diplomatie – Ministry for Europe and Foreign Affairs, February. Available from: https://www.diplomatie.gouv.fr/en/french-foreign-policy/security-disarmament-and-non-proliferation/crises-and-conflicts/g5-sahel-joint-force-and-the-sahel-alliance/ [accessed 3 April 2020].

National Consortium for the Study of Terrorism and Responses to Terrorism (START). (2020). Global Terrorism Database. Available from: https://www.start.umd.edu/gtd/ [accessed 4 April 2020].

Ndiaga, T. (2020). Burkina Faso Approves State Backing for Vigilantes Fighting Jihadists. Reuters, 23 January. Available from: https://www.reuters.com/article/us-burkina-security/burkina-faso-approves-state-backing-for-vigilantes-fighting-jihadists-idUSKBN1ZL1UT [accessed 3 April 2020].

Okello, C. (2020). France Aims to Legitimise Sahel Anti-Jihad Fight at Pau Summit. *Radio France Internationale*, 12 January. Available from: http://www.rfi.fr/en/international/20200112-france-macron-seeks-legitimise-Sahel-anti-jihad-fight-Pau-summit [accessed 3 April 2020].

Østby, G., Nordås, R. & Rød, J.K. (2009). Regional Inequalities and Civil Conflict in Sub-Saharan Africa. *International Studies Quarterly*, 53(2), pp. 301-324.

Oxford Reference. (2019). Westphalian State System. 3 November. Available from: https://

www.oxfordreference.com/view/10.1093/oi/authority.20110803121924198 [accessed 3 April 2019].

Pellerin, M. & Guichaoua, Y. (2018). Making Peace, Building the State. Relations between Central Government and The Sahelian Peripheries in Nigeria and Mali. International Security Sector Advisory Team (ISSAT), Geneva Centre for Security Sector Governance (DCAF). Available from: https://issat.dcaf.ch/Learn/Resource-Library2/Policy-and-Research-Papers/Making-Peace-Building-the-State.-Relations-between-Central-Government-and-The-Sahelian-Peripheries-in-Nigeria-and-Mali [accessed 3 April 2020].

RESOLVE Secretariat. (2020). Community-Based Armed Groups in Sub-Saharan Africa. 31 March. Available from: https://resolvenet.org/projects/community-based-armed-groups-sub-saharan-africa [accessed 4 April 2020].

SABC News. (2019). IS Jihadists Kill Seven Tuareg Leaders in Sahel. 16 July. Available from: http://www.sabcnews.com/sabcnews/is-jihadists-kill-seven-tuareg-leaders-in-sahel/ [accessed 3 April 2020].

Thurston, A. (2018). *Boko Haram: The History of an African Jihadist Movement.* Princeton, Oxford: Princeton University Press.

United States Institute of Peace. (n.d.). Justice and Security Dialogues: USIP Brings Communities Together to Strengthen the Rule of Law. Available from: https://www.usip.org/programs/justice-and-security-dialogues [accessed 4 April 2020].

Zielcke, J. (2018). UN Support Plan for the Sahel: Working Together for a Prosperous and Peaceful Sahel. United Nations, May. Available from: https://www.un.org/africarenewal/sahel/documents/un-support-plan-sahel-working-together-prosperous-and-peaceful-sahel [accessed 3 April 2020].

Endnotes

1. Africa Center for Strategic Studies, 2020.
2. Kishi, 2020; Dewast, 2020.
3. In discussing Burkina Faso with Dr Molly Ariotti, she noted in particular the rapidity with which the Burkinabe community has collapsed in on itself, having previously demonstrated an unusual level of consolidation in terms of national Burkinabe identity.
4. Kishi, 2020.
5. The G5 Sahel was created by the region's leaders as a way of taking their security into their own hands and encouraging regional development by coordinating their efforts (Ministère de l'Europe et des Affaires étrangères, 2019).
6. This data reflects numbers reported at the time of writing this chapter. In the intervening period, conditions on the ground across the Sahel have further deteriorated. Violence in the region left just under 1 million people displaced at the end of 2019, with over 500,000 fleeing their homes in Burkina Faso alone (BBC News Africa, 2020a).
7. Finnegan & McLaughlin, 2020.
8. As discussed in a June 2018 report by International Crisis Group, local communities in the border area, armed and mobilised as far back as the 1990s, have now become increasingly polarised and warlike amid recent military operations because they are often forced to choose between siding with the state or with jihadists (Armstrong, 2019).
9. Leroux-Martin & O'Connor, 2017.
10. The term 'hybrid governance' has emerged to refer to these new organisational arrangements, incorporating local institutions and popular organisations, which fill gaps in state capacity (Meagher et al, 2014). I contend that there is nothing new about the organisational arrangements for Sahelian governance.
11. "As the jihadist groups have implanted themselves deeper into communal conflicts, they have developed systems of coercion and control over populations that Sahelian governments struggle to cope with by military means." (Armstrong, 2019)
12. Grant, 2018.
13. Africa Faith & Justice Network, 2018.
14. Lewis, 2012.
15. Cooke, 2016.
16. Thurston, 2018.
17. Boukhars, 2018.
18. Zielcke, 2018.
19. Madowo, 2018.
20. Foreign Assistance, 2020.
21. Østby et al, 2009.
22. Menastream, 2018.
23. ACLED, 2020a.
24. Freeman, 2018.
25. Mahmood & Ani, 2018.
26. START, 2020.
27. Agbiboa, 2019.
28. Hauer, 2018.
29. Friend, 2018.
30. Chauzal & Van Damme, 2015.
31. Fessy, 2013.
32. Chauzal & Van Damme, 2015.
33. McAllister, 2018.
34. Cocks, 2018.
35. Meagher et al, 2014.
36. Idrissa et al, 2019.
37. Since independence, in Mali and to a lesser extent in Niger, state power, which has its political and social bases in the southern parts of both these countries, is struggling to establish its legitimacy in the north (Pellerin & Guichaoua, 2018).
38. The Nigerien integration system goes beyond this. Built around the existing government – the Nigerien Party for Democracy and Socialism (PNDS) – it operates by controlling dissenting voices, and by distributing government revenue which it monitors closely. (Pellerin & Guichaoua, 2018)
39. Pellerin & Guichaoua, 2018.
40. Meagher et al, 2014.
41. Grant, 2018.
42. These trafficking economies are inherently volatile and require careful management – new shocks can prove extremely disruptive. Furthermore, Niger's approach to trafficking is not without its own set of risks. (Armstrong, 2020)
43. "Although ethnic groups have competed for decades over rights and resources in the Mali-Niger border zone, fighting there has risen to unprecedented intensity over the past several years, with armed factions keen to control valuable cross-border trafficking routes." (Armstrong, 2019)

44. Armstrong, 2020; International Crisis Group, 2020.
45. Pellerin & Guichaoua, 2018.
46. Guichaoua, Y. as quoted in Pellerin & Guichaoua (2018).
47. Kleinfeld, 2018.
48. Agbiboa (2019) notes that "a definition of CBAGs has proven difficult due to their many types and characteristics, and the fact that they are often located in zones of ambiguity between the presence and absence of law and order".
49. "Niger and the commanders of Operation Barkhane should not think that by returning to the use of proxy militias to go against the Islamic State and its local allies, they can remotely defeat them. Doing this would more likely aggravate communal conflicts even further and give the Islamic State more opportunities to expand its foothold in North Tillabery." (Armstrong, 2019)
50. "Term used in international relations, supposedly arising from the Treaties of Westphalia in 1648 which ended the Thirty Years War. It is generally held to mean a system of states or international society comprising sovereign state entities possessing the monopoly of force within their mutually recognized territories." (Oxford Reference, 2019)
51. Since Mali's government relies on majority support to stay in office, political leaders must think strategically about building alliances that can keep them in power (Ariotti, 2019).
52. "In May 2017, faced with the Islamic State threat emanating from Mali, authorities in the Nigerien capital Niamey initiated cooperation with Malian Tuareg and Daosahak armed groups, the Imghad Tuareg Self-Defence Group and Allies (GATIA) and Movement for the Salvation of Azawad (MSA), both of which have ties to the Malian government and drew upon France's military venture in the Sahel, known as Operation Barkhane, for support." (Armstrong, 2019)
53. "The Nigerien state attempted to extend patronage to the Tuareg and Peul by absorbing young men into the armed forces, but this effort has served to further provoke the Islamic State." (Armstrong, 2019)
54. Given that the state is the highest form of organisation an armed group can achieve, the conditions of relationships between political security and communal polarities exhibit similar currencies of authority, legitimacy and exercises of violence (RESOLVE Secretariat, 2020).
55. "Their sweeps in North Tillabery (the region surrounding Inates) seemed to halt the jihadist threat in the short term but also caused tit-for-tat ethnic massacres and drove even more Peul and other fighters to ally with the Islamic State" (Armstrong, 2019).
56. Meagher et al, 2014.
57. Many donors are likely to reject a non-state security-sector-reform strategy because it precludes the venerated state monopoly of legitimate force; this ideal, however, has proven highly elusive in many state-building programmes (Lawrence, 2017).
58. Meagher et al, 2014.
59. While France has a legal mandate from the five Sahel countries justifying its presence in the region, it now wants these countries' populations to recognise its legitimacy as well (Okello, 2020).
60. Meagher et al, 2014.
61. Ndiaga, 2020.
62. Picking sides and intervening via local proxies often makes matters worse, not better, in the countries of the Sahel (Lebovich, 2020).
63. The significant involvement of international actors in hybrid governance processes further complicates assumptions that messy hybrid arrangements can lead to positive processes of state formation (Meagher et al, 2014).
64. Cote d'Ivoire, with its history of recent civil conflict, large caches of weapons, and countrywide networks of decommissioned combatants with links to elites in political and security institutions, is a strong candidate to receive support under the new framework.
65. The 2020 Global Fragility Act dedicates $1,15 billion over the next five years for conflict prevention and peacebuilding, to be implemented by the US Department of State, US Department of Defense, and US Agency for International Development (Alliance for Peacebuilding, 2020).

66 Finnegan & McLaughlin, 2020.
67 McCullough & Papoulidis, 2020.
68 SABC News, 2019.
69 Armstrong, 2020; International Crisis Group, 2020.
70 The US Institute of Peace has engaged in justice security dialogue programming for over a decade, focused on countries in Southeast Asia, the Middle East, and the Sahel and West Africa. The goal of justice security dialogue programming is to assist communities in developing locally informed accountability mechanisms for security actors. Learn more from United States Institute of Peace (n.d.).
71 Devermont, 2019.

CHAPTER 14

Using Evidence-Based Research to Directly Improve P/CVE Programming: A Case Study of a Social Network Analysis in Somalia

Fatma Ahmed, Laura Nettleton and Jem Thomas

Introduction

Across the community of practitioners, policymakers, researchers and academics involved in Preventing/Countering Violent Extremism (P/CVE) laments are often heard of a paucity of deep research in the discipline. There are claims that projects are too often conduced by a weak solid-evidence base, that researchers are too removed from practitioners (and vice versa), and that research is often unrelated to realities on the ground.

More specifically, although it can be seen that there has been an increase in primary data-driven, qualitative research over the past decade, many have claimed that P/CVE research is still based predominantly on secondary data, which is often reliant on literature reviews and documentary analysis,[1] whereas clinical, psychological and psycho-social research remains relatively rare.[2] Compared with other wider social science research fields, methodological issues are often apparent, such as informed consent, confidentiality of data and researcher security, pointing to a need for more robust research designs. Further, researchers often work alone, or as one-off contributors, in a field that exhibits relatively little genuine collaboration, with data stove-piped, due mostly to political and funding issues.[3]

This snapshot appears to be a harsh indictment of the P/CVE field, and neglects to account for much excellent work done in the field and many cases of effective coordination and collaboration between researchers and practitioners. However, the broader claims cannot be ignored, notably one that there is too often a disconnect between primary evidence-based research and P/CVE programming.

Using Evidence-Based Research to Improve P/CVE Programming

With regard to such research, we consider three issues to be prevalent within P/CVE programming:

1. Approaches are often based on 'western-centric' analyses, with not enough local input.
2. Campaigns are often focused on violent extremism itself (pull factors) as opposed to potential deeper causes (push factors), requiring significant research and analysis.[4]
3. Media, including social media, are often employed without consideration and understanding of the deeper psycho-social, relational and communicative aspects of local societies, not least power, identity and trust.

However, we have also considered recommendations that have been articulated by Alastair Reed and others, which largely point to three main factors in designing effective P/CVE programmes. First, projects must be based on a clear theory that outlines what effect the project is intended to have and the causal process by which it is believed this will happen. Increasingly, this is encapsulated in a Theory of Change – a management tool that emerged from the development community in the 1990s and is now a bedrock of international development agency programmes. The second, closely related to a Theory of Change, is that monitoring and evaluation provisions must be hardwired into all projects. It is only through vigorous monitoring and evaluation that we can hope to identify which approaches work and which do not, and, crucially, why they do or do not work. Finally, these lessons learned must be fed back into the research and development of the next round of projects.[5]

To this end, this chapter aims at examining the utility of such research to directly inform P/CVE programmes, and to address the programming issues above by focusing on a specific case study. This study looks at the use of a Social Network Analysis (SNA), which is "a tool which maps and measures relationships and flows between people, groups, organisations, computers, URLs, and other connected information/knowledge entities".[6] The study used its empirical data and the resultant analysis to inform a programme on socio-cultural relationships – power, identity, communication and trust – to better conduct P/CVE campaigns. The research and subsequent project design and activities were conducted by Albany Associates, funded by the United States (US) Department of

State. No further programme details will be disclosed, for security reasons, except to state that the backdrop to the case study was Somalia.

A Brief Synopsis: Violent Extremism in Somalia

After 25 years of civil war, Somalia has been gradually and deliberately emerging out of its failed-state status, with the support of regional actors and international partners. However, this transition has not been without challenges. Security is uneven, with all the regional capitals secured while large areas in south-central Somalia remain occupied by Al-Shabaab. In those areas, the Somali National Army and regional forces are operating with varying capacity and effectiveness.

Somalia's historical, political and social dynamics have been exploited by groups such as Al-Shabaab and the so-called Islamic State in Iraq and Syria (ISIS), which remain a dominant threat to the country's security and overall development. Significant efforts have been made towards the traditional military approach (hard approach) to countering violent extremism (CVE) and terrorism in Somalia. Although the hard approach has been effective in the recovery of Al-Shabaab/ISIS-held territory, it is expensive and has negative effects, such as causing further grievance among communities already affected by previous injustice. A balance must be struck between hard interventions and soft, community-oriented interventions that are geared towards increasing the overall understanding of the causes of violent extremism in Somalia, and building awareness of, and confidence in, local governance.

Albany Associates has been working in Somalia continuously for more than a decade. It therefore has the institutional knowledge on Somalia and violent extremism to design a programme that addresses the structural motivators of violent extremism while taking into consideration the bottom-up initiatives that communities have applied to resist Al-Shabaab. It is in this complex and ever-changing context that we operationalised a pilot project between September 2018 and February 2020. The project intervention and activities were focused on areas that were at the epicentre of insecurity – Jubaland State and Southwest State – and areas vulnerable to attacks and recruitment – Benadir region and Puntland. Project design was informed and shaped by a comprehensive Theory of Change, which helped design the SNA.

Social Network Analysis

Within the past decade, as social media has increasingly been embedded into public utility, and radical politics has resurged in the west, social science research has examined the deeper relationships between the public and technology. Psycho-social and cultural studies, behavioural economics and sociology are fields that have been central in this research. The nature of societies and communities is subject, as ever, to social interactions and group dynamics, and responsive to information passed within and outside of these interactions and dynamics. Research is able to examine how the basic, non-physiological fundamentals of human existence – morality, purpose, trust, identity and belief – are affected by technological changes and affect wider society. Importantly, SNAs focus more on the human and his or her groups, rather than on the technology itself, which is where project research may tend to focus. The answers are not necessarily found in the viral mechanics of memes within Instagram, or within individual psychology, but rather in the multi-layered and complex modes of relationships between humans, some primevally hardwired, others adaptive to 21st century circumstances.

When analysing violent-extremism groups, an increasing appreciation of the nature of organisational dynamics (as opposed to focusing on the individual) has allowed for a better understanding of ties between group members and their impact on group identity, radicalisation and engagement in violence. SNA has thus become a key feature when studying violent-extremism groups.[7]

In the wider sense, SNA can be seen as a valuable tool for understanding societies and communities that may be vulnerable to recruitment and radicalisation. By focusing on such groups, as opposed to the violent-extremism groups themselves, such understanding is seen as assisting in developing stronger community resilience and more effective campaigns, albeit of an alternative-narrative nature.[8] For example, as Berger states: "Social network analysis can also be used to pare less relevant followers from the target audience, for instance separating fully engaged ISIS users from people in the early stage of curiosity."[9]

Despite these considerations, in the East African region, a search for research using SNA in P/CVE highlighted few results; the most recent was a 2017 study carried out by Search for Common Ground in Kenya and Tanzania.[10]

To understand the inter-relational factors at play throughout local communication factors within Somalia, and to use this knowledge to inform campaigns contributing to P/CVE, we conducted an SNA. As explored below, this allowed for the development and delivery of alternative-narrative campaigns that addressed push factors. They focused on relevant groups of actors (not necessarily the violent-extremist groups themselves), their power structures, identity factors, trust networks and communicative channels, and thus leveraged more effective social relationships, as opposed to using entities and channels that are less trusted.

The Case Study Social Network Analysis

The methodology used for this assessment was a mixed-methods approach, combining qualitative in-depth interviews with the use of a quantitative SNA tool in key informant interviews.

Given the nature and sensitivity of the research, Albany Associates partnered with civil society organisations (CSOs) in the following four districts: Garowe, Mogadishu, Baidoa and Kismayo. They helped find research participants and assess the validity of the data, and helped with wider project implementation. These CSOs had the task of selecting research respondents among the youth aged 18 to 35 years, both employed and unemployed.

The CSOs interviewed 35 youth from each of these districts (with 70 in Mogadishu, where Albany Associates partnered with two CSOs). In this study, 175 youth who had homogeneous characteristics (aged between 18 and 35 years, some employed and others unemployed, male and female) were selected using purposive sampling, and their responses were taken as a representation of the general view regarding social networks in the aforementioned regions of Somalia. We were unable to reach an equal gender split. We believed this was due to both a higher fear of discussing such topics among women, as well as inaccessibility to phones for women. In total, 48,6% of respondents in Baidoa were female, 27,1% in Mogadishu, 37,1% in Kismayo, and 34,3% in Garowe.

After the selection of youth in these districts, the researchers engaged enumerators who had experience working in fragile contexts, and they were given refresher training in conflict and gender sensitivity over a two-day period. The enumerators set out to conduct the research with the approval of the CSOs who had mobilised the selected participants. All respondents were contacted, and participants in Baidoa, Kismayo and Garowe proved relatively simple to reach with few challenges, as expected. Four respondents selected by the CSO in Garowe were replaced due to their unavailability. Mogadishu proved more challenging, as most of the respondents did not pick up or answer their phones due to the risks associated with unknown numbers. Seven respondents had to be replaced with respondents from the researchers' network in the city. The researchers processed the data and fed it back to the Albany Associates team, who conducted a thorough analysis.

This study faced a number of limitations, as summarised below.

- As CSOs selected the participants, there could have been bias in the selection that prevented a thorough representation of the Somalis in the region. Due to the high security risks in the region, we deemed it an unavoidable and necessary limitation.
- Given the highly personal nature of this research, in which respondents were asked about employment, religion, CVE, communication, their movements and personal frustrations, respondents might not have been as forthcoming as desired, with some respondents refusing to answer several questions in the quantitative survey. However, this was rather minimal across the board.
- The security risks for both the researchers and the respondents, especially in Mogadishu and Baidoa where Al-Shabaab threats are still high, caused some respondents to fear discussing CVE issues as this could make them a target.
- Some of the respondents were unavailable – either their phones were off, or they were unable to answer calls from the enumerators. This is common due to the security situation in Somalia, and replacement respondents were contacted in such cases.
- The research was conducted by a Kenya-based research firm, which could limit understanding on the ground. However, the research firm selected work on numerous projects in the region, so this was not seen as a significant limitation.

The research provided significant insight into the nature of a society facing prolonged violent extremism, and the findings have been, and will be, applied to the design and delivery of our programming. To demonstrate the utility of SNAs within P/CVE programming, this chapter will explore three specific themes: power and identity, communication, and trust.

Power and Identity

The process of radicalisation is complex, and academics across multiple disciplines have debated the subject extensively in literature. It is now widely agreed that the process of radicalisation is context-specific, and that identity and power are factors often exploited in the process.[11] Indeed, as Freestone attests:

"The search for identities that offer coherent answers to the problems of modern life is more than simply 'discontent': it is an essential process fulfilling a human need. To understand and combat violent radicalisation, therefore, it is important to look beyond psycho-pathology and exceptionalism and situate the radicalisation process in context."[12]

For the context of radicalisation in Somalia, the 2014 work of Botha and Abdile is instructive on the importance and complexity of identity, both religious and collective.[13] When analysing ISIS recruitment techniques and narratives, it is clear that they have used, and abused, grievances related to identity and power to recruit new members. The SNA offered clear insight into individuals' major concerns on a daily basis, which can intrinsically be said to be linked to both themes. Although the SNA sample was small, the answers are complementary to existing reports, as well as consistent with previous findings on radicalisation processes within the country. It is important to note that not all individuals who have power struggles and/or identity crises in their lives will be radicalised. Indeed, the large majority of individuals who go through this will never consider joining an extremist group. However, when certain micro-, meso- and macro-factors come together, some individuals might become radicalised, and identity and power might be a vehicle through which this happens. As such, it is important to look at.

It is difficult to collect data on why an individual has joined Al-Shabaab, but some reports have provided an indication. In 2017, the United Nations Development Programme (UNDP) published the results of an extensive two-year study. It interviewed more than 700 individuals who had joined an extremist group; more than 450 of them were voluntary recruits from Somalia, Nigeria, Kenya, Sudan, Cameroon and Niger.[14] From this study, the largest percentage was from Somalia and they had joined Al-Shabaab (41%). The report identified economic factors (particularly unemployment), familial circumstances, religious ideologies, and the role of the government as leading reasons for radicalisation. Further, a United Nations Office for the Coordination of Humanitarian Affairs (OCHA) report demonstrated that both conflict, or fear of conflict, and a lack of livelihood opportunities were the dominant reasons for internally displaced persons within the country.[15]

These two reports stood out due to their relevance to the SNA. Unemployment and insecurity were the two concerns most mentioned by the individuals. Unemployment was discussed the most – by 55,4% of participants from Mogadishu, 77,1% from both Kismayo and Garowe, and 60% from Baidoa. The major concerns of the participants are shown in Figure 1. The nodes represent the concerns and frustrations mentioned by the participants. They are sized by degree of centrality; each point represents a participant, with the lines linking to the concerns they mentioned.

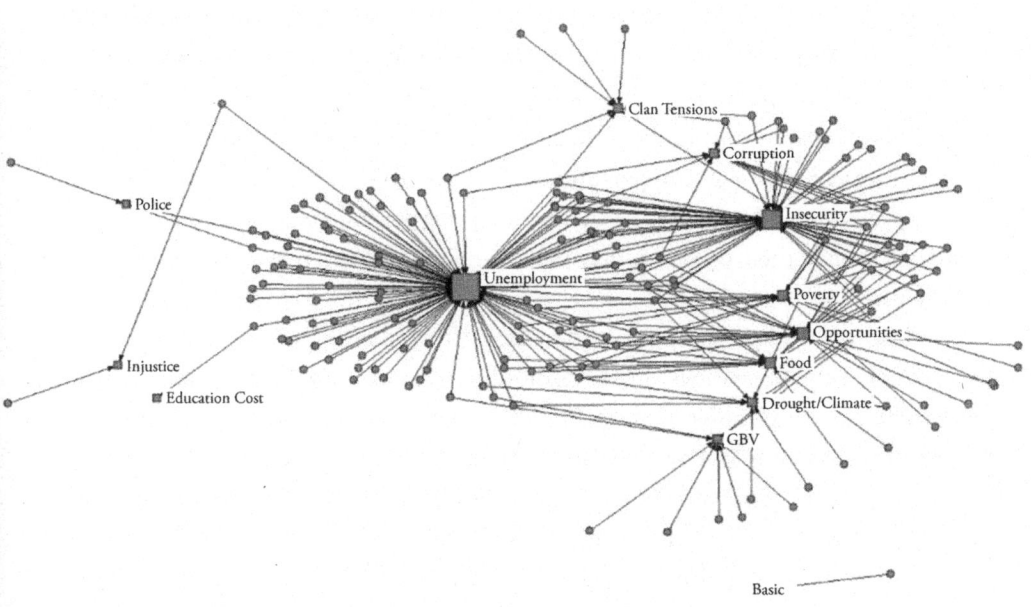

Figure 1: What are the top frustrations and concerns in your day-to-day life?

Our findings demonstrate that there has not been a large shift in the situation on the ground, with unemployment and insecurity still mentioned as the highest concerns by far for the participants. Unemployment can often be intertwined with identity and a sense of self-worth;[16] contributing to society can assist in avoiding a sense of marginalisation from a community. In Somalia, youth unemployment is one of the highest in the world. Exact statistics are difficult to ascertain due to the lack of nationally produced, systematic statistics on the matter, and therefore the results found can vary widely.[17] However, the World Bank, in 2018, marked youth unemployment in the country at 75%.[18] The World Bank stated that youth unemployment contributed to "illegal migration, organised crime, and/or violent extremism".[19] Al-Shabaab has regularly used unemployment to its advantage to recruit new members.

Back in 2010, when Al-Shabaab was at the height of its power, it is estimated that it offered recruits a salary of $500 a month – four times the national average at the time.[20] Although it is estimated that this figure is much lower now (closer to $30 a month), many choose to still join the group instead of the military (which offers $100 a month) as Al-Shabaab tends to be more consistent in its payments than the government.[21] Al-Shabaab has also been known to offer material goods, such as motorcycles[22] or free phones,[23] which are then used to disseminate propaganda, and it also often disseminates propaganda videos about members' extravagant lifestyles. In a situation where youth need to compete for employment, and where opportunities are limited, this offer of employment and the promise of a lavish lifestyle can be tempting for onlookers. It can give them status within their communities, power and an identity previously missing in their lives.

Through a combination of the findings from the SNA, desk research, and findings from interviews on the ground, the concept of identity, although a reasonably well-trodden path in P/CVE programmes, emerged as a prominent factor to address in our programming. Alongside this, power, in the Foucauldian sense,[24] was considered largely through the lenses of security (or rather, insecurity) and participation (or rather, representation).

Insecurity was cited more times by participants in Mogadishu than in other regions, at 61,5%, likely due to the number of attacks that take place in the capital. When it came to Baidoa, 33,3% of participants mentioned insecurity as a concern, whereas this figure dropped for participants from both Kismayo and Garowe (at 15,8% and 14,3%, respectively). At the time this study was conducted, Garowe and Kismayo had not experienced an attack for several years. Unfortunately, after the study took place, Kismayo experienced a deadly attack that killed at least 26 people.[25] This event may have led to different results were the study to have taken place again. Al-Shabaab can use this fear of reprisal and attacks as a way to recruit new members. Indeed, joining Al-Shabaab, or being an ally of the group, can ensure the safety of an individual. Although Al-Shabaab is the main conduit of the attacks within the country, it exploits security to lure recruits into the group.

Insecurity can also be linked to government action or inaction. Indeed, extremist groups and terrorism in general can be used as a means of effecting change within society. As Hoffman states, "terrorism is designed to create power where there is none or to consolidate power where there is very little".[26] To assess whether the participants of our SNA felt such a lack of power, we asked questions relating to the political environment in the country and their representation within it. Only in Mogadishu did a majority of participants feel represented within their political system (54,3%). As the central government is located in Mogadishu, this might explain why there is a stronger belief in the governmental environment there. In Kismayo, only a slight majority said that they did not feel represented (51,4%). However, in both Baidoa and Garowe, participants offered a much starker reality of political discontent, with 62,9% of participants in Baidoa and 80% in Garowe stating that they did not feel represented in the political system. Of those who did not feel represented, the majority of individuals stated that they felt excluded from opportunities because their clan was not the dominant one. The role that clan structure and dynamics have within Somali society is critical to better understanding how Al-Shabaab exploits these to further its cause. Although not part of the SNA, Bincof's study of the role of youth in Somali politics also demonstrates a desire for greater participation in the democratic process.[27]

Members of minority groups are known to be at a disadvantage within the country in governing institutions, and are subject to discrimination in employment opportunities and in access to public services.[28] When looking at the potential for clan divisions to lead to violence, a majority of respondents from

Kismayo (65,7%), Mogadishu (52,9%) and Baidoa (51,4%) alleged that they did. Garowe was the only region where the majority of participants believed that clan-based divisions did not lead to violence. It was also the region where the most people were indecisive about this issue. Extremist groups, including Al-Shabaab, use these feelings of powerlessness, arguing that politicians divide the country and distribute resources unevenly depending on clans.[29] Al-Shabaab has gone so far as to accuse the Kenyan government of reigniting clan tensions to benefit from their fighting.[30]

These forms of narratives and disinformation can create anger within clans, and build a desire for revenge and equality for the clan. By offering them a judicial system perceived as fair towards all clans and an unbiased conflict-resolution mechanism, Al-Shabaab is giving individuals opportunities to feel empowered. Further, Al-Shabaab exploits the injustices these individuals may have suffered at the hands of government representatives or dominant clan members by offering a chance for revenge through violence. This gives new recruits a sense of power over their own lives and trajectory, as well as representation in their society.

By examining the main concerns individuals mentioned in our SNA, to see how Al-Shabaab shapes their narratives around these concerns and how individuals and groups respond, the research gleaned a sense of the roles of power and identity played within the social fabric. Note that there are many other micro-, meso- and macro-factors that will come into play during the radicalisation and recruitment process, as well as numerous other forms of narratives that Al-Shabaab disseminates, so this is by no means a comprehensive representation. Understanding that Al-Shabaab indeed abuses these main concerns meant that our programme needed to carry out activities that would both empower individuals and give them a sense of identity. The majority of activities undertaken following the research achieved just this, as will be seen below.

Communication

When conducting communication campaigns of any sort, it is vital to understand how and where individuals communicate, consume and share information. Our SNA findings provided a baseline for just that; it offered an understanding of the information ecology of our audience across the four regions in Somalia. It is often presumed that, in fragile countries, access to information and technology is limited. We wanted to challenge this idea and better understand the access our target group had to mobile phones, radio, television and other traditional media to identify the most appropriate and effective means to disseminate content. The SNA found that across the four regions, a majority of respondents had access to smart phones, 94% of whom used them daily. Radio is also commonly used across the four regions; in Baidoa, 82,9% of participants listen to radio on a daily basis, while participants in other regions stated that they listened less frequently, with Garowe at 62,9%, and Kismayo and Mogadishu slightly lower.

Overall, the SNA found that social media pages (specifically Facebook) are popular across all regions. Respondents in Mogadishu, Garowe and Kismayo all use social media pages frequently, with 100% in Kismayo stating that they use them every day, 92,9% in Mogadishu and 88,6% in Garowe. The Baidoa respondents use them less frequently, with 65,7% stating that they use them on a daily basis.

These insights into communication channels allowed us to target our communication interventions, and ensured that they reached our audience through the appropriate means and mediums. These findings positively impacted the programme as they allowed us to build activities, using Facebook as a means to amplify our offline activities, and radio to disseminate further dramas, public service announcements and live debates.

A wider debate within the P/CVE field is focused mainly around the effectiveness of communication efforts to counter and prevent violent extremism, especially when discussing counter-narratives and counter-messaging efforts.[31] Indeed, much literature explores the effectiveness of communication campaigns, particularly counter-narratives, when aiming at reducing or preventing radicalisation. There is a need to shift the conversation to examining, with robust evidence, which alternative or counter narratives work, and why.

Archetti has argued that the current approaches to communication in counter-messaging campaigns are outmoded and based on a misunderstanding that narratives are simply stories or messages.[32] The critique of the current approaches is that P/CVE interventions rarely take into consideration the perceptions of local communities and involvement in understanding their societal and cultural experience. Rather, narratives have deep social, religious and cultural roots, which arise from a specific constellation of relationship – a social network.[33] As communicators who have worked in Somalia for more than a decade, we would agree with Archetti; narratives have deep roots and therefore it is critical for us to understand not only the prevailing narratives of Al-Shabaab, but also the social networks that disseminate these messages, and to whom. The SNA is able to provide a solid basis to do this, understanding what drives networks within communities to build narratives that are most relevant to them.

For example, participants stated that youth were the most at-risk target group for violent extremism, most visibly in Mogadishu and Baidoa, where 93,8% and 97,1% of participants, respectively, claimed this. In Kismayo, youth were still mentioned as the most at-risk group, but at a lower percentage (74,3%). Participants from Garowe were not as united on who the most at-risk group was, with 54,8% of respondents naming women to be most at-risk, and youth as the second category coming in at 51,6%. In both Kismayo and Mogadishu, women were also considered a high-risk group (with 60% in Kismayo mentioning them, and 32,3% in Mogadishu). Although we were not able to conduct follow-up research to understand the role of women in relation to Al-Shabaab, we stressed the importance of including women specifically in our interventions in these two regions. In Baidoa, this was much lower, at 8,8%. This information allowed our activities to be built on the basis that within these regions, these groups needed to be the focus. The offline and online activities discussed topics and issues faced by youth and women within the regions, as will be further detailed below.

Our SNA also found that there is a high reliance on friends and families, not only to voice concerns and frustrations, but also as people to turn to for advice and information. From our analysis, it is clear that Al-Shabaab exploits these family and friend networks to recruit and radicalise vulnerable communities; the group is infiltrating well-trodden and trusted communication channels.

At the onset of our efforts, we conducted an analysis around the tools used to recruit and the types of narratives used to communicate with vulnerable groups. Groups like Al-Shabaab do not use a one-size-fits-all approach to their communication, but rather tailor their tactics to specific vulnerable groups and individuals. Our analysis found that Al-Shabaab used six types of narratives: political and military, social and personal, ethnic and clan-based, religious and ideological, economic and, finally, integrity narratives.[34] Being able to couple this information with the findings from the research allowed a greater understanding

Using Evidence-Based Research to Improve P/CVE Programming

of how the CSOs could effectively build resilience to extremism and those narratives in communities. The extremist group disseminates its messages through various media, with both the radio and networks of family and friends the most commonly used. As seen above, our SNA found that the most central and frequently used channels include television, social media, mobile phones and FM radio in tandem and, thus, our activities had to ensure that we used these spaces too. There was no discernible difference by gender, age or district.

The research also explored which physical or digital places the participants used most frequently. The three places individuals in our target group used most frequently were the digital space (93,1%), family space (80,6%) and religious space (78,9%). Despite the aforementioned research that tends to dismiss technology in these contexts, it showed the importance it holds in these regions. This was a critical insight, which shaped the communication platforms used to engage with the target groups. This is shown in Figure 2, where each node represents the communication channels mentioned by the participants. They are sized by degree of centrality, meaning that the bigger the node, the more times it was stated as a channel of communication. Each point represents a participant, with the lines linking to which communication channel they mentioned.

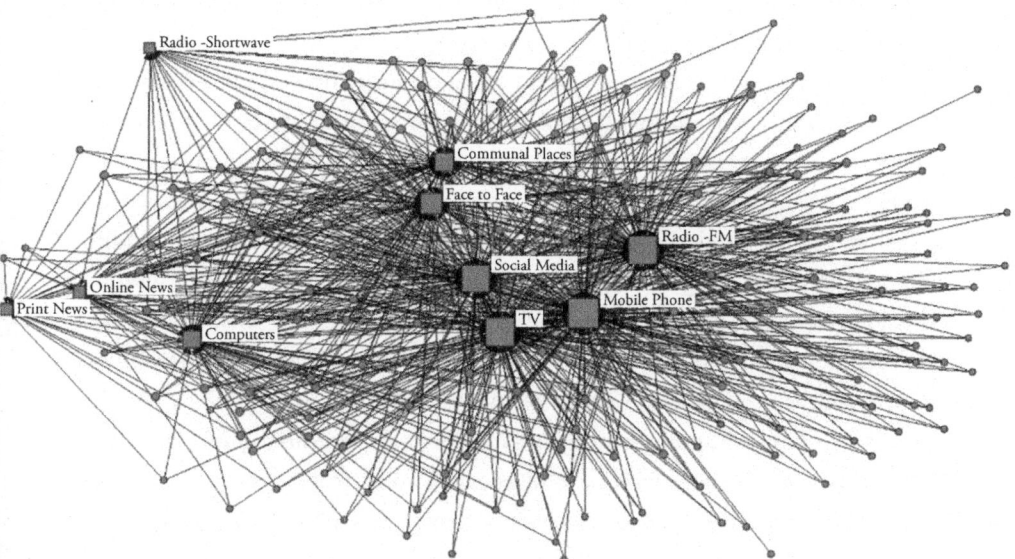

Figure 2: Which communication channels do you use most frequently?

An interesting observation was that when the CSOs were initially presented with the SNA findings and insights, they were unable to apply all of them due to sensitivities around the findings, but also as a result of the lack of trust and a relationship with the media. However, when the SNA findings were revisited towards the end of the project, many of the contentious discussions were willingly adopted into the new campaigns. The relationships with media partners, specifically radio, allowed for difficult conversations to be had and for addressing the genuine concerns and frustrations of the target group.

Insight from our SNA on the most-used mediums and spaces for communication also allowed us to shape the perception of our audience by providing a contrasting reality and accessing positive stories. However, groups like Al-Shabaab continue to have an intuitive understanding of the grievances and aspirations of their potential recruits. We have observed a timely increase in Al-Shabaab propaganda and messaging around political and military narratives to influence the population's perception of the authorities and security forces, further fuelling grievances of marginalisation and neglect. Understanding the concerns and frustrations of the target groups allowed the creation of spaces to discuss these in an open and healthy manner. For example, in Mogadishu, the findings demonstrated that there was a prevalent belief that the media and local journalism offer insights into topics relating to the participants' concerns and frustrations. This allowed the programme team to use radio as a means to open discussions around unemployment and insecurity. Allowing this to happen narrows Al-Shabaab's ability to distort these grievances and shape its own solutions to them.

Our SNA approach reinforced the notion that an individual's social network – that is, ties to family, friends and acquaintances – is one of the most influential factors impacting the trajectory of an individual's path to radicalisation. This idea has been explored by numerous authors, including Woodhams, who explored how social networks affected the pathway to radicalisation. Woodhams also looked at the challenges faced by the relationship connections within an individual's and community's social and terrorism-prevention support network.[35] This holds true for those who have disengaged and left Al-Shabaab – a process wherein they used their social networks of family to defect and leave the group. An informed understanding of the social networks of individuals within our target group has a positive impact in reducing vulnerabilities to violent-extremist narratives and propaganda. The research carried out within this programme gave us insights into such networks and an understanding of how they could be used to build effective alternative narratives.

Trust

Trust, much discussed in contemporary western discourse, is still something of a mystery for researchers from many fields: evolutionary psychology, economics, genetics and anthropology.[36] Regardless, Lieberman captures an essence of the concept: "While trust can be promised and earned, it cannot be ordered or demanded."[37]

Social science research into trust has grown significantly since the 1980s.[38] It is generally accepted that society is utterly reliant on trust, as it allows that society to make judgements on reality and thus make decisions. Without it, societal development would remain in paralysis. Trust is key to enabling predictability, community and collaboration, and is seen, from Hobbes to Locke to De Tocqueville, as a prerequisite for social order.[39] At this societal level, trust is seen as a public good, a measure of social capital, a key part of the institutional fabric of society, and essential for communication processes. It operates as an inherent, habitual mechanism; as a cohesive bond within family, friends and social groups; and as a macro-level foundation of collaborative solidarity.[40]

Trust is a concept very much wrapped up in future predictions on the actions of others. As such, it involves risk. In a general sense, it has been claimed that trust should become more valued as uncertainty increases – a notion connected with Beck's "risk society"[41] as a mechanism for managing risk. Further, as Luhmann attests: "One should expect trust to be increasingly in demand as a means of enduring the complexity of the future which technology will generate."[42]

It can thus be argued that in societies where certainty is low, as in conflict or post-conflict states, trust, especially social trust, is a highly critical factor in navigating daily social existence, more valued than in developed, relatively peaceful and ordered societies.

Within the research community, there are mainly two theoretical approaches, based on either a micro- or a macro-generative perspective. The dominant school tends to see trust created, maintained and developed within interpersonal and group dynamics, which then form the basis of cultural frameworks for political and economic systems. On the other hand, an alternative view is that trust is promoted, even imposed, by a "civilised public sphere"[43] through rational organisation and the rule of law, the gift of state, organisations and institutions. It can be recognised, however, that the two approaches should be considered as complementary rather than competing.[44] However, in areas of limited statehood, the former is seen as the prime factor, manifested in social trust, even if other structures, such as clans and tribes, may reflect a version of cultural 'institutions' impinging upon the social space.

With regard to the wider psycho-social frameworks, replete with trust networks, in some cases the failure to fully investigate such dynamics in relation to key CVE topics (as a result of being CVE-blind) may reduce the effectiveness of holistic approaches. Of course, this can often be attributed to specific donor requirements, lack of resources, or the absence of CVE input in programme design.[45]

Networks of Trust

The contemporary, digitally connected society has seen significant shifts in trust networks, not least a depletion of institutional trust. It could be argued that Somalia never really, certainly within the past 30 years, mirrored the state-led institutionally trust-based system. However, it could also be argued that Al-Shabaab could be seen as offering a framework something akin to it. The clan system, as an 'institution', has held sway, with a strong degree of religious underpinning. Both clan leaders and religious scholars and clerics have maintained a significant degree of 'personalised' trust, attached to the individual. However, in areas of limited statehood, this system or framework is often limited in scale, and prone to instability.

Equally, the clan system can be seen as encompassing 'particularised' trust networks, relying on widespread shared norms and values. Often compared to mafia-style organisations, familial ties – often widely extended – are key to these networks. Somalia is cited as a prime example.[46] This network system can be highly effective in maintaining social order, but also harbours potential for conflict. This potential for mistrust is a major feature of violent extremism. Research for the United States Agency for International Development (USAID) has confirmed that long-standing clan conflicts cause severe mistrust, and Al-Shabaab is regarded by some as a 'manipulator' of these sentiments.[47]

A third level of trust, 'generalised', wrapped up in the concepts of social capital and civil society, is seen as relatively weak in areas of limited statehood, according to the World Values Survey,[48] although admittedly the research is sparse.

However, as has been recognised in the West, growing societal expectations (or, more accurately, their failure to be met) and technology have enabled, at the cost of institutionalised and generalised trust, a mechanism of 'distributed' trust, where thin but real fibres of trust are built and maintained between a wide variety of actors. Such trust "flows laterally between individuals, enabled by networks, platforms and systems",[49] and its rise explains why we are now much more likely to 'phone a friend' than consult official sources, make judgements based on consumer feedback, and why faith in 'experts' is waning. Although many point to the West, often without clan-like 'institutions', as an exemplar of this phenomenon, Somalia is not immune. Comments from respondents to our SNA (see below) indicated that personalised trust, such as towards religious leaders, was far from guaranteed in certain circumstances, and some were reticent to place trust in anyone or anything. The point here is that trust networks, in whatever form, matter. Too often, we are concerned with how people obtain information for decision-making as opposed to who they are, how and why they trust that information, and the communication channels used to obtain it.

Trust in Communication

Having said that, media, notably social media (and to a degree more mainstream communication), are often employed within P/CVE programmes without consideration of the deeper relational and communicative aspects of local societies, not least trust. It is also recognised that such communicative aspects are under-represented areas within the field of P/CVE research.[50] Indeed, the effectiveness of counter-narratives, essentially responding to pull factors of violent extremism, has been widely called into question, as explored above.[51]

The issue of trust is relevant here. As many commentators have pointed out, fake news and disinformation are rife within Africa. More interestingly, or worryingly, is the differing perceptions of such between western audiences and African ones. A 2018 study indicated that audiences in Nigeria, Kenya and South Africa were more sceptical about their news sources than those in the US, with many fewer expressing complete faith (as in, never having identified fake news) in the media in African states (see Figure 3).[52] Although there are no trust barometers akin to the Edelman Trust Barometer covering Africa, this study does suggest that there are serious trust issues regarding the media in many African countries, with greater numbers distrusting their news.

Figure 3: How often do you come across news stories about politics and government online

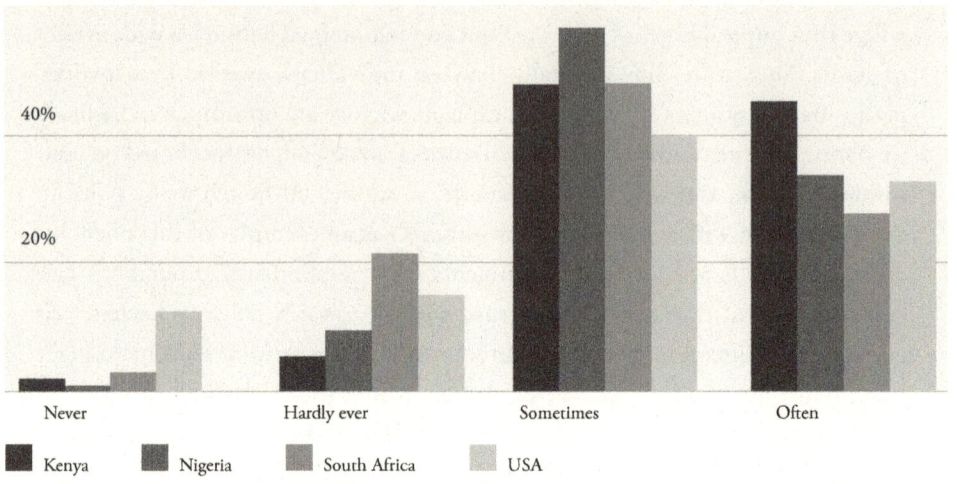

that you think are completely made up?[53]

Admittedly, Figure 3 applies to relatively media-savvy African nations. However, Somalia is also afflicted by the usual political chicanery attached to the disinformation phenomenon, as well as by poor standards of journalism education.[54] Although radio and television remain a major source of information, social media is also a key feature. Precise figures for media and information literacy in Somalia are scant, but qualitative research does indicate an appreciation of disinformation, propaganda and fake news – what one could assess as a healthy scepticism or mistrust of media.[55] However, as the study above indicates, there will undoubtedly be huge differences, dependent on context. Further, as seen below, media is only one facet of the communicative mix, alongside people's own interpersonal network and actual experience, which humans selectively trust and thus use to assess, analyse, decide and act.

The detail with which modern consumer campaigns are conducted account for many variables to not only grab attention but to capture such trust, albeit briefly. As such, an understanding of how, when, in what circumstances, in relation to what, and by whom – in other words, the "thick description"[56] at a micro-level – information is communicated is vital for influence. Also, an understanding of psycho-social dynamics and network effects is central to this endeavour, enabled through SNA.

Who is Trustworthy?

By examining patterns of which influencers are connected (or not), it is possible to infer an underlying pattern of advice-seeking relationships, and hence a degree of trust, among the respondents. The closer the influencers appear together on Figure 4, and the thicker the line between them, the more likely they are to be used by the same individual for advice. Figure 4 thus provides direction as to which influencers are more likely to be used in concert, as they share similar issue positions and focus.

Figure 4: One-mode representation (strength of ties between network nodes) – trusted

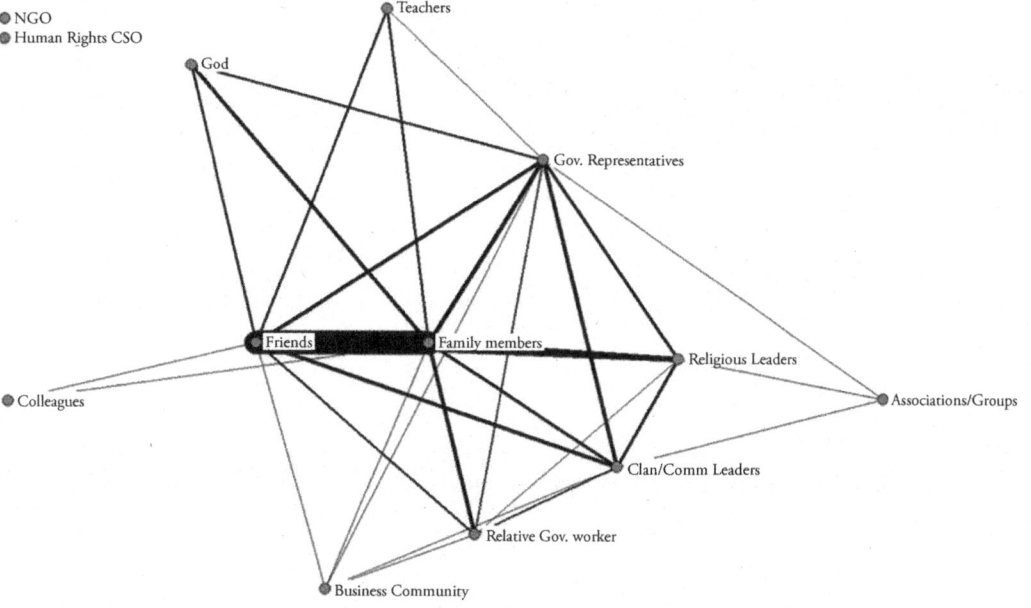

advice – all regions

As can be clearly seen, the strongest relationship is between friends and family members. Put another way, individuals are more likely to turn to both friends and family members in combination when seeking advice. There is also a strong relationship between family members and religious leaders. Conversely, Figure 4 also helps to show which sources or advice are not related. For example, individuals are not at all likely to seek advice from friends as well as associations/groups. Not one respondent cited non-governmental organisations (NGOs) and human rights CSOs in combination as sources of advice.

With regard to Figure 5, individual respondents were asked to identify which sources they turned to for advice as trusted sources. The nodes in the networks are sized by degree of centrality; in other words, the number of incoming ties to a particular node.

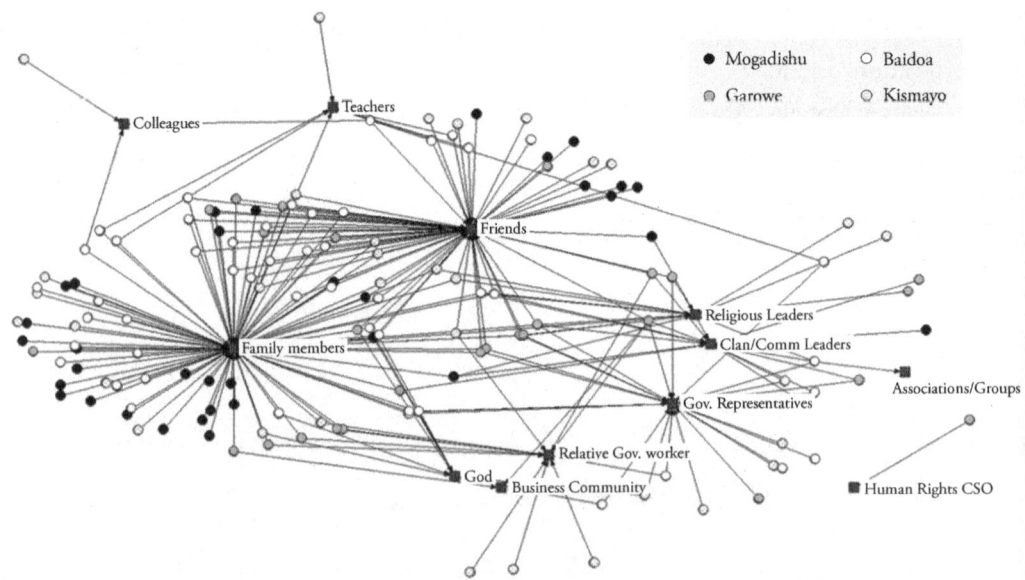

Figure 5: Two-mode representation (ties between individual nodes) – trusted advice

As can be seen once again from Figure 5, family members and friends were by far the most commonly selected sources of advice, and the remaining sources were selected with far less frequency. Figure 5 clearly illustrates the importance of friends and family to the respondents in seeking trusted advice. Associations

Using Evidence-Based Research to Improve P/CVE Programming

and NGOs have little to no influence in this space. However, separate research indicates that, in certain areas (Lower Juba/Kismayo), despite their advice not necessarily being sought, there is evidence that NGOs and the private sector are more trusted in assisting communities in managing assets collaboratively.[57]

The value-add of SNA can be highlighted in the fact that we can see that, in Baidoa (unlike other districts), trusted advice is almost exclusively limited to family and friends. In fact, the data showed a considerable difference in trust networks in Baidoa compared to the other regions, where government representatives enjoyed a modest degree of trust.

The SNA data itself threw light on other trust issues, once again with some differences across regions. As can be seen in Figure 6, a stark and direct closed question on the trustworthiness of information from religious leaders is highly informative, indicating that trust in religious leaders is markedly less in regions outside Mogadishu.

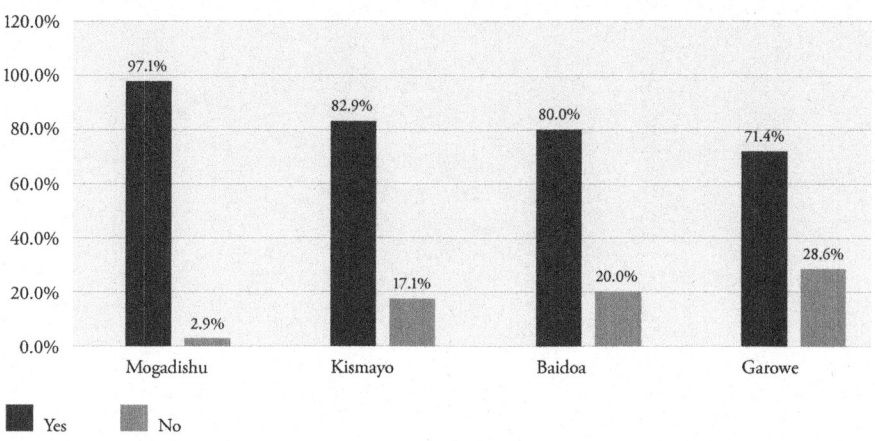

Figure 6: Would you consider the information provided by your religious leaders as trustworthy?

Which Channels and Sources are Trustworthy?

As is seen above, CSOs and NGOs are not necessarily key influencers in the Somali context. Tighter trust networks around family and friends are much more vibrant. Yet, in defining what information is discussed within these tight networks, media plays a role, inferring that a degree of trust is afforded to such media.

In Figure 7, the nodes represent the most trusted source of information mentioned by the participants. They are sized by degree of centrality, meaning that the bigger the node, the more times it was stated as a trusted source. Each point represents a participant, with the lines linking to the trusted source they cited. Figure 7 clearly shows a core group of trusted information channels, including religious leaders, family members, friends, social media, television and radio. The remaining information channels are used with far less frequency and are not often used together.

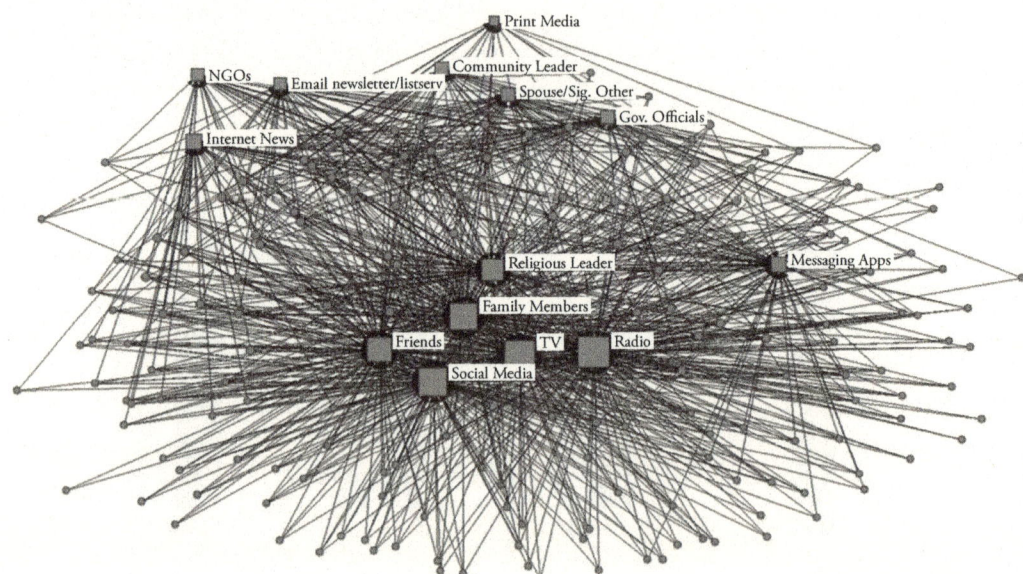

Figure 7: Two-mode representation (ties between individual nodes) – channels of reliable (trusted) information – all regions

Having mentioned clan-based 'particularised' trust networks at play in Somalia, further research indicates that the current Somali media landscape is no longer dominated by clan influences, with most media outlets operating to more corporate market-driven forces. That said, through funding, clans do maintain some limited control over local media.[58] Communications research also points to a complex and highly contextual inter-relationship between traditional communication and media, both local and international.

Although media has overtaken traditional sources of information, these nonetheless remain important. Indeed, despite the fact that most would turn to the radio for information about a serious event, Somalia's strong oral culture means that people constantly share information across their personal network, which is highly trusted.[59] Indeed, although interaction between media and consumers (polls, phone-ins, etc.) is limited, largely through lack of interest in doing so rather than a lack of ability, media content does filter through to, and to a degree drive discussion within interpersonal, traditional networks.

However, when respondents were asked what sources they go to first when a serious political event arises, modern media outlets came far ahead of informal, interpersonal sources of information.[60] Even so, international media are generally much more trusted than local media (except for highly local events), as shown in Figure 8. This assertion itself presents just one example of the necessity of highly localised understanding – there are significant disparities regarding trust in international media, with almost 80% trusting international media more than local in Barawe, compared with less than 40% doing so in Baidoa.[61] Similar notable contextual differences occur across demographics, such as region, gender, age, the urban/rural divide, etc.

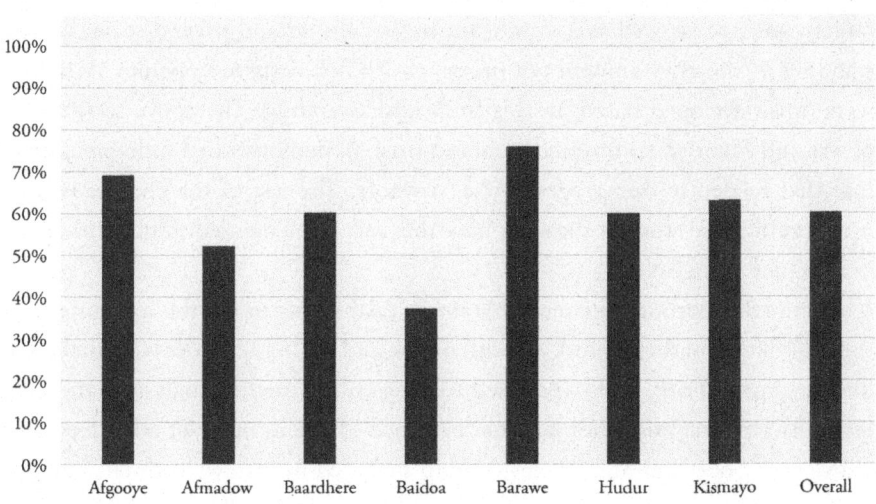

Figure 8: Share of respondents who trust international media more than local ones, per district[62]

Generally, trust in media is directly related to perceptions of completeness and accuracy, more than impartiality and timeliness, although once again there are variations between regions. Also, those with higher degrees of trust in their clans, with more closed trust networks, tend to be less connected via any media. Indeed, Somalia presents a complex framework of trust and communication networks, demanding highly localised understanding of those networks.

> "Despite the rise of various media platforms, traditional sources are likely to remain crucial to the spread of information as they are deeply embedded in Somali culture and operate in parallel to the media. Indeed, as revealed by case studies and field research, traditional networks combine with media platforms to shape the spread of information. What people hear on the radio or see online is quickly spread throughout the community as information [which] is then quickly spread through traditional networks. Reporters and social networks therefore act as gatekeepers of knowledge as they have considerable influence on what enters the community discourse."[63]

The Impact of Social Network Analysis on Programming

The SNA gave the programme designers a deep, contextually rich sense of the target audience, as well as a significant socio-cultural and psycho-social understanding of the environment within which P/CVE activities operate. Activities were thus developed based on this fresh understanding. The above sections on power and identity, communication and trust all demonstrated individual findings that related to our programme as a whole. The rest of the chapter will go into specific case studies, showing how this was implemented, highlighting the importance of an SNA.

Monitoring throughout the programme enabled us to see the real impact of these activities on the ground. As both online and offline activities were included, different monitoring tools were used such as online metrics analysis, radio call-ins transcript analysis, photographic evidence of the number of attendees, and videography observations. The evaluation included interviews with all the partner organisations and analysis of their own monitoring datasets. Overall, the results were positive. Feedback collected at events from participants was clearly in line with the overall objectives of the activities. Beneficiaries who previously were afraid to speak out about Al-Shabaab decided to dedicate themselves to it, and imams who initially refused to speak openly on the radio about topics relating to violent extremism requested to do so by the end of the project. One partner organisation trained youth to become peace ambassadors. They received more applications than needed, and are therefore planning to run similar programmes in the future to meet the demand. This feedback allowed us to understand which activities were most effective within each region, and to share lessons learned across the project. The final evaluation of datasets has allowed the project to demonstrate its effectiveness, relevance and impact.

Messaging alone will not prevent the radicalisation and recruitment of violent extremists. It is critical to adopt a holistic approach that is reinforced by offline action, as violent-extremist groups successfully offer a pathway of action through their messaging.[64] This includes, for example, using those most trusted to spread information relating to identity and power, as discussed above. In the design of our project, we took into consideration Hamid's thesis that counter-messaging needs to be coupled with counter-engagement; that it is ineffective to "[offer] alternative messages only, these efforts should shift towards offering alternative things to do as well".[65] Our efforts aimed to have a holistic strategy that connected our online messages directly to offline actions so the two reinforced one another.

Drawing on two successful examples of our holistic approach provides the evidence to examine what counter- and alternative narratives worked and why, while also taking into consideration the wide criticism of counter-narrative projects: that they are not informed by contextual research or even designed with local input.[66] The first example was undertaken in an area with a noticeable Al-Shabaab presence, the Jubaland region. The second example, in stark contrast, was carried out in an area which is relatively secure and with a strong government presence, the Benadir region. Although with contrasting profiles, the methodology for designing our interventions would remain the same, but be tailored to a hyper-localised solution and communication.

In the Jubaland region, the approach was focused on peacebuilding and stability through a community-based and multidisciplinary approach that included sports and dialogues. These activities were built to empower those participating in the activities. As seen in the SNA, unemployment was one of the main grievances expressed by youth in the region, and it was also clear from the findings that a lack of access to education was prevalent in this area. The online campaign and offline action were designed to provide a space for youth to come together to express themselves through a shared interest in sports, music and culture, and to offer them support in their interaction with one another to promote integration, peaceful coexistence and friendship. The activities were specifically designed to offer a sense of identity and belonging to the youth groups through trusted networks. Factoring in the criticism that these types of initiatives often do not guarantee that they will reach the target audience,[67] we began mobilising unemployed youth who were not enrolled in school between the ages of 15 and 25 from Kismayo district, and notably three remote villages in Jubaland that were newly liberated from Al-Shabaab control.

Since the SNA revealed that radio was still a highly popular communication mechanism, we partnered with two local radio stations that had a high listenership and were popular among the target audience. Through these, we created a space for two-way dialogues to take place. The radio campaigns aimed to ensure that youth and the larger communities had access to peace messaging that diminished the influence of extremist narratives and created more trust in positive influential figures such as imams.

Another activity undertaken was the creation of a five-episode radio drama series developed with local input and insights from the SNA, which followed five characters faced with tough choices and circumstances. Each episode had an underlying message driven by the characters as they tackled themes such as the quest for empowerment, handling choices and dilemmas, and identity crises.

Some of our work is sensitive and has security implications for the participants, so we are unable to delve into detail. However, in the Benadir region, particularly vulnerable youth were identified within the community. These youth were seen to be marginalised, disenfranchised and excluded from everyday life in the region. Their lives had been directly impacted by Al-Shabaab actions. As the findings of the SNA identified insecurity and unemployment as major issues facing our target audience, we decided to go with these youth who were directly affected by the topics.

The designed online campaign and offline action focused around an outreach campaign to encourage these marginalised youth to engage in positive activities in their region that aimed to empower them. Activities included mobilising youth to clean up their community, collect trash and plant flowers as a means of beautifying their surroundings. The aim was to create ownership of their environment and empower them in their communities. Following the clean-up campaign, a one-day event was held, which brought youth from numerous backgrounds together to encourage integration among the community. By facilitating and promoting social cohesion, the campaign aimed to reduce the sense of marginalisation and thus help reduce vulnerability to extremist messaging by offering an alternative pathway. This created a sense of trust among youth from different backgrounds, and a sense of belonging together, helping to forge an identity as a Somali.

The local partner organisations were in charge of data collection during these activities. Feedback collected during the first event had participants claiming the importance of safeguarding and protecting their communities, and emphasising the importance of empowerment. A photographer and film crew attended the second activity to capture the feedback and understand the atmosphere on the ground. The footage was to be used for feedback and internal project monitoring. From the footage and feedback collected, it was clear that being able to mix with groups of youth whom they would not normally interact with helped them achieve a sense of belonging. Crew from a local television station also attended the event to amplify the activities. Here, both young men and women were happy to hold up signs of peace to the camera without covering their faces, and spoke of the importance of achieving peace in their country. Speaking so openly about such topics is uncommon in Somalia due to the threat that might be linked to doing so. Seeing this develop naturally across these events demonstrated the sense of empowerment these youth experienced through the activities.

Effectively, the radio campaigns aimed to engage and entertain the target audience through a story that revolved around the lives and struggles of four young people in Mogadishu. Each episode had an underlying message driven by the characters, who take a prominent role as they tackle themes such as the risk of limited knowledge and misinformation, the quest for empowerment, choices and dilemmas, identity crises, and the struggles of living in marginalisation.

In our programming, the elements that worked were largely a result of understanding the target audience and their information ecology, and tailoring campaigns for each geographic region, drawing on the insights of the SNA. Understanding the prevailing Al-Shabaab narrative, but offering an alternative action and pathway, was crucial in this programme. In all, our research enabled a hyper-localised campaign that was credible, coordinated and consistent – a factor that led to the success of the campaigns.

Conclusion

Our SNA insights and wider project approach placed grassroots input and in-depth analysis of the socio-economic and societal factors within our campaign planning, engagement and evaluation. The SNA proved to be a highly useful research tool, especially when focused on aspects critical to social interaction, notably the nature of trust enabling such networks. The value of understanding why, or why not, trust is afforded to certain actors within a network, as opposed to merely identifying them, can be crucial in the development of P/CVE campaigns. For example, trust in religious leaders is often taken for granted, and thus these figures feature prominently in P/CVE campaigns. However, in certain circumstances, as seen above, such trust is not necessarily robust. This proves that a one-size-fits-all approach is susceptible to the risk of failure. Further, the SNA enabled us to understand how concerns and frustrations interlink and are fed back to trusted sources. This information not only helps understand how they can be abused by extremist groups, but also allows offline activities to tackle these issues head-on.

The focus on counter-narratives is often borne out of a straightforward focus on the networks, narratives and contexts of violent-extremist groups themselves. This is often an approach based on 'pull' factors in society, which can be easier to grasp and tackle. It is vital to engage with, and build programmes around, the often more politically unpalatable 'push' factors based on social science research, such as an SNA. Based on the results of the programming of activities, reported from the ground, the latter can provide for highly successful interventions.

Although such an approach may produce a longer-term endeavour than many donors and governments are comfortable with, investment in developing research and evaluation skills on the ground will significantly enhance how to understand social factors. Such an approach should address the three issues raised in the introduction: issues of psycho-social understanding, the need for local expertise and knowledge, and an increasing focus on 'push' factors. With this approach, much more targeted, evidence-based and effective alternative-narrative campaigns will arise.

Crucially, local knowledge, via respondents, was sought to build the evidence base for the pre-campaign analysis. Although, as of 2012, there were some 40 universities in Somalia,[68] it is considered that there is limited or no capability specifically focused on research or evaluation.[69] This reiterates the crux of the issue. If it is seen that social science research, such as SNA, can provide significant advantages in addressing 'push' factors and informing alternative-narrative campaigns within the rubric of P/CVE, then local expertise and knowledge are critical. As Albany Associates has long championed, "make it theirs" – empower local people to engage with and solve their own issues in their own contexts.[70]

Select Bibliography

Albany Associates. (2018). Conflict Mapping and Analysis Report: Baseline Study. Unpublished. London: Albany Associates.

Altai Consulting. (2019). Somalia Media Mapping and Landscape Survey – *2019*. Paris: Altai Consulting.

Anzalone, C. (2016). Continuity and Change: The Evolution and Resilience of Al-Shabab's Media Insurgency, 2006-2016. Hate Speech International. Available from: https://www.hate-speech.org/wp-content/uploads/2016/11/email_722762_Readers.pdf [accessed 22 February 2020].

Archetti, C. (2015). Terrorism, Communication and New Media: Explaining Radicalization in the Digital Age. *Perspectives on Terrorism*, 9(1). Available from: https://www.jstor.org/stable/26297326?seq=1#metadata_info_tab_contents [accessed 7 April 2020].

BBC News. (2019). Kismayo attack: At least 26 dead as gunmen storm Somali hotel. Available from: https://www.bbc.com/news/world-africa-48969781 [accessed 7 March 2020].

Beck, P.U. (1992). *Risk Society: Towards a New Modernity*. London: SAGE.

Bedig, A., Siddiq, H. & Norton, A. (2015). *A new frame for CVE:* Analyze beliefs, but counter behavior. Brookings. Available from: https://www.brookings.edu/blog/markaz/2015/03/17/a-new-frame-for-cve-analyze-beliefs-but-counter-behavior/ [accessed 13 March 2020].

Berger, J.M. (2016). Making CVE Work: A Focused Approach Based on Process Disruption. ICCT Research Papers. Available from: https://doi.org/10.19165/2016.1.05 [accessed 22 February 2020].

Bincof, M.O. (2018). The Role of Youth in Political Participation in Somalia. *IOSR Journal of*

Humanities and Social Science (IOSR-JHSS), 23, pp. 64-74.

Borino, F. & Saget, C. (2019). Employment programs and conflict in Somalia. Working Paper no. 51. Geneva: International Labour Office. Available from: https://www.ilo.org/wcmsp5/groups/public/---dgreports/---inst/documents/publication/wcms_734237.pdf [accessed 7 March 2020].

Botha, A. & Abdile, M. (2014). Radicalisation and al-Shabaab recruitment in Somalia. ISS Paper 266. Pretoria: Institute for Security Studies.

Botsman, R. (2017). *Who Can You Trust?: How Technology Brought Us Together and Why It Might Drive Us Apart*. London: Penguin Portfolio.

Brett, J., Eriksen, K.B. & Sørensen, A.K.R. (2015). *Lessons learned from Danish and other international efforts on Countering Violent Extremism (CVE) in development contexts*. Copenhagen: DANIDA.

Cooper, T. & Thomas, J. (2019). *Nature or Nurture: A Crisis of Trust and Reason in the Digital Age*. London: Albany Associates.

Davis, P.K. (2009). Representing Social-Science Knowledge Analytically. In Davis, P.K. & Cragin, K. (eds.). *Social Science for Counterterrorism*. Santa Monica, California: RAND Corporation, pp. 401-452.

Draude, A., Holck, L. & Stolle, D. (2018). Social Trust. In Risse, T., Borzel, T.A. & Draude, A. (eds.). *The Oxford Handbook of Governance and Limited Statehood*. Oxford: Oxford University Press, pp. 353-372.

Ferguson, K. (2016). *Countering violent extremism through media and communication strategies: A review of the evidence*. Cambridge: Partnership for Conflict, Crime and Security Research.

Freestone, M. (2017). Personality, identity, risk and radicalisation. *International Review of Psychiatry*, 29, pp. 310-312. Available from: https://doi.org/10.1080/09540261.2017.1344395 [accessed 13 March 2020].

Geertz, C. (1973). *The Interpretation of Cultures*. New York: Basic Books.

Gini, A. (1998). Work, Identity and Self: How We Are Formed by the Work We Do. *Journal of Business Ethics*, 17(7), pp. 707-714. Available from: www.jstor.org/stable/25073117 [accessed 19 March 2020].

Hamid, N. (2018). Don't Just Counter-Message; Counter-Engage. International Centre for Counter-Terrorism (ICCT) – Publications. Available from: https://icct.nl/publication/dont-just-counter-message-counter-engage/ [accessed 9 March 2020].

Haselock, S. (2010). Make it Theirs: The Imperative of Local Ownership in Communications and Media Initiatives (No. SR253). Washington, D.C.: United States Institute of Peace.

Hoffman, B. (2006). *Inside Terrorism*. New York: Columbia University Press.

Horgan, J. (2012). Interviewing the terrorists: Reflections on fieldwork and implications for psychological research. *Behavioral Sciences of Terrorism and Political Aggression*, 4, pp. 195-211. Available from: https://doi.org/10.1080/19434472.2011.594620 [accessed 26 February 2020].

IGAD Centre of Excellence for Preventing and Countering Violent Extremism (ICEPCVE). (n.d.). Gap Analysis of CVE Literature Relevant to the Eastern Africa Region. Djibouti:

ICEPCVE.
Independent Advisory Group on Country Information. (2019). Country Policy and Information Note Somalia: Majority clans and minority groups in south and central Somalia. London: United Kingdom Home Office. Available from: https://assets.publishing.service.gov.uk/government/uploads/system/uploads/attachment_data / file/773526/Somalia_-_Clans_-_CPIN_V3.0e.pdf [accessed 3 March 2020].

Jegede, O. (2012). The Status of Higher Education in Africa. Presented at the Weaving Success: Voices of Change in African Higher Education, New York, p. 5.

Lieberman, J.K. (1983). *The Litigious Society*. New York: Basic Books.

Luhmann, N. (1979). *Trust and Power*. New York: John Wiley & Sons.

Misztal, B. (1996). *Trust in Modern Societies: The Search for the Bases of Social Order*. Cambridge: Polity Press.

Mohamed, S.S. & Affan, M.U.I. (2012). Evaluating Quality Performance of Somali Universities. *Arabian Journal of Business and Management Review*, 1(16).

Nettleton, L. (2018). *Al-Shabab recruitment tools and narratives and the struggle to counter them*. London: Albany Associates.

Orgnet.com. (n.d.). Social Network Analysis: An Introduction. Available from: http://www.orgnet.com/sna.html [accessed 19 March 2020].

Papakostas, A. (2012). *Civilizing the Public Sphere: Distrust, Trust and Corruption*. London: Palgrave Macmillan.

Perliger, A. & Pedahzur, A. (2011). Social Network Analysis in the Study of Terrorism and Political Violence. *Political Science and Politics*, 44, pp. 45-50. Available from: https://doi.org/10.1017/S1049096510001848 [accessed 2 March 2020].

Reed, A. (2018). *An Inconvenient Truth: Countering Terrorist Narratives – Fighting a Threat We Do Not Understand*. International Centre for Counter-Terrorism (ICCT) – Publications. Available from: https://icct.nl/publication/an-inconvenient-truth-countering-terrorist-narratives-fighting-a-threat-we-do-not-understand/ [accessed 9 March 2020].

Reinares, F., Della Porta, D., Coolsaet, R., Khosrokhavar, F., Lohlker, R., Ranstorp, M., Schmid, A.P., Silke, A., Taarnby, M. & De Vries, G. (2008). Radicalisation Processes Leading to Acts of Terrorism: A Concise Report prepared by the European Commission's Expert Group on Violent Radicalisation. Gent: Universiteit Gent. Available from: https://biblio.ugent.be/publication/446365/file/6814706 [accessed 3 March 2020].

Rosand, E. & Winterbotham, E. (2019). Do counter-narratives actually reduce violent extremism? Brookings. Available from: https://www.brookings.edu/blog/order-from-chaos/2019/03/20/do-counter-narratives-actually-reduce-violent-extremism/ [accessed 9 March 2020].

Schuurman, B. (2018). Research on Terrorism, 2007-2016: A Review of Data, Methods, and Authorship. *Terrorism and Political Violence Online*, pp. 1-16. Available from: https://doi.org/10.1080/09546553.2018.1439023 [accessed 22 February 2020].

Stewart, F. (2005). Horizontal Inequalities: A Neglected Dimension of Development in Wider Perspectives on Global Development. In Shorrocks, A.F. (ed.). (2005). *Wider Perspectives on Global Development: Studies in Development Economics and Policy*. Basingstoke:

Palgrave Macmillan, pp. 101-135.

Sztompka, P. (1999). *Trust: A Sociological Theory*. Cambridge: Cambridge University Press.

Sztompka, P. (2016). Two Theoretical Approaches to Trust; Their Implications for the Resolution of Intergroup Conflict. In Alon, I. & Bar-Tal, D. (eds.). *The Role of Trust in Conflict Resolution*. Cham: Springer International Publishing, pp. 15-21.

United Nations Assistance Mission in Somalia (UNSOM). (2015). Countering Al-Shabaab propaganda and recruitment mechanisms in South Central Somalia. Mogadishu: UNSOM.

United Nations Development Programme (UNDP). (2017). Journey to Extremism in Africa. New York: UNDP. Available from: http://journey-to-extremism.undp.org [accessed 26 February 2020].

United Nations Office for the Coordination of Humanitarian Affairs (OCHA). (2018). Humanitarian Needs Overview: Somalia 2019. Mogadishu: OCHA. Available from: https://reliefweb.int/sites/reliefweb.int/files/resources/Somalia_2019_HNO.PDF [accessed 4 February 2020].

Wahlberg, H. (2017). "Right now, the lies are ahead of us" – Maneuvering in fake news in Kenya and Somalia. International Media Support. Available from: https://www.mediasupport.org/right-now-the-lies-are-ahead-of-us-maneuvering-in-fake-news-in-kenya-and-somalia/ [accessed 24 February 2020].

Wasserman, H. & Madrid-Morales, D. (2018). Study sheds light on scourge of 'fake' news in Africa. *The Conversation*. Available from: http://theconversation.com/study-sheds-light-on-scourge-of-fake-news-in-africa-106946 [accessed 3 March 2020].

Wood, S., Malla, L., Okwarah, P., Omar, S. & Kjaer, M. (2019). Somalia Program Support Services (SPSS), Transition Initiatives For Stabilization Plus (TIS+) Synthesis Report (No. IDIQ AID-623-I-14-00009). Vienna, Virginia: International Business & Technical Consultants, Inc.

Woodhams, K.M. (2016). Connections among communities: preventing radicalization and violent extremism through social network analysis in the Threat and Hazard Identification and Risk Assessment (THIRA) framework. Monterey, California: Naval Postgraduate School. Available from: https://calhoun.nps.edu/handle/10945/51640 [accessed 26 February 2020].

World Bank. (2018). Youth as Agents of Peace: Somalia (No. P152600). New York: World Bank. Available from: http://documents.worldbank.org/curated/en/463921526414702925/pdf/126251-WP-P152600-PUBLIC-Youth-As-Agents-of-Peace-Somalia.pdf [accessed 8 March 2020].

Youngman, M. (2018). Building "Terrorism Studies" as an Interdisciplinary Space: Addressing Recurring Issues in the Study of Terrorism. Terrorism and Political Violence Online. Available from: https://doi.org/10.1080/09546553.2018.1520702 [accessed 22 February 2020].

Zeiger, S. (2018). *Undermining Violent Extremist Narratives in East Africa – A How-To Guide*. Abu Dhabi: Hedayah.

Using Evidence-Based Research to Improve P/CVE Programming

Endnotes

1. Schuurman, 2018.
2. Horgan, 2012.
3. Youngman, 2018.
4. This is possibly a symptom of CVE-blindness, in which wider societal programmes, potentially dealing with push factors, are not necessarily cognisant of the relevance or potential of CVE within such programmes. See Brett et al (2015:29).
5. Reed, 2018.
6. Orgnet.com, n.d.
7. Perliger & Pedahzur, 2011.
8. See Davis (2009) and Woodhams (2016).
9. Berger, 2016.
10. ICEPCVE, n.d. (available through the ICEPCVE Digital Portal – registration required).
11. Reinares et al, 2008.
12. Freestone, 2017.
13. Botha & Abdile, 2014:10-11.
14. UNDP, 2017.
15. OCHA, 2018.
16. Gini, 1998.
17. Borino & Saget, 2019.
18. World Bank, 2018.
19. Ibid.
20. Zeiger, 2018:14.
21. Albany Associates, 2018.
22. Zeiger, 2018:2.
23. UNSOM, 2015.
24. Foucauldian in as much as power is seen as a function of social relations or linkages (not necessarily groups themselves), dependent on the knowledge of actors and working through discourses.
25. BBC News, 2019.
26. Hoffman, 2006.
27. Bincof, 2018.
28. Independent Advisory Group on Country Information, 2019.
29. UNSOM, 2015:10.
30. Anzalone, 2016:33.
31. ICEPCVE, n.d.:5 (available through the ICEPCVE Digital Portal – registration required).
32. Archetti, 2015.
33. Ibid, 39.
34. Nettleton, 2018.
35. Woodhams, 2016.
36. Cooper & Thomas, 2019.
37. Lieberman, 1983:134.
38. Sztompka, 1999.
39. Misztal, 1996.
40. Ibid, 101.
41. Beck, 1992.
42. Luhmann, 1979:16.
43. Papakostas, 2012.
44. Sztompka, 2016.
45. ICEPCVE, n.d.:27 (available through the ICEPCVE Digital Portal – registration required).
46. Draude et al, 2018:360.
47. Wood et al, 2019:108.
48. See http://www.worldvaluessurvey.org/wvs.jsp.
49. Botsman, 2017:257.
50. ICEPCVE, n.d.:27 (available through the ICEPCVE Digital Portal – registration required).
51. See, for example, Rosand & Winterbotham (2019), Reed (2018) and Ferguson (2016).
52. Wasserman & Madrid-Morales, 2018.
53. Ibid.
54. Wahlberg, 2017.
55. Altai Consulting, 2019.
56. Geertz, 1973.
57. Wood et al, 2019:150.
58. Altai Consulting, 2019:82-83.
59. Wood et al, 2019:80.
60. Ibid, 90-91.
61. Ibid, 86.
62. Altai Consulting, 2019:86.
63. Ibid, 91.
64. Hamid, 2018.
65. Ibid.
66. Rosand & Winterbotham, 2019.
67. Ibid.
68. Jegede, 2012:5.
69. Mohamed & Affan, 2012.
70. Haselock, 2010.

CHAPTER 15

Disentangling Violent Extremism in Cabo Delgado Province, Northern Mozambique: Challenges and Prospects

Blessed Mangena and Mokete Pherudi

Introduction

Radicalisation and violent extremism in Mozambique's Cabo Delgado province[1] are on the rise and are posing a major threat to human security and development in the region. This study sought to investigate the nature of the challenges that the Mozambique government is encountering in addressing the violent extremism posed by Ansar al-Sunnah (also sometimes referred to as Ahlu Sunna Wa-Jama, Ansar al Sunna or Al-Shabaab)[2] as well as its prospects in addressing the threat.

The study established that Mozambique's wholly militarised approach to addressing violent extremism in the province, marred by human rights abuses, could worsen the problem. The country is at risk of following the path of Nigeria, where a ham-fisted government response to a radical sect led to a surge in support for the group that became Boko Haram.[3] However, there is a good chance that the insurgency in Mozambique might be contained if the government embraces holistic, comprehensive and integrated counter-extremism strategies that encompass dynamic military approaches fused with sustained efforts that are aimed at effectively addressing the root causes of extremism in the province.

The Mozambican government also has a better chance of containing the threat if it can curb the extremist group's source of funding, which has enabled it to expand its war chest. Basically, there are two factors driving the conflict in Cabo Delgado province. The first is insurgency capacity to recruit more militants through enticing them with financial incentives that are donated by sympathisers, who donate via electronic payments. The second is recruitment conducted through family ties and radical mosques, where funds are also provided to new recruits. Government's militarised approach is misplaced as it alienates itself from the rest of the population in the province.

History of Ansar al-Sunnah in Cabo Delgado

The birth of Ansar al-Sunnah in Cabo Delgado province dates back to 2014[4] when the first signs of extremism came to light in the Mocímboa da Praia district among youths, who were influenced by a combination of push factors such as bad governance, social fragmentation and economic marginalisation, as well as pull factors, notably the inspirational extremist teachings of a Tanzanian radical preacher, Adbul Chacur, and the now deceased charismatic Kenyan imam Aboud Rogo Mohammed. The spread of external fundamentalist ideas in the province, as well as the material and emotional benefits generated from affiliation with Ansar al-Sunnah, contributed to the growing number of youths who were mobilised into violent extremism in Cabo Delgado province. Opportunistic criminals and army defectors have also joined the extremist group.[5]

Most of Ansar al-Sunnah's core militants have come from the Mwani ethnic group in Cabo Delgado. This ethnic group has traditionally been politically, socially and economically marginalised by Mozambique's ruling Frente de Libertação de Moçambique (FRELIMO) government and, consequently, their livelihoods are based mostly on informal and illegal trading. The Mwani are distrustful of the local police and military, who mostly come from Maputo and are of a different ethnicity.

During Mozambique's fight for independence against the Portuguese between 1964 and 1974, which was primarily fought in Cabo Delgado, the majority of the largely Christian Makonde ethnic group aligned with FRELIMO to fight the Portuguese, and they have continued to be rewarded by the government through pensions and political concessions. A large portion of the Mwani people remained in Portuguese camps or fought with them against FRELIMO during the war of independence. Consequently, after independence, the FRELIMO government sidelined the Mwani in favour of the Makonde and other ethnic groups.

Many Makondes and other Mozambicans view the Mwani as backward or irredentist for supporting, or at a minimum living among, the Portuguese and eventually supporting the opposition Resistência Nacional Moçambicana (RENAMO) party.[6] The Mwani are largely recognised as the original occupants of coastal Cabo Delgado, but their current social status and economic standing are not reflective of their past.[7] The war furthered ethnic tension between the Mwani and other coastal ethnic groups, including the Makondes. These divisions have been kept alive by the memories of war and the ruling party's policies of excluding the Mwani. Ansar al-Sunnah attacks have demonstrated this division, with Mwani people being spared in many instances.

Ansar al-Sunnah also refers to itself as Swahili Sunna, suggesting a reference to the Mwani's past as the original people of northern coastal Mozambique.[8] The group's claim to the coastal region and their former glory, together with their current marginalisation, contributed to the group's discontent with oil exploration in the region and the resultant targeting of foreign oil workers in February 2019.

The group's militants are predominantly young Muslim Mwani youths ranging from 18 to 35 years of age.[9] Signs of discontent and radicalisation have included abandoning Islamic customs and practices traditionally followed in the region. They have also abandoned traditional mosques, and have built their own where a fundamentalist interpretation of Islam is espoused. The group has also refused to recognise the Mozambican government as the legitimate authority in the province. The penetration of Wahhabism[10] in the province, which is an austere form of Islam that insists on a literal interpretation of the Qur'an, has shaken the tradition of religious tolerance in Cabo Delgado. The imported radical religious ideas espoused by Wahhabism, and justifying the recourse to armed struggle, have contributed to the radicalisation of religious discourse and rising intra- and inter-communal tensions in Cabo Delgado.

Wahhabism was introduced in northern Mozambique in the 1960s by graduates from Saudi Arabia and other Gulf schools who began to challenge the country's traditional Sufi customs, which had long been practised in the province. In recent years, the Islamic Council in northern Mozambique, which is heavily influenced by Wahhabism, tapped Gulf nongovernmental organisations to provide scholarships for students to study abroad. It is these returning students who make up the core of Ansar al-Sunnah, and who have capitalised on the grinding poverty and other grievances in the province to recruit more followers. It is from the Islamic Council's activities and its sub-organisations that Ansar al-Sunna has emerged.[11]

Ansar al-Sunnah is inspired by international jihadism, including the establishment of an Islamic state under sharia law, the rejection of formal education and healthcare, as well as the rejection of state taxes and other state authority. For the politically disgruntled and economically marginalised Mwani ethnic group, 'purified' Islam, as opposed to the more traditional Sufism, holds out the promise of decisive answers to northern Mozambique's inequities and marginalisation.[12] Although Ansar al-Sunnah has operated under the guise of wanting to establish an Islamic caliphate based on sharia law, socio-economic grievances play an important role, especially in attracting followers.[13]

Although the Mozambican authorities had intelligence on the activities of Ansar al-Sunnah, they failed to act decisively to contain the group during its nascent stages, until its first attacks in October 2017 targeting police and military posts in the coastal town of Mocímboa da Praia. The group had "at least three years of social and psychological work to recruit, indoctrinate, brainwash and transform the youth"[14] before its first attack. This is because, over the past several years, religious leaders have taken a more active role in governance while the central government's presence in the region has remained limited. Northern Mozambique has experienced growing migration from neighbouring Tanzania, including Islamic preachers who were influenced by radical clerics in East Africa, such as Kenyan-born Sheikh Aboud Rogo who was killed in 2012. These religious clerics have established mosques that preach anti-government ideology, denounce western education, and call for moving away from the existing moderate form of Islam. By 2014, they had capitalised on the long-standing feelings of resentment and marginalisation to build up military cells.

The insurgency group used various methods to further its activities, including radicalisation, recruitment, training, logistical acquisition and the execution of attacks. With regard to radicalisation, Ansar al-Sunnah used a number of methods, which included openly preaching its extremist ideology in mosques, secret places, round meetings (*darasa duara*), madrassas, social media and Qur'anic schools, where DVDs and CDs containing extremist messages are distributed.

Ansar al-Sunnah also manipulated four legal Islamic concepts – *jihad, kufar, shahid* and *hijrah* – to justify its violent actions. In line with its Wahhabist beliefs, the extremist group is waging a jihad as proclaimed in the Qur'an, and fighting against *kufar* (non-believers). The group members also believe that if they die in *jihad* (holy war) they will be *shahid* (martyrs).

Recruitment into Ansar al-Sunnah

Ansar al-Sunnah has skilfully exploited the underlying societal vulnerabilities of inequity, pervasive poverty, social exclusion, widespread unemployment, insecure land rights, and excessive use of force by the military and police during their counterinsurgency operations to secure local support and boost its recruitment drive. Recruitment takes place through clandestine operations in mosques, madrassas, prisons and social media platforms. The group also leveraged social and familial networks to recruit new members, not only through the offer of wages or bounty, but also by providing recruits with capital to enter into both the illicit and licit economy, as well as offering study bursaries.[15]

A close look at the profiles of some of the insurgents reveals how important their entry into the local economy was to both recruitment and funding. In Mocímboa da Praia, Nuro Adremane and Jafar Alawi, who were early leaders of the group, each owned a small shop with an equally small local customer base. They travelled regularly to Tanzania for business, and their small shops became big ones, bringing in large sums of money. Adremane and Alawi both bought expensive cars and houses in Palma, which raised their standing with the town's youth. After the October 2017 attacks, the two sold many of these assets, which had been powerful tools for recruitment.[16]

As mentioned, youth unemployment in Cabo Delgado is high, and financial benefits from illegal activities such as drug trafficking have been a key tactic of recruitment. In fact, there are few alternatives that produce similar profits and rapid enrichment in Cabo Delgado, and this has encouraged a large number of youths to join the extremist group to tap into this lucrative criminal economy.

Indirect recruitment is also done through videos obtained from radical movements in Kenya and Tanzania. Some of the popular narratives that the group has used for recruitment include the following:

> "Participating in jihad provides one with a purpose in life and is a means to a better life in the holy Islamic land governed by sharia laws and is also a way of freeing one from *kuffars* (non-believers). Taking part in jihad will contribute to the liberations of the world from the 'unholy' western culture. Dying as a martyr enables an individual to liberate seven closest members of one's family who will directly go to paradise."[17]

These extremist ideas, espoused by Wahhabism, have provided a default form of salvation from relative deprivation, dispossession and the fragmentation of social relations. Due to a number of structural factors, mentioned above, Ansar al-Sunnah's activities have found resonance among some segments of the youth. All of this is against a backdrop of a local population that has been sidelined and marginalised in the wake of considerable investment in infrastructure in the area to support the extraction of petroleum, natural gas, and large deposits of pink sapphires and rubies. The local population, most of whom are unskilled, have been sidelined from employment opportunities in infrastructural development projects such as roads; such employment opportunities have gone mostly to expatriates.

Furthermore, foreign multinational companies, with the aid of the government, have expropriated land from locals without proper compensation. Private security guards employed by these companies, particularly the British-based Gemfields, as well as Mozambique's security forces have forcibly removed the community from their land and displaced a number of local miners. This has created consternation and social stress among the population, providing fertile ground for militant recruitment. Subsequently, the group has grown exponentially, from about 30 to 40 militants in early 2018 to 1,000 multinational fighters in 2019.[18] The militants are from Tanzania, Uganda, Gambia and Somalia, although the majority are Mozambican. The militants are organised into small autonomous cells along the coast of northern Mozambique and neighbouring Tanzania's Kibiti region.[19]

Ansar al-Sunnah Strategies

Most of Ansar al-Sunnah's members have received military training in the Cabo

Delgado districts of Mocímboa da Praia, Macomia and Montepuez, where the group established clandestine training camps and cells. Former Mozambican police, army deserters and ex-frontier guards, as well as Al-Shabaab mercenaries from Somalia and Kenya, have trained militants in the province.[20] Other group members have received military training in Tanzania and the Great Lakes region.[21] In 2018, Tanzania arrested 104 Ansar al-Sunnah militants who were undergoing military training in the country's Kibiti region.[22] In the same year, the Mozambican government put 189 alleged militants on trial in Pemba for their involvement in violent acts – 50 of them were Tanzanian.[23] This is a clear indication of the strong links that exist between extremist groups in Tanzania and Mozambique.

During its initial stages, Ansar al-Sunnah predominantly used machetes and a few guns to carry out attacks. The group seized these firearms, grenades and military uniforms by overrunning police and military posts in the province. The group has now acquired a substantial number of firearms, enabling it to attack multiple places at once. Initially, Ansar al-Sunnah members were armed with knives and machetes,[24] but their weaponry is improving after targeting police stations in the area and confiscating weapons and heavy artillery. Some used knives to inscript drawings on their weapons, while others made wooden weapons similar to the ones they confiscated from the police or government forces as a sign of supremacy.

Transnational organised crime and illicit trade are thriving in Cabo Delgado due to a limited state presence. The illicit economy has fostered corruption in the province, which has played a vital role in the breakdown of law and order, allowing the insurgency to establish itself locally and across the region. As a result, security forces, government officials and their cronies who are benefiting from the illicit economy ensure that borders are kept porous and coastlines unmonitored.

Ansar al-Sunnah has taken advantage of the illicit economy to finance its operations through transnational criminal activities, notably heroin, timber, wildlife and gemstone trafficking, as well as internal and external financial donations from sympathisers from across northern Mozambique, including Nampula and other parts of the country. Vietnamese and Chinese nationals are part of an intricate web of criminals involved in transnational organised crime,[25] which has helped to finance Ansar al-Sunnah's activities. Funds are used to maintain group members and their families, to recruit new members, for propaganda, and to purchase guns. Robberies, extortion, cattle rustling, charcoal trade, artisanal mining, human trafficking to South Africa, and looting food from villagers are also economic lifelines for the group. Travel documents are acquired by recruiting and bribing immigration officers. Some civilians, fearful of the group's growing strength, also provide them with supplies, medical care, and intelligence on the movements of the security forces.

Before executing an attack, Ansar al-Sunnah conducts reconnaissance missions to acquire intelligence on when to time an attack and how to inflict maximum damage, as well as mapping out escape routes. To avoid detection, reconnaissance missions are conducted by small groups of no more than three cadres, who use machetes and assault rifles.[26]

During the initial stages of the insurgency, Ansar al-Sunnah targeted mostly security installations to acquire weapons. However, after indiscriminate counterinsurgency operations by government security forces, the extremists' *modus operandi* has evolved to include beheadings, mostly of male civilians and community leaders accused of collaborating with security forces.[27] The insurgency group's tactics have also morphed to match the brutality of the security forces, and now include indiscriminate attacks on villages, setting homes alight, looting, plundering, pillaging, widespread intimidation, and attacks on women, children and the general civilian population – a new trend not previously experienced. In most of these attacks, the Mwani ethnic group is spared.

In March 2019, the group used an improvised explosive device to attack the Mozambican military, suggesting an evolution in tactics.[28] The insurgency group also shifted its operations from night-time attacks on isolated homes to coordinated day-time attacks, as well as attacks on foreign employees working for gas exploration companies in the province. The attacks in 2019 on foreign employees of the United States (US) oil conglomerate Anadarko Petroleum Corporation (since replaced by French oil company Total), currently leading the biggest liquefied natural gas project in the country worth $20 billion,[29] is a case in point. This was an indication that Ansar Al-Sunnah was becoming more extremist.

By February 2020, the attacks had spread across nine of the 16 districts in the province, with most attacks concentrated on the coast of Cabo Delgado, from Pemba to the Tanzanian border. Consequently, villages have been completely abandoned, and hunger is growing as people abandon their farms and other economic activities. Many people, some of them women and children, have taken refuge on the small islands that dot the coast, with no access to clean water. Some have been forced to live in public buildings or even under trees. By February 2020, at least 100,000 people had been internally displaced, with more than 300 killed, and, since 2017, more than 1,000 properties have been destroyed.[30] The United Nations High Commissioner for Refugees has provided $2 million to respond to the growing humanitarian catastrophe.[31] Many areas affected by the attacks were also devastated by Cyclone Kenneth in April 2019, compounding the already dire humanitarian situation.

It is pertinent to note that Ansar al-Sunnah has also targeted its own members who took loans from the group to start small businesses but later deserted or failed to cooperate when they were needed to launch attacks. This is why attacks on whole villages result in only a few deaths; the men who have defaulted are beheaded – and if they cannot be found, family members are made to pay the price.[32]

Challenges in Combating Ansar al-Sunnah

The Mozambican government is facing a number of challenges in dismantling Ansar al-Sunnah due to a multiplicity of factors. The extremist group's diversified funding portfolio and ability to raise money through transnational organised criminal activities have enabled it to survive and expand its war chest. Since political corruption related to the illegal drug industry is high in Mozambique, with proceeds often used to fund election campaigns, there is little incentive for politicians to clamp down on the militants.[33]

The government's counter-extremism efforts have failed to effectively tackle the group's funding mechanisms due to the province's highly informalised economy, which makes it extremely difficult to track illicit financial flows to Ansar al-Sunnah. Terrorism financing in Mozambique is also difficult to track because the country's Financial Intelligence Unit is too weak to track funds from Cabo Delgado's predominantly cash-based economy, where cash is transferred outside the formal financial sector via telecommunications companies, transport companies, bus services or other businesses.

Ansar al-Sunnah has continued its recruitment drive as a result of the government's failure to address the root causes of the crisis, particularly poverty, inequality, unemployment, social exclusion and disputed land resettlement schemes, whereby locals were removed from their land to pave way for multinational corporations' mining concessions. For instance, Anadarko Petroleum Corporation's development of a $20 billion liquefied natural gas project has led to the forced resettlement of thousands of farmers and fishermen from the Afungi peninsula in the Palma district of Cabo Delgado. There is widespread dissatisfaction with the implementation of the resettlement programme, which is characterised by the diversion of funds intended to assist the displaced population, inadequate compensation for lost land, and lack of compensation for what the communities have invested and done on the land.[34] Some resettled households, particularly fishermen, were settled inland and have lost their livelihoods.[35] Despite the billions of dollars invested by major oil and gas companies in the province, there has been little benefit to local communities, and this has aggravated local grievances and fuelled the insurgency.

Furthermore, the heavy-handed responses of Mozambique's security forces, including extra-judicial killings, an extra-judicial state of emergency, the closure of mosques, as well as arbitrary detentions and harassment, have forced more people to join the group, either out of fear or to avenge human rights abuses which they have suffered. Mozambique's security forces have consequently lost legitimacy and local support, creating more grievances against the government. Seventy-one percent of former Ansar al-Sunnah members say that they joined the extremist group in response to violent or repressive government actions against them or those close to them.[36] The ongoing heavy-handed intervention by government security forces will likely lead to more radicalisation and tension, and risks further alienating a population that already feels that the government has abandoned them. The pattern of escalating violent extremist attacks, followed by indiscriminate security responses, has played out repeatedly elsewhere in Africa, notably in Somalia, Nigeria, the Lake Chad Basin, the Sahel and the Maghreb.

Ansar al-Sunnah's use of guerrilla tactics and ability to melt into the population after attacks have led the military to indiscriminately target whole villages,[37] which has deepened local grievances against the government. Since most of the militants come from local communities, residents are reluctant to provide intelligence to the security forces for fear of reprisal, while others are sympathetic to the group. In this regard, poor civil-military cooperation has reduced the security forces' ability to collect intelligence about the group's activities.

The Mozambican government's ineffectiveness in countering Ansar al-Sunnah's extremist narrative, as well as downplaying the situation as mere 'banditry', ignoring the broader narrative of socio-economic grievances, also risks aggravating the problem. An understanding of the deadly interplay of push and pull factors is therefore necessary for tackling the underlying causes of militancy and criminality in the province.

Scant information about the group's membership base, as well as a lack of a clear-cut leadership structure which the security forces could identify and target, has equally constrained the Mozambican government's counterinsurgency operations. Mozambican President Filipe Nyusi expressed his frustration at a political rally he addressed in the Chiure district of Cabo Delgado ahead of the October 2019 elections by saying "if they show their face, we will go and meet them",[38] an indication that his government was finding it difficult to negotiate with an insurgency group whose leaders are unknown.

By February 2020, the Mozambican security forces had arrested hundreds of Ansar al-Sunnah militants, but security-force interrogations have failed to yield substantial intelligence because those arrested have been reluctant to release any information on the group's activities – a sign of extreme radicalisation.

Porous borders between Mozambique and its neighbours, particularly Tanzania, make it easy for Ansar al-Sunnah militants to cross the border. Fragile loyalty to the central state is further weakened in Cabo Delgado, where the Mwani ethnic group straddles the border between the two countries. Identities there are forged on a local rather than a national level, and frequent trans-boundary movements reinforce this disconnect from the central state. Daily life is regulated in an ad hoc, informal manner built around ethnic or local customs. Border porosity has also enabled militants to sneak out of the country to undertake military training in the Great Lakes region with few constraints. Criminal groups also use the porous border with Tanzania to export drugs and minerals. Efforts to limit smuggling and the free flow of people and goods in the region of Mocímboa da Praia and the Tanzanian border have failed.

Mozambican security forces also lack key skills in counter-extremist operations. Infantry forces deployed by the government have proved to be very weak in combating violent extremist groups on the continent. The Mozambican security forces also lack force enablers and multipliers, as well as adequate organic human intelligence,[39] to effectively counter the extremist group. This is reflected in the fact that the insurgents are attacking administrative centres, even those protected by the army.[40] The security forces also lack discipline; its command structure "often releases suspected extremists from custody in exchange for large amounts of money".[41] Consequently, many soldiers have avoided handing suspected extremists over to their superiors, preferring to collect the cash payments from the suspects themselves.

The government has also not put in place population-centric programmes to enhance governance and development to address the structural causes of the insurgency. In addition, the security forces have failed to put measures in place to protect members of the civilian population who have provided them with intelligence against reprisal attacks. Ansar al-Sunnah has targeted informers, which has frightened other civilians out of providing intelligence against the insurgency group.

The terrain and isolated nature of the five districts where most of the attacks have taken place – Mocímboa da Praia, Macomia, Nangade, Palma and Quissanga – has provided a safe haven for the insurgency group. All of these districts, with the exception of Nangade, are on the coast overlooking the Mozambican Channel, and Macomia has a large plateau area that stretches into the interior.[42] It is also pertinent to note that, with a population of 24,7 people per square kilometre, Cabo Delgado is the fourth least-populated of Mozambique's 10 provinces.[43] The largely uninhabited landscape is characterised by wetlands, undulating hills and ridges, and flat-bottomed valleys, speckled with small villages and settlements. Cabo Delgado also has a tropical savanna climate with a wet season from October to March. Combined, these factors make reconnaissance by the security forces challenging.

Recommendations

There is a chance that the insurgency could be addressed if the Mozambican government first acknowledged the real nature of the problem. Ansar al-Sunnah has genuine grievances to which the government should be paying attention. The government should embrace a holistic, comprehensive and integrated counter-extremism strategy, encompassing dynamic and selective military approaches fused with sustained efforts aimed at effectively addressing the root causes of the problem. A hard-line response that depends solely on repression will only make things worse. Improving the quality of life for Cabo Delgado's residents, particularly its youth, is an essential first step in improving trust between the government and local communities. This trust will provide tactical advantages to the government, such as intelligence on militant movements, members and activities, as well as strategic gains. The British counterinsurgency effort in Malaya from 1952 to 1955 featured increased efforts to improve the quality of life of civilians, including initiatives to accelerate self-government and increase access to economic opportunities, community halls and medical assistance – programmes that helped increase civilian support for the counterinsurgents.[44]

A more comprehensive approach, which focuses on shared socio-economic development and leverages international partnerships, would be more effective in fighting extremist groups such as Ansar al-Sunnah. There are prospects that if the government develops a holistic security, community engagement and communication approach, the insurgency might be contained. This strategy would include investigating allegations of abuse by multinational mining interests, and offering compensation to the aggrieved if abuse is established.

The Mozambican government, with the help of the international community, should train the national police, other state actors and private-sector security forces to carry out their responsibilities in ways consistent with international standards of human rights in conflict settings. This should be accompanied by providing the means to hold security forces accountable. Such actions are important not only on their own merit, but also because the failure to uphold human rights standards is recognised as one of the strongest drivers of militant recruitment on the continent. For instance, the killing of Boko Haram's charismatic founder, Mohamed Yusuf, in police detention in 2009 was a trigger in turning the group into an indiscriminate violent insurgency in Nigeria.

The Mozambican government also has better prospects of countering the insurgency if it addresses Ansar al-Sunnah's sources of funding. If the government manages to counter the group's funding, it would have solved 90% of the insurgency.[45] In this regard, the Mozambican government should intensify the specialised training of people engaged in counterterrorism financing and anti-money laundering, especially in the sphere of financial intelligence gathering, analysis and investigation, as well as the interoperability of agencies engaged in the implementation of counterterrorism financing and anti-money laundering regimes. The unregulated informal sector should be brought into the formal sector, and financial inclusion should be promoted in the province.

The security forces involved in counterinsurgency should improve civic-military relations and work closely with local communities to obtain intelligence; counterinsurgency is an intelligence war that puts much more emphasis on human intelligence sources to infiltrate and weaken the group. According to Williams and Hashi, "locals are best placed to identify insurgents and inform counterinsurgency operations of militants' movements and routines".[46] Short of these, it is most likely that the group will continue to launch more deadly attacks because its strength is steadily increasing. There is also a possibility that its capacity will be enhanced through foreign fighters relocating from Iraq and Syria.

Multinational companies that have been given mining concessions in the province could positively impact on local communities and contribute to long-term stability through social corporate responsibility in community development, such as in health, agriculture, fishing and skills training. This would address some of the local grievances about marginalisation and unemployment. The government should also ensure that local youths benefit from the multi-billion-dollar natural gas projects in the province through massive infrastructural development that could create employment for the large number of unemployed young people.

Community dialogues between a broad spectrum of traditional, faith-based (Muslim and Christian) community leaders – which should include women and youth, government and administrative officials, educators, security personnel and health providers – are equally key in disentangling violent extremism in Cabo Delgado. Likewise, local media, especially community radio stations, are critical in promoting civic engagement and disseminating counter-extremist messages and alternative narratives that are credible and persuasive among the

Mozambican youth who are being recruited. Without the support of local people, Ansar al-Sunnah will not survive. Mao Tse Tung famously observed that a guerrilla swims among the people like a fish swims in the sea; without the support of the people, the guerrilla is a fish out of water and it cannot survive.[47] Ansar al-Sunnah is also vulnerable to internal divisions as it lacks a charismatic leader who can set clear goals. The government could leverage that weakness.

Regional and international cooperation with Mozambique on countering violent extremism has been limited in scope to only intelligence-sharing.[48] However, if cooperation was widened to include other areas of countering violent extremism, there is a good chance that the insurgency could be addressed. Close collaboration with Tanzania, to at least reduce access to safe havens abroad, will be an important factor in putting pressure on the insurgents. Enhancing maritime monitoring of the area, paired with joint operations and patrols along the border, would help to increase pressure on the militants. These operations would be especially effective if supported by actionable intelligence that prevents the security forces from targeting civilians. Enhanced border security and regional cross-border cooperation, especially in tracking illicit financing, could undercut the financial resources Ansar al-Sunnah requires for its growth.

The government, in line with the Africa Amnesty Month for the surrender and collection of illegally owned weapons/arms, should also accelerate its amnesty programme for youth who have taken up arms. As part of the programme, the government should offer rehabilitation with skills training and employment opportunities.

Community policing through the development of close-knit neighbourhood-watch associations and peace-and-security committees could prevent clandestine operations and serve as an early-warning network against violent extremism.

Conclusion

Addressing violent extremism in Cabo Delgado requires concerted efforts from all stakeholders. A security-oriented approach is not the answer. There are specific remedies that the Mozambican government could undertake to alleviate push and pull factors of violent extremism in the province. Some are developmental in nature and require a governance-oriented response, along with a determined effort to invest in neglected geographic areas and ensure equal access to economic opportunity for aggrieved youth. These responses should be people-centred, comprehensive, context-specific and prevention-oriented.

According to the United Nations Global Counter-Terrorism Strategy, there are eight interlinked processes that create a development pathway for preventing and addressing the growth of violent extremism in Africa. These include strengthened socio-economic conditions, effective rule of law and security, disengagement and reintegration strategies with a development lens, efficient leveraging of media and technology to counter extremist narratives, resilient and cohesive communities, and gender-specific engagements that take into account the differential impacts of violent extremism on men, women, boys and girls.[49] Taken together, these elements form a comprehensive and inclusive development response to violent extremism.

If the government fails to take into consideration the factors listed above, there is a likelihood that violent extremism in Cabo Delgado will escalate and have a negative impact on food security and economic development in the province.

Select Bibliography
Annette, H. (2007). *Terrorist Financing in Southern Africa*. Institute for Security Studies, Volume 10.
Assaye Risk. (2018). Al Sunnah wa Jama'ah (ASWJ) updated threat overview. 21 November. Available from: https://www.assayerisk.com/wp-content/uploads/2018/11/20181121_Al-Sunnah-wa-Jama%E2%80%99ah-ASWJ-updated-threat-overview.pdf [accessed 12 April 2020].
Bande, A. & Alfroy, P. (2019). Jihadist Insurgency Grows in Northern Mozambique. *Agence France-Presse*. Available from: https://news.yahoo.com/jihadist-insurgency-grows-northern-mozambique-140639893.html [accessed 10 November 2019].
Boukhars, A. (2015). Corridors of Militancy: The Sahel-Sahara Border Regions. FRIDE Policy Brief, 206, July. Available from: https://www.files.ethz.ch/isn/192724/Corridors%20of%20Militancy_%20the%20Sahel-Sahara%20Border%20Region.pdf [accessed 12 April 2020].
Columbo, E. (2019). Northern Mozambique at a Crossroads: Scenarios for Violence in the Resource-rich Cabo Delgado Province. Center for Strategic and International Studies, 7(8).
Committee of Intelligence and Security Services of Africa (CISSA). (2017). Radicalisation and de-radicalisation efforts in the Horn of Africa. *Journal Towards Enhancing Stability, Peace, Security and Development in Africa*, 4(17), pp. 149-160.
Dausen, N. (2018). Tanzania: 104 Suspected Islamist Militants Arrested. *Reuters*. Available

from: https://www.reuters.com/article/us-tanzania-mozambique-violence/tanzania-arrests-104-people-for-plotting-radical-camps-in-mozambique-idUSKCN1MU0N3 [accessed 9 November 2019].

Fabricius, P. (2018). Is Another Boko Haram or al-Shabaab Erupting in Mozambique? Institute for Security Studies, 61(02). Available from: https://issafrica.org/iss-today/is-another-boko-haram-or-al-shabaab-erupting-in-mozambique [accessed 20 November 2019].

Habibe, S., Forquilha, S. & Pereira, J. (2019). Radicalização Islâmica no Norte de Moçambique Institutode Estudos Sociais e Economicos. *Cadernos*, 17. Available from: http://www.iese.ac.mz/wp content/uploads/2019/09/cadernos_17.pdf [accessed 23 November 2019].

Haysom, S. (2018). Where Crime Compounds Conflict: Understanding Northern Mozambique's Vulnerabilities. Geneva: Global Initiative against Transnational Organized Crime.

Kajjo, S. & Solomon, S. (2019). Is IS Gaining Foothold in Mozambique? *Extremism Watch*, 10(23).

Mahecic, A.J. (2020). Fresh violence in northern Mozambique forces thousands to flee. United Nations High Commissioner for Refugees, 0205(16). Available from: https://www.dallassun.com/news/263950111/fresh-violence-in-northern-mozambique-forces-thousands-to-flee [accessed 7 February 2020].

Matsinhe, D.M. & Valoi, E. (2019). The Genesis of Insurgency in Northern Mozambique. *Institute for Security Studies*, 27(2), pp. 1-24.

Morier-Genoud, E. (2018). Mozambique's own version of Boko Haram is tightening its deadly grip. Quartz Africa. Available from: https://qz.com/africa/1307554/mozambiques-boko-haram-al-sunnah-is-tightening-its-deadly-grip/ [accessed 24 November 2019].

Paul, C., Clarke, C.P., Grill, B. & Dunigan. M. (2013). Paths to Victory: Detailed Insurgency Case Studies. Santa Monica, California: RAND Corporation. Available from: https://www.rand.org/pubs/research_reports/RR291z2.html [accessed 24 November 2019].

Perkins, B.M. (2019). Evaluating the Expansion of Global Jihadist Movements in Mozambique. *Terrorism Monitor*, 17(10).

Pirio, G., Pittell, R. & Yussuf, A. (2019). The Many Drivers Enabling Violent Extremism in Northern Mozambique. Africa Center for Strategic Studies, 3(6).

Rogers, J. (2019). Ahead of Elections: Mozambique grapples with violent insurgency. *Africa Source*, 4(7).

Tse-tung, M. (1961). *On Guerrilla Warfare*. New York. Praeger.

United Nations Development Programme. (2014). Preventing and Responding to Violent Extremism in Africa: A Development Approach. New York: United Nations.

Vicente, P.C. & Vilela, I. (2019). *Preventing Violent Islamic Radicalization: Behavioral Evidence from Northern Mozambique*. London: Weaver and Press.

West, S. (2018). Ansar al-Sunna: A New Militant Islamist Group Emerges in Mozambique. *Terrorism Monitor*, 16(12).

Williams, P.D. & Hashi, M. (2016). Stabilising Somalia: The African Union Mission and the Next Stage in the War against Al-Shabaab. *The RUSI Journal*, 159(2), pp. 52-60.

Endnotes

1. Cabo Delgado, with Pemba as its capital, is the northern-most province in Mozambique, bordering Tanzania and the provinces of Nampula and Niassa.
2. Ansar al-Sunnah began as a religious organisation in Cabo Delgado in 2014 and only later became militarised. Its early members were followers of Aboud Rogo Mohammed, the radical Kenyan cleric who was shot dead in 2012, possibly by the Kenyan security services. Continuing Rogo's work, the early Ansar al-Sunnah members first settled in Kibiti, in southern Tanzania, before entering Mozambique. Cabo Delgado, with its large Muslim population, high youth unemployment and marginal economic development, provided a suitable environment for the militant group to grow its membership.
3. Boko Haram was founded in 2002 in Maiduguru, northern Nigeria, by the late religious leader Ustaz Mohammed Yusuf. In 2004, it moved to Kunama, Yobe State, close to the border with Niger, where it set up a base dubbed 'Afghanistan' from where it attacked nearby police outposts. The group draws its membership from religious zealots.
4. Fabricius, 2018:23.
5. Perkins, 2019:12.
6. Ibid.
7. Ibid.
8. Morier-Genoud, 2018:9.
9. Vicente & Vilela, 2019:56.
10. Wahhabism is the Saudi Arabian version of Islam. It is the product of mid-18th century fundamentalist theologian Muhammad Abd al-Wahhab. He preached a strict interpretation of Islam and condemned other interpretations. He saw western values and civilisation as abhorrently evil.
11. Perkins, 2019:13.
12. Boukhars, 2015:6.
13. Ibid.
14. Matsinhe & Valoi, 2019.
15. Habibe et al, 2019:9.
16. Haysom, 2018:10.
17. CISSA, 2017.
18. Assaye Risk, 2018.
19. Ibid.
20. West, 2018:5.
21. Ibid.
22. Dausen, 2018:6.
23. Haysom, 2018:11.
24. West, 2018:6.
25. Ibid.
26. Ibid.
27. Ibid.
28. Columbo, 2019:12.
29. West, 2018:23.
30. Ibid.
31. Mahecic, 2020:43.
32. Haysom, 2018:17.
33. Ibid.
34. Pirio et al, 2019:26.
35. Ibid.
36. Columbo, 2019:25.
37. Ibid.
38. Rogers, 2019:23.
39. Bande & Alfroy, 2019:5.
40. Ibid.
41. Ibid.
42. Matsinhe & Valoi, 2019.
43. Ibid.
44. Paul et al, 2013.
45. Annette, 2007:13.
46. Williams & Hashi, 2016.
47. Tse-tung, 1961.
48. Kajjo & Solomon, 2019:76.
49. United Nations Development Programme, 2014:45.

CHAPTER 16

The Libya Crisis and the Need for African Ownership of Peace and Security Processes on the Continent

Lebogang Seshoka

Introduction

While some have argued that the Libyan civil war that started in February 2011 was an example of a popular uprising (supported by benevolent international military powers) to overthrow a corrupt dictatorship and establish basic human rights and democracy, the reality was very different. Rather, the Libyan uprising and subsequent international intervention were the result of a myriad domestic politics and international relations.

The fall of Libya's former leader Muammar Gaddafi ushered in a period marked by protracted instability defined by frequent clashes between rival armed groups, massive human rights violations, and economic and political instability. Armed-group activity and the damage done to basic infrastructure by a decade of conflict has been profound, deeply impacting the livelihoods and economic prospects of Libyans. The United Nations Office for the Coordination of Humanitarian Affairs reported that by the end of 2019, 1,6 million people had been impacted by the current crisis in Libya, with 823,000 people in need of humanitarian assistance, 248,000 of whom were children.[1]

For decades, due to its geographic location (with six bordering countries) and its strategic position between Africa and Europe, Libya has been a popular transit route for migration flows.[2] However, since 2014, mixed migration (asylum seekers, economic migrants, unaccompanied and separated children, environmental migrants, victims of trafficking and stranded migrants) has increased by 33%.[3] A video of men being sold for $400 at a modern slave market in Libya shocked the world when it aired on CNN in 2017, and there has been regular press coverage of tragedies unfolding at sea as migrants take the dangerous journey by boat between the Libyan coast and the islands of Malta and Lampedusa.

Chronic instability in Libya has created a complex security environment, which continues to threaten the region and has broader implications for both the African and global struggle against violent extremism. In particular, Al-Qaeda and the Islamic State (IS) have been able to capitalise on the fractured ethnic and political environment, as well as a thriving illicit black-market economy, to entrench themselves.[4]

Libya's challenges are multifaceted and will likely take several years to be resolved. However, it is important that in doing so, local negotiations are allowed to take place, free from the self-interest of major powers. This chapter will argue that foreign military intervention in Libya has, and continues to have, a largely negative impact on peace and security in the country – by enabling a disorganised, ill-equipped faction to prevail in the war, and by continuing to prevent organic negotiation and conflict-resolution practices from taking place.

17 February Revolution and the Fall of Gaddafi

In early 2011, anti-government protests were held in the port city of Benghazi in response to the arrest of human rights lawyer Fethi Tarbel, calling for Gaddafi to step down and the release of political prisoners. Inspired by a wave of popular protests happening across the Middle East, protests quickly spread to Tripoli and other cities. Trying to quell the protests, security forces responded with violence, firing live ammunition at civilians. The government's extreme use of force against the protests drew international condemnation and led to the resignation of several high-level officials within the Libyan government, including the justice minister and the Libyan ambassador to the United Nations (UN).[5]

Support among segments of the military also began to waver, and some units began to side with protestors. As demonstrators started acquiring weapons from government arms depots and merged with defected military units, local militias and Islamist militants, the protest morphed into an armed rebellion. Rebels were able to expel most of Gaddafi's forces from the eastern areas of Libya, but pro-Gaddafi paramilitary units were able to hold the capital, Tripoli, where Gaddafi and his family remained.

As the violence increased, international pressure on Gaddafi to step down continued. The United Nations Security Council (UNSC) imposed sanctions, travel bans and arms embargoes on the regime, and referred the Libyan situation to the International Criminal Court. In March 2011, the Transitional National Council (TNC) was formed by a coalition of rebel leadership and declared itself the official voice of the Libyan opposition, with the aim of providing services in rebel-held territory and guiding the country's transition to democratic governance.[6]

While rebel forces were able to take control of much of eastern Libya, Gaddafi's forces still had the loyalty of enough soldiers and access to arms to hold Tripoli and battle for control of the lucrative oil-export terminals on the Gulf of Sidra.

The international community continued to debate possible diplomatic and military responses to the crisis but remained divided, while rebel groups continued to call for the implementation of a no-fly zone over the country to stop Gaddafi loyalists from launching air attacks on their positions. The African Union (AU) rejected any military intervention in Libya, calling for further negotiations to resolve the conflict. The Arab League, however, pushed for a UNSC resolution to implement a no-fly zone, in opposition to the AU position.[7]

On 17 March 2011, the UNSC adopted Resolution 1973, authorising a no-fly zone as well as the use of force to defend civilians under attack. Bosnia and Herzegovina, Colombia, Gabon, Lebanon, Nigeria, South Africa, and permanent members France, the United Kingdom (UK) and the United States (US), voted in the affirmative. Brazil, Germany, India, and permanent members China and Russia, abstained. No country opposed the resolution. The language of the resolution was aligned to the Responsibility-to-Protect mandate, authorising the use of force only to protect civilians who were attacked, but forbade foreign occupation of Libyan territory. The UK and France were joined by the US in pushing for a further mandate to use force from the air to defend civilians.[8] The North Atlantic Treaty Organization (NATO) and western diplomats were firm in their commitment to the rebels' position that Gaddafi should leave immediately.

However, even with a no-fly zone and NATO attacks on pro-Gaddafi forces, it became apparent that Libyan rebels would be unable to achieve a decisive victory. Diplomatic efforts to end the crisis intensified.

The AU Peace and Security Council proposed a high-level ad hoc committee made up of heads of state to facilitate a negotiated solution in Libya and to rally the international community behind the AU's efforts.[9] South Africa's former president Jacob Zuma was appointed chairperson, with the heads of state of Uganda, the Democratic Republic of Congo, Mauritania and Mali comprising the other members. The committee's official mandate was "to engage with all the relevant actors to facilitate dialogue" among the parties, and to work with "the UN, regional organisations such as the League of Arab States, the Organisation of the Islamic Conference and the European Union to facilitate a non-violent resolution of the conflict".[10]

The most substantive element of the AU's communiqué in this regard was paragraph 7, which became known as the 'roadmap':

> "The current situation in Libya calls for an urgent African action for: (i) the immediate cessation of all hostilities, (ii) the cooperation of the competent Libyan authorities to facilitate the timely delivery of humanitarian assistance to the needy populations, (iii) the protection of foreign nationals, including the African migrants living in Libya, and (iv) the adoption and implementation of the political reforms necessary for the elimination of the causes of the current crisis."[11]

The committee met in Nouakchott, Mauritania, on 19 March 2011, hosted by President Mohamed Ould Abde Aziz, who provided them a plane to fly to Tripoli the following day. However, this was the same day on which the no-fly zone came into effect, and the AU received a curt message from the US and UN saying that should it proceed with its visit, its security could not be guaranteed.[12]

The AU high-level committee's shuttling took place as military measures were being effected, and on 9 April 2011 the committee again met in Nouakchott, but this time were given UN permission to fly to Tripoli. On 10 April 2011, the committee met with Gaddafi and presented the AU roadmap, which was designed in such a way that it would enable Gaddafi to step down within a stipulated timeframe, handing over power to an inclusive interim government that would pave the way for elections. While the committee was encouraged by Gaddafi's initial acceptance of the plan, it did not gain support when presented to the Libyan opposition. On 11 April 2011, the AU committee flew to Benghazi, where the TNC leadership rejected the plan. Mustafa Abdel Jalil – chairperson of the TNC from 5 March 2011 until its dissolution on 8 August 2012 – announced that the roadmap was unacceptable because it did not include the immediate departure of Gaddafi or explicitly state the timeframe for his departure.

Although South Africa initially supported UNSC Resolution 1973, which called on member states to use "all necessary means" to end the conflict and authorised a no-fly zone over Libya to protect civilians, the country began to question NATO members' interpretation of the resolution, saying that they were using the resolution as a pretext for regime change.

The AU argued that its proposal was unfairly derided and dismissed by the western powers, and that its roadmap was based on a realistic appreciation of the perils of civil war in Libya and the shortcomings of forcible regime change. The AU consistently spoke of an inclusive transition to democracy in Libya, meaning a process in which Gaddafi would step aside peacefully, while the UNSC prioritised an immediate end to loss of life.[13]

However, Africa itself was divided. While it appeared that most of the continent's leaders wanted Gaddafi removed with minimal disruption, a few leaders were still sympathetic to 'Brother Leader', among them Uganda's President Yoweri Museveni and the now late Zimbabwean president Robert Mugabe, while South African President Jacob Zuma's position was more ambiguous. Other African leaders were antipathetic towards Gaddafi and actively sought his overthrow. For instance, Sudan under former president Omar al-Bashir was heavily involved in supporting the TNC. The late Ethiopian prime minister, Meles Zenawi, not only nurtured personal disgust towards Gaddafi, but was also furious over Libyan support for Eritrea, and he insisted that Gaddafi should step down immediately. Former Nigerian president Goodluck Jonathan was also eager to see Gaddafi's departure.[14]

Ultimately, the AU was unable to convince Libyans, Africans or the rest of the world that it was a credible interlocutor for peace. Africa did not present a united position, and did not provide the financial, military or diplomatic resources necessary for the AU initiative to prevail. The AU's efforts in Libya were largely undermined by its own division from early 2011, when the A3 (South Africa, Nigeria and Gabon) endorsed military intervention, contrary to the position of the AU Peace and Security Council. Additionally, the AU did not provide a good account of its intent and strategy to the general public, and as a result the AU position remained largely misunderstood.

Towards the end of 2011, the no-fly zone and an intensified NATO bombing campaign on Tripoli allowed rebel forces to break through the city's defences. By the end of August 2011, Tripoli was largely in rebel hands, and Gaddafi's remaining forces were under siege in cities scattered across the west of the country, primarily Sirte and Beni Walid. Some members of Gaddafi's family fled the country in late August and September 2011. Gaddafi's sons continued to lead loyalist forces during September and October, and were eventually captured, killed, or killed in captivity.[15] On 20 October 2011, Gaddafi himself was captured and killed during the Battle of Sirte after TNC forces found him hiding in a culvert.

South Africa found itself in a diplomatic predicament, oscillating between two differing strategic pathways: those of the AU and UN. As a member state, South Africa supports the Constitutive Act of the African Union, which establishes the right of the union to intervene in a member state to prevent grave violations of human rights.[16] Similarly, during the 23 July 2009 UN General Assembly debate on the secretary-general's report on the topic, the South African ambassador, Baso Sangqu, declared that his country welcomed the report and acknowledged the centrality of the UN, particularly the UN General Assembly, in developing the concept. On the other hand, Sangqu was critical of the UNSC and argued that its failure to prevent mass atrocities and its inability to act on behalf of all humankind rather than a select few had caused the demand for new measures.[17] Nonetheless, the failure to implement the AU roadmap, in the public perception, reflected poorly on South Africa, given the prominent role the country played in promoting 'African solutions to African problems'.

To this end, in January 2012, the UNSC unanimously adopted Resolution 2033, which urged enhanced cooperation between the UNSC and sub-regional organisations, particularly the AU, in peace and security matters.[18] South Africa initiated Resolution 2033 as a way of harmonising the work of various stakeholders in the conflict. The resolution also encouraged the improvement of regular interaction, consultation and coordination between the two bodies on matters of mutual interest. It was South Africa's intention to continue to advocate for multilateralism and to ensure that any conflict resolutions in Africa represent the interests of the continent.

After the Fall

Despite wide international recognition of the TNC as the only legal regime in Libya, violence continued to evolve after Gaddafi's fall as various militias, Islamist groups and new security state forces battled for power. On 7 July 2012, the General National Congress (GNC) was elected by popular vote and took over from the TNC. Lacking the ability to disband the various militias operating across the country, the GNC tried to incorporate them into the state security structure but with limited success, generating a climate of lawlessness across the country and sharp economic decline.

In February 2014, Khalifa Haftar, a former lieutenant-general in the Libyan army under the TNC, appeared on television to urge Libyans to revolt against the democratically elected GNC, which he believed had been overtaken by a coalition of Islamists, members of the Berber ethnic group, and former revolutionaries from Misrata (the Islamist-Misrata bloc).

While initially unsuccessful, Haftar embarked on a series of meetings around Libya and, with the support of fellow ex-officers from the military, began to build an army and local support. On 16 May 2014, Haftar launched Operation Dignity in Benghazi. Operation Dignity-aligned forces stormed the parliament building in Tripoli and called for the dissolution of the GNC. On 20 May 2014, four days after the Benghazi assault, the GNC announced that it had finally scheduled the long-postponed national elections that were to replace the then-interim legislature (the Tripoli-based GNC) with the Tobruk-based House of Representatives.

While all candidates ran as independents, the elections saw nationalist and liberal factions win the majority of seats, with Islamist groups being reduced to some 30 of the 200 seats. The election turnout was low, and the Islamist-Misrata bloc's greatest fears were realised as a nationalist-federalist coalition hostile to its agenda made large electoral gains.

The loss of the parliament, coupled with the growing threat posed by Haftar's offensive, prompted the Islamist-Misrata bloc to launch a military campaign of its own named Operation Dawn, aimed at seizing control of Tripoli.[19] Rather than accept the election results, Islamist leaders accused the new parliament of being dominated by Gaddafi supporters.

After a five-week campaign to capture Tripoli in late August 2014, Operation Dawn succeeded in gaining control of the airport in fierce fighting against pro-government militias. The victory secured Islamist control of Tripoli, in the bloc's eyes, making amends for its loss in the parliamentary elections. The House of Representatives in the eastern city of Tobruk denounced the attack as illegal, branding the group behind Operation Dawn a 'terrorist organisation' and announcing a state of war against the group. This resulted in Libya having two de facto governments, one in Tripoli and one in the east of the country, each battling for the hearts and minds of the country's myriad militias.

As the Dignity and Dawn campaigns gained momentum, political divides in Libya deepened. The factors underpinning the civil war are complex, involving regional, tribal, political and religious fault lines that often both overlap and conflict with one another to create a dizzying array of allegiances and rivalries.[20]

Today, war continues to rage in Libya, especially in its western region. On one side is the internationally recognised Government of National Accord (GNA), heavily dependent on armed groups and increasingly reliant on Turkey, which has provided military assistance and sent thousands of Syrian mercenaries to support the defence of Tripoli.[21]

The primary opposing force of the GNA is Haftar's Libyan National Army (LNA), comprised of an alliance of armed groups and foreign mercenaries from Russia, Sudan and Chad, while supported primarily by the United Arab Emirates. Between 2019 and March 2020, fighting between these groups led to the death of an estimated 6,000 fighters and hundreds of civilians, and displaced 140,000 people. While Haftar's LNA has slowly gained territory in western Libya, Turkey's growing support for the GNA-aligned armed groups has diminished the chances of a total victory for the LNA. However, by marketing himself and the LNA as essential for countering Islamist extremist groups, Haftar retains significant international support.[22]

Islamist Extremism in Libya

Libya's Islamist extremist networks can be divided along generational lines, beginning with those that emerged in the 1980s with the return of fighters who had answered the call to jihad against the Soviet-backed forces in Afghanistan. On their return, these veterans created a number of groups in opposition to Gaddafi, the largest of which was the now-defunct Libyan Islamic Fighting Group. Several former figures in this group played key roles in the 2011 uprising and went on to participate in the country's democratic transition, forming political parties, running in elections, and serving as deputy ministers in government, as in the case of Khaled Sherif who became minister of defence.

This did not sit well with the second and third generation of jihadists, the former having fought in Iraq after 2003, and the latter in Syria after 2011, who tended to take a more radical position and rejected outright the idea of participating in democratic processes, which they viewed as unIslamic. Libyans who joined Islamic State in Iraq and Syria (ISIS) tend to come from the second and third generations.[23]

Libya's instability and insecurity have allowed extremist groups to thrive. They have been able to capitalise on the political and security vacuum to consolidate influence and control of certain geographic areas. ISIS has been active in Libya since at least 2012. However, on 13 November 2014, Abu Bakr al-Baghdadi, the former leader of IS, released an audio recording accepting pledges of allegiance from supporters in five countries, one of which was Libya. He also went on to announce the creation of three provinces *(wilayah)* in Libya: Wilayah al-Fizan (Fezzan in the desert south), Wilayah al-Barqah (Cyrenaica in the east) and Wilayah al-Tarabulus (Tripolitania in the west).

In 2016, the UN-backed GNA in Tripoli, supported by US airpower and western special operations forces, scored a hard-won victory against IS's Libyan stronghold in the central city of Sirte. This battle was pronounced as the group's 'last stand' in the country. Some IS fighters fled to the desert valleys south of Sirte, where they have tried to regroup in small encampments. Its underground cells are still capable of attacking in and around Tripoli, but they currently lack a clear leadership structure. While the group is no longer a territorial force in Libya in any meaningful sense, it may well be able to reconstitute itself or its members, to sow political discord.[24]

In Benghazi, Haftar's LNA has largely defeated IS and other jihadist groups, but at significant cost. The fighting displaced thousands of families, and the city has seen an increase in sectarian conflict. Haftar has replaced elected municipal councils with military governments, and has cracked down on civil society and freedom of the press. Disturbing evidence has surfaced of war crimes committed by soldiers under his command, such as the exhumation and abuse of enemy corpses. The campaign against ISIS has helped encourage Haftar and his supporters to make a renewed push for national domination with the capture of major oil facilities in Sirte (though not uncontested) and repeated threats to invade Tripoli.[25]

Haftar has no realistic prospect of stabilising Libya through military rule. His LNA is neither national nor an army. The bulk of the LNA's forces are drawn from civilian fighters. In the west and south, LNA units have a distinctly tribal composition, provoking suspicion among neighbouring communities who view them as tribal militias.[26] The idea that Haftar's forces could take over Tripoli and rebuild the Libyan state is highly implausible. Encouraging Haftar to expand his reach towards Tripoli risks triggering a war over the capital that could drag on for years. A third of the country's population is living in the greater Tripoli area, and such a conflict would undoubtedly cause massive displacement and human suffering. Moreover, a push towards the capital may also have the counter-productive effect of causing Islamist factions to reconstitute themselves to confront his advances.

Libya's Oil Industry Caught in the Middle of a Power Struggle

Prior to the February 2011 uprising and subsequent civil war, Libya was one of the most developed countries in Africa. Much of Libya's considerable wealth stems from its vast oil reserves. The government used oil revenue to build an impressively developed social welfare state. Oil is the cornerstone of the Libyan economy and the country's only real source of revenue. Oil is marketed by the state-run National Oil Corporation (NOC), and money flows through the Central Bank of Libya in Tripoli. The bank distributes public salaries across the country, which account for more than half of all public spending. However, groups in eastern Libya have long complained that they get less than their fair share of this revenue. Previous fluctuations in oil production have crippled Libya's economy and contributed to a rapid downward slide in living standards.[27]

In January 2020, tribal forces loyal to Haftar seized control and closed several large oil-export terminals along the eastern coast of Libya, as well as some of the country's southern oil fields. The move came ahead of an international peace summit on Libya in Berlin, and was designed to strengthen Haftar's position against the UN-backed but weak rival government in Tripoli. Haftar's armed forces ordered five subsidiaries of the NOC to halt exports from over 50 key oil fields and multiple port terminals surrounding Sirte. The suspension leaves only two oil fields operational in the country, which produce only enough power to cover a quarter of Libya's domestic needs.[28] Before the blockade, production was about 1,2 million barrels per day; within six days of the blockade, it had cost Libya $255 million in revenue.[29]

Further complicating matters are infighting and divisions within the NOC itself. On 26 December 2018, Almabruk Sultan replaced Faraj Said as the new chair of the NOC – an appointment made by the interim government. On 12 May 2019, a letter signed by a board of directors of the NOC based in eastern Libya was sent to market operators. The letter stated that the current chair of the corporation was now Almabruk Sultan, and that the NOC headquarters were in Benghazi. In response to this communication, the Permanent Mission of Libya to the UN reiterated that the sole legitimate authority to export crude oil is the NOC based in Tripoli and chaired by Mustafa Sanalla.

On 2 August 2019, the UN Panel met with Sultan, who indicated that the Benghazi-based NOC would persist in trying to obtain recognition as a legitimate institution, with the ultimate goal of gaining control over all Libyan oil. On 9 October 2019, the UN Panel of Experts on Libya received a letter from a board of directors of the Benghazi-based NOC, the contents of which continued to challenge the legitimacy of the Tripoli-based NOC.

Sultan was confident that the current dynamics in the country would pave the way for a situation in which the eastern authorities would at some point be able to export crude oil. Although the NOC in Tripoli retains its leading institutional role, and still controls the exploitation of natural resources, the eastern NOC's recent decisions are a clear threat to the overall integrity of the company. This institutional split is eroding the NOC's capacity to perform its oversight duties over the export of crude oil.[30]

What is the Future Role of the African Union in Libya?

On 19 January 2020, the parties in Libya's civil war gathered in Berlin, Germany, to discuss peace negotiations in Libya. The summit was mostly an effort to plead with foreign powers to halt military support, which has turned a local conflict into a global proxy war. Days after the conference, foreign cargo planes were once again shuttling military supplies into the war-torn country.

The continued violation of the UN-imposed arms embargo by foreign actors in Libya will make it impossible for Africa to achieve its 2020 goal of 'silencing the guns'. The Libyan crisis also reveals the complexity of Africa's security environment, and the challenges faced by organisations working for peace on the continent.

NATO's decision to escalate its intervention from a Responsibility-to-Protect mandate to regime change, while options for a negotiated settlement were still available, could be seen as the cause of the country's continued instability over the past decade. Ultimately, however, the AU had little choice but to accept the military involvement of outside parties due to its own financial weaknesses and internal divisions. Hopefully, lessons have been learnt from this experience.

In this respect, South African Minister of International Relations and Cooperation Naledi Pandor recently emphasised the need for the AU to be more proactive in responding to conflicts instead of leaving the job to outside powers. One priority for the new chair of the AU, South African President Cyril Ramaphosa, is to have the AU playing a bigger role in Libya-related peace processes, which to date have been led primarily by the UN. On 12 March 2020, in Oyo in the Democratic Republic of Congo, Ramaphosa had this to say in his speech at the inaugural meeting of the AU Contact Group on Libya:

> "The ongoing strife in Libya has dangerous repercussions for the security and stability of the region and the continent in general. Furthermore, continued political and military interference by external actors in the affairs of Libya undermine the fundamental interests and rights of the Libyan people and their aspirations for freedom, peace, democracy and development. As the African Union we note with mounting concern the devastating impact of the conflict on the lives of Libyan civilians, particularly on women and children.
>
> In this regard, we call for a ceasefire to be implemented with urgent and immediate effect. We are disappointed that the much-anticipated ceasefire talks of the Libyan Joint Military Group in Geneva, Switzerland, from the 18th to the 24th of February 2020 did not result in a positive outcome. In spite of this, we continue to stress the need for inclusive dialogue between all Libyan parties to the conflict, in recognition that it is only by sitting around the negotiating

table that a durable solution can be reached. In this, the year that the African Union has dedicated to Silencing the Guns in Africa, we must be at the forefront of efforts to bring the warring parties together. We must be firm and resolute that Africa's problems must be solved by Africans. We must continue to advance AU-UN collaboration as we work towards a political solution, reconciliation process and lasting peace; a process that must be led by the Libyan people, driven by the Libyan people and upheld by the Libyan people...

We emphasise Libyan ownership of this process without the interference of external actors. We reaffirm the decision of the 33rd Ordinary Session of the Assembly of the AU calling on all outside actors to immediately and permanently put an end to their interventions that continue to undermine the sovereignty, unity and territorial integrity of Libya. In this regard, we view the implementation of the arms embargo as an important instrument to stem the illicit flow of arms into Libya and the Sahel region.

We wish to reiterate that there can be no military solution to the conflict in Libya. All Libyan parties, community leaders and nongovernmental organisations should commit to dialogue. The parties must urgently commit to a ceasefire and thereafter work towards securing a political agreement...

We further support the goal of unification of the country's institutions, the holding of national elections, and enhancing security, stability and living conditions for the Libyan people. This includes the unification and integration of the Libyan armed forces.

In conclusion, I wish to stress that the negotiation of a ceasefire, its enforcement and observation is the critical first step in creating conducive conditions for a lasting peace. It will pave the way for an all-inclusive inter-Libyan dialogue, and lead to national reconciliation and unity. It is a goal we all share, and it is a goal we must all work together to see realised."

The Way Forward

The ongoing Libyan crisis is not only causing massive suffering to the country's population, but also has profound implications for countering extremism on the continent. Regional and international proxy battles and contestation over control of Libya's oil resources have pushed the country to the brink of civil war.[31]

The Libya Crisis and the Need for Ownership of Peace

A solution through military action in Libya is unrealistic. The international community needs to make a renewed push for a political settlement which focuses on deterring any military escalation through the exertion of credible pressure on the warring parties. Pressure must also be put on Haftar to pull back his forces from Tripoli and ensure that the UN arms embargo is enforced. While the UN's track record in facilitating political negotiations in Libya thus far provides some reason for pessimism, dialogue is still the correct course of action when compared to taking sides, even if ultimately some 'irreconcilables' remain.

The rebuilding of Libya is something in which the international community will be involved for a very long time, and any short-term measures to fight terrorism should also reinforce longer-term goals of encouraging political unity and good governance. Many tasks remain that will require support, including the demobilisation of armed combatants, stopping the flow of arms in the region, rebuilding damaged infrastructure, diversifying the economy, advancing the rule of law, promoting a political culture of tolerance, and holding inclusive elections.

While world leaders remain confused and divided over the future of Libya, the country's municipal leaders point the way forward. Aided by non-governmental organisations such as Humanitarian Dialogue, many are doing what outside powers have so far failed to accomplish through organic conflict-resolution solutions that speak to their local realities.

To this end, the focus of outside assistance and internal Libyan governance should shift to local municipalities (which are more legitimate political units today than the national government) so that they can pursue a realistic governance and security model that builds on current realities at the local level.

A series of national dialogues with security actors from across the country on a roadmap for reconstituting the security sector should be supported. National consensus is needed on what kind of military the country needs. Special consideration should be given to harnessing the strength of existing municipal and provincial security actors, while also tethering them to a national command.[32] Such a dialogue among security actors could help to develop this vision while also identifying actionable steps and building trust among warring parties.

The south's security-sector challenges are especially complex and will likely take several years to resolve. There should be a slow implementation of a phased withdrawal of non-southern security actors, and an agreed-upon transitional roadmap developed for handing over policing functions to a locally recruited and municipally controlled force, which is tethered to the Interior Ministry. A provincially constituted force may prove to be the most beneficial solution to give local communities ownership of security.[33] These initiatives should also be enhanced by the authorisation and deployment of a UN-approved observation force.

Nothing is guaranteed, of course, and ultimately Libyans will need to be willing to take the brave steps necessary for such a strategy to have a chance, but there is a realistic possibility of peace if regional and international actors prioritise genuine support over self-interest.

Select Bibliography

Al Jazeera. (2016). Libya, extremism and the consequence of collapse. 28 June. Available from: https://www.aljazeera.com/indepth/opinion/2016/01/libya-extremism-consequences-collapse-160128054629594.html [accessed 12 April 2020].

AP News. (2020). Libya's eastern-based forces move to halt oil exports. 18 January. Available from: https://apnews.com/fd51f5b71d90e7ea76d973640e8bfdf2 [accessed 12 April 2020].

Apuuli, K.P. (2017). The African Union's Mediation Mandate and the Libyan Conflict (2011). *African Security*, 10(3-4), pp. 192-204. DOI: 10.1080/19392206.2017.1360095.

BBC. (2019). Libya: Timeline. 9 April. Available from: https://www.bbc.com/news/world-africa-13755445 [accessed 12 April 2020].

Dewaal, A. (2012). The African Union and the Libya Conflict of 2011. 12 December. Available from: https://sites.tufts.edu/reinventingpeace/2012/12/19/the-african-union-and-the-libya-conflict-of-2011/ [accessed 12 April 2020].

Encyclopedia Britannica. (2012). Libya Revolt of 2011. 8 February. Available from: https://www.britannica.com/event/Libya-Revolt-of-2011 [accessed 19 March 2020].

European Council on Foreign Relations. (2020). A Quick Guide to Libya's Main Players. Available from: https://www.ecfr.eu/mena/mapping_libya_conflict [accessed 17 March 2020].

Gartenstein-Ross, D. & Barr, N. (2015). Dignity and Dawn: Libya's Escalating Civil War. 20 February. The Hague: International Centre for Counter-Terrorism.

Herbert, M. (2020). What would Khalifa Haftar's Libya look like? Institute for Security Studies, 4 March. Available from: https://issafrica.org/iss-today/what-would-khalifa-haftars-libya-look-like [accessed 12 April 2020].

Organization of African Unity (OAU). (2000). Constitutive Act of the African Union. 1 July. Available from: https://www.refworld.org/docid/4937e0142.html [accessed 12 April 2020].

Reuters. (2020). Factbox: Libya's oil industry caught in middle of power struggle. 24 January. Available from: https://www.reuters.com/article/us-libya-oil-factbox/factbox-libyas-oil-industry-caught-in-middle-of-power-struggle-idUSKBN1ZN23A [accessed 12 April 2020].

Siebens, J. & Case, B. (2012). The Libyan Civil War: Context and Consequences. August. THINK: International and Human Security. Available from: http://citeseerx.ist.psu.edu/viewdoc/summary?doi=10.1.1.462.690 [accessed 12 April 2020].

TRT World. (2020). Libya says oil shutdown caused over $225 million in losses. 25 January. Available from: https://www.trtworld.com/middle-east/libya-says-oil-shutdown-caused-over-255m-in-losses-33222 [accessed 12 April 2020].

United Nations Children's Fund (UNICEF). (2019). UNICEF Libya Humanitarian Situation Report. January–June. Available from: https://reliefweb.int/report/libya/unicef-libya-humanitarian-situation-report-january-june-2019 [accessed 12 April 2020].

United Nations High Commissioner for Refugees (UNHCR). (2013). Mixed Migration: Libya at the Crossroads. Available from: https://www.refworld.org/pdfid/52b43f594.pdf [accessed 12 April 2020].

United Nations Security Council (UNSC). (2011). Security Council Resolution 1973 (2011) [on the situation in the Libyan Arab Jamahiriya]. 17 March. Available from: https://www.refworld.org/docid/4d885fc42.html [accessed 12 April 2020].

United Nations Security Council (UNSC). (2012). Security Council Resolution 2033 (2012) [cooperation between the United Nations and regional and subregional organizations in maintaining international peace and security]. 12 January. Available from: https://www.refworld.org/docid/5824774e7.html [accessed 12 April 2020].

United Nations Security Council (UNSC). (2019). Letter dated 29 November 2019 from the Panel of Experts on Libya Established pursuant to Resolution 1973 (2011) addressed to the President of the Security Council. Available from: https://digitallibrary.un.org/record/3838591?ln=en [accessed 12 April 2020].

Wehrey, F. (2017). The Challenge of Violent Extremism in North Africa: The Case of Libya. 29 March. Testimony: US House Sub-Committee on Counterterrorism and Intelligence. Available from: https://carnegieendowment.org/2017/03/29/challenge-of-violent-extremism-in-north-africa-case-of-libya-pub-68446 [accessed 12 April 2020].

Endnotes

1. UNICEF, 2019.
2. UNHCR, 2013.
3. UNICEF, 2019.
4. Al Jazeera, 2016.
5. Encyclopedia Britannica, 2012.
6. BBC, 2019.
7. Encyclopedia Britannica, 2012.
8. UNSC, 2011.
9. Dewaal, 2012.
10. Apuuli, 2017.
11. Dewaal, 2012.
12. Ibid.
13. Ibid.
14. Ibid.
15. Siebens & Case, 2012.
16. OAU, 2000.
17. Statement delivered by Sangqu in 2009 during the General Assembly debate on the secretary-general's report on implementing Responsibility to Protect.
18. UNSC, 2012.
19. Gartenstein-Ross & Barr, 2015.
20. Ibid.
21. Herbert, 2020.
22. Ibid.
23. European Council on Foreign Relations, 2020.
24. Ibid.
25. Wehrey, 2017.
26. Ibid.
27. Reuters, 2020.
28. AP News, 2020.
29. TRT World, 2020.
30. UNSC, 2019:44.
31. Wehrey, 2017.
32. Ibid.
33. Ibid.

CHAPTER 17

The Escalation of Extremist Violence in Southern Africa and the Need for More Collaborative Security Responses

Stephen Buchanan-Clarke

Introduction

The year 2021 marks 20 years since the 11 September attacks on the United States (US) by Al-Qaeda, in the wake of which the country launched an international war on terrorism defined by military intervention, nation building, and efforts to reshape the politics of the Middle East and elsewhere.[1] Legislation and military initiatives under the umbrella of the Global War on Terror have proliferated in the intervening years, creating a web of conventions, laws and institutions that define the ways in which states react to terrorism in the 21st century.

Nonetheless, over the past two decades, extremism and associated acts of terrorism, whether perpetrated by fundamentalist Islamist, white-supremist or far-right nationalist organisations, have continued to spread globally. Military operations at massive financial and human cost have provided territorial victories over groups such as Islamic State (IS) and Boko Haram, consecutively lowering the annual number of terrorist deaths from a high point in 2014. However, extremist movements continue to spread internationally, and 2019 saw the highest number of countries (103) since 2000 record at least one terrorist incident.[2]

Southern Africa, in particular, has seen an escalation of extremist activity in recent years. The price of inaction on the part of the region's governments and the Southern African Development Community (SADC) has been a deepening insurgency in northern Mozambique with potentially profound consequences for the region. In part, this failure is the result of political leadership and policymakers not learning from both the successes and the many mistakes made in efforts to address extremism internationally over the past two decades.

The objectives of this chapter are to (1) report on recent developments in extremist activity in South Africa and the wider southern African region, including responses by governments and regional bodies; (2) discuss some of the regional dynamics of security challenges in southern Africa; and (3) synthesise lessons learned throughout the *Extremisms in Africa* series to provide recommendations on how extremisms can be better addressed in both South Africa and the wider region.[3]

As outlined below, South Africa has a particular responsibility in the region to take a leading role in efforts to fight extremism in southern Africa, both because of its relative wealth and resources, and due to its function as a node for illicit transnational networks, which support extremist movements. Moreover, the country currently sits as a non-permanent member of the United Nations Security Council, and in February 2020 South Africa's President Cyril Ramaphosa took over chairmanship of the African Union (AU). South Africa has stated that the primary focus of its chairmanship will be on the AU Silencing the Guns by 2020 initiative.[4] However, this can only be achieved by addressing the continued spread of extremist movements on the continent, many of which are at the core of Africa's most intractable conflicts.

Extremism and Terrorism in South Africa

Currently, in terms of legislation and law enforcement, South Africa's law enforcement and judicial response to terrorist activity occurs through the Protection of Constitutional Democracy Against Terrorist and Related Activities Act (POCDATARA), which criminalises acts of terrorism, as well as the financing of terrorism, and sets out specific obligations for international cooperation.[5] The Crimes Against the State unit within the Directorate for Priority Crime Investigation (Hawks) in the South African Police Service (SAPS), the SAPS Crime Intelligence Division, as well as the State Security Agency, are tasked with detecting, deterring and preventing acts of terrorism within South Africa, while the SAPS Special Task Force is specifically trained and proficient in counter-terrorism, counterinsurgency and hostage rescue.[6]

South Africa is a major international transit hub on the continent, and as such is an important node for both transnational extremist and criminal networks. However, in recent years, the country has also seen an increase in the threat of direct terrorist attacks on its soil from both Islamist and far-right, white extremist movements. This is not uncommon, and countries across the world have similarly seen a local rise in movements emboldened by a range of extremist ideologies.

Over the past decade, for example, populism has become a defining political movement across the globe. The decade has seen the election of American President Donald Trump on a populist agenda, the Brexit vote in Britain, and ascendant far-right parties in Austria, Germany, Brazil, Italy, India and Indonesia, to name a few. There is scarcely a region in the world that has not seen a rise in populist movements and associated political parties, which build their platforms on the basis of national identity, immigration and race.

In South Africa, identity and race still play a central role in politics. Centuries of racial segregation have not been undone in the 25 years since the end of apartheid. While the Democratic Alliance and African National Congress have largely attempted to promote non-racialist party rhetoric, the Economic Freedom Fighters (EFF), Black First Land First, Freedom Front Plus, and social movements such as AfriForum, Rhodes Must Fall and Fees Must Fall place race and identity front and centre in their rhetoric.

One illustrative example from the 2019 election is the largely unexpected success of the Freedom Front Plus, whose party platform rallied against perceived victimisation of white South Africans by affirmative action and land expropriation policies. The party was formed in 1994 as a break-away group from the Afrikaner Volksfront (a separatist umbrella organisation of right-wing nationalist parties) under the leadership of former South African Defence Force military commander Constand Laubscher Viljoen. In 1994, its main policy objective was to establish a volkstaat or independent state, and that year it received 2,2% of the popular vote. In 1999, this declined to 0,8%, where it remained in all subsequent elections until 2014. In 2019, however, the party returned to its 1994 support level, capturing 2,5% of the popular vote and six more parliamentary seats, making it the fifth-largest political party in the country.[7]

From a national security perspective, questions remain around the degree to which an increasingly charged political atmosphere and toxic rhetoric on race and identity will fuel extremist narratives and translate into militancy. Posts about 'reverse apartheid', white genocide and land grabs are fairly common on social media platforms in South Africa, fuelling feelings of white victimhood.[8] This is given further oxygen by divisive political figures such as EFF leader Julius Malema and others who have used explicitly racial rhetoric for political gain and public appeal, and by farm murders, which remain ongoing.

Historically, the most significant terrorist incidents and biggest threats to peace in South Africa have come from the far right. During the 1994 multi-party negotiations process to end the apartheid system, members of the Afrikaner Volksfront, Afrikaner Weerstandsbeweging and other far-right paramilitary groups, led by Eugène Terre'Blanche, in armed vehicles stormed the Kempton Park World Trade Centre where negotiations were taking place. In 1996, members of the Boere Aanvalstroepe, an offshoot of the Afrikaner Weerstandsbeweging, detonated two bombs, killing a woman and three children, while injuring another 67 people, in an attempt to start a 'race war'. Similarly, in 2002, members of the Boeremag detonated eight bombs in Soweto and had formed a plot to assassinate President Nelson Mandela in an attempt to start a race war, during which they would seize power and reinstate 'white rule'.

There are several far-right extremist groups currently active in South Africa. While some exist largely online, there are others such as the Suidlanders[9] and Kommandokorps[10] which have a greater organisational structure and pose a threat large enough to be actively monitored by security services.[11]

There have been no coordinated attacks by a far-right organisation in South Africa over the past decade. However, in November 2019, the Hawks' Crimes Against the State unit and National Crime Intelligence arrested the professed leader of the National Christian Resistance Movement (NCRM, also known as the Crusaders), Harry Johannes Knoesen, in Mpumalanga, South Africa, for alleged terrorist activities. In the weeks following, three more alleged Knoesen accomplices were arrested in Johannesburg, and a fourth in Cape Town. The arrests followed an extensive two-year, intelligence-led investigation into an alleged terrorist plot coordinated by the group to bomb national key points, shopping malls and informal settlements. During raids on the homes of two members of the group, police uncovered firearms, ammunition and bomb-making equipment. Knoesen and his accomplices have been charged with terrorism-related activities in contravention of the POCDATARA.[12]

The Escalation of Extremist Violence in Southern Africa

Knoesen is a retired pastor and former member of the South African National Defence Force. He was elected leader of the NCRM in 2012 and has been known to law enforcement for some time, having publicly released a series of controversial videos in which he calls for white South Africans to take up arms and declare war on the black majority. As discussed in Volume 1 of *Extremisms in Africa*, in a chapter on identity politics and the re-emergence of South Africa's far right, social media platforms have helped disparate far-right movements to connect and rally around common narratives containing themes of white supremacy, white victimhood, isolationism, 'reverse apartheid' and divine calling. Some of these themes can be seen in Knoesen's social media posts:

> "[South African Defence Force] and [South African Police]...Brave veterans. Precious pensioners. Young people and not so young...Business persons and farmers....If you are experiencing the Oppression and Hate of Reversed Apartheid [Black Economic Empowerment], [Affirmative Action], and the ill treatment because you are White...Stand by me and do as I say...work with me. I have Godly instruction to take back what Satan has stolen from us through clever, sly Money Powers and Politics and given to the North African settlers and Land Invaders...our God Given Country. In return I PROMISE YOU a Safe, Secure country where criminals fear to walk our streets. Your colour will count in your favour for jobs. I will reinstate the Death Penalty and punish those already judged and sentenced. Prison will be a feared place. I PROMISE to secure the Future of our Race. Permanently...our neighbours will fear to illegally cross our borders. We will again be proud of our Race."[13]

To date, the absence of a unified organisational structure, strong leadership and, from a cost-benefit analysis, the outcomes of engaging in acts of terrorism, have likely prevented far-right organisations from escalating their cause through violence. Knoesen, however, broke from this trend, explaining his reasoning in a video posted to social media:

> "It's important for us to stay together as a white nation. I know there are many movements. I met with some of the leaders around the table and we sat and we spoke, and halfway into speaking I told them we're not on the same page.

The reason being they want to defend and see what happens…Reality is, you cannot wait to see what the enemy does to you. You cannot wait for the enemy to wake up. It's too late already. The Crusaders haven't got a waiting plan, we've got an attack plan. The only way to win the situation and turn the tables is by attacking. Yes, I'm talking war."[14]

In the week following the arrests in November 2019, Harry Knoesen, brothers Eric and Errol Abrams, and Riana Heymans made a brief appearance together in a Middelburg court, where the magistrate was told that they would not be applying for bail. Randall Esau, who was apprehended in Cape Town, was released on R1,000 bail.[15] In November 2019, police publicly released a picture of a woman who is being sought for questioning in relation to the case, asking for public support in establishing her whereabouts.[16] Hawks spokesperson Hangwani Mulaudzi stated: "We know they are in their hundreds if not their thousands. It is a matter that is of very serious concern in the country, hence it has taken some time for us to be able to come to this stage. We will continue to monitor others."[17] The investigation is ongoing and based on the extensive evidence gathered on the organisation over the past two years, implicating up to 100 members in terrorist activity, the Hawks expect to make more arrests in 2020.[18]

In addition to far-right extremist movements, the threat of IS and associated Islamist extremist networks in South Africa remains. In July 2016, brothers Brandon-Lee and Tony-Lee Thulsie were arrested during raids in Newclare and Azaadville, west of Johannesburg, on evidence that they were linked to IS and planned to bomb the US embassy, Jewish institutions and several other targets in South Africa. This was allegedly after Tony-Lee had discussed plans for the attacks online with an undercover agent from the US Federal Bureau of Investigation. Being a Schedule 6 offence, their defence was unable to provide evidence of exceptional circumstances for them to be granted bail, and the twins have remained in prison for more than four years. The case has had several false starts as the state and the Thulsies' defence argue over what evidence can be heard in court. In January 2020, the case was again postponed, to April, after it emerged that some of the state's evidence had accidentally been wiped from a laptop by the information department at the National Prosecuting Authority.[19]

In early 2018, Sayfudeen Aslam Del Vecchio, his wife Fatima Patel, a Malawian national living with them named Ahmad 'Bazooka' Mussa, and their teenage neighbour Temba Xulu, were caught by police in connection with the murder of two British citizens, botanists Rod and Rachel Saunders, in KwaZulu-Natal, South Africa. In addition to kidnapping and murder charges, the state has charged them with contravening the POCDATARA, alleging that the three were in communication with IS and planning terrorist attacks on South African targets when they stumbled across the couple (Xulu was released with a suspended sentence after being found in possession of the Saunders' cell phones and turning state witness). Again, due in part to challenges experienced by the state in collecting and storing evidence, the case remains at the pre-trial phase after several delays. The defence team has argued that should the state again request a delay in the trial, the co-accused should be granted a new bail application.[20]

In October 2019, the Hawks arrested 19 suspects during a raid on a residence outside Durban, South Africa. The state alleges that, led by businessman Farhad Hoomer, the residence was being used as an IS training facility. Eleven of those arrested have been charged with contravening the POCDATARA, among other crimes, in connection with an attack on a local Shia mosque in which one person died, the planting of a series of incendiary devices in shopping malls and other public locations across the province, extortion and kidnapping. Alleged ringleader Hoomer was released on $10,000 bail and, despite concerns over their potential flight risk, his co-accused on lesser amounts.[21] The case has also seen several delays, and Hoomer is expected back in court on 21 May 2020.

While the incidents outlined above are relatively isolated for the most part, South African law enforcement has successfully detected, monitored and apprehended individuals before they could launch attacks on local targets. Some of the cases have seen multiple delays, and the state is yet to successfully secure their prosecution under the POCDATARA. This could signal a need for improved coordination between prosecutors and law-enforcement agencies, as well as indicating the urgent need for special prosecutorial skills. Many of the country's law-enforcement units, such as the SAPS Special Task Force, are particularly well regarded and trained in counterterrorism, counterinsurgency and hostage rescue. Ultimately, however, to sustainably prevent local acts of terrorism in the long term requires inter-agency collaboration between prosecutors, law-enforcement agencies and the intelligence community, guided by an integrated national strategy to address extremism and associated acts of terrorism.

Extremism and Terrorism in Southern Africa: A Multiform Security Challenge

In addition to the South African-based cases outlined above, southern Africa as a region has seen a recent rise in terrorist activity, and increased collaboration and coordination between extremist organisations. Empirical research shows that extremist organisations tend to take root in areas where the state is unable or unwilling to provide effective governance, or where socio-economic grievances and perceptions of political neglect and marginalisation are present. Furthermore, 95% of the world's annual terrorist attacks take place in countries with ongoing armed conflict.[22]

While southern Africa is more politically stable than some other regions on the continent, it has not been without incidents of armed conflict and political upheaval, and has recently seen a concerning regression in democratic gains and good governance practices. An improvement in both would help to insulate against the spread of extremism in the region.

For example, since the forced resignation of Robert Mugabe in 2017, President Emmerson Mnangagwa has failed to stabilise Zimbabwe's economy or control hyperinflation. The country has also seen widespread protests, many of which have turned violent, and generated tens of thousands of economic migrants. In 2014, Lesotho went through a *coup d'état* and has continued to be marred by political intrigue and instability. In 2009, Madagascar went through a political crisis that had severe economic consequences for the country – the impact of which is still felt. The Democratic Republic of Congo remains mired in political upheaval and widespread violence, and Tanzania, once perceived as one of the most stable democracies in Africa and a strategically vital part of the region, has seen increasingly authoritarian rule in recent years under President John Magufuli. South Africa has seen bouts of xenophobic violence, political killings and gender-based violence against a backdrop of economic stagnation and failing state-owned enterprises.

These political crises and governance challenges arise over and above the ongoing socio-economic and environmental issues across the continent, such as a population youth bulge and youth unemployment, slow economic growth, climate variance and environmental degradation.

Mozambique has seen an alarming increase in extremist activity and associated acts of terrorism. The origins and extent of the insurgency[23] have been documented in detail in chapters by Linos Mapfumo as well as Blessed Mangena and Mokete Pherudi in this volume. However, the situation in the region is extremely fluid and changing daily. While writing this chapter, Alu Sunna Wa-Jama (ASWJ) insurgents surrounded the town of Mocímboa da Praia, ransacked government buildings, and overtook a barracks, where they raised the black flag of IS. The following day, IS released a statement claiming responsibility for the attack through its Amaq news agency. On 25 March, the group staged another attack on the town of Quissanga, seizing and looting significant caches of arms and ammunition from the Quissanga police station. The group released footage from the incident in which masked fighters can be seen waving IS flags and calling for the imposition of sharia rule across the country. The total number of civilian deaths from these attacks is still unknown, but early reports indicate that at least six members of the Mozambican security forces were killed during fighting in Quissanga alone.[24]

Reporting indicates that insurgents have recently changed tactics, moving away from the targeting of civilians to government and security forces. On 6 April 2020, ASWJ insurgents staged attacks in Miengueleua and Bilibiza, and on 7 April an attack took place in Ntchinga. During these incidents, the insurgents made public declarations calling for an Islamic state, urged citizens to build mosques, and promised to attack only the government and its representatives. There are also reports of more public support for the group, and a recently released video shows local townsfolk cheering for the group. These reports indicate a significant escalation in the insurgency and its potential intractability.

While the nature and extent of the relationship between ASWJ and IS has been debated over the past year, it now seems clear that the organisations are at the very least attempting to align and are almost certainly in communication. By raising the IS flag, ASWJ gains more global recognition (thereby strengthening its fundraising and recruitment prospects), while IS gets to boost its image as a global jihadist force, which is still powerful despite the loss of its primary territory in Syria and Iraq.[25] The organisational structure and internal leadership dynamics of the group are still largely unknown. There could, for example, be multiple factions vying for power, in so doing attempting to leverage IS affiliation. Several of the organisation's leaders have been killed or captured in police and military operations over the past two years, which may have had an impact on its structure.

The insurgency in northern Mozambique is fuelled by a variety of regional factors that require understanding to build a holistic and collaborative response by governments. In an extensive study into the origins of the insurgency, Haysom[26] argues that the large and dynamic illicit economy in northern Mozambique, which has its markets in South Africa and other countries in the region, is not only how the group derives funds but has itself generated the conditions for the insurgency to emerge by fostering corruption, undermining state legitimacy, providing livelihoods and local investment, and keeping borders porous and the coastline unmonitored.

Migration Routes
Over the past decade, before the recent large-scale liquefied natural gas investments, Mocímboa da Praia had already emerged as a key node of criminal activity in the southern African region, particularly in heroin and human smuggling. Recent external investments into oil and gas exploration and the mining of rubies and other minerals have, however, created 'boom times' for the area and allowed for increased opportunity for both licit and illicit revenue streams.

Mocímboa da Praia lies on the 'southern migration route' that starts in Somalia and enters Mozambique across the Rovuma River, then exits to South Africa via the Ressano Garcia border.[27] While most irregular migrants from East Africa and the Horn are simply trying to escape political, economic and food crises in search of a better life, their movement is usually facilitated by criminal networks.[28] To enter a country without the requisite permission requires contravention of the law and usually involves an assortment of parties offering illegal services, from lorry drivers willing to smuggle migrants over an international border, to document forgers, logisticians and handlers – many of whom are likely involved in a range of criminal activities.

The International Organization for Migration (IOM) identifies four established migration routes in East Africa and the Horn of Africa. The Horn route consists of circular migration movements between countries in the region, particularly Djibouti, Eritrea, Ethiopia and Somalia. The eastern route consists of migration movements from East African and Horn countries towards the Arab peninsula, along which Saudi Arabia and Yemen are the most common destinations. The northern route comprises migration movements from Ethiopia and Somalia towards Sudan and Libya, and then on to Europe, while the southern route runs from Horn countries to South Africa (see Figure 1).

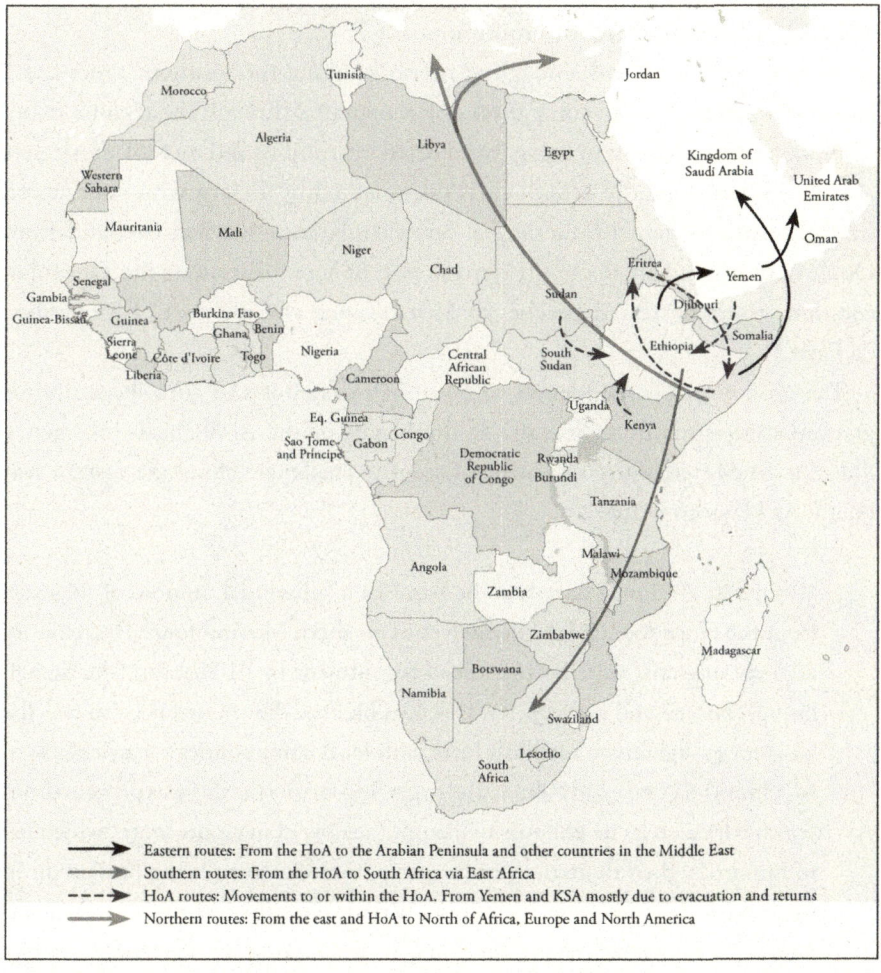

Figure 1: Main migration routes in East Africa and the Horn of Africa as of December 2018[29]

In a 2018 study, the IOM tracked 47,545 migrant movements along the southern route. The data showed that the majority of tracked movements along this route were mainly towards Kenya from Somalia (71%) but also included a substantial (8%) number of migrants heading to South Africa through Mozambique. Of those 8% tracked to South Africa, 85% were Ethiopian and 11% were Somali. The majority (94%) were young males, which was much higher than the average found on other routes. While the exact number of migrants who use this route is difficult to measure and will fluctuate depending on conditions of instability in the region, in 2017, the Mixed Migration Centre estimated that between 14,750 and 16,850 migrants travel this route annually.[30]

Human trafficking and smuggling networks along the southern route use a chain of *mukulas* (human smugglers) to get migrants through the region's many jurisdictions. In addition to being transported by minibus and on foot, smugglers also use dhows along the coastline. As documented by Gerety, who interviewed smugglers in northern Mozambique, Somali migrants travelled overland from Doble in southern Somalia to the Kenyan port of Mombasa, along the Tanzanian coastline, to the northern beaches of Mozambique and the port of Mocímboa da Praia.[31]

The unintended consequences of South Africa's efforts to curb illegal immigration southwards from Somalia at the height of the Al-Shabaab insurgency illustrates the interconnected nature of security challenges along the eastern seaboard. As Haysom writes:

> "Events in 2010 may have laid the basis for a substantial number of migrants from the Horn to establish themselves in northern Mozambique. The majority of these migrants were fleeing forced recruitment by Al-Shabaab (the Somali group), famine and poverty, but it is possible that these networks also laid the basis for ex-fighters to establish links with local communities – particularly in Mocímboa da Praia and Palma. The triggering factors for this was pressure from South Africa on its neighbours to disrupt the flow of migrants south, which led to hundreds, then thousands, of migrants from the Horn being bottled up in the north of Mozambique, including a period where they were effectively abandoned (by smugglers) along the Cabo Delgado coast where dhows dropped them off."[32]

A similar security crackdown by Tanzania on human smuggling routes during this period meant that the thousands of migrants in northern Mozambique were unable to return north or complete their journey south, and became a vulnerable population from which both criminal and extremist actors could recruit. Unsurprising, then, that by early 2015 radical imams from Somalia, Kenya and Tanzania had moved into Mocímboa da Praia and surrounding towns, took control of existing mosques or established their own, began to preach radical ideologies, which challenged both the state and the existing Muslim religious establishment, and started to establish military cells.[33] Following the initial attacks by ASWJ insurgents on police stations in Mocímboa da Praia in October 2017, the Mozambican government quickly closed two of these mosques, which were known to take in Kenyan, Tanzanian and Somali migrants and had become a hotbed of extremist activity.

The Heroin Trade

In recent years, the volume of heroin shipped from Afghanistan along a network of routes in east and southern Africa has increased considerably. In particular, northern Mozambique has served as a conduit for heroin coming from other countries in transit to South Africa before being transported to Europe and other international markets. The same criminal networks that engage in human smuggling have also been implicated in the heroin trade.

In a 2018 study based on 240 interviews across seven countries, Shaw et al[34] provide an outline of how heroin is shipped from Afghanistan to the east coast of Africa along a maritime route known as the 'southern route'. In reality, this is a network of routes stretching along the east and southern African seaboard, with drug consignments eventually making their way to countries in Asia, Africa, Europe and, to a limited extent, North America.

Similar to the mukulas who smuggle people along the eastern seaboard of Africa, heroin is shipped to Africa on motorised seagoing dhows built in the United Arab Emirates. The dhows are loaded with heroin shipments off the Makran coast of southern Pakistan. From there, the dhows cross the Indian Ocean and anchor off the coast of Africa in international waters, while flotillas of small boats collect the heroin and offload it at small harbours and various beaches along the coasts of Somalia, Kenya, Tanzania and Mozambique.

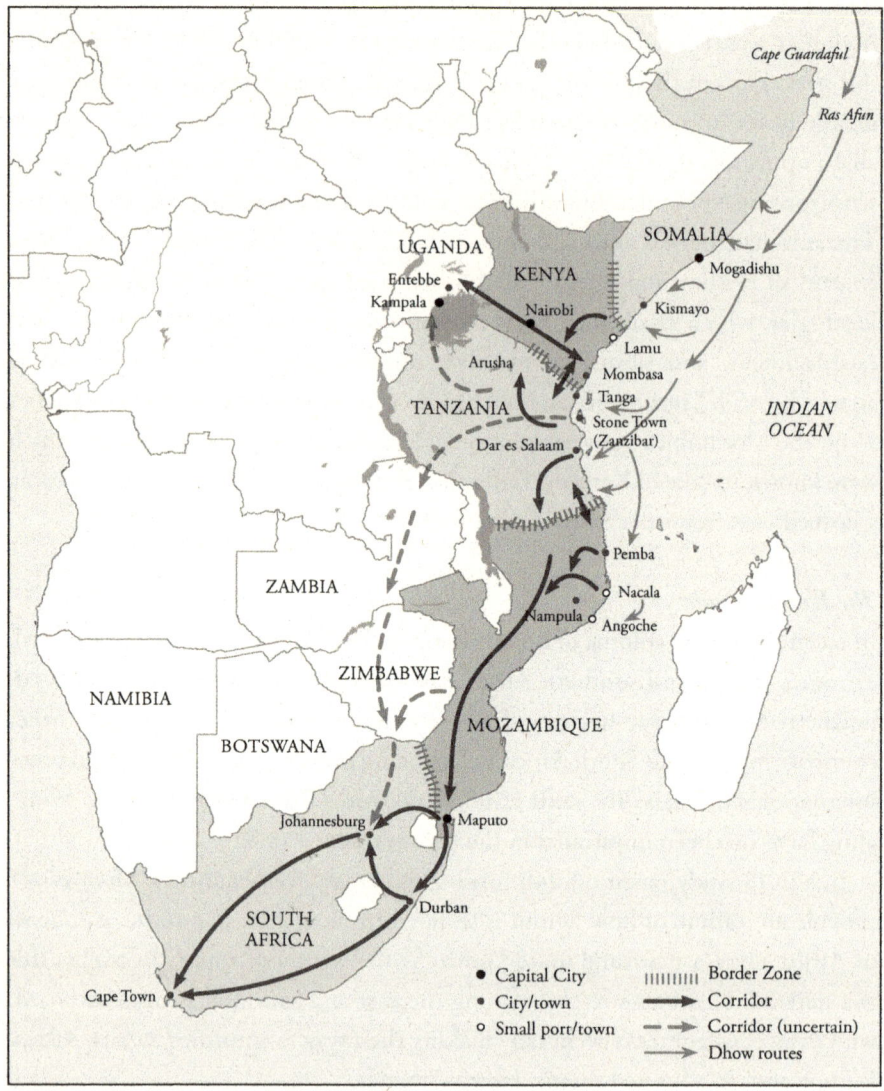

Figure 2: Sea- and land-based heroin routes across East African coastal states[35]

In the case of Mozambique, heroin is transferred from these dhows onto small fishing vessels off the port of Mocímboa da Praia and the coastal town of Pemba. Once on land, the heroin is taken by road to Nampula for processing and onward shipment to South Africa. There are no verified figures to estimate how much heroin arrives in northern Mozambique in this manner. However, dhows arrive weekly, except during the three-month monsoon season, each carrying between 100 kg and 1,000 kg of heroin. This would suggest that between 10 tons and 40 tons of heroin move through Mozambique annually, a figure that has been corroborated by the Combined Maritime Force, which has made several large heroin seizures in recent years.[36]

South Africa is the primary destination for most of the heroin that enters the region, both as an end destination for local sale and consumption, and for onward shipping to Europe and other international markets. In addition to its developed aviation sector relative to other African countries, South Africa is considered to be at lower risk of containing contraband, and there is a large volume of licit trade between South Africa and Europe in which to hide illicit products.[37]

In Nampula, drugs are hidden in motor vehicles and shipped by road to South Africa, or are smuggled by sea. Several large heroin seizures hidden in motor vehicles coming from Mozambique have occurred in the past five years. However, likely due to poor resources and corruption, none have occurred on the Mozambican side of the border. As Shaw et al write: "In South Africa the number of ports of entry and long international borders mean that there are a range of entry options available to those involved in trafficking illicit goods, and these routes can be changed and shifted should the risks associated with a particular route become too high."[38] Once in South Africa, heroin is consolidated for smaller shipments and repackaged for onward transport by air or sea.

As the above examples illustrate, the insurgency in northern Mozambique cannot be successfully addressed only at the national level. Up until recently, however, this was the approach taken by the Mozambican government. It will require collaboration and a coordinated policy response from states in southern and eastern Africa. Failing to do so will ensure that the heroin trade can sustain itself indefinitely.

Mozambique's Response
The response to the insurgency in northern Mozambique by governments in southern Africa illustrates some of the political challenges that undermine collaborative security-policy coordination on the continent. As argued by Ewi and Louw-Vaudran,[39] the Mozambican government reacted to the insurgency by first denying its existence and attempting to downplay the extent of the problem.

This saw the barring of media access to the region, the intimidation of journalists, and a crackdown on civil society and human rights organisations. After the extent of the insurgency became clear, the government made strong public statements promising to deal harshly with anyone suspected of terrorist activity. This was bolstered by a strong military response by police and the military, which included mass arrests, the closure of mosques where radical elements were seen to be congregating, and the destruction of two ASWJ training facilities.[40] However, as detailed above, the insurgency in northern Mozambique has many transnational components. The military crackdown in Cabo Delgado on places of worship, and the mass arrests, has likely done little to stem the trafficking of people and drugs, and other illicit activities, which ensures ASWJ's funding and continued survival.

In August 2019, President Filipe Nyusi signed energy and security agreements with Russian President Vladimir Putin in Moscow, in the first visit by a leader from the country in two decades. A month later, on 13 September, 160 Wagner Group Russian military contractors arrived in Mozambique on a Russian Antonov An-124. Twelve days later, another Antonov An-124 touched down at Nacala airport carrying military equipment, including a Mi-17 attack helicopter. At least one of the Antonovs that flew into Mozambique belonged to the 224th Flight Unit of the Russian air force.[41]

In November 2019, several Wagner contractors were killed in fighting in Cabo Delgado province. Reports indicate that Wagner soldiers suffered a surprise attack when insurgents entered their camp dressed in Mozambican army uniforms. The total number of casualties suffered by the Wagner Group is disputed, and reports on the specific details of the operation are scant.[42] Despite close links between Wagner Group financier Yevgeny Prigozhin and the Kremlin, Russian presidential spokesperson Dmitry Peskov has stated that "as far as Mozambique is concerned, there are no Russian soldiers there".[43] The Mozambican government has also been reluctant to speak about the presence of foreign military contractors in the country. There are, therefore, still differing reports on whether the Wagner Group is still operating in Mozambique and, if so, to what extent.

It was only in late 2018 that President Nyusi began to publicly acknowledge the need for regional support to deal with the escalating insurgency. However, the messaging of the Mozambican government was mixed and at times contradictory.

Some statements indicated that the situation was under control, the instability was simply banditry, and Mozambique did not need or desire 'foreign intervention'. Other statements directly mentioned the extremist ideology espoused by ASWJ, its transnational links and the need for international support. In September 2018, at the 73rd Plenary Assembly of the United Nations, Nyusi stated: "We count on everybody's cooperation in measures against these evildoers, because this is a heinous crime of a global nature involving both nationals and non-nationals still unidentified and of who-knows-what motivation, which will tend to spread to neighbouring countries."[44]

More than two years into the insurgency and the Mozambican government's messaging remains no less confusing, alternating between referring to the insurgents as criminals and sometimes as extremists, and alluding to the potential for dialogue while emphasising a strong military and police crackdown on anybody seen as supporting the movement.[45] While the actions and public messaging by the Mozambican government taken since the start of the insurgency have been erratic and variable, it is clear that the government grossly underestimated the extent of the security challenge and failed to appreciate its transnational links. Similar heavy-handed militaristic responses by governments to emerging extremist threats in Nigeria, Kenya and north Africa have had disastrous long-term consequences. Either lessons from these contexts are not being learned, or governments are failing to consider, develop and implement alternative strategic responses.

SADC and the AU's Response

SADC has not made any public statements regarding the insurgency in northern Mozambique. The SADC Organ on Politics, Defence and Security, responsible for promoting peace and security in the SADC region, has neither tabled any meetings on the topic nor issued any communiques. In 2015, SADC heads of state drafted a sub-regional response to terrorism known as the SADC Regional Counterterrorism Strategy and Action Plan. On handing over the chairpersonship of the SADC Organ to Nyusi in 2015, former South African President Jacob Zuma stated that the counterterrorism strategy "ensured preparedness in confronting these threats facing our continent and the world".[46]

Furthermore, in addition to SADC protocols relevant to the insurgency in northern Mozambique, such as regional responses to drug trafficking, small-arms trafficking and human trafficking, the SADC Organ's Regional Early Warning Centre is mandated to strengthen SADC mechanisms for conflict prevention, management and resolution through the compilation of strategic assessments and analysis of regional security threats, information sharing and policy recommendations.

Despite this, SADC faces a number of structural and capacity challenges that constrain the organisation from taking a more proactive role in efforts to address extremism in the region. In the case of its procedures, the Mozambican government needs to bring the issue to SADC before it is officially tabled for discussion. As outlined above, Mozambique chose first to deny the severity of the problem before seeking outside bilateral security arrangements.

Historically, during political crises in the region, SADC has been reluctant to intervene in matters of its member states unless explicitly called on to do so by a ruling party. Being comprised largely of member states governed by liberation parties that share a common history, SADC tends to support incumbents in power, and the presidents and states act in mutual support of one another.

Furthermore, at the core of relations between the AU and the Regional Economic Communities (RECs) is the principle of subsidiarity, which encourages regional structures to take the lead on situations occurring in their region or under their political jurisdiction.[47] Therefore, SADC would likely first need to give approval before the topic could be tabled at the AU's Peace and Security Council.

It is only recently that Mozambique has solicited the support of SADC and the AU in addressing the insurgency.[48] This despite repeated calls by Africans to their leaders to avoid outsourcing national security responsibilities to foreign powers, and to build the capacity of African regional bodies to handle their own security challenges.

The insurgency in northern Mozambique began more than two years ago, while a strong early warning system and good analysis may have been able to identify early markers of instability even further back. The ongoing escalation highlights the changes required in the African Peace and Security Architecture to encourage less bureaucratic and more dynamic responses to peace and security challenges as a whole.

South Africa's Response

South Africa has not yet provided military or other forms of support to the Mozambican government to address the insurgency. Defence analyst Helmoed Heitman[49] outlines several military options available to South Africa should the insurgency continue to escalate, and containment and diplomatic efforts fail. These include, for example, support in logistics, training, communications intelligence, and interdiction patrols off the coast. If the South African military did choose to become engaged, support could include aerial reconnaissance, air transport, communications intelligence, the deployment of special-forces teams, and close air support. However, as Heitman notes, effective military interventions in Mozambique will require the participation of other countries in the region. Tanzania would have to close its borders to guard against resupply through its territories, and Malawi would need to deploy forces along its border with Mozambique to prevent spill-over.

However, foreign military interventions against extremist organisations across the continent should serve as a warning to South Africa, which to date has largely avoided engaging militarily in counterterrorism operations. Many troop-contributing countries to the African Union Mission to Somalia (AMISOM) have experienced blowback attacks on their own territories by Al-Shabaab, in Kenya and Uganda in particular.

There are a variety of ways in which South Africa could provide assistance to Mozambique short of military intervention. The government, however, has made no explicit public statements on the insurgency. During President Ramaphosa's AU chair acceptance speech on 9 February 2020, he stated:

> "South Africa will also host the Extraordinary Summit on Silencing of the Guns in May 2020 to look at the implementation of the AU Master Roadmap, and at the same time respond to emerging circumstances on the African peace and security landscape. The summit must come up with real actions we, as Africans, must take to end conflicts, and deal with acts of terrorism that are raging in many countries and regions such as the Sahel, the Horn of Africa and now spreading to other parts of southern Africa as well."[50]

However, at the African Heads of Mission Conference in January 2020, which is a closed meeting for ambassadors and regional representatives, South Africa's

Minister of International Relations and Cooperation, Dr Naledi Pandor, seemingly made a point of mentioning both instability in northern Mozambique and the presence of IS in southern Africa. She stated:

> "Trends in conflict and violent events during 2019 have indicated an increase in the number of conflict actors and the transnational nature of threats and vulnerabilities. Datasets and analyses point to the proliferation of rebel and extremist groups, bolder linkages between transnational organised crime and violent extremists in Africa and the Middle East, and a rise in the frequency and scale of riots and protests. Attacks by militants affiliated with the Islamic State and Daesh in the northern Mozambique province of Cabo Delgado have raised concerns about an IS presence in new territories where it has drawn allegiance from local militant groups. We should be worried, given that the attacks on Mozambique point up the presence of IS in the SADC region. History has shown that poorer regions are most vulnerable to violent external incursions as material incentives are easily disbursed to attract young people to these negative activities."[51]

Hopefully, recognition by the South African Department of International Relations and Cooperation (DIRCO) of both the threat that instability in northern Mozambique poses to the entire region, as well as of the operation of IS in southern Africa, indicates movement towards action.

Towards a More Collaborative Security Paradigm: Recommendations to Southern African States

Pan-African and regional solutions to peace and security challenges on the continent are especially important today, particularly in a global context of declining multilateralism where developing nations are increasingly seeking bilateral security arrangements. The past two decades have shown that foreign military interventions in conflicts involving extremist actors often serve to rally support behind these movements and elevate their standing among international jihadist networks. The potential for creative diplomatic solutions to resolving conflicts with extremist actors diminishes when foreign militaries become involved in African conflicts. The use of private military companies, especially the Wagner

Group, which is so closely tied to the Kremlin, oftentimes introduces opaque foreign-policy objectives into conflict situations, complicating peacebuilding efforts. It is also an outsourcing of national security responsibilities, which should be fulfilled through training and capacity development.

Today, more than ever, security cannot be seen as the internal affairs of a state, and where a government's handling of an extremist threat will impact a region it is up to regional organisations to intervene.[52] The spread of extremist organisations and transnational criminal networks does not fall neatly within the boundaries of RECs, and in many cases stretches across regions. Inter-REC cooperation should be encouraged as a matching response to this, particularly on topics of migration and trafficking. There is also potential for the sharing of important lessons learned from regions that may have more experience in dealing with extremist violence.

The capacity of states in southern Africa to deal with the unique challenges posed by transnational extremist groups differs, and it is therefore important that platforms be created to encourage capacity-building and the exchange of expertise across nations. States in the region must work to review and strengthen counterterrorism legislation in compliance with international legal frameworks against terrorism, and in compliance with human rights and the rule of law. The nature of extremisms, and associated acts of terrorism, has changed considerably over the past two decades in virtually all its aspects, from the way groups recruit and disseminate propaganda, to how they plan and stage attacks. States' counterterrorism legislation, such as South Africa's 2004 POCDATARA, must be reviewed and, where necessary, strengthened to reflect these changes.

In addition, where necessary, states must bolster mutual legal-assistance laws to enable regional and international cooperation in the investigation, prosecution and adjudication of terrorism and terrorism-financing cases. As demonstrated by ongoing delays in current terrorism cases in South Africa, in addition to strengthening mutual legal-assistance laws, states must develop standard operating procedures to ensure that cooperation takes place in a timely and coordinated manner.

Across southern Africa there is a need for increased awareness among parliamentarians, policymakers, legislative drafters and civil society organisations of strategies to help citizens, especially young people, identify divisive extremist narratives, propaganda and fake news online, as well as the establishment of programmes to promote tolerance, civic education and social cohesion.

Efforts must be made to build and/or strengthen the capacity of special investigative units, financial investigative units, prosecutors and judges to better deal with terrorism cases. This would include training on the collection and preservation of physical and electronic data, and the use of the internet for terrorist purposes. This should be done through enhanced engagement between governments, both within the region and internationally, and through the development and use of regional networks and platforms where expertise in the field and best practices can be shared.

Southern African states must develop national strategies to address extremism based on the dynamics unique to their region, their national capacities, and their realistic ability to implement these. The all-too-common copy-and-paste approach to developing national counterterrorism and Preventing/Countering Violent Extremism (P/CVE) strategies has proven ineffective and a wasteful use of resources. In reality, most such strategies function simply as a set of goals rather than a clear set of choices that define what a government is going to do (and not do) based on the resources available. Where international nongovernmental organisations and the international donor community are involved, states must be given the room to develop unique approaches to addressing extremism based on local knowledge and expertise, augmented by international best practices.

In developing national strategies to address extremisms in southern Africa, it has become overwhelmingly clear that good governance must be prioritised, since perceptions of marginalisation, corruption, nepotism and a lack of service delivery are what extremist actors exploit to garner support. In the southern African context in particular, efforts must be made not to strengthen the core of government at the expense of the periphery. Local elites in these regions often play a significant role in initiating or preventing conflict, and they should be included in the state-building process rather than being alienated.

Furthermore, states must move from reactive to preventative measures to address the spread and emergence of extremisms and associated terrorism violence. As the case of northern Mozambique illustrates, an early warning system that identified the movement of known Islamist extremists into Mocímboa da Praia, coupled with the town's location as a node for regional illicit trafficking and an understanding of the widespread perceptions of marginalisation by the local population, may have helped to prevent the insurgency.

Consultations with local communities to understand their security needs are paramount. Ultimately, the state's relationship with these communities will help to determine whether an extremist threat will escalate into a full-blown insurgency. Local communities can be an important source of intelligence to the state, or can choose to provide material and other forms of support to insurgents.

In Mozambique, as is the case with almost every major Islamist extremist organisation operating in Africa today, the roots of the insurgency can be traced back to individuals who received scholarships and religious education in Saudi Arabia and other Gulf nations. In addition, Gulf funding towards mosques, madrassas, youth centres, humanitarian organisations and civil society organisations across the continent is often contingent on the receiver's compliance with a particular Islamist agenda. African nations should not tolerate the export of fundamentalist ideologies that are disrespectful of local norms and customs, and that are socially divisive. Extensive research should be carried out into Gulf funding patterns and appropriate measures taken to ensure that any funding received is not predicated on such ideological commitments.

Policy planning to address the threat of extremisms should be informed by evidence-based research. However, a vast amount of the most cited current research in the field of terrorism studies focuses on radicalisation and the individual's reason for joining an extremist organisation. While useful, this research often ends up producing policy options that are not scaleable, and can turn attention away from larger socio-economic challenges, the potentially negative role of the state, or negative externalities produced by government security policy. In this regard, more innovative research is required which examines the relationship between extremisms and wider social, political and economic trends. It is our hope that the *Extremisms in Africa* anthology series has contributed to these efforts.

Select Bibliography
African Union. (2020). Summit Orientation Concept Note on the AU Theme of the Year 2020 – Silencing the Guns: Creating conducive conditions for Africa's Development.
Al Jazeera. (2020). 'We are dying': Residents lament attacks in Northern Mozambique. 24 March.
All Africa. (2020). Mozambique: Nyusi ready for dialogue – but also will hunt down insurgents. 3 February.
Bonate, L. (2018). Roots of diversity in Mozambican Islam. *Lusotopie*, 14(1), pp. 127-150.

Castle, T., Kristiansen, L. & Shifflett, L. (2020). White Racial Activism and Paper Terrorism: A Case Study in Far-Right Propaganda. *Deviant Behavior*, 41(2), pp. 252-267. Available from: https://www.tandfonline.com/doi/abs/10.1080/01639625.2018.1557380?tab=permissions&scroll=top [accessed 9 April 2020].

Club of Mozambique. (2018). President Nyusi warns that Cabo Delgado terrorists "can spread to neighbouring countries". 26 September.

Crawford, N.C. (2018). United States Budgetary Costs of the Post 9/11 Wars Through FY2019: $5.9 Trillion Spent and Obligated. Providence: Watson Institute for Public Affairs, Brown University.

DefenseWeb. (2015). SADC counter-terrorism strategy in place. 18 August.

DefenseWeb. (2019). Another drug seizure for Combined Maritime Forces. 7 January.

Dlulane, B. (2019). Hawks launch hunt for suspected terrorist in Mpumalanga. *Eyewitness News*, 30 November.

Ewi, M. & Louw-Vaudran, L. (2020). Insurgents change tactics as Mozambique seeks help. Institute for Security Studies, 1 April.

Fabricius, P. (2019). Wagner private military force licks wounds in northern Mozambique. *Daily Maverick*, 29 November.

Fabricius, P. (2020). Is Islamic State taking charge of Mozambique's jihadist insurgency? Institute for Security Studies, 10 January.

Frouws, B. & Horwood, C. (2017). Smuggled South: An updated overview of mixed migration from the Horn of Africa to southern Africa with specific focus on protections risks, human smuggling and trafficking. Danish Refugee Council.

Gottschalk, K. (2019). Race still permeates South Africa's politics 25 years after apartheid's end. *Quartz Africa*, 3 May.

Habiba, S., Forquilha, S. & Pereira, C. (2019). Islamic Radicalization in Northern Mozambique: The Case of Mocímboa da Praia. Institute for Social and Economic Studies.

Haysom, S. (2018). Where crime compounds conflict: Understanding northern Mozambique's vulnerabilities. The Global Initiative Against Organised Crime.

Heitman, H. (2020). SA needs to keep an eye on escalating terrorism in Mozambique. DefenseWeb, 25 February.

Human Rights Watch. (2018). World Report 2018 – Mozambique. 18 January. Available from: https://www.refworld.org/docid/5a61ee49a.html [accessed 7 April 2020].

Institute for Economics and Peace. (2017). Global Terrorism Index 2017.

Institute for Economics and Peace. (2019). Global Terrorism Index 2019.

International Organization for Migration (IOM). (2019). A Region on the Move.

Lauren, I. (2019). Alleged 'Crusaders' terror group member gets bail in CT. *Eyewitness News*, 6 December.

Lister, T. & Shukla, S. (2019). Russian mercenaries fight shadowy battle in gas-rich Mozambique. *CNN*, 29 November.

McKenzie, D. & Swails, B. (2018). They're prepping for a race war. And they see Trump as their 'ray of hope'. *CNN*. Available from: https://edition.cnn.com/interactive/2018/11/africa/south-africa-suidlanders-intl/ [accessed 9 April 2020].

Mokhoali, V. (2019). Hawks believe more arrests imminent in NCRM 'terror' case. *Eyewitness News*, 2 December.

Pandor, N. (2020). Welcome Remarks by Minister of International Relations and Cooperation (DIRCO), Dr Naledi Pandor, at the DIRCO-Hosted Africa Heads of Mission Conference. 28 January, OR Tambo Building, Pretoria. Available from: http://www.dirco.gov.za/docs/speeches/2020/pand0128.htm [accessed 9 April 2020].

Pirio, G., Pitelli, R. & Adam, Y. (2018). The Emergence of Violent Extremism in Northern Mozambique. 25 March. Africa Center for Strategic Studies.

Powell, A. (2019). Right wing rises in rainbow nation. *VOA*, 8 June.

Ramaphosa, C. (2020). Acceptance Statement by South African President H.E. Cyril Ramaphosa on assuming the Chair of the African Union for 2020. 9 February, African Union. Available from: https://au.int/en/speeches/20200209/acceptance-statement-south-african-president-he-cyril-ramaphosa-assuming-chair [accessed 9 April 2020].

Reuters. (2020). Islamic State claims Mozambique attack close to gas projects. 25 March.

Russian News Agency. (2019). No Russian military servicemen in Mozambique, Kremlin says. 8 October.

Saur, P. (2019). In push for Africa, Russia's Wagner mercenaries are 'out of their depth' in Mozambique. *The Moscow Times*, 19 November.

Shaw, M., Haysom, S. & Gastrow, P. (2018). *The Heroin Coast: A Political Economy Along the Eastern African Seaboard*. Enact.

Singh, O. (2020). Suspected 'Isis trio' to be tried for botanists' murder in high court. *Dispatch Live*, 4 March.

Somduth, C. (2018). 'Terror' suspects are flight risk: state. *IOL*, 25 October.

South African Police Service. (2019). Media Statement from Directorate of Priority Crimes Investigation (HAWKS): South African Police Service. Available from: https://www.saps.gov.za/newsroom/msspeechdetail.php?nid=23522 [accessed 9 April 2020].

The Citizen. (2019). 'Racist Man of God' Harry Knoesen calls for war while 'enemy' sleeps. 4 January.

The Conversation. (2020). The who, why and what of South Africa's minority Afrikaner party. 10 May.

United States Department of State. (2017). Country Reports on Terrorism 2017 – South Africa. 19 September. Available from: https://www.refworld.org/docid/5bcf1f8021.html [accessed 6 April 2020].

Van Gelder, E. (2015). How a Right-Wing South African Group Incites a New Wave of White Fear. *Timeslive*, 26 June.

Wicks, B. (2020). Thulsie 'terror' twins to launch fresh bid for bail. *The Citizen*, 23 January.

Wright, J. (2013). Transnational Organised Crime in Eastern Africa: A Threat Assessment. United Nations Office on Drugs and Crime.

Endnotes

1. Between 2001 and 2019, the US government has appropriated and spent an estimated $5,9 trillion on the War on Terror – roughly $32 million per hour. See Crawford (2018).
2. Institute for Economics and Peace, 2019.
3. As lead researcher on the National Security Programme at Good Governance Africa, the author has been involved in the editing of all three volumes of *Extremisms in Africa*, in addition to contributing a chapter to each. The anthology includes 44 chapters on a variety of topics relating to understanding and addressing extremism and associated acts of terrorism on the continent. In total, more than 45 authors based across Africa, Europe and the US, and drawn from a variety of fields, have contributed to the anthology.
4. African Union, 2020.
5. South Africa also has acts relevant to counterterrorism, such as the Regulation of Foreign Military Assistance Act of 1998, which applies to nationals who may have left South Africa to join extremist movements abroad, such as IS. The country is a member of the Financial Action Task Force, the Eastern and Southern Africa Anti-Money Laundering Group, and the Global Counterterrorism Forum. It is a signatory to a number of acts and protocols relating to terrorism and trafficking developed and promulgated by the AU, SADC and United Nations.
6. United States Department of State, 2017.
7. The party's platform found success in vocally challenging calls for land expropriation without compensation and affirmative action policies, with an aggressive *Slaan Terug* (Fight Back) slogan and media campaign (coloured blue, orange and white, to mimic the old South African flag). See *The Conversation* (2020) and Gottschalk (2019).
8. For a discussion of 'white victimhood' and the role it plays in white supremist propaganda, see Castle et al (2020).
9. The Suidlanders – roughly translated from Afrikaans as 'southerners' or 'south-landers' – are an all-white, Christian group who believe that a race war is imminent, and that white South Africans are in mortal peril. Founded in 2006, the group claims to have over 130,000 members, but these numbers are difficult to verify as the group does not keep a public membership list. Rather than looking to commit acts of terrorism, the group prepares itself with survival and weapons training, and is planning to withdraw to a sparsely populated area in the Kalahari Desert and establish a refugee settlement for white South Africans. See McKenzie & Swails (2018).
10. Van Gelder, 2015.
11. Powell, 2019.
12. South African Police Service, 2019.
13. *The Citizen*, 2019.
14. Ibid.
15. Lauren, 2019.
16. Dlulane, 2019.
17. Mokhoali, 2019.
18. Ibid.
19. Wicks, 2020.
20. Singh, 2020.
21. Somduth, 2018.
22. Institute for Economics and Peace, 2017.
23. In October 2017, 30 militants attacked three police stations in Mocímboa da Praia, a district in the Cabo Delgado region. Since then, the ASWJ, which alternatively goes by the moniker Ansar al-Sunnah or Ahlu Sunnah Wal-Jamâa, has launched increasingly violent attacks on villagers, security installations and liquefied-natural-gas companies, ostensibly with the goal of overthrowing the old order of the National Islamic Council, which it views as having been coopted by the government, and building an Islamic state. The number of those killed in the insurgency is difficult to determine, but estimates vary from anywhere between 300 and 900.
24. Reuters, 2020; Al Jazeera, 2020.
25. Fabricius, 2020.
26. Haysom, 2018.
27. See Habiba et al (2019).
28. Frouws & Horwood, 2017.
29. IOM, 2019.
30. Ibid.
31. As cited in Haysom (2018).
32. Ibid, 12.
33. See Bonate (2018) and Habiba et al (2019).
34. Shaw et al, 2018.

35 Shaw et al, 2018:9.
36 DefenseWeb, 2019.
37 Wright, 2013.
38 Shaw et al, 2018:14.
39 Ewi & Louw-Vaudran, 2020.
40 Pirio et al, 2018.
41 Lister & Shukla, 2019.
42 See Saur (2019) and Fabricius (2019).
43 Russian News Agency, 2019.
44 Club of Mozambique, 2018.
45 See All Africa (2020).
46 DefenseWeb, 2015.
47 In July 2004, the AU adopted the Protocol of the Algiers Convention, which recognised the "linkages between terrorism and mercenarism, weapons of mass destruction, drug trafficking, corruption, transnational organised crimes, money laundering, and the illicit proliferation of small arms" as increasingly prevalent risks associated with terrorism. The protocol mandated the AU's Peace and Security Council to monitor and facilitate implementation, and to encourage RECs to play a more active role.
48 Ewi & Louw-Vaudran, 2020.
49 Heitman, 2020.
50 Ramaphosa, 2020.
51 Pandor, 2020.
52 The African Peace and Security Architecture provided a strategic shift away from non-interference in the internal affairs of member states to include the responsibility to protect; conflict prevention, management and resolution; and post-conflict reconstruction.

INDEX

9/11 attacks 159, 163–165, 203, 383

A

Adremane, Nuro 102, 352
Africa
    countries in *see* countries and regions
    crime-terrorism nexus *see* crime, organised
    international military partnerships with *see* partnerships, international military
    regions *see* countries and regions
    technology in *see* technology
    terrorism in *see* terrorism
    Africa CDC *see* organisations
African Union (AU) 6–8, 27n24, 67, 113, 131–132, 167, 254, 368–371, 376–378, 384, 399–400
    role in Libyan conflict *see* Libya
aircraft 34–35, 48, 107, 159 *see also* weapons
Al-Baghdadi, Abu Bakr 156n49, 270, 374
Al-Qaeda and Al-Qaeda in the Islamic Maghreb (AQIM) *see* extremist groups
Al-Sahrawi, Adnan Abu Walid 270–272
Al-Shabaab *see* extremist groups
Alu Sunna Wa-Jama (ASWJ) *see* extremist groups
Amadu, Sheku 266–268
Ambazonia *see* countries and regions
Anadarko *see* business and businesses
Angola *see* countries and regions
antiquities, trafficking in *see* trafficking
apartheid 32, 126, 242, 385–387 *see also* race and racism; South Africa
armed forces *see* security forces
armed non-state groups (ASNGs) 202–205, 209–211, 214–218, 222, 225–227, 298 *see also* extremist groups
    Community-based armed groups (CBAGs) 291–292, 296, 312n48
    disarmament, demobilisation, repatriation, reintegration and resettlement process (DDRRR) 223, 227
    separatist groups 12, 244, 253, 287–289, 292–293, 385
artificial intelligence (AI) 53–68
    automated weapons systems 53, 61–62 *see also* weapons
    facial recognition *see* technology
    history of 55–58
    machine learning 53, 57–59
    militarisation of 60–64
    regulation of 53–54, 60–61, 66
    technology of 56–59
    uses for 56–58, 65–66
    vulnerabilities of 59–60
Asa'ib Ahl Al Haq *see* extremist groups
atrocities *see* crime
Azambonia *see* countries and regions

B

Benin *see* countries and regions
bioterroism *see* terrorism
Boko Haram *see* extremist groups

borders
  between countries *see* countries and regions
  nature reserves and national borders *see* conservation, nature
  transnational (cross-border) extremism *see* extremism
Botswana *see* countries and regions
Bourdieu, Pierre 206, 234n36 *see also* habitus
Burkina Faso *see* countries and regions
business and businesses 102–111, 124, 137–141, 160–173, 355–357, 360–262, 408n23
  Anadarko 96, 101, 105–106, 355, 357
  business travellers *see* business travellers
  cost of terrorism to 161–163, 170–173
  counter-terrorist methods for 164–168 *see also* counterinsurgency and counterterrorism
  duty of care 168–173
  industrial *see* industry and industries
  multinational and international 96–97, 105–106, 112, 159, 166–168, 202, 353, 356–357, 360–362
  National Oil Corporation (NOC), Libya 375–376
  risk management by 164–166 *see also* risk management
business travellers 158–173 *see also* business and businesses
  female 160–161
  impact and cost of terrorism on 158–163
  kidnapping of *see* kidnapping

C
Cabo Delgado *see* Mozambique
Cameroon *see* countries and regions
Chacur, Abdul 99, 349
children 75, 84, 191–193, 210–211, 220–221, 366, 377 *see also* youth
  child soldiers 215, 221
  trafficking in *see* trafficking
China *see* countries and regions
Christianity 103, 112, 203, 213–214, 274–276, 349, 408n9 *see also* religion

and religions
civil society 131, 248, 250, 256, 262–266, 298, 331, 374
civil society organisations (CSOs) *see* organisations
colonialism 32, 239
  anti-colonial warfare *see* warfare
  colonial militarisation *see* militarisation
  decolonisation *see* decolonisation
  direct 238, 254–255
  liberation movements *see* liberation movements
  neocolonialism 238–239, 246, 253–255
  occupation *see* occupation and anti-occupation movements
  resistance to *see* resistance
communication 112, 177–179, 187–196, 315, 318–320, 324–329, 331–333, 337–340 *see also* media
  in military partnerships *see* partnerships, international military
community-based armed groups (CBAGs) *see* armed non-state groups (ASNGs)
companies *see* business and businesses
conservation, nature 29–49, 52n2
  boots on the ground *see* rangers
  canine support 32–35, 41, 48
  community involvement in 30, 32, 35, 39–40, 46–47
  cross-border 42–45
  green militarisation of *see* militarisation
  hunting and *see* hunting
  Kruger National Park 34, 39–43, 52n2
  models of 32–38, 42
  National Integrated Strategy to Combat Wildlife Trafficking (NISCWT) *see* policy and strategy
  poaching 29, 32–36, 39–48, 87, 96
  protected areas for 29–32, 37–43, 47–48
  rangers *see* rangers
  use of technology in 33–34, 36
  wildlife trafficking *see* trafficking
contractors, private military *see* military forces
conventions *see* diplomacy
corruption 36, 40–44, 75–83, 107–113,

Index

128–132, 142–144, 182, 292, *321*, 354–356, 392, 397, 404
United Nations Convention against Corruption (UNCAC), *see* diplomacy
counter-extremism *see* counterinsurgency and counterterrorism
counterfeit goods *see* trafficking
counterinsurgency and counterterrorism 35–38, 63, 88–89, 110–111, 178, 198n4, 217, 293, 303–305, 352, 355–362, 384, 389, 397–405 *see also* risk management
counter-narratives 111, 325, 331, 339, 342
for businesses *see* business and businesses
Preventing/Countering Violent Extremism (P/CVE) 314–343, 404
counter-narratives *see* counterinsurgency and counterterrorism
counterterrorism *see* counterinsurgency and counter-terrorism
Counter-Terrorism Monitoring, Reporting and Support Mechanism *see* policy and strategy
countries and regions
  Ambazonia (Anglophone Cameroons) 12, 238, 242–244, 249–257, 293 *see also* Cameroon
  Angola 12, 16, 126, 178, 198n7, 227
  Benin 135, 143, 146–151, 264
  borders between 37, 42–48, 79–81, 84, 112, 120–130, 236, 246–253, 285–290, 294–295, 299–300, 354, 358–363, 392, 397
  Botswana 12, 33, 41, 43, 46, 48, 396
  Burkina Faso 17–18, 143–151, 273–278, 285–290, 299
  Cabo Delgado *see* Mozambique
  Cameroon 12, 148, 243–244, 249–254, 271, 290, 293, 321 *see also* Ambazonia
  China 1, 4, 6–8, 14–21, 40, 59–64, 109, 239–241, 354–355
  Djibouti 124, 178, 393 *see also* Horn of Africa
  East Africa 87, 101–103, 125–126, 264, 317–318, 351, 392–393, 396
  Eritrea 16, 121–126, 393 *see also* Horn of Africa
  Ethiopia 121–126, 244, 393–394 *see also* Horn of Africa
  Europe 79, 82, 86, 265–267, 393, 395–397
  France 64, 221, 254, 285, 293, 301–302, 312n52, 312n59, 368
  Gabon 16, 46, 368, 370
  Germany 6–7, 18–19, 27n24, 64
  Ghana 16–18, 143–145, 237–238
  Guinea 135–136, 266, 274 *see also* Gulf of Guinea
  Gulf of Guinea 136, 142, 147–150 *see also* Guinea
  Gulf states 100–102, 126, 134n21
  Horn of Africa 29, 38, 81, 118–132, 136, 244, 293, 401
  Iran 124, 126, 138, 198n4
  Kashmir 243–244, 254
  Kenya 29, 46–48, 81–84, 107, 178, 331–332, 352–354, 395
  Kismayo 127, 218, 318–326, 334–340
  Korea, South and North 7, 61–62
  Libya *see* Libya
  Malawi 12, 18, 46, 401
  Mali 79–80, 85–88, 266–277, 285–304 *see also* West Africa
  Mexico 138, 142
  migration between 244–245, 265, 322, 351, 366–367, 392–394
  Mocimboa da Praia *see* Mozambique
  Mozambique *see* Mozambique
  Namibia 12, 16, 33, 43, 48, 396
  Niger 271, 285–290, 295, 299, 302
  Niger Delta 148–149, 288 *see also* Nigeria
  Nigeria 16, 84–86, 135, 142–151, 215–217, 250–253, 262–266, 270–276, 288–290
  Non-Self-Governing Territories (NSGT) 239–240
  Palestine 243, 254
  Puerto Rico 240–241, 245, 254
  Qatar 100, 124–125, 138
  Russia 62–64, 107, 162, 244, 292, 398, 408
  Sahara *see* Sahel-Sahara region

413

Sahel-Sahara region 80–88, 134n6, 146, 271–273, 284–306, 378, 401
Sahrawi Arab Democratic Republic 246–247
Saudi Arabia 100–102, 107, 124–126, 350, 393, 405
Senegal 143–146, 264–265 *see also* West Africa
Sierra Leone 190, 201–202, 220, 225
Somalia 81, 87, 121–129, 218–219, 314–343, 353–354, 392–396, 401 *see also* Horn of Africa
Somaliland 242–244
South Africa 5–6, 12–13, 16–19, 31–49, 246–247, 369–371, 383–403
Southern Africa 43, 96, 108, 383–405, 408n5
South Sudan 16, 84, 121–122, 129, 131, 134n22, 254 *see also* Sudan
sovereignty 238–239, 242, 246–247, 254–256, 292, 378
Soviet Union *see* Russia
stateless nations 244–245
Sudan 102, 107, 121–122, 126–131, 134n22, 264–265, 321, 370, 393 *see also* South Sudan
Tanzania 12, 33, 46–48, 99–108, 126, 178, 351–362, 365n1, 390, 394–396, 401
Togo 148–149
Turkey 88, 124–126, 138, 373
Uganda 5–6, 97, 120–121, 126–127, 214, 353, 396, 401
United Arab Emirates (UAE) 124, 126, 373, 393, 395
United States 61, 124, 158–159, 177–178, 301–302, 383
Vietnam 177, 198n2, 251, 354
West Africa 8, 79–81, 135–151, 156n1, 262–277, 286–306
Western Sahara 237–239, 242, 246–249, 254–257, 272 *see also* Sahrawi people
Yemen 126, 129, 292, 393
Zimbabwe 12, 34, 43, 48, 67, 105, 210, 220, 225, 390, 396
COVID-19 *see* pandemics

crime
  atrocities 118, 134n5, 225, 276, 371
  corruption *see* corruption
  crimes against humanity 190–191, 201, 276
  genocide 190, 238, 276 385–386
  kidnapping *see* kidnapping
  organised *see* crime, organised
  trafficking *see* trafficking
crime, organised 73–90, 96–113, 354–357 *see also* trafficking
  anti-money laundering and combating the financing of terrorism frameworks (AML/CFT) *see* policy and strategy
  extremism and terrorism nexus 73–90, 96–113, 165, 202, 322, 354–355, 402, 409n47
  money laundering 74, 84, 87–88, 119, 123–125, 128–132, 361, 408n5, 409n47
  transnational 40, 47–48, 296, 300, 304–305, 354, 392, 403
cross-border (transational) terrorism *see* terrorism
cultural property, trafficking in *see* trafficking
culture
  and military partnerships *see* partnerships, international military
  theories of *see* theory and theoretical approaches

D

data *see* research and methodologies
decolonisation 178, 237–240, 243–245, 254–256 *see also* colonialism
  decolonisation listings *see* United Nations (UN)
democracy 13, 17, 255, 366–374, 390
democratic insecurity *see* security and insecurity
development *see also* economics
  Brundtland Commission on *see* diplomacy
  socio-economic 2, 29, 38, 46–49, 63, 97–98, 111, 126, 178, 288–289, 360,

Index

363, 365n2
sustainable 38, 47, 172
Sustainable Development Goals (SDGs) *see* United Nations (UN)
diplomacy 60–64
  Algiers Convention 73, 409n47
  Berlin Conference (1884) 31
  Brundtland Commission 38–39
  in Libya *see* Libya
  Smuggling of Migrants Protocol 75
  Trafficking in Person Protocol 75, 81
  United Nations and *see* United Nations (UN)
  United Nations Convention against Corruption (UNCAC) 75
  United Nations Convention against Transnational Organized Crime (UNTOC) 75
direct colonialism *see* colonialism
disarmament, demobilisation, repatriation, reintegration and resettlement process (DDRRR) *see* armed forces
diseases and viruses *see also* pandemics
  bioterrorism and *see* terrorism
  COVID-19 *see* pandemics
  health-care and *see* healthcare
  human immunodeficiency virus (HIV) *see* pandemics
  Middle East Respiratory Syndrome (MERS) *see* pandemics
  SARS-CoV-2 virus *see* pandemics
  severe acute respiratory syndrome (SARS) *see* pandemics
  weaponising of *see* bioterrorism
displaced persons *see* refugees and displaced persons
Djibouti *see* countries and regions
drones *see* technology
drug smuggling *see* trafficking
duty of care *see* business and businesses

E

East Africa *see* countries and regions
East African Community *see* organisations
economics *see also* finance
  companies *see* business and businesses
  development *see* development
  economic insecurity *see* security and insecurity
  economic marginalisation *see* marginalisation
  employment and unemployment *see* employment and unemployment
  illicit economies *see* crime
  political economy 97–98, 238, 242–243, 297, 300–301
education 45, 66, 105, 112, 179–181, 187–189, 194, 224, 321, 340, 351, 404–405 *see also* skills and skills development
employment and unemployment
  job losses 15–16, 321–322
equality and inequality 120, 126, 130, 192, 266–267, 271–272, 288–289, 324, 357
Eritrea *see* countries and regions
Ethiopia *see* countries and regions
ethnicity 99, 102–104, 120, 125, 183, 189–192, 201–207, 244–245, 262–269, 272–278, 299–302, 311n43, 349–358
Europe *see* countries and regions
European Union *see* organisations
expert systems *see* artificial intelligence (AI)
extremism 29, 73–90, 96–113, 118–132, 158–159, 262–263, 272–277, 300–306, 314–343, 348–363, 373–375, 383–405 *see also* extremist groups; ideology and ideologies; terrorism
  counter-extremism *see* counterinsurgency and counter-terrorism
  cross-border 120, 124, 290–291, 299–300
  jihadism *see* jihad and jihadist movements
  organised crime nexus *see* crime, organised
  radicalisation 89, 100, 125–129, 253, 271, 317, 320–321, 324–325, 328, 348–351, 357–358, 405
  transnational *see* terrorism
  violent extremism 96–113, 118–132, 158–160, 272–275, 277–278, 300–306, 314–343, 348–363, 367, 404

415

extremist groups 14–15 *see also* armed non-state groups (ASNGs); extremism; terrorism
Abu Sayyaf Group (ASG) 139
Al-Qaeda and Al-Qaeda in the Islamic Maghreb (AQIM) 73, 79–87, 159, 218, 262, 270–271, 287–288, 290, 367, 383
Al-Shabaab 81–90, 117, 121–129, 218–219, 316–331, 339–342, 348, 354, 394, 401
Alu Sunna Wa-Jama (ASWJ) 96–113, 117n5, 391–399, 408n23 *see also* Islamic State (IS)
Ansar al-Sunnah (Ansar al Sunna) 117n5, 348–362, 365n2, 408n23
Asa'ib Ahl Al Haq (AAH) 137–140
atrocities by *see* crime
Boko Haram (Islamic State West Africa Province - ISWAP) 84–86, 147, 215–218, 251, 270–275, 287–293, 305, 360, 365n3, 383 *see also* Shekau, Abubakar; Yusuf, Mohammed
children and child soldiers *see* children
far-right 383–388
financing of 90, 96–97, 110–112, 118–132, 146, 212, 218, 304, 348–349, 354–363, 384, 403
Islamic State *see* Islamic State (IS)
Islamist 102, 106–107, 146, 250, 262–263, 269, 276, 293, 372–375, 383, 385, 388–389, 404–405
Jama'a Nusrat ul-Islam wa al-Muslimin (JNIM) 147, 270–273, 287–288, 290
jihadists *see* jihad and jihadist movements
Lord's Resistance Army (LRA) 84, 87, 126–127, 134n22, 205, 211, 214–215 *see also* Kony, Joseph
magic and *see* magic
Mai-Mai 210–212, 220, 223, 225
National Christian Resistance Movement (NCRM) / Crusaders 386–387
National Movement for the Liberation of Azawad (MNLA) 293
recruitment and retention of members *see* military forces

Revolutionary Armed Forces of Colombia (FARC) 83, 89
right-wing and white supremacist 383–388, 408n8
Sudan People's Liberation Army (SPLA) 121, 134n22
tactics of *see* tactics
Taliban 73, 82–85

F

field (game) rangers *see* rangers
finance *see also* economics
    financial institutions 88, 119–122, 134n5, 167
    financing of extremist and terrorist groups *see* extremist groups
Fodio, Uthman Dan 262, 266–268 *see also* Sokoto Caliphate
force, use of *see* violence
fragmentation *see* governance
framing *see* theory and theoretical approaches
France *see* countries and regions
Freedom Front Plus *see* organisations
FRELIMO *see* organisations
Fulani people 262–278, 282n10, 290, 299 *see also* Sokoto Caliphate
    Fulfulde linguistic family 263–264, 267, 274
    links to jihadist movements *see* jihad and jihadist movements
Fulbe people *see* Fulani people
funding
    of extremist groups *see* extremist groups

G

Gabon *see* countries and regions
Gaddafi, Muammar 83–84, 200–201, 366–373 *see also* Libya
gender *see also* women
    conflict-related sexual violence (CRSV) *see* military forces
    conflict-related sexual violence (CRSV) framework *see* policy and strategy
gender-based violence 190–193
genocide *see* crime

INDEX

Germany *see* countries and regions
Ghana *see* countries and regions
Global Counter-Terrorism Strategy (United Nations) *see* policy and strategy
governance 46–49, 60, 67–68, 89–90, 97–98, 104–105, 149, 167, 286–306, 349–351, 359–362, 379, 390–391, 404
   collaborative 398
   fragmentation of 285–286, 297–301
   hybrid 284–289, 294–298, 305, 311n10, 312n63
   theories of *see* theory and theoretical approaches
green militarisation *see* militarisation
Guinea *see* countries and regions
Gulf of Guinea *see* countries and regions
Gulf states *see* countries and regions

H
habitus *see* psychology
Haftar, Khalifa 372–376, 379
healthcare 1, 17, 53, 65–68, 251, 351
Horn of Africa *see* countries and regions
hostages 74, 140, 149, 156n21, 156n49, 198, 384–385, 389 *see also* kidnapping; negotiations
human rights *see* rights, human
Human Rights Watch *see* organisations
human security *see* security and insecurity
human trafficking *see* trafficking
hunting 30–31, 48, 217–218
hybridity *see* governance

I
identity 248, 264–267, 276–277, 289, 292, 302–303, 315–317, 320–324, 338–341, 385–387
ideology and ideologies 75–82, 100–106, 136, 140, 146, 256–257, 267–269, 274, 284–285, 290–291, 351–352, 359, 399, 405
   extremist 351, 385, 399 *see also* extremism
   Islamic *see* Islam
industrial revolutions 62, 68, 265

industry and industries 53–59, 65–67, 104–106, 141, 159–166, 375–376 *see also* business and businesses
inequality *see* equality and inequality
insecurity *see* security and insecurity
international military partnerships *see* partnerships, international military
intimidation *see* psychology
invincibility and invulnerability *see* magic
Iran *see* countries and regions
Islam 99–102, 106–107, 124–125, 146–147, 201, 213–216, 262–278, 350–353, 365n10, 372–375 *see also* religion and religions
   Islamist groups *see* extremist groups
   jihadism *see* jihad and jihadist movements
   Salafism 81, 216, 272, 275, 277
   Sufism 85, 100–102, 272, 277, 350–351
   Wahhabism 99–103, 350–353, 365n10
Islamic State (IS) 84, 101, 145, 159, 262, 367, 383, 389, 402 *see also* extremist groups
Islamic State in Iraq and Syria (ISIS) 14, 19–21, 54, 290, 316–320, 374–375
Islamic State in the Greater Sahara (ISGS) 147, 270–273
Islamic State West Africa Province (ISWAP) *see* extremist groups
ivory *see* natural resources
   poaching of *see* conservation, nature
   trafficking in *see* trafficking

J
jihad and jihadist movements 79–81, 100–102, 166, 215–216, 262–278, 285–286, 290–292, 300–306, 311n11, 312n55, 351–353, 373–374 *see also* extremism; extremist groups; Islam; terrorism
   18th and 19th centuries 265–269
   21st century 269–275
   Fulani Jihad 262, 266, 272–277

K
Kamajors *see* military forces
Kashmir *see* countries and regions

Kenya *see* countries and regions
kidnapping 84–86, 135–151, 156n19, 159–160, 165, 216–217, 270, 299, 302, 309, 389 *see also* crime, organised; trafficking
    by criminal groups 135–151
    by militant groups 135–151
    hostages *see* hostages
    kidnapping for ransom (KFR) 76–77, 81, 86, 101, 135–151
    maritime *see* pirates and piracy
    negotiations with kidnappers *see* negotiations
    ransoms 86, 137–146, 149–150, 156n21
    reasons for 143–150
    risk management of *see* risk management
Kismayo *see* countries and regions
Knoesen, Johannes 386–388
Kondewa, Allieu 201, 210, 212
Kony, Joseph 214–215, 235n104
Korea (North and South) *see* countries and regions
Kruger National Park *see* conservation, nature

L

law and legislation 60
    law enforcement 29–30, 34–47, 52n2, 78–80, 88–90, 127–129, 150–151, 384, 387–390
    Law Enforcement and Anti-poaching Strategy *see* policy and strategy
    Presidential Commission on the Fourth Industrial Revolution 65
    Protection of Constitutional Democracy Against Terrorist and Related Activities Act (POCDATARA) 384, 386, 389, 403
    states of emergency and disaster 6, 8–14, 276, 357
liberation movements 237, 241, 243, 247
Libya 83–85, 200–201, 366–380, 393 *see also* Gaddafi, Muammar
    17 February revolution, 2011 367–372
    African Union ad-hoc committee 368–371
    African Union Roadmap for 369–371
    diplomacy in 368–371
    General National Congress (GNC) 372
    Government of National Accord (GNA) 373–374
    Libyan National Army (LNA), 373–375
    no-fly zone over (UNSC Resolution 1973) 368–371
    oil industry 375–376, 379
    Operation Dawn and Operation Dignity 372–373
    role of the African Union in 368–371, 376–378
    Transitional National Council (TNC) 368–371
lockdowns *see* pandemics
Lord's Resistance Army (LRA) *see* extremist groups

M

machine learning *see* artificial intelligence (AI)
Macina caliphate 266, 273
magic 200–228 *see also* religion and religions
    amulets, charms and talismans 200–201, 206–209, 211, 215–217, 224, 235n123–124
    belief in 200–201, 213–214, 221
    failure of 211–212
    habitus and *see* psychology
    invincibility and invulnerability 205–207, 209–210, 219
    magicians, shamans and witchdoctors 200–201, 204, 212, 220
    psychological impact of 204, 209–218, 226–228 *see also* psychology
    rationality and *see* psychology
    strategic, tactical and operational use of 203–213, 219–227
Makonde people *see* Mozambique
Malawi *see* countries and regions
Mali *see* countries and regions
marginalisation 30, 102–106, 120, 126, 130, 288–293, 328, 340–342, 349–353, 365n2, 404
media 15, 40, 76, 110–112, 315, 325–328, 330–332, 336–338, 361 *see also*

Index

communication
    radio and television *see* radio and television
    social media *see* social media
Mexico *see* countries and regions
migrants and migration *see* countries and regions
militarisation 60–64, 129–130, 255, 284, 348–349
    colonial 30–32
    of artificial intelligence *see* artificial intelligence (AI)
    of nature conservation (green militarisation) 29–49
military forces 30–48, 53–62, 100–110, 121–129, 178–196, 200–228, 238, 249–257, 284, 297–307, 348–363, 367–380, 393–405 *see also* security forces
    Africa 177–196
    atrocities by *see* crime
    change management in 187–188
    conflict-related sexual violence (CRSV) 190–193
    discipline and punishment in 183, 195, 207–215, 227, 359
    extremist groups *see* extremist groups
    Forces Armees de la Republique Democratique du Congo (FARDC) 223–224
    foreign internal defence missions (FID) 223–224, 227, 236n159
    international partnerships *see* partnerships, international military
    Kamajors 201, 207, 210–212, 225
    militarisation *see* militarisation
    military information support operations (MISO) 224–225
    North Atlantic Treaty Organization (NATO) 177, 199n20, 200, 218, 287, 368–371, 377
    paramilitary forces 32–33, 38, 46–47, 138, 201, 367, 386
    partner forces *see* partnerships, international military
    power relations within 180–181
    private military contractors 46–47, 105, 398–399
    recruitment and retention 67, 79–90, 100–107, 125–128, 166–168, 210–218, 225–227, 263, 273–277, 316–328, 348–363, 391, 394–395 *see also* extremism; radicalisation
    tactics of *see* tactics
    technology and equipment for *see* technology
    training of 181–196, 301–303, 318, 351–358
    uncertainty management *see* tactics
    United States Africa Command (USAFRICOM) 223–224
    use of magic *see* magic
    Wagner Group 398–399, 402
    women in 190–193
mining *see* natural resources
Mocimboa da Praia *see* Mozambique
models *see* theory and theoretical approaches
Mohammed, Sheik Aboud Rogo 99–100, 349, 351, 365n2
money laundering *see* crime, organised
morale *see* psychology
Mozambique 41–48, 96–113, 166–167, 211–214, 348–363, 363n1–2, 383, 391–405
    Cabo Delgado province 96–112, 348–363, 365n1–2, 394–398, 402, 408n23
    counterinsurgency *see* counterinsurgency and counterterrorism
    Frente de Libertacao de Mocambique (FRELIMO) *see* organisations
    Makonde people 99, 102–104, 349–350
    Mocimboa da Praia 96–110, 349–359, 391–396, 404, 408n23
    Mwani people 102–104, 349–351, 358
    Nacala 96, 108, 396, 398
    Northern 96–113, 348–363, 383, 392–405
    Pemba 96, 108, 354–356, 365n1, 396
    Resistencia Nacional Mocambicana (RENAMO) *see* organisations
Muslims *see* Islam
Mwani people *see* Mozambique

N

Namibia *see* countries and regions
National Integrated Strategy to Combat Wildlife Trafficking (NISCWT) *see* policy and strategy
natural resources 30, 39, 45, 82, 86–88, 97–98, 104–105, 129, 247–249, 254, 291–292, 376
    trafficking in *see* trafficking
nature conservation *see* conservation, nature
necolonialism *see* colonialism
negotiations 77, 196, 243–244, 358, 367–369, 376–379, 386
    to release hostages *see* hostages
    with extremist groups and terrorists 137–138, 140–141, 358
    with kidnappers 136–141, 146, 149–151
nexus of crime and extremism / terrorism *see* crime, organised
Niger *see* countries and regions
Niger Delta *see* countries and regions
Nigeria *see* countries and regions
non-governmental organisations *see* organisations
Non-Self-Governing Territories (NSGT) *see* countries and regions
North Atlantic Treaty Organization (NATO) *see* military forces

O

occult *see* magic
occupation and anti-occupation movements 125, 238, 241, 243, 246–249, 254, 368
organisations
    Africa CDC 6–9
    African Parks 34, 47–48, 52n2
    African Union (AU) *see* African Union (AU)
    centres for disease control and prevention (CDC) 6, 8–9
    civil society organisations (CSOs) 131, 288, 318–319, 327–328, 334–336, 398, 403–405 *see also* non-governmental organisations
    East African Community 47, 131
    Environmental Investigation Agency (EIA) 109
    European Union (EU) 74, 177, 218, 369
    extremist groups *see* extremist groups
    financial institutions *see* finance
    Freedom Front Plus 242, 385–386
    Frente de Libertacao de Mocambique (FRELIMO) 97–104, 109, 349
    G5 Sahel 285, 311n5
    Human Rights Watch 249, 252–253
    International Union for Conservation of Nature (IUCN) 38
    non-governmental organisations (NGOs) 30, 33, 38, 47–48, 191, 333–336 *see also* civil society organisations (CSOs)
    North Atlantic Treaty Organization (NATO) *see* military forces
    Peace Parks Foundation 34, 47–48
    Polisario Front 247–248, 256
    Regional Economic Communities (RECs) 9, 131, 400, 403, 409n47 *see also* African Union (AU)
    Resistencia Nacional Mocambicana (RENAMO) 103–104, 211, 350
    Southern African Development Community (SADC) 9–10, 12, 39, 45–48, 97, 112–113, 383, 399–400
    United Nations (UN) *see* United Nations (UN)
    United States Africa Command (AFRICOM) 46, 223–224
    Unrepresented Nations and Peoples Organization (UNPO) 241–242
    World Health Organisation (WHO) *see* United Nations (UN)
organised crime *see* crime, organised

P

Palestine *see* countries and regions
pandemics 3–4 *see also* diseases and viruses
    as threat to security 6–10, 14–15
    centres for disease control and prevention (CDC) *see* organisations
    COVID-19 disease 1–21
    Ebola 4–6, 27n23
    economic and political impact of 15–18

Index

see also security and insecurity
human immunodeficiency virus (HIV) 1, 4–6
lockdowns 5, 11–13, 20
Middle East Respiratory Syndrome (MERS) 1, 4, 14
responses to 3, 6–12, 18–20
SARS-CoV-2 virus 1–2
severe acute respiratory syndrome coronavirus 2 *see* SARS-CoV-2 virus
severe acute respiratory syndrome (SARS) 1–2, 4, 14–16, 165
Pandor, Naledi 377, 402
paramilitary forces *see* military forces
paranormal beliefs *see* magic
parks, nature (protected areas) *see* conservation, nature
partnerships, international military 177–196
change management in 187–188
communication between partners 179–180, 187–190, 195
culture and 178–188, 195–196
discipline and punishment in *see* military forces
education and training in 179–180
individualism versus collectivism in *see* theory and theoretical approaches
partner forces 177–199
power relations within *see* military forces
psychology of 193–196
time management and 181–182
training and *see* military forces
Peuhl people *see* Fulani people
pirates and piracy 136, 142–151, 165, 218–219
risk management of *see* risk management
poaching *see* conservation, nature
police forces 13, 18–19, 41–49, 100–102, 109–111, 142, 193, 201–202, 288, 349–354, 360, 384–399 *see also* security forces
Directorate for Priority Crime Investigation (Hawks) 41, 384, 386, 388–389
Policia da Republica de Mocambique (PRM) 96
South African Police Service (SAPS) 384, 388–389
policy and strategy 402–405
anti-money laundering and combating the financing of terrorism frameworks (AML/CFT) 128–129
artificial intelligence 53
conflict-related sexual violence (CRSV) framework 190–193
Counter-Terrorism Monitoring, Reporting and Support Mechanism (CT MORSE) 74, 123
Global Counter-Terrorism Strategy (United Nations) 123, 363
Law Enforcement and Anti-poaching Strategy (LEAP) 45–46
National Integrated Strategy to Combat Wildlife Trafficking (NISCWT) 41, 44–46
Prevent, Disrupt, Deny framework 303–305
Sahel Summit 285
Southern Africa 402–405
War on Terror *see* War on Terror
Polisario Front *see* organisations
political economy *see* economics
population growth 29, 39, 65
power, personal *see* psychology
Preventing/Countering Violent Extremism (P/CVE) *see* counterinsurgency and counterterrorism
private military contractors *see* military forces
protected areas *see* conservation, nature
Protection of Constitutional Democracy Against Terrorist and Related Activities Act (POCDATARA) *see* law and legislation
protocols *see* diplomacy
psychology 56, 168, 179, 193–196, 203–204, 210, 219–222
habitus 206, 208, 210, 219–220, 222–223, 227–228 *see also* Bourdieu, Pierre
identity, psychology of *see* identity
morale 85, 171, 209–210, 215, 218

of communication *see* communication
of interrogation and interviewing 222
of intimidation 36, 74, 84, 209–210, 219, 272, 375, 398
power, personal 315, 320–324
psychological trauma 21, 36, 156n19, 191
psychological warfare (PSYWAR) 193–196, 203, 205, 209–212, 219–222, 225–227, 351
rationality 76, 143–148, 151, 204, 208, 219
superstition *see* magic
trust *see* trust
Puerto Rico *see* countries and regions

Q
Qatar *see* countries and regions

R
race and racism 385–387, 408n9 *see also* apartheid; ethnicity
radicalisation *see* extremism
radio and television 112, 325–328, 332, 336–341, 361–362 *see also* communication; media
Ramaphosa, Cyril 5, 8–11, 27n32, 65, 377–378, 384, 401
rangers 30–41, 48–49, 52n2
  boots on the ground 32–33, 41
  psychological pressures on 36–37
  training of 32–34
ransom *see* kidnapping
rationality *see* psychology
recruitment and retention *see* military forces
refugees and displaced persons 29, 47, 52n2, 96, 101, 120–121, 246–247, 251–253, 299–300, 311n6, 354–357, 373–375, 408n9
Regional Economic Communities (RECs) *see* organisations
religion and religions 68, 82, 103, 111, 120, 168, 201–214, 225, 271, 274–277, 320–337, 350–351, 361–362
  Christianity *see* Christianity
  Islam *see* Islam

magic *see* magic
RENAMO *see* organisations
research and methodologies 314–404 *see also* theory and theoretical approaches
  case studies 315–316, 318–320, 338
  counter-terrorist *see* counterinsurgency and counter-terrorism
  data 33, 43, 56–67, 130, 135–136, 141–142, 150–151, 156, 173, 314–320, 404
  data collection 33, 141, 150, 341
  psychological 314
  social network analysis (SNA) 40, 314–343
  Theory of Change 315–316
resistance 219, 222, 237, 305
  civil 240, 243, 246–250, 253, 255–256
  Lord's Resistance Army (LRA) *see* extremist groups
resolutions of the United Nations *see* United Nations (UN)
resources, natural *see* natural resources
rhino horn
  poaching *see* natural resources
  trafficking in *see* trafficking
rights, human 13, 61, 67–68, 105, 111, 178, 191–192, 241–242, 249–257, 333–334, 357–360, 366–367
right-wing groups *see* extremist groups
risk management 135, 141, 158, 160, 164–168, 171–172, 207, 219–220 *see also* counterinsurgency and counter-terrorism
  for businesses *see* business and businesses
Russia *see* countries and regions

S
Sahara *see* countries and regions
Sahel (Sahel Sahara) *see* countries and regions
Sahrawi Arab Democratic Republic *see* countries and regions
Sahrawi people 246–249, 256, 272
Salafism *see* Islam
Saudi Arabia *see* countries and regions
securitisation 2–6, 9–13, 21, 293, 303–305
  democracy and *see* democracy

security and insecurity 60–62, 322–323 *see also* marginalisation
  democratic and political 16–18, 286–294, 303–305
  economic 15–16, 97, 321–322
  food security 2, 39, 68, 97–98, 363
  human 2–3, 6–21, 27n6, 39, 124–125, 190, 348
  social 16–18
security forces
  child soldiers in *see* children
  human rights abuses 13–14, 357–362
  interrogation by *see* psychology
  military *see* military forces
  morale of *see* psychology
  police *see* police forces
  relationship with communities 110–112, 288–289, 303–305, 357–359, 402–405 *see also* armed non-state groups; community-based armed groups (CBAGs)
self-determination 238–245, 255
Senegal *see* countries and regions
separatist groups *see* armed non-state groups (ASNGs)
service delivery 65, 89, 90, 97, 404
shamans *see* magic
Shekau, Abubakar 270–272 *see also* Boko Haram
Sierra Leone *see* countries and regions
skills and skills development 32–33, 47, 66–67, 111–112, 179–180, 195, 342–343, 362, 389 *see also* education
slaves and slavery 31, 84, 267, 366–367 *see also* trafficking
smuggling *see* trafficking
social and economic development *see* development
social media 53–54, 63, 88, 315–317, 325–327, 331–332, 336, 386–387 *see also* media
social network analysis (SNA) *see* research and methodologies
Sokoto Caliphate 262, 266–267, 274–275 *see also* Fodio, Uthman Dan; Fulani people

Somalia *see* countries and regions
Somalia and Eritrea Monitoring Group (SEMG) *see* United Nations (UN)
Somaliland *see* countries and regions
South Africa *see* countries and regions
Southern African Development Community (SADC) *see* organisations
South Sudan *see* countries and regions
sovereignty *see* countries and regions
speech act theory *see* theory and theoretical approaches
stateless nations *see* countries and regions
states of emergency and disaster *see* law and legislation
strategy and strategies *see* policy and strategy
Sudan *see* countries and regions
Sufism *see* Islam
superstition *see* magic; psychology
sustainable development *see* development

T
tactics 32–34, 77–90, 96, 101, 110–111, 159–160, 180–181, 186–196, 204–206, 213–214, 219–227, 246–257, 302–306, 355–360, 391
  flexibility and management of uncertainty 185–188
Taliban *see* extremist groups
Tanzania *see* countries and regions
technology 14, 34–48, 53–68, 76, 167–168, 317, 327–331, 363
  Africa 64–67
  artificial intelligence (AI) *see* artificial intelligence (AI)
  drones 35–36, 54, 66–67
  facial recognition 63, 67
  Fourth industrial revolution *see* industrial revolutions
  mobile communications 64–65
  skills required to use *see* skills and skills development
  use in nature conservation *see* conservation, nature
television *see* radio and television
terrorism 73–90, 118–132, 159–163, 289–291 *see also* extremism; extremist

groups
bioterrorism 1, 3, 14–15, 21
counterterrorism *see* counterinsurgency and counterterrorism
financing of *see* extremist groups
impact on businesses *see* business and businesses
organised crime nexus *see* crime, organised
tactics used in *see* tactics
transnational 73, 76, 159, 293, 385, 403
theory and theoretical approaches *see also* research and methodologies
competition versus collectivism 184–185
framing 5–6, 10–11
governance 98
individualism and collectivism 182–185
securitisation models *see* securitisation
speech act theory 5, 10–11, 20
Sustainable Development Conservation models 38–41
Togo *see* countries and regions
tourism 38, 48–49, 52n2
trafficking 107–110, 288–289, 295–296, 303
antiquities and cultural property 82, 84–85
counterfeit goods 80, 82, 85–86
drug smuggling 74, 77, 80–85, 107–109, 123, 138, 295–296, 352, 356–358, 395–400
human trafficking 82, 84, 107, 124–125, 136, 191, 295, 355, 394–395, 400 *see also* kidnapping; slaves and slavery
natural resources 45, 77, 81–82, 86–88, 96–97, 107–108, 129, 335
weapons 83–84, 107, 123–124 *see also* weapons
wildlife 37–48, 81
training
in nature conservation *see* rangers
military *see* military forces
skills 111, 361–362
transnational activities
transnational crime *see* crime, organised
transnational (cross-border) extremism *see* extremism
transnational terrorism *see* terrorism
travellers, business *see* business travellers
treaties *see* diplomacy
trust 98, 111–113, 177–180, 288, 300, 315–320, 329–338, 340–343, 360
Tuareg people 79, 81, 272, 287, 292–293, 299, 312n53
Turkey *see* countries and regions

U

Uganda *see* countries and regions
uncertainty management *see* tactics
United Arab Emirate (UAE) *see* countries and regions
United Nations (UN)
Committee of 24 (Special Committee on Decolonisation) 239
decolonisation listings 239–240
Global Counter-Terrorism Strategy *see* policy and strategy
Multidimensional Integrated Stabilization Mission in Mali (MINUSMA) 293
Office for the Coordination of Humanitarian Affairs 321, 366
resolutions by 6, 73, 121, 123, 368–371
Responsibility-to-Protect mandate 368, 377
Silencing the Guns 377–378, 384
Somalia and Eritrea Monitoring Group (SEMG) 122–123
Special Court for Sierra Leone 201–202 *see also* Kondewa, Allieu; Sierra Leone
Sustainable Development Goals (SDGs) 172
United Nations Convention against Transnational Organized Crime (UNTOC) *see* diplomacy
United Nations Development Programme (UNDP) 2, 320
United Nations Environment Programme (UNEP) 38
United Nations Office on Drugs and Crime (UNODC) 38
United Nations Security Council (UNSC) 6, 73–74, 81, 84, 121–123, 368–371

Index

World Health Organization (WHO) 2, 6, 20
United States Africa Command (AFRICOM) *see* organisations
United States (US) *see* countries and regions
Unrepresented Nations and Peoples Organization *see* organisations

V
Vietnam *see* countries and regions
violence 29–31, 36–37, 60–61, 272–273, 289–290, 303–305 *see also* warfare
    gender-based *see* gender
    violent extremism *see* extremism
viruses *see* diseases and viruses; pandemics

W
Wagner Group *see* military forces
Wahhabism *see* Islam
warfare *see also* terrorism; violence
    anti-colonial 98–99
    psychological *see* psychology
    use of magic in *see* magic
War on Terror 107, 202, 269, 383, 408n1
weapons 31, 53–54, 107, 123–124, 354
    autonomous *see* artificial intelligence (AI)
    trafficking of *see* trafficking

West Africa *see* countries and regions
Western Sahara *see* countries and regions
white supremacist groups *see* extremist groups
wildlife
    poaching of *see* conservation, nature
    trafficking in *see* trafficking
witchdoctors *see* magic
women *see also* gender
    conflict-related sexual violence *see* military forces
    female travellers *see* business travellers
    in military forces *see* military forces
World Health Organization (WHO) *see* United Nations

Y
Yemen *see* countries and regions
youth 105–106, 111–112, 127–131, 210–211, 216–218, 221–222, 272, 318, 322–323, 326, 339–343, 349–353, 360–363, 391 *see also* children
Yusuf, Mohammed 216, 270, 360, 365n3

Z
Zimbabwe *see* countries and regions
Zuma, Jacob 369, 399